The Mainstream of Civilization

Second Edition

To 1715

The Mainstream

Second Edition

JOSEPH R. STRAYER
Princeton University

HANS W. GATZKE
Yale University

E. HARRIS HARBISON
Late of Princeton University

# of Civilization

To 1715

Harcourt Brace Jovanovich, Inc.

New York / Chicago / San Francisco / Atlanta

The Mainstream of Civilization   To 1715
Second Edition

Cover: ceiling of Hypostyle Hall, Temple of Denderah, Egypt. © Henri Stierlin.

Maps by J. P. Tremblay

ISBN: 0-15-551556-X

Library of Congress Catalog Card Number: 73-19410

Printed in the United States of America

Preface

It requires a certain amount of courage to attempt to write a history of civilization in one volume. Once the task has been accomplished, however, it is easier to do it a second time. As before, we have deliberately omitted certain details so that we could discuss as fully as possible the basic characteristics of each civilization and of different periods in the history of each civilization. We have tried to emphasize connections and interrelations—the ways in which politics, economics, art, scholarship, and religion all influence one another. We have tried to capture the flavor of each age—the unique combination of beliefs, activities, and institutions that distinguishes one society from another. In choosing the illustrations and the inserts in the text we have tried to give some idea of the diverse and ever-changing ways in which men have looked at and lived in their world. Finally, we have tried to consider the most difficult of all historical questions—the nature of and the reasons for change in human communities. Why and how do new institutions, new activities, new ideas rise and flourish? Why do they fade away? There are no easy answers to these problems; all we can do is suggest lines of inquiry that the reader may wish to pursue.

Obviously, it is easier to assess the characteristics and achievements of earlier periods than those of the age in which we live. The English Revolution of the seventeenth century ended long ago; the communist revolutions of the twentieth century continue to develop in unpredictable ways. Obviously also, it is more important to know details about the nature and background of problems that are still with us than details about problems that have been solved (at least partially). For these reasons the book broadens as it reaches the nineteenth century. More information is provided and more state of the world.

We trust that no one will passively accept our interpretations or believe that our book is an adequate summary of human history. Our work is only an introduction, an attempt to persuade the reader to think deeply about history and to study it in detail. We are convinced that historical-mindedness is a necessity of human life. Consciously or unconsciously, we all base our estimates of the future on our knowledge of the past. It is important, then, that our knowledge of the past be as accurate and as deep as possible.

We lament the untimely death of one of the original members of the group, Professor E. Harris Harbison. His material has been revised to include the results of recent

v

research, but we have built on the foundation that he gave us. We have also found the contribution of our former collaborator, Professor Edwin L. Dunbaugh, to be helpful in our revision.

The authors are greatly indebted to the following historians, who critically read *The Mainstream of Civilization* and made many valuable comments and suggestions: Jeremy Adams, Yale University; William Allen, University of Connecticut; John Eadie, University of Michigan; Erich S. Gruen, University of California at Berkeley; William W. Hallo, Yale University; Ramsay MacMullen, Yale University; Richard Marius, University of Tennessee; and Raphael Sealey, University of California at Berkeley.

J. R. S.
H. W. G.

Foreword *The Study of History*

Consciously or unconsciously, all of us are historians. We can plan for the future only because we remember the past. We can add to our knowledge only because we do not lose memory of former experiences. Everyone, from the peasant to the scholar, tries to meet new situations by discovering familiar elements that make it possible to evoke analogies with the past. An individual who has lost his memory, who has forgotten his own history, is helpless until he has recovered his past or has slowly built up a new past to which he can refer.

What is true of individuals is also true of societies. No community can survive and no institution can function without constant reference to past experience. We are ruled by precedents fully as much as by formal laws, which is to say that we are ruled by memories of the past. It is the memory of common experiences that unites individuals into communities, and it is the memory of his own experiences that makes a child into an adult. Some of the memories may not be happy ones, but in reacting against them we are still linked to the past that produced them.

If everyone is his own historian, if individuals and societies necessarily draw on their memories of the past in order to deal with the present, then what is the need for formal, scholarly history? Isn't it enough to remember only the history that serves our immediate needs?

It is not enough, for two reasons. Human memory is fallible; individuals and societies forget many things that might be useful in solving their problems. This is why we have written records (which are a kind of formal history); this is why illiterate peoples try to preserve their customs and traditions through repeated oral recitations by the elders of the tribe. Second, the more complicated a society becomes, the narrower the range of individual experience in proportion to the total of possible experiences. A peasant living in a medieval village shared most of the experiences of his neighbors, and village custom gave solutions of a sort even to rare and unusual problems. No one living in an urbanized society shares many of the experiences of his neighbors, let alone the experiences of the millions of people throughout the world with whom he is connected by political and economic ties. No one can sum up the past experiences of his society, and of the societies with which his own interacts, with a few customary formulas; and yet these past experiences place a heavy burden on the present. In facing any problem, we look for familiar elements; if these are lacking, we feel fearful and helpless. Knowledge of history increases the chance of finding something familiar in a new and difficult situation.

Certain card games show how this process works at an elementary level. There is almost no chance that one distribution of cards will be repeated in a subsequent deal in bridge. Yet a person who has played several thousand hands of bridge should be able to make intelligent decisions and predictions even though every deal presents a new situation. He should be able to use his high cards and long suits effectively; he should be able to make some shrewd guesses about the location of cards in other hands. Not every experienced player will develop these skills. Some people are unable to generalize from their past experiences, and others cannot see analogies between the present and the past. But, generally speaking, an experienced player will make better use of his cards than a person who has played only ten hands. There is such a thing as a sense of the realities and possibilities of social activity, which can be developed from a knowledge of history.

At the very least, the past has left us the problems that we are trying to solve and the patterns of living that we are seeking to modify. At the most, we may find in the past suggestions for understanding and coping with the present. It is the historian's task to study the behavior of man in the past, to uncover facts, sort them, mass and link them, and so provide connections between past and present.

At the same time the historian must avoid certain pitfalls along the way. Connections with the past cannot be broken, but they can be misrepresented or misunderstood. Primitive peoples have little sense of chronology; they are apt to stir all their memories into a timeless brew of legend. At a more sophisticated level, the past has been used as a means of justifying present values and power structures. Many writers, from ancient times down to the present, have found historical examples to prove that their people were specially favored by the gods, that their state was founded and strengthened by heroes of superhuman ability, that virtue and wisdom (as defined by the author) have always brought success while folly and vice have led to disaster. "History is philosophy teaching by example," said an ancient Greek (Dionysius of Halicarnassus), and it was more important for the examples to be edifying than for them to be true.

But it is not difficult to avoid deliberate distortions of the past. What *is* difficult is to avoid distortions caused by the incompleteness of our knowledge of the past. Many human activities have left few traces, especially in written records. For example, for thousands of years agriculture has been the chief occupation of the human race, but there are still serious gaps in our knowledge of the history of agriculture. "The short and simple annals of the poor" are short because information is scanty. If we had better information we would probably find that the life of a poor man in any period was anything but simple; it must have been filled with an unending series of nagging problems. In general, we know more about political history than social history, more about the privileged few than the unprivileged masses, more about the history of art than the history of technology, more about the ideas of philosophers and religious leaders than about the beliefs of the common people.

Historians have become more skillful in recent years in finding material that gives a better-balanced picture of the past. Archeology reveals not only the palaces of kings, but the homes of ordinary people with their tools, their toys, their cooking utensils, and even fragments of their food. Gods and heroes may dominate the great works of art, but the common folk going about their ordinary business are there too—on Greek vases, Roman tombs, and portals of Gothic cathedrals. Discoveries of hoards of coins reveal unexpected trade relations. Aerial photography can bring out traces of ancient methods of plowing land and dividing fields. Even the written records, which have been studied for centuries, contain hitherto unused facts about such things as family life, migrations, and changes in economic patterns. There are still many holes in the record, but there is no reason to complain about lack of material.

The historian's greatest difficulty is not in discovering facts, but in deciding what facts can be ignored, or merely sampled, or clumped together in a single generalization. No one could master all the facts in yesterday's issue of the *New York Times,* and there are files of newspapers that run back to the eighteenth century. No one could master all the facts brought out in a single session of the Supreme Court, and the records of American courts and of the English courts from which they were derived go back to the twelfth century. To deal with the overwhelming mass of facts, historians have to arrange them, link them together, establish meaningful sequences of causes and effects.

The massing and linking of facts is not only essential, if history is to rise above the level of a catalogue; it is also inevitable, since it is the way the human mind deals with past experience. We do not recall every word we have exchanged when we decide that a certain person is a good friend. We do not remember every paragraph we have read when we decide that we like a certain book. But, while the process of massing and linking is essential and inevitable, this operation is the point of greatest danger in any kind of historical thinking. Consciously or unconsciously, one can mass facts to produce a misleading impression, even though each individual fact is true. Any governmental system can be made to appear obnoxious by discussing only the cases in which there is clear evidence of corruption or oppression. Any society can be wreathed in a golden haze by dwelling only on its accomplishments in art, literature, and scholarship. Individuals and communities can become convinced that the whole world is conspiring against them if they remember only the occasions when they were treated unjustly. The nature of the sources themselves may cause distortion. For example, it is very easy to find material on political life in the city of Rome during the first century of the Roman Empire. It is difficult to collect evidence on provincial government or on social and economic development. The natural tendency is to overemphasize court intrigues and to pay little attention to such topics as economic growth or the spread of Latin culture throughout the West.

There is no easy way to overcome these problems, but an understanding of the principle of interconnectedness will help. No one is a purely political, or economic, or ideological being, and societies are composed of such varied human beings. Historians must look for the ways in which these (and other) forces interact. For example, the kind of food men eat can affect their whole social structure: a society dependent on olive oil for its fats will differ in many ways from one that depends on animal products such as lard, butter, and cheese. Religion can have an influence on trade: medieval churchmen aided the growth of Mediterranean commerce by importing silk for their vestments, incense for their ceremonies, and precious stones for their altar vessels and relic boxes. Trade in turn can influence the development of a religion: often it has been the merchant who prepared the way for the missionary. Ideas, technologies, institutions, social patterns, shifts in consumer preferences interact in complicated and bewildering ways. For example, increased use of easily washable cotton clothing in modern Europe improved personal hygiene and thus may have reduced death rates and contributed to growth of population. At the same time, increased demand for cotton encouraged the extension of slavery in the United States and thus was one of the causes of the Civil War.

Full realization of the connections among all human activities should lead to three conclusions. First, there are multiple causes for every event; single explanations for change are almost always wrong. Second, change in any one part of the social pattern may affect any other part of the pattern. Finally, the connections lead back into the past and therefore the past influences the present.

The relationship between continuity and change is an interaction that the historian must watch with special care. All societies change and yet all societies retain some connection with the past. The most "traditional" society is less traditional than it realizes; the most "modern" society is more influenced by tradition than it would like to believe. The Anglo-Saxons, theoretically bound by immemorial custom, invented the office of sheriff about the year 1000 A.D. The Americans, theoretically free to create an entirely new political structure, have preserved the office of sheriff with many of its original powers. Conquests and revolutions do not break all the connections with the past. Even where there has apparently been a complete break, the roots of a society may again grow down into its past. Roman law practically vanished from the West after the fifth century A.D.; it reappeared as a powerful force in the thirteenth century.

If there were no continuity, there would be no use in studying history, since nothing in the past would have any bearing on what is done today. If there were no change, there would be no history; a few years of practical experience would teach anyone all he needed to know about human behavior in society at any time and in any place. But, in the world as it is, the forces that make for change are modified and even distorted by habit and custom, the forces that make for continuity are weakened and limited by new desires and new ideas. It is of some importance to understand where, why, and to what degree the desire for change prevails.

It is easy to see multiple, interlocking activities and rapid rates of change in the modern world. It is less easy to get a sense of the complexity and capacity for change of premodern and non-European societies, which is why the history of such societies often seems flat and uninteresting. The European Middle Ages are summed up as an "Age of Faith"; the history of much of Asia is dismissed with talk of the "unchanging Orient." Yet the Middle Ages were also a period of state-building, economic growth, and technological invention—activities that have influenced the modern world fully as much as the Christian Church. The "unchanging Orient" produced all the great world religions, and each of these religions was a powerful force for change. Moreover, there are advantages in studying societies that are less complex and in which rates of change are less rapid than in our own. It is easier to observe and to draw conclusions about human behavior when the number of variables is small and changes do not come so fast that their effects are blurred.

A good historian, then, will try to give adequate attention to a wide variety of human activities, to discuss the interactions among these activities, and to trace the connections between past and present. But these principles cannot be applied mechanically. A writer who is careful to give an exactly equal amount of space to politics, economics, religion, the arts, and scholarship will probably not produce an adequate description of a society. The importance and even the identity of each of these activities varies with time and place. Religion had more influence on Indian than on Chinese society. Economics and politics merge in primitive societies, such as that of the early Germans. It is probably true that the vast majority of the world's scientists were born in the twentieth century; this could not be said of theologians. Thus the impact of scholarship on early societies is different from its impact on modern societies. To understand such variations and transformations, the historian must be more than a meticulous scholar. He must develop a feel for the period he is writing about, a sense of how people lived and worked and thought. It takes time and experience to acquire this feeling for the past, but once it has been acquired historians can give reasonably accurate, and occasionally penetrating, descriptions of earlier societies.

It is this understanding of the development of human society that gives history its chief value. History, even at its worst, gives us the comforting and necessary feeling that there are some familiar elements in a changing world and that there is some hope of understanding the changes that do occur. History at its best gives us a chance of reacting sensibly to problems as they arise. It does not guarantee the correctness of our responses, but it should improve the quality of our judgment. Good judgment about human behavior in society is badly needed today.

A Note on the Paperbound Edition

This volume is part of a variant printing, not a new or revised edition, of *The Mainstream of Civilization,* Second Edition. Many of the users of the first edition found the two-volume paperbound version of that edition useful because it enabled them to fit the text into the particular patterns of their teaching and scheduling. The publishers have continued that format in preparing this printing, which exactly reproduces the text of the one-volume version of *The Mainstream of Civilization,* Second Edition. The first of these volumes starts with the beginnings of western civilization in the ancient Middle East and continues to the eighteenth century. The second volume, repeating two of the chapters on the seventeenth century (Chapters 20 and 21), carries the account forward to the present day. The variant printing, then, is intended as a convenience to those instructors and students who have occasion to use either one part or the other of *The Mainstream of Civilization.* Consequently, the pagination and index of the one-volume version, as well as its illustrations, maps, and other related materials, are retained in this printing. The difference between the one-volume and the two-volume versions of the book is a difference only in form.

Contents

3

4

5

6

7

14

15

16

17

18

List of Maps

Introduction

This is a history of civilization, with emphasis on the civilization developed by the peoples of Europe. Like all histories, it must be selective. Incomplete as our record of the past is, it is still too full to permit discussion in a single book of all civilizations or even of all events in the history of one civilization. The principles that have guided our selection of topics may be indicated by a definition of our subject. We must answer two questions: What is civilization, and what has been the role of western civilization in creating the conditions that we find in the world today?

Civilization is derived from the Latin word for city, *civitas.* There is reason to emphasize this derivation, for every great civilization has had great cities, and the basic characteristics of civilization are easiest to observe in cities. Civilization is first of all *cooperation*—men working together to satisfy their material and spiritual needs. It requires *organization*—as soon as several people start working together there must be some sort of social, political, or economic pattern to regulate their activity. It encourages *specialization*—as soon as several people begin to cooperate in an organized way there are obvious advantages in dividing the work so that no one man has to do everything for himself. The character of a particular civilization is determined by the type and degree of the organization and specialization of that civilization. Ten thousand Greeks living in a small city-state could accomplish much more than ten thousand Indians scattered through the forests of North America. A few hundred men specializing in science have done more to change our civilization in the last few centuries than millions of artisans working through past ages. Intensive organization and specialization can produce spectacular results, and they can also create spectacular problems.

Civilization requires faith in certain ideals and values as well as skill in organization and techniques. The immediate and direct advantages of organization and specialization are not very apparent to most people. Organization sets limits on personal freedom, and specialization makes a man dependent on other men who may not be wholly trustworthy. In the long run the advantages are greater than the disadvantages, but farseeing, enlightened self-interest is a very rare human quality, probably rarer than altruism. And if men hesitate to give up present benefits for advantages in their own future, they will be even more hesitant if the advantages are to be gained only by their descendants. There is always resistance to increasing the scale and scope of organization; there is usually resistance to new types of specialization. This resistance can be overcome only by belief that there is something more important than the individual—a religion that emphasizes cooperation, a divinely appointed ruler or ruling class, a nation that has become almost a divinity, a theory of society that has taken on the aspects of a religion. There is a close connection between the dominant beliefs of a people and the kind of civilization it creates.

This history of civilization examines, more than anything else, how and why people have worked together. It is concerned with political history because the political record helps us to understand why people have been more successful at some times than at others in organizing on a large scale, and why some types of organization have proved more effective than others. It is concerned with economic and social history because economic and social organization has a direct effect on both political organization and the type and degree of specialization. It is concerned with the history of ideas and their manifestations in art and literature because organization and specialization are possible only within a framework of accepted beliefs. The interactions among political organizations, economic institutions, and dominant beliefs determine the character and development of a civilization.

Western civilization is only one, and by no means the oldest, of the civilizations that have left a historical record. The earliest civilizations touched Europe and the West only slightly; they centered in the river valleys of Egypt, the Near East, and China. Only with the appearance of the Greek city-states after 1000 B.C. can we see the beginnings of a civilization that belongs to the same family as our own. The Greeks drew heavily on the older civilizations of their neighbors, but they reorganized their borrowed materials and added significant elements to them. Ideas and forms of organization that have remained important in western civilization for over twenty-five hundred years first appear in ancient Greece. The Romans followed the Greeks as the dominant people in the Mediterranean basin. Like the Greeks, they borrowed from their predecessors, rearranged the old materials in new ways, and added ideas of their own, especially in government and law. Roman civilization is the direct ancestor of the civilization of modern European countries. There has never been a time, from the first conquests of the Roman Republic down to the present, when Roman law and Roman political ideas were not being dicussed in some parts of the Continent.

Yet, while there is unbroken continuity between the civilization of the Greeks and the Romans and that of the modern West, it is well to remember that continuity is not identity. Much has been added—for example, the ideas brought in by Christianity—and much has been changed. Greco-Roman civilization was neither western nor European; it was Mediterranean. It was most highly developed on the eastern shores of the Mediterranean, and it was greatly influenced by the Orient. France and Spain were colonial outposts that contributed little to Greco-Roman civilization; Germany, Scandinavia, and the Slavic countries were outside the limits of the civilized Mediterranean world.

This Mediterranean civilization ran into trouble in the fourth and fifth centuries A.D. The economic organization proved unsatisfactory, and loyalty to the political organization weakened. As the Roman Empire slowly crumbled, the unity of the Mediterranean basin was destroyed, never to be restored. The southern and eastern shores became part of an Arab empire, part of the non-European Moslem civilization. A remnant of the old Roman Empire, centering around Constantinople, became the Byzantine Empire. This empire developed its own civilization—Christian in belief, Greek in language, but strongly influenced by the East in organization. Byzantine civilization made a great impression on the Slavic peoples of Eastern Europe and had some influence on the Latin and Germanic peoples of the West. But it was never fully integrated with the civilization that grew up in western Europe. The western Europeans thought of the Byzantines as remote and somewhat untrustworthy relatives, who might hand out valuable gifts from time to time but who were too eccentric to live with. This attitude, in turn, has made it difficult to integrate eastern and western Europe, since the eastern countries borrowed much more from Byzantium than did those of the West.

With the Arab and Byzantine empires developing separate civilizations, the western European remnant of the old Mediterranean world was thrown back on its own resources. These were at first not very great. Western Europe saved only a fragment of its Roman inheritance, and this Roman inheritance was itself only a fragment of the old Mediterranean civilization. Moreover, the Germanic peoples of northern and central Europe, who had never been included in the Mediterranean world, were for a time dominant in western Europe. They brought in some new ideas and institutions, but they were backward in both political and economic organization. They were slow in assimilating the fragments of Roman civilization that remained, and even slower in developing effective types of organization. In the same way, the Christian religion, which eventually had great influence on European civilization, was only slowly absorbed by the half-barbarized Latins and the half-civilized Germans. For six centuries Europeans struggled with the problems of assimilating the Roman inheritance, integrating Latin and Germanic peoples, and implementing the basic ideas of Christianity. Only when this triple task was done did western Europe at last achieve an independent and consistent civilization. Only then could it profit from its contacts with the more highly developed civilizations of the Arab and Byzantine worlds.

Once it was established as a separate and viable entity, western European civilization developed rapidly. Many of our basic institutions and ideas, such as universities and representative assemblies, were worked out in the twelfth and thirteenth centuries. But this western European civilization was confined to a very small area. Its center was in the North, in a triangle bounded by Paris, Cologne, and London. The peripheral countries—Spain, Ireland, Norway, Sweden, Poland, Bohemia, and Italy—did not share in all the manifestations of this civilization, though they accepted its basic ideas. And beyond these countries the influence of western European civilization dropped off sharply. It had little effect on the Moslem world and none whatever on the peoples of Africa and Asia who lived beyond the limits of Moslem influence. It had some impact on Byzantium, but not enough to erase the differences that separated Byzantium from the West. There were some contacts with Russia, but the Russians were probably more influenced by the Byzantines. And the Mongol conquest of the thirteenth century weakened the ties that the Russians had with the West and forced them to face east for two centuries.

Meanwhile, another group of civilizations had developed in the Far East, in India, China, and Japan. Each had its own characteristic values—religious in India, secular and political in China, military in Japan. All three tended to become somewhat self-satisfied and isolated; neither India nor China, for example, was as interested in foreign voyages in the sixteenth century as it had been earlier. In all three the economic system was still based largely on village agriculture. Finally, in spite of promising beginnings, none of the Far Eastern civilizations had developed a strong scientific tradition. These characteristics put the Far Eastern countries at a disadvantage in dealing with Europeans, who were deeply interested in strange lands and peoples, were beginning to develop an economy based on machine production, and were just about to make their first important scientific discoveries.

The great voyages of exploration and the great mechanical inventions, both of which began in the fifteenth century, enabled western European civilization to emerge from its narrow corner and to spread throughout the world. Eastern Europe gradually accepted much of the civilization of the West, though the process was never complete. Three new continents—North America, South America, and Australia—were occupied by Europeans, and a fourth, Africa, was dominated by them. Asia, with its old civilizations and its dense population, was not so easily overrun, but even Asia was profoundly influenced by the European impact. Thus, for the first time, all the peoples of the world were brought into contact with a single civilization. The results of this great experiment are only beginning to be apparent.

There is some justification, then, for the conventional division of history into Ancient, Medieval, and Modern. Ancient history deals with the period in which some of the basic elements of western civilization were developed and passed on to later peoples. But Ancient history must be focused on the Near East and the Mediterranean, not on Europe. It must give greater weight to Greece, Asia Minor, Syria, Mesopotamia, and Egypt than to Gaul, Britain, or Germany. Medieval history deals with the period in which a distinct western European civilization appeared. But this civilization was confined to a small part of the European peninsula, and it had little influence outside that area. During the Middle Ages each great region of the world had its own civilization, and no one civilization was able greatly to modify another. Modern history deals not only with the rapid development of western European civilization in its old homeland but also with relations between that civilization and the rest of the world.

This growth and diffusion of western civilization has gone so far that we have perhaps entered a fourth period in its history. This period is marked by the appearance of distinct types of western civilization in the different areas occupied by Europeans, and, even more, by the revitalization of other civilizations following their contact with the West. Both the appearance of different types of western civilization and the revival of old civilizations are stimulating factors; they should help to prevent ossification and decay. Unfortunately, a stimulus can also be an irritant, and the reactions among competing civilizations may lead to efforts for mutual destruction rather than for mutual instruction.

The history of civilization begins in obscurity and ends with a question mark. Yet past experience is our only guide in solving present and future problems, and knowledge of our history may help us answer the great question with which we are faced today, that of the survival of civilization in any form.

EXPLORATION IN SPACE

SATURN 886,000,000 miles from sun

PLUTO 3,606,000,000 miles from sun

VIKING (projected 1975) USA First soft landing on Mars (1976)

URANUS 1,783,000,000 miles from sun

NEPTUNE 2,793,000,000 miles from sun

MARINER 10 (1973) USA To fly within 3300 miles of Venus and 625 miles of Mercury in 1974

MARS 142,000,000 miles from sun

JUPITER 483,000,000 miles from sun

VENUS 67,000,000 miles from sun

MERCURY 36,000,000 miles from sun

MARINER (projected 1977) USA To fly within 270,000 miles of Jupiter (1979) and within 125,000 miles of Saturn (1981)

SUN

MARINER 4 (1965) USA Passed within 6118 miles of Mars

PIONEER 5 (1960) USA First solar orbit

PIONEER 10 (1972-73) USA To pass within 87,000 miles of Jupiter (December 1973). Fastest object to leave Earth and first object to leave our solar system.

RINER 2 (1962) USA Passed within 22,000 miles of Venus

MARINER 9 (1971-72) USA Orbited Mars and took pictures for a year

VENERA 4 (1967) USSR Parachuted through atmosphere of Venus

EARTH 93,000,000 miles from sun

VOSTOK 1 (1961) USSR First man in orbit

LUNA 2 (1959) USSR First probe to impact on moon's surface

SPUTNIK 1 (1957) USSR First satellite to orbit Earth

APOLLO 11 (1969) USA First men on moon

MOON 238,900 miles from Earth

LUNA 10 (1966) USSR First lunar orbit

Asteroid Belt

ORGE V. KELVIN

EAST AND WEST
Second century

Deserts   Principal trade routes

MILES
0   500   1000

J. P. TREMBLAY

P
A
C
I
F
I
C

O
C
E
A
N

SEA
OF
JAPAN

EAST
CHINA SEA

SOUTH
CHINA SEA

HUNS

ALTAI MTS.

GOBI DESERT

GREAT WALL

L A T E   H A N

E M P I R E

Yellow River

Loyang

Hankow

Amur River

IEN SHAN MTS.

Kashgar

Yarkand

Khotan

Yangtze River

AN

RE

Brahmaputra River

HIMALAYA MTS.

Ganges River

Pataliputra

EMPIRE
OF THE
ANDHRAS

A

Mangalore

BAY
OF
BENGAL

NDIAN OCEAN

THE SPREAD OF CHRISTIANITY IN EUROPE To 1417

ATLANTIC OCEAN

NORTH SEA

St. Andrews

York

Bremen

Elbe River

Magdeburg

Salisbury
London
Winchester
Canterbury

ENGLISH CHANNEL

Rhine R.

Cologne
Aachen

Fulda

Amiens

Rouen
Bec
St. Denis
Laon
Reims
Trier

Mainz
Worms

Seine
Paris

Chartres

River

Strasbourg

Loire River

Clairvaux

Tours
Bourges

Cîteaux

St. Gall

Cluny

BAY OF BISCAY

Clermont
Lyons
Le Puy
Vienne

Milan

Aquileia

Bordeaux

Garonne River

Po River

Santiago de Compostela

Toulouse

Albi

Rhône R.

Bobbio

Ravenna

Ebro R.

Avignon
Arles

Pisa
Florence

Duero River

Narbonne

Siena

Tagus River

CORSICA

Rome

Lisbon

Toledo

Monte Cassino

Seville

BALEARIC IS.

SARDINIA

Naples

Monreale
Palermo

SICIL

MEDI

	Christianity to 600
	to 900
	to 1200
	to 1417
	Temporarily lost to Islam

♀ Principal cathedral cities
✝ Principal monasteries

MILES
0   100   200   300

la +

BALTIC SEA

Gnesen

Vistula River

River

Cracow

enna

Gran

Danube River

ROMAN CHURCH
GREEK CHURCH

Novgorod

Moscow

Volga River

Kiev

Dnieper River

Don River

BLACK SEA

Tigris River

Constantinople +

Thessalonica

AEGEAN
SEA

Euphrates River

CRETE

CYPRUS

ANEAN SEA

Nile R.

J. P. TREMBLAY

NORWAY

NORTH
SEA

DENMARK

ATLANTIC OCEAN

SCOTLAND

Edinburgh

IRELAND

Dublin

ENGLAND

Oxford   Cambridge

London

ENGLISH CHANNEL

Hamburg   Lübeck   Elbe River

Bremen

Brunswick   Magdeburg

Leiden
Rotterdam

Bruges
Ghent
Brussels
Louvain

Antwerp

Rhine

Leipzig

Cologne   Erfurt

HOLY   RO

Prague

Noyon

Paris

Seine River

B
U
R
G
U
N
D
Y

Trier   Mainz

Nuremberg
Regensbur

Fontainebleau

Loire River

EMPIRE

Tours

F
R
A
N
C
E

Dijon

Augsburg

Basel

Zurich   Constance

BAY OF
BISCAY

Angoulême

Lyons

Geneva

Bordeaux

Dordogne River

Rhône River

Avignon

Milan

Po River

Trent

Venice

PORTUGAL

Duero River

Ebro

N
A
V
A
R
R
E

Marseilles

Genoa

Ferrara
Bologna

ADR

Lisbon

Tagus River

Escorial
Madrid

C
A
S
T
I
L
E

A
R
A
G
O
N

Barcelona

CORSICA

Pisa
Florence   Siena

PAPAL
STATES

Perugia

N
A

Rome

Seville

GRANADA

SARDINIA
(ARAGON)

Palermo

SICILY
(ARAGO

EUROPEAN CIVILIZATION Fifteenth century

MEDI

BALTIC SEA

Novgorod

Moscow

Königsberg

anzig

Thorn

Vistula River

Volga River

POLAND – LITHUANIA

Kiev

Cracow

Dnieper River

Don River

Buda

UNGARY

Danube River

BLACK SEA

O
T
T
O
M
A
N

Constantinople

Sálonika

AEGEAN

SEA

Tigris River

E
M
P
I
R
E

Euphrates River

RHODES

CYPRUS

CRETE

ANEAN SEA

Nile R.

J. P. TREMBLAY

khotsk,
1648

JAPAN

*EAST
CHINA
SEA*

P A C I F I C

Amur River

*Lake
Baykal*

Yellow River

Yeniseisk, 1618

O C E A N

C H I N A

Yangtze River

**A
S
I
A**

*PHILIPPINE
IS.*

*SOUTH
CHINA
SEA*

*ARAL
SEA*

*SPICE IS.
(MOLUCCAS)*

AMBOINA

Brahmaputra R.

HIMALAYA MTS.

EAST INDIES

*SPIAN
SEA*

Indus River

Ganges R.

Calcutta,
1690

INDIA

*BAY OF
BENGAL*

JAVA

A U S T R A L I A

Bombay,
1661, 1665

Madras, 1639
Pondicherry, 1674

ARABIAN SEA

I N D I A N   O C E A N

J. P. TREMBLAY

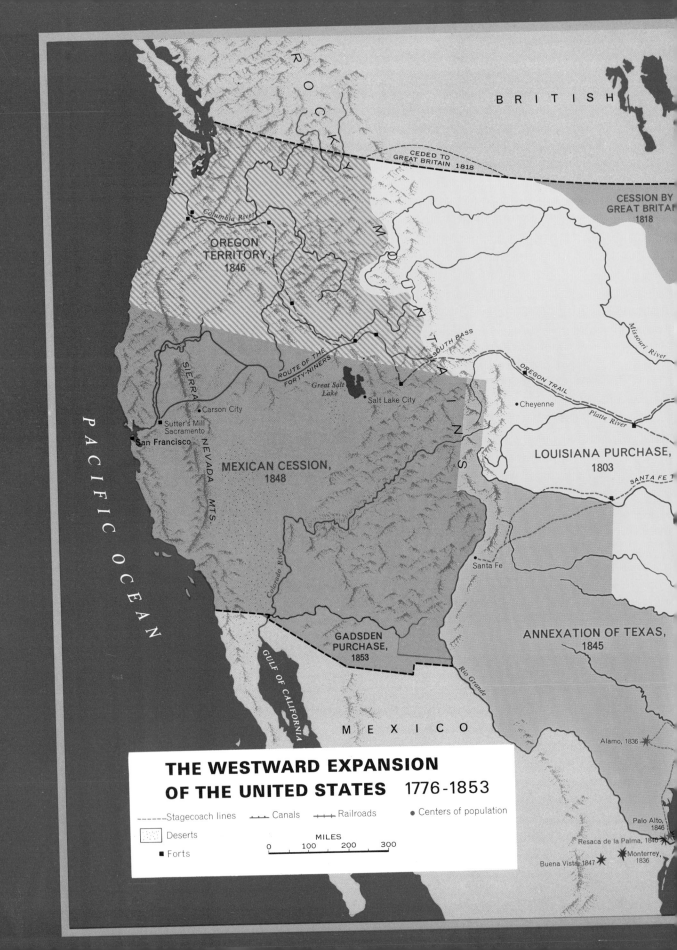

THE WESTWARD EXPANSION
OF THE UNITED STATES 1776-1853

----- Stagecoach lines   ⊣⊣⊢ Canals   +++ Railroads   • Centers of population

Deserts

■ Forts

MILES
0   100   200   300

BRITISH

CEDED TO
GREAT BRITAIN 1818

CESSION BY
GREAT BRITAIN
1818

OREGON
TERRITORY,
1846

Columbia River

ROCKY

MOUNTAINS

SOUTH PASS

OREGON TRAIL

Missouri River

ROUTE OF THE
FORTY-NINERS

Great Salt
Lake

• Salt Lake City

• Cheyenne

Platte River

PACIFIC

SIERRA

• Carson City

Sutter's Mill
Sacramento
• San Francisco

NEVADA

MTS

MEXICAN CESSION,
1848

LOUISIANA PURCHASE,
1803

SANTA FE T

OCEAN

Colorado River

• Santa Fe

ANNEXATION OF TEXAS,
1845

GADSDEN
PURCHASE,
1853

GULF OF CALIFORNIA

Rio Grande

M E X I C O

Alamo, 1836 ✳

Palo Alto,
1846

Resaca de la Palma, 1846

Buena Vista 1847 ✳   ✳ Monterrey,
1836

NORTH AMERICA

St. Lawrence River

LAKE SUPERIOR

Northwest

LAKE MICHIGAN

LAKE HURON

Plattsburg, 1814

VT. N.H.

MASSACHUSETTS

Boston

NEW
YORK

Albany

Lundy's Lane
1814

L. ONTARIO

CONN. RHODE ISLAND

Battle of Lake Erie 1813

Chippewa, 1814

Buffalo

New Haven

Territory

Detroit

LAKE ERIE

Cleveland

PENNSYLVANIA

New York

Chicago

Toledo

Harrisburg

Trenton

NEW JERSEY

Philadelphia

1800

1810

Springfield

ROAD

Columbus 1840

1820

DEL.

Baltimore

CUMBERLAND

Indianapolis

1850

1830

Washington, 1814

MD.

sas City

St. Louis

Ohio River

VIRGINIA

Richmond

WESTWARD
EXPANSION
TO 1783

APPALACHIAN

Mississippi River

NORTH
CAROLINA

Memphis

SOUTH
CAROLINA

Charleston

Atlanta

GEORGIA

Savannah

Mississippi Territory

New Orleans, 1815

New Orleans

lveston

FLORIDA
PURCHASE,
1819

ATLANTIC OCEAN

GULF OF MEXICO

J. P. TREMBLAY

ATLANTIC OCEAN

NORTH SEA

KINGDOM OF DENMARK AND NORWAY

KINGDOM OF SWEDEN

UNITED KINGDOM
OF
GREAT BRITAIN AND IRELAND

Hanover

WESTPHALIA

CONFEDERATION

OF THE

RHINE

Ber

Leipz

Jena SAXON

London

ENGLISH CHANNEL

Waterloo

Paris

Seine

River

Valmy

Rhine R.

Elbe River

1809

1805

Loire River

NAPOLEONIC

EMPIRE

SWITZERLAND

BAY OF
BISCAY

Garonne River

Rhône R.

1814–15

KINGDOM

OE

1797

Duero River

1808

Ebro

Po River

Marengo
1800

ITALY

Salamanca

Madrid

Toulon

KINGDOM OF PORTUGAL

Tagus River

Lisbon

KINGDOM OF SPAIN

ELBA

CORSICA

Rome

KINGDOM
OF
SARDINIA

Trafalgar

KINGDOM
OF
SICILY

NAPOLEONIC EUROPE 1812

Napoleonic Empire
States under French control
States allied to France
Routes of Napoleon

MED

MILES
0   100   200   300

BALTIC SEA

Moscow

Borodino

Tilsit

1812

Friedland

DOM
RUSSIA

DUCHY

OF

Vistula River

WARSAW

RUSSIAN EMPIRE

Volga River

Dnieper River

Don River

-07

Austerlitz

agram

TRIAN EMPIRE

BESSARABIA

na

Danube River

BLACK SEA

Tigris River

O T T O M A N

E M P I R E

Euphrates River

AEGEAN

SEA

ES

1798

ANEAN SEA

1799

Abukir Bay

Nile R.

J. P. TREMBLAY

RUSSIAN EXPANSION To 1914

Russia in 1533
Acquisitions to 1689
Acquisitions to 1801
Acquisitions to 1914

MILES
0   500

OCEAN

ALASKA
(Russian, 1787?–1867)

BERING SEA

PACIFIC

OKHOTSK SEA

SAKHALIN
Russian,
(1875–1905)

KURILE IS.
(Russian, 1711–1875)

EMPIRE

Lena River

Yenisei River

Amur River

Lake Baykal

ALTAI MTS.

RUSSIAN SPHERE OF INFLUENCE

OUTER MONGOLIA

MANCHURIA

Vladivostok

SEA
OF
JAPAN

JAPAN

Tokyo

Peking

KOREA

Seoul

Port Arthur
(Russian, 1898–1905)

Yellow River

CHINA

EAST
CHINA SEA

Shanghai

OCEAN

Yangtze River

MALAYA – MOUNTAINS

BHUTAN

Brahmaputra River

River

Calcutta

BURMA

SIAM

Mekong River

FRENCH
INDO-CHINA

Hong Kong

SOUTH
CHINA SEA

BAY OF
BENGAL

J. P. TREMBLAY

WORLD POPULATION

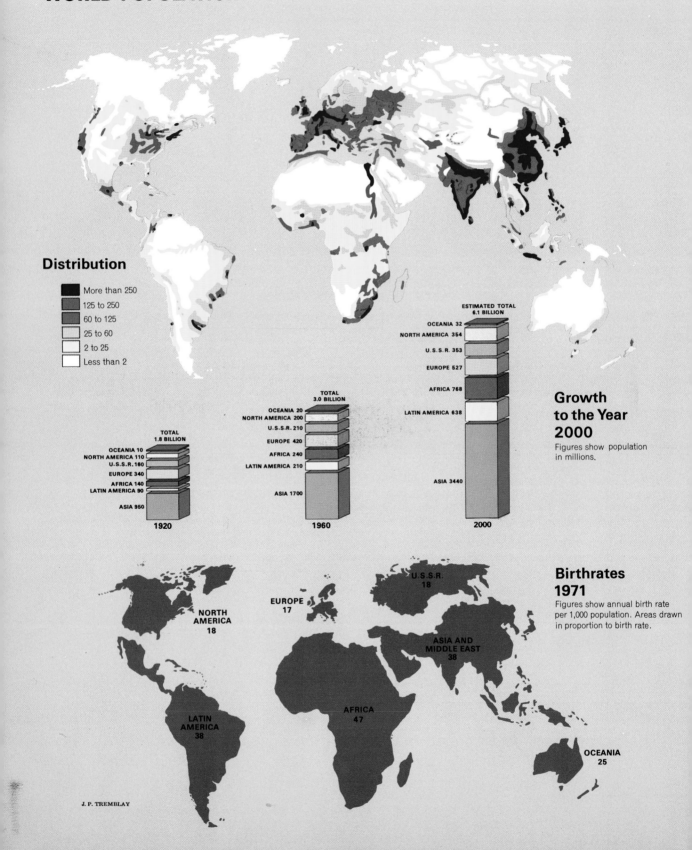

Distribution

- More than 250
- 125 to 250
- 60 to 125
- 25 to 60
- 2 to 25
- Less than 2

Growth to the Year 2000

Figures show population in millions.

ESTIMATED TOTAL 6.1 BILLION

- OCEANIA 32
- NORTH AMERICA 354
- U.S.S.R. 353
- EUROPE 527
- AFRICA 768
- LATIN AMERICA 638
- ASIA 3440

2000

TOTAL 3.0 BILLION

- OCEANIA 20
- NORTH AMERICA 200
- U.S.S.R. 210
- EUROPE 420
- AFRICA 240
- LATIN AMERICA 210
- ASIA 1700

1960

TOTAL 1.8 BILLION

- OCEANIA 10
- NORTH AMERICA 110
- U.S.S.R. 160
- EUROPE 340
- AFRICA 140
- LATIN AMERICA 90
- ASIA 950

1920

Birthrates 1971

Figures show annual birth rate per 1,000 population. Areas drawn in proportion to birth rate.

- NORTH AMERICA 18
- EUROPE 17
- U.S.S.R. 18
- ASIA AND MIDDLE EAST 38
- AFRICA 47
- LATIN AMERICA 38
- OCEANIA 25

J. P. TREMBLAY

The Mainstream of Civilization

Second Edition

1

The Ancient Middle East to *ca.* 500 B.C.

Men have long been interested in their past. But for most peoples the remote past has been very difficult to recover. A few undated monuments, confused mixtures of ancient utensils and ornaments, groups of often contradictory legends were all that was available. As recently as 200 years ago—or about the time of the American Revolution—western scholars knew almost no history before that of the classical age of Greece (*ca.* 500 B.C.). True, there was some understanding of the historical passages of the Hebrew scriptures, and some awareness that the colossal monuments along the Nile were the remnants of a very early Egyptian civilization. But little attention was given to these evidences of the existence of preclassical societies.

Just at this time, however, the excavations at Pompeii began, and the discoveries made there gave a tremendous impetus to the development of the science of archeology. During the past two centuries it has become clear that thousands of years before the Greeks there were highly developed civilizations in many parts of the Old World. About the year 1800, archeologists and historians began to reconstruct the long and fascinating history of ancient Egypt. More recently, in the nineteenth and twentieth centuries, they uncovered many other civilizations—notably in Mesopotamia, in India, and on the island of Crete—whose existence had not been known before.

Although great cities long unknown have been unearthed and whole libraries and archives discovered, the pace of new excavations continues unabated. The historian of the preclassical civilizations must be constantly prepared to revise his interpretations in the light of new evidence.

Human skull from the ruins of Jericho, *ca.* 7000 B.C. The inhabitants of this town developed the art of "portraiture" by modelling the features in plaster and inlaying the eyes with shell in an attempt to reconstruct the face of the dead man.

PREHISTORY TO
ca. 3000 B.C.

Man, or something akin to man, has inhabited the earth for at least a million years and perhaps more. All but the last

Boatmen struggling on the Nile. Relief from a tomb in Sakkara, Old Kingdom (*ca.* 2470–2270 B.C.). The relief shows scenes of life on the Nile.

Art of the Old Stone Age:

Harpoon

Dart thrower of reindeer antler

Baton de commandement of reindeer antler, showing wild horses

5,000 years of this span is regarded as prehistory, since it antedates the invention of writing. The vast sweep of human prehistory from its clouded beginnings to about 7000 B.C. is known as the Old Stone Age because of the primitive stone tools used by manlike animals and by men throughout this era. During the Old Stone Age many species of manlike creatures appeared and disappeared. It was not until about 20,000 B.C. (a relatively recent date in prehistory) that Cro-Magnon man, the species from which all modern men are descended, first wandered into Europe, though we cannot know where or for how long this species may have existed before that time.

The New Stone Age
ca. 7000–3000 B.C.

It took tens of thousands of years to advance from the first crude stone hammers to the precisely made tools characteristic of the New Stone Age. But in the relatively short span of about 4,000 years, there were two basic changes in man's way of life: the introduction of agriculture about 7000 B.C. and the emergence of early cities sometime before 3000 B.C. Both steps seem to have been connected with the drastic changes in climate between about 10,000 and 3000 B.C. that followed the last of the four great Ice Ages and the subsequent melting of the glaciers that had covered much of the Northern Hemisphere.

By about 10,000 B.C. human life seems to have been concentrated in a wide belt embracing southern Europe and northern Africa and extending eastward through Palestine, Syria, Mesopotamia, and Persia to the Indus River and Yellow River valleys. These regions were fertile then and abounded in the animal life on which men fed. But, as the glacier gradually retreated northward, the rainfall decreased and the land became dry. The animals either migrated northward or died out. Man's response was the invention of agriculture—the domestication of plants and animals. Recent historians of agriculture have suggested that the first attempt to plant and harvest grain took place somewhere between Palestine and the upper Tigris-Euphrates Valley about 7000 B.C. Over the next two or three thousand years, the knowledge of farming, and later of animal breeding, spread throughout the areas of human habitation, though many primitive peoples in the hills and hinterlands continued to live only by hunting and food gathering.

As hunters, men had moved about as freely as the animals on which they preyed and as widely as the plants that they foraged, traveling in small bands that needed relatively little organization. As farmers, men had to settle down, at least temporarily. The oldest human settlements uncovered by archeologists date from about 7000 B.C., approximately the same time as the introduction of agriculture. Although little is known about life in these early villages, we can make certain assumptions. With larger numbers of people living and working together, life became more complex and more organization was needed. Men had to find regular patterns of behavior. They had to guide and regulate their relations with one another. These patterns gradually hardened into fixed customs, which replaced whim and violence in settling disagreements. Some sort of chieftain and a council of advisers were needed to enforce these customs and to maintain order; this was the basis of village government. Living in villages, men gave up some of their freedom in return for better protection against human and natural enemies, a more regular supply of food, and a more ordered life. This was, in short, man's first step toward civilization.

EARLY CIVILIZATIONS
ca. 3000–1500 B.C.

With improved food supply and better protection, the number of humans increased rapidly. But at the same time the lands they inhabited continued to dry up. Once again, men found that they would have to develop new techniques if they were to survive. In time some human communities found that they could assure themselves a larger and more regular food supply by cultivating the fertile soil in the valleys of large rivers. But the low-lying lands near the larger rivers provided a far from satisfactory environment. The river banks were too marshy to build on. The steaming swamps along the rivers bred disease.

And the floods that came every spring were often strong enough to sweep away whole villages. If men were to make their homes along the rivers, they would have to learn to drain the swamps, control the floodwaters, and irrigate the higher land away from the river beds. To carry out such projects, men would first have to organize into larger communities, accept more complex and more authoritarian forms of government, and acquire greater technical skills than they then had. It was in valleys of the Tigris-Euphrates, Nile, Indus, and Yellow rivers that the first cities and the first civilizations appeared.

Mesopotamia

The earliest evidences of civilization were found in Mesopotamia (Greek for "between the rivers"), the valley of the Tigris and Euphrates rivers, in what is now Iraq. This Babylonian civilization—as it is often called after the city

THE ANCIENT MIDDLE EAST

Civilization *ca.* 2000 B.C.

Civilization *ca.* 1000 B.C.

Areas of greatest fertility

Desert

0 MILES 300

of Babylon that later dominated the valley—began about 3000 B.C. when a people known as the Sumerians established several city-states in the combined delta of the two rivers. It is still not known where the Sumerians came from. Some historians believe that they migrated into the delta region from much older agricultural villages in the hilly country further up the valley. More likely, they came to Mesopotamia from somewhere else—perhaps by sea, as their own myths suggest.

The Sumerian cities were united in a loose league. They shared a common culture, they spoke a common language, and they worshiped the same gods. A typical Sumerian city-state consisted of the city proper and as much of the surrounding population as the city walls could accommodate in times of crisis. The focal point of each city was a great platform raised above the surrounding residential areas. On it were erected the

A Babylonian boundary stone, *ca.* thirteenth to tenth century B.C., showing an example of cuneiform writing.

places of worship, including ultimately the many-storied temples (ziggurats) that became the typical form of Babylonian monumental architecture.

Writing, in the strict sense of the term, was first invented and employed in Mesopotamia about 3100 B.C. If the Sumerians did not actually originate it, they very soon took it over to represent their language. Most of the earliest examples of Sumerian writing are business records. But school texts appeared almost at once as a means of educating specialists in the new technique. Literary texts and historical records followed in due course. The Sumerians wrote by pressing split reeds on wet clay that was then baked until it was hard. Originally quasi-pictographic, Sumerian writing soon lost all resemblance to pictograms and developed the characteristic symbols called cuneiform (from the Latin word for "wedge-shaped").

The advantages of civilization could not be contained within the confines of the Sumerian city-states. By about 2500 B.C., cities on the Sumerian model had appeared throughout the area from the Tigris-Euphrates Valley to Syria and Palestine on the eastern coast of the Mediterranean—the so-called Fertile Crescent. The people of these newer cities were not Sumerian but Semitic. The Semites, a number of different peoples speaking similar languages, seem to have originated in the Arabian peninsula where they had been nomads who lived by breeding animals. As they recognized the superior attractions of the urbanized area of the Fertile Crescent, Semites moved in several waves into Palestine, Syria, and the parts of Mesopotamia north of the Sumerians. By about 2300 B.C. the old Sumerian cities were merely the core of a much larger civilization that embraced the entire Fertile Crescent and whose population was primarily Semitic.

A Semitic warrior named Sargon (*ca.* 2300 B.C.) was the first to unite the city-states of Mesopotamia into a single empire, though the union survived him by little more than a century. There followed an era of about 150 years when the Sumerians again controlled Mesopotamia. But about 2000 B.C. the valley was conquered by a newly arrived

Hammurabi, *ca.* 1765 B.C.

Semitic people called the Amorites ("westerners"). Under the Amorites the Sumerian Empire at first dissolved into a number of small kingdoms. But in time the city-state of Babylon, under its greatest ruler, Hammurabi (*ca.* 1792–50 B.C.), briefly reunified the entire valley under a single empire.

After Hammurabi's death, Babylon lost its supremacy and Mesopotamia was again divided into a number of small states. The situation was complicated by the appearance of the Kassites, a people of unknown origin. Babylon itself fell to the Kassites soon after 1600 B.C., and southern Mesopotamia was ruled by the Kassites for more than four hundred years. Little is known about this period; what evidence we have suggests a rather stagnant, if peaceful, civilization. Upper Mesopotamia had a more eventful existence, but Babylonia did not resume its primary role in the development of Mesopotamian civilization until the eighth century B.C.

The economy of the pre-Kassite Babylonian civilization was based on commerce as well as agriculture. There was so much buying and leasing and trading that the Babylonians, earlier than most other peoples, developed a system of commercial law. Over the centuries, many Babylonian rulers attempted to collect the laws of the various cities and collate them into a single legal code. The

most extensive and comprehensive of them was the Code of Hammurabi.

Babylonian laws seem harsh today. Some offenses called for the loss of the tongue or a hand. Many were punishable, at least in theory, by death. But we must remember that the Babylonian codes represented an early stage in the evolution of law and that they reflected an even more primitive era when violence was the only recourse for a man who had been offended or cheated. The very creation of written laws, impossible before there were governments strong enough to enforce them, was a major advance toward justice and order.

The Babylonians produced the first known mathematics. They handled rather complicated problems in arithmetic and geometry; they also had some understanding of algebra. Babylonian numbers were ordered on multiples of sixty (unlike our own, which are ordered on multiples of ten), and such Mesopotamian units of measure as the sixty-minute hour and the 360-degree circle are still in use.

Although urban life brought many advantages and a higher level of living for part of the population, no region in Mesopotamia enjoyed long periods of peace and prosperity. The rival states were frequently at war, and often whole cities were razed to the ground. Devastating floods and plagues swept through

Ziggurat of Ur, *ca.* 2250 B.C.

ca. 3100 B.C.	ca. 2700	ca. 2150	ca. 2050	ca. 1650	ca. 1550	ca. 1100	ca. 650	525
Proto-Dynastio	Old Kingdom		Middle Kingdom		New Kingdom		3rd intermediate period	

1st intermediate period   2nd intermediate period   Saïte Dynasty

the lands. These uncertainties were especially shocking to business-oriented communities in which men were seeking individual profit rather than group survival. The Babylonians took a gloomy view of life, seeing their gods as selfish beings who paid little heed to men except to deliver an occasional blow, apparently out of sheer caprice. Babylonian religion was roughly like a business arrangement: The Babylonians believed that if they performed certain ceremonies the gods would leave them in peace. There was a great deal of magic and very little morality in their religious observances. To appease the gods, it was more important to know the right prayers and the appropriate sacrifices than it was to lead an upright life. And yet these same people set very high standards in their business dealings with one another.

The Emergence
of Egyptian Civilization

In the same era in which the Mesopotamian city-states were battling the elements, one another, and a succession of foreign invaders, another civilization appeared, matured, and flourished in relative serenity only 900 miles away, in Egypt. The Nile Valley, seat of the ancient Egyptian civilization, extends about 600 miles into Africa; although in Upper (southern) Egypt the fertile belt along the river is rarely more than ten miles wide. The Delta in Lower (northern) Egypt forms a large triangle that widens steadily until it reaches the sea, but much of the land in the Delta is swampy because the Nile splits into many branches. Primitive agricultural communities appeared along the banks of the Nile as early as 5000 B.C. when a variety of peoples, including both Negroes and Semites, sought refuge there from the encroaching deserts. About 4000 B.C. these communities began to consolidate into a series of small kingdoms, and by 3000 B.C. the entire Nile

Valley had been united under a single monarch.

The civilization that began to appear in Egypt shortly before 3000 B.C. may have received an initial stimulus from Mesopotamia. But Egypt, unlike Mesopotamia, was rapidly united under a single political and economic system, and Egyptian civilization matured more rapidly than that of Mesopotamia. Once established, Egyptian civilization endured as a separate and clearly identifiable entity until Egypt was absorbed by the Persian Empire in 525 B.C.—a span of 2500 years, as long a period as that from 525 B.C. to the present.

Egypt had many advantages over Mesopotamia, most of them derived from the peculiar nature and position of the Nile Valley. The flooding of the Tigris and Euphrates rivers was irregular and unpredictable. Sometimes there was not enough water to irrigate the crops; at other times heavy floods might wipe out a whole year's harvest. But the Nile flooded every year at the same time and rose to very nearly the same level, and Egyptian life could be geared to the rhythmic regularity of the river. Also, the Mesopotamian plain was open to invasion on all sides, and the frequent incursion of new peoples helped to keep the region divided into warring states. The Nile Valley was exposed to invasion only at its northern and southern extremities. Invasions were less frequent than in Mesopotamia, and when they did occur they could be dealt with easily by a unified military effort.

Thus, it was relatively easy and obviously useful for the small kingdoms along the Nile to consolidate into the large states of Upper (southern) and Lower (northern) Egypt. Some sort of struggle obviously preceded the unification of the "Two Lands" (as Egypt was named by its contemporaries), but it occurred so early that only traces of it remain in religious legends. During almost all its history, ancient Egypt was ruled by kings who wore the double crown of the North and the South.

The long expanse of ancient Egyptian history can be divided into four eras, each preceded by a period of transition that began with internal weakness and ended with national consolidation and expansion. Thus the first four centuries of proto-dynastic unification (*ca.* 3100–2700 B.C.) were followed by the Old Kingdom (or the Pyramid Age) from about 2700 to 2150 B.C. Collapse of central power (*ca.* 2150–2050 B.C.) was rapidly reversed by the rise of the Middle Kingdom (*ca.* 2050–1650 B.C.). This era ended with another weakening of central authority and the conquest of Egypt by the Hyksos (*ca.* 1650–1550 B.C.). The expulsion of the Hyksos led to the period of Egypt's greatest expansion under the New Kingdom (*ca.* 1550–1100 B.C.). The next decline was longer (*ca.* 1100–650 B.C.), and the brief revival under the Saïte dynasty (*ca.* 650–525 B.C.) was only a pale reflection of former glories. The Persian conquest of 525 B.C. ended the independence of ancient Egypt.

The Old Kingdom and Middle Kingdom in Egypt ca. 2700–1550 B.C.

The era of the Old Kingdom in Egypt was one of the most dynamic periods in the history of man. Within three or four centuries after civilization first appeared in the Nile Valley, some of the most notable achievements of the Egyptian civilization had already been realized: the erection of a strong monarchy and a complex bureaucracy capable of maintaining peace and order throughout the country; the introduction of hieroglyphics, a very complicated system of writing based on pictographs; the development of sufficient engineering skill to erect large stone structures (including the pyramids) for the first time in the history of man; and the invention of a calendar so accurate that, with minor modifications, it is still in use.

The most important factor in the rapid progress of Egyptian civilization was that all the abundant agricultural resources and ample manpower of the Nile Valley were controlled by a single divine and absolute ruler, known to us,

from the Hebrew scriptures, as the pharaoh. The Egyptians believed that the land belonged to the gods. They were grateful to the gods for the gifts of water and grain; and they were beholden to them for the use of the land. They worshiped their pharaoh as one of their gods and as the earthly representative of all the gods, a status accorded to very few Mesopotamian kings. With this unquestioning loyalty of their subjects, the powerful pharaohs of the Old Kingdom were able to administer Egypt almost as a private estate. Agents of the pharaoh—using their calendars to predict the regular rise and fall of the Nile—told the Egyptian peasants when and where to plant their seed and when to harvest their crops. Such a planned economy ensured a maximum yield, and much of the profit was used to enrich and strengthen the government.

Egyptian peasants seem not to have objected to their servile status. Rather

Egyptian Religion   Fourteenth century B.C.

Morality and the Last Judgment in the Book of the Dead.

Hail to you, ye gods. . . . Behold, I came to you without sin, without evil, without wrong. . . . I gave bread to the hungry, water to the thirsty, clothing to the naked, and a ferry to him without a boat. I made divine offerings for the gods and food offerings for the dead. Save me! Protect me!

Monotheism in the hymn to the sun-god (Aton). This was written during the brief period when King Akhnaton (1376–1362 B.C.) was trying to establish the cult of a single sun-god.

How manifold are thy works!
They are hidden before men.
O sole God, beside whom is no other,
Thou didst create the earth according to thy heart . . .
Thou didst make the distant sky in order to rise therein,
In order to behold all that thou hast made
While thou wast yet alone.
Shining in thy form as living Aton,
Dawning, glittering, going afar and returning.
Thou makest millions of forms
Through thyself alone.

From James H. Breasted, *The Dawn of Conscience* (New York: Scribner, 1934), pp. 259, 284–85.

Ramses II, ruler of the Egyptian Empire at its height, built this temple to Amon at Karnak. Below is a colossal statue of Ramses at Karnak. At his knees is his queen, Nefertari.

they accepted the authority of the pharaoh as necessary to their well-being. Unlike the Mesopotamians, who feared the caprice and ill will of many of their deities, the Egyptians thought of their gods—including the pharaoh—as well disposed toward men.

Because the Egyptians buried their dead on the fringes of the desert, in places that were never cultivated, thousands of their tombs have survived. From the contents of these tombs we can get a clearer view of Egyptian religious beliefs than those of other ancient peoples. It is evident that the Egyptians were tremendously interested in the afterlife and that they devoted much of their energy and wealth to assure survival in the next world. Other peoples believed that the soul might linger in some shady nether world, but the Egyptians were convinced that man participated in the same life-death-rebirth cycle they observed in nature. In Egypt's clear, dry air, dead bodies did not decompose; they turned brown and brittle like the grain stalks. Thus it seemed natural to the Egyptians that if the soul of a man—like the seed of a plant—could be preserved through the human equivalent of a "dry" season, he would be restored to life in another world when the time came for his rebirth.

The Egyptians gave considerable attention to the problem of providing the soul with a suitable place to reside when the body died. In the era of the Old Kingdom, the Egyptians apparently believed that only the pharaoh's soul had to be preserved and that he would take care of the rest of his subjects in the afterworld. It was to provide an elaborate palace for their afterlives that some of the earlier pharaohs built the pyramids between about 2700 and 2200 B.C. In later eras more individualistic views prevailed and even people of moderate means built tombs for themselves, furnished with texts to guide them to the next world and with provisions for the journey.

The pyramids are only the most impressive examples of the remarkable engineering skill of the ancient Egyptians. The concentration of wealth and manpower under a single strong government made it possible for the Egyptians to build many magnificent temples, tombs, and statues on a scale that could be rivaled only in the greatest states of Mesopotamia. Although even the Egyptians did not attempt to build anything so large as the pyramids after the era of the Old Kingdom, structures like the temple at Karnak, built in the era of the New Kingdom, are still awe-inspiring in their size and artistic perfection. The pharaohs, who were gods, built like gods; their temples dominated space just as their statues dominated representations of ordinary men.

Egypt's first long period of peaceful development, under the Old Kingdom, ended about 2150 B.C. when a series of weak pharaohs permitted the government to fall into the hands of powerful local administrators. Without centralized supervision, Egypt experienced an era of local famines and civil wars. After a century of turmoil, the country was reunited under the Middle Kingdom (*ca.* 2050–1650 B.C.). But toward the end of this era, Egypt again experienced a time of troubles, caused largely by foreign invaders. The invaders were known as the Hyksos, and their origin is still not exactly clear. They were probably a Semitic people (perhaps Amorites) whose kinsmen had already conquered the eastern arm of the Fertile Crescent. Aided by their horse-drawn chariots, they gained control of Egypt and then established themselves strongly in the Delta. Elsewhere they were weaker, and they were unable to govern all Egypt for more than a century. Native armies began to push them back and by about 1550 B.C. the Hyksos had been expelled from Egypt.

It was perhaps no accident that Mesopotamia was overrun by the Kassites at just about the same time that the Hyksos attacked Egypt. Growth of population created pressures for expansion, and new military techniques, such as the horse-drawn chariot, facilitated conquest. But Egypt recovered much more rapidly from the Hyksos domination than Mesopotamia did from the Kassite conquests.

Crete

The island of Crete stretches for over 150 miles across the entrance to the Aegean Sea. The Greeks preserved leg-ends about a great King Minos of Crete who was so powerful that even the city of Athens had to send him an annual tribute. But since the sandy soil of Crete has barely been able to sustain its small population throughout historical times, no one was inclined to take the legend of a powerful kingdom on the island very seriously. Then in 1900 Arthur Evans, an English archeologist, dug into a mound on the northern coast of Crete and uncovered a magnificent palace, the size of a small city, which he assumed to be Knossos, the ancient capital of King Minos.

In addition to the palace at Knossos, Evans and his successors discovered many other sites. They were able to show that a civilization, separate from those of Egypt and Mesopotamia, had flourished on the island from about 2000 to 1400 B.C. This civilization had a style of its own, not monumental like the Egyptian nor stolid like the Mesopotamian, but delicate and cheerful, made for men and not for gods. Evans called it the Minoan civilization after the legendary King Minos. During this era the Minoans seem to have prospered not by farming, but by dominating the trade of the Aegean and the eastern Mediterranean.

The archeologists found that the

Ceremonial axe of victory over Hyksos showing the pharaoh Ahmose smiting an enemy.

Cretan fresco of court ladies seated around a pillar shrine at a public festival, from the palace at Knossos.

At top is a seal stone impression of earliest form of Minoan writing, from which Linear A developed. Below is Linear A tablet. At bottom is Linear B tablet.

Minoan civilization must have succumbed to some great catastrophe, for virtually every settlement they discovered showed evidence of violent destruction dating from about 1480 B.C. The palace at Knossos was rebuilt after the catastrophe, but Evans concluded that it was occupied by a people other than its original inhabitants. His main proof was that in the palace he discovered examples of tablets inscribed with two distinct scripts. One of them, which he called Linear Script A, was used throughout the island during the whole era of the Minoan civilization. The second, Linear Script B, was used only at Knossos and only after the rebuilding of the palace.

Many questions still remain unanswered: Who were the Minoan people? Where did they come from and how did their civilization originate? What was their society like? What form of government did they have? What great disaster overtook the island of Crete about 1480 B.C.? And who were the people who occupied the palace at Knossos after that time?

Two recent discoveries provide some clues to these questions. In 1954 an Englishman named Michael Ventris showed that Linear Script B was actually an old way of writing Greek, which means that the people who occupied the palace after its original destruction were probably Greeks. Then in 1966 a group of American oceanographers discovered a thick layer of volcanic ash at the bottom of the eastern Mediterranean. They were able to demonstrate that around 1480 B.C., on an island about one hundred miles north of Crete, there had been a volcanic eruption four times more violent than any ever recorded. Such a disaster could well account for the destruction of Knossos and other sites on the island of Crete at about that time.

Linear Script A has not yet been conclusively deciphered; until it is most of the story of the Minoan civilization must remain a mystery. But with the few clues now available we can attempt a reconstruction, however hypothetical, of Minoan history.

Archeological evidence indicates that the first civilized settlers on Crete arrived from Asia Minor some time after 3000 B.C., that they were at least partly Semitic, and that they had already learned some of the elements of civilization from Mesopotamia. The island of Crete was ideally situated for controlling the commerce between Mesopotamia or Egypt and the more primitive peoples on the shores of Europe. Thus it has been assumed that the Minoan civilization that emerged was based on trade.

The greater part of Minoan trade was apparently with the villages located around the Aegean Sea. The populations of these settlements began to increase rapidly after about 2000 B.C. when the Greeks, migrating south from central Europe, began to settle in the lands around the Aegean (see p. 28). Minoan trade increased proportionately, so that the height of Minoan prosperity, and of Minoan civilization, came after 2000 B.C.

In time the Greeks created a civilization of their own, known as the Mycenaean civilization, which owed a good deal to the Minoan example (see p. 28). By 1500 B.C. Greek traders were competing with the Minoans in the markets of the Aegean and also in Syria and Egypt.

Greeks apparently occupied the palace at Knossos after the Minoan civilization had been weakened by disaster about 1480 B.C. They probably attempted to dominate the island and to take over its commerce. About 1400 B.C. the palace was again destroyed, possibly as a result of a revolt of the Minoans against their Greek rulers. At any rate the Minoan civilization declined rapidly after this time. By about 1200 B.C. it had virtually disappeared and the island of Crete was nothing more than a part of the Greek civilization.

The Indo-Europeans

The Greeks were but one of several peoples known collectively as Indo-Europeans. The term *Indo-European*, like the term *Semitic*, does not refer to a race of related peoples. Rather it describes a mixture of peoples speaking similar languages. Their ancestors may have come from various parts of the earth, but at some stage in their histories—the stage in which their languages took form—they apparently lived close to one another. For this reason, their cultures as well as their languages developed certain common characteristics.

Shortly before they first appear in history—about 2000 B.C.—the Indo-European peoples seem to have been concentrated somewhere north of the Black Sea between the Danube and the Volga rivers. From this center, as their numbers grew, they spread out in all directions. In the era between about 2000 and 1000 B.C. several waves of Indo-European peoples migrated southward toward the Mediterranean. The western-most branch—consisting of several separate tribes (including the Latins)—crossed the Alps and settled in Italy.

We have already seen that the Greeks, whose language was similar to Latin, settled in the Aegean area at about the same time. Still further east were the Hittites, who ruled an empire in Asia Minor from about 1800 to 1200 B.C. The Hittites were among the first people to use horses and iron weapons in combat and were one of the most feared military powers of their time. The easternmost branch of the Indo-Europeans occupied northern India, also in the same era.

By 1000 B.C. Indo-European peoples had occupied all of the continent of Europe. It is from their languages that most tongues spoken in the western world today are derived, including the Romance languages (such as Italian, Spanish, and French), the Germanic lan-

Race

Race and language are not the same. This should be obvious, for not all who speak Arabic are Arabians and not all who speak English are of the White race. . . . A man's hereditary features and the language he speaks depend on two different sets of circumstances. His hereditary anatomy depends upon his remote ancestors, and his language depends upon the speech he heard as a child.

A race does not move forward as a whole. . . . Race is not a touch-stone by which civilized people can be separated from uncivilized. . . . The lesson of history is that pre-eminence in cultural achievement has passed from one race to another, from one continent to another; it has embraced not whole "races" but certain fragments of an ethnic group which were for certain historical reasons favorably situated at the moment.

From Ruth Benedict, *Race: Science and Politics* (New York: Viking, 1945), Ch. 2, pp. 9, 18.

guages (such as English, German, and Dutch), the Celtic languages (such as Gaelic and Welsh), and the Slavic languages (such as Russian, Polish, and Czech). The Persian and Sanskrit languages spoken in Asia are also of Indo-European origin.

The Spread of Civilization

Before 2000 B.C. civilization was still not very widespread even in the Middle East, where Egypt, Mesopotamia, and Crete were fairly close and had some contacts with one another. There was a civilization in the Indus Valley that traded with Mesopotamia and an even more isolated civilization in the Yellow River Valley of China (see p. 133). The rest of the Middle East and East Asia was still inhabited by peoples who had not gone much beyond the village level of organization. But the wealth and skills of Egypt, Mesopotamia, and Crete impressed their neighbors and encouraged them to build more complex societies. By 2000 B.C. Mesopotamian civilization, the most dynamic because of its active trade beyond its own frontiers, had spread throughout the Fertile Crescent to include Syria and Palestine as well as the Mesopotamian valley. It became almost contiguous with Egypt.

By about 1500 B.C. the Greeks and the

The Tomb of Tutankhamon

The English archeologist Howard Carter writes of the excitement of uncovering the tomb of the pharaoh Tutankhamon in 1922.

Slowly . . . the remains of passage debris that encumbered the lower part of the doorway were removed, until at last we had the whole door clear before us. The decisive moment had arrived. With trembling hands I made a tiny breach in the upper left hand corner. Darkness and blank space, as far as an iron testing-rod could reach, showed that whatever lay beyond was empty, and not filled like the passage we had just cleared. Candle tests were applied as a precaution against possible foul gases, and then, widening the hole a little, I inserted the candle and peered in. . . . At first I could see nothing, . . . but presently, as my eyes grew accustomed to the light, details of the room within emerged slowly from the mist, strange animals, statues, and gold—everywhere the glint of gold.

From Howard Carter and A. C. Mace, *The Tomb of Tut-ankh-Amen* (London: Cassell, 1923), I, 95–96.

The gold-plated inner coffin of the pharaoh Tutankhamon (*ca.* 1340 B.C.).

Hittites were also building cities, organizing states, and engaging in wide-ranging trading ventures. Thus a civilized world extended without a break from the Aegean Sea to the Persian Gulf. With the influx of new peoples and the steady increase in the populations of the older centers, the number of people in this civilized area was probably four or five times greater in 1500 B.C. than it had been in 2000 B.C. Trade increased proportionately, and with it the general standard of living. In the prosperous period between about 1500 and 1200 B.C., the leading power of the ancient world was Egypt. The Minoan civilization disappeared shortly after 1500 B.C., and much of the Mesopotamian world was still under the control of less advanced northern peoples.

THE NEW KINGDOM IN EGYPT
ca. 1550–1100 B.C.

Egypt had been freed from foreign domination about 1560 when an Egyptian nobleman named Ahmose led a successful revolt against the Hyksos rulers and established himself as pharaoh of all Egypt. The reign of Ahmose marked the beginning of the New Kingdom, the most glorious phase of Egypt's long history.

The Egyptian Empire

Ahmose not only expelled the hated Hyksos; he pursued them across the desert to Palestine and Syria. To prevent further invasions, he placed both of these lands under Egyptian protection. Thus for the first time the Egyptians abandoned their centuries-old tradition of isolation and extended their rule to areas beyond their borders. The Egyptian Empire inaugurated by Ahmose later included not only Palestine but also Libya to the west and Nubia to the south.

Under the New Kingdom, Egypt also began to take an active part in the Mediterranean trade that had already enriched the Minoan and Mesopotamian civilizations. After the fall of Crete, Egypt dominated the commerce of the eastern Mediterranean for several centuries.

With tribute from their empire and

with commerce to convert their bounteous grain supply into cash, the wealthy and powerful pharaohs of the New Kingdom created the most elaborate architectural monuments in Egyptian history. These pharaohs were no longer content with stark pyramids for their graves; instead, they carved lavishly decorated tombs out of the sandstone cliffs of the Upper Nile. The discovery in 1922 of the tomb of Tutankhamon (*ca.* 1340 B.C.)—the only tomb that had not been completely sacked by thieves over the centuries—provided historians with an invaluable source of information on the life and tastes of the upper classes of the New Kingdom.

Akhnaton, ca. 1363–1347 B.C.

Through most of the history of the New Kingdom, Egypt was at war with the

Head of a colossus of Akhnaton at Karnak (*ca.* 1370 B.C.).

THE HITTITE AND EGYPTIAN EMPIRES *ca.* 1450 B.C.

Hittites over the control of Syria and Palestine. Thus most of the pharaohs of the era were warriors. One exception was Akhnaton, who was a religious reformer. Akhnaton tried to superimpose on the ancient and complex religious traditions of Egypt the worship of Aton, god of the sun-disk, whom he believed to be the supreme and perhaps even the only god. This is the first instance in history of something close to the concept of pure monotheism: the belief in one god. But Akhnaton's religion was never popular in Egypt. The old religious beliefs were deeply ingrained in the thinking of the Egyptian people, and the priests of the old gods, who guarded the formulas for entrance into the afterlife, were far too powerful to be bypassed, even by the pharaoh. As a result, soon after Akhnaton's death the old religion was restored.

Akhnaton was a sensitive man given to writing poetry but little interested in affairs of state. Largely as a result of his negligence, Egypt lost Syria to the Hittites and declined as a military power. Akhnaton's immediate successors proved as weak as he, and the dynasty founded by Ahmose ended ignominiously with a military coup. Subsequent pharaohs regained some of the territory and prestige that Egypt had lost, but a series of protracted wars between Egypt and the Hittites over control of Syria resulted in the exhaustion of both these powers by about 1150 B.C.

THE ERA OF SMALL KINGDOMS
ca. 1250–750 B.C.

Between about 1250 and 900 B.C. new Indo-European invasions upset the stability of the ancient world. In the Aegean area the invaders were another wave of Greeks, called Dorians (see p. 29), who nearly destroyed the struggling Mycenaean culture that had survived the fall of Crete three centuries earlier. Other Indo-Europeans moved into Asia Minor. They overthrew the Hittite Empire, already weak after its wars with Egypt, and established several smaller kingdoms in its place. Many people of the Aegean area, mostly Greeks, fled from the invaders in fleets of small boats. Ostensibly, these "sea-peoples" were looking for new homes, but they were quite ready to engage in piracy and plundering along the way. Their attacks on Egyptian shipping and their raids in the Nile Delta contributed to the decline of the New Kingdom and ended Egypt's role as a commercial power.

After the decline of the Hittite and Egyptian empires, no strong power appeared in the Middle East until the rise of the Assyrian Empire about four centuries later. During those centuries several small kingdoms and city-states emerged in the lands at the eastern end of the Mediterranean now occupied by Syria, Lebanon, and Israel. Before about 1200 B.C. these lands had been occupied by a Semitic people known as Canaanites, whose culture was derived from that

THE MIDDLE EAST *ca.* 800 B.C.

of Mesopotamia. But Ahmose, as we have seen, had placed this area under Egyptian protection. When Egypt declined as a world power and Egyptian garrisons were withdrawn, the Canaanite cities were left defenseless. In the period between about 1200 and 1000 B.C., the "sea-peoples" attacked them from the Mediterranean, while two new waves of Semitic peoples, first the Hebrews and later the Aramaeans, attacked them from the east and south.

Eventually most of the Canaanite cities succumbed to the invaders. The "sea-peoples," now known as the Philistines, established a string of independent city-states along the coast of the Mediterranean. Inland, the Aramaeans settled in what became the kingdom of Syria, with its capital at Damascus. South of Syria were the two smaller Hebrew kingdoms of Israel and Judah, of which more will be said later.

The Phoenicians

The only Canaanite cities to survive the invasions were those along the rocky coast of Syria that were relatively easy to defend. The inhabitants of these cities were a mixture of Canaanites and "sea-peoples" and were known as Phoenicians. When the raids of the "sea-peoples'' subsided, Phoenician ships were the first to venture into the Mediterranean. By about 1100 B.C. the Phoenicians had begun to revive the trade routes abandoned by the Minoans and the Egyptians, and for the next three centuries they controlled Mediterranean commerce.

The ancient trade routes from India and the East were still funneling goods into Mesopotamia. From there, the eastern wares, along with local Mesopotamian produce, moved along the Aramaean caravan routes to one of the Phoenician cities. Here they were loaded onto small ships bound for Egypt, Asia Minor, North Africa, or even western Europe. Returning ships carried raw materials from the western Mediterranean back to the Phoenician cities, where they were fashioned into finished products and sent to the markets of Mesopotamia.

The Phoenicians were better sailors than any other ancient peoples, even the Greeks. They were the first people from the Middle East to trade and colonize in western Europe. They were also the first on record to venture beyond Gibraltar into the Atlantic, for their ships sailed regularly to Brittany and Cornwall to obtain the tin needed in the manufacture of bronze. Egyptian sources suggest that the Phoenicians may have sailed around Africa, a feat that would not be repeated until the fifteenth century A.D. Some scholars believe that the Phoenicians may even have reached America.

The largest Phoenician city was Tyre. But by far the oldest—dating from before 2000 B.C.—was Byblos, which specialized in the manufacture of writing materials. It was from Byblos that the Greeks took their word for "book"—*biblion*—and it is from *biblion* that we get such English words as *Bible* and *bibliography*. The Phoenicians also helped to refine and to spread the use of the West Semitic system of writing. Ultimately reduced to only twenty-two letters that could be drawn and recognized without difficulty, the Phoenician alphabet was much easier to use and to understand than cuneiform or hieroglyphic writing. For the first time in history it was possible for almost anyone to learn to read and write without long years of training. Learning could be

more widely diffused and more men could enter administrative careers. The Phoenician alphabet provided the basis for all three of the major alphabets now in use in the western world: the Hebrew, the Latin (which we use), and the Greek. The Greek alphabet, in turn, is the basis for the Cyrillic alphabet used in Russia and much of eastern Europe. And an Aramaic version of the West Semitic script formed the basis for the writing systems of India. It is curious that so useful a discovery was never duplicated, even by such ingenious people as the Chinese.

Just as the merchants of Europe later brought their civilization to America in their search for new markets and raw materials, the Phoenician traders carried the civilization of the Middle East to the western Mediterranean. They established colonies and trading posts in many places, particularly on the island of Sicily and in North Africa. The largest Phoenician colony was at Carthage, located near the site of modern Tunis. Here the Phoenician settlers were able to make serfs of the natives and to put them to work on large plantations growing agricultural products for the home markets.

The Phoenician cities came under the domination of the Assyrian Empire after about 750 B.C., and declined rapidly thereafter. At that time the leading merchant families emigrated to Carthage, which became the center of the Phoenician world until it was destroyed by the Romans in 146 B.C.

The Hebrews

Among the peoples of the ancient world, the Hebrews played a relatively unimportant political role. If one were to consider only their significance to their contemporaries, one might dismiss them with a few sentences or perhaps not mention them at all. But during the years from about 1200 to 400 B.C. the Hebrews developed a religion that was unique among ancient peoples and that has given their history enormous significance to the modern world. Their religion has helped the Hebrews to maintain their identity, even to the present day, whereas most ancient peoples mixed

Typical letters of the alphabet in Phoenician, Greek, and Roman forms. The final Greek letter, Omega, is pronounced like the Roman long *o*.

Phoenician	Greek	Roman
𐤀	A	A
𐤁	B	B
𐤂	Γ	G
𐤃	Δ	D
𐤄	E	E
𐤅	[Y]	F
𐤆	Z	Z
𐤇		H
𐤈	I	I
𐤉	K	[K]
𐤋	Λ	L
𐤌	M	M
𐤍	N	N
𐤏	O	O
𐤐	Π	P
𐤒		Q
𐤓	P	R
𐤔	Σ	S
𐤕	T	T
	Υ	U,V
	X	X
	Ω	

A God of Social Justice

with one another or with successive waves of conquerors. Moreover, because the ancient Hebrews maintained a detailed record of the evolving relationship between themselves and their God, Jahweh, their scriptures constitute one of the richest original sources for ancient history. The religion developed by the ancient Hebrews provided the basis for three of the major religions of the modern world: Judaism, Christianity, and Islam.

Most of the Hebrew scripture (that part known to Christians as the Old Testament) was written down by many different authors between about 1000 and 150 B.C. It includes rules of law and religious behavior, legend, history, poetry, prophecy, and apocalyptic visions. But it is given unity by the firm belief in an enduring relationship between God and His people. The first several books recount the stories preserved by the Hebrews about their early history. Although recent archeological discoveries show that many of these stories may well be based on actual historical events (just as archeologists have shown that the poems of Homer, written at about the same time, are probably based on actual events in Greek history), there is not enough evidence to reconstruct the history of the Hebrews before about 850 B.C. with any certainty.

According to their scriptures, all Hebrews were descended from Abraham, who migrated westward from Ur in Mesopotamia when Jahweh promised him and his descendants the land of Canaan (Palestine). Abraham's grandson Jacob (also called Israel) had twelve sons who were believed to be the progenitors of the twelve tribes into which the Hebrews were later divided. Joseph, one of Jacob's sons, was taken to Egypt as a slave but later rose to a high position in the pharaoh's government. His father and his brothers then joined him in Egypt. The second book of the Old Testament, *Exodus,* explains that a new pharaoh arose who "knew not Joseph," and who reduced the children of Israel (by then a sizable tribe) to slavery. It is here that we are introduced to Moses, one of the most impressive figures in all literature.

Moses was an Israelite who, according to the account in *Exodus,* was raised by a daughter of the pharaoh. One day when Moses was alone in the wilderness, Jahweh, the God of Abraham, called to him. While Moses listened in awe and terror, Jahweh renewed His Covenant with the children of Israel: to guide and protect them as long as they worshiped Him and Him only and obeyed His laws. Jahweh then ordered Moses to lead His people back to the land of Palestine. Moses led the Israelites out of Egypt into the Sinai Desert, where they remained for forty years before trying to enter Palestine. During this sojourn in the desert, Jahweh gave Moses the Law, which included the Ten Commandments and a long catalogue of religious, ethical, and juridical regulations.

Two books, *Joshua* and *Judges,* give differing accounts of the Hebrew attack on Palestine after the death of Moses. Here we are on somewhat more solid historical ground, since Egyptian records show that the Canaanite cities were attacked by tribes from the desert during the thirteenth century B.C. Archeological evidence also shows that Jericho and several neighboring cities were besieged and destroyed at about that time. The Hebrew conquest was complicated by the more or less simultaneous arrival of the Philistines, who attacked from the sea. For about a century a three-way battle took place among the Hebrews, the Canaanites, and the Philistines.

In the final stages of the conquest of the Canaanites, the Hebrew tribes decided to unite under a king. Samuel, a religious leader, chose Saul (*ca.* 1000 B.C.) as the first king and later designated David (*ca.* 1000–960 B.C.) as Saul's successor. It was King David who completed the conquest of the Canaanites and the Philistines and united the Hebrew people under a single kingdom with its capital at Jerusalem. The Philistines were permitted to maintain their independent cities along the coast but the Canaanites were eventually absorbed by the Hebrews. Since the Canaanites had been exposed to Mesopotamian influence, they may have been the source of the many Mesopotamian elements in the Hebrew culture, such as the story of the Flood.

Solomon (*ca.* 960–930 B.C.), David's son and successor, built an impressive royal palace and a temple to Jahweh in Jerusalem and established commercial and diplomatic relations with neighboring states. The Hebrew people, however, whose memory of tribal independence was still fresh, resented Solomon's royal pretensions and high taxes. At Solomon's death, the northern tribes seceded and created the new kingdom of Israel under another dynasty. From about 930 B.C. on, there were two Hebrew kingdoms: Israel in the north, the larger and more prosperous of the two; and Judah in the south, a smaller agricultural kingdom that remained loyal to the house of David.

According to the Bible, the Hebrew concept of monotheism goes back at least to the time of Moses. But monotheism—the worship of one god—does not necessarily imply that this god is sovereign over the entire earth and is to be worshiped by all peoples. When they first entered Palestine the Israelites believed that, according to their Covenant, they were to worship only Jahweh and to obey His laws, but that other people might worship other gods. They seem to have conceived of Jahweh as being rather like the gods of other nomadic desert peoples: He protected them from their enemies, He took their side in battles, and He provided them with food and water.

Once the Hebrews had ceased to be desert nomads and had settled down as farmers in Palestine, the worship of a desert god had less meaning for them. Although Jahweh remained the official national god of the Hebrews, many of them turned also to the Baalim, the Canaanite version of the Mesopotamian fertility gods. The conflict between the Baal-worshipers and the defenders of Jahweh produced the first Hebrew prophets, such as Elijah and Elisha. These peripatetic preachers warned that Baal-worship was a breach of the Covenant and would bring the wrath of Jahweh down upon all the Hebrew people. The recorded versions of their preaching include some of the most stirring passages in any literature.

The teaching of the prophet Amos (*ca.* 750 B.C.) marks a turning point in the evolution of the Hebrew religion. In powerful measured verse, Amos named the various neighboring peoples known

Semite prisoner inscribed on a relief at the temple of Luxor (perhaps dating from period of Hebrew residence in Egypt).

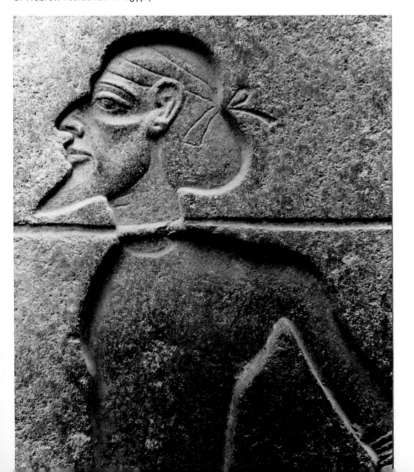

to the Hebrews, listed their sins, and promised that Jahweh would punish them. Although Amos himself may not have realized it, in so preaching he became the first Hebrew teacher—as far as written records show—to speak of Jahweh not merely as the God of the Hebrews but as a god whose law extended to all people.

Amos did not stop, however, after he had listed the sins of Israel's neighbors. He reached a crescendo of fury when he spoke of the sins of the Hebrews themselves. In the time of Amos, many Hebrews were beginning to live in cities and to engage in trade. They were beginning to learn, as the Greeks were learning at the same time, that when a society first turns to a money economy, some men become very rich while others are reduced to poverty or even servitude. The Greeks considered the problem a political matter to be solved through consti-

tutional reforms. For Amos, as for most Hebrews, it was a religious matter. The Hebrews were sinning against Jahweh, he warned, when they sold "the righteous for silver, and the needy for a pair of shoes." Amos gave a new dimension to the worship of Jahweh by stating explicitly something that was already implicit throughout the Law of Moses—namely, that Jahweh was a god of social justice. Thus in Amos we find the first clear expression of the concept of ethical monotheism that made the Hebrew religion unique in the ancient world.

The teachings of such later prophets as Hosea, Isaiah, and Jeremiah reflect a continuing evolution in the Hebrew concept of Jahweh. They presented a universal abstract God, who could be reached by his worshipers wherever they were; a God possessed of infinite power, and infinite sanctity, and infinite love; a God far above the need for the petty

THE ASSYRIAN EMPIRE   *ca.* 700 B.C.

sacrifices of the Baal-worshipers; a God whose relationship to His people was that of a loving father.

The repeated warnings of the prophets that Jahweh would punish the Hebrews for their sins were reinforced by the growing danger from the Assyrians to the east. By the eighth century this militaristic people had gained control of most of Mesopotamia and had already begun to threaten the small states along the Mediterranean coast. There could be no doubt in the minds of the Hebrews just what form Jahweh's punishment would take should it ever come.

A NEW AGE OF EMPIRES
ca. 750–333 B.C.

Such small states as the Phoenician cities and the Hebrew kingdoms had been able to survive only because there were no major powers to threaten them in the period from about 1150 to 750 B.C. Between about 750 and 333 B.C., however, three successive empires dominated the entire Fertile Crescent. These empires brought all the small states of Mesopotamia, Syria, and Palestine under their control and at times even extended their power over Egypt.

The Assyrian Empire
ca. 750–612 B.C.

The first of the new empires was created by the Assyrians, a Semitic people living in the hilly country of the upper Tigris Valley. Located at the northern extreme of the Mesopotamian world, the Assyrians were generally the first to feel the blows of the repeated invasions from the north. They had to become militarily strong in order to survive. In time they built up the most efficient army the ancient world had seen, with long-service professional soldiers and what were probably the first effective cavalry units. About 900 B.C., when barbarian threats

from the north temporarily subsided, the Assyrians began to use their army to terrorize and conquer their Mesopotamian neighbors. By about 750 B.C. their empire included the whole Mesopotamian valley. Then in a series of swift and devastating thrusts to the west, they conquered Syria, the Phoenician cities, the Kingdom of Israel, and finally even Egypt.

The Assyrians enforced their rule with cruelty, enslaving and deporting whole peoples and torturing and killing thousands of captives. A large part of the population of Israel, for instance, was either killed or deported and the land was resettled with people from other parts of the empire. The ten northern Hebrew tribes lost their identity forever. The only Hebrews left were the two tribes of the southern Kingdom of Judah, which survived as an Assyrian dependency.

Assyrian art (expressed mostly in sculptured reliefs) reflects many of the characteristics of these fierce people. Strong, harsh, and realistic, it abounds in scenes of war, torture, and death. The human figures are somewhat stiff, but no artists have ever surpassed the Assyrians

An alabaster relief showing an Assyrian king on a hunt.

in depicting animals fighting, charging, and writhing in their death agonies.

There were simply not enough Assyrians to garrison a territory stretching from the Nile to the borders of Persia, and the systematic cruelty of the Assyrians made it impossible for them to control conquered peoples except by force of arms. The Babylonians, eager to regain their old supremacy, launched an uprising and were enthusiastically supported by other subject peoples. Nineveh, the Assyrian capital, fell in 612 B.C., and the great Assyrian Empire crumbled overnight.

The Chaldean Empire
ca. 626–539 B.C.

After the fall of Assyria, most of Mesopotamia came under the short-lived Chaldean Empire, which had its capital in the ancient city of Babylon. Trying to avoid domination by the Chaldeans, the small Kingdom of Judah joined a coalition led by Egypt. But in 587 B.C. Nebuchadnezzar, the Chaldean king, overran Judah, devastated the land, destroyed Solomon's temple in Jerusalem, and led the king and several thousand leading citizens back to Babylon as captives. During this "Babylonian Captivity," the Hebrews came to believe that Jahweh had a divine plan for His people that was being worked out through history. At first their fate had perplexed them. If Jahweh was the only true God, and if the Hebrews were the only ones to worship Him and follow His laws, why had they been subjected to conquest and cruelty at the hands of nonbelievers? The answer was provided by the new prophets of the period of exile, such as Joel. The day would soon come, they believed, when Jahweh would reveal Himself to all peoples and institute His rule of righteousness. When that time came, the Hebrews would lead the nonbelievers into the paths of Jahweh. Meanwhile, the Hebrews would have to be educated and purified through suffering. Their numbers would be reduced by conquest and slaughter until only a "saving remnant" of dedicated souls was left to carry out the will of Jahweh.

The book of *Daniel* gives a dramatic account of the fall of Babylon in 539 B.C. According to this version, a spectral hand began to write on the wall during a banquet given by the crown prince Belshazzar. Only Daniel, a Jew, was able to interpret the message for Belshazzar and his terrified guests. The Chaldean Empire would fall that night. According to other sources, the handwriting on the wall was unnecessary, for the Persian troops were already at the gates, and the citizens of Babylon, frustrated by the weakness of their rulers, were offering no resistance.

The Persian Empire
549–333 B.C.

The Persians, an Indo-European people, lived in a loose federation with the Medes and other neighbors in the hilly

Babylonians and Syrians paying tribute to the Persian emperor Xerxes.

THE PERSIAN EMPIRE *ca.* 500 B.C.

region east of Mesopotamia. In 549 B.C., Cyrus, a very able military leader, established himself as king. This was the beginning of the great period of Persian expansion. In 543 B.C. Cyrus conquered and annexed all of Asia Minor. With his victory over the Chaldean Empire in 539 B.C., he added Mesopotamia, Syria, Palestine, and the Phoenician cities to his empire. When his son conquered Egypt in 525 B.C., the Persian Empire embraced almost all of the Middle East.

The organization of the Persian Empire was so successful that it was later used by both the Greeks and the Romans. The Persian system combined a large measure of local autonomy with careful supervision by the central government. Each of the subject peoples was allowed to keep its own customs, its own religion, and often even its own local government. The Hebrews, for instance, were allowed to return to Judah, to re-establish their kingdom, and to rebuild the temple in Jerusalem. A Persian governor and a Persian garrison were as-

signed to each of the provinces to maintain order and to supervise the collection of taxes. When faced with rebellion, however, the Persians did not hesitate to take extreme military measures.

One result of the Persian conquests was that Persian religious concepts left a strong mark on the later religions of the western world. The Persian religion, in its earliest known form, was essentially the deification of natural forces. It gave special prominence to Mithra, the sun-god. By the time of the Persian conquests, however, the king and most of the leading families had embraced a newer creed based on the teachings of the prophet Zoroaster. According to Zoroaster there were two gods. Ahura-Mazda, the god of good and light, was engaged in a perpetual struggle with Ahriman, the god of evil and darkness. Man had free will and could ally himself with either side. After thousands of years, there would be a final struggle in which the good would triumph. Those who had chosen to fight on the side of good would go to paradise (a Persian word); the rest would be consumed in eternal fire. Although Zoroastrianism never spread far beyond Persia, it must be counted as one of the most influential religions of history. Its dualism explained one of religion's most difficult problems: How can a good god permit the existence of evil? Although the belief in two separate gods has never been accepted by Christians, popular concepts of the devil in the Middle Ages were not much different from Zoroaster's description of Ahriman. Even more influential on both Christianity and Islam were Zoroaster's teachings about paradise, hell, and the Last Judgment.

Persian gold cup, fifth century B.C.

The Persians first tasted defeat at the battle of Marathon in 490 B.C. when they failed in their attempt to subdue the Greek city-state of Athens (see pp. 38–39). The reason for Persia's defeat was probably not the superior fighting ability of the Athenians, as Greek historians would have us believe, so much as a combination of weaknesses in the Persian system. It placed too much power in the hands of the king. Such a system can succeed only under a man who is both a good administrator and a good general. During the fifth century B.C. the Persian Empire was ruled by a series of men who were neither. Other factors contributed to a general decline of the eastern civilizations under Persian rule. The Persians were not originators or intellectual leaders; they accepted with little change most of the cultures of their subjects. The Persians created favorable conditions for trade, but they were not themselves great traders. High taxes and subjection to a foreign power apparently dampened the initiative of such trading people as the Phoenicians, whose economic activity declined. The Persians never learned to use their manpower efficiently. In fact, under Persian rule opportunities for the ordinary man decreased. He became a peasant, bound to the soil, rather than a free farmer or a free warrior. This change had a bad effect on the army, which became more and more dependent on mercenaries, many of whom were barbarians from areas outside the Persian Empire.

During the fifth century B.C., the most important advances in commerce, philosophy, art, letters, and the organization of society were not made in the older civilizations that had come under Persian rule. They came from that small part of the eastern world that had escaped Persian domination: the city-states of the Greek peninsula, whose histories will be examined in the next chapter. Greek strength grew as the Persian Empire decayed, until finally, in 333 B.C., the Greek king Alexander defeated the Persian armies and added all of the Persian Empire to his own domains.

Suggestions for Further Reading

Note: asterisk denotes a book available in a paperback edition.

General   Several good texts are devoted specifically to ancient history. Among those recently published are W. E. Caldwell and M. F. Gyles, *The Ancient World,* 3rd ed. (1966), and C. G. Starr, *A History of the Ancient World* (1965). W. H. McNeill, *The Rise of the West** (1963), is more successful than most in placing ancient western history in a framework that includes the ancient world as a whole. For a detailed study, see J. B. Bury *et al.,* eds., *The Cambridge*

Ancient History (1923–29). The first two volumes have been issued in a paperback edition. Three recent works on the ancient world before the Greeks are G. V. Childe, *What Happened in History** (1964); H. Frankfort, *The Birth of Civilization in the Near East** (1956); and S. Mascoti, *The Face of the Ancient Orient** (1962). L. Cottrell, *The Anvil of Civilization** (1957), is shorter but scholarly and informative.

Archeology and Prehistory

There are two works that recount recent archeological discoveries: C. W. Ceram, *Gods, Graves, and Scholars,* rev. ed. (1967), and L. Woolley, *Digging Up the Past** (1940). Ceram is especially helpful in giving references to the work of the great archeologists. R. J. Braidwood, *Prehistoric Men** (1963), and J. Hawkes and L. Woolley, *Prehistory and the Beginnings of Civilization** (1963), are interesting summaries of what is known of the story of man before the invention of writing.

Mesopotamia

A good summary is W. W. Hallo and W. K. Simpson, *The Ancient Near East: A History* (1971). A. L. Oppenheim, *Ancient Mesopotamia* (1964), and H. W. F. Saggs, *The Greatness That Was Babylon* (1962), are detailed surveys of Mesopotamian history. S. Mascoti, *Ancient Semitic Civilizations** (1960), is shorter and includes Syria and Palestine. S. N. Kramer, *History Begins at Sumer** (1959), contains excellent source material for the political, social, and religious thinking of the Sumerians, the first people to keep written records. L. Woolley, *Ur of the Chaldees** (1950), is one of many books by a leading authority on Mesopotamian archeology. An interesting description of the Mesopotamian world may be found in G. Contenau, *Everyday Life in Babylon and Assyria* (1954).

Egypt

There are two good surveys of ancient Egypt. Of them, A. H. Gardiner, *Egypt of the Pharaohs** (1961), is more factual; J. A. Wilson, *The Culture of Ancient Egypt** (1963), more interpretive. For a study of Egyptian monuments, see either I. E. S. Edwards, *The Pyramids of Egypt,** rev. ed. (1961), or W. S. Smith, *Art and Architecture of Ancient Egypt** (1958). H. Frankfort, *Ancient Egyptian Religion** (1948), largely replaces some of the older standard works on this subject. P. Montet, *Everyday Life in Egypt in the Days of Ramses II* (1958), is a counterpart to Contenau's book on Babylon.

Crete

There is no complete and generally accepted history of the Minoan culture, though most of the texts on Greek history mentioned at the end of the next chapter have short surveys. A recent study of the archeological discoveries on Crete is R. W. Hutchinson, *Prehistoric Crete** (1963). L. Cottrell, *The Bull of Minos** (1953), is shorter and more readable.

The Indo-Europeans

The best general account is V. G. Childe, *The Aryans: A Study of Indo-European Origins* (1926). O. R. Gurney, *The Hittites** (1952), is a good introduction to the study of the Hittites, and C. W. Ceram, *The Secret of the Hittites* (1956), gives a fascinating account of the archeological expeditions that uncovered the Hittite civilization.

Syria and Palestine

Informative studies of the non-Hebrew peoples who inhabited Syria-Palestine can be found in J. Gray, *The Canaanites* (1964), D. Harden, *The Phoenicians* (1962), and R. A. H. Macalister, *The Philistines* (1913). There is such a wealth of material on the ancient Hebrews and their religious evolution that any short list must omit even many standard works. Among the better general histories are W. F. Albright, *The Biblical Period from Abraham to Ezra** (1963); J. Bright, *A History of Israel* (1959); C. H. Gordon, *The Ancient Near East** (1965); A. Lods, *Israel* (1932); and the early chapters of A. L. Sachar, *A History of the Jews** (1966). For a briefer treatment, see E. J. Ehrlich, *A Concise History of Israel** (1965), or H. Orlinsky, *Ancient Israel** (1964).

Assyrians, Chaldeans, and Persians

The Assyrians and the Chaldeans are both treated in the general histories of Mesopotamia mentioned above. For studies of the Persians as well as of the diverse peoples they ruled, see either R. N. Frye, *The Heritage of Persia* (1963), or A. T. Olmstead, *A History of the Persian Empire** (1959).

2

Greek
Civilization

Even though Persia was weakening when it met its first defeats at the hands of the Greeks, it is still surprising that a few small, loosely allied Greek cities could resist the professional army of a great empire. The Greek success is even more astonishing when we consider that many Greek cities were so afraid of Persia that they took no part in the war. The Greek victories were won by a minority of the Greek people.

The same paradox appears in other Greek achievements. The Greeks were very conscious of their identity, very proud of being Greek, very scornful of the barbarians who did not share their culture. They worshiped the same gods, revered the same oracles, spoke what was basically the same language, met and competed with one another at great festivals such as the Olympic Games. Yet Greece was divided into many quarreling states, and most Greeks were peasant farmers who contributed little to and were little influenced by the high culture of the Greek world. That culture was created by a few men living in a few cities scattered around the rim of the Aegean Sea. It was a long time before it penetrated very far inland; Boeotia, only thirty miles from Athens, was notorious among the Greeks as the home of dull, ignorant, blundering yokels. Greek culture eventually spread throughout the Mediterranean world, but the Golden Age of Greece was a golden age for only a few hundred thousand men.

Geography helps explain the divisions and the uneven development of the Greek people. Rocky mountains enclose fertile plains, emerge from the Aegean Sea to form countless islands, and rise again to form the craggy promontories of Asia Minor. The best harbors were usually not near the best farming land. It was in the seaports that new ideas and new patterns of social organization were most likely to emerge, either through contact with other cities or because of the pressure of growing population. The more fertile areas of Greece, such as Thessaly, had fewer outside contacts and were under less pressure to make innovations.

Geography made it easy for many small states to emerge and to survive. It was not impossible to unite Greece, but it was far more difficult than it had been to unite Egypt, and the task took many centuries. Meanwhile the Greeks lived in small, independent communities, each of

which developed its own pattern of life. Obviously some patterns would be more likely to encourage writers, artists, and philosophers than others. Cities that had an active intellectual and artistic life attracted capable men from other parts of the Greek world. Thus small differences became magnified with the passage of time. Early Athens and early Sparta had a good deal in common but by the middle of the fifth century B.C. Sparta was a garrison state and Athens was the cultural center of the Greek people.

EARLY GREEK HISTORY TO *ca.* 800 B.C.

The Greeks knew little about their own past and were apt to exaggerate the originality and the rapidity of development of their civilization. Their oldest historical records were the two epic poems of Homer—the *Iliad* and the *Odyssey*. These poems celebrate the siege of Troy by a league of Greek warriors. The siege probably took place about 1250 B.C., and its memory was probably preserved in legend, but Homer (or the two or more poets whose work was ascribed to

Gold and silver decoration on this Mycenaean dagger shows early Greeks fighting a lion (*ca.* 1700 B.C.).

The earliest representation of Homer, on a fourth-century B.C. coin.

Homer) did not write the epics before 750 B.C. and perhaps not until a half century or so later. The Greeks were not very conscious of or concerned by these dates. For them, Homer's epic poems were like the first books of the Old Testament for the Jews—a record of their early history, a guide to right conduct, and a foundation for their religion. The epics were works of timeless value, and all of early Greek history was typified by Homer's heroes.

Nineteenth-century European scholars saw little historical value in the Homeric legends, except as evidence about early Greek society and religion. But a German businessman named Heinrich Schliemann was convinced that there had been a siege of Troy. In 1870 he began to excavate a mound near the Dardanelles in Asia Minor that was the traditional site of Troy. To the astonishment of the scholarly world, he found layer after layer of ancient settlements, one of them a large fortified city that had been destroyed about 1200 B.C., and an-other older and very rich town that had fallen earlier. He assumed that the older city was Homer's Troy; actually, layer 7a (the city that fell in 1250) was the one he should have selected. He then went to Mycenae in southern Greece, the legendary home of the Greek leader Agamemnon, and began a search for the king's palace. Here he found evidence of a surprisingly advanced civilization whose roots went back at least as far as 1800 B.C.

Schliemann's successors found similar sites, and it became evident that this Mycenaean civilization was fairly widespread throughout the Greek peninsula. It seemed probable that the Mycenaeans were early Greeks; the decipherment of Linear Script B in 1952 (see p. 12) strengthened this hypothesis. We know that the Greeks reached the Aegean area about 2000 B.C., that they had contacts with the Minoan civilization, that they traded and raided in the Aegean Sea, and that they finally settled in the Greek peninsula, the Aegean islands, and along the coast of Asia Minor. These early Greeks spoke an Indo-European language, knew the use of bronze, and were strong enough and numerous enough to conquer and assimilate the earlier inhabitants of the region.

The Mycenaean Civilization ca. 1650–1150 B.C.

By about 1600 B.C., or soon thereafter, this early Greek, or Mycenaean, civilization had reached a fairly advanced state. As was to be the case for centuries, there were many small independent political units, each one based on a strongly fortified citadel and ruled by a king and his band of warriors. The Greek city of later centuries did not exist then, but a fairly large merchant class traded throughout the Aegean and with Crete. There was certainly some competition (perhaps violent) with the Minoans for trade, but there must have been periods of peaceful cooperation as well. The great palaces of Mycenae, Tiryns, and Pylos show Minoan influence, and the enormous wealth of the rulers of Mycenae must have come largely from trade.

The Mycenaean Greeks may have

The Discovery of Troy

Heinrich Schliemann's discovery of Troy in 1873 helped trigger further archeological expeditions.

He struck into the mound, boldly ripping down walls that to him seemed unimportant. He found weapons and household furnishings, ornaments and vases, overwhelming evidence that a rich city had once occupied the spot. And he found something else as well. . . . Under the ruins of New Ilium he disclosed other ruins, under these still others. The hill was like a tremendous onion, which he proceeded to dismember layer by layer. Each layer seemed to have been inhabited at a different period. Populations had lived and died, cities had been built up only to fall into decay. Sword and fire had raged, one civilization cutting off another, and again and again a city of the living had been raised on a city of the dead.

. . . The question now arose which of these nine cities was the Troy of Homer, of the heroes and the epic war. . . .

Schliemann dug and searched. In the second and third levels from the bottom he found traces of fire, the remains of massive walls, and the ruins of a gigantic gate. He was sure that these walls had once enclosed the palace of Priam. . . .

From C. W. Ceram, *Gods, Graves, and Scholars*, rev. ed. (New York: Knopf, 1967), pp. 36–37.

contributed to the downfall of Minoan Crete about 1480 B.C.; certainly the Greeks attempted to profit from the disaster. As we have seen in Chapter 1, they probably took over and rebuilt the palace at Knossos; they also must have hoped to take over Minoan trade routes. If so, they were disappointed. It was Egypt under the militant pharaohs of the New Kingdom that became the dominant commercial power of the eastern Mediterranean. The Mycenaeans continued to trade in the Aegean and eastern Mediterranean, and began to penetrate the Black Sea. This may have stirred up rivalry with Troy, which was well placed to block the entrance to the Straits, though the legendary wealth of Troy could also have been a cause of conflict. If there was a Trojan War it must have taken place after the fall of Crete and before the collapse of the Mycenaean civilization—that is, very near the traditional date of 1250 B.C.

The Greek Dark Ages
ca. 1150–800 B.C.

The Mycenaean world was wracked by a series of violent attacks from unknown invaders soon after 1200 B.C. Royal palaces were burned, towns destroyed, and kingdoms overthrown. A few places escaped with little damage, notably Athens, and many Mycenaean Greeks were able to flee to islands in the Aegean or to Greek settlements in Asia Minor. Nevertheless, the Mycenaean ruling class was wiped out and with it Mycenaean art and the Mycenaean system of writing.

The downfall of the Mycenaean civilization was followed by a new invasion of Greek-speaking people, the Dorians. The Dorians may have completed the destruction of the fragments of Mycenaean civilization that had survived the attacks of the earlier invaders; certainly they did nothing to rebuild the old way

Scene from Greek vase (*ca.* 550 B.C.) showing merchants weighing produce. As trade routes multiplied, Greek merchants and wine and oil producers prospered.

routes throughout the eastern Mediterranean. For example, Miletus and eleven other cities had a seaport in the Nile Delta. Miletus also had a string of trading posts along the shores of the Black Sea where goods from Egypt and western Asia could be sold to the peoples of eastern Europe.

Trade was greatly stimulated by the invention of coined money, which occurred in Asia Minor (probably in the kingdom of Lydia) in the late seventh century B.C. Gold and silver had long been prized, and the value of other goods had often been expressed in terms of specific weights of these precious metals. But testing, weighing, and cutting a bar of gold or silver was too tedious for ordinary small transactions. Men eventually discovered that the metal could be cut up into many small bits, stamped to show that a ruler guaranteed their weight and fineness, and then be used repeatedly for any sort of business. By making it easier to buy and sell goods of all kinds, this discovery increased the volume of trade.

As Greek trade expanded, towns on the western shore of the Aegean (such as Corinth) began to prosper. Population increased, both in Ionia and in the Greek peninsula. The commercial cities became crowded, and few of them controlled enough agricultural land to guarantee an adequate food supply for all their people. Fortunately, the Mediterranean region was still thinly settled, and there were many districts where small native populations could be subdued or displaced by colonists from the Greek shores of the Aegean. Just as the Phoenicians had taken over North Africa, so, from 750 B.C. on, the Greeks took over southern Italy and eastern Sicily; Naples and Syracuse were both founded by Greeks, and other Greek cities in the region were so numerous that the Romans later called southern Italy Magna Graecia or Great Greece. Other Greek colonies were even more remote, such as Marseilles in southern France, trading posts in Spain, and Tanais on the north shore of the Black Sea. Greek colonies usually maintained cultural and religious ties with their mother-cities, but they were fully independent and owed no political or military support to their founders.

of life. They were a rustic people who had had little contact with the civilizations of the eastern Mediterranean; their communities were composed of small farmers dominated by groups of warriors. The Dorians were especially numerous in the Peloponnesus, the old center of Mycenaean civilization. As a result, memories of the past faded, especially since there were no written records to preserve old traditions and to report the activities of the new ruling class. Very little is known about Greece during the "Dark Ages" that followed the Dorian invasions.

THE GREEK WORLD
ca. 800–500 B.C.

After 800 B.C. a little more information is available about the Greek world and especially about the Greeks of Ionia, the western coast of Asia Minor. It is evident that an economic revival had occurred and that a number of trading cities had emerged. Some commerce must have existed even during the "Dark Ages," and with both Egypt and the Phoenician cities under Assyrian control, the Greeks had a new opportunity to expand their trade

ca. 2000 B.C.	ca. 1700	ca. 1480	ca. 1100	ca. 800	ca. 600	404	323	Conquest by Rome 146 B.C.
Minoan Civilization on Crete			"Dark Ages"	Dominance of City-states of Asia Minor	Dominance of Athens and Sparta		Hellenistic Era	
Arrival of Greeks	Mycenaean Civilization in Aegean Area							

Decline of
City-state System and
Conquest by Macedon

Cultural Development

Prosperity, as it often does, encouraged cultural development. It was in Ionia that the Greeks rediscovered the art of writing by adapting the Phoenician alphabet to the Greek language in the eighth century B.C. This discovery encouraged poets to put orally transmitted legends into permanent written form, as Homer did with the story of the Trojan War. In the same way, the works of lyric poets could now be preserved. Writing spread rapidly throughout the Greek-speaking communities, and, as will be seen, Ionia was not the only region that produced famous poets in the seventh and sixth centuries B.C. Nevertheless, as long as they preserved their independence, the Ionians remained the intellectual leaders of the Greeks.

Throughout the Greek world there was a rapid development of literature

and the arts. Not long after the Homeric epics were composed, Hesiod, a small landowner in Boeotia, wrote his long didactic poems describing the origins of the gods and the hard life of the farmer. The first famous woman poet was Sappho of Lesbos; the author of the martial songs that inspired the Spartan soldiers was the Athenian Tyrtaeus. Even the remote and newly colonized cities of Sicily produced their poets. And in Ionia the foundations were being laid for work in philosophy and natural science.

Some remarkable works of art were produced during the seventh and sixth centuries B.C. The Greek temple began to take on its characteristic form—an oblong building framed by pillars with sculptured figures on the doorposts and along the upper walls. Early Greek sculpture clearly owed much to the Egyptians; the figures are stiff and tense, ritualistic rather than realistic. But the

GREEK AND PHOENICIAN COLONIZATION AND TRADE   ca. 750–550 B.C.

Greeks had already learned to show figures in full profile (which the Egyptians could not or would not do), and they were already showing interest in the beauty of the human figure. Most typical because most common were the vase paintings, on which it is still possible to see lively and realistic pictures of all sorts of human activities.

Greek vase of late sixth century B.C. depicting a foot race. The vase was awarded to the winner of the foot race contest at the Panathenaic festival in Athens.

Social and Political Change

The rapid growth of trade and population put serious strains on the old political and social system. The *Iliad* and other early Greek writings suggest that a typical Greek community of the "Dark Ages" was ruled by a king or chieftain, who was advised and often contradicted by a council of very independent warriors. The warriors in turn held most of the land and dominated the peasant farmers and herders. The petty kings of the Homeric Age had very little power compared to an Egyptian pharaoh or a Persian emperor, and as time went on they tended to lose what power they had. The community was controlled by the land-holding aristocracy; if the king survived at all it was only because he was needed to perform certain religious rites, or because it was convenient to have a predesignated war-leader ready for sudden emergencies.

In communities with adequate amounts of good land, slow-growing populations, and relatively little commercial activity, this pattern of aristocratic government persisted throughout the period of independent Greek states. But in the trading cities there was more reason for the aristocracy to break up into factions and more friction between rich and poor. Some of the aristocrats became traders and joined forces with merchants of humbler origin; some continued to draw most of their income from their estates. There could be serious policy differences between those who sought to protect and extend trade routes and those who sought to protect and extend their lands. But even those in the latter group were involved in commerce, since they discovered that there was a market for wine and olive oil throughout the Mediterranean. Only a rich landowner could afford the initial investment needed to start a vineyard or an olive grove; the peasants continued to grow grain. But the profits on wine and oil exports could be used to buy cheap grain in Egypt or Sicily where the soil was more productive. Thus while small farmers and day laborers suffered, landlords, merchants, shipbuilders, and skilled artisans like those who made the great pottery jugs for wine and oil prospered.

With grain prices low, peasants fell into debt, and with interest rates running at 16 percent or more, they seldom were able to repay their loans. At best they lost their land and had to join the casual labor force in the city; at worst they and their children were sold into slavery.

The logical outcome of this crisis would have been either a bloody rebellion or else the establishment of a society in which a few masters dominated thousands of slaves. But the Greeks had always lived in small tight-knit communities in which every family had its place and every man was known to most of his fellows. Such communities could not fully accept the depersonalizing effects of a commercial economy based on formal business contracts. If anything, economic growth forced people closer together as villages became cities and as the rural population became more dependent on the urban nucleus. The old sense of mutual responsibility and individual dignity persisted and was reinforced by a growing realization that these emerging city-states must make the best use they could of the limited manpower at their disposal. Enslaving half the population was not a good use of manpower; neither was a rebellion that might have killed off most of those who had military, political, and commercial skills. Most Greek cities avoided both these extremes and gradually satisfied the protests of debt-ridden farmers and laborers by a long drawn-out series of political reforms.

One of the first reactions to social strains was the establishment of tyrannies. A tyrant was usually a colorful politician who gained enough support by vague promises of better government to make himself a dictator. Most tyrants were aristocrats with considerable political experience; many of them were quite capable rulers. They usually tried to weaken the landed aristocracy, and in doing so they favored commercial interests and allowed a somewhat larger group of citizens to take part in the political process. For a time they seem to have succeeded in reducing social tensions, but they did not solve the problems of slavery and land reform. Although some tyrants managed to pass their power on to their sons, no tyranny persisted for any significant length of time. The

Greeks disliked the idea of tyranny, not because the tyrants were evil men (though a few of them were), but because they had seized power illegally and behaved arrogantly. The Greeks could accept class differences, but to the very end they remained suspicious of a single man who tried to dominate his fellow-citizens. Thus tyranny did not become accepted as a new and desirable form of monarchy; instead it gained a reputation for oppressiveness that has persisted to the present day.

The seventh and sixth centuries B.C. were an age of tyrants, but they were also an age of law-givers. The latter were rather more successful than the former. Old customs had to be adapted to new conditions, and the ruling classes gave full support to (and usually chose) men who tried to bring the laws up to date. Early laws were rigid and severe (the word "draconian" is still a memorial to the harsh code of the Athenian Draco) but, even so, fixed rules had advantages over decisions based on obsolete customs or whims of kings or aristocratic councils. And later law-givers were less severe and were more concerned with the welfare of the poorer part of the population. About 590 B.C., for example, Solon of Athens reduced the burden of debt on small farmers and forbade enslavement for debt. Though he was followed by a tyrant, his laws remained in force and formed the basis for a new constitution at the end of the sixth century. Other cities had similar experiences. In time it became a matter of pride to the Greeks that while other peoples were ruled by the will of kings, the Greeks were ruled by laws, not by men. Every Greek knew the laws of his city; they determined and protected his rights; they bound aristocrats and public officials as well as the poor and private citizens. And because the law was known, it was always possible to consider ways in which it could be changed and reformed.

The City-State

By 500 B.C. most of the tyrannies had ended and many significant codes of law had been drafted. The worst of the social crisis caused by rapid changes in the economy was over, although many reforms were still needed. The Greeks were ready to try their great political experiment, the establishment of basically secular governments in which power and responsibility were shared by a considerable part of the citizenry. The kings were gone and religion was becoming a form of civic patriotism. Basic loyalty went to the *polis*—the city-state—and the *polis* was a republic. It might be controlled by a handful of aristocrats, but it might also allow most or all of the citizens to participate in the work of government. Whatever the distribution of power, the peak of Greek civilization was reached during the period in which the city-state, like an early Greek kingdom, controlled only a limited area, usually no more than that of a small American county. Much of the land was devoted to farming, but the center of the *polis* was the city itself with its marketplace, its citadel, and its temples. No city-state had a very large population: with more than one hundred thousand inhabitants, Athens was probably the biggest, but many cities had only ten thousand or so.

The smallness of the population was compensated for by the intensity of communal life. The citizens knew one another better and shared one another's experiences more fully than in any modern city of comparable size. Most activities took place in the open since Greek houses were small and simple—places to eat and sleep, but not to live. Public and private business was transacted on the streets or on the porches of temples and law courts. Artisans and merchants worked in small shops open to the street. Actors gave their performances in unroofed theaters; teachers met their pupils in public gardens; politicians argued in the public squares. Everyone had a chance to know everything that was going on in the city; there was little privacy and apparently little desire for it.

In such close-knit communities it was easy to judge the character and ability of every citizen. And with such small populations it was essential to make the most of these human resources, especially in time of war. The days when a few aristocratic warriors with horses and chariots could carry the main burden of combat were long since gone. Greek armies were now composed of heavy-armed infantry fighting in close formation; all but the very poorest citizens were supposed to provide their own weapons and serve in the ranks. And when, as in the case of Athens, it was necessary to man a fleet of warships as well as provide an army, even the poorest citizens were needed for

This stele informed the Athenians of the Law Against Tyranny in 336 B.C.: "Should anyone, in an attempt at absolute power, rise up against the people or try to overthrow the democracy of Athens— whoever kills him shall be blameless."

Athena, goddess of wisdom, protector of the home and the citadel, is shown here in military dress (bronze statue, *ca.* seventh century B.C.).

service. They could pull an oar even if they could not afford shields and weapons.

Men who served in the armed forces at their own expense could scarcely be barred from the political activities of the community. The tendency was to increase the power of the general assembly, to admit more and more citizens (in some cases all citizens) to the assembly, and to increase the number of men eligible for political office. In many cities the officials, or a governing council, were elected by the assembly.

Even at their greatest extent, these concessions did not produce pure democracy. Slaves, who were numerous in every Greek city, had no rights, and immigrants from other Greek states, who formed a large part of the population in various trading cities such as Athens, could not vote even after many years of residence. Moreover, the aristocratic type of government persisted, with slight modifications, in many states. Overall, however, by the end of the sixth century B.C., a larger percentage of the male citizen population (varying from 100 percent in Athens to 10 percent in Sparta) participated in the political process than in any earlier period.

This increasing participation in politics strengthened the bonds between the citizen and his city. The *polis* was not just an area of land or a group of buildings; it was a way of life that shaped every human activity. As Socrates once put it, the laws and customs of Athens were his parents; they had raised and nurtured him. He was the kind of person he was because he had been born a citizen of Athens. But if the *polis* shaped the lives of its citizens, the citizens also shaped the life of the *polis.* Even in aristocratic states the rulers had to pay some attention to public opinion; elsewhere very little could be done without the approval and active assistance of a considerable part of the body of citizens.

Approval and assistance went far beyond the making and enforcing of laws. The adornment of the city with public buildings, the encouragement of poetry and drama, the support of teachers and scholars all were influenced by public opinion; and all were, to some degree, dependent on the support of the wealthier classes. Peasants and day laborers were probably not greatly interested in art and literature, but men who had a little money and some leisure could argue endlessly about esthetic and intellectual problems. In fact, one of the arguments for slavery was that it made it possible for the citizen to participate fully in the cultural and political life of his city by freeing him from the routine of daily work. Not all citizens took advantage of their opportunities, even in the most enlightened cities, but enough of them did to enable a sophisticated civilization to develop on a very small population base.

This discussion of life in the Greek city-state has focused exclusively on men. But society then was thoroughly male-dominated (which may be why homosexuality was so rampant). Women stayed home, unless they were courtesans or lesbians, as Sappho reputedly was.

Greek Religion

The religion of the Greeks both bound them together and encouraged strong local patriotisms. Some of the Greek gods probably go back to the religion of pre-Greek inhabitants of the Aegean area; some certainly came in with successive waves of invaders; but by Homeric times they had been combined into a family of twelve major gods who lived on Mount Olympus. Zeus was ruler of the gods and wielder of the thunderbolt; his wife, Hera, was goddess of women and marriage. Strangely enough, Ares, the god of war, was not especially honored by the Greeks, in spite of their belligerent spirit.

Each city gave special honor to one divinity, who was its protector and patron. Thus Athena, goddess of wisdom, was greatly revered in Athens, even though this meant giving second place to Poseidon, god of the sea and the chief god of many communities in Attica. Artemis, the twin sister of Apollo, was worshiped at Sparta as the spirit of bravery and courage. Apollo, god of prophecy, was not so closely tied to any one city; people came from all parts of

Gorgon from the Temple of
Artemis, goddess of the hunt,
at Corfu, 600 B.C.

the Greek world to seek guidance from his oracle at Delphi, and his shrine on the island of Delos was a center of religious life for many of the Greek islands. Zeus was also widely worshiped. In their great festivals, such as the Olympic or Isthmian Games, the Greeks honored all the gods in competitions to determine who was the best poet, the fastest runner, the ablest playwright, the strongest wrestler. But in their frequent wars, the Greeks expected each god to defend his own city, even to the extent of fighting with the god of the opposing city. Religion gave the Greeks cultural but not political unity.

The early Greek religion was not very edifying or inspiring. The gods were simply human beings on a large scale. They had great power and were immortal, but they were also quarrelsome, lustful, and prejudiced. They lied to and cheated one another; they interfered in human affairs in unpredictable and whimsical ways; they were completely undisciplined. Zeus had no real control over them (especially when he was off on one of his amorous adventures), and men could never be sure what would please them. One could only sacrifice and hope for the best.

Educated Greeks tried hard to draw some moral lessons from the confused stories of the gods, but with little success. Something could be done with Apollo as the god of reason and light, and Zeus could be reverenced as the Father of all by ignoring the scandalous stories about him. But while the Greeks were reasonably sure that there were supernatural beings, they were not very sure that they knew much about them. The official religious cult was an excuse for festivals and parades, for building temples and carving statues, for writing poems and plays. It furnished an outlet for civic patriotism. The basic problems of the meaning of life and of the right conduct of life had to be solved in other ways.

As for the common people, it is doubtful that they had ever been wholly devoted to the Homeric gods, who were the gods of the old aristocracy. The pre-Greek fertility cults, centered on the worship of Demeter, goddess of grain and fertility, and Dionysus, god of wine and ecstasy, remained popular with them. Both involved secret rituals; both gave some promise of immortality. Through ritual and moral purity the initiate could be united to Demeter and be assured of lasting bliss. Through drink-

A procession recorded in marble at the Parthenon (fifth century B.C). The paraders on their way to the Acropolis carry jars containing sacrificial gifts.

Minoan Civilization on Crete

Arrival of Greeks — Mycenaean Civilization in Aegean Area — "Dark Ages" — Dominance of City-states of Asia Minor — Dominance of Athens and Sparta — Hellenistic Era

Decline of City-state System and Conquest by Macedon

ing wine mixed with sacrificial blood, the followers of Dionysus could rise from the dead, as their god had done. Often the two fertility cults were combined, and they spread throughout the Greek world. The most famous Greek dramas were written for the annual festivals of Dionysus, one of the great religious events at Athens.

THE PERSIAN WARS
499–478 B.C.

In the last decades of the sixth century B.C. the Greeks were clearly ready for "take-off"; they had the economic, political, and intellectual base on which to build a great civilization. Precisely at this point came the crisis of the Persian Wars. War can ruin a civilization that is fully developed and set in its ways, but it can stimulate a civilization that is still in its early stage of development. Victory over the Persians confirmed the belief of the Greeks in their uniqueness and in their destiny; the wars were followed immediately by the Golden Age of Greece.

The immediate cause of the wars was the conquest of the Ionian cities by the Persian Empire about 543 B.C. The Greek world was shocked by this calamity, but an effective response to Persian aggression could come only from the mainland of the Greek peninsula. And leadership there had gradually concentrated in two cities, Athens and Sparta. If they could cooperate, Persia might be resisted; if not, the prospects were dim. But cooperation was not easy, for Athens and Sparta stood at the two extremes of the Greek political system.

Sparta

Sparta in the early period of its history was not very different from other Greek states; like them, it took a prominent part in the early development of

Greek art and literature. But Sparta was situated in a fertile agricultural region, one that was not greatly concerned with commerce. It sought to make the most of its favorable agricultural position by dominating other grain-producing communities in its neighborhood. About 650 B.C. one of these neighboring communities, Messenia, revolted and almost destroyed the Spartan state. By 600 B.C. the Spartans were victorious, but they had been badly frightened. They decided to turn the entire male population of their *polis* into a standing army and to suppress any activity that might interfere with military efficiency.

When the reorganization had been completed the population of the Spartan state (called Lacedaemon) was divided into three groups. First were the Spartan male citizens (less than 10,000 men) who had all political rights and enjoyed full equality among themselves. Then came the free citizens of the neighboring communities, who could manage their own affairs but who had nothing to say about decisions of the ruling city. Third were the *helots,* serfs who worked the lands of Lacedaemon for the benefit of Spartan citizens.

The citizens paid a high price for their political and economic privileges. At the age of seven they were taken from their homes to be trained for military service. They entered the army at twenty and were allowed to marry then, but they could not live with their wives until they were thirty. They remained liable for military service until they were sixty.

It is easy to see how this system created the best-disciplined army in the Greek world and how it enabled Sparta to control most of the Peloponnesus, either directly or through an alliance with other cities known as the Peloponnesian League. It is less easy to understand why other Greeks, even in the liberal-minded and unregimented city of Athens, admired the Spartans so greatly. Bravery, discipline, frugality, scorn of luxury were characteristic of the Spartans, and it may be that the many Greeks who lacked these qualities found some satisfaction in seeing them embodied in at least one *polis.* Even so, self-discipline is more attractive than discipline imposed by the state; it seems likely that for most people Spartan success was more impressive than Spartan virtue.

Athens

Athens was more like an Ionian city than most of the other states of the Greek peninsula. Dependent on commerce rather early (seventh century B.C.), the Athenians aimed to suppress or control trade rivals rather than add agricultural regions to their holdings. Athens had one asset that most other cities lacked—the silver mines of Laureium, which for many generations yielded enough to pay for great expenses, such as the building of a fleet.

As we have seen, Athens had its early law-givers (Draco and Solon) and its sixth-century tyrants. The net result of these experiences had been to increase somewhat the number of citizens eligible to take an active role in government, although the wealthy still retained control. A sharp change came after the last tyrant was overthrown in 510 B.C., when the reformer Cleisthenes put through some basic constitutional reforms. Cleisthenes divided the citizens into ten tribes, so arranged that each tribe was a cross section of the whole population, rich and poor, rural and urban. Fifty citizens chosen by lot from each tribe made up the Council of Five Hundred, which prepared business for the assembly. A general assembly of all citizens passed the laws, as had long been customary. The top civil and military offices were open only to the wealthier citizens, and the old Council of the Areopagus or council of ex-archons (the highest civil officials) had considerable power for a generation or more after Cleisthenes' reforms. But even these officials were elected by popular vote, and since they were not paid, the poorer citizens had no great desire anyway to become archons or generals or treasurers.

The Athenian constitution thus gave every citizen the right to influence the government and to participate in its activities. Almost every citizen took a passionate interest in politics, education, art, and literature. There were, of course, private interests and political factions; the Athenians could be as shortsighted, selfish, and unreasonable as many modern voters. But for almost a century the Athenian system succeeded in releasing the energy of all citizens and in concentrating a good part of it on the common welfare.

The Defeat of Persia

When the Greek cities of Asia Minor revolted against Persia in 499 B.C., Athens sent a fleet to assist them. After the revolt had been put down, the Persian king Darius dispatched a punitive force by sea to Attica. But this force was repulsed by a small Athenian army at Marathon in 490 B.C. The Persian king, unwilling to let such a humiliation go unpunished, planned a full-scale campaign against the cities of the Greek peninsula. Fortunately for the Greeks, Darius died before he could begin his attack. It was only in 480 B.C. that his successor, Xerxes, and a Persian army of over 100,000 men crossed the Dardanelles and marched down the Greek peninsula. Faced with such an overwhelming force, most of the rural cities north of Athens declared their neutrality. Athens and the Peloponnesian League were left to defend what remained of Greek civilization from envelopment by the Persian Empire.

The Peloponnesian League formed the basis of the Greek defense against the Persians. The Athenians had hoped for Spartan help at Marathon and were quite ready to form a new league in alliance with the Peloponnesians, although in so doing they were forced to accept the leadership of Sparta. As the Persian forces moved southward, a small Spartan detachment at the head of some 6,000 Greeks attempted to hold the pass at Thermopylae, north of Athens, until a decisive naval battle could be fought. This battle, which took place off the coast, was a draw. The Greek forces withdrew to take up new positions at the

Head of Spartan warrior believed to be King Leonidas, who commanded the Greek force at Thermopylae. (Early fifth century B.C.)

Isthmus of Corinth and the Bay of Salamis. Meanwhile, the Persians broke through the pass at Thermopylae after the entire Spartan detachment had been killed trying to defend it. With Thermopylae unguarded, the Persians had an open road into Athens. The Athenian citizens were quickly evacuated to nearby islands, where they watched in horror as the Persians looted and burned their city.

Though the city was destroyed, Athens was not defeated. Before the Persian attack, Themistocles, an ambitious but farsighted politician, had persuaded the Athenian assembly to put all the income of the silver mines into building a fleet far larger than a city the size of Athens would normally require. He realized that, while the Greeks could not

expect to defeat the massive Persian armies in battle, the Greek peninsula with its islands and inlets could never be conquered except by sea. Shortly after the Persians occupied Athens, a Greek fleet, at least two-thirds of which was Athenian, met the Persian navy in the Bay of Salamis and destroyed it in a single engagement. Cut off from supplies coming by sea from Asia Minor, the Persians were badly crippled. After a final defeat at Plataea by a Spartan-led force (479 B.C.), they retired permanently from the Greek peninsula.

The defeat of Persia in 479 B.C. meant that the Greek world remained outside Persian control. Since Persia no longer had a strong navy, the Greek cities of Asia Minor were also able to reassert their independence, though they never regained their former strength. The Persian Empire was not completely defeated, however. For the next century and a half, Persia retained its control over the rest of the eastern Mediterranean—Egypt, Palestine, Syria, most of Asia Minor, and Mesopotamia. And the Persian king was able, at times, to influence Greek politics by siding with one or another group of quarreling states.

The victory over the Persians was to the Greeks what the American Revolution was to the colonists, an inexhaustible source of pride and confidence. A few small states had defeated a great empire. Now the Greeks were more sure than ever that they were destined for greatness, that their way of life was superior to that of all other peoples, that they could succeed in any enterprise they undertook. The century following the Persian Wars was the Golden Age, in which the Greeks made their indelible mark on the history of civilization.

THE AGE OF ATHENIAN DOMINATION, 478–431 B.C.

As soon as the Persians retreated, the Athenians rebuilt their city on an even grander scale. Proud of their city, proud of their democracy, proud of their victory over Persia, and prosperous beyond all expectations, the Athenians of the fifth century B.C. not only dominated the Aegean but created one of the most striking cultural patterns in the history of western civilization.

The Athenian Empire

A basic factor in Athens' rise to power and cultural supremacy was wealth. A century earlier, most of the commerce in and out of the Aegean had gone to Miletus or one of the other Greek cities of Asia Minor. But as these cities declined during the late sixth century, enterprising Athenian merchants began diverting trade to Athens. After the Persian Wars, the Athenians used their large navy to bring former Milesian trading stations—on the Black Sea and in Syria—under their own control.

In the vast expansion of their trading

Four drachma coin from Athens showing Athena and her owl (*ca.* sixth century B.C.).

empire, the Athenians took advantage of their position as leaders of the Delian League. This league was an alliance of the Greek maritime cities around the Aegean. Its original purpose was to continue the naval war against Persia until all Persian forces had been chased from the Aegean Sea and all Greek cities had been freed of Persian control. Delegates met first in 478 B.C. on the island of Delos, from which the league took its name. Each member state was to contribute an annual quota of ships or money. Since Sparta was of no use in naval affairs, the Athenians had no rival power to face in the league. And because they contributed by far the largest fleet, they were given the right to name the admiral and the administrators of the common treasury.

In time, the navy of the Delian League became almost exclusively Athenian. Other members, with only a few exceptions, contributed cash rather than ships. Naturally, the navy of the league was soon being used primarily to protect and even extend the Athenian economic empire. When one of the member cities resigned in protest, the league's navy appeared in its harbor, besieged the city, and dismantled its fortifications. From that time on, the city was governed by Athens, and the other league members were made to understand that a similar fate awaited other defectors. Finally, in 454 B.C., when the league's treasury was moved from Delos to Athens, it was clear that the league had become an Athenian Empire and that the members were little more than Athenian dependencies.

Although the cities comprising the league had no choice but to remain in it, the other cities of the Greek peninsula became increasingly alarmed at the growth of Athenian power and began to seek closer ties with Sparta and the Peloponnesian League. Between 454 and 431 B.C. most of the cities of the Greek peninsula and around the Aegean became associated with one of the two alliance systems: the Delian League dominated by Athens or the Peloponnesian League dominated by Sparta.

During this time the productive power of Athens was enriched by the

Ostraka, or broken pieces of pottery, on which citizens wrote the names of those they wished to ostracize from Athens, *ca.* 470 B.C. The names on these pieces are Themistocles, who was later recalled, and Cimon.

influx of thousands of artists, artisans, and merchants from the more sophisticated Greek cities of Asia Minor, who saw greater opportunities in Athens than in their home cities. These immigrants, known as *metics* (that is, Greeks who were not Athenians), provided a labor supply for the expanding Athenian economy. And the many artists, poets, and philosophers among them deserve much of the credit for making the fifth century Athens' Golden Age.

Another source of Athenian postwar prosperity was the large number of prisoners-of-war brought to Athens as slaves. With *metics* to help produce and sell their wares and with slaves to labor in their shops and mines, all but the poorest Athenian citizens could participate fully in the cultural and political life of the city. And with the wealth derived from tribute paid by the Delian League, plus the income from commerce and mining, the life of the Athenian *polis* was remarkably rich and complex.

Politics

The Athenian constitution, by the middle of the fifth century B.C., gave almost equal rights to all citizens; only a few vestiges of aristocratic privilege remained. In fact, in some areas even the privileges of merit were avoided; for example, the members of the Council of Five Hundred were chosen by lot. The Greeks called this system "democracy," and many modern writers have echoed the phrase. But in a population of around 100,000, there were about 20,000 *metics* and about 40,000 slaves. Neither *metics* nor slaves could vote, nor could the wives and daughters of citizens. Thus only about 20,000 male citizens (one-fifth of the population) had political rights.

This was a high proportion, by standards of the ancient world, but it was not what we would call democracy.

The really significant change in the fifth century was not an increase in the number of voters, but an increase in the political power of the lower classes. These men manned the fleet, which was the source of Athenian wealth and power. Leaders of political factions had to seek the favor of the mass of common citizens, and the favor of the masses could shift with alarming rapidity. To prevent a revival of tyranny, the Athenians had invented a device known as ostracism: a majority of citizens could vote the exile for ten years of any politician who seemed to be gaining too much power. Many of the ablest leaders of the city were ostracized, including Themistocles who had built the fleet that preserved the liberty of Athens. The system of government was unwieldy; the general assembly was too large and the Council of Five Hundred changed its leadership each month. Policy had to be decided in private conferences among politicians and then be sold to the citizens. It took an extremely able leader to give consistency to Athenian policy without falling into demagogy on the one hand or self-righteous disdain of public opinion on the other. It is remarkable that several men in the fifth century succeeded in this difficult task and that one man, Pericles, was a powerful politician from 463 to 429 B.C. and unchallenged leader of Athens for the last fifteen years of this period.

The issues discussed by the people ranged all the way from charges of corruption and excessive ambition to basic questions of foreign policy. There were conservatives who feared that the growth of Athenian power was alienating friends of Athens and forcing them to ally with

Pericles, from a Roman copy of a Greek bust of the fifth century B.C.

Sparta; there were expansionists who wanted to grab everything in sight. But there were not two organized political parties. The Athenians were too individualistic to fall into rigid political allegiances, and as long as the expansionist policy was successful, the majority did not really want to drop it. Thus in his early years Pericles' chief opponent was not a conservative, but Cimon, who was even more of an imperialist than Pericles. Only when they were faced with the disaster of a losing war did the Athenians think seriously about modifying their constitution and their basic policies.

Art and Architecture

The destruction of Athens by the Persians meant that the city had to be rebuilt, and the new wealth of Athens allowed it to be rebuilt splendidly. Construction was rather haphazard until Pericles became "boss" of the city and put his friend Phidias, a sculptor, in charge of what might be called city planning. With plenty of money at their disposal, Pericles and Phidias were able to attract architects, sculptors, and painters from all over the Greek world. There was nothing at Athens that could not be found in other Greek cities, but there was more of it and, on the whole, it was better arranged.

Greek art of the fifth century B.C. was an art that had solved its technical problems. Greek architects could construct imposing and well-proportioned buildings; Greek sculptors could represent all the details of the human body with absolute accuracy. It was also an art with definite and limited goals. Greek artists were interested in the finite, not the infinite; they never undertook the hard task of giving concrete form to visions. They idealized life here on earth, not life in a heaven about which they thought little. The ideal man was a demigod, and the god was simply an idealized man. There is little sense of conflict in the Greek art of this period, no antagonism between the real and the ideal. Life in this world at its best could be beautiful and satisfying, and this is what the artists sought to represent.

These characteristics of Greek art are evident in the crowning achievement of the rebuilding of Athens—the temple of the Parthenon,* dedicated to Athena, the patron goddess of the city. The Parthenon did not attempt to impress the beholder through mere size as Egyptian structures had done. Though the Parthenon is almost as large as a football field, its basic qualities are harmony and proportion; it is constructed on a scale that can be measured and understood by the human eye. The Parthenon stands on the crest of the Acropolis, the hill that dominates Athens, but it does not reach toward heaven like a Gothic cathedral. It is the crown of an earthly city, not the gateway to a heavenly one.

The sculpture of the Parthenon, carved by Phidias and his followers, represents the gods as well as the people of

Pericles on Athens and Sparta

This oration, inserted by the Greek historian Thucydides in his *History of the Peloponnesian War*, does not give Pericles' exact words, but it does express admirably the pride of the Athenians in their city and its form of government.

We are called a democracy, for the administration is in the hands of the many and not of the few. But . . . the claim of excellence is also recognized, and when a citizen is in any way distinguished, he is preferred to the public service, not as a matter of privilege, but as the reward of merit. . . . Our city is thrown open to the world, and we never expel a foreigner or prevent him from seeing or learning anything of which the secret, if revealed to an enemy, might profit him. . . . In the matter of education, whereas the Spartans from early youth are always undergoing laborious exercises which are to make them brave, we live at ease, and yet are equally ready to face the perils which they face. . . . For we are lovers of the beautiful, yet simple in our tastes, and we cultivate the mind without loss of manliness. . . . Such is the city for whose sake these men fought and died; . . . and every one of us who survive should gladly toil on her behalf.

From Pericles' Funeral Oration, in Thucydides, *The History of the Peloponnesian War,* trans. by B. Jowett in Francis R. B. Godolphin, ed., *The Greek Historians* (New York: Random House, 1942), Vol. 1, pp. 648–50.

---

* The Parthenon served as a place of worship for over 2,000 years; it was a temple to Athena, then a Christian church, and finally a mosque. It was almost intact until it was blown up in a minor war 300 years ago. Today only the outer row of columns is standing, though many of the sculptures were saved.

The Acropolis at Athens.

the city in their processions, their athletic contests, and their military exercises. Here again, the Greeks did not distinguish between the religious and the secular, or, put another way, the noblest and best secular activity was also a religious act.

Drama

Built into the side of the Acropolis sloping away from the city was an outdoor amphitheater dedicated to the god Dionysus. Here, during the two annual festivals of Dionysus, the Athenians attended a series of plays. These plays were not staged for amusement. An important part of the religious festival, they were presented by the city to instruct and purge the citizens before they attended the sacred Dionysian rites.

The Greeks had long celebrated religious festivals with semidramatic performances in which a single speaker told a story to which a chorus offered responses. But during the Golden Age the Athenian dramatists transformed these rituals into full-fledged drama by adding a second and then a third speaker. The stories were not new to the audience. Playwrights used themes drawn from ancient Greek legends to illustrate the religious and ethical problems of the present world. What is right conduct? Can a man avoid the fate decreed him by the gods? What course can an individual take when civic and religious laws conflict? These are some of the questions posed by the great Athenian dramatists of the Golden Age: Aeschylus (525–456 B.C.), Sophocles (496?–406 B.C.), and Euripides (480?–406? B.C.).

Running through all the Greek tragedies is the theme that man must remain in harmony with the universe. The Greeks admired a man who was strong and self-sufficient. But the Greek ideal was "moderation in all things," and—as might be expected in a society where most people knew one another—the Greeks could not tolerate a man who believed that he was superior to other men. Thus the greatest fault was *hybris,* or pride. Specifically, *hybris* meant assuming a role reserved for the gods, particularly in taking the life of another human being, even by accident. Thus most Athenian tragedies deal with guilt and expiation—the misfortunes that must come to a man who defies the gods by not accepting the limitations placed upon him as a human.

Best known of the plays of Aeschylus are the blood-chilling tales of the *Oresteia* trilogy, which examine the religious aspects of justice through the story of the downfall of the house of Agamemnon. Agamemnon, betrayed by his wife, is avenged by his son, but the son must suffer for presuming to deal out the retribution reserved for the gods. In *Oedipus the King,* Sophocles, the most popular playwright of the period, deals with the problem of the man who has unwittingly done wrong. Not knowing who his parents were, Oedipus killed his own father and married his own mother. In his *Antigone* Sophocles portrays a conflict that is still acute today—the conflict between the demands of the state and the desire of the individual to follow a higher moral law. Creon, King of Thebes, forbids the burial of his nephew, who had been killed in an unsuccessful rebellion. The body must be left to rot in the fields; anyone who touches it will be put to death. Antigone, sister of the victim, defies the king, for no human order can justify breaking the laws of the gods. Creon decrees that Antigone be confined in a rocky vault and she kills herself. Creon's subsequent remorse is not enough to save him. His son, who had loved Antigone, commits suicide; his wife kills herself in despair. Human pride, which had defied religion and conscience, has been punished.

Euripides was the youngest of the three great tragedians of the Golden Age. Unlike his predecessors, he was more interested in human emotions than in the problems of sin. His plays were not always well received, for they frequently dealt with unpopular themes. In *Medea,* for instance, Euripides elicits the sympathy of his audience for a half-crazed foreign woman who murders her own children to spite the Greek husband who

had abandoned her. And in *The Trojan Women,* presented when Athens was at war and bursting with pride, Euripides made the Athenians watch a play about the inhuman atrocities perpetrated by a people at war and passed off as patriotic acts.

The writers of comedies were at least as popular as the writers of tragedies, and they probably came closer to reflecting the ideas of ordinary citizens. The only fifth-century comedian whose works have survived was Aristophanes (448?–380? B.C.). Many of his plays were lost, but those that we possess are witty commentaries on the events of his own day. At times he seems to have been seeking the applause of the low-brows; for example, the philosopher Socrates appears in one of his plays, *The Clouds,* as a ridiculous figure who talks learned nonsense. But Aristophanes had an honest dislike of humbug and pomposity and a sincere aversion to war. One of his most effective plays is *Lysistrata,* an antiwar comedy in which the women of Athens persuade their husbands to make peace by refusing to sleep with them.

History and Philosophy

Sculpture and architecture, tragedy and comedy, reached their peak in the Athens of the fifth century B.C. History and philosophy, which started later, naturally attained their highest level at a later date. The foundations for both disciplines were laid during the period when Athens was rising to greatness, but the most influential books on these subjects were written after the collapse of the Athenian Empire.

Little is known of the first Greek historians; they seem to have been interested chiefly in genealogies. But with Herodotus of Halicarnassus (*ca.* 490?–430? B.C.), one of the many scholars who migrated to Athens, we find the historian who is a storyteller and who is interested in the curious differences among the customs of peoples. Herodotus' theme was the war between the Persians and the Greeks, which he saw as the culmination of a long struggle between the culture of the Orient and the culture of Greece. He therefore felt that he should

Sophocles, popular fifth-century B.C. playright.

describe the development of all the peoples of the Persian Empire, including the Egyptians and the Babylonians. Herodotus had traveled through these countries and had talked to many well-informed men. He preserved many useful facts, but he himself knew that there were as yet no techniques for separating facts from legends. Even his account of the Persian War is so influenced by national pride that it is not entirely reliable, but it is still exciting reading.

Philosophy and science had their roots in the learning of Egypt and Babylonia. In both countries there had been accurate astronomical observations, development of basic principles of mathematics, and some speculation about the nature of the physical world. The Greeks of Ionia, who were a gifted people, probably had ideas of their own about such matters, but they were enormously stimulated by the material they received from the older civilizations of the East. By the sixth century B.C. the Ionians were attempting to organize scattered facts and ideas into coherent systems, to discover first principles and general laws, to express the difference between things as they are and things as they seem. They were somewhat too ready to generalize from insufficient data, somewhat inclined to oversimplify complex problems, somewhat too willing to ascribe human values to mere abstractions (e.g., "lucky" or mystical numbers, such as seven). But in beginning to develop the idea of laws of nature, in looking behind appearances to reality, in seeing mathematics as a powerful tool for solving problems, the early Greek philosophers laid the foundations for all later scientific thought in the West.

The search for a single first principle was not very successful as long as it was confined to purely physical entities, such as "water" or "fire." But several Greek philosophers, notably Heraclitus and Anaxagoras, reached the idea of a *logos* or a Mind that governed and permeated the world. Pythagoras, an Ionian who migrated to southern Italy, saw the organizing principle in numbers, naturally enough, since he was a distinguished mathematician. The appearance of change also perplexed early philoso-

phers: How can a flowing river remain the same river? Anaxagoras resolved the paradox by arguing that the world was made up of countless tiny particles, unchanging themselves, but constantly rearranged to give the appearance of change. This was a forerunner of the "atomic" theory of Democritus, rejected by most of the Greeks but revived by modern scientists.

Athens attracted scholars just as it did artists. The intellectual climate was stimulating, and the Athenians could afford to hire teachers for their youth and to support distinguished writers. By the fifth century B.C. Athens had become the center for the teaching of philosophy, which it remained for many centuries. With so many men arguing about basic truths, opinions were bound to be voiced that shocked conservative citizens. For example, Anaxagoras was accused of atheism because he taught that the sun was simply a ball of fire and that the earth rotated around it. Since Pericles was a patron of Anaxagoras, charges against the philosopher could be used to discredit the statesman.

Even more annoying to many Athenians were the Sophists (the "Wisdomers"), a group of wandering teachers primarily interested in problems of human reason and behavior. They tried to make students think for themselves by asking questions without giving answers. The naive responses of the students were then demolished by logical arguments, so that eventually (at least in theory) the students would begin to think logically themselves and discard prejudices and outworn dogmas.

Teaching students to think for themselves and opposing time-honored beliefs with logic are always dangerous occupations. The Sophists made things worse by being relativists. "Beauty," said one Sophist, "is in the eye of the beholder." If beauty is relative, so is truth, so is justice. And if justice is relative, why should not a bright young man trained in logic and rhetoric go to the law courts and win bad cases with clever arguments?

This is precisely what the enemies of the Sophists feared. Their concern was not unjustified. The Sophists did develop

An actor wearing a mask, in a declamatory pose (bronze statue from Graeco-Roman period).

an excellent technique of logical analysis, used by all succeeding Greek philosophers, but they also developed a number of tricks of argument that could thwart the simple, honest, uneducated man. The Athenians did believe in justice, even if they could not define it logically, and the Sophists offended their civic and religious beliefs. Men of the lower and middle classes, who could not afford to hire tutors for their sons, were also offended by the fact that the Sophists sold "wisdom" for money.

Socrates (469–399 B.C.), one of the few native Athenian philosophers, shared the dislike of many of his fellow-citizens for the Sophists. He would not take money for his teaching, and he spent his life trying to prove that the Sophists were wrong. He believed that truth, beauty, and justice were eternal and existed independently of man. If an object was beautiful, it would be beautiful whether or not a human being was there to see it. Similarly, if an action was a crime, it was wrong for all people and for all time.

Socrates taught that each man was born with an innate knowledge of eternal truth, but that this knowledge became clouded by his experiences in a selfish and materialistic world. To know the truth, a man must clear away the misconceptions acquired in this world and discover the spark of eternal truth that was in his own soul. To make his point, Socrates borrowed the techniques of the Sophists, asking questions to make people see for themselves where their thinking was unclear or illogical. Although Socrates was beloved by his immediate followers, his methods did not endear him to the populace, most of whom classed him with the Sophists. And in one of the great ironies of history, this opponent of the Sophists was finally executed on charges that, like the Sophists, he was corrupting the youth of the city (see p. 48).

THE PELOPONNESIAN WAR 431–404 B.C.

The Peloponnesian War has been viewed as a Greek tragedy that was acted out in history. It was caused by *hybris*—the ambition of Athens and of Sparta, the desire of politicians for renown, the deliberate renouncement of justice and reason. It was a curse that passed from one generation to the next, an evil that endured when it could soon have been stopped. It ended with the humiliation of one "actor" and the realization by the other that victory led only to new suffering. One might easily see in this tragedy the downfall of classical Greece.

Such a view is, of course, a gross exaggeration. Life is less logical and less coherent than a classical tragedy. Actually, some of the greatest achievements of Greek culture came during and after the war—the plays of Euripides and Aristophanes, the philosophy of Plato and Aristotle. And while the war weakened many Greek city-states, especially Athens and Sparta, the Greek world of competing city-states had always been insecure. It could endure only so long as no great power existed in the eastern Mediterranean. Once the decaying Persian Empire was replaced by new and

The Trial of Socrates

Plato, in his dialogue *The Apology,* reported the trial of Socrates. In this passage Socrates explains why he cannot change his ways.

Suppose . . . you said to me "Socrates, we shall disregard Anytus and acquit you, but only on one condition, that you give up . . . philosophizing. If we catch you going on in the same way, you shall be put to death." . . . I should reply, "Gentlemen, . . . I owe a greater obedience to God than to you; and so long as I draw breath and have my faculties, I shall never stop practising philosophy and exhorting you and elucidating the truth for everyone that I meet." I shall go on saying . . . , "My very good friend, you are an Athenian and belong to a city which is the greatest and most famous in the world for its wisdom and strength. Are you not ashamed that you give your attention to acquiring as much money as possible, . . . and give no attention or thought to truth and understanding and the perfection of your soul? . . . Wealth does not bring goodness, but goodness brings wealth and every other blessing, both to the individual and to the State." Now if I corrupt the young by this message, the message would seem to be harmful. . . . And so, gentlemen, I would say, "You can please yourselves . . . whether you acquit me or not; you know that I am not going to alter my conduct, not even if I have to die a hundred deaths."

From Plato, *The Last Days of Socrates,* trans. by Hugh Tredennick (Baltimore: Penguin Books, 1959), pp. 61-62.

Socrates, statuette from Hellenistic period.

powerful kingdoms, the Greek cities, strong or weak, could exist only on sufferance. The Peloponnesian War simply underlined a fact that had long been apparent: the Greeks could not unite into a single state. If they could not unite, they were doomed to lose their independence.

The immediate causes of the war were quarrels with Corinth over the colonies of Corcyra and Poteidaea and the decision of Athens to exclude the merchants of Megara from Athenian markets. These acts did no real damage to Corinth or to Sparta and its allies—none of the disputed cities had great military strength or important trade connections—but they seemed one more proof of the dangers of Athenian imperialism. Sparta and the Peloponnesian League declared war in 431 B.C.

Pericles' war plan was to abandon the Athenian rural areas, concentrate the population inside the city walls, and rely on his navy to harass the enemy and keep open the sea lanes. Since Sparta had no navy, Athens could be sure of an adequate supply of imported food and thus could hold out indefinitely. But in the second year of the war a plague broke out in Athens, killing a considerable part of the population, including Pericles himself. No one could really take his place. There were still able leaders in Athens, but none of them could gain the support of the people long enough to follow a consistent policy. The Athenians did well enough in the early fighting, and Sparta made peace in 421 B.C. But ambitious politicians seeking to gain power by a victorious war reopened the conflict, and from that point it was all downhill. The Athenians took greater and greater risks, such as their disastrous attempt to conquer Syracuse in 415-413 B.C., and in the end their naval power was completely destroyed. In 404 B.C. they surrendered to Sparta.

For a brief period Sparta dominated the Greek world. The Spartans put Athens under the control of a brutal oligarchy and tried to set up similar governments in other enemy states. But Sparta also was suffering from the effects of the war, and political dissension at home weakened its power abroad. Athens soon threw off the harsh government imposed by Sparta and reverted to its old political system. Other cities followed the Athenian example. Although Sparta struggled for several decades to maintain its hegemony, its army, never very large, steadily dwindled in a series of losing battles. By 370 B.C. Sparta had become so weak that it could not even defend the Peloponnesus.

The great war between Athens and Sparta produced a great historian, Thucydides (ca. 460-400 B.C.). An Athenian general who had been deprived of his command, Thucydides very early began to collect material for a history of the conflict. He wanted to be absolutely accurate, to write only from his own experience or from the testimony of eyewitnesses. But even more, he wanted to describe the behavior of politicians and states in terms that would have meaning for all future generations. In his own words, his history was to be "an everlasting possession." He succeeded in this high endeavor as few other historians have. The Funeral Speech that he ascribed to Pericles describes what a democratic community can be at its best. The Melian dialogue shows Athens descending to naked imperialism in dealing with a small city. This dialogue portrays so accurately the behavior of a scienceless conqueror that it was reprinted without changing a word to describe Hitler's takeover of Czechoslovakia in 1938.

GREECE IN THE FOURTH CENTURY B.C.

The Peloponnesian War and the subsequent struggles against Spartan hegemony created a confused political situation in which there was no real center of power in the Greek world. The King of Persia interfered again in Greek affairs and established a loose and intermittent control over the Greek cities of Asia Minor. Athens rebuilt its naval empire, but it was a much weaker one than that of the fifth century. Syracuse dominated the Greeks of Sicily and Italy, but it could not intervene in the Aegean area.

Plato (426–347 B.C.), Socrates' favorite pupil.

Aristotle (384–322 B.C.), pupil of Plato and organizer of Greek thought.

None of these states had a political future; in the end the great power of the Near and Middle East was to be the half-Greek, almost unknown, Kingdom of Macedon.

Plato and Aristotle

Political confusion did not destroy Greek culture; it simply gave the Greeks something more to talk about. The greatest Greek orators were men of the fourth century. They urged the Greeks, eloquently but vainly, to forget their petty quarrels and to unite against common enemies. More lasting than oratory, however, was the work of the philosophers who taught at Athens, the city that had been, and was long to remain, the center of Greek culture.

The beginning was not auspicious. The citizens of Athens, humiliated by their defeat, looked for a scapegoat and picked on the philosopher Socrates. Some of his pupils had been leaders in the unfortunate expeditions that crippled Athenian naval power; moreover, in his persistent questioning Socrates had challenged many accepted dogmas. He was accused of sacrilege (he believed in "eternal truth" rather than in the gods of the city) and of corrupting the youth. He was arrested in 399 B.C. and condemned to death by a narrow vote of a citizens' court. He could easily have escaped from his prison (which is probably what the authorities wanted him to do) but he refused to renounce his city or to disobey its laws. He died bravely, even

cheerfully, and set an example for all his successors.

His memory lived on in his devoted students, and especially in Plato (426–347 B.C.). Most of what we know of Socrates comes from Plato's Dialogues, and Plato's own work was founded on that of his teacher. He took Socrates' concept of the eternal good and expanded it into a more complex philosophy of his own. According to Plato, the only reality was the world of "ideas" where all things had existence in an abstract and perfect form. In the world of ideas the perfect "house" or "table" existed forever as a concept, not as a material object. Here on earth we have but poor and temporary copies of these things. Earthly houses are not true houses. They are but wood or stone that men have tried to shape into a copy of the true and eternal house; they can burn, blow apart, or deteriorate. The real house—in the world of ideas—can never change or deteriorate. The same, according to Plato, is true of "beauty" and "justice." True justice can exist only in the world of ideas; man may come closer to true justice by contemplating this ideal, but his efforts will always be subject to error. Plato thus provided a solution to the paradox posed by the teaching of Heraclitus, who said that all things were constantly changing, and the teaching of Parmenides, who held that change was impossible and therefore illusory. According to Plato, change was a characteristic only of the physical world. In the World of Ideas, all things remain eternally the same.

Like almost all Greeks, Plato believed that the city-state was the best form of political organization and that the character of the citizen was determined by the laws of his city. Plato was an intellectual aristocrat; he disliked Athenian democracy and doubted that the poor and half-educated lower classes could ever be virtuous unless they were controlled by an intellectual elite. His plan for an ideal city-state in the *Republic* showed a clear preference for the Spartan rather than the Athenian example. Each individual's life was to be carefully regulated from birth for the benefit of the whole community. Justice, of course, must be the basis of society, but justice belongs to the eternal world of ideas. It can be understood only by the most intelligent and most carefully educated citizens. Thus the heart of the *Republic* is the description of the training of the "philosopher-kings" who would rule and lead all other citizens to the good life.

Aristotle (384–322 B.C.), Plato's most famous pupil, was the great organizer of Greek thought. By his time the Greeks had accumulated a large amount of information and were trying to arrange it in meaningful order. Aristotle provided a powerful tool for classifying and deriving general propositions from scattered facts. This tool was logic, which he distilled from the somewhat erratic arguments of the Sophist school. Aristotle developed rigorous, consistent, and intellectually honest rules of logic and thus gave western thinkers an instrument that could be used for intellectual exploration of any field. Aristotle himself wrote treatises on everything from biology through political theory to poetics, and he supplied the vocabulary and the basic ideas that were used for centuries in almost every field of learning.

Aristotle was less of an idealist than Plato and was more concerned with observing actual facts. For example, he studied the constitutions of hundreds of Greek cities and came to the conclusion that pure monarchy, pure aristocracy, and pure democracy were good in themselves but were apt to degenerate; democracy, for example, easily falls into dictatorship. Thus the most stable government is a mixed government, in which a strong executive, an aristocratic council, and a democratic assembly balance one another. This idea still influences western society. But Aristotle applied it only to the city-state, in spite of the fact that in his later years the Kingdom of Macedon had gained control of almost all the Greek cities.

Aristotle, unlike Plato, did not believe that ideas were independent entities. He believed in the value of general propositions, but he felt that they grew out of concrete experiences. And in his distinction between Form and Matter he stimulated thought about developmental processes in the universe. Thus the sculptor imposes Form on the Matter of a piece of clay; the Matter of the acorn contains within it the Form of an oak.

Aristotle's logic was not entirely free from flaws; it depended a little too much on words with overtones that went beyond pure description. Yet western theology, law, mathematics, and science were all marked in their formative periods by strict applications of Aristotelian logic. Like all Greeks, Aristotle tended to generalize too rapidly, and difficulties in taking exact measurements vitiated some of his facts. These weaknesses were especially apparent in his works on the physical sciences; some of his guesses were helpful, but some, such as his theory of motion, were stumbling blocks for centuries. Even at his worst, however, Aristotle posed fundamental problems. For centuries western scholars began their work with a study of his books.

The Rise of Macedon

During the fourth century most of the cities of the Greek peninsula came under the domination of the Kingdom of Macedon. Macedon was a country of peasants ruled by crude, hard-living warriors who formed a loose federation under a king. Its culture was not much above the level of that described in the *Iliad*. These primitive people posed no threat to the Greeks in earlier periods. During the fourth century, however, when the Greek city-states were weak, the remarkable King Philip (359–336 B.C.) managed to organize the Macedonian warriors into a powerful and unified fighting force. Once his control of Macedon was secure, Philip began to extend his control over the city-states of the Greek peninsula. Once again, as during the Persian threat more than a century earlier, there was a great debate among the Greek city-states on how best to meet the danger. Demosthenes of Athens, the most famous orator of the golden age of Greek oratory, vainly warned his countrymen of the danger from Macedon, and urged them to unite. But, as so often before, the Greek cities were unable to support any single policy. Enough of them resisted to provoke a war with Macedon, but they could not cooperate to the extent of presenting a unified defense. As a result, Philip defeated the Greek city-states in 338 B.C. and turned the Greek peninsula into a Macedonian protectorate.

Greek coin bearing the likeness of King Philip, conqueror of Athens.

Alexander the Great
336–323 B.C.

Two years later, before Philip could complete his project by reconquering the Greek cities of Asia Minor from Persia, he was assassinated. He was succeeded by his twenty-year-old son, Alexander (336–323 B.C.). Conceited, overbearing, undisciplined, and wildly temperamental, Alexander was also brilliant and could display a mesmerizing charm. He was idolized by his soldiers—no small factor in his military success—and even among his enemies he became a legend in his own short lifetime.

Before his death, Philip had planned to unify the Greeks and rally them to his banner by leading a combined Greek army in a war of revenge against the Persians. Determined to carry out his father's plan, Alexander crossed the Hellespont with a Greek army in 334 B.C. and soon proved himself one of the most successful military strategists in history. At the very beginning of his campaign, he won a decisive battle against a Persian force in Asia Minor. The following year he moved eastward into Syria where he met and routed an army under the Per-

sian king himself. In 332 B.C. Alexander invaded Egypt. After conquering the country he took two momentous steps. He founded the city of Alexandria, which soon became the leading seaport of the eastern Mediterranean and a center of Greek scholarship. And he visited the famous oracle of Ammon in the Libyan desert, where he persuaded the priests to greet him as son of the god. Much of the Middle East had long been ruled by god-kings, and Alexander's prestige and authority were increased by this act. Even the Greeks may have gained some consolation by believing that Alexander was the son of Zeus (whom they identified with Ammon) and therefore their rightful ruler.

From a military point of view the rest was easy. Alexander proclaimed himself King of Persia, defeated the last Persian army without difficulty, and took his troops on a wild march north to Turkestan, south into the Indus Valley, and back to Babylon. The real problem was political, not military. How could this vast empire, inhabited by such different peoples, be made into a unit? Alexander apparently hoped to use Greek culture to control Asian manpower. Greek colonies were founded everywhere, even in western India; Greeks were encouraged to marry Asian women, and Greek was to be the common language of all the upper classes. Alexander died of fever in 323 B.C., at the age of thirty-three, before he could see how his plan worked. The amazing thing is that even without his guiding hand, even during the bitter quarrels among his successors, his plan did work. For eight hundred years Greek culture was the dominant and unifying culture of the Middle East.

THE HELLENISTIC ERA
323–*ca.* 30 B.C.

Alexander's sudden death meant that he had had no time to consolidate his empire or to arrange for an orderly succession. His Macedonian generals fought among themselves for his conquests. Ptolemy took Egypt immediately and Seleucus eventually gained control of most of the old Persian Empire, which became known as the Seleucid Empire. Matters could not be arranged so neatly in the old Greek heartland. Antigonus became king of Macedon and protector of the city-states of the Greek peninsula. But he could not hold Asia Minor, where many of the cities were united in the Kingdom of Pergamum and where the island of Rhodes became an independent naval power. And as time went on, Macedon's control over the southern Balkans and the Greek peninsula steadily diminished.

Political disunity, however, did not interfere with Alexander's vision of a commonwealth of peoples united by Greek culture. All the successor states were dominated by Greeks and by natives who imitated the Greek way of life. Of course the peasants and much of the urban population of the Middle East held fast to their native cultures and native languages. But scholars, administrators, and businessmen all used Greek and were guided, to some degree, by Greek ideas and customs. This era, in which the Middle East was permeated by Greek

Idealized statue of Alexander, probably the work of an artist of Pergamum in Asia Minor.

THE PARTITIONING OF ALEXANDER'S EMPIRE   *ca.* 300 B.C.

549 B.C.   338 323   ca. 30 B.

| Persian Empire |
| Independent Greek City-states |

Hellenistic Era

Rise and Dominance
of Macedon

influence, is known as the Hellenistic period.* It ended politically in 30 B.C. when Rome annexed Egypt, the last nominally independent Hellenistic state. But the cultural unity of the Middle East lasted far longer; it was broken only when the Moslems conquered Syria and Egypt in the seventh century A.D.

Egypt was probably the region in which Hellenistic culture flourished most. Alexandria, the capital of the Ptolemies, had a population of about a million; Athens in its prime had had about one hundred thousand. Alexandria profited from the boom in international trade that was one of the great unifying forces of the Hellenistic period. Into its harbor came ships from all parts of the Mediterranean; its caravans crowded the routes that led to Syria, Mesopotamia, and the Red Sea ports that traded with India. Alexandria imported ideas as well as merchandise. Next to the palace of the Ptolemies was a magnificent temple to the muses (called the Museum) for the study of the arts and sciences, and next to the Museum was a remarkable library. These facilities attracted scholars from all parts of the Hellenistic world and helped make Alexandria the only Greek city that could rival Athens as a cultural center. But Alexandria was more than a Greek city. Native Egyptians made up most of the laboring class, and in its streets one might hear almost any language of the ancient world. There were more Jews in Alexandria than in Jerusalem; it was in Alexandria that the Old Testament was translated into Greek.

Alexandria was by far the largest Hellenistic city, but Antioch, the capital of the Seleucid Empire, was also a great trade center. Rhodes and Pergamum prospered as transshipment points for goods headed for the Aegean and Black Seas. Pergamum also attracted a group of very able artists. Dozens of other

*The Greeks called themselves Hellenes; Hellenistic means "Greek-like."

Hellenistic cities took part in commercial, intellectual, and artistic activity of the period.

Art and Literature

Hellenistic art naturally differed from that of the fifth century; it had lost the serenity and security of the work of Phidias. It was more emotional and at times almost too emotional in depicting pain and suffering. Occasionally it sought to impress by mere size, as in the statue that stood astride the harbor of Rhodes or the Mausoleum at Halicarnassus. But at its best it created works that are still impressive. The Winged Victory of Samothrace, the Venus of Milo, the Dying Gaul of Pergamum are probably better known than the statues of the Parthenon.

Hellenistic art turned more and more toward realism as time went on. Paintings, mosaics, and statues in this style are not great art, but they are remarkably helpful to the historian. They show men and women as they were, and life as it was lived.

The literature of the period is not as well known. Theocritus was a lyric poet of merit; unfortunately so many followers imitated his pastoral settings that his originality has been forgotten. Apollonius wrote an epic in the Homeric style, and he too might be better remembered if so many later poets had not done the same thing. Certainly the writer whose influence has lasted longest was Menander. Although his comedies lack the bite of Aristophanes, his plots have amused audiences for two thousand years. Picked up by the Romans and passed down to Shakespeare, they still inspire modern musical comedies.

Science

Many scholars would say that the most striking achievements of the Hellenistic age were in science. Hellenistic

"Old Market Woman." Sculpture from the Hellenistic era was more emotional and realistic than art of the fifth century.

scientists performed some remarkable experiments and developed theories that foreshadowed the discoveries of the sixteenth and seventeenth centuries. But science did not have the same significance in the Hellenistic world that it has in ours. It was only an aspect of philosophy, a speculative pastime with little effect on ordinary life. Herophilus came very close to a theory of the circulation of the blood, but his work did little to change the practice of medicine. Aristarchus of Samos developed a theory of a solar system with planets revolving about the sun, but most people, even scholars, clung to the belief that the earth was the center of the universe. Eratosthenes made an estimate of the circumference of the earth that was very nearly correct, but it was centuries before anyone acted on this proof that the world was not impossibly large and that a voyage from Europe to the Far East would not take an impossible length of time. On the whole, Hellenistic science was not incorporated into the intellectual tradition of the Mediterranean world. Men reverted to the older doctrines of Aristotle, which remained the standard explanations of natural phenomena throughout the Roman and much of the medieval period. The first to take up the work of the Hellenistic scientists were Moslem scholars, and their writings did not reach western Europe until the thirteenth century A.D.

The most important exception to this rule was mathematics. Even practical-minded people could see the value of geometry, and Euclid (*ca.* 300 B.C.), who built scattered propositions about geometry into a coherent system, has been studied from his day to our own. Archimedes of Syracuse (278?–212 B.C.) worked out basic problems concerning mass and motion; he also perfected the theory of machines, such as the compound pulley. Again, there was a practical side to this work: missile-throwing machines built on his principles nearly defeated a Roman attack on Syracuse. This was remembered, but his more theoretical work was long neglected. One of the best tests of a scientific revival in thirteenth-century Europe was the degree to which the works of Archimedes were used.

Philosophy and Religion

Hellenistic philosophy and religion reflected the great problem of the age: What part could an individual play in a society in which individual effort seemed useless? In a small city-state of the fifth century the individual had an important role in his community; he could find meaning and purpose in his life and work. But in the great kingdoms of the Hellenistic world and in the huge cities that were the centers of Hellenistic culture, what could one man do? Would his greatest efforts have any impact on his society? Because of this problem, the three most popular schools of philosophy of the period emphasized private virtues and self-discipline, not participation in public life. The Stoics, whose influence lasted longest, believed in a universal law, which bound all men. Since all men were subject to this law, all men were brothers. Everyone from slave to king must do his duty in the position in which he found himself. Power and wealth, human desires and affections, were dangerous distractions. Public office was not to be sought, though it might be one's duty to accept it. The ideal existence was that of the private citizen, unaffected by external events. The Epicureans went even further. The wise man sought pleasure, but real pleasure came from right conduct, serenity of mind, and moderation in all things. Political ambition and pursuit of wealth caused more pain than they were worth, and the wise man avoided strong attachments to family, friends, or country. The Cynics doubted the possibility of any true knowledge and saw no sense in trying to save a world sunk in hopeless ignorance. Thus the wise man should not worry about wealth and power; he should find peace of mind by withdrawing from worldly concerns.

The philosophers spoke mainly to the middle and upper classes. The mass of the population sought spiritual satisfaction in the mystery cults, with their exotic ceremonies and mystic symbolism. With the active cross-fertilization of culture made possible by trade, new religions traveled from one part of the Hellenistic world to another, and all borrowed concepts and ceremonies from one another. Especially popular were the Dionysian rituals from the Greek cities, Isis-worship from Egypt, and the cult of the Great Mother from Asia Minor. Most of these cults offered their initiates a ceremonial purification from earthly sins, the comforts of a personal and loving god or goddess, a mystic brotherhood that gave each member a sense of security and personal worth, and a promise of eternity for the soul. The cults did not try to reform the world any more than the philosophies did; they helped the initiate to forget his miseries by giving hope that he would be compensated for present sufferings in a future life.

The Fall of the Hellenistic States

The Hellenistic states were never very strong militarily; and they were further weakened by wars and rebellions. For example, the Seleucid Empire soon lost Bactria and Persia, and in 167 B.C. the Jews, led by the Maccabees, regained their independence. It was easy for Rome, which became the dominant state in the Mediterranean by 200 B.C. to take advantage of quarrels among the fragmented states of the Hellenistic world and to annex them one by one. Rome had effective control of the region by 146 B.C.; with the seizure of Egypt in 30 B.C. it had acquired all of Alexander's empire, except Persia. But the Romans admired Hellenistic culture and, as far as they could, spread it to the West in Latin forms. Greek remained the language of the upper classes in the East, and Athens and Alexandria were the cultural centers of the Roman Empire. In a sense, the Hellenistic culture never ended, though its sphere of influence began to shrink after 500 A.D. It gradually and imperceptibly changed into Byzantine culture, and Byzantine culture ended only after the fall of Constantinople in 1453 A.D.

Suggestions for Further Reading

Note: Asterisk denotes a book available in paperback edition.

General　J. B. Bury, *A History of Greece,* remains the most thorough history of the ancient Greeks. Originally published in 1901, it is now available in a Modern Library edition (1972). G. W. Botsford and C. A. Robinson, *Hellenic History,* 5th ed., rev. by D. Kagan (1969), the standard text, is also excellent. Among the shorter treatments, M. I. Finley, *The Ancient Greeks** (1963), makes an interesting introduction to Greek history. A. Andrewes, *The Greeks* (1967), and F. J. Frost, *Greek Society* (1972), are interpretive rather than chronological. A representative selection of historical sources can be found in M. I. Finley, ed., *The Greek Historians** (1959). Complete texts of all the Greek writers are available in Greek and English in the *Loeb Classical Library.*

The Mycenaean Era and the Dark Ages　The most thorough study of the Greek world before the Golden Age is C. G. Starr, *Origins of Greek Civilization, 1100–650 B.C.* (1961). For the early period, see A. E. Samuel, *The Mycenaeans in History* (1966). There have been several recent studies of the Greek world at the time of the Trojan Wars: C. W. Blegen, *Troy and the Trojans* (1963); M. I. Finley, *World of Odysseus** (1954); and D. L. Page, *History and the Homeric Iliad* (1959).

The Greek World from 800 to 500 B.C.　A. R. Burn, *The Lyric Age of Greece* (1960), presents a detailed and factual history of the politics and literature of this era. The Greek cities of Ionia and of Sicily and Italy respectively are studied in J. M. Cook, *Greeks in Ionia and the East* (1962), and A. G. Woodhead, *Greeks in the West* (1962). F. de Coulanges, *Ancient City** (1956), is the classic study of the development of the city-state. H. Michell, *Sparta** (1952), helps explain the evolution of Sparta's unique institutions. On political change, see W. G. Forrest, *Emergence of Greek Democracy* (1966), and A. Andrewes, *The Greek Tyrants* (1965).

The Fifth Century	Recent studies of the Persian Wars include A. R. Burn, *Persia and the Greeks* (1962), and C. Hignett, *Xerxes' Invasion of Greece* (1963). For the political history of Athens in the Golden Age, see A. E. Zimmern, *The Greek Commonwealth** (1956), considered the classic work on the subject, or one of the excellent shorter treatments such as A. R. Burn, *Pericles and Athens** (1962); C. A. Robinson, *Athens in the Age of Pericles* (1959); V. Ehrenberg, *From Solon to Socrates* (1968); and W. R. Connor, *The New Politicians of Athens* (1971). H. Michell, *Sparta** (1952), deals with Sparta in the same period. A discussion of Athenian economics may be found in H. Michell, *The Economics of Ancient Greece*, 2nd ed. (1963), or W. S. Ferguson, *Greek Imperialism* (1913). A comprehensive study of the Peloponnesian Wars is B. W. Henderson, *The Great War Between Athens and Sparta* (1927). See also D. Kagan, *The Origins of the Peloponnesian War* (1969).
Art, Literature, and Drama	Excellent introductions to Greek art are J. Boardman, *Greek Art** (1964); G. M. A. Richter, *A Handbook of Greek Art* (1959); and T. B. L. Webster, *Greek Art and Literature** (1939). G. Murray, *The Literature of Ancient Greece* (1956), is standard. Among the many studies of Greek drama, H. D. F. Kitto, *Greek Tragedy** (1954), and D. L. Page, *History of Greek Tragedy** (1951), are particularly well-written introductions.
Greek Religion	A good account is M. Nilsson, *A History of Greek Religion*, 2nd ed. (1949). Robert Graves, *The Greek Myth** (1961), presents a new and exciting version of Greek mythology. Two excellent studies of Greek religious beliefs and practices are W. K. C. Guthrie, *The Greeks and Their Gods** (1950), and M. Hadas and M. Smith, *Heroes and Gods* (1965). E. R. Dodds, *The Greeks and the Irrational** (1951), examines Greek religion in the era before and during the Golden Age, and F. C. Grant, *Hellenistic Religions* (1953), covers the era after the Golden Age.
Science and Philosophy	The best introductions to Greek philosophy are to be found in general works on the history of philosophy. One of the best is F. Copleston, *A History of Philosophy*, Vol. I (1946). W. Jaeger, *Paidaea* (1944–45), is a remarkable book. The most useful recent summaries of Greek philosophy are W. K. C. Guthrie, *The Greek Philosophers from Thales to Aristotle** (1950), and B. Snell, *Discovery of the Mind: The Greek Origins of European Thought** (1953). G. S. Kirk and J. E. Raven, *Presocratic Philosophers** (1957), and F. M. Cornford, *Before and After Socrates* (1932), both have well-written accounts of the philosophers of the Milesian school. There are many excellent scholarly studies of Socrates, Plato, and Aristotle; for the interested student, A. E. Taylor, *Socrates** (1933), G. M. A. Grube, *Plato's Thought** (1935), and W. Jaeger, *Aristotle** (1962), are recommended.

L. Robin, *Greek Thought and the Origins of the Scientific Spirit* (1948), and B. Farrington, in both *Greek Science* (1949) and *The Origins of Scientific Thought** (1961), trace the development of Greek scientific inquiry. |
| Alexander the Great and the Hellenistic Era | The chief source for the career of Alexander the Great is the *Anabasis of Alexander* by Flavius Arrian, a Greek historian. From this Plutarch drew his *Life of Alexander,** of which there are many editions. Two scholarly but readable modern studies of Alexander are A. R. Burn, *Alexander the Great and the Hellenistic Empire** (1947), and U. Wilcken, *Alexander the Great* (1967).

No writer on the Hellenistic Era has successfully disentangled himself from the complexities of the politics of the period. For the reader who has learned the art of selectivity in studying political and diplomatic history, however, there are several useful and interesting works. The two standard works on the period are M. Cary, *A History of the Greek World from 323 to 146 B.C.* (1932), and M. I. Rostovtzeff, *Social and Economic History of the Hellenistic World* (1941). W. W. Tarn and G. T. Griffith, *Hellenistic Civilization** (1952), is shorter but thorough. M. Hadas, *Hellenistic Culture: Fusion and Diffusion* (1959), emphasizes the effect of Hellenistic culture on the Jews. |

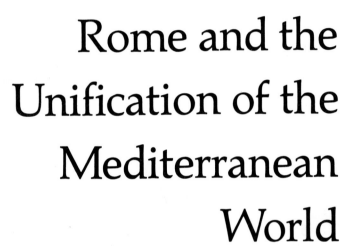

Rome and the Unification of the Mediterranean World

Rome succeeded in unifying the ancient world, a feat that neither Darius the Persian, nor Alexander of Macedon, nor the Hellenistic kings had accomplished. In the days of Darius and Alexander, Rome would have seemed a very unlikely candidate for this role. It was a small city without a good harbor and not much given to commerce; it controlled only a part of the Italian peninsula; its inhabitants were, from a Greek point of view, uneducated, unsophisticated barbarians. Even in the western Mediterranean there were cities that were richer, that possessed a higher culture, and that seemed as strong as Rome. The eastern cities and kingdoms were even more advanced. The rise of

Rome has puzzled historians in all ages. The Greek Polybius, who witnessed the crucial period of Roman expansion and was the first to ask what made the expansion possible, gave an answer framed largely in terms of politics. Rome conquered because it had a good constitution, knew how to keep the loyalty of its allies, and played the game of international politics with tenacity and ruthless determination. This is not a complete explanation, but it contains enough of the truth to warrant giving more attention to Roman politics than to the politics of earlier empires.

Linguistically the Romans and their Italic allies were closely related to the Greeks. Both were branches of the

Etruscan warrior (bronze,
early sixth century B.C.).

Indo-European-speaking peoples who had moved toward the Mediterranean from the interior of Europe in the period after 2000 B.C. But the Romans, unlike the Greeks, were far removed from eastern civilizations, and the geography of the Italian peninsula did not encourage long-distance commerce. There were few good natural harbors on either coast; those that did exist, such as Naples, were soon occupied by Greek colonists. On the other hand, there was more good farmland in the Italian than in the Greek peninsula; for a long time expansion could be inland rather than overseas. Rome and its Italic neighbors thus tended to resemble the Greek communities that were based on control of agricultural land rather than those based on control of trade routes. Early Rome was more like Sparta than it was like Athens.

The Italian peninsula, though a clearly delimited geographic entity, has never been difficult to invade. It was occupied by a mixture of peoples when the ancestors of the Romans arrived about 2000 B.C., and while these peoples were gradually assimilated by the invaders, other groups continued to try to conquer or to settle in Italy. The Romans were not entirely hypocritical when they claimed that some of their wars were forced on them by the continual influx of aggressive newcomers.

THE ITALIAN PENINSULA TO *ca.* 500 B.C.

By 1000 B.C. most of Italy was held by tribes that spoke Latin or one of the related Indo-European dialects. Soon after 800 B.C., however, two new peoples appeared in Italy, the Greeks who settled to the south of Rome and the Etruscans who settled to the north. Both built walled cities and subdued neighboring Italic tribes; both were active in Mediterranean commerce and brought Italy into closer contact with eastern civilization.

The Etruscans

The Etruscans had a more immediate impact on the Romans and their Latin neighbors than did the Greeks. Unfortu-

nately, it is not known who the Etruscans were and only a few elements of their language have been deciphered. They probably originated in Asia Minor. Although they certainly acquired some of their religious and artistic ideas from other peoples in that area, in Italy they developed an independent and highly sophisticated culture of their own. Their art was as remarkable as that of the Greeks, and sometimes more powerful. Their religion, especially their devices for forecasting the future, long influenced the Romans and other peoples of Italy. By acting as middlemen in trade between the Greek world and the peoples of central Europe, they became very wealthy. Wealth supported their high civilization and enabled them to dominate Italy from the Po Valley down into Latium (the region around Rome). The peak of Etruscan power and culture coincided fairly closely with the great age of Athens (600–400 B.C.). And like the Athenians, the Etruscans were to be subjugated by a semibarbarous neighboring state.

The Origins of Rome

In 600 B.C. Rome was only the largest of several fortified villages in Latium. According to Roman legend, the city was

Detail from Etruscan sarcophagus (mid-sixth century B.C.). The deceased couple was shown reclining on a couch, pouring libations as if at their own funeral banquet.

Etruscan kitchen utensils:
a spoon and a water bottle.

founded by the twins Romulus and Remus in 753 B.C. The site had been occupied long before that date, but archeology suggests that some sort of consolidation or rebuilding did take place in the eighth century B.C.

The early government of Rome resembled that of the Greek states of the eighth and early seventh centuries B.C. A king ruled with the help and advice of a council of leading citizens (the Senate). Major decisions, such as a declaration of war, had to be ratified by an assembly, composed of all citizens old enough for military service.

There were two classes of citizens: patricians and plebeians. The patricians owned most of the larger farms and formed a social elite; some of them came from leading families in other Italian communities, perhaps as the result of intermarriages. Almost all members of the Senate were patricians, and only patricians could hold public office. A few plebeians were well-to-do, but most of them were small landholders, tenant farmers on patrician estates, and artisans and shopkeepers. There must have been some inhabitants who were not citizens, such as slaves and foreign merchants, but little is known about them in the early period.

Rome came under Etruscan control around 600 B.C., when an Etruscan aristocrat managed to get himself accepted as king. He and his Etruscan successors raised Rome from a citadel and small market-town to a city. Greek and Etruscan merchants frequented the town, and the Romans acquired some understanding of the culture and institutions of the civilized world. Cultural benefits, however, seldom make a people grateful for foreign domination, and the Romans were no exception to this rule. About 509 B.C. (this traditional date is as good as any) a group of Roman patricians drove out the Etruscan king and proclaimed Rome an independent republic.

Rome then went through a stage very like that of the Greek cities a few centuries earlier: aristocracy replaced monarchy. All power passed into the hands of the patricians, and these Roman aristocrats were much more careful than their Greek counterparts to make sure that power could never again be concentrated in the hands of a single man. All administrative functions were performed by committees of at least two men, whose term of office, with few exceptions, was limited to one year. Thus the supreme executive authority was given to two consuls, who served both as chief magistrates and as commanders of the army. In times of crisis a single man could be named dictator with absolute authority, but his power lasted only for the duration of the emergency, and in no case for more than six months.

This was a republic, not a democracy. If one man could not rule, neither could the multitude. It is true that officials were elected by the assembly, but only patricians were eligible for office. Moreover, officials serving for only one year were always influenced by the wishes of the Senate, a body that included all former officials. It was hard for anyone to disregard the advice of such an experienced and prestigious group of men.

TERRITORIAL EXPANSION AND POLITICAL REFORM
ca. 500–265 B.C.

The early Roman constitution might have produced complete chaos, with its division of power among short-term officials, an assembly, and a Senate, and with flagrant discrimination against a majority of its citizens. Rome was saved by the good sense of its leaders, who always made concessions in time to avert collapse, and by the patriotism of its citizens, who were willing to accept gradual reform rather than risk open rebellion. One may wonder whether there would have been so much good sense and so much patriotism if the very life of the community had not been constantly threatened by outside enemies during the first two centuries of the Republic. Nevertheless, the Romans behaved better under pressure than most of their contemporaries; neither internal grievances nor external defeats destroyed the coherence and stability of the community. They were cautious in exploiting their victories and, at least in their early years, skillful in gaining the friendship of defeated enemies. These qualities gave them security at home and, by 265 B.C., control of all the Italian peninsula except for the Po Valley.

Threats from outside enemies began almost as soon as the Etruscans had been expelled. Under the Etruscans Rome had dominated the other cities of Latium, but with Rome independent these Latin cities wanted independence too. They formed a Latin League to challenge Roman domination and were thoroughly defeated by the Roman army (*ca.* 496 B.C.). Rome, however, realized that it had other neighbors who were more dangerous than the Latins; the Roman government wanted Latin support, not sullen enmity. Instead of destroying or annexing the cities of the Latin League, Rome made treaties with the League that formed a pattern for Roman control of other defeated Italian states. The Latin cities retained full rights of local self-government, but in time of war they had to supply troops for the Roman army. This formula worked well for many generations. Defeated Italian cities remained independent enough to satisfy local pride, while the Roman army acquired practically inexhaustible supply of troops.

Plebeian Activity and Political Reform

The Roman leaders had shown that they could conciliate outside enemies; they soon had the task of conciliating their own citizens. The plebeians, who formed the bulk of the army, suffered many political and social disabilities. Probably toward the end of the Latin War, and certainly during the fifth century B.C., the plebeians staged a series of sit-down strikes; if they were denied political rights they would not serve in the army. The Romans, like the Athenians in the same period, realized that they needed the full cooperation of all citizens in order to survive. Little by little the plebeians gained most of their demands.

The first concession, and one of the most important, was the election of five (later ten) tribunes to protect the interests of the plebeians. The persons of the tribunes were inviolate; to attack a tribune meant death without trial. A tribune could veto the acts of a consul or any other official, and his veto could not be overridden. Equally important was the fact that the tribunes were elected by an assembly of tribes, not by the old assembly in which citizens were divided into groups based on their wealth. Because the tribes were based on geographical districts, the patricians could not dominate this assembly. Resolutions passed by the assembly of tribes and approved by the Senate had the force of law. It was always difficult for the Senate to withhold such approval, and eventually the requirement was removed (287

Cities of the Latin League, *ca.* 400 B.C.

From Livy, *The Early History of Rome*, trans. by Aubrey de Sélincourt (Baltimore: Penguin Books, 1960), pp. 113–16.

Plebeian Reforms

Enslavement for debt was a constant threat to the poorer peasants of the ancient world. In this passage, the Roman historian Livy (59 B.C.–17 A.D.) shows how the plebeians gained constitutional safeguards against enslavement for debt by refusing to fight in a time of emergency.

An old man suddenly presented himself in the Forum. . . . Though cruelly changed from what he had once been, he was recognized, and people began to tell each other, compassionately, that he was an old soldier who had once commanded a company and served with distinction. . . . "While I was on service," he said, "during the Sabine War, my crops were ruined by enemy raids, and my cottage was burnt. Everything I had was taken, including my cattle. Then, when I was least able to do so, I was expected to pay taxes, and fell, consequently, into debt. Interest on the borrowed money increased my burden; I lost the land which my father and my grandfather had owned before me, and . . . I was finally seized by my creditor and reduced to slavery. . . ."

The man's story . . . caused a tremendous uproar, which spread swiftly from the Forum through every part of the city. . . .

On top of this highly critical situation came the alarming news . . . that a Volscian army was marching on Rome. . . . For [the plebeians] it seemed like an intervention of providence to crush the pride of the Senate; they went about urging their friends to refuse military service. . . . [One of the consuls then issued] an edict, to the effect that it should be illegal . . . [to] imprison a Roman citizen. . . . As a result of the edict, all "bound" debtors who were present gave their names on the spot, . . . and in the ensuing fight with the Volscians no troops did more distinguished service.

Founding of
City of
Rome
ca. 750 B.C.   *ca.* 600   *ca.* 500   265   146   27

| Independent Roman Kingdom | Etruscan Dominance | Rome Conquers Italian Peninsula | Punic Wars | Rome Conquers Entire Mediterranean Area |

B.C.), but long before that date resolutions of the assembly of tribes had become a normal form of Roman legislation. Consuls and other high officials, however, continued to be elected by the older form of assembly, which was led by the wealthier classes.

Like the Greeks, the Roman plebeians wanted written laws to protect them against arbitrary decisions of patrician officials. About 450 B.C. a committee was sent to Greece to investigate the laws of Solon and other codes. Subsequently, all power in the Roman state was temporarily turned over to a commission of ten men, who drew up the basic laws of Rome, the Twelve Tables. It proved somewhat more difficult to get rid of the commission than to establish it, but its work endured even when its members were driven from power. The Twelve Tables were a rather rudimentary set of laws, but through skillful judicial interpretation they satisfied the needs of the Roman people for many generations. They set the tone and marked the beginning of the greatest Roman intellectual achievement, the Roman law.

Finally, the plebeians gradually gained access to all public offices. This took a little longer than the other reforms; it was only in the fourth century B.C. that restrictions on secular offices were removed and only *ca.* 300 B.C. that plebeians were admitted to the priesthood. This last concession was more important than it seems, since a priest could block many political acts by declaring that the auspices were unfavorable.

Rich plebeians gained the most from these reforms: only they could afford the time and money to play the political game. Officials were unpaid, and a seat in the Senate, which regularly followed the holding of high office, was a time-consuming honor. But the plebeians as a whole seem to have been satisfied by their gains. Their tribunes and tribal assemblies gave them considerable power

when crucial political decisions had to be made; invidious legal distinctions had been removed; and theoretically all careers were open to all citizens. In actual fact, the Roman ruling class did what many ruling classes have done—it drew the ablest plebeians into its own ranks, accepted them as part of a new senatorial aristocracy, and so deprived poorer citizens of their natural leaders. But during the crucial years of Roman expansion the different Roman classes cooperated enough to avoid serious difficulties.

Rome's Conquest of Italy

The first real test of the Roman system came about 400 B.C. when the Romans decided to end the Etruscan threat to central Italy. After a long and difficult siege (*ca.* 405–396 B.C.) the Romans captured Veii and pushed the Etruscans back from the region of the Tiber, permanently shifting the balance of power between the two peoples. One reason, however, for Etruscan weakness was that they were also being attacked in the North by a new group of invaders, the Gauls. The Gauls were a branch of the Celts, another one of those Indo-European-speaking peoples who had been striking at the civilizations of the Mediterranean, the Middle East, and India ever since 2000 B.C. By the fifth century B.C. the Celts had occupied Germany, the British Isles, and what is now France but was then called Gaul from the name of the Celtic group that had settled there. The Gauls then crossed into Italy and drove the Etruscans out of the Po Valley. They moved south rapidly, and only a few years after the fall of Veii they destroyed a Roman army on the Tiber (*ca.* 390 B.C.). Rome was abandoned; only the citadel held out. Fortunately for Rome, this was only a raid, and the Gauls withdrew after sacking the city. Rome barely survived this catastrophe; some of its allies fell away, and

This head of a statue of Hermes (*ca.* 500 B.C.) was part of a group of terra cotta figures that adorned the roof of a temple of Apollo in Veii. It became a spoil of war when Veii fell to beseiging Romans in 396 B.C.

expansion almost ended for a generation. But the Romans were tough enough to rebuild their city and their power. By the 360s B.C. they were attacking both the Gauls and the Etruscans, and by about 350 they had annexed southern Etruria. The danger from the North had been greatly lessened.

After 350 B.C. the chief threat to Rome came from other Italic peoples, whose populations and territories were expanding rapidly. Even the Latin allies resented Roman hegemony, and the more distant cities saw no reason to allow Rome to expand indefinitely. Rome, on the other hand, wanted to stop the growth of potential rivals. The situation was complicated by the weakening of the Greek cities of southern Italy. Their trade had declined as a result of wars in Greece and the occupation of western Europe by the Celts, but they were still rich prizes. No Italic people would willingly let one or more of the Greek cities go to a rival. Finally, the more or less Hellenized inhabitants of the Balkans were beginning to cross the Adriatic and mix in Italian affairs, a course that reached its peak with the invasions of King Pyrrhus of Epirus in the years after 280 B.C.

The strongest Italic people were the Samnites, who held much of south-central Italy, including most of the fertile plain of Campania. They were in a much better position to take over Greek cities than the Romans, and they could count on the help of many of the other peoples of Italy. But before Rome could fully concentrate on the Samnites, it had to suppress a rebellion of its own allies. The Latin cities demanded complete equality with Rome, including an equal voice in the federal government. When this was denied, the Great Latin War (ca. 340–338) began. The Romans crushed the Latins, dissolved the Latin League, and instituted a new and harsher system for controlling subject cities. Most of the Latins had the duties of Roman citizens without the vote or the right to hold office. Some municipalities were governed directly from Rome; others retained limited rights of self-government. Still others became Roman colonies; that is, portions of their land were granted to Roman citizens, who became the ruling class of the city.

The lid of a bronze container from Praeneste, in Latium, fourth century B.C. The handle represents two warriors carrying a slain comrade.

Rome also retained the system of free, allied cities with full rights of self-government and limited military obligations, but there had to be strong political reasons and a good prospect of faithful cooperation to put a city in this category.

With the Latins under control, the Romans could turn on the Samnites. In a long series of wars (ca. 325–290 B.C.) the Romans finally defeated the Samnites and their allies. It was not an easy task; the Samnites won most of the early battles and, through an alliance with the Etruscans, forced Rome to fight on two fronts. But Rome's superior military organization and tight system of control of subject and allied cities prevailed over the loose Samnite and Etruscan confederacies. After the last Samnite War (298–290 B.C.), there was still a little mopping up to do, but the Romans basically controlled all Italy except for the Gauls in the Po Valley and the Greeks in the South. Some of the Greeks prudently allied themselves with Rome; others, led by Tarentum, called in King

EARLY ITALY   *ca.* 275 B.C.

Roman territory ca. 326 B.C.

Rome and its allies at the start of the
Second Punic War, 218 B.C.

MILES
0   100

Pyrrhus of Epirus to protect their liberties. Like most of Rome's enemies, Pyrrhus won many battles but lost the war.* By 265 B.C. the Greek cities of the peninsula had accepted Roman domination.

*In 279 B.C. Pyrrhus gained a victory over the Romans that cost a ruinous loss of his forces. Hence the term "Pyrrhic victory."

Rome's success in war was due to the remarkable staying power of its army. Roman generals were not infallible, but the Roman military system was unbeatable in the long run. The consuls enforced stern discipline: there was no straggling on the march or wavering on the battlefield; disobedience was punished with death. The basic military unit,

Founding of
City of
Rome
ca. 750 B.C.   *ca.* 600   *ca.* 500   265   146   27 B.C.

| Independent Roman Kingdom | Etruscan Dominance | Rome Conquers Italian Peninsula | Punic Wars | Rome Conquers Entire Mediterranean Area |

the legion of 6,000 men, had great striking power and at the same time great flexibility, for it was divided into smaller units that could maneuver independently. Most important of all was Rome's control over its subject and allied cities. The Romans never accepted defeat, not only because they were courageous, but also because they could always raise new armies. Stubborn perseverance won more for Rome than brilliant strategy. Even the strongest states of the Mediterranean world could not hold out against the steady pressure that Rome could exert.

ROMAN EXPANSION OVERSEAS, 264–146 B.C.

In acquiring the Greek cities of southern Italy, Rome inherited their struggle with Carthage for the control of Sicily. The resulting "Punic" Wars (Latin *Poenicus* = Phoenician = Carthaginian) tested Rome's staying power even more severely than had the Samnite Wars; several times Rome came close to total defeat. Since Carthage had been the strongest naval power in the Mediterranean, Roman victories over Carthage meant that Rome became dominant on sea as well as on land. This made it easy for Rome to intervene in the eastern Mediterranean, and long before the destruction of Carthage in 146 B.C., Rome had begun to dominate the Hellenistic world.

The Punic Wars, 264–146 B.C.

The first war with Carthage started in 264 B.C., only a year after Rome's final conquest of southern Italy, and lasted until 241 B.C. Without a fleet, Rome could not contest Carthaginian control of western Sicily, much less attack the center of Carthaginian power in North Africa. With characteristic confidence in their ability to master any military problem,

the Romans built a fleet, and made up for lack of naval experience by constructing ships that would let them profit from their skill in hand-to-hand combat. Grappling irons and movable boarding bridges locked hostile ships together and so enabled the Romans to convert a sea battle into something like a land engagement. Even with these advantages, Rome came close to losing the war. After initial victories, the Romans lost three fleets in succession, not to the enemy but to shipwreck and storm. It was all they could do to build a fourth fleet, but this one was victorious in a battle off western Sicily. Carthaginian naval superiority was permanently broken, and Carthage surrendered Sicily to the Romans in 241 B.C.

To make up for the loss of Sicily the Carthaginians decided to take over the rich mines and farmlands of Spain. Under the leadership of one of its best generals, Hamilcar Barca, Carthage gained control of southern and eastern Spain. This region was soon producing more revenue for Carthage than Sicily ever had. When Hamilcar died he was succeeded as governor of Spain first by his son-in-law and then by his twenty-five-year-old son Hannibal (221 B.C.).

Roman legend has it that Hannibal as a child swore to his father that he would avenge the Sicilian defeat by destroying Rome. For their part, the Romans were clearly annoyed by Carthaginian success in Spain and were furious when Hannibal crossed the Ebro River in northeastern Spain and attacked a city allied to Rome. They determined to crush Carthage in Spain as they had in Sicily. But the fighting had scarcely begun in Spain when Hannibal made one of the most daring strategic moves in all history. In 218 B.C. he left Spain, marched through southern Gaul, and crossed the Alps with a large army including fifty war-elephants. Cut off from his supplies, usually outnumbered, Hannibal repeatedly defeated the massive Roman armies sent against him. For fifteen years he

Symbol of Sicily, found in Ostia, chief port of Rome. The symbol's three legs correspond to the three points of Sicily.

This third-century B.C. coin bears one of the few known contemporary portraits of Hannibal. The elephant appears on the reverse.

ravaged the Italian countryside and on one occasion came close to Rome. In this desperate war, Rome was saved by the loyalty of its allies in Latium, Samnium, and Etruria, who made it impossible for Hannibal to establish himself in central Italy. In the south, through fear or favor, more of the allied and subject municipalities went over to Hannibal, and it looked as if he could maintain himself there indefinitely.

The deadlock was not broken until the Romans were able to field a first-rate general, Scipio Africanus. Scipio first went to Spain, where an indecisive war had been dragging on for years, and conquered the province for Rome. He then led a Roman army to North Africa and laid siege to Carthage itself. As he had anticipated, the Carthaginians recalled Hannibal, thus ending his Italian adventures. Losses in Italy and Spain had weakened the Carthaginian army; when Scipio met Hannibal at Zama, a few miles from Carthage, he won a decisive victory (202 B.C.). Carthage had to accept a harsh treaty: Spain was ceded to Rome; a heavy war indemnity was levied; and the Carthaginian fleet was limited to ten ships. Carthage had ceased to be a first-rate power.

Rome and the Hellenistic East

Unlike the Roman conquest of Sicily and Spain, it is hard to find a consistent pattern in Roman expansion in the East. Roman generals certainly wanted triumphs, and Roman businessmen wanted profit from eastern trade. Rome sought stability in the area and a recognition of its dominant position. On the other hand, it did not have a definite plan for conquest and expansion, nor was it even sure that it wanted to annex much eastern territory.

As we have seen, the Hellenistic kingdom of Epirus had tried to block Roman expansion in South Italy, and Macedon gave some assistance to Hannibal when he was operating in the same region. Rome had defeated both kingdoms and in the process had learned a good deal about the richness and the weakness of the Hellenistic world. Because there was no strong state in the

area, there was constant bickering among Egypt, the remnant of the Seleucid Empire, the little kingdoms of Asia Minor, Macedon, and leagues of Greek cities. Everyone sought the aid of Rome in their quarrels, but every peace settlement imposed by Rome collapsed. Rome soon found itself hopelessly entangled in a political mess. Roman leaders naturally became exasperated; they could neither keep order in the Hellenistic world nor get out of it.

When the Romans were exasperated they became brutal. Macedon and Epirus were plundered in 167 B.C.; thousands of their inhabitants were sold as slaves. Growing admiration for Greek culture did not keep the Romans from turning savagely on Greek cities that disobeyed Roman orders. Corinth was destroyed; Athens was plundered; and thousands more young men were sent to Italy as slaves. The net result was that Macedon became a Roman province; Rome controlled the Greek cities, allowing them a good deal of autonomy in internal affairs; Asia Minor became a sort of protectorate. Rome was less interested in ruling Syria and Egypt (in fact, the Romans had favored Egypt more consistently than any other Hellenistic state), but Rome made it clear that neither country was to take any initiative without its approval. Most of the Hellenistic world was now in Roman hands.

In the same year that Corinth was destroyed (146 B.C.) the Romans for no apparent reason turned again on Carthage. Carthage had regained some of its wealth but not its military power. Although no threat to Rome, its very existence offended men who remembered stories of the desperate battles against Hannibal. Carthage fell after a six-month siege; every inhabitant was slaughtered or enslaved, and the city was destroyed stone by stone. North Africa became a Roman province.

CONSEQUENCES OF EXPANSION

By 146 B.C. Rome controlled Italy, Sicily, Spain, North Africa, Sardinia, and Corsica in the West, and Illyria, Macedon, and Greece in the East. During the next century the gaps in this ring around the Mediterranean were filled in, but the problems of empire existed long before the empire was complete. How could the institutions of a city-state be used to govern the vast territories now ruled by Rome? How could leaders be found who could keep the confidence of the Roman people and gain the obedience of Roman subjects? How could Rome and Italy adjust to the drastic social and economic changes caused by the growth of Roman commerce and banking, the influx of wealth from plundered enemies and tribute-paying provinces, the importation of hundreds of thousands of slaves? How could one find a focus of loyalty in an empire that was also a republic, that had no dominant religion, no god-king, not even a chief of state? These were the questions that the Romans struggled with in the last two centuries before Christ. They found only partial answers at best. The resulting dissatisfaction destroyed the Roman Republic with its multiple leadership and led to the creation of an Empire with a single head.

Governing the Provinces

One problem could not be postponed—the government of the provinces. It soon received a workable if not entirely satisfactory answer. The Romans had long found it necessary to use former officials as military commanders. For example, Rome had only two consuls, but it might well have four or five theaters of military operations; in that case former consuls (proconsuls) would command some of the armies. Since most provinces had Roman garrisons, it seemed natural to make the military commander (the proconsul) the governor. This was not an ideal solution. Backed up by an army an unscrupulous governor could easily enrich himself. In fact, in 149 B.C. the Romans had to establish a special court to try corrupt governors. But not all governors were corrupt, and the mere existence of the court shows that there was some feeling against exploiting the provinces. Moreover, since there were repeated rebellions in some provinces, notably in Spain,

military governors were needed to hold the empire together.

The governors usually had very small staffs and left local affairs to the leaders of local communities. A few allied cities had complete autonomy; elsewhere Roman officials could intervene when they felt it necessary or profitable. The inhabitants of the provinces paid regular taxes to Rome, which, added to the money extorted by corrupt officials, imposed a heavy burden on the provincial economies. Earlier rulers, however, had been no less greedy, and Rome did put an end to the wars that had devastated many parts of the Mediterranean world. After the initial shock of conquest and after the penalties for unsuccessful rebellions had been dealt, the provinces seem to have adjusted fairly well to their new situation.

Changes in Religion, Literature, and Art

Closer contacts with the Hellenistic world brought about changes in Roman art, literature, and religion. Even before the eastern wars, educated Romans had known and been influenced by Greek models, but the sudden arrival of tens of thousands of Greek slaves and hostages in Rome came very close to producing culture shock. Some Romans were horrified at the idea of imitating despised foreigners; they wanted to be more Roman than ever: severe, warlike, unbending lovers of the simple life. Others felt that there was little that was good in the old Roman cultural tradition, and that only the Greek style was worthy of respect. Most men, of course, accepted neither of these extreme points of view, but the disagreement ran deep enough to have repercussions in politics. Conservative senators were sure that Greek influence caused political unrest, and this was one of the reasons why they opposed reform movements.

In religion, the Romans identified Greek gods with their own; for example, Zeus was Jupiter and Hera was Juno. Historically, these identifications had a foundation in fact: both sets of gods went back to early Indo-European divinities. But in their Greek form the gods were more human and more wayward than the stern, rather impersonal gods of Rome. In Rome as in Greece, the official religion had been controlled by the aristocracy, and it was already losing its hold on the masses, but it is probable that the introduction of Greek myths made it seem even less applicable to the needs of the people. In any case, the Romans turned, like the Greeks before them, to the mystery religions of the East. During the dark days of the Second Punic War, the Senate itself introduced the Asian cult of Cybele, the Great Mother, in order to bring good fortune to Rome. The cult of Dionysus came in about the same time, even though the Senate disliked its uninhibited ceremonies. Other Oriental religions soon followed.

In art, and especially in literature, Greek influence was so great that it is difficult to discover material that does not show signs of Roman imitation of Greek models. The Romans had certainly written poetry and composed some kinds of histories in the early period of the Republic, but one of the first long poems written in Latin was a translation of the *Odyssey*, and around 200 B.C. Romans writing history used Greek. As was pointed out (p. 56), an excellent account of Rome's rise to dominance in the Mediterranean was written in Greek by Polybius, one of the Greek hostages held in Rome. Polybius was deeply impressed by Roman power and by the Roman constitution, but he imitated Thucydides rather than Roman historians. Only with Cato's book on early Roman history (*ca.* 168 B.C.) was a solid historical work attempted in Latin. Cato, who was one of the anti-Greek senators, made a deliberate effort to bring Latin prose up to the Greek level.

The Romans thoroughly enjoyed Greek drama, and the first plays given at Rome were written in Greek. Later the playwrights Plautus and Terence satisfied the Roman desire for amusement by writing comedies in excellent Latin based on earlier works by Hellenistic authors. Little is known about early Roman architecture and not much more about early Roman sculpture, but in both fields a rough, vigorous native style was being replaced by imitation of Greek originals

This fresco found in a villa on the outskirts of Pompeii depicts initiation rites of a Dionysiac mystery cult, but they are rendered in such a way as to make precise interpretation difficult for the outsider.

before 200 B.C. Only in works on law was Greek influence minimal. This was the area in which Roman thinkers excelled. Soon after 200 B.C. they were writing solid treatises on basic legal texts and their interpretation. But even in fields related to law, it was only in the first century B.C. that the Romans began to produce important books on political theory and philosophy.

Social, Economic, and Political Change

In addition to providing a constant stream of wealth flowing toward Italy, the provinces supplied Rome with cheap labor. Each conquest and each rebellion was followed by the enslavement of a large part of the defeated people. The result of this influx of money and men was to change the nature of the Roman social and economic system. The upper classes could profit from the new opportunities offered by the acquisition of an empire; the lower classes could not. The gap between rich and poor grew steadily wider. And gaps appeared among the rich as well. War was no longer a fight for existence but a hunt for plunder; public office was no longer a burden but a chance to acquire wealth. As a result, competition for magistracies, army commands, and contracts for public works became intense, and factional struggles among the governing class eventually made it incapable of governing.

The upper classes included the senators and the *equites,* or equestrians. The senators belonged to families, both patrician and plebeian, that had held high public office and hence were entitled to seats in the Senate. Most officials, and consequently most senators, came from old senatorial families; only occasionally could a new man break into this privileged group. It cost a good deal of money to campaign for public office, and the profits began coming in only when a man had reached the higher ranks (certain lower officials had to provide amusements for the public at their own expense). Moreover, the great noble families felt that they alone were worthy of office; they used all their influence to exclude lesser men.

The equestrians were those who, in the early years of the republic, had had enough money to provide their own horses for service in the army. As a class, they were less wealthy than the senators, although the richer equestrians were better off than the poorer senators. Most equestrians were substantial landowners, but some of them were merchants, bankers, and bidders for public contracts. Custom and law forbade senators to engage in these activities, though they often did so by making secret arrangements with businessmen. On the whole, the interests of the senatorial and equestrian classes coincided fairly closely, and each political faction that struggled for office had both senators and equestrians in its ranks.

A major impetus to social and political change was agricultural change. At the beginning of Roman expansion there was a considerable amount of uncultivated land in Italy. Most of this land, as well as cultivated land confiscated from defeated enemies, fell into the hands of the Roman government. Ordinary citizens, especially those who went out to found colonies in the peninsula, received some of the new lands, but the largest part went to the upper classes. They discovered, as rich men in other societies have discovered, that a large estate can be run more efficiently than a small farm, especially when cheap labor is available. The Roman conquests provided them with an almost inexhaustible supply of slaves. Slaves cost little, were given a minimum of food and clothing, and were at times literally worked to death.

Free peasant farmers found it difficult to compete with plantations using slave labor. They also lost their best market when the city of Rome began to import cheap grain from Sicily by sea, rather than purchase higher-priced grain trundled across the hills in ox-carts. Rich landlords could compensate for this shift by going in for stock raising or wine growing; poor men could not make such investments and were bought out by the rich. Finally, since all landholders owed military service, peasants were frequently called away from their farms at inconvenient times. The result of all these pressures was that a considerable number of small farmers were forced to sell their lands to the owners of the great estates. Those who sold out seldom found work in the countryside, but drifted to Rome where work was equally scarce. The city was growing rapidly; it had no major export industry, and most of the poor had no permanent jobs. They became "clients" of the rich and especially of the senators. Their duties were to run errands, act as bodyguards, applaud speeches, and start riots when it seemed helpful to their boss or to his faction.

Thus there were two depressed classes in Roman society: the slaves and the poor freemen. Of the two, the slaves caused the less trouble. The agricultural slaves, who were treated most harshly,

Scenes from everyday life in first-century Rome. Above right: a Greek slave appears to be tutoring his master and mistress. Above left: grain from African colonies is being unloaded. Below: a goldsmith practices his trade, and a stooped farmer takes his produce to market.

were carefully watched, even to the point of being locked in underground dungeons at night. Household slaves, such as the educated Greeks who acted as tutors for rich young Romans, had an easier life. They were often allowed to go into business for themselves and could then buy their freedom, or they might be freed simply because in their long service they had practically become members of the family. Thus the slaves, already divided by race and language, were still further divided by occupation and level of living; it was difficult for them to form an organized resistance. There were remarkably few slave rebellions in the history of the Roman Republic. They tried twice in Sicily, in risings that swept across the island like grass-fires and died down as quickly. The rebellion of Spartacus in Italy (75–71 B.C.) was more dangerous, but it also failed. Thereafter the brutality of masters and the hopes of slaves lost their edge, and the "peculiar institution" was absorbed into Rome's social structure.

The poor freemen, however, were a constant problem. If they lived in Rome they could vote, and their votes were not always predictable. If they remained on the land as farmers, they were expected to be the backbone of the army, but military requirements were growing while the number of peasant farmers was probably deceasing. This particular difficulty was resolved in 101 B.C. by permitting landless men to enlist. Such an action, however, merely intensified the problem: the most discontented part of the citizen body now had military as well as political power. Obviously some form of government intervention was needed to save the small farmers and improve the lot of the proletariat, but in spite of long discussions, the ruling class could never agree on a policy. In the end the poorer classes put their faith in soldiers rather than in politicians. The rival generals whose quarrels destroyed the Republic kept the loyalty of their troops by promises of bonuses and grants of land, not by appeals to political programs.

THE COLLAPSE OF THE REPUBLIC 146–59 B.C.

The Gracchi

Tiberius and Gaius Gracchus were the first members of the senatorial class to realize that the problem of the poorer citizens was becoming serious. Even these enlightened men did not fully understand the crisis. They thought more in terms of an idealized early republic than in terms of an empire facing a social crisis. They believed in the old Roman virtues of honesty, self-sacrifice, and devotion to the public welfare, which they thought were incarnate in the class of small farmers. They also believed, more realistically, that the army would be weakened by a decline in the peasant population. Finally, they may have felt that their political group could profit from popular support. The Gracchi were members of the highest aristocracy, grandsons of the great Scipio who had conquered Carthage, but while their birth ensured them high office, it did not confer control of policy. As events were to prove, the Gracchi could never bring many senators to their side; their tragedy was that they could not develop a solid base of political power in any other section of the population.

Tiberius Gracchus was elected tribune in 133 B.C. His first step was to demand that land owned by the state but controlled by senators be broken up into small farms. He succeeded in getting the popular assembly to pass a law limiting the amount of public land held by one family, but this action outraged the senators. It not only hurt their interests; it violated recent constitutional conventions that left legislative initiatives to the Senate. The Senate persuaded another tribune to veto the act; Gracchus, in an unprecedented move, had the tribune voted out of office. To make sure that his reform would endure he ran for a second term as tribune, a violation of custom if not of law. This was more than some senators could swallow; they used their clients to organize a riot in which Gracchus was killed.

Some ten years later (123 B.C.) Gaius Gracchus, the younger brother of Tiberius, managed to get himself elected tribune in spite of the hostility of many of the senators. Gaius tried to find a wider political base than his brother had, and for a time he had more success. He gained the support of the impoverished proletariat by providing for state distribution of grain at half-price. This law was so necessary and so popular that no succeeding politician dared to repeal it. He tried to win over the equestrians by giving them control of the juries that judged official corruption. This was a sensible move, since the senators (who had furnished the juries before) held all important offices, and the equestrians, as government contractors, were often the victims of extortion. He continued his brother's policy of land reform and tried to increase the number of small farmers by establishing new colonies.

Gaius also saw a danger that Tiberius had ignored, the discontent of the Italian municipalities. These cities had given Rome faithful service during the Punic and the eastern wars, but they were still treated as inferiors. Their inhabitants could not vote in Roman elections and they received few material benefits from Roman victories. Although they faced many of the same social and economic problems that Rome did, no one was worrying about them.

Gaius proposed to give Roman citizenship to the Italian municipalities. This would have relieved them of some of their financial burdens and gained Gracchus a great deal of good will, but it would have been difficult to transform that good will into votes: a citizen could vote only by going to Rome. It is curious that Rome, with its genius for law, never thought of the principle of representation, by which each community could have participated in political decisions by sending one or two men to a central assembly. In any case, his proposal was not accepted. Senators, equestrians, and lower classes agreed in rejecting the law, revealing the weakness of his support. Gaius defended his legislation during two terms as tribune, but in the end was lynched like his brother. His death sharply increased tension in Italy and laid the foundation for the bitter civil wars of the next generation.

During the second century B.C., Roman leaders seem to have lost the gift for compromise and accommodation that had held the state together during its early history. Attempts to solve social and economic problems by legal and peaceful means had broken down. A new series of wars, beginning in 107 B.C., was to put still further strains on the Roman system of government and give increasing power to military commanders. Ultimately, decisions would be made and enforced by the generals.

A coin minted in 137 B.C. celebrates the private ballot. A Roman is shown dropping a stone tablet into a voting urn.

Marius and Sulla

The military difficulties that led to the downfall of the Republic began with a long and bitter war in western North Africa against a recalcitrant ally. As usual, the Romans made a bad start. They began to win only after they discovered a very capable general in an army officer from rural Italy named Marius. Elected consul in 107 B.C., Marius ended the African war with a complete victory. It was high time that he did, because a new Indo-European invasion, this time by the Germans, was throwing all of Europe north of the Alps into confusion. Two German tribes appeared in Gaul, raided Spain, and then threatened Italy. After they won several victories over Roman armies, Marius was again called to the rescue. He was reelected consul in 104 B.C., as well as in each of the next four years (103–100 B.C.). Such a series of reelections was unprecedented, but the need to preserve continuity in command was obvious, and there was no real opposition to the break with tradition. Marius justified the confidence placed in him: he annihilated the German armies in two hard-fought battles (102 and 101 B.C.). Thus ended the first, but by no means the last, of the Roman-German wars.

It was during this crisis that the old connection between ownership of land and military service was broken. Marius had to recruit landless men in order to have sufficient forces. Since the state could not pay these men, Marius rewarded them with bounty from the defeated enemies and grants of land in occupied territories. Most of his successors followed this pattern, but while it provided necessary manpower it introduced two dangers that endured to the end of Roman history. Troops who received their reward from their general were loyal to that general, not to the state. If land or a substantial bonus was the chief reward for service, then enlistment would be most attractive to the poor and disadvantaged. Over the centuries, fewer and fewer Romans or Italians joined the armed forces. Their places were taken first by provincials, and then by barbarians, men who had little understanding of or loyalty to the Roman state.

Marius was in a strong position after his defeat of the Germans, but he had no political program of his own. Some of his associates wanted to revive the Gracchan policy of land reform; Marius turned against them and helped suppress their movement. This equivocal behavior thoroughly discredited Marius, although other leaders proved no wiser. Nothing was done to allay the grievances of the Italian cities, or the discontent of provincial subjects. As a result two dangerous uprisings occurred almost simultaneously in Italy and in the East.

The so-called Social War (that is, the war with the Italians) began in 90 B.C. The Italian cities formed a confederacy, created their own Senate, raised an army, and held out against Rome for over two years. Marius defended the North, on the whole successfully, but one of his former officers, Sulla, made an even better record in the South. The Romans realized that they had little to gain by devastating Italy, especially since they needed to free their armies for war in the East. They ended the Social War by offering full citizenship to all Italians who would lay down their arms, an act that could have prevented the civil war had it been adopted earlier.

The eastern uprising was led by Mithridates, king of a small Hellenistic state on the Black Sea, who hoped to create a new Greek empire. Most of the Greek cities, including Athens, gave him enthusiastic support. They were so embittered by Roman bankers, soldiers, and

Sulla, dictator of Rome from 82 to 79 B.C.

tax-collectors that in 88 B.C., when Mithridates gave the signal, they murdered 80,000 Romans and Italians in the Greek cities of Asia Minor.

No Roman army was immediately available to avenge this massacre, and a bitter struggle broke out over who was to command an expeditionary force. Sulla, consul in 88 B.C., had the best claim, but Marius still had supporters who tried to vote him the command. Sulla marched on Rome, drove out his opponents, and eventually got control of the eastern army as proconsul. After three years of hard fighting, he defeated Mithridates and his Greek allies and restored Roman control in Greece and Asia Minor. Sulla demanded an enormous indemnity from his conquered enemies but otherwise was fairly lenient. Mithridates was even allowed to retain his kingdom.

One reason for his leniency was Sulla's eagerness to return to Rome. During his absence opponents had taken over the government and had once more attempted to deprive him of his military command. But when Sulla landed in Italy in 83 B.C. with an army of veterans the opposition collapsed. Scattered armies were defeated one by one, and when Sulla took Rome in 82 B.C. he was named dictator for an unlimited period. He proscribed his enemies; that is, he put a price on their heads and confiscated their property. Thousands of "bad citizens," as he called them, were put to death. The property seized from his enemies and from Italian towns that had supported the opposition was distributed among his soldiers. Sulla established military colonies throughout Italy and filled them with his supporters.

Although Sulla had full power to revise the Roman constitution, he found no way of overcoming its basic weaknesses. His plan seems to have been to weaken the popular assembly and concentrate power in the Senate, stacked with his own supporters. Once this was done, he retired to his country estate (79 B.C.), where he died the following year. But the new senators were not very different from the old ones; the restrictions on the assembly and the tribunes were gradually removed; and the Roman political system remained inherently unstable.

The New Leaders:
Pompey, Crassus, and Cicero

As before, the chief goal of ambitious politicians was to gain the overseas commands that would give them money and control of a loyal army. Danger spots throughout the Roman world offered opportunities for establishing such commands. The East was restless; a bitter opponent of Sulla controlled much of Spain; piracy was rampant in the Mediterranean. The ablest and most popular Roman general was Pompey, who had helped Sulla gain control of Sicily and North Africa, but Pompey had some respect for constitutional procedures and some willingness to compromise with his rivals. Thus for almost three decades no one man dominated Rome. Power was held by shifting coalitions of leading politicians, and in a good many cases unaligned majorities in the Senate still had a decisive voice.

Pompey's chief rival was Crassus, a man who had made a fortune in questionable real estate operations. He was never a very good general, but he acquired some military reputation when the one great slave rebellion in Roman history broke out. Led by the gladiator Spartacus, the slaves at first won several victories, but were finally defeated by Crassus in 71 B.C. Pompey meanwhile had been ending the rebellion in Spain, and there was some danger of a collision between the two victorious generals. They settled their differences, however, and both men were elected consul for the year 70 B.C.

The third political leader to emerge at this time was Cicero, the only civilian in the group. Cicero gained public favor when he secured the conviction of a Roman provincial governor on charges of corruption; his whole career depended on his skill as a lawyer, orator, and writer. Although he came from a wealthy equestrian family, it is not remarkable that he was able to enter the Senate—a good many men of similar background did. But the old senatorial families looked down on these "new men," and most of them went no farther. It was only his extraordinary ability that carried Cicero to the highest office, the consulship.

Bust of Pompey late in his life.

Cicero was far more honest than most men in that age of corruption. He tried to avoid violence at a time when most problems were settled by civil war. The Romans had already developed a powerful style of oratory; Cicero perfected this style to the point where one of his speeches could sway the entire Senate. As one who thought deeply about Rome's constitutional problems, he tried to halt the drift toward the concentration of powers in the hands of rival politician-generals. Like most intellectuals, Cicero could see so many sides of a question that he was often indecisive, and he knew enough about Roman politics to find it difficult to commit himself to a single faction. In a pinch, he was apt to favor Pompey, who had some of his own qualities (or defects), but as the crisis in Roman government deepened, both men became unable to control events. Cicero was respected to the end, but at the end he had lost most of his political influence.

In 74 B.C. Mithridates again tried to rally the Hellenistic world against Rome, and this time he kept the war going for a decade. Some Roman commanders were incompetent; some conducted brilliant operations; but none of them was able to end the war. This gave Pompey a chance to shine once more. In 66 B.C. the Senate passed a law giving Pompey extraordinary powers (Cicero made a great speech supporting the proposal), which allowed Pompey to end the eastern problem that had plagued Rome since the third century B.C. Mithridates was defeated; parts of Asia Minor and Syria were annexed and the rest put under the control of subject kings. The Jewish kingdom of Palestine was one of these vassal kingdoms. When Pompey returned to Rome in 62 B.C. he had acquired more territory for his country than any previous general.

The Senate gave Pompey a splendid triumphal procession and a cool reception. He had committed Rome to a series of treaties with the eastern kingdoms, and he had promised his soldiers grants of land. The Senate hesitated to ratify these acts, even though Pompey had been given extraconstitutional power to end the war. Pompey was determined to have his promises honored; when the senators refused to satisfy him he had to find ways of putting political pressure on them. The means to do so lay in the person of Gaius Julius Caesar.

THE RISE OF CAESAR 59–44 B.C.

Caesar was a young aristocrat with political ambitions, popularity with the masses—and huge debts. Crassus, who still hoped for power, was aware of his own lack of popularity both in the Senate and with the people, so he decided to back Caesar. By paying off the debts Crassus gained a hold on Caesar; by using Crassus' money Caesar gained an enthusiastic personal following and rapid political advancement. He had a reputation as a reformer, although his plans for reform were far from clear; those who knew him best realized that he also had a tremendous desire for power. By 60 B.C. he was ready to run for consul.

The First Triumvirate 59–53 B.C.

Caesar found it an easy matter to bring together Crassus and Pompey, who was still furious with the Senate. Pompey's prestige, Crassus' wealth, and Caesar's popular following made an almost unbeatable combination. The three bosses, or First Triumvirate (to give them their more dignified Roman appellation), had about the same degree of power that a similar coalition would have today. They could get most of what they wanted for themselves, and some of what they wanted for their followers, but they were far from having absolute power. And they had to threaten the Senate with force in order to get as much as they did.

The first thing the Triumvirs wanted was Caesar's election to the consulship for the year 59 B.C. As consul, Caesar saw to it that Pompey's promises were honored, and he distributed land not only to Pompey's veterans, but also to other citizens. Caesar also tried to curb corruption in provincial government by expanding measures taken by Sulla and earlier leaders. He was not entirely successful, but he may have gained some popularity in the provinces.

Two busts of Caesar: early in his political career, and at the time of his assassination.

What Caesar wanted most of all was a military command that would give him a reputation equal to that of Pompey. The one weak link in Rome's control of the Mediterranean was in southern Gaul, where the Romans held only a thin strip of territory linking Italy to Spain. The rest of Gaul was held by Celtic tribes, who were relatively civilized, but who were constantly at war with one another or with Germans pushing in from the East. These wars had a nasty way of spilling over into Roman territory or the territory of Rome's allies. Clearly, it would help Rome if the political situation in Gaul could be stabilized, but it seemed an unrewarding task. Gaul had neither the wealth nor the splendor of the East. Would a victory over a few Celtic tribes be equivalent to Pompey's triumph over the kings of Asia? Nevertheless, in 58 B.C., Caesar made his choice: a proconsulship of Gaul for five years, a term later extended to ten. His command included the old Gallic settlements in the Po Valley—a region that was largely Romanized—and Transalpine Gaul, roughly the French Riviera.

It is difficult to say what Caesar's plans were when he first went to Gaul. Certainly he wanted to pacify the tribes living near the Roman frontier and protect the Gauls who seemed friendly to Rome. Probably he wanted to enlarge the Roman province of Transalpine Gaul.

But, as often happens in such a situation, one war of pacification led to another, and every time the zone of Roman-protected territory moved northward new enemies appeared. In the end, Caesar conquered all of Gaul and made it a Roman province. As a warning to neighboring peoples, he invaded Britain twice

CAESAR IN GAUL   58–49 B.C.

Richly embossed helmet of aristocratic warrior of Gaul, at the time of Julius Caesar's conquest.

and crossed the Rhine to fight the Germans. All these accomplishments Caesar described in clear terse style in his *Commentaries on the Gallic War.* Any Roman who heard of this book would be convinced that Caesar was a great general and a first-rate administrator.

While Caesar was conquering Gaul, Crassus, still seeking a military reputation, led an army against the Parthians, a people who had taken over Persia. His army was cut to pieces and Crassus himself was killed (53 B.C.). Meanwhile, Caesar and Pompey had begun to drift apart. The First Triumvirate had come to an end.

Caesar and Pompey

Of the two surviving Triumvirs, Pompey in Rome seemed to have the better position. Mob violence in the city had made orderly government impossible; it created such a dangerous situation that

in 52 B.C. Pompey was elected sole consul with practically dictatorial powers. He dominated the Roman government; he was hailed as *Princeps,* or First Citizen. Yet he was not secure as long as Caesar commanded an intensely loyal army in Gaul and northern Italy.

Pompey's obvious move was to try to deprive Caesar of his military command, an act that would have ended Caesar's political career and probably his life. But Caesar had friends in Rome, and the Senate was afraid of starting a civil war. It tried to arrange a compromise by which both Caesar and Pompey would give up their armies, but Pompey would have been perfectly safe in Rome without an army and Caesar would not. Caesar therefore refused to give up his command. In 49 B.C. the Senate ordered Pompey to march against him.

Caesar's outstanding quality as a general was his ability to make quick decisions and to carry them out rapidly. There was no real army in Italy; Pompey's military supporters were mainly in Spain and in Greece. Caesar had to strike at once to avoid being caught in a pincers. He marched his army across the Rubicon, a little river marking the boundary between his province of Cisalpine Gaul and Italy, and thundered down on Rome. Pompey, unable to defend the city, fled to Greece with most of the Senate. Caesar had to spend a year securing his position in Italy, which gave Pompey time to build up a large and well-trained army. When Caesar followed him to Greece, the fighting at first went in Pompey's favor, but Caesar finally won a decisive victory at Pharsalus in 48 B.C. Although Pompey managed to escape to Egypt, he was murdered there by order of the king. Caesar and his lieutenants spent the next three years overcoming supporters of Pompey in Spain, North Africa, and the East. By 45 B.C. Caesar was master of the Roman state.

Caesar on the Origins of the Civil War

Caesar no sooner heard of these proceedings [the raising of a senatorial army against him] than he appealed to his troops. After recounting in detail the wrongs he had suffered at the hands of his political opponents, he charged Pompey with having allowed his mind to be misled, and his judgement to be warped by the pernicious influence these men exerted upon him, owing to the petty jealousy he felt at his rival's reputation. . . . He called upon them now to protect from political adversaries the honor and good name of their commander, under whose leadership for nine long years they had fought with such brilliant success the battles of their country, during which time they had gained such numberless victories, and subjugated the whole of Gaul and Germany [west of the Rhine]. . . . Assured of the temper of his troops Caesar began his advance . . . as far as Rimini . . . [thus crossing the Rubicon, the frontier of his province, and defying the Senate].

From Julius Caesar, *De bello civili,* trans. by F. P. Long (Oxford: Clarendon, 1906), p. 7.

Caesar's Rule, 48–44 B.C.

Caesar's rule was too short for us to know what his plans were, and it is likely that he himself was not very sure what was to be done. It was clear that the old constitution had collapsed, and that the Roman state must be led by one man, but the Romans still hated the idea of a king and Caesar had to combine several offices to get the power he needed. He was *imperator* (whence our word "emperor"); that is, he had the *imperium,* the full right of military and civil command. He was, in effect, dictator for life, and enjoyed the privileges and immunity of a tribune.

With personal command of the army it was not too difficult to restore order in Rome and in the provinces. Beyond this, Caesar's program was not unlike the programs of Sulla and Pompey, though it was carried out on a larger scale. More land was distributed to veterans, and Roman colonies were established in the provinces. The Senate was enlarged again; this time a few provincial leaders were given seats. Caesar, like his predecessors, tried to lessen corruption in provincial administration, but since he did not change the basic system of giving short-term appointments to proconsuls and other ex-officials, he did little to suppress the temptation to loot and run. Although Caesar managed to speed up the Latinization of the western provinces and gained the support of some of the upper classes in Gaul and Spain, the full incorporation of the provincials into Roman society was still a long way in the future. Caesar's most lasting reform was a reform of the calendar. By adopting the 365-day Egyptian year, with an extra day every four years, he introduced the system that, with minor modifications, is still in use.

Many senators were unhappy about Caesar's accumulation of power, and they were even more upset by rumors that he wanted to be king. The rumors were probably false, but they provided a good excuse for a conspiracy. When Caesar entered the Senate on the Ides of March (March 15), 44 B.C., the conspirators, led by Brutus and Cassius, stabbed him to death.

The Murder of Caesar, 44 B.C.

The *Lives,* written by the Greek historian Plutarch around 100 A.D., supplies valuable information on Greek and Roman history, particularly on the confusing years of the late Republic. As may be seen from this passage, Plutarch's *Lives* served as a source of Shakespeare's play *Julius Caesar.*

When Caesar entered, the senate stood up to show their respect to him, and of Brutus's confederates, some came about his chair and stood behind it. . . . Tillius, laying hold of his robe with both his hands, pulled it down from his neck, which was the signal for the assault. Casca gave him the first cut in the neck. . . . Those who were not privy to the design were astonished, and their horror and amazement at what they saw were so great that they durst not fly nor assist Caesar, nor so much as speak a word. But those who came prepared for the business enclosed him on every side. For it had been agreed that they should each of them make a thrust at him, and flesh themselves with his blood; for which reason Brutus also gave him one stab in the groin. Some say that he fought and resisted all the rest, shifting his body to avoid the blows, and calling out for help, but that when he saw Brutus's sword drawn, he covered his face with his robe and submitted, letting himself fall . . . at the foot of the pedestal on which Pompey's statue stood. . . .

From Plutarch, *The Lives of Noble Grecians and Romans,* trans. by John Dryden, rev. by Arthur Hugh Clough (New York: Modern Library, n.d.), pp. 892–93.

THE SECOND TRIUMVIRATE 44–36 B.C.

Men like Brutus, who represented the best of the old senatorial class, were convinced that by killing Caesar they could restore the old Republic. But the old system had broken down completely, and the Senate had little popular support. The trouble was that no one else had much support either. Brutus and Cassius left Rome to take up military commands in the East. Mark Antony, who was consul at the time, was loyal to Caesar's memory; he gained the support of the veterans and some of the lower classes by his famous oration at Caesar's funeral. His position was challenged by Octavian, Caesar's grand-nephew and adopted son. Octavian, a frail and sickly lad of eighteen, had very little popular support. Cicero and other senators, thinking that it was safe to use him against Mark Antony, accepted him as Caesar's true

Coin commemorating the death of Caesar. One side bears the portrait of Brutus; the other side shows the assassins' daggers.

successor. But Octavian, even at eight-een, was an astute politician and knew where the real power lay. When he had gained all he could from the Senate, he switched sides suddenly and joined Antony and Lepidus (another of Caesar's lieutenants). With Caesar's armies be-hind them, the three men formed the Second Triumvirate, and marched on Rome in 44 B.C. There the assembly granted them full power for five years.

The first act of the Second Trium-virate was a bloody proscription in which thousands of political opponents were put to death. Cicero, a personal as well as a political enemy of Antony, headed the list. While terrifying the opposition, the Triumvirs divided confiscated lands among veterans and won the support of a new class of landholders. Next, the Triumvirate took its armies across the sea to Macedonia, where they won a quick victory over Brutus and Cassius in 42 B.C.

The three men now divided the Roman world among themselves. Antony had the largest army and controlled both Gaul and the East. Italy was common ground to all three Triumvirs. As neither Octavian nor Lepidus had much military power, Antony paid little attention to his colleagues. In a series of struggles Oc-tavian crushed Lepidus and gradually united Italy behind himself. Lepidus was driven into retirement, but Antony still seemed secure in the East, with its wealth and its tradition of one-man rule.

Antony began to lose support when he became the lover and then the con-sort of Cleopatra, Queen of Egypt. Al-though Caesar had also had an affair with Cleopatra, he did not let it interfere with serious business. Antony did: he lived with Cleopatra at the court in Alexandria and rather neglected his other territories. Like many other ill-advised Roman generals, he started a war with the Parthians; nothing of any value was gained and thousands of Roman soldiers were killed. By 32 B.C. Octavian felt strong enough to move against Antony. He exaggerated and exploited reports that Antony wanted to give Rome's eastern province to Cleopatra's children. Then he secured a decree depriving Antony of his command. It took some time for each side to marshal its strength, but the two rival forces finally met in the naval battle of Actium in 31 B.C. Octavian's fleet, commanded by his very capable lieutenant, Agrippa, won a decisive victory. Antony fled and later committed suicide; Cleopatra followed his example when she found that she could strike no bargain with Octavian. Egypt was annexed by the victor.

The battle of Actium ended the long period of civil war. Octavian was the master of the Roman world. He proclaimed the restoration of the Republic, but, like Caesar, he occupied all the positions of power. Unlike Caesar, he was able to make his monopoly of power acceptable to the vast majority of citizens and subjects. No military commander opposed him; no politician roused the discontented; no political theorists complained about the break with old traditions. Octavian was to be chief of state for over forty years, and during those years the Roman Empire was born.

Suggestions for Further Reading

Note: Asterisk denotes a book available in paperback edition.

General

The surveys of ancient history mentioned at the end of the first chapter have sections on the Roman era. There are also many reliable texts devoted specifically to Rome, of which one of the best is H. H. Scullard, *History of the Roman World from 753 B.C. to 146 B.C.*, 3rd ed. (1961). A. E. R. Boak's *A History of Rome to A.D. 565* has been revised by W. G. Sinnigen (1965), and is useful and clear. Shorter but more vivid are M. I. Rostovtzeff, *Rome** (1964), and D. R. Dudley, *The Civilization of Rome** (1962). M. Grant, *The World of Rome** (1964), emphasizes Roman institutions, customs, and attitudes. A very rich sampling of source readings is collected in the first volume of N. Lewis and N. Reinhold, eds., *Roman Civilization** (1951).

Early Italy, Roman Political Evolution, and Roman Expansion

H. H. Scullard, *The Etruscan Cities and Rome* (1967), and R. Bloch, *The Etruscans* (1958), provide up-to-date accounts of a period still quite obscure and complicated. Bloch carries the story further in his *The Origins of Rome* (1966). On the evolution of Rome's constitution, L. Homo, *Roman Political Institutions** (1929, 1962), needs up-dating but is still the best. Expansion throughout Italy is described in great detail by E. T. Salmon, *Samnium and the Samnites* (1967) and *Roman Colonization under the Republic* (1969). Two recent works unfold Rome's developing power overseas against Carthage and the Hellenistic states: R. M. Errington, *The Dawn of Empire* (1972), and E. Badian, *Roman Imperialism in the Late Republic* (1968).

The Last Century of the Republic, 146–30 B.C.

There is such a wealth of material on this complex and chaotic century that only a sampling can be mentioned here. Students interested in a detailed account of the period may consult either F. B. Marsh, *History. of the Roman World from 146 to 30 B.C.*, 2nd ed. (1953), or H. H. Scullard, *From the Gracchi to Nero: A History of Rome from 133 B.C. to A.D. 68* (1959). L. R. Taylor, *Party Politics in the Age of Caesar** (1949), gives a clear, concise picture of Roman politics in the later years of this era. R. Syme, *The Roman Revolution** (1939), a classic, offers a detailed but exciting account of the social as well as the political changes that accompanied the failure of the Republic and the creation of the Empire. See also R. E. Smith, *The Failure of the Roman Republic* (1955).

For a description of Roman society in the late Republic, see T. Frank, *Life and Literature in the Roman Republic** (1930). The best studies of Cicero are R. E. Smith, *Cicero the Statesman* (1966), and D. Stockton, *Cicero* (1971). F. R. Crowell, *Cicero and the Roman Republic** (1956), combines a short, lively biography of Cicero with a discussion of the politics of the era. There are many excellent biographies of Caesar as well as many that are not. The most valuable is M. Gelger, *Caesar, Politician and Statesman* (1968). D. Earl, *The Moral and Political Tradition of Rome* (1967), offers striking insights into the culture and psychology of the times.

4

The Early Roman Empire,

27 B.C.–284 A.D.

Returning in triumph to Rome after his victory at Actium, Octavian worked carefully and cautiously to solidify his position. He was quite willing to conciliate the upper classes by preserving old institutions. Consuls were elected every year; the Senate, purged of its recalcitrant members, continued to meet; even the popular assembly was summoned from time to time to give formal approval to Octavian's proposals. But no one can have been deceived by this façade of republican respectability. Octavian had been given full powers to restore order and stability, and he made all the important decisions. Like Caesar, he was *imperator*, commander of all the armies. Like Caesar, he had the power and immunities of a tribune, including the right to propose laws. He spoke first in the Senate, where no one ever dared contradict him; he had his own staff of officials and advisers. He was not quite a sovereign, since theoretically the Senate or the assembly could have voted him out of power if he had ever lost his ability to control them. But he was more than a political boss, because he was surrounded by an aura of sanctity and infallibility that no boss has ever enjoyed.

Octavian himself preferred to be called "Princeps" or First Citizen and his government is often called the "Principate." But in 27 B.C. the Senate gave him the title of Augustus, and from that time on he was usually referred to by that name. *Augustus* is a word with several layers of meaning. Anyone who was *augustus* was to be looked on with awe and reverence. It was a title that could be used of gods as well as men; it carried overtones of holiness, dignity, wisdom,

and authority. Thus, to oppose Augustus was not only politically inexpedient; it was also immoral.

THE PRINCIPATE OF AUGUSTUS, 27 B.C.–14 A.D.

Augustus could not have had a very clear concept of the form and extent of imperial authority, since he had only begun the process of developing that authority. But he did have a clear idea of what he wanted to do with his power: there was to be security, a revival of the old Roman virtues, and stability throughout the Roman world.

A battleship like this won the battle of Actium in 31 B.C.— and the Roman world for Augustus. (Detail from Arch of Titus, 81 A.D.)

Theoretically, the Senate was to help Augustus in this task. Rome and Italy would be governed by the Senate and the elected magistrates, and provincial districts that were completely pacified and needed no armies would be governed by senatorial representatives (proconsuls and the like). Augustus, with permanent proconsular power, had authority over all the provinces in which armies were stationed. These provinces were far more numerous than those that were entrusted to senators.

In practice, the division of power did not work very well. To be secure Augustus had to control Rome and Italy. Many senators, unhappy about their reduced role in government, secretly intrigued against the emperor. At the same time, the Senate could not take any initiatives. Augustus formulated the program of the government. Some of his projects, such as a reform of morals and a revival of the old Roman religion, though they were supported by the upper classes, had little effect. Rome was a cosmopolitan city; even Augustus could not make it revert to the idealized social patterns of the early Republic.

In the provinces the old problem of an inadequate and untrained bureaucracy continued to exist. There were few Roman officials in any province, and most of them served only for short periods. It is probable that the lieutenants of Augustus who administered his provinces were somewhat more honest than senatorial governors; on the other hand, imperial provinces had to support a Roman army while senatorial provinces did not. In general, Augustus would not permit the flagrant maladministration that had recurred in the last century of the Republic and under his rule provincial grievances were lessened, though not ended.

Even with all these strains, there was no danger that the Roman Empire would fall to pieces. In the first place, there were no longer independent armies, each loyal to its own general. Augustus was commander-in-chief, and his close friend Agrippa was his chief of staff. The army was more or less insulated from the rest of the population, since enlistments were for a period of twenty years. About half of the army was made up of Roman citizens, enrolled in some twenty-five legions of (theoretically) 6,000 men each. At the end of their service these men were given large cash bonuses, and occasionally plots of land. The rest of the army was made up of provincials who served as auxiliary troops. The legions were usually under full strength, so Augustus had about 250,000 soldiers. This army was completely loyal to him and numerous enough to put down any uprising.

The second factor that made the inadequate Roman administrative system viable was that it actually had very little administrative work to do. In one way or another, most of the details of government were turned over to local authorities. On the fringes of the Empire were semi-independent kingdoms, like that of Herod in Judea, which controlled their own internal affairs. Even more numerous were the city-states, which administered rural districts from an urban center. As long as local aristocracies kept order in these city-states there was relatively little interference from Roman authorities. In fact, the system worked so well that it was transferred to the less developed parts of the Empire. The Gauls, for example, were encouraged to develop cities that could act as administrative centers for each tribe.

The Frontiers

Augustus wanted to round out the holdings of the Empire in order to make his frontiers more defensible. In most places this was done fairly easily. The border with the Parthians was fixed at

Augustus issued these coins to proclaim the submission of Egypt and Armenia to Roman power.

the Euphrates, thus ending for a time the Parthian wars. It took only a little fighting to establish firm boundaries between Judea and Arabia, Egypt and Ethiopia, and North Africa and the Berber desert tribes.

The one frontier that was never certain and never secure was the frontier with the Germans. The Rhine was not a good boundary. As Caesar had discovered, the Germans frequently pushed across the river into Gaul. The Rhine also made an awkward angle with the Danube, which was a possible frontier against the eastern Germans. It was clearly desirable to push the Germans back from the Rhine, but when an attack was made in 9 A.D. the German chieftain Arminius (Herman) annihilated three Roman legions. Though Arminius became a national hero for modern Germany, his fellow chieftains killed him soon after his great victory. Augustus did not try to take advantage of this act; Germany was not worth risking another three legions. His stepsons, Tiberius and Drusus, did advance toward the Danube line in what are now Switzerland and Austria, and later in the first century, the middle Rhine and the upper Danube were linked by a fortified wall. But on the whole little German territory was permanently annexed by Rome.

Augustus acquired a considerable amount of territory in creating defensible boundaries for Rome. The lands he acquired, however, had more strategic than economic value. The conquest of Alpine territory, for example, did not produce the flood of gold and highly skilled slaves that had come from the conquest of Asia Minor. There were no magnificent triumphs, such as those celebrated by Pompey. Except for the island of Britain, which was to be conquered in 43 A.D., Rome had reached the limits of its expansion.

Augustus' Rule

Augustus had not been very popular as a young man, and the Senate was never entirely happy about his dominant position. But, as in many other cases, the mere length of his reign enhanced his popularity; one could scarcely imagine

THE GERMAN PROBLEM
First and second centuries B.C.

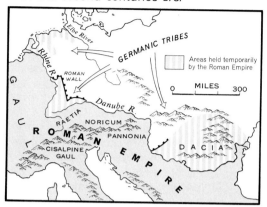

Rome without Augustus. Moreover, Augustus deliberately tried to build up support for his government. New official positions were created for the equestrians, and the class as a whole profited from an increase in commerce and in financial transactions. The lower classes of Rome were kept quiet by increasing

The Deeds of Augustus

This excerpt is from a long epitaph that Augustus composed for himself in his old age, and that was inscribed on brazen columns at Rome and copied in stone in many provincial cities. The only relatively complete copy that has survived is at Ankara (Ancyra). Note how Augustus poses as the preserver of the old Roman Republic.

In my twentieth year, acting upon my own judgment . . . I raised an army by means of which I restored to liberty the Republic which had been oppressed by the tyranny of a faction. . . . Those who killed my father [Julius Caesar], I drove into exile . . . and when they waged war against the Republic I twice defeated them in battle. . . . I have extended the boundaries of all the provinces of the Roman people. . . . I have reduced to a state of peace . . . the lands enclosed by the ocean from Gades [Cadiz] to the mouth of the Elbe. . . . I have added Egypt to the empire of the Roman people. . . . I accepted no office which was contrary to the customs of the country. . . . When I had put an end to the civil wars . . . I transferred the commonwealth from my own power to the authority of the Senate and the Roman people. In return for this favor I was given by decree of the Senate the title Augustus. . . . After that time I excelled all others in dignity, but of power I held no more than those who were my colleagues in any magistracy.

From Augustus, quoted in *Monumentum Ancyranum: The Deeds of Augustus*, ed. and trans. by William Fairly, *Translations and Reprints* (Philadelphia: University of Pennsylvania Press, 1898), Vol. V, No. 1, pp. 12ff.

the dole of grain and by lavish public entertainments. The inhabitants of Italy had an opportunity to take part in the establishment of new colonies in the thinly settled western provinces. Non-Roman subjects still bore heavy burdens, but at least their lands were no longer ravaged by civil wars, and Augustus had made some effort to improve provincial administration.

Augustus also tried to build up an all-inclusive patriotism that would override local loyalties. Worship of the "spirit" of Rome became an official cult. To this was added worship of the "genius" of the emperor. This was not quite the same thing as saying that the emperor was a god, but it certainly implied that he was guided and imbued by a divine spirit. Such nice distinctions were not important in the East, where rulers had long been worshiped as gods, but they were essential in Italy, which was definitely hostile to the idea of a god-king.

The Golden Age of Latin Literature

In the last years of the Republic and during the first years of the Empire Latin literature reached its peak. Prose writers dealt mainly with history, political theory, and philosophy. Cicero covered the

Contemporary bust of Cicero, the great orator of the first century B.C.

widest range—he published his orations and letters as examples of an elegant and polished style, and wrote extensively on ethics, rhetoric, philosophy, and political theory. Caesar's accounts of his wars showed that military communiqués could have both style and political purpose. Sallust (86–34 B.C.) was an enemy of Cicero, and his account of Cicero's consulship is just about as biased as Cicero's defense of his actions. But Sallust was an excellent prose writer and could be a good historian, as he showed in his account of the *Jugurthine War* (a campaign in North Africa). The most influential historian of this period was Livy (59 B.C.–17 A.D.), who summed up the books of earlier writers in a monumental history of Rome. Most of this work has been lost, but enough survives to show that he was chiefly interested in celebrating the piety, civic spirit, and heroism of the early Romans. He accepted legends uncritically, but he retold them splendidly. More than anyone else, Livy created the tradition that Roman character was the source of Roman strength, a tradition that has impressed historians for almost two thousand years.

The poets of the late Republic avoided politics. Catullus (87–54 B.C.) wrote graceful lyrics about his love affairs. The greatest poet of the Republic, and perhaps the most original of all Latin authors, was Lucretius (99–55 B.C.). In his *De rerum natura* he expressed his personal philosophy and his view of the universe in verses of remarkable beauty and power. Although he drew many of his ideas from Hellenistic philosophers, the synthesis was his own. But Lucretius was too speculative to appeal to the practical Roman mind; he had little influence and no successors.

The poets of the early Empire, unlike their predecessors, were deeply involved in politics. Vergil and Horace were not wealthy men; they could devote themselves to writing only because they were patronized by the emperor, or rather by one of his chief advisers, Maecenas. As a result, some of their work has an official flavor. Thus when Vergil (70–19 B.C.) wrote his epic, the *Aeneid,* he was careful to include compliments to the imperial family. The poem itself argues that Rome was founded under divine auspices, that its glorious destiny had long been predicted, and that its brilliant success was due to the virtue of its founders. Vergil imitated the Homeric model, but imitation did not keep him from being a great poet; he wrote some of the most effective lines that appear in the literature of any country.

Horace (65–8 B.C.) wrote official poems for Augustus' religious festivals and celebrated the virtue of the early Romans. But he was much more than an official poet. He was a shrewd and experienced man, a keen observer of human behavior, and a master of summing up his observations in brief and striking verses.

The fate of Ovid (43 B.C.–17 A.D.) shows why it was well to pay some attention to pleasing the emperor. Drawing on Greek mythology for much of his material, Ovid could tell a good story in graceful verse. But there was little morality in his sources, and Ovid did not bother to add any, which may explain why Ovid was banished from his comfortable life in Rome to a very uncomfortable life on the shores of the Black Sea. His work remained popular, however, and was the chief source of knowledge of Greek mythology during the Middle Ages and the Renaissance.

With the exception of Lucretius, these Latin authors contributed few new ideas to the intellectual tradition of the ancient world. But they did perfect the Latin language by fixing its grammatical rules and by increasing its vocabulary. In their hands Latin became a precise and efficient language. Since much of the world's thinking was to be done in Latin for the next fifteen hundred years, this was no mean achievement. They also introduced eastern ideas to the West in a form in which they could be easily assimilated. Something was lost in the process: Latin was never able to reproduce all the subtle distinctions that could be made in Greek, and the Romans had little interest in Greek scientific work. But by borrowing from the Greeks, and by putting what they borrowed into enduring form, Latin authors laid the foundations for much of the later literature of the West.

SUCCESSORS TO AUGUSTUS 14–68 A.D.

It was clear long before Augustus died that his system of government would endure. But who was to succeed him? He was not a hereditary monarch and he had no son. On the other hand, his own career had shown the value of family connections; he owed his position to the fact that he was the grandnephew and adopted son of Caesar. Therefore, Augustus looked around the circle of his relatives and, after a long series of intrigues and premature deaths of possible successors, settled on his stepson, Tiberius. He made Tiberius his associate in the tribunician power and in the *imperium*, so that Tiberius had no trouble in taking over the government when the old emperor died in 14 A.D. But the episode revealed a weakness in the imperial system that was never cured: the absence of a fixed rule of succession and the danger that the title could be seized through intrigue and violence. The Julio-Claudian emperors* (the first four successors of Augustus) all shared these problems.

*These men were all related, by blood or by marriage, to the great Roman families of the Julians and the Claudians.

Relief of a figure thought to be Horace (fragment of a marble frieze, Greco-Roman period).

Lucretius on Atoms

If you think that basic particles can stand still, and by standing still can beget new motions among things, you are astray and wander far from true reasoning. For since basic particles wander through the void, they must needs all be carried on either by their own weight or by a chance blow from one or other. For when in quick motion they have often met and collided, it follows that they leap apart suddenly in different directions. . . . And to show you more clearly that all the bodies of matter are constantly being tossed about, remember that there is no bottom in the sum of things, and the first bodies have nowhere to rest, since space is without end or limit. . . . Beyond doubt no rest is granted to the first bodies, . . . some after being pressed together then leap back with wide intervals, some again . . . are tossed about within a narrow compass. And those which being held in combination more closely condensed collide and leap back through tiny intervals, . . . these constitute the strong roots of stone and . . . iron and others of this kind. . . . The rest leap far apart and pass far back with long intervals between; these supply thin air for us and the gleaming light of the sun.

From Lucretius, *De rerum natura*, trans. by W. H. D. Rouse (Cambridge, Mass.: Harvard University Press, 1937). Book II, ll. 80–108.

Tiberius (14–37 A.D.) and Caligula (37–41 A.D.)

Tiberius was an able administrator and a good general, but he had been embittered by the fact that Augustus had passed him over repeatedly in his search for a successor. Though he came from one of the most distinguished families in Rome (his father was a Claudian), many senators resented his supremacy and intrigued against him. He made more enemies by weeding out subordinates who seemed dishonest or incompetent. Quarrels in his own family over the succession led to several suspicious deaths. Disgusted with Rome and fearful for his life, Tiberius took refuge on the island of Capri near Naples. This move made it easier for intrigue to flourish in Rome. Suspicious of everyone around him, Tiberius ordered the execution of many officials and senators on charges of treason. There was general relief when he died in 37 A.D.

He was succeeded by his grandnephew, Caligula, who seemed as attractive as Tiberius had been morose. Unfortunately, Caligula was also insane. His whimsical cruelty and his lack of military

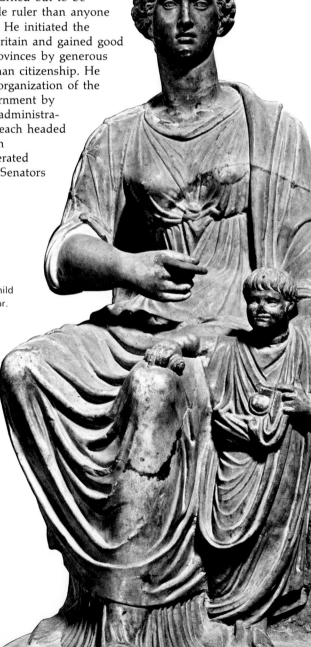

sense disgusted the army and led to a conspiracy in which Caligula was put to death.

Claudius (41–54 A.D.) and Nero (54–68 A.D.)

With the death of Caligula, the Senate hoped to abolish the position of emperor and restore the Republic. They had forgotten that for more than a century real power had rested in the army, and that the army had no great respect for the Senate. While the senators were debating, the palace guard found Caligula's sickly uncle Claudius and proclaimed him emperor.

Claudius turned out to be a more capable ruler than anyone had expected. He initiated the conquest of Britain and gained good will in the provinces by generous grants of Roman citizenship. He started the reorganization of the imperial government by creating four administrative bureaus, each headed by a freedman (usually a liberated Greek slave). Senators

A family portrait. Above: Claudius (*ca.* 50 A.D.); right: Agrippina, Claudius' wife, with her child Nero; left: Nero as emperor.

still commanded armies and governed provinces and equestrians handled most of the financial affairs of the Empire, but a new imperial bureaucracy was to grow out of Claudius' group of freedmen.

Claudius married his niece, Agrippina, an evil and ruthless woman who persuaded him to disinherit his son by an earlier marriage and to give the succession to her own son, Nero. Nero was self-indulgent and unstable, but at first he left the government of the Empire to his mother and his tutor, the philosopher Seneca. When he decided to take power into his own hands he offended most of the leading men of the Empire by his lack of dignity and his cruelty. Believing that he was a great poet and musician, he traveled about the Empire performing his works. When a disastrous fire almost destroyed Rome in 64, there were rumors, almost certainly not true, that Nero had set the blaze to provide a brilliant background for a recitation of his poetry. Seeking a scapegoat, Nero blamed the fire on Rome's small community of Christians and put many of them to death.

Naturally there were plots against such a man, and naturally Nero imagined plots where none existed. He condemned to death his mother, his old friend Seneca, the poet Lucan, and the brilliant general Corbulo, who had defended the eastern frontier against the Parthians. He executed many senators and confiscated their property. And while he was building up a mountain of resentment against himself, he was paying no attention to the administration or to the army.

This time the legions led the rebellion, not the palace guard. This was a new and ominous development. The guard had been able to agree on one man; the scattered legions could not. Each group advanced the claims of its own general, and the result was the famous "year of the four emperors" (68–69). Nero, easily overthrown, committed suicide; then three army commanders in succession marched on Rome, claimed the imperial title, and promptly lost it to the next aggressor. The commander in the East, Vespasian, was wiser: he consolidated his hold on his own region and waited for his rivals to kill each other off. When Vespasian's troops gained control of Rome in 69 A.D., little opposition remained and he was to hold the imperial title until his death ten years later.

THE EMPIRE AT ITS HEIGHT 69–180 A.D.

Vespasian's rule marked a change in the character of the Empire. His predecessors had all come from the old aristocratic families that had held the highest offices in Rome for the last three centuries. Vespasian was not an aristocrat; he came from a middle-class family (the Flavians) in a small Italian town. He had become emperor through his own efforts, not through family connections and palace intrigues. He knew the provinces better than he knew Rome, and he relied on the Roman or Romanized inhabitants of the provinces more than any of his predecessors had done. He maintained correct relations with the Senate, but the Senate with which he had to deal was more and more a new Senate. Proscriptions, executions, and lack of heirs were extinguishing the old Roman aristocratic families. The new senators were drawn from all parts of Italy and eventually of the Empire. Senators as individuals occupied high administrative posts, and served the emperor on various advisory committees. But the Senate as a corporate body had long lost its independent authority.

These tendencies continued under Vespasian's successors. Most of them had had some administrative or military experience. Most of them came from new families. Most of them knew and were concerned with the provinces—two of them were born of Roman families that had settled in Spain.

The Flavian Emperors, 69–96 A.D.

Vespasian was an excellent administrator. The Empire was deeply in debt after Nero's extravagances; he made it solvent by reforming the tax structure. The practice of farming taxes to corporations of bankers, which had already been

Vespasian, founder of the Flavian dynasty.

Trajan (*ca.* 100 A.D.)

Inscription from Trajan's column in the Roman forum, *ca.* 114 A.D., celebrating his victories over the Germans and Dacians: "The Senate and the Roman people to the imperator Caesar, son of the deified Nerva, Nerva Trajan Augustus conqueror of the Germans and the Dacians. . . ."

cut back by earlier emperors, was eliminated by Vespasian and his sons. Procurators appointed by the emperor took over financial administration in the provinces. The vast amounts of land owned by the state or confiscated from alleged traitors were organized to produce maximum revenues. The frontiers of the Empire were strengthened in places where defense was difficult.

Vespasian was succeeded by his two sons, Titus (79–81) and Domitian (81–96). Titus was as capable as his father and, with the financial crisis over, could avoid the unpopularity caused by some of Vespasian's financial practices. Domitian seems to have ruled the provinces well, but he was disliked in Rome. The cult of the Republic was about dead, but philosophers were now arguing that the "best man" should rule. Domitian did not seem the best man to many of his subordinates, and he grew more autocratic as he grew older. Writers accused him of wishing to be addressed as "lord and god"; whatever the truth of this accusation, he certainly executed a number of men of high rank on flimsy charges. A palace conspiracy was formed, and Domitian was assassinated in 96 A.D. The armies were taken by surprise and made no move, so that for once the Senate was able to act. With the approval of the palace guard, it chose one of its own members, Nerva, as emperor.

The "Five Good Emperors" 96–180 A.D.

Nerva was an upright and distinguished senator, but he knew that he needed military support. He designated Trajan, commander of the armies on the Rhine, as his successor. With Nerva and Trajan began the era of the "five good emperors," which lasted from 96 to 180 A.D. Gibbon once wrote that this was the happiest period in the history of the human race; certainly it was the most prosperous and least troubled period in the history of the Roman Empire. Partly because of a lack of direct heirs, partly because they shared belief in the rule of "the best man," four emperors in succession passed their power on to adopted sons, and each of the men they chose proved worthy of ruling. The old problem of the succession seemed to be solved; the old jealousy between emperor and Senate almost disappeared; the old distinction between privileged Italy and oppressed provinces was practically eliminated; and the imperial administrative system was greatly improved.

SENATVSPOPVLVSQVEROMANVS
IMPCAESARIDIVINERVAE·F·NERVA
TRAIANOAVGGERM·DACICOPONTI
MAXIMOTRIBPOTXVIIIMPVICOSVIP
ADDECLARANDVMQVANTAEALTITVDINI
MONSETLOCVSTAN   IBVSSITEGESTV

This is not to say that there were no problems or no mistakes on the part of the emperors. The Germans along the lower Danube and the Parthians on the eastern frontier were a constant menace. Trajan (98–117) tried to end this danger by annexing enemy bases. He took Mesopotamia from the Parthians and Dacia (roughly, modern Romania) from the Germans at great cost in both money and manpower. Under Trajan the Empire reached its greatest extent, but even Trajan could not hold all of Mesopotamia, and Dacia was a battlefield for the next century and a half.

Hadrian (117–138) was less a soldier and more an administrator. He abandoned what was left of Mesopotamia and strengthened fortifications along the frontiers. One example of these efforts is Hadrian's Wall, much of which is still visible; it was built to protect northern Britain from raids by the inhabitants of Scotland. But Hadrian's real interest was in perfecting the imperial civil service. He continued earlier trends by appointing equestrians as bureau chiefs instead of freedmen, by organizing a regular hierarchy of positions, and by developing a group of career officers who could be advanced from post to post until they reached the highest positions in the government. He kept careful watch over these men and made long trips through the Empire to inspect provincial government. His success may be measured by the fact that the reign of his successor, Antoninus Pius (138–160), was so uneventful that contemporary writers have little to say about it. The reign of Marcus Aurelius (161–180), the last of the "good emperors," was not uneventful, but his problems are discussed in a later section.

The Empire in the Second Century

From the time of Vespasian to the death of Marcus Aurelius, most inhabitants of the Empire could go about their business without fearing invasion and without suffering from misgovernment. The letters exchanged by Trajan and the younger Pliny, who was a provincial governor in Asia Minor, show the high standards set for administrators and a real concern for the welfare of the governed. Certainly there were some corrupt officials and some cases of undue severity, but on the whole the provincials could at last feel that they were members of the Roman commonwealth, not subjects of a foreign conqueror.

The distinction between senatorial and imperial provinces had become meaningless; all provincial administration was controlled by the imperial bureaucracy. And while that bureaucracy occasionally interfered in local affairs, the city governments still had most of the

Roman soldier fighting on the Danube frontier (108–09 A.D.).

responsibility for administering their towns and the surrounding countryside. The city-state was the natural unit of local government in the East, and Rome had tried to build similar units in the western provinces. By the middle of the second century almost all the Empire was divided into these city-states, which proved to be powerful instruments for spreading a common Greek or Latin culture and common loyalties. All offices in the cities were reserved for men from the upper middle classes, who were expected to set an example of good citizenship to the rest of the community. They collected the taxes and made up any deficits in the assigned quota from their own pockets; they erected public buildings and monuments in the Roman style; they supported the official religion of Rome and the emperor. But to become one of these local notables a man had to accept Latin culture in the West and Greek culture in the East. The imperial government did not trust people who clung to old customs and spoke odd languages.

This gradual assimilation of Greco-Roman culture worked better in the West than in the East. The memory of earlier cultures had almost disappeared in the West; either one learned Latin and adopted Roman customs or one remained isolated from the mainstream of life. Even so, the process took time: Gaul and Spain became thoroughly Latinized, whereas Britain, which was conquered late and lost early, did not. The East had plenty of time to assimilate Greek culture, but stronger survivals with which to contend. Even though Hellenization had been going on since the third century B.C., Egyptian and Syrian traditions persisted. Most business, public and private, was conducted in Greek, but the old Oriental languages did not vanish, as Celtic gradually vanished in Gaul.

The Roman authorities, like the Hellenistic rulers of the earlier centuries, had encouraged assimilation and were reasonably satisfied with the results. Roman citizenship was given to the ruling classes of provincial cities and to provincials who served in the Roman army. By the end of the second century, most men of any standing in provincial society were citizens. When, in 212, the emperor Cara- calla extended Roman citizenship to all free men in the Empire, he was only giving legal sanction to an already existing psychological reality.

The Jews

Two groups seemed deliberately to avoid assimilation, the Jews and the Christians. The Jews' concept of Jahweh as the one universal God made it impossible for them to accept the idea that in their devotion to Jahweh they were simply worshiping another manifestation of Zeus-Jupiter. The Jewish scriptures gave them an acute sense of their own identity as a people. To be integrated into Greco-Roman culture was to deny the whole meaning of their history and their special relationship with Jahweh.

Most Jews lived together in Judea. Many, however, lived in Hellenistic cities outside Judea, especially in Alexandria. These Jews of the Diaspora (scattering) admired some elements of Greco-Roman culture, but even they remained a people apart. They could not take part in the sacrifices and rituals that demonstrated allegiance to the government. They had to be exempted from the state cults and military service and allowed to live by their own law.

When Rome took over the Hellenistic kingdoms, the special privileges of the Jews were confirmed and Judea was made a client kingdom. But the client kings were not very satisfactory. After wavering back and forth for several generations, Judea became a Roman province. This aroused resistance, especially in Galilee, where a group called the Zealots used terrorist techniques. Resistance stirred up a counter-terror by the Romans, which in turn precipitated an open rebellion in 66 A.D. The Jews fought heroically, but in the end the Romans sacked Jerusalem (70 A.D.), destroyed the temple, and slew thousands of Jews.

The final blow came under Hadrian. With the best of intentions, but with less than his usual sensitivity, he tried to rebuild Jerusalem as a Greco-Roman city, with a temple dedicated to Roman gods. Again Judea rebelled and again the Jews were slaughtered by the thousands. With Judea largely depopulated, the Jewish

Spoils taken by the Romans from the temple in Jerusalem (detail from Arch of Titus, Rome, 81 A.D.).

communities around the Mediterranean became the centers of Jewish culture. Although there were no more rebellions, there did remain an overwhelming desire to preserve the Law of Moses (the *Torah*) with the teachings concerning the Law (the *Mishna*) and interpretations of the Law (the *Talmud*).

The Beginnings of Christianity

The religion that was eventually accepted by most inhabitants of the Empire was founded in the reigns of Augustus and Tiberius. Jesus of Nazareth was born about 4 B.C.;* his brief period of active teaching and the conversion of the first disciples came during the years from 26 to 30 A.D. Shortly after the birth of Jesus, Augustus had taken direct control of Judea from a client king. Many Jews dreamed of a Messiah who would free

* Jesus' birth should, of course, have begun the year 1 A.D. But the reckoning of years from the birth of Jesus did not begin until the sixth century, and by that time errors had crept into the generally accepted chronology.

them from this foreign rule and prove that theirs was the only true religion. When Jesus began teaching, some Jews accepted him as the Messiah, especially since he quoted passages from the prophets that seemed to refer to such a mission. But most of these followers became discouraged when Jesus made it clear that his kingdom was "not of this world," that he was interested in a new view of the relation between God and man, and not in earthly politics. On the other hand, those who really understood his message were convinced that he was the Christ, the Son of God, and that his teaching of the love of God and the brotherhood of man was the most important revelation that the human race had ever received.

The dominant group among the Jews at this time was the sect of the Pharisees, strict upholders of the Jewish Law. They were shocked by Jesus' claim that he bore a new revelation that superseded the Law and even more by his assertion that he was the Son of God. They accused Jesus of blasphemy and denounced him to the Roman governor,

Pontius Pilate. Pilate was not very sure what he should do, but Judea was a troubled area, and anyone who stirred up strong popular feelings might be dangerous to Roman authority. So about 30 A.D. Jesus was crucified—a Roman form of execution reserved for criminals of the lowest classes.

Pilate and the Pharisees thought that this was the end of the matter. But the disciples remained faithful, for they were convinced that Jesus had risen from the dead and had repeatedly appeared to his followers. The Resurrection gave them courage and confidence. They began to understand the divine purpose: God had become man and had suffered on earth to redeem the sins of mankind. All who believed in Jesus would be saved by his sacrifice. Strong in their faith, they began to make converts among the Jews of Palestine and Syria. At this time they began to be called Christians.

The new religion was at first only a Jewish sect, ignored by the rest of the world and bitterly opposed by many Jews. At this critical point the conversion of Saul of Tarsus enabled Christianity to broaden its appeal. Saul, though Greek in education and Roman in citizenship, was a fiercely orthodox Jew who felt it was his duty to attack the Christians. In the midst of his campaign he suffered a physical collapse (in the *Acts of the Apostles* it is said he was blinded); on his recovery he announced his conversion to the faith he had opposed. He took the new name of Paul and began preaching Christianity in the cities of Asia Minor and Greece, and eventually in Rome itself.

It was Paul who made Christianity attractive to the non-Jewish inhabitants of the Roman world. He persuaded early Christian leaders that many Jewish ritual practices could be abandoned; one could be a Christian without first having to become a Jew. He also explained Christian doctrine in terms that were understandable to men thinking in terms of Greek philosophy. In his *Epistles,* he began the work of building a Christian philosophy and theology that could appeal to men of all races.

Meanwhile, other disciples were spreading the faith outside Palestine. Peter, the leader of the group, probably came to Rome; very early tradition holds that he was head of the Roman Church and was martyred there. Other churches were established in Egypt, Asia Minor, Greece, and later in Gaul and in Spain. Stories of the sayings and doings of Jesus were collected and by the end of the first

This marble relief pictures a small Italian city as it looked in the days of the early Caesars. Blocks of two- and three-story tenements are enclosed by the ancient town wall. At the right, the country villas of the wealthy, with their gardens and colonnades, sprawl across the nearby hillsides.

century began to take shape as the Gospels. To these were added the letters and acts of the apostles, and so the New Testament was formed.

Christianity was a vigorous, active faith at a time when the old state religions were losing their credibility and the mystery cults were not very precise about their doctrines. Its appeal was greatest among the poor and, in the West, among eastern slaves and laborers. There were enough Christians in Rome by 64 A.D. so that they could be blamed for burning down the city, and during the second century they began to cause problems for imperial governors. Like the Jews, they were a people apart who refused to take part in the public rituals honoring the state and the emperor. Unlike the Jews, the Christians were not protected by ancient privileges. Their religion was an unknown quantity and

their exclusiveness made them objects of suspicion. They were persecuted sporadically, although the most serious attacks against them came only in the third century.

Society and Economy

By the time the Empire had reached its height, Rome and its environs had a population somewhere around a million. Other great cities, especially in the East, had a hundred thousand or more. The rich could live luxuriously in their town houses, or suburban villas, but without public transportation the poor had to be crowded into tenements which rose to five or six stories in Rome. The ground floor was used for small shops; the upper stories were divided into small, dark apartments. There was no window glass, so all openings had to be narrow in order

THE ROMAN EMPIRE AT ITS HEIGHT   117 A.D.

A gladiator contends with a wild animal. Detail from a fourth-century mosaic.

was an absolute necessity. The old Roman Forum was lined with temples and shops; the emperors built several new forums nearby. They also provided the people with arenas for public spectacles. The Colosseum, started by Vespasian and dedicated by Titus, held 50,000 spectators. It was used chiefly for combats between gladiators or between slaves, criminals, and wild beasts. The Circus Maximus, which could seat about 150,000 persons, was the center for chariot racing. There were also elegant public baths, though the largest ones were not built until the third century.

Most of the western cities were like Rome—they had forums, temples, arenas, and baths. The eastern cities, with older traditions, had more individuality. But, as the literature of the period shows, there was enough resemblance among the cities so that a man traveling through the Empire found himself at home wherever he went.

The class structure was as rigid as it had been under the Republic. Although few of the old Roman senatorial families had survived the civil wars and the

to keep out cold and rain. Roman engineers knew how to bring water into a city by aqueducts, but they did not know how to raise it to the upper stories of a tall building. It is not surprising that most people spent as much time in the street as possible. The emperors had to forbid vehicular traffic in Rome during the day; all deliveries were to be made at night when the streets were less crowded.

For the Romans, as for the Greeks before them, the existence of public buildings, market squares, and gardens purges of the early emperors, a new senatorial class had replaced them. This class had little political power, but it enjoyed great wealth and held vast estates in Italy and in the provinces. The equestrians, as before, were not far behind the senators. Next came the municipal aristocracies. Far below these privileged groups were the country-folk (small farmers, tenants, and laborers), and in the cities, shopkeepers, workers, and unemployed freedmen. And at the very bottom, as in the days of the Republic, were the slaves, who worked in chain gangs in mines and on the great Roman estates.

The imperial government in various ways increased the rigidity of the class structure. By the second century the law made a strict distinction between upper and lower classes, not only in office-holding but also in judicial procedure. Only the *humiliores* (the more humble) could be tortured or executed in cruel ways, such as by crucifixion. On the other hand, some attempts were made to improve the lot of the slaves: they could not be treated as cruelly as they had been

under the Republic, and the freeing of slaves was favored. The very poor could improve their position by enlisting in the army.

Internal peace stimulated commerce, especially in the eastern cities. Greeks, Syrians, and Egyptians brought their wares to western markets in Gaul and in Britain. They also went far beyond the borders of the Empire. There was an active trade with India and indirectly with China, since Chinese merchants brought their silk to Indian markets. There were expeditions into central Africa in search of wild animals to stock the arenas. Germany furnished amber, furs, hides, and slaves.

This prosperity, however, rested on very narrow foundations. The chief occupation of most inhabitants of the Empire was agriculture, which was not very profitable. Slave labor was disappearing, both because slaves were more expensive in time of peace than during the wars of conquest and because many slaves were liberated and given land as tenant-farmers. Many free peasants were also tenant-farmers, and veterans who acquired land

Greek and Roman merchants traveled freely in the stable world of the first two centuries A.D. Their ships could average more than 100 miles a day. (Sarcophagus from Ostia, *ca.* second or third century A.D.)

The abundance of labor discouraged Roman invention of labor-saving devices. The crane pictured here required the use of many slaves to operate the treadmill. (Detail from tomb relief, first century A.D.)

metalwares, and pottery. It was easy for each region to become relatively self-sufficient in goods for ordinary consumption. Luxury goods were another matter, but producers and traders who dealt in these goods formed a very small part of the population.

The Romans were backward in finding new sources of energy. They never learned how to harness horses so that they could pull heavy loads. As a result, land transport was limited to small, two-wheeled carts, usually drawn by oxen. Although water mills were used to grind grain in places like Rome, elsewhere grain was ground by hand. True, the flow of Mediterranean rivers is irregular, but not all Romans lived on the shores of the Mediterranean. The rainy regions of Gaul had few water mills in Roman times, whereas there were thousands of them in the Middle Ages. In a subsistence economy, with a surplus of manpower (at least until the third century), there was no need for labor-saving devices, and Roman conservatism made innovation even more difficult.

Art and Literature of the Silver Age

The same conservatism may be found in Roman architecture of the second century. The Romans had made the round arch—little used by the Greeks—an essential element in their building. The arch was needed to bridge rivers and to carry aqueducts across deep valleys. With the arch and its logical development in the third dimension—the vault —they could construct huge buildings, such as the Colosseum or the Pantheon, a temple dedicated to all the gods. So enamored were the Romans of this architectural form that they constructed triumphal arches to stand by themselves as signs of glory and of victory. The use of concrete gave the architect more freedom to vary the rigid composition of Greek buildings (again the Pantheon is an example). Roman architecture may not have been as well proportioned as the Greek, but it had more variety and it expressed the power and magnificence of the Roman state.

Roman sculpture and wall-painting picked up the Hellenistic tradition of

on leaving the army usually had small holdings. The plantation run by slave labor had probably been more efficient than these groups of small farms. Even worse, the market for farm products was declining. When olive trees were planted in Spain and vineyards in Gaul, there was no reason to export oil or wine from Italy or Greece. Imperial domains in Egypt and elsewhere supplied Rome with grain. Agriculture supported the upper classes in luxury and the lower classes at a subsistence level, but it did not produce very much of a surplus for investment.

Industrial production was even less profitable. A promising start had been made around the Bay of Naples, but this center declined as Roman techniques spread to the provinces. When southern Gaul could produce pottery indistinguishable from Neapolitan ware, there was no reason to pay the cost of transport from Italy. Roman manufactures were not very complicated—textiles, realism. At times it was merely decorative, as in many of the houses of Pompeii. But at their best, Roman sculptors went beyond realism and expressed the inner character of the people they were portraying.

The literature of the late first century and second century A.D.—sometimes called the Silver Age—gave the Latin style its highest polish. Pungent epigrams and pithy sayings mark the work of the leading writers. The poets Martial (*ca.* 40–102) and Juvenal satirized the corruption and selfishness of Roman society. Tacitus (55–118), the greatest of the Roman historians, was also a master of the epigrammatic style. He was strongly prejudiced in favor of the old aristocracy and against the emperors, and he attached too much importance to gossip about intrigues at court. But few historians have written so well or have been so skilled in characterizing their subjects. His description of one of the ephemeral emperors of 69 A.D. as a man who in everyone's opinion was qualified to rule if only he hadn't tried it would fit a good many subsequent politicians. We still see the emperors of the first century through Tacitus' eyes.

Other writers of the period have had somewhat less influence. Seneca (*ca.* 4 B.C.–65 A.D.), Nero's tutor and victim, was a Stoic philosopher; he wrote the only Roman tragedies that have survived— very noble and rather cold. Seneca's nephew and fellow-victim Lucan (39–65 A.D.) composed the *Pharsalia*, an epic on republican resistance to Caesar, which has some memorable lines. Suetonius (*ca.* 75–110) in his *Lives of the Twelve Caesars* regaled his readers with amusing anecdotes about Julius Caesar and the emperors through Domitian. Josephus (*ca.* 37–100), a Jewish army officer during the rebellion of 66 A.D. who went over to the Roman side, tried to explain the peculiar history and nature of his people in his *Jewish Antiquities.*

Two promising starts were made at creating the literary form we know as the novel. One was the *Satyricon* by Petronius (d. 65 A.D.), an elegant courtier at the time of Nero. The other was the *Golden Ass* by Apuleius (*ca.* 125–180), who lived in North Africa. Both works bear an extraordinary resemblance to the first novels in modern European languages. Each describes the adventures of a hero whom misfortune dooms to wander among strange, often disrespectable, people. But while Petronius and Apuleius had a few successors, the novel never became an established branch of ancient literature.

Pliny (61–113?) was a cultivated gentleman and an honest and conscientious public servant. His *Letters* (modeled

The writer's tools: wax tablet, papyrus scroll, ink pot.

Imperial Administration

The letters between the emperor Trajan and Pliny the Younger, his representative in one of the provinces of Asia Minor, suggest that imperial administrators, however severe, were generally more concerned with achieving justice than in following the letter of the law.

Pliny to Trajan:

> . . . Having never been present at any of the trials of the Christians, I am unacquainted with the method and limits to be observed either in examining or punishing them. Whether any difference is to be made on account of age, or no distinction allowed between the youngest and the adult; whether repentance admits to a pardon, or if a man has been once a Christian it avails him nothing to recant. . . .

> In the meanwhile, the method I have observed . . . is this: I interrogated them whether they were Christians; if they confessed it I repeated the question twice again, adding the threat of capital punishment; if they still persevered, I ordered them to be executed.

Trajan to Pliny:

> The method you have pursued, my dear Pliny, in sifting the cases of those denounced to you as Christians is extremely proper. It is not possible to lay down any general rule which can be applied as the fixed standard in all cases of this nature. No search should be made for these people; when they are denounced and found guilty they must be punished; with the restriction, however, that if the party denies himself to be a Christian, and shall give proof that he is not (that is, by adoring our Gods) he shall be pardoned on the ground of repentance. . . .

From Pliny, *Letters,* trans. by William Melmoth, rev. by W. M. L. Hutchinson, The Loeb Classical Library (Cambridge: Harvard University Press, 1953), pp. 401, 407.

somewhat on those of Cicero) show that he knew how to tell a story, as in his description of the eruption of Vesuvius that buried (and so preserved) the towns of Pompeii and Herculaneum. His correspondence as governor of Bithynia with the emperor Trajan shows the extent of imperial control and some lack of initiative on Pliny's part. Pliny asked Trajan's advice on every difficult question—for example, on how to deal with the Christians—and the emperor seems to have been wearied by all these questions.

The scholarly traditions of the Hellenistic era continued under Roman rule. Athens was still the center for the study of philosophy and Alexandria of science. During the second century the Greek physician Galen wrote his treatises on medicine and Ptolemy his studies in astronomy. Both were regarded as basic texts well into the sixteenth century. Unfortunately, both contained serious errors mixed with useful information. Thus Ptolemy's system made it possible to predict the position of the planets with accuracy, but it was based on a belief that the earth was the center of the solar system.

Plutarch (46?–120?) wrote a series of short biographies in Greek—*Parallel Lives of Famous Greeks and Romans.* Plutarch had little primary source material on men such as Pericles or Pompey, but he used, and thus preserved, stories from earlier histories that have since been lost. His biographies are lively reading and are often our only source of information about a good number of episodes in ancient history.

Philosophy and Theology

Hadrian's reign (117–138) marked a turning point in the history of literature, as in many other activities. For writers in Latin, especially, there was a tendency to imitate past masterpieces and to write in a deliberately archaic style. Poetry, history, and oratory never fully recovered from this blight. At the same time, a tremendous amount of intellectual energy was poured into philosophy and theology. The second century was a century of religious searching, and some of the searchers were able to put their beliefs into words that made a lasting impression on Mediterranean and European societies.

It was in the second century that the first Church Fathers, writing in Greek, increased the appeal of Christianity to the educated classes by deriving a theology and a philosophy from Biblical texts. And by the end of the century neoplatonism was revived more as a religion than a philosophy. Starting with Plato's belief in eternal, incorporeal Ideas (see p. 48), the neoplatonists developed a system in which God, who was pure Spirit, generated lesser spirits through whom the physical world was created and through whom the spirit in man could reach out toward God. In its lower forms, neoplatonism came close to magic (which was very popular at this time); in its higher forms, it had some influence on Christian philosophy.

During the second century Stoic philosophy was given its highest expression in the writings of the slave Epictetus (60–140) and the emperor Marcus Aurelius (121–180). The careers of these two men illustrate the basic Stoic doctrine: whether slave or emperor, a man must follow the eternal law. But Stoicism appealed mainly to the upper classes. The masses clung to their traditional and regional religions of infinite variety, in which the worship of Zeus or Jupiter jostled Celtic or semitic cults.

Roman Law

The long period of political stability and the interest of the emperors in good administration made the second century the decisive period in the formulation of Roman law. The Romans, like most other peoples, had started with a few simple rules of law that had been expanded and amended until they covered most of the ordinary problems of Roman citizens. But the Romans also had allied and subject cities, each with its own law. Since inhabitants of different cities often had legal dealings with one another, Roman judges had to discover equitable principles that would be accepted by all reasonable men. Stoic philosophy, which influenced most Roman jurists, helped in this quest. It was easier to discover principles that were valid at all times and in all places if one was first convinced, as the Stoics were, that such principles existed. And as Roman jurists began to formulate these principles in the late Republic and early Empire it seemed reasonable to apply them to all kinds of cases. Rules derived from the common experience of all peoples must be closer to the eternal law of nature than the peculiar and imperfect laws of a single city. Thus the Romans themselves began to prefer the general principles of the law of nations to their own municipal law, which in many respects was out of date.

This process was speeded up in the second century as the emperors began to take increasing responsibility for the administration of justice. The concentration of judicial authority in the hands of the emperor and his appointees naturally led to a greater uniformity in interpreting the law. Able jurists began to produce textbooks that the courts accepted as authoritative. Some emperors, such as Hadrian, asked for official formulations of some parts of the law. This process of putting the law into enduring form continued for many generations; some of the most eminent Roman lawyers wrote in the first half of the third century.

The formulation of Roman law was one of the great achievements of Western man. It was not perfect—no law is—but it was a great improvement over all earlier legal systems. It was consistent, logical, and complete, and it was based on principles of justice and equity. The Romans themselves described it as "the art of goodness and fairness," or "a continuing desire to give every man his due." Roman law did not quite reach this standard; for example, the courts treated the poor much more harshly than the rich, and there were practically no restrictions on the power of the state. These weaknesses were due in part to the fact that Roman law was almost entirely civil law. Criminal law remained crude and harsh. But the majesty of the law impressed even the emperors. They admitted that they should follow the law rather than their own whims, even if they did not always live up to this principle. Roman law, comprehensive and flexible enough to be adapted to any situation, survived all the misfortunes of the Late Empire; Justinian's great compilation in the sixth century (see p. 165) was based

Ulpian on Justice

Ulpian was one of the great Roman jurists of the early third century A.D. These passages were quoted by Justinian's lawyers at the beginning of the *Digest,* an authoritative treatise on Roman law (see p. 165).

Justice is a constant and perpetual will to give every man his due. The principles of law are these: to live virtuously, not to harm others, to give his due to everyone. Jurisprudence is the knowledge of divine and human things, the science of the just and the unjust.

Law is the art of goodness and justice. By virtue of this we [lawyers] may be called priests, for we cherish justice and we profess knowledge of goodness and equity, separating right from wrong and legal from the illegal. . . .

largely on the work of Roman jurists of the second and third centuries. Through Justinian's compilation, Roman law has affected the jurisprudence of every country in the world.

THE CRISIS OF THE THIRD CENTURY

During the second century the Roman Empire seemed to have found a permanent solution to many of the problems that had long plagued the ancient world. By uniting the peoples living around the Mediterranean into a single state the Empire had given peace and security to a vast area. Improvements in imperial administration and the granting of Roman citizenship had almost ended the resentment that subject peoples had felt toward their conquerors. Millions of people shared a common culture and had the same tastes; they offered a huge market to enterprising businessmen. The third century should have seen an ever more prosperous and powerful Empire. Instead, it witnessed a series of catastrophes from which the Empire never fully recovered.

Political Weakness

The obvious cause of the troubles of the third century was the old problem of the succession. When Marcus Aurelius died in 180 he was succeeded by his son, Commodus, thus breaking the long chain of adoptions that had produced the "good emperors." Commodus was rather like Nero, vain and capricious, though he fancied himself as a gladiator rather than as a poet. When Commodus was assassinated (192 A.D.) the Senate once more tried to name an emperor, but its nominee was swept away and the army again divided, with each group of legions supporting a rival emperor. The shrewdest of the generals, Septimius Severus, came out on top; he and members of his family ruled from 193 to 235. Their reign resembles the history of Vespasian and his

The emperor Marcus Aurelius (160–80) entering Rome in triumph. Detail from the column of Marcus Aurelius in Rome.

sons, and Septimius Severus, like Vespasian, began a basic reconstruction of the Empire. But when the last of the Severi was assassinated, the Senate and the army could not agree on a successor; there was no Nerva, no Trajan. Instead, the army made and unmade emperors with appalling rapidity. Between 235 and 285 there were twenty-six emperors and at least as many unsuccessful pretenders. Many of these emperors were men of real ability, but few of them remained in power for as long as five years. Rulers whose reigns began with a civil war and ended with assassination could do little to solve the problems of the Empire.

Military Weakness

Behind the problem of the succession lay a very serious military problem. Trouble had begun early in the reign of Marcus Aurelius, when the Parthians attacked in the East while the Germans pushed across the Danube. It took years of fighting to drive back these enemies, and the peace won by Marcus Aurelius lasted less than a generation. The Germans, especially the Goths, renewed their attacks on the Rhine-Danube frontier. In the East the Sassanid ruler of Persia overthrew his overlord, the Parthian emperor, and established a revived and militant Persian Empire. The Parthians had been bad enough; the Sassanids were even more dangerous. They plundered the eastern provinces, while the Goths pushed into the Balkans and even built a pirate fleet that disrupted Mediterranean commerce.

The long wars put a severe strain on the finances of the Empire and on the morale of the army. The fighting was desperate, often hopeless. The soldiers, long-term professionals who were out of touch with the civilian population, tended to magnify the virtues of their own general if he were successful, and to despise and rebel against generals or emperors whom they did not know, especially if they seemed incompetent or cowardly. These soldiers led a hard life; they expected bonuses when they completed a campaign or helped their general to become emperor. If money was not available—and often it was not—there would be a mutiny. But not all third-cen-

Third-century tomb relief showing an affluent banker and two struggling Roman laborers. The Roman economy was weakened by this gap between the wealthy few and the poor masses.

unfortunate that civilians found it necessary to take on military posts. Two of the greatest Roman jurists, Papinian and Ulpian, became commanders of the palace guard, and—like most men who rose to that dangerous eminence—died in palace rebellions led by their own troops.

Economic Weakness

Economic as well as military problems forced the emperors to militarize the state. As we have seen, even in the second century there were weaknesses in the Roman economy. In a sense, the Empire had simply lived off the profits made by the conquests of the Republic. Areas annexed after the beginning of the Christian era probably never yielded a profit because of the cost of defense. In the third century this cost rose sharply. Army pay had to be increased and the size of the army doubled. Frontier and civil wars devastated many areas and impoverished others. Mediterranean commerce was declining even before the appearance of Gothic pirates on the sea; most economic historians agree that it never regained its earlier level. Great landowners, high public officials, and a few dealers in luxury goods still had comfortable incomes, but small farmers and middle-class businessmen found it hard to meet extraordinary expenses, and even harder to accumulate capital for new enterprises. The situation was aggravated by the government's policy of meeting its debts by devaluating the currency.

Weakness in Municipal Government

All these forces tended to weaken local governments. In some respects, the early Empire could have been described as a federation of cities, each responsible for the political and economic welfare of the surrounding territory. During the third century these cities lost population and income. General insecurity affected both local and long-distance trade. Cities far from the frontier had to be fortified; even Rome was protected by encircling walls in the reign of Aurelian (270–275). Municipal government began to break down as the local aristocracies could no

tury emperors were assassinated or executed by their soldiers: a good many fell in battle or died on campaigns. Even if the army had been completely united and loyal, there would have been many short reigns.

A considerable part of the army was permanently stationed in frontier provinces and was recruited from the poorest groups in the population. These characteristics were accentuated when Marcus Aurelius began the practice of inviting Germans into the Empire, giving them land, and enlisting them in the army to defend the frontier against their fellow tribesmen. Such soldiers probably understood little about the institutions or the values of the Empire. But they do not seem to have been any more irresponsible than the crack troops of the imperial bodyguard, who murdered more emperors than did the provincial soldiers.

More and more the quality of the army determined the character of the Empire. Beginning with Septimius Severus, the Roman state became increasingly militarized. Army officers took over civilian tasks, such as tax collection and some kinds of legal jurisdiction. Italy, which was more closely supervised by the emperor in the third century, had a garrison of regular troops. This militarization was necessary in a period in which the Empire was on the defensive, and military men were not necessarily bad administrators. It was, perhaps, more longer afford to hold office and to be responsible for the full payment of local taxes. The imperial government had already found it necessary to intervene in municipal affairs toward the end of the second century; during the third century it had to take over most of the responsibility for local government. All authority became concentrated in the hands of imperial officials, and in many places this meant that authority was in the hands of military governors.

Weakness in Society

The Empire shrank in upon itself during the third century. Physically, it lost some of its outposts, such as Dacia; spiritually, it lost some of its vigor and confidence. The ordinary man had long ceased to have political significance, but even well-to-do citizens now had little influence on policy, either in Rome or in provincial cities. Neither the upper nor the lower classes felt much responsibility for the general welfare: that was the business of the emperor and his officials. In a declining economy there was little that anyone could do to improve his lot

or to increase productivity; great increases in wealth came largely from service to or favors from the emperor. Repeated outbreaks of plague, beginning in the reign of Marcus Aurelius and continuing through the first half of the third century, may not have greatly reduced the population, but they certainly weakened morale.

Unable to understand or to influence events in this world, a considerable part of the population looked to the next world for hope and consolation. The mystery religions continued to grow. The number of Christians increased enough to worry the emperors; the first large-scale persecutions took place in the third century. None of the eastern religions advocated open opposition to the state, although many of them considered that service to the state was unimportant at best, and an obstacle to salvation at worst. The Empire continued to exist, but it had only the passive loyalty of many of its citizens. And those who were galvanized into resistance were often interested only in their own districts, not in the Empire as a whole. Thus Gaul had its own emperor for some fourteen years: he defended only Gaul, not the Danube line or the East.

The Establishment of Military Absolutism

Even its most disillusioned inhabitants could not conceive of a world in which the Empire did not exist. They proved wise in their own generation. After 270 the emperors were still short-lived, but they did their job better. Outside invaders were gradually beaten back, and internal rivals for power were eliminated. Aurelian restored the unity and security of the Roman world; he might have been the founder of the Late Empire if he had not been assassinated in 275. But less than ten years later, in 284, another victorious general, Diocletian, began the reforms that held the Roman world together for another century. Thus, in the end, the generals saved the Empire—by making themselves absolute sovereigns and by imposing a strict, almost military, discipline on their subjects.

The Empire in Decline

This passage, the musings of a trader as he revisits a provincial city in Switzerland in the third century, is from a modern historical novel.

It was a pleasant town. Demetrius paused to look at the Treasury inside its stone wall, and the villas scattered within shady gardens. Yet each year they were a little more neglected; the temple yard had not been properly swept, a latch was hanging loose from a shutter, the gutter was choked by a dirty mass of what had once been somebody's garland. He wondered why the place had changed so much during the six years since his first visit. Then there had been chariots on the streets, and many wagons, an indefinable sense of the city being alive. Was the Empire too big? Yet it had been larger, and nobody had counted the provinces. Were the young so ungrateful? It seemed to him that there was just the same proportion of honest men and rogues as in his childhood. There was constant talk about invasion; nobody now was certain as to who was emperor of what, but the Treasury still functioned reasonably well, most roads got mended, trade went on, yet he could not deny the change. Something had happened; it was as if a sentry had been asked to keep one watch too many, and his fibre had snapped.

From Bryher, *Roman Wall* (New York: Pantheon, 1954), p. 124.

Suggestions for Further Reading

General

Note: Asterisk denotes a book available in paperback edition.

The texts mentioned at the end of the preceding chapter will also serve as introductions to the era of the Roman Empire. A reader seeking a more detailed discussion of the imperial period should consult M. Cary, *History of Rome*, 2nd ed. (1954). Somewhat shorter is J. Wells and R. H. Barrow, *A Short History of the Roman Empire* (1931). Since this book ends with the death of Marcus Aurelius, one might read H. M. D. Parker, *History of the Roman World from A.D. 138 to 337* (1935) or M. Grant, *The Climax of Rome* (1968), for the later period. The classic nonpolitical history of the era is M. I. Rostovtzeff, *The Social and Economic History of the Roman Empire,** rev. ed. (1957). Two short studies of the Roman Empire, both extremely well written, are M. P. Charlesworth, *The Roman Empire** (1951), and H. Mattingly, *Roman Imperial Civilization** (1959). An excellent collection of original source material may be found in N. Lewis and M. Reinhold, *Roman Civilization* (1955), Vol. II.

Government

There are two exhaustive studies of the creation of the Roman Empire: F. B. Marsh, *Founding of the Roman Empire* (1927), and M. Hammond, *The Augustan Principate in Theory and Practice* (1933). See also R. Syme, *The Roman Revolution* (1939), and H. T. Powell, *Rome in the Augustan Age* (1962). The best biography of Augustus is T. R. Holmes, *The Architect of the Roman Empire,* 2 vols. (1928–31), which contains a thorough description of the Empire in the Augustan era. There are many good studies of the individual reigns of the later emperors. V. Scramuzza, *Claudius* (1940), and R. Seager, *Tiberius* (1972), are the best biographies of these two emperors. B. W. Henderson's two lengthy studies, *Life and Principate of the Emperor Nero* (1903) and *Life and Principate of the Emperor Hadrian* (1932), are old but still unsurpassed on these two controversial emperors. For the second century, see M. Hammond, *The Antonine Monarchy* (1959); B. W. Henderson, *Five Roman Emperors* (1927); and A. Birley, *Marcus Aurelius* (1966) and *Septimius Severus* (1970).

The Provinces, Provincial Administration, and Roman Law

T. Mommsen, *The Provinces of the Roman Empire,* 2 vols. (1909), is monumental in size and scope and remains the classic, though outdated, study of economic, social, and political life in the Roman provinces. On provincial administration, the most thorough treatment is found in W. T. Arnold, *The Roman System of Administration* (1914). A later, and excellent, survey is G. H. Stevenson, *Roman Provincial Administration* (1939). F. F. Abbott and A. C. Johnson, *Municipal Administration in the Roman Empire* (1926), and A. H. M. Jones, *The Cities of the Eastern Roman Provinces* (1937), both have valuable information on the municipal administrations that were the basis of the Roman provincial administration.

The standard introduction to Roman law is R. W. Buckland, *A Manual of Roman Law* (1925). See also J. A. Crook, *Law and Life of Rome* (1967). A good study of the army is G. Webster, *The Roman Imperial Army* (1969).

Society, Literature, and Religion

A comprehensive and interesting description of the society of the early Roman Empire may be found in S. Dill, *Roman Society from Nero to Marcus Aurelius** (1925). Another useful study is J. P. V. Balsdon, *Life and Leisure in Ancient Rome* (1968). Two good introductions to the literature of the era are M. Grant, *Roman Literature** (1954), and M. Hadas, *A History of Latin Literature* (1952). See also the two books by J. W. Duff, *A Literary History of Rome to the Close of the Golden Age,* 3rd ed. (1963), and *A Literary History of Rome in the Silver Age,* 3rd ed. (1964). For the arts, M. Wheeler, *Roman Art and Architecture* (1964), is excellent.

The most thorough treatment of Roman religion is F. Altheim, *A History of Roman Religion* (1938). The effect of the spread of Hellenistic religions is treated in T. R. Glover, *The Conflict of Religions in the Early Roman Empire** (1960), while the best study of eastern mystery religions in the era of the Roman Empire is F. Cumont, *Oriental Religions in Roman Paganism** (1956). A good recent book is J. Ferguson, *The Religions of the Roman Empire* (1968).

5

The Late Roman Empire, 284–476

Even after the crisis of the third century, the Roman Empire still had two great assets: a formidable army and a well-organized bureaucracy. These two institutions proved strong enough to restore order and unity to the Roman world for another century. The revival of the Roman state had a profound effect on the history of civilization, for it was during the fourth century that Christianity became the official religion of the reunited Roman Empire. Christianity thereby won for itself a firm foothold in the western world.

THE RESTORATION OF ORDER: THE REIGN OF DIOCLETIAN, 284–305

The work of restoration was begun by Aurelian (270–75), who checked the civil wars within the Empire and started the drive to push the Germans and the Persians back to their old frontiers. Aure-

lian's work was carried on by his successors, even though the army was still making and unmaking emperors at its usual rate. It was not until Diocletian became emperor in 284 that internal stability was fully restored.

Political and Military Reorganization

Diocletian's success was due first of all to his character. Shrewd, tough, and determined, he dominated rival generals as no emperor had been able to do for a century. He was able to keep most of the army on his side and to put down the few commanders who tried to rebel.

In an effort to improve the defense of the borders, Diocletian increased the size of the army, and also built up a mobile reserve of picked troops, under his personal command, which could be rushed to any threatened frontier. This army was also effective in putting down revolts by provincial commanders. To make his personal command over these troops effective, however, Diocletian had to abandon Rome as his official residence and rule from capitals set up in cities nearer the frontiers. From this time on the city of Rome declined steadily in size and importance.

Just as ingenious, but less successful, were Diocletian's attempts to solve the problem of succession. He realized that the troubled Empire needed more than one high-ranking commander, and he realized that some potential revolts could be warded off by sharing power with

Romans battling barbarians (from a third-century Roman sarcophagus).

able generals. Almost as soon as he was established as emperor, Diocletian named a fellow officer, Maximian, as coemperor. Later, each of the two emperors selected an assistant with the title of Caesar. It was understood that when the emperors retired or died, the Caesars would succeed as emperors and designate new Caesars in turn.

The system of divided authority was also helpful in Diocletian's reorganization of the imperial government. For purposes of administration, each emperor became responsible for half of the Empire: the western half, under Maximian, encompassed Italy, North Africa, Spain, Gaul, Britain, and northern Illyria. The eastern half, under Diocletian himself, consisted essentially of the provinces that had formerly made up the Hellenistic world. Each half was divided into two prefectures, one of which was administered by the Caesar. Consequently, the administrative workload was shared among the emperors and their assistants, and decisions could be made rapidly and intelligently. Diocletian, however, did not give his corulers an entirely free hand; there was never any doubt that he was the senior emperor and that it was he who made the decisions that applied to the Empire as a whole.

In a further effort to increase stability and forestall rebellion, Diocletian emphasized the divine and autocratic nature of the emperor, completing a process that had been going on for generations. By the third century all pretense that the emperor was merely the First Citizen had long been abandoned. But Diocletian became *dominus et deus,* lord and god. Everything that pertained to his household or administration was sacred, and he adopted many of the symbols and ceremonies of the eastern monarchies. Anyone granted an audience with Diocletian was required first to prostrate himself and then to kiss the hem of the emperor's garment.

Diocletian and his coemperor Maximian, each embracing his appointed Caesar (St. Mark's Cathedral, Venice).

Economic Reform

Diocletian tried to stabilize the economy as well as the politics of the Empire. He was almost the only Roman emperor who realized the need for economic planning. Some of his reforms were successful, such as the issue of a new and much improved currency. Some were less successful, such as his attempt to stem inflation by freezing prices and wages. Because he lacked the bureaucracy to enforce the new regulations, his edict soon became a dead letter.

The realization that something should be done about the Roman economy shows Diocletian's perceptiveness, but the means he used to carry out his ideas were harsh and often ineffective. Diocletian was a soldier who believed that a state could be run like an army. He was convinced that an unhealthy economy could be cured by edict, that men could be commanded to produce goods at fixed prices just as troops could be commanded to charge an enemy. Since most of Diocletian's successors were also military men with similar approaches to political and economic problems, almost all private activities came under the control of the state during the fourth century.

RELIGION IN THE LATE ROMAN EMPIRE

One of the most baffling problems faced by Diocletian, and one he could not solve, was the growing popularity of the many eastern mystery religions that had first appeared in the Hellenistic era (see p. 54) and of Christianity. All these religions emphasized the afterlife and discouraged the vigorous participation in the affairs of this world on which Diocletian's program of restoration depended. The Christians were particularly offensive to Diocletian, for they continued to refuse to recognize the divine aspect of imperial authority.

The Eastern Mystery Religions

During the first three centuries of the Roman Empire many people in the Mediterranean world had been seeking a faith by which to live. The appeal of the older Greco-Roman gods had been declining since the Hellenistic era; the rituals were still performed, but few people really believed in Jupiter and his fellow gods. The attempt to institute a state religion based on the worship of "the spirit of Rome and the genius of the emperor" had failed when the population lost the intense patriotism that might have given the cult meaning. In the first and second centuries the upper classes had turned to Stoicism. But to the ordinary man Stoicism offered cold comfort. It was too intellectual and too impersonal; it valued eternal law, human brotherhood, and devotion to duty, but it elicited no strong emotional response. There was no individual salvation, no promise of a better life for the poor and the oppressed. Although the Stoics would have denied it, their main motivation was probably pride—pride in doing one's duty for duty's sake, pride in remaining unbroken by worldly problems. During the troubled third century even the upper classes began to abandon Stoicism, and by the end of the century a large part of the population had accepted one of the mystery cults.

Most of the mystery religions were based on very ancient beliefs, though they took on their characteristic forms during the Hellenistic era and the early years of the Roman Empire. Their gods were not the carefree deities of the Greek and Roman pantheons. Instead, they were semidivine heroes who had suffered as men suffer in the age-long struggle against darkness and evil. Most of them had been killed in the conflict but had returned to life, thus prefiguring victory over death and eternal life for the souls of their followers.

The worship of the Egyptian Isis was widespread throughout the Empire, but even more widespread was Mithraism, a

THE ADMINISTRATIVE DIVISIONS OF DIOCLETIAN   Fifth century

popular form of the Zoroastrian religion of Persia. Mithra was a warrior-god who had been killed by the god of darkness but who rose again and was thus able to bestow immortality on converts who would join him in the eternal war against evil. Mithraism was popular among soldiers and became almost the official religion of the Roman armies. It remained a competitor of Christianity all through the fourth century and its dualistic theology (a god of good fighting a god of evil) was picked up again by the Manichean heresy that was to trouble medieval Christendom.

A person could join one of these mystic brotherhoods by participating in rituals that cleansed him of the sins of the physical world and ensured that his unstained soul would become a part of the eternal world of the spirit. An Isis-worshiper was purged of his sins and prepared for his reception by the pure and loving mother-goddess by being immersed in water that symbolized the sacred Nile. An initiate into the religion of Mithra stood beneath a platform on which a bull was being sacrificed; the blood that dripped down washed and regenerated him.

For many people these religions satisfied a genuine need. The individual felt helpless and insecure in a society over which he had no control, in which his economic and political welfare was determined by remote and unapproachable authorities. He often felt a deep sense of sin, not so much because of personal misconduct as because he was convinced that the misery of the human condition could be explained only by a fundamental blemish on the soul of each man. The eastern religions assured men of their importance as individuals and promised them forgiveness of sin and a happy future life. It is not surprising that these religions won adherents in every part of the Roman world.

The Triumph of Christianity

Another religion that gained large numbers of adherents in the third century was Christianity. Although the Christian refusal to worship "the spirit of Rome and the genius of the emperor"

was technically the equivalent of treason, the imperial government was scarcely aware of the existence of the sect in the first and second centuries. Most Christians belonged to the lower classes during this period, and the government took note of them only when there was political or social unrest (as in Rome under Nero or in Bithynia under Trajan). Even then, it persecuted Christians largely for political reasons; it made no attempt to wipe out the religion.

As a result the early Church had been able to develop its theology and to create a remarkable administrative system, modeled more or less on the administrative system of the Empire. It was important for the scattered members of the new faith to keep in touch with each other and to preserve uniformity of doctrine. The most respected members of each congregation became priests ("elders"), and in each city one priest was designated as bishop ("overseer"). The bishop was responsible for supervising all the Christian congregations in his city and in the surrounding villages. By the second century the bishop of the capital city of each Roman province was recognized as an archbishop, with authority over the other bishops in his province. The systematic organization of the early Church was an innovation in the ancient world and helped establish the supremacy of Christianity over the many other religions of the Empire. No similar system existed for the pagan or mystery cults; the priests of Jupiter in one city, for example, were entirely independent of those in other cities.

During the third century Christianity began to attract members from all classes. Earlier, the educated classes of the Empire, broadminded by tradition, had been offended by the exclusiveness of the Christians, by their unwillingness to admit that there might be truth in other religions. Many people preferred to hedge their bets, so that devotees of the Great Mother (the goddess Cybele) might also join the Isis cult just to play safe. But in the troubled third century— when economic decline, civil war, barbarian raids, and plague affected nearly every family and signaled confusion and decay in almost every aspect of civilized

The young boy in this painting (*ca.* 300–350) is an acolyte of the Isis cult. The cup and garland are emblems of his religious belief; the side hairlock was long associated with the child-god Horus.

Colossal head of Constantine, from his basilica in Rome, *ca.* 320.

Diocletian, who hated any kind of disobedience. But Diocletian does not seem to have reduced the number of Christians greatly, even in the East, where he ruled directly instead of through a colleague.

THE REIGN OF CONSTANTINE, 307–37

Diocletian, an innovator to the end, abdicated in 305 and became one of the few Roman emperors to die peacefully. But his elaborate provisions for an orderly succession were soon disregarded, and a series of civil wars put five different generals in control of various parts of the Empire. One of these generals was Constantine, who completely reversed Diocletian's policy of persecuting Christians.

The Conversion of Constantine

Scholars have long argued about the reasons for and the sincerity of Constantine's conversion to Christianity. His mother is said to have been a Christian, and certainly he had some idea of the doctrines and the power of the religion before he became emperor. On the other hand, he had held command in Gaul, where Christians were neither numerous nor influential. Constantine cannot have believed that there were enough politically motivated Christians in his part of the Empire to make any difference in the struggle for power with rival generals. When he invoked the help of the Christian God, he must have been motivated by religious conviction, not by political expediency. Perhaps he thought that he was only tapping a new source of semi-magical power, but he surely did not think that he was gaining thousands of Christian recruits for his army. The decisive moment in Constantine's religious life came just before he was to meet his strongest opponent for the imperial title at the battle of the Milvian Bridge (near Rome) in 312. Just before the battle Constantine is said to have had a vision of a cross in the sky surrounded by the words *"in hoc signo vinces"* ("in this sign shalt thou conquer"). Convinced that the Christian God had helped him to victory,

life—the very firmness of Christian beliefs began to make them attractive. Similarly, the unswerving morality of the Christians and their belief in the fatherly love of God offered security in a time of confusion. Finally, the extreme otherworldliness of the Christians, which had seemed mere foolishness to all but the slaves and the poor in the affluent second century, fitted well with the intense desire for future happiness in the chaotic third century.

Christianity grew rapidly enough during the third century to alarm some of the emperors. They were annoyed by Christian lack of patriotism; these zealots would neither sacrifice to the emperor nor serve the state. This disregard of religion (it was even called "atheism") was sure to rouse the anger of the gods. There were some severe and prolonged periods of persecution during the century. The worst and longest came under he ordered his troops to carry Christian insignia from that time on. Soon, in 313, Constantine (and the remaining co-emperor who still ruled with him) issued the Edict of Toleration ending the persecution of Christians.

Constantine himself received baptism only on his deathbed, a not uncommon precaution at that time. But, though not a full member, he supported the Church throughout his reign, thus enabling it to become the dominant religion of the Empire during the fourth century. And he apparently hoped that the Empire would be strengthened by strengthening the position of Christianity. Certainly the Empire was stronger in the fourth century than it had been during much of the third century, but quarrels among theologians proved almost as dangerous as quarrels among generals.

In the face of persecution, the Christians had managed to suppress their differences. After the Edict of Toleration, however, Christian leaders fell into such bitter doctrinal disputes that the unity of the Church was threatened. But Constantine wanted Christianity to promote unity, not destroy it. And since, like any good Roman, he was sure that there must be some single legal formula that would be acceptable to all reasonable men, he often used the force of his imperial office to bring the Church to agreement.

One of the earliest controversies concerned the doctrine of the Trinity. A priest named Arius taught that the Son and the Holy Spirit had been created by, and were therefore subordinate to, God the Father. Other churchmen attacked his teachings, insisting that the three aspects of God must be equal. The quarrels that sprang up were so bitter that Constantine called a council of bishops at Nicaea (in Asia Minor) in 325 to settle the matter. After some argument, the Council of Nicaea produced a confession of faith that completely rejected the teachings of Arius. The Arians were not cowed by this action and remained a powerful force in the Empire (and even more among the Germans) for many generations. And new doctrinal disputes continued to emerge so that councils of bishops had to meet at frequent intervals. The decisions of a majority of a general council were held to be binding on the whole Church. Those who would not accept them were excommunicated—that is, cast out from the Church and the communion of the faithful.

The Extension of Military Absolutism

After his victory at the Milvian Bridge in 312, Constantine established his rule over the western half of the Roman Empire. In 324 he defeated his coemperor and thus gained full control over the entire Empire. Constantine, like Diocletian, was a tough-minded soldier who maintained the order and stability of the Empire with military discipline. Experience, however, had taught him the dangers of sharing the imperial power with generals. So, although Constantine retained most of Diocletian's reforms, he did not revive the practice of dividing his authority with coemperors.

Realizing, as had many earlier emperors, that the economic and military

Constantine's Religious Beliefs

The official policy of the Empire after 312 was toleration, as shown in a letter sent in the name of both Constantine and his coemperor to the governor of Bithynia in 313.

. . . we resolved to make such decrees as should secure respect and reverence for the Deity; namely, to grant both to the Christians and to all the free choice of following whatever form of worship they pleased, to the intent that all the divine and heavenly powers that be might be favorable to us and all those living under our authority.

But Constantine showed stronger personal convictions in a letter written only a year later to the governor of Africa, dealing with the problem of schism in that province.

Since I am assured that you are also a worshipper of the supreme God, I confess to your Excellency that I consider it absolutely wrong that we should pass over in insincerity quarrels and altercations of this kind, whereby perhaps the supreme divinity may be moved not only against the human race, but even against me myself, to whose care He has entrusted rule over all earthly affairs. . . . For then, and only then, shall I be able truly and most fully to feel secure . . . when I shall see all men, in the proper cult of the Catholic religion, venerate the most holy God with hearts joined together like brothers in their worship.

From *Great Problems in European Civilization*, ed. by K. M. Setton and H. R. Winkler (Englewood Cliffs, N.J.: Prentice-Hall, 1954), pp. 75, 79.

strength of the ancient world lay in the East—the former Hellenistic world—Constantine sought a new capital that would be easy to defend, that would have access by sea to the commercial routes of the Aegean and the Mediterranean, and that would be near enough to the frontiers for the emperor never to be too far from either his administration or his armies. He chose the site of the ancient Greek city of Byzantium on the Bosporus. He named his capital New Rome, but after his death it became known as Constantinople (and after its occupation by the Turks in 1453, as Istanbul).

Constantine's efforts to make his new city prosper were successful. He had picked an excellent location, he coerced wealthy men to build there, and he plundered much of the Empire to embellish his new capital. Constantinople soon became one of the leading commercial and cultural centers of the Greco-Roman world. But this move to the East was one more step in downgrading the importance of the western provinces (including Italy) and in leading to a separation between the two sections of the Empire.

THE EMPIRE IN THE FOURTH CENTURY

So towering was Constantine's prestige that for several decades after his death members of his family retained the imperial throne. Except for the brief reign of Julian (361-63), all of Constantine's descendants were Christians. Therefore Christianity came to be more and more the official religion of the Empire. But imperial protection meant imperial intervention in the affairs of the Church. Thus, caesaropapism—the control of the Church by the emperor rather than by the bishops—developed. It was to cause many conflicts between church and state in later periods. Though Constantine's successors quarreled bitterly among themselves over both politics and religion, most of them were men of military ability, a quality that was badly needed in the fourth century. They succeeded in holding the Empire together and protecting its frontiers.

This silver and gold horse adorned the throne of the king of the Persians (*ca.* fourth or fifth century).

The Barbarian Threat

Trouble was brewing almost everywhere along the eastern and northern frontiers. The Persians, the oldest and most dangerous of the enemies of the Empire, once more moved to attack the eastern provinces, and the best Roman troops had to be used to repel them. At the same time the Germanic tribes were in turmoil along the Rhine and the Danube. Large groups were migrating in search of better lands or more secure homes, and each migration touched off a series of tribal wars. The victors often raided Roman territory; the vanquished begged permission to settle in Roman frontier zones (as they had done since the time of Marcus Aurelius). Moreover, individual tribes banded together in more or less permanent confederations with such huge reserves of manpower that they could eventually challenge the Roman defenses.

Meanwhile, the Roman army was running short of manpower just when it needed to expand. There was never a time when the inhabitants of the Empire did not outnumber all their barbarian enemies put together. But more and more Roman citizens were being excluded from military service. Senators were barred from army posts because they were needed for civilian jobs; members of the urban aristocracies, because they were needed for local administration. Landlords (and tax collectors) felt that peasants could not be spared from the land, and the city proletariat was useless for military purposes. The frontier provinces still supplied troops, but, since those troops were used almost entirely as border guards, they could not be used as mobile armies to ward off sudden attacks.

To overcome this lack of officers and men, the Empire drew recruits from among the barbarians themselves. The barbarian soldiers acted as the shock

Head of a barbarian found in Gaul, probably representing one of the Helvetian (Swiss) peoples.

Silver-gilt spear mount made for a barbarian warrior, found in a tomb in northern France (*ca.* fourth century).

troops of the Empire, and for the first time in the long history of Rome armies composed of foreigners were valued more highly than armies composed of Roman citizens. But except for a better-organized top command, these barbarian troops were very like the armies of the enemies they were opposing. Consequently, in a battle between armies of equal size it was by no means certain that the barbarized Roman army would prevail. The process that had created this dangerous situation was irreversible, for by the fourth century it was too late to rebuild the army with Roman citizens. There were no mass levies of inhabitants of the Empire and no spontaneous organizations for defense. If barbarian armies could not defend the Empire, then there was no one left to defend it.

Economic and Social Problems

The growing apathy of the people of the Empire was even more dangerous than the barbarizing of the army. Even the upper classes seem to have assumed that the Empire would survive without any great effort on their part. Citizens obeyed orders and paid taxes when they could not evade them, but they showed no readiness to sacrifice life or property to save the state.

As if to reinforce this political apathy, the Roman economy continued to slump. Some parts of the Empire were reasonably prosperous in the fourth century, but in many provinces the depression that had begun in the third century persisted without relief. Population declined in many regions. The towns became less and less able to discharge their economic functions. Large amounts of arable land were permitted to slip out of cultivation, and the burden of taxes forced many peasants to become tenants or laborers on the estates of the wealthy.

Least affected by the depression were the great landlords, especially those of the western provinces. These men were able to ignore the world around them by operating their estates as independent social and economic units. By using the simple home manufactures of their peasants to supply the needs of the estate, they reduced contacts between town and countryside. This was especially disruptive in the West, where the cities were not very strong to begin with. As the cities weakened the landlords took over much of the responsibility for local government, a practice that weakened the authority of imperial officials and eventually led to the autonomous lordships of the early Middle Ages.

Most citizens had long ago given up hope of controlling their political future. During the fourth century they began to give up hope for their economic future as well. They saw no prospect of rising in the world, nor even any assurance that they would be able to hold on to what little they had. This feeling of discouragement was especially strong in the West, and it is not surprising that in that region devotion to the Roman state and to the principles of the Greco-Roman civilization tended to decline.

A State-controlled Economy

From the time of Diocletian the emperors had been aware of these problems, but they could not trace back through five centuries of history to find the roots of the people's indifference. They could deal only with the current symptoms. And since many of them were military men and all of them were occupied with military affairs, they tried to solve their problems by running the Empire like an army. If the people failed to do their duty voluntarily, they would have to do it under compulsion. If self-interested economic motivations were no longer enough to get essential work done, then it must be done under state control.

The emperors' treatment of municipal governments offers a good example of their attitude. The chief function of municipal government was to collect taxes for the imperial government. These taxes were not high by today's standards, but in a declining economy even low taxes placed a heavy burden on many communities. The city officials were responsible for collecting the taxes in their communities; if some inhabitants failed to pay, then the officials had to dig into their own pockets to make up the lack. Predictably, well-to-do town-dwellers tried to avoid municipal office. But the central government, instead of easing their burden, simply ruled that all municipal officials had to stay in office and that their sons had to succeed them when they died. Thus the government attempted to keep the municipalities operating through sheer compulsion. This policy alienated the landholding class of officials, who had formerly been generous contributors to civic projects. It did nothing to halt the decline of commerce. Many western cities were dwindling away by the end of the fourth century.

At the same time the government passed laws to bind the peasants to the soil. The number of slaves had decreased since the wars of conquest, while the number of poor but free farmers had increased. During the third and fourth centuries these farmers were often forced by the depression and high taxes to give up their small plots of land and become tenants on the great estates. Many of them found such an existence unsatisfactory and sought other employment. But the central government, worried lest a decrease in the amount of land under cultivation might lead to a decrease in tax revenues, forbade tenant farmers to leave the estates they were working on. In the end, the tenant farmer became something more than a slave but something less than a freeman; to use the later medieval expression, he became a serf. Though not bound to personal service, he was tied to a particular piece of land, and he and his heirs were bound to cultivate that land forever.

Some groups of artisans suffered a similar fate. Bakers in Rome and Constantinople, for instance, were bound to remain in their trade and to furnish a son to succeed them. In fact, by the middle of the fourth century much more than half of the population of the Empire was

Symbol of Christianity, incorporating the Greek letters for Chi and Rho (the monogram for Christ that forms the shape of the cross) and for Alpha and Omega (meaning beginning and end).

probably frozen in permanent hereditary occupations. The laws could be evaded, but economic decline reduced opportunities, and so reinforced the effects of legislation.

The Church

We are apt to exaggerate the number of Christians in the Empire during the fourth century. There were wide areas, especially in the West, where Christianity had scarcely penetrated. Christianity was at first a city religion; it had yet to develop the parish organization that was later to make it successful in rural areas. The cities of the predominantly rural West were smaller, fewer, and weaker than those of the East. Thus hundreds of thousands of country-dwellers had little contact with the new religion. As late as the early sixth century missionaries could still make numerous converts in Italy and southern Gaul.

At the same time, to the detriment of both literature and politics, theological controversies absorbed the energies of the best thinkers and the ablest writers of the more urban and urbane East. Good Christians might, and did, say that this was only right, that it was better to study the things of God than the problems of the world, but concentration on theological disputes stirred up passions that injured both the Church and the Empire. This was especially true in the East, where there was strong rivalry among the religious leaders of Constantinople, Antioch, and Alexandria. The people of these cities supported their own clergy and argued vehemently over disputed doctrines. The Syrians and the Egyptians voiced their resentment against centuries of Greek domination by adopting theologies that infuriated the Greeks. Religious separatism and local patriotism went hand in hand, and during the next two centuries the loyalty of the eastern provinces to Constantinople diminished steadily.

The West, with the exception of North Africa, was less shaken by religious controversy. Beginning with Tertullian in the second century, Latin theologians had shown a tendency to make clear and simple definitions rather than to speculate on fine points of doctrine. Fortunately, the definitions they made proved acceptable to the church councils. The bishop of Rome, now regularly called the pope, was the heir to this Latin tradition and was therefore always on the side of orthodoxy. Since no other bishop in the West had anything like the pope's authority, his interpretation of doctrine was usually accepted in the Latin-speaking provinces. The doctrinal unity of the West, as opposed to the diversity of the East, was one factor that led to the separation of the two parts of the Empire.

THE END OF THE EMPIRE IN THE WEST

In the last quarter of the fourth century the threat to the Rhine and Danube frontiers of the Empire reached a new intensity. To the familiar German raids was added a fresh menace: the advance of the Huns from Central Asia.

The Huns

The Huns were typical of the Asian nomads who for centuries threatened the civilized peoples of the Eurasian continent. These nomads lived in a harsh land of scant rainfall and great extremes of temperature. Often the distance between their summer and winter pastures was over a thousand miles, so they had to become expert horsemen. Living in the saddle, they invented most of the equipment that made cavalry an effective fighting force. For example, they used horseshoes and stirrups long before these devices were known in the West. If one imagines riding a horse into battle without stirrups, one can see why the Asian nomads long had supremacy in cavalry fighting. But even after their equipment was adopted by other peoples the nomads were still almost unbeatable as horse soldiers; they were unafraid of death and as pitiless as the land in which they lived.

Fortunately for their neighbors, the nomads usually lived in small bands of no great striking force. But every now and then bands threatened by a common danger would join together, or a leader of genius would manage to unite several groups. Once this process started, it was almost irreversible. The ruler of some thousands of nomads could force all the smaller groups in an area of thousands of square miles either to join him or perish. Thus were built up the great human avalanches that thundered down from the high plateaus of Central Asia onto the coasts of China, Europe, and India.

The Huns who attacked Europe were a part of one of these avalanches. As they moved west across the steppes their army snowballed until at last they broke out onto the Russian plain in the second half of the fourth century. No Germanic people could withstand them. Some of the resident population joined the Huns as satellite troops; others fled in terror to the shelter of the Empire.

The Goths

The first Germanic people to be struck by the Huns were the Goths, who had come from the north and had settled around the Black Sea. Since they were on reasonably good terms with the Romans, they turned to Rome for aid. The East Goths (Ostrogoths) were overrun by the Huns, but the West Goths (Visigoths) managed to cross the Danube and take refuge in the Empire. Unfortunately, some imperial officials regarded the West Goths as a new source of forced labor, and mistreatment soon led to revolt. After routing a hastily gathered Roman army in the battle of Adrianople (378), the Goths occupied a large part of the Balkan peninsula.

This was not the first time that Germans had defeated a Roman army and

THE GERMANIC MIGRATIONS   Fourth to sixth centuries

occupied Roman territory. The time-honored tactic in such a case was to settle the invaders in a frontier province, and to integrate them gradually into Roman society. This was the policy adopted by the emperor Theodosius (378–395), and it very nearly succeeded. He concentrated the Goths in a small strip of land south of the Danube in the Balkans, where they lived as Roman allies under their own kings. Their most promising young men were sent to Constantinople for education; some of them received posts in the army. For the remainder of Theodosius' reign the Goths remained quiet.

Theodosius tried to preserve the religious as well as the political unity of the Roman state, but here again he ran into the problem of the barbarians. After a half-century of conflict, Arius and his followers had been crushed by the authorities of the Empire, but before their final defeat Arian bishops had converted some of the Goths. One of these Goths, Ulfila, translated the Scriptures into Gothic and so gave the Arians an advantage in missionary work among the Germans. By the time of Theodosius most of the Goths, and an increasingly large number of other Germans, had accepted the Arian form of Christianity. Theodo-

Roman soldier and barbarian warrior (detail from a third-century Roman sarcophagus).

sius tried to suppress Arianism among his own subjects, but he could not interfere with the religious beliefs of his allies. Most German settlers and most German soldiers were Arians. Their heretical belief offended the Romans and was one of the factors that delayed the merging of the two peoples.

Although Theodosius was a defender of the orthodox faith, he was the first European ruler to do public penance for offending the Church. He had ordered a massacre of the people of Thessalonica because they had killed one of his officers. St. Ambrose, bishop of Milan, refused to give Theodosius communion until he had done penance, and, in spite of threats, forced the emperor to admit his fault. Theodosius' submission demonstrated the growing power of the Church. Medieval popes were to use the event as a precedent in their struggles with lay rulers.

Theodosius was the last emperor to control the whole Roman world and the last to keep the frontiers reasonably intact. He achieved this success, however, only by strengthening the barbarian element in the army and in the border regions. Theodosius himself was strong enough to control his generals, but his weak successors were puppets of the army commanders, most of whom were of Germanic origin.

The Division of the Empire

When Theodosius died in 395, he was succeeded by his two sons, Arcadius in the East and Honorius in the West. This division of the Empire was not meant to be permanent; during the last century there had usually been more than one emperor. While each ruler had been primarily responsible for one part of the Empire, the coemperors had always cooperated to some extent and in emergencies had acted in each other's territories. But the division between Arcadius and Honorius proved to be rather different. The army commanders who held real power under the two young emperors were suspicious of each other and would not cooperate. The Germans (both those in the army and those pushing across the frontiers) grew so strong in the West that the eastern ruler

Arian and Catholic in Gaul

This letter was written by Sidonius Apollinaris (a Roman aristocrat living in southern Gaul) to Bishop Basilius (472–73).

I must confess that formidable as the mighty Goth may be, I dread him less as the assailant of our walls than as the subverter of our Christian laws. They say that the mere mention of the name Catholic so embitters his heart that one might take him [Euric, king of the Visigoths] for the chief priest of his Arian sect rather than for the monarch of his nation. . . . For these reasons I would have you consider the secret malady of the Catholic Church that you may hasten to apply an open remedy. Bordeaux, Perigueux . . . and many another city are all like bodies which have lost their heads through the death of their respective bishops. No successors have been appointed to fill their places. . . . Do your best, as far as the royal condescension lets you, to obtain for our bishops the right of ordination in those parts of Gaul now included within the Gothic boundaries, that if we cannot keep them by treaty for the Roman state, we may at least hold them by religion for the Roman Church.

The Letters of Sidonius, trans. by O. M. Dalton (Oxford: Clarendon Press, 1915), Book VII, p. 6.

Alaric, "King of the Goths," depicted in a seal contemporary with the sack of Rome in 410.

A Vandal general in the service of Rome. Note that although he is a barbarian, he wears Roman clothing. (Ivory diptych, *ca.* 400.)

could not step in and reunite the two halves of the Empire when his western colleague died.

Theoretically, the Empire remained one state, but in fact it was permanently divided after 395, and each half had a different fate. The West fell completely under the power of the Germans and for centuries remained backward in political organization and economic activity. In the East the Empire continued, and though it gradually became quite un-Roman it was far more stable and prosperous than the barbarian kingdoms of the West.

The Sack of Rome

When Theodosius died, the Visigoths left their Balkan reservation and began raiding again. They might have been crushed if the western and eastern army commanders had cooperated, but each was afraid the other might gain an advantage. In fact, it seems likely that the eastern government persuaded the Goths to move west in order to spare the Balkans from further looting. When the Visigoths stormed down into the Italian peninsula, the emperor Honorius shut himself up in the fortified city of Ravenna and made no move to stop them. The Goths occupied Rome in 410—a catastrophe that sent a last feeble impulse of patriotism through the Empire.

True, Rome had not been the real capital for many years, but it was still the symbol of the Empire. No enemy had touched it for almost eight centuries, and its fall shocked men who otherwise cared little about imperial affairs. Adherents of pagan religions said bitterly that this disaster occurred only after the Empire had forsaken its old, protecting deities for the powerless Christian God. St. Augustine, the ablest Christian writer of the period, was spurred into writing his most famous book, *The City of God* (see p. 119), in order to refute this argument. He insisted that the eternal City of God inhabited by the saints was far more important than any earthly city of sinners. Yet even St. Augustine admitted that the Romans had created the best secular government that had ever existed, and less devout Christians must surely have been worried by signs that this government was failing.

The Visigoths, perhaps seeking more fertile land, abandoned Italy and moved to southwestern Gaul. Here they settled permanently, gradually occupying Spain as well. They remained allies of the Empire and helped the Romans repel a dangerous Hun invasion in 451. But as the western Empire weakened, the Goths grew more independent; by 500 they were entirely free from imperial control. The Visigothic king ruled his own realm, and the authority of Rome was only a distant memory.

Other Germanic Migrations

Shortly after the Visigoths started their long march to the west, other Germanic groups pushed across the frontiers. The Romans had neither the troops nor the will to stop the invaders, but they were able, in most cases, to reach an accommodation with them. They granted the Germans the status of allies and allowed them to set up kingdoms in Roman territory. By thus regularizing the occupation, the Romans avoided much violence. The Germans, who were not very numerous, had no desire to destroy the Romans and their cities; all they wanted was a reasonable share of the land. The Romans, with a declining population, had land to spare; so long as they could keep some of their property, they could tolerate the rule of barbarian kings. Thus in most of the western Empire there was no catastrophic loss of life or property as the Germans moved in. The one great exception was Britain, where the imperial government had collapsed so completely that no peaceful settlement could be worked out with the invading Anglo-Saxons.

One of the longest, and in the end the most unsuccessful, of the Germanic migrations was that of the Vandals. This coalition of peoples moved from North Germany through Gaul into Spain. Attacked by the Visigoths, they abandoned Spain and finally settled in North Africa. Here they built a fleet with which they dominated the western Mediterranean for half a century. They even managed to seize Rome briefly in 455, but although they plundered the city they were not guilty of the kind of wanton destruction that has become associated with their name. The Vandals did not try to hold Italy, and even in North Africa they grew so weak that they were easily crushed by the Eastern Roman Empire in the sixth century.

More typical of the German migrants were the Franks and the Burgundians. They made a shorter journey and established a successful and permanent settlement. Until the death of Theodosius both peoples had been confined to border territories along the Rhine and in northeastern Gaul. The Franks then began to move south and west, while the Burgundians settled in the Rhône valley. Neither people was ever again brought under control of the imperial government.

At about the same time the Angles and the Saxons began to raid Britain from their homes along the North Sea. Rome had withdrawn its army and its officials from Britain, and the invaders, crossing the sea in small flotillas, were unable to concentrate their forces. With no unified command on either side, negotiations were almost impossible. Small groups of native Britons fought small groups of Anglo-Saxons in a bloody war that lasted for over a century. In the process Roman civilization was wiped out. Cities and villas were destroyed, and the Britons, driven back into Wales or Cornwall, gave up the use of Latin and reverted to their native Celtic. The larger part of Britain became England, a land of Germanic speech and customs.

By the middle of the fifth century all that was left of the Empire in the West was Italy and a fragment of Gaul. Even this remnant was threatened by a new advance of the Huns under their famous king Attila, the "Scourge of God." A first attack on Gaul was defeated in 451 by Aëtius, the "last general of the Empire," with the help of Visigothic and Frankish allies. Attila invaded Italy the next year, but he found the peninsula too barren to support his army. He was persuaded to withdraw by an embassy led by Pope Leo I, an episode that gave great prestige to the papacy. With Attila's death in 453 his empire disintegrated and the Huns no longer menaced the West.

Aëtius' victory gained him only the jealous suspicion, not the thanks, of the emperor. The general was put to death; his followers retaliated by assassinating the emperor. For a while German army commanders governed Italy behind a façade of puppet emperors. At last, in 476, Odovacar, the leader of a band of German mercenaries, tired of the pretense. He deposed the last emperor and became king of Italy. All Roman territories west of the Adriatic were now under barbarian rulers.

Zeno, the emperor in Constantinople, promptly regularized the situation by naming Odovacar his representative in Italy. Thus the fiction of imperial unity was preserved, though Zeno had no real authority in the West. A decade later the imperial government tried to turn fiction into fact by sending a new group of Germans to attack Odovacar. These Germans were the Ostrogoths, who had finally escaped Hunnish domination after the death of Attila. Like the Visigoths, they had settled in the Balkans; and like the Visigoths, they were so unruly that the emperor was delighted to speed their way to Italy. After several years of fighting, the Ostrogoths defeated and killed Odovacar and by 493 had full control of Italy.

The Ostrogothic king, Theodoric, was one of the ablest of the Germanic rulers. Having lived several years at the court of Constantinople, he made a greater effort than most barbarian kings to preserve the forms of Roman government. He always acknowledged the formal sovereignty of the emperor, but in fact he was just as independent as Odovacar. Theodoric had no intention of restoring imperial rule in the West.

The "Fall of the Roman Empire"

The deposition of the last western emperor in 476 is often referred to as the "Fall of the Roman Empire." Taken literally, this is a meaningless phrase. There was almost nothing left to fall in the West, and in the East the Empire survived as a powerful state. No inhabitant of the Mediterranean world could believe that the Empire had "fallen" in 476, though he might have good reason to feel that the western part of it was decrepit.

Still, the passing of the Latin-speaking part of the Empire under Germanic rule was a watershed in history. Basic ideas of government and law had come from the Latin West; an Empire that was largely Greek could not remain a Roman Empire, even though it kept the name. The Latins became barbarized under Germanic rulers; the Greeks became Orientalized as their contacts with the West decreased. Thus the two halves of the Roman world drifted apart, preparing the way for the later split between eastern and western Europe.

This divergence between the two parts of the Empire raises a question that has puzzled generations of historians. Why did the Empire and the civilization it embodied collapse in the West and survive in the East? The East suffered the same social illnesses as the West; why did they do less damage? About all that can be said is that the East was favored by geography and that it had more economic and spiritual vitality than the West. The richest eastern provinces were protected by impregnable Constantinople; the exposed Balkan provinces did not attract permanent German settlement. In the West it was easy to attack and occupy the rich farmlands of Gaul and the Po Valley. Commerce and industry were concentrated in the East; the wealth of eastern cities could be used to hire armies and bribe enemies. The West had no such resources.

Finally, Christianity had cut deeper and spread more widely in the East than in the West, and zeal for the faith often led to support of the state that protected the faith. This identification of religion with patriotism was not universal—nor was it always helpful. Heretics often bitterly opposed the imperial authorities. But at least in the East some people felt strongly enough about their beliefs to fight for them; in the West Christians were as apathetic as pagans. Western bishops disliked the Arian Goths, but they did not fight them, either to preserve the true faith or to save the eternal Empire. During the fifth century the eastern emperor was able to recruit soldiers from among his subjects, while in the West the Roman population hardly lifted a finger to protect itself.

But these were differences in degree and not in kind. The East was only a little more stable than the West; it saved itself from the Germans but could not repel the next great attack, that of the Arabs (see p. 173). The basic trouble was that very few inhabitants of the Empire believed that the old civilization was worth saving. As we have seen, there never was a time when the Romans did not greatly outnumber the invaders. A reasonably trustworthy source numbers the entire Vandal people—men, women and children—at about eighty thousand when they crossed the Straits of Gibraltar. Yet this small group overran all North Africa. The "Fall of the Empire" was not a political episode of the year 476; it was a deadly crisis in the history of a civilization.

ART AND LITERATURE DURING THE MIGRATIONS

Secular Art and Literature

Officially sponsored literature, education, and art were as decadent as imperial politics during the time of the Germanic migrations. The blight of imitation lay heavily on all secular thought and literature. Overrefinement of earlier techniques had produced a style that was

---

Capella on Geographic Zones

Martianus Capella's *Satyricon*, from which the following was taken, was written in the early fifth century. It was one of the typical encyclopedic digests of the late Empire.

The round world may be divided into five zones or bands of different characteristics. Of these, great excesses of heat or cold force three to be abandoned. The two zones which touch either end of the earth's axis, dominated by terrible cold, are deserted because of frost and snow, while the middle zone, baked by flames and breath-taking heat, scorches all living things that come near. The two other zones, tempered by the breath of life-sustaining air, offer a habitation to living things. These zones, curving around the sphere of the earth, go around both the upper and the lower hemisphere. . . . Those who live opposite us are called "antipodes." . . . For when we roast in summer, they shiver with cold; when spring here begins to cover the fields with flowers, there worn-out summer is passing into sleepy autumn.

From Martianus Capella, *De nuptiis philologiae et Mercurii* (Leipzig: Teubner, 1866), Book VI (on Geometry), p. 252.

Art of the fourth and fifth century declined from the elegant work of the first and second century. Contrast the fine modeling of the coin of Tiberius (14–37 A.D.) with the crude portrait of Honorius (395–423) below it. The same contrast can be seen on the fourth-century Arch of Constantine, below. The four circular medallions were carved for Hadrian 200 years earlier.

involved, ornate, and often deliberately obscure. Greek was seldom studied in the West—another sign of the drawing apart of the two halves of the Empire—and the Greek scientific tradition was scarcely known to men of Latin speech. A final sign of the degeneration of secular studies was the making of digests—handy collections of familiar quotations, one-volume encyclopedias, summaries of the rules of grammar in a few pages. Men studied these digests more than the original works from which they were drawn; they were to become the basic textbooks of the Middle Ages.

Official art, like secular literature, was heavy and imitative. Few new buildings or monuments were constructed. Those that were built often were decorated with materials taken from earlier works. For example, on the Arch of Constantine there is a striking contrast between the crude work of the fourth century and the elegant sculptures borrowed from a second-century monument. The same decline is evident in the coins of the period. The Romans had been masters of realism, if not of the higher forms of art,

and the coins of the emperors of the first and second centuries carry striking portraits. By the end of the fourth century the coins are less well made and the portrait is becoming a symbol—the emperor as a type rather than as an individual.

Thus wherever one turns in the fourth and early fifth centuries one sees apathy on the part of the multitude and a lack of creativeness among the upper classes. The framework of imperial government held the Roman world together long after Roman civilization was dead, but it could not support a corpse indefinitely. New forms of organization and new beliefs were needed before civilization could revive.

Christian Art and Literature

The new beliefs and many of the new forms of organization were developed by the Christian Church, the only segment of late Roman society that still had any vitality and originality. Christian literature and Christian art of the fourth century stood at the beginning of a new tradition rather than at the end of the old classical tradition. But the old tradition had to die before the new tradition could reveal its full potential. Christians could no more preserve classical literary and artistic forms than they could preserve the political organization of the Empire.

The career of St. Augustine, the greatest Christian theologian of the period, illustrates this point. Augustine (354–430) was born in what is now Tunisia, the only son of a well-to-do family. He received a good classical education and could have had a profitable career as a lawyer or as a member of the imperial bureaucracy. But Augustine, like many of his contemporaries, was concerned about religion and salvation. He was not at first a Christian—one more proof of the slow spread of the faith into the West. As a young man he turned to neoplatonism and then to Manicheanism to satisfy his spiritual interests. When he finally accepted Christianity he abandoned public life entirely and dedicated his remarkable intellectual gifts to the service of the Church.

Augustine was not greatly concerned by the troubles of the Empire, though at the time of his death the Goths had seized Rome and the Vandals were attacking Hippo, the city where he was bishop. Pagan charges that neglect of their gods had caused the sack of Rome did inspire him to write *The City of God*, but only to prove that the fate of Rome was unimportant compared to the preservation of the holy community of saints and angels. His real concern was with God's ways toward man, and especially with the problems of free will and predestination, of evil and sin. If God is all-wise and all-powerful, does man really have free will? How can such a God allow man to sin and condemn himself to endless suffering? How can a merciful God countenance the existence of evil? These were the questions Augustine wrestled with in his *Confessions*, one of the most remarkable autobiographies of all time. He dealt with them again in *The City of God* and in the innumerable treatises that made him the most influential theologian of the West.

By avoiding extreme answers Augustine found solutions that have appealed to Christian scholars of all times and all

St. Augustine on the City of God

Accordingly, two cities have been formed by two loves: the earthly by the love of self, even to the contempt of God; the heavenly by the love of God, even to contempt of self. The former glories in itself, the latter in the Lord. For the one seeks glory from men, but the greatest glory of the other is God, the witness of conscience. . . . In the one, the princes and the nations it subdues are ruled by the love of ruling; in the other, the princes and the subjects serve one another in love, the latter obeying, while the former take thought for all. The one delights in its own strength, represented in the persons of its rulers; the other says to its God: "I will love Thee, O Lord, my strength." And therefore the wise men of the one city, living according to man, have sought for profit to their own bodies or souls, or both, and those who have known God "glorified him not as God, neither were thankful, but became vain in their imaginations, and their foolish heart was darkened. . . ." For they were either leaders or followers of the people in adoring images, "and worshipped and served the creature more than the Creator." But in the other city there is no human wisdom, but only godliness, which offers due worship to the true God, and looks for its reward in the society of the saints, of holy angels as well as holy men, that God may be all in all.

From St. Augustine, *City of God,* in *Basic Writings of St. Augustine,* ed. by Whitney J. Oates, Vol. II, p. 274. Copyright 1948 by Random House, Inc. Reprinted by permission.

sects. Thus he argued that evil is not an independent power (as the Manicheans taught) nor yet the creation of God; it is merely the absence of good. Man has free will, but this free will is ineffective without the assistance of divine grace. Augustine made his points emphatically, sometimes too emotionally, but he was writing about subjects that were important to him.

The other chief Latin Christian authors of the fourth century were St. Jerome and St. Ambrose. Jerome (335–420) was a better scholar than Augustine; he knew both Greek and Hebrew. He spent much of his life translating the Bible into Latin, a translation on which the Vulgate—the official Catholic text—was based. Ambrose (d. 397) was an administrator and preacher rather than a scholar. He had had a successful career in the imperial civil service before he became bishop of Milan. He was involved in a long quarrel with Arian heretics, and, as we have seen, he forced the emperor Theodosius to do public penance for his sins. During these disputes he encouraged his flock by writing sermons, and even more by writing hymns for them to sing. This was a rather new idea; Ambrose did much to popularize hymn singing in the West, and his hymns are still sung in the Catholic Church.

Christian art of the late Empire showed the same vigor as Christian literature. The trend away from realism to symbolism was entirely appropriate for religious art. During this period some of the most persistent symbols for representing Christian ideas were developed, such as the dove to represent the Holy Spirit. Christian painting and sculpture of the late Empire are sometimes crude, but never flaccid.

It was also during this period that the basic patterns for church architecture were developed. In the West, the model was the Roman law court, or basilica, a long rectangular room with two sets of pillars dividing the room into a central hall, or nave, flanked by two side aisles. The roof over the nave was elevated to admit light through windows set above the side aisles. Eventually the far end of the nave was rounded into an apse that held the altar and seats for the clergy. Later a transept was inserted between nave and apse. This was a hall that crossed the nave at right angles and protruded beyond the aisle walls, thus giving the church the form of a cross. There were basilicas in the East as well, but the most typical form for eastern churches was a round or polygonal structure with

The church of Santa Sabina, built in 425, incorporates the characteristics of a Roman basilica—a long, rectangular nave divided from two side aisles by rows of pillars.

a dome over the central portion. This pattern still characterizes churches of the Greek rite.

Christian art and Christian literature were to have their fullest development in later centuries. But even before 500 two things had been demonstrated: first, that under the inspiration of Christian doctrine new styles were arising to replace those that had dominated the Mediterranean world for centuries; second, that the people of the Greco-Roman world, despite all their troubles, were still capable of creative activity.

Suggestions for Further Reading

Note: Asterisk denotes a book available in paperback edition.

The Late Empire   There are many fine histories of the late Roman Empire. Perhaps the best one-volume study is the masterly synthesis by F. Lot, *The End of the Ancient World** (1931), which shows the causes of the political ruin and economic weakness that Diocletian attempted to check. Another excellent survey is A. H. M. Jones, *The Later Roman Empire* (1964); an abridged version came out in 1966. Both S. Dill, *Roman Society in the Last Century of the Empire** (1910), and M. Rostovtzeff, *Social and Economic History of the Roman Empire* (1926), discuss the reforms of Diocletian. Rostovtzeff is more thorough and is useful as a reference, but Dill is more readable. P. Brown, *The World of Late Antiquity** (1971), is a brilliant recent study. See also J. Vogt, *The Decline of Rome* (1967).

The Spread of Christianity

One of the great problems in European history is that of the conversion of the Emperor Constantine. R. MacMullen, *Constantine* (1969), in his good short biography of the emperor is inclined to see a semimagical, semireligious impulse. The Swiss historian J. Burckhardt, in his influential book *The Age of Constantine the Great,** trans. by M. Hadas (1952), sees Constantine's conversion as completely an act of political expediency. A. H. M. Jones, *Constantine and the Conversion of Europe* (1948), interprets the conversion as religious in motivation. Both scholars base their arguments on the writings of the court bishop Eusebius and the scholar Lactantius, significant parts of which are in K. Setton and H. R. Winkler, eds., *Great Problems in European Civilization* (1954). This book has excellent source material on the spread of Christianity. J. Lebreton and J. Zeiller, *The Emergence of the Church in the Roman Empire* (1962), discuss the spread of Christianity. The short monograph of E. R. Goodenough, *The Church in the Roman Empire* (1931), presents Christianity as a summation of various religious ideas of the Roman environment. Goodenough is a useful introduction to the study of Christianity in this period. On the persecutions, see W. H. C. Frend, *Martyrdom and Persecution in the Early Church** (1967).

The Goths and the Huns

H. Mattingly, *Tacitus on Britain and Germany** (1952), is a rich mine of information about the political, social, and economic conditions of the Germanic peoples at the time when they first came in contact with the Roman Empire. There is a good picture of the Germanic migrations and warlike spirit in Jordanes, *Origins and Deeds of the Goths,* trans. by C. C. Mierow (1908). J. B. Bury's *The Invasions of Europe by the Barbarians** (1928) has valuable material on the barbarian impact on Europe, while L. Halphen, *Les Barbares* (1930), traces the beginnings and spread of the Germanic peoples down to the eleventh century. Halphen has good bibliographic material. Another good book in French is E. Demougeot, *La formation de l'Europe et les invasions barbares* (1969). The old study of P. Villari, *The Barbarian Invasions of Italy,* 2 vols. (1902), is still valuable. See also E. A. Thompson, *The Visigoths in Spain* (1969).

The Fall of the Empire in the West

E. Gibbon's monumental work, *The History of the Decline and Fall of the Roman Empire,* ed. by J. B. Bury (1896–1900), presents an answer to this problem in a book that has stood as a classic in English literature since 1776. A leading French medievalist, F. Lot, in *The End of the Ancient World** (1931), attributes the decline largely to economic causes, while H. L. B. Moss, *Birth of the Middle Ages** (1935), interprets the problem from a more political and military point of view. C. Dawson, *The Making of Europe** (1934), shows the importance of religious developments. See also W. C. Bark, *Origins of the Medieval World** (1960).

Art and Literature

From its beginnings Christianity has inspired art in the pictorial form. C. R. Morey, *Early Christian Art** (1942), is an interesting introduction. W. Lowrie, *Art in the Early Church* (1947), is an excellent study of early Christian art, with fine reproductions and a critical bibliography. The broad survey of W. R. Lethaby, *Medieval Art from the Peace of the Church to the Eve of the Renaissance, 313–1350,* rev. by D. Talbot-Rice (1947), covers all art forms and has considerable material on the early Church.

Perhaps the greatest thinker the Western Church produced in the Middle Ages was St. Augustine of Hippo. *The Confessions of St. Augustine** (many editions) is one of the most remarkable accounts of a spiritual pilgrimage ever written. St. Augustine's *City of God** (many editions), which deals with such basic theological questions as the nature of God, the will, sin, and salvation, played a large part in the evolution of Roman Catholic and Protestant thinking. P. Brown, *Augustine of Hippo** (1967), is the best work in English. The writings of most of the early Church Fathers have been collected and translated in *The Fathers of the Church* series, ed. by R. J. Deferrari (1947 ff.).

H. Marrou, *History of Education in Antiquity** (1948), which carries the reader down to 700 A.D., has good material on Christian literature. A. Alföldi, *A Conflict of Ideas in the Later Roman Empire* (1932), is a short and brilliant book.

6

Ancient India and China

The civilizations we have discussed so far were all in direct and constant contact with one another. The peoples of the ancient Middle East had exchanged techniques and ideas from the second millennium B.C.; Greece had drawn heavily on these older civilizations; Rome had received the Greek heritage and had also had close relations with all the cultures of western Eurasia, from the Celts in the West to the Persians in the East. The Romans were familiar with the religions, the social and political organization, the agricultural and industrial techniques, the science, the literature, and the art of the vast region that stretched from Spain and Gaul to Egypt and Mesopotamia. They were more interested in some aspects of older civilizations than in others; for example, they accepted Oriental religions but tended to

Scene of the life of the Buddha, from a section of the North Gate to the Great Stupa at Sanchi (first century B.C.). Buddha is represented by the tree in the center.

neglect Hellenistic science. Neglect was not the same thing as total ignorance, however; the works of Archimedes were available even if few inhabitants of the Roman world chose to study them, and any educated Roman knew who Archimedes was.

The two great civilizations that arose in East Asia had only intermittent contacts with each other and even less with the Middle East and the Mediterranean. India and China were cut off from each other by jungles and mountains and from the rest of the Eurasian continent by vast deserts and thousands of miles of semiarid steppes. Some trade was carried on in these forbidding regions, even in the third millennium B.C. But on the whole, for many centuries China and India had little influence on each other and cast only vague shadows on the life of Mesopotamia, Egypt, and the Mediterranean. After 500 B.C. merchants, missionaries, and conquering armies brought the peoples of Eurasia into closer association. Trade between China and India grew, and one of the great Indian religions, Buddhism, penetrated the region north of the Himalayas. Greek soldiers of fortune, following Alexander's footsteps, built states in central Asia from which Greek ideas and forms of art were disseminated to both China and India. At the height of the Empire the Romans traded directly by sea with India and Ceylon, and indirectly with China through middlemen who carried silk across Asia to the Black Sea and Syria. The many Roman coins found in India testify to the extent of that trade.

These contacts, however, were tenuous and easily disrupted by political or economic disasters. Even in the second century A.D., the time of Rome's closest contact with East Asia, the Romans knew little of the civilizations of China and India and were scarcely influenced by them. Neither Buddhism nor Confucianism had any impact on the Mediterranean world. The Romans could incorporate the temple-states of Syria and the semidivine monarchies of Asia Minor into their society, but they never understood the caste system of India or the imperial institutions of China. Even in the field of technology, where innovations spread most rapidly because they have no ideological flavor, the Romans ignored such significant Asian innovations as the stirrup and the horse collar. And yet East Asia probably had more influence on the West than the West had on East Asia.

Relations between India and China were closer than those between East Asia and the West, but there was no wholesale borrowing between the two countries. Each region developed its own way of life, very different from the other and equally different from the world the Romans knew.

This relative isolation of India and China from the West makes it hard to describe their civilizations in terms understandable to a western reader. There is bound to be some distortion when English words are used to describe Asian ideas and institutions, for there are no exact parallels in western experience to the intellectual and social patterns that developed in India and China. But it is worth making an effort to understand the early civilizations of East Asia. From time to time events in this region exerted a powerful influence on the peoples of the West. Some of the basic differences between East and West that still cause difficulties in relations between the two areas were already evident in the early history of India and China. Finally, it is well to remind ourselves of the fact that there are other solutions to the perennial problems of mankind than those devised by the peoples of the West. History has shown that the most enduring and successful of these alternative solutions have been formulated by the Indians and the Chinese.

INDIA

As we have seen, India, like the ancient Middle East, had a very early river-valley civilization, centered in the basin of the Indus. This Indus Valley civilization, however, was first weakened and then destroyed by a series of disasters after 2500 B.C. Decline may have begun with climatic changes that led to repeated floods, but the final collapse was probably caused by invasions of northern peoples. Little is known about conditions in India between 2500 and 1500 B.C. When the darkness lifts there has been a great change. The early inhabitants of India— the Dravidians—have been enslaved or driven south by the conquerors from the north, a group who speak an Indo-European language and who seem to be related to the Greeks and even more closely to the Aryans of Persia. These Indo-Aryans were far less advanced than the builders of Mohenjo-Daro. They had no cities; they were herdsmen and farmers living in scattered villages. But they were excellent fighters, and they gradually occupied first the Indus Valley, then the Ganges Valley, and finally the central part of the Indian peninsula. As the dominant race, they established the religious concepts and the social institutions that have persisted in India to the present day.

Statuette of a man, perhaps a priest, wearing an ornamental robe, from Mohenjo-Daro, *ca.* 2500 B.C.

Early Indo-Aryan Society

The language of the Indo-Aryan invaders, Sanskrit, resembled Greek in many ways, and there is other evidence that the two peoples were related. They worshiped similar gods; they accorded special honor to the warrior class; and they were organized in many small states instead of one unified kingdom. A Heroic Age in northern India, commemorated in their epics, seems to have been very similar to the Greek heroic age described by Homer. But there were also significant differences between the Greeks and the Indo-Aryans. In the first place, the Indo-Aryans created a literature that gave enduring form to their ideals far earlier than the Greeks. Their oldest works, the Vedas, go back at least to 1400 B.C. The Vedas are religious rituals or hymns to the gods, not accounts of worldly adventures such as the *Iliad* or the *Odyssey*. It was many centuries before the Vedas were written down, but oral transmission through carefully trained priests seems to have preserved much of the original text. This difference in the character of their early literature illustrates another divergence between the two peoples: religion and an organized priesthood were far more important among the Indo-Aryans than among the Greeks. Finally, the Indo-Aryans developed race and class distinctions that were far sharper than those of the Greeks.

These peculiarities of early Indian society tended to reinforce one another. The fact that the language had been fixed for religious purposes at such an early date meant that there was a growing discrepancy between the sacred and the vulgar tongue. In the end the only people who could still understand and interpret the early religious literature were the priests, who thereby assumed added authority. Tendencies toward a caste system were reinforced by the differences between the conquering Aryans and the subjugated Dravidians. Because the Dravidians were shorter and darker than the Aryans, they were readily distinguishable from the ruling group. And because they were obliged to work at the dirtiest jobs, the conquerors had good reason to remain aloof from them. Though differences between conqueror and conquered eventually disappeared in other societies—as in the Roman Empire, for example—in India they were given a religious sanction and so became permanent. And if one caste barrier could be justified by religion, then other barriers could be instituted among the members of the ruling group. Eventually each principal occupation formed a caste, and intermarriage among these castes was forbidden.

Ultimately a society emerged that was dominated by religion, unlike the secular societies of ancient Greece and Rome. Early Indian religion, like that of Greece, was based on carefully formulated rituals. When the Greeks became dissatisfied with the intellectual content of their religion, they developed philosophies

(३) सूर्याविवाहः ।

ऋग्वेदः, म. १०, सू ८५

४७ सावित्री सूर्या ऋषिका । १–५ सोमः, ६–१६, १७ देवाः, १८ सोमार्काँ, १९ चन्द्रमाः २०–२८ नृणां विवाहमन्त्रा आशीःप्रायः, २९–३० वधूवासःसंस्पर्शनिन्दा, ३१ दम्पत्योर्यक्ष्मनाशनं, ३२–४७ सूर्या सावित्री । अनुष्टुप्; १४, १९–२१, २३–२४, २६, ३६–३७, ४४ त्रिष्टुप्; १८, २७, ४३ जगती; ३४ उरोबृहती ।

सत्येनोत्तभिता भूमिः   सूर्येणोत्तभिता द्यौः ।
ऋतेनादित्यास्तिष्ठन्ति   दिवि सोमो अधि श्रितः   ॥ १ ॥

Manuscript of the Rig-Veda (hymns to gods).

Vedic Hymns

ORIGINS OF CASTE

When they [the gods] divided the Man,
  into how many parts did they divide him?
What were his mouth, what were his arms,
  what were his thighs and feet called?

The brahman [priest] was his mouth,
  of his arms were made the warrior.
His thighs became the vaisya [merchants and cultivators],
  of his feet the sudra [servants] was born.

The moon arose from his mind,
  from his eye was born the sun,
from his mouth Indra and Agni [the war god and the fire god],
  from his breath the wind was born. . . .

HYMN OF CREATION

Then even nothingness was not, nor existence,
There was no air then, nor the heavens beyond it.
What covered it? Where was it? In whose keeping?
Was there then cosmic water, in depths unfathomed?

Then there was neither death nor immortality,
nor was there then the torch of night and day.
The One breathed windlessly and self-sustaining.
There was that One then, and there was no other. . . .

But, after all, who knows and who can say
whence it all came, and how creation happened?
The gods themselves are later than creation,
so who knows truly whence it has arisen?

Quoted in A. L. Basham, *The Wonder That Was India* (London: Sidgwick and Jackson, 1954; New York: Macmillan, 1954), pp. 241, 247–48.

that were completely divorced from their old faith. In India there was also a shift from empty ritual to philosophical speculation, but Indian philosophy always remained closely associated with religious faiths. Philosophy and religion combined to produce pantheism, a belief that all living things were part of a world-soul (Brahma) from which they emanated and to which they returned. A natural result of this doctrine was belief in the transmigration of souls. Each individual soul, before its final absorption in the world-soul, might inhabit many bodies in many lifetimes. But these individual existences and the world of the senses were mere illusion; the one reality was the world-soul. Thus death was not to be feared and worldly misfortune could be endured in the hope that the next reincarnation would be happier.

These ideas were expressed in the Upanishads, a series of religious treatises written in the eighth and seventh centuries B.C. They also appear in the epic of the Mahabarata, which was probably first written down in the fifth century B.C. and then reedited and expanded until it reached its final form about 200 A.D. The Mahabarata is a story of wars leading to the creation of a vast empire under the hero Krishna, but the narrative is frequently interrupted by discussions of right conduct and proper belief. The best-known section of the epic is a religious poem called the Bhagavadgita, which closes with a strong affirmation of belief in the immortality of the soul through transmigration. "Never was there a time when I was not, nor thou . . . and never will there be a time when we shall cease to be. . . . Just as a person casts off worn-out garments and puts on new, so does the soul cast off worn-out bodies and put on others. . . ." The other great Indian epic, the Ramayana, was written about 200 A.D. It also discusses the relation between religious belief and right conduct, but its principal theme is the devotion of a faithful wife to the hero Rama, who is trying to regain his rightful position as a ruler.

During the Heroic Age (*ca.* 1000–*ca.* 500 B.C.), a split developed between the religious concepts of the leading thinkers and those of the people. The philosophers still saw universal truths behind the bewildering variety of gods and rituals, but the mass of the population became content with external observances. The number of gods increased; ceremonies and offerings were substituted for the inner enlightenment that the great religious leaders had sought; and caste lines became increasingly rigid. The Brahmans, as the priests were called, profited from the heightened formalism of religion; since they alone knew what was pleasing to the gods, they became the dominant caste. Next to them in the caste scale were the kings and warriors, while farmers and artisans filled lower ranks. Almost at the bottom were the laborers, who performed humble tasks and whose very shadow would defile a Brahman. Most miserable of all were the outcastes—men who had no caste at all and who could not participate in the religious or social activities of their villages. These unfortunates were to become the untouchables of modern India. Every man was supposed to stay in his caste and to perform the duties appropriate to it, since his fate had been determined by the will of the gods. Social

The Buddha often was not pictured in human form in early representations; his presence here is indicated by the tree in the upper left corner. Detail from pillar at Sanchi, first century B.C.

mobility was not completely blocked, especially for men who left their native villages and went to the towns, but the great majority of the people could not change their occupations. This waste of human resources slowed down economic development and explains, to some extent, India's economic backwardness.

The Buddha

Before the sixth century B.C. there were from time to time kings who united most of northern India under a single ruler. But none of their ephemeral empires had much influence on the development of Indian society. The real genius of India lay not in politics but in religion. And about 580 B.C. India produced one of the great religious leaders of all time, Sakyamuni the Buddha. The Buddha, son of a petty Indian king, at first led the normal life of a wealthy aristocrat. He became convinced of the futility of worldly pleasure, but he was repelled by the formalism and superstition that had crept into the official religion. Renouncing the world, he spent many years seeking enlightenment through fasting and self-discipline. Finally he saw the true path. All man's troubles spring from his attachment to the things of this earth. So long as a man craves pleasure, or even merely existence, he is condemned to be reborn again and again, in higher or lower form, depending on his behavior in his last reincarnation. The only escape from this dreary repetition of sorrow and pain is to renounce all worldly desires. Then the individual soul will be freed from the Wheel of Things and can achieve nirvana. The term *nirvana* is hard to define; it means a complete cessation of worldly cares, an end to the cycle of birth and rebirth, and complete absorption into the Universal Soul that is God.

Though the final goal of Buddhism was the loss of individual consciousness, it was an intensely individualistic religion for those who wanted to follow its teachings in this world. No ritual or priesthood could save the individual who was seeking enlightenment; salvation depended on his own thoughts and actions. He must follow the Eightfold Path of right views, thought, and action; he must

The Basic Doctrines of Buddhism

The following is part of a sermon of the Buddha.

There are two ends not to be served. . . . The pursuit of desires and of the pleasure which springs from desires . . . leading to rebirth, ignoble and unprofitable; and the pursuit of pain and hardship, which is grievous, ignoble and unprofitable. The Middle Way . . . avoids both these ends; it is enlightened, it brings clear vision, it makes for wisdom, and leads to peace, insight, full wisdom and Nirvana. . . .

This is the Noble Truth of Sorrow. Birth is sorrow, age is sorrow, disease is sorrow, death is sorrow, contact with the unpleasant is sorrow, separation from the pleasant is sorrow, every wish unfulfilled is sorrow.

This is the Noble Truth of the Arising of Sorrow. [It arises from] thirst, which leads to rebirth, which brings delight and passion, and seeks pleasure now here—now there—the thirst for sensual pleasure, the thirst for continued life, the thirst for power.

This is the Noble Truth of the Stopping of Sorrow. It is the complete stopping of that thirst, being emancipated from it, being released from it, giving no place to it.

This is the Noble Truth of the [Middle] Way that Leads to the Stopping of Sorrow. It is the Noble Eightfold Path—Right Views, Right Resolve, Right Speech, Right Conduct, Right Livelihood, Right Effort, Right Recollection and Right Meditation.

Quoted in A. L. Basham, *The Wonder That Was India* (London: Sidgwick and Jackson, 1954; New York: Macmillan, 1968), p. 271.

observe a strict moral code; above all else, he must never relax in his personal quest for salvation.

Buddhism was a reformation rather than a renunciation of the principles of the old Indian religion. The Buddha disdained the elaborate rites and rituals of the Brahmans and the worship of a multiplicity of gods. He also opposed the rigidities of the caste system; according to legend, he had eaten with a poor laborer just before he died. But while the Buddha wanted to purify Indian religion he accepted its basic doctrines of the one world-soul, the illusory nature of the world of the senses, and transmigration of souls. Unlike most of the Brahmans, however, he held these beliefs with such intensity that he could convince many of his hearers that renunciation of the world was happiness and that beyond illusion was true wisdom. He attracted a devoted group of disciples who lived together in monastic dwellings and helped in turn to convert others. During his lifetime, the Buddha's ideas spread rapidly through the north of India, where he had begun his teaching, and some Buddhists could be found in every part of the peninsula.

In the years that followed, Buddhist monasteries developed into notable centers of learning and stimulated the growth of the new religion. For a while it seemed that the whole subcontinent might become Buddhist. The future of Buddhism seemed especially bright under the Mauryan dynasty, which lasted from 322 to about 184 B.C. The first king of this dynasty, Chandragupta Maurya (322–298 B.C.), came closer to uniting India than had any earlier ruler; only the extreme south escaped his domination. The third Mauryan king, Asoka (ca. 273–ca. 232 B.C.), became a Buddhist, and with his support Bud-

dhism developed into the first great missionary religion. The only other faiths that have spread as widely are Christianity and Islam. In Asoka's day Buddhism was accepted in most parts of India and throughout Ceylon. Later it spread to the countries of Southeast Asia and across the mountains into China. And with Buddhism went Indian art, literature, and philosophy. The influence that India still exercises in eastern Asia began with this cultural expansion under Asoka.

The Mauryan Empire

The Mauryan Empire was a strong state; it had a reasonably advanced civil service and an adequate financial system. Asoka, a more benevolent ruler than most of his predecessors, tried to soften the harsh penalties of earlier laws and to improve the lot of the poor through extensive charities. Though a Buddhist

THE SPREAD OF BUDDHISM Sixth century B.C. to seventeenth century A.D.

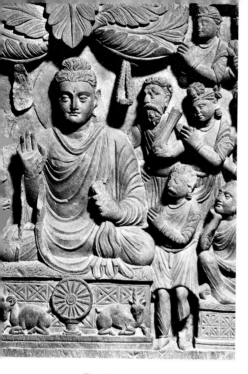

The Buddha, second century A.D.

kings of his house devised frightful tortures for rebels and traitors. Fear was a poor means of creating loyalty to the dynasty, as future events demonstrated.

Asoka sought to show his devotion to Buddhism by supporting a magnificent program of religious building. During his reign and the reigns of his immediate successors, Indian art developed some of its most typical forms. Stupas, or burial mounds with elaborately carved stone gateways, were erected over the relics of Buddhist leaders. At Ajanta a series of immense cave temples was built, with gigantic columns and carvings that imitated woodwork. In these cave temples of Ajanta some of the earliest Indian painting is found, though the finest examples there were created a few centuries later. But Indian painting had already acquired some of its chief characteristics—an emphasis on rhythmic, curving lines and the absence of any light-shadow pattern.

himself, he was tolerant of other faiths and never tried to convert his people by force.

Yet there were two serious weaknesses in the empire, even at the height of its power. The first was economic. Both internal trade and external trade with the Hellenistic states of Egypt and Syria were taxed heavily. But the economy was still based on agricultural villages rather than on trade centers. The government owned most of the land and took large shares of the peasants' income. The resulting hardships meant that there was no real loyalty to strong centralized rule.

The second weakness was that the Mauryan government was a depotism, enlightened at times but always arbitrary. The *Arthasastra*, a manual of statecraft written under the Mauryans, reads very much like an Indian version of Machiavelli:

> With increasing strength, make war; when you have a clear advantage over a neighbor, march against him; do not disturb the customs of a newly conquered people.

But the most revealing statement is this: "Government is the science of punishment." Even the kindly Asoka invoked the death penalty freely, and the other

The Great Stupa at Sanchi, first century B.C.

Capital on a column erected by Asoka (242–232 B.C.) to commemorate the Buddha's preaching of the First Sermon in Sarnath.

begun in the Mauryan period enabled it to survive elsewhere in Asia. But the decline of Buddhism in India meant that a gap was opening between northern Buddhists, such as those in the sub-Himalayan kingdoms, and southern Buddhists, such as those of Ceylon. In the second century A.D. the religion split into two branches, Hinayana Buddhism in the south and Mahayana Buddhism in the north. The Hinayana version is still the principal religion of Ceylon, Burma, Thailand, Cambodia, and Laos, and in these areas it has remained fairly close to the ideals of its founder. The northern version dominates Tibet and has many followers in China and Japan. This form of Buddhism has become more like other religions; in it Buddha is a savior who renounced nirvana in order to redeem mankind. A cult of saints (bodhisattvas) grew up around him, and emphasis on ritual and ceremony increased.

With the establishment of the Mauryan Empire, a period of close contacts between India and its western and northern neighbors began. The most significant relations were by land, for the

Soon after Asoka's death the Mauryan Empire disintegrated, and for several centuries no ruler held more than a fraction of the territories Asoka had controlled. It is curious that India should have split into small states just at the time when Rome was uniting the Mediterranean world and the Han emperors were building an empire in China. But separatist tendencies were always strong in India, where people felt that cultural unity was far more important than political unity. Governors of outlying provinces threw off the control of Asoka's weaker successors and set themselves up as independent rulers. It is possible that the Buddhist doctrine of nonviolence weakened the military strength that had created the Mauryan Empire. Asoka, after his early conquests, gave up war as an instrument of policy, and his successors, though not going so far, did not show much capacity for organizing military operations.

The collapse of the Mauryan state had serious consequences for Buddhism. Deprived of the support of kings like Asoka, the religion began to decline in India, although the missionary work

THE MAURYAN EMPIRE *ca.* 250 B.C.

322 B.C.   ca. 225   184   ca. 1 A.D.   ca. 225   ca. 320   ca. 500 A.D.

| Mauryan Empire | | Kushan Dynasty—Northwestern India | Period of Political Disorder | Gupta Dynasty |

Andhra Dynasty—Central India

Seleucid Empire and certain of its successor states bordered on northern India. From these countries Indian artists learned something about Greek sculpture and thus were able to incorporate elements of Greek style into their work. It was also by the land route through western Asia that Indian philosophy and science reached the Greeks. The sea route was important for the exchange of goods between India and the West but was far less effective than the land route for the exchange of ideas. The chief Indian ports for western commerce were in the extreme south, a region that lay outside the main centers of Indian culture, and seaborne commerce declined rapidly after 200 A.D., when the Roman Empire was weakened by civil war.

The Kushan and Andhra Dynasties

The Kushan state, established in the first century A.D., was even more effective than the Mauryan Empire in establishing relations with China and with the West. The Kushans, a nomadic people of central Asia, gradually took over the northwestern corner of India. Since they also retained their old holdings in central Asia, their empire provided a channel through which Indian ideas and Indian goods could flow northeast toward China and northwest toward Rome. The most famous example of Kushan influence occurred when their king Kanishka was converted to Buddhism soon after 120 A.D. Kanishka, concerned about disagreements among Buddhist teachers, called a council to clarify and reconcile their statements of belief. This council defined the doctrines that became those of the northern, or Mahayanan, school of Buddhism.

The Andhra dynasty of central India (*ca.* 225 B.C.–*ca.* 225 A.D.) began earlier than the Kushan but reached the peak of its power at about the same time. Control of the Ganges Valley gave the Andhras a dominant position in eastern India, where the people were more inclined to preserve ancient traditions than those of the northwest. Though tolerant, the Andhras favored the Brahmans, and Buddhism lost ground under their rule.

The Gupta Period

Both the Andhra state and the Kushan Empire disintegrated during the first years of the third century. A period of disorder followed, until northern India was finally reunited under the Gupta dynasty, which was founded in 320. The Guptas never held as much of India as the Mauryans had, but the region they controlled prospered under their rule.

During the Gupta period (*ca.* 320–*ca.* 500) Buddhism almost vanished from India. The collapse of the Kushans weakened the religion in the northwest, the last region in which it had had any real strength. The chief centers of Buddhism were now outside India, and the Indians began to feel that a religion taught by outer barbarians was un-Indian and unacceptable. The Guptas themselves were tolerant, but they clearly preferred the old Indian religion, which had now settled into the form known as Hinduism. Buddhism withered away and Hinduism, with the support of the Gupta kings, became the religion of the vast majority of the inhabitants of India.

The central beliefs of Hinduism—the unity of all life and the need to recognize and feel this unity as the highest good —had come down through the centuries unchanged. Indian philosophers and religious leaders still taught the necessity for meditation, renunciation, and union with the world-soul. But the common people of India could not understand these remote ideals; they needed visible images to worship and fixed rules to obey. They needed gods who watched over human activities and who could be placated by sacrifices. Their chief gods constituted a trinity—Brahma the creator, Vishnu the preserver, and Shiva the destroyer. But the Indians worshiped innumerable other divinities, each with his own special temples and forms of worship. As the gods multiplied, the caste structure also became more complicated: the large, original castes broke up into many subcastes. Growing rigidity in caste and social structure led to a deterioration in the position of women. Most well-to-do men took many wives, a practice that had been rare in earlier times. It was during the Gupta period that suttee, the custom of widows burning themselves on their husband's funeral pyres, became common, though it was not obligatory.

Indian mathematics and astronomy probably reached their height under the Guptas. The Indians had long been interested in these subjects and surpassed even the Greeks of the Hellenistic period in some branches of mathematics. For example, the Greeks tried to solve their problems by the visible demonstrations of geometry, but the Indians, using the abstract principles of algebra, could cope with much more difficult concepts. Greek algebra was rudimentary, but the Indians invented the concept of negative quantities, solved quadratic equations, and found the square root of 2. They knew that the earth was round and that it rotated, and they had some understanding of gravitation. Their most famous invention, however, was the system of so-called Arabic numerals, which first appeared in India in the third century B.C. By the time of the Guptas, Indian mathematicians were using a form of decimal system. The final and most important innovation, the zero, may or may not have resulted from the work of Indian mathematicians. But it is significant that the zero first appears in the works of scholars familiar with Indian numerals. It is also significant that Christian Europe did not know of Indian-Arabic numerals until the twelfth century and did not use them extensively until the sixteenth. The two civilizations were too far apart and contacts between them too infrequent for even such obviously useful ideas to travel quickly from one region to the other.

Gupta literature influenced the West somewhat more rapidly than Gupta science. The Gupta age was an age of short stories, fables, and fairy tales, some of which reached the Middle East, and then Europe, in a relatively short time. The Indians, endowed with remarkably fertile imaginations, invented situations and plots that have been borrowed by writers in all other languages. The story of Sinbad the Sailor, for example, is drawn from Indian sources. The best-known collection of Hindu tales—the Panchatantra—has had a direct and continuing effect on other literatures. For example, the basic pattern of many fables—stories of animals acting like human beings—comes from this source. Famous poets and playwrights such as Kalidasa (ca. 395–450) remained unknown outside India; their poems and plays were too thoroughly Hindu to be understood elsewhere.

During the Gupta period classical Indian art reached its highest level. Before the Gupta period Greek influence on Indian art had been noticeable, but after 300 that influence declined and Gupta art

THE GUPTA EMPIRE   *ca.* 400 A.D.

reverted to the basic Indian patterns that had taken form in the Mauryan period. Indian art was essentially religious in purpose and symbolic in form. Restrained and dignified, it tried to express the eternal truths of the Indian religions. The finest paintings at Ajanta are from this period, as are some of the last great Indian sculptures representing scenes from the life of the Buddha.

The Gupta state, which never controlled more than half of India, was constantly threatened by enemies along the frontiers. Its administrative system was simpler and less bureaucratic than that of either of the great contemporary empires—the Roman and the Chinese. The relative weakness of centralized control may have made life easier for the people, but it made the kingdom vulnerable to internal disorder and attack from aggressive enemies. The Gupta state probably had less income than the Mauryan empire because the peasants now owned their own land and gave less to the state. With the death of Chandragupta II in about 412, the Gupta state began to decline. The Huns, whose depredations had weakened Han China and imperial Rome, also contributed to the fall of the Guptas. The Huns, or a people associated with the Huns, invaded the Punjab late in the fifth century and held northwest India for a time. But the invaders were driven out after a few decades, and an outbreak of rivalry among local princes was probably the chief cause of the disintegration of the state. By the sixth century the Gupta kingdom had collapsed, and it was generations before any large state was to emerge again.

For the next six centuries India suffered an endless succession of internal wars and foreign invasions. Unlike the Chinese, who always managed to build a new empire on the ruins of the old, the Indians seemed unable or unwilling to replace their small, warring states with larger political units. They were more interested in religion than in politics, and the overwhelming influence of the Brahman priests made it difficult for secular rulers to exercise effective political control. When a new Indian Empire finally appeared it was ruled by Moslems, not by Hindus.

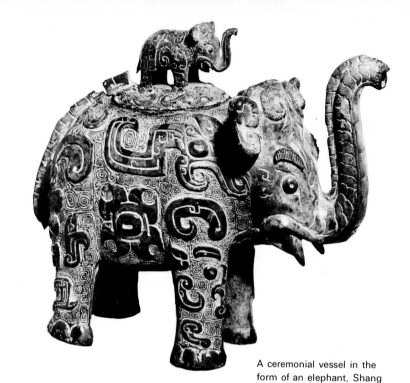

A ceremonial vessel in the form of an elephant, Shang dynasty (*ca.* 1500–1100 B.C.).

CHINA

If Indian civilization was predominantly religious, Chinese civilization was predominantly secular. In the earliest periods of Chinese history this secularism is less noticeable than it is later, but it still can be observed. The early Chinese attached great importance to religious rituals and ceremonies. They worshiped a god of Heaven, an Earth-god, and lesser divinities, and they made sacrifices and consulted oracles; but they never brooded over religious problems as did the Indians, nor did they develop a powerful priesthood. True, they long believed that the ruler held his power through the Mandate of Heaven. But when he lost his power it was usually because of a rebellion led by some political subordinate rather than because of a pronouncement by a group of religious leaders. For the Chinese the most urgent problems were good crops and good government, not salvation and immortality.

Even though some of the oldest human fossils have been found near Peking in North China, very little is known about the first stages of Chinese civilization. Agricultural settlements certainly existed in the Yellow River region at an early date; it is difficult, however, to determine when the Chinese began to

Confucius on Government

Duke Ting [d. 495 B.C.] asked if there were any one phrase that sufficed to save a country. Master K'ung [Confucius] replied, saying, No phrase could ever be like that. But here is one that comes near it. There is a saying among men: "It is hard to be a prince and not easy to be a minister." A ruler who really understood that it was "hard to be a prince" would have come fairly near to saving his country by a single phrase.

Duke Ting said, Is there any one phrase that could ruin a country? Master K'ung said, No phrase could ever be like that. But here is one that comes near to it. There is a saying among men: "What pleasure is there in being a prince, unless one can say whatever one chooses, and no one dares to disagree?"

From *The Analects of Confucius*, trans. by Arthur Waley (London: Allen and Unwin, 1938), p. 175.

develop more elaborate forms of political organization and economic specialization. It seems likely that the first cities arose somewhat later in China than in Egypt or Mesopotamia—considerably after, rather than before, 3000 B.C.

At any rate, the Shang dynasty (*ca.* 1500–*ca.* 1100 B.C.) presents firmer ground. Early Chinese historians preserved stories about the remarkable accomplishments of the Shang which were once thought legendary but which we now know had a solid basis in fact. It was under the Shang that the Chinese began to use bronze, a development that may have contributed to the power and splendor of the dynasty. The Chinese rapidly acquired great skill in casting this metal, and some of the sacrificial vessels of this period show remarkably fine workmanship. Another sign of advancing civilization was the appearance of the first specimens of Chinese writing—pictographs, which, like early Egyptian hieroglyphs, represented words, syllables, or ideas rather than sounds. Finally, though most of the people were still peasant farmers, industry and commerce had developed to a point where they could support many artisans and traders, who lived in the walled cities of the Shang rulers.

Soon after 1100 B.C. the Shang dynasty was succeeded by the Chou. The Chou domain stretched from the area around Peking to parts of the lower Yangtze Valley, but the heart of the state was the lower valley of the Yellow River. The Chou did not rule a unified kingdom; they were merely the heads of a confederation of peoples who spoke the same language and lived more or less the same way. The Chou kings did not have the military strength to dominate the local rulers. The relationship between the Chou king and local lords was somewhat like the feudal relationship that later developed in western Europe; each lord was to aid the king in time of war, but he was almost independent in his own region. Eventually the local rulers became less and less submissive to central control; principalities increased in size and power and engaged in incessant war, so that during the third century B.C. the Chinese lands were divided among a group of warring, regional states.

Confucius

It was during the later years of the Chou dynasty that China's great philosopher, Confucius (K'ung Fu-tzu, 551–479 B.C.), was born. A scholar, and for a while an official of one of the local rulers, he eventually retired from public life to teach sons of aristocrats and devote himself to the development of an ethical system. The Chinese, as we have seen, had never been particularly concerned about religion and had developed no systematized theology. Nor had they been especially interested in political theory; they simply accepted the fact that there always had been, and always would be, rulers and subjects. But they were greatly concerned with human conduct, with the problems of how a man should adjust to the world in which he lived and to the society of which he was a member. Such problems became especially acute during the disorders of the late Chou period. Confucius taught respect for authority, for tradition, and for custom. He was rather skeptical about religion—"If you do not know about the living," he asked, "how can you know about the dead?" But he believed that at all levels of society there was a guiding force that should be honored and

Ancient symbol "Yi" for "Changes." One of the five Confucian classics is the "Book of Changes."

obeyed: the father guided the family, the ruler the state, and Heaven the universe. By accepting such guidance, man could achieve both harmony with himself and harmony with his environment.

This doctrine, with its emphasis on self-control, conformity, and obedience, created a strongly conservative force in Chinese society. It strengthened existing tendencies toward ancestor worship, the veneration of ancient customs, and the acceptance of authority. This outcome was not wholly contrary to Confucius' own desires; and yet we should remember that Confucius saw himself as a reformer trying to bring stability to a turbulent society and that his teachings were opposed by many rulers of his own time. His ethical principles may have been conservative, but he insisted that they applied to nobles and kings as well as to commoners, and one of his successors, Mencius (*ca.* 372–288 B.C.), logically concluded from this that a bad ruler could be deposed by the people.

Moreover, the conservatism that flowed from Confucius' teaching was neither arrogant nor obscurantist. It was tempered by punctilious respect for good manners, which Confucius felt were as important as good institutions. This emphasis on courteous behavior proved a precious lubricant as the Chinese population grew. It enabled millions of people with limited resources to live close together without developing dangerous social tensions. And with good manners went an admirable ethical code. The "superior man repays evil with uprightness and kindness with kindness." He treats others as he himself would be treated.* Confucius also stressed the value of education in developing men worthy to rule—a lesson the Chinese upper classes never wholly forgot. True, education in China became highly formalistic and traditional, and the ability to quote extensively from ancient texts came to be regarded as the essence of scholarship. Nevertheless, Chinese education did produce men with disciplined minds trained to think clearly. And during most of China's history this educated class held key positions in the government; periods in which the military enjoyed complete domination were exceptional and brief.

Confucius never claimed divine inspiration, and he had little influence on Chinese society during his lifetime. But his ideas survived and gradually, through the efforts of several generations of disciples, became the philosophy—almost the religion—of the ruling classes. Eventually, sacrifices were offered to the spirit of Confucius and he was venerated as the chief religious teacher of China. More than any other man, he gave permanent form to ideas that the Chinese people had been working out for many centuries. The early codification of these ideas gave enduring strength to Chinese society. From the time of Confucius down to this century, despite the impact of foreign ideas and the rule of barbarian conquerors, the Chinese were able to maintain their way of life because they had standards to which they could make both foreign ideas and foreign rulers conform.

* See Charles A. Moore, *Philosophy: East and West* (Princeton: Princeton University Press, 1946), p. 28.

THE CHINESE STATES AT THE TIME OF CONFUCIUS *ca.* 500 B.C.

Chinese calligraphy. Left: a rubbing from one of the ten "Stone Drums," an example of the Great Seal style of writing, which evolved in the latter part of the Chou dynasty (1111–221 B.C.). Right: a rubbing from a stone inscription of the Han dynasty (first century A.D.), inscribed in the Official Style.

Divine seal of Lao-Tzu, used in Taoist magic.

Taoism

The ethical code of Confucius was based on a rational analysis of Chinese society, but there was another side to Chinese thought. This side was represented by Lao-Tzu, a shadowy figure, who probably lived at about the same time as Confucius. Lao-Tzu's doctrine was intuitive and mystical, and even Chinese scholars are not in full agreement on its meaning. At least this much is clear: while Confucius believed that man could achieve harmony with the world by making an effort to think rightly, act rightly, and organize society properly, Lao-Tzu believed that harmony came from renunciation and passivity. Man should allow the forces of nature to work on him as they do on all other material things; feeling is more important than thinking; harmony with the guiding world-principle is more desirable than action. This philosophy was called Taoism—the Way—and there are obvious resemblances between it and the Way of Buddha. Taoism, in fact, made it easier for Buddhist doctrines to spread into China, and Chinese Buddhism was colored by Taoist thought.

Though Taoism never became the dominant philosophy in China, it was highly influential for centuries. Politicians and scholars tended to be Confucianists, while painters and poets were more likely to have Taoist leanings. By seeking harmony with nature, by allowing the inner essence of things to penetrate their minds, Chinese artists and writers achieved remarkable results with remarkable economy of effort. They avoided direct, literal representations of reality; instead, with a few strokes of the brush, or in a short poem, they evoked the mood occasioned by some event or some natural object.

Chinese Art and Literature

The Chou dynasty was a period of rapid development in Chinese art and literature. Bronze works of high quality continued to be made, and some of the earliest and finest jade carvings were created in this era. The peculiarly Chi-

Taoist Teaching

The following is ascribed to Chuang Tzu (*ca.* 320 B.C.).

I first learned to consider myself as an external object, then I no longer knew if I were dead or living. . . . After having seen the One [*tao*] he [the disciple] is able to attain a state where there is neither past nor present, and then a further state where he is neither dead nor living. . . . Were the thunder to bring down the mountains or the hurricane to spill the ocean, he would not care. He is borne up by the air and the clouds; he rides on the sun and moon and frolics beyond the limits of space.

How can we know if the self is what we call the self? Once I dreamed that I was a butterfly . . . and I felt happy. I did not know that I was Chuang Tzu. Suddenly I awoke and was myself, the real Chuang Tzu. Then I no longer knew if I were Chuang Tzu dreaming that he was a butterfly or a butterfly dreaming that he was Chuang Tzu.

From René Grousset, *The Rise and Splendour of the Chinese Empire* (London: Bles, 1952; Berkeley: University of California Press, 1953), pp. 32–35.

nese art of calligraphy also became prominent at this time. The Chinese had developed a written language very early that used a separate symbol for each word or idea. By the time of the Chou dynasty there were about 4,000 such symbols, many of them very intricate. It was difficult enough to write these characters accurately, especially as a soft brush was the most common implement; it was even harder to write them with style and elegance. Anyone who could do so has always been admired by the Chinese; over the centuries they have regarded fine calligraphy as satisfying as a beautiful painting.

It was also during the Chou period that the Five Classics of Chinese literature were compiled from earlier writings. These books include history, philosophy, poetry, and rules for religious ceremonies. Tradition has always given Confucius credit for these compilations, but he almost certainly did not do the actual editorial work. The books are in harmony with his philosophy, however, and two were quoted in his own teachings. For centuries the Five Classics served as the foundation of Chinese education; all students had to study them thoroughly before attempting anything else.

The First Emperor

The struggle among the states that developed in the late Chou period was checked about the middle of the third century B.C., when the rulers of Ch'in, one of these states, undertook the unification of all China. Tough, cruel frontiersmen who measured their victories by the number of enemy heads cut off, they created a strong, disciplined army. About 221 B.C. King Sheng of Ch'in subdued the last of the rival kingdoms and took the title of First Emperor. He was, in fact, the first real emperor in Chinese history. He ruled directly through provincial governors instead of depending on the doubt-

ful cooperation of semi-independent local rulers, and he instituted uniform laws and weights and measures throughout the empire. His authority and income must have been substantial, for he was able to build the Great Wall, stretching 1,400 miles across North China, to protect his country from barbarian invaders. This work included sections of earlier fortifications, but its completion required tremendous human suffering. Whole families were uprooted to work on the wall, and food was scarce in the barren regions through which it was built. Sheng also tried to destroy all copies of the Confucian classics because opponents of his absolutism cited them to support their criticisms. Memories of the harshness of the First Emperor may explain why his heir was quickly overthrown. The general who succeeded the Emperor's heir founded the Han dynasty, which was to rule China from 202 B.C. to 220 A.D.

Bronze wrestlers and a bear tamer, from Chou dynasty, *ca.* fifth century B.C.

The Great Wall of China, completed in 204 B.C.

The Han Period

The Han emperors, who extended the boundaries of their realm to Turkestan in the west and to Canton in the south, strove to understand the ways of foreign peoples and to open up trade with them. A substantial trade in silk with Persia and Rome was developed, though it was carried on almost entirely by middlemen. Far more direct and influential were Chinese contacts with India. Buddhism began to find acceptance in China during the Han period, and with it came a host of intellectual and artistic concepts. The Chinese pagoda, for example, is modeled on Indian Buddhist shrines.

The Han emperors expanded the centralized administrative system that had been instituted by the Ch'in. China was relatively peaceful and prosperous under their rule, and the doctrines of Confucius were nationally honored. All officers of government, including the emperor himself, paid reverence to the philosopher's spirit, and an official Confucian cult was supported by the state. The Han emperors had copies made of all the Confucian texts that could be found, a task that was simplified by the invention of paper making early in the first century A.D. They honored scholars and made scholarship a means of access to high official positions. The Han also encouraged the writing of history, both of the ancient past and of the Han period itself. This emphasis on history tended to reinforce the Confucian emphasis on tradition and continuity.

During the Han dynasty vast water-control projects were undertaken in an effort to expand the economic resources

Pottery tile rubbing depicting hunters and peasants (Han dynasty).

Terra cotta figure of warrior in leather armor (fourth or fifth century A.D.).

of the country. The North China plain is subject to flooding in seasons of heavy rainfall and to disastrous droughts at other times of the year. The local princes of the area had made some effort to control the floods and to build irrigation systems, but none of them had controlled enough territory for their programs to be effective. The Han rulers, however, could plan on a larger scale, and their water-control projects added substantially to the productivity of Chinese agriculture. These projects also served to increase the prestige of the imperial government, since they were more successful than those that had been attempted by local lords.

In the Chinese Empire, as in the Roman Empire, a rather narrow economic base supported an elaborate political structure. The Chinese peasant had to support the governing classes, the scholars, the writers, and the artists. It is not surprising that he became discontented at times. Toward the end of the Han period that discontent manifested itself in a series of peasant revolts. Moreover, localism, which is usually strong in an agricultural society, had been only temporarily suppressed. It revived in the second century A.D. and began to impair the unity of the Han Empire. Finally, palace intrigues among members of the imperial family weakened the central government. In China, as in Rome, the third century was a period of civil war.

The Han dynasty was overthrown in 220 A.D., and for generations no one ruler proved powerful enough to reunite the country.

This period of disintegration was especially dangerous because China, like Rome, had a long, vulnerable northern frontier to defend. Chinese settlement had stopped at a line where diminishing rainfall made agriculture impossible. Beyond that line lay the vast, arid reaches of central Asia. These were the domains of nomad tribes, who were the most dangerous barbarians the civilized world has ever known. In their wide-ranging raids these nomads struck at Europe and India, and they were always an immediate threat to China. In order to protect the border zone where the nomads threatened Chinese outposts, the First Emperor built the Great Wall and the early Han rulers subdued Turkestan. When China was strong, the nomads were content to trade peacefully with the Chinese; but when China was weak, they were quick to renew their assault. Such a period of weakness came at the end of the Han dynasty. The Huns made several attacks on China, but in the end it was a group related to the Tartars who overran North China in the fourth century. For the next three hundred years most of the Chinese were ruled by barbarian dynasties.

These nomad rulers gradually accepted Chinese civilization. In the end they became far more Chinese than their contemporaries, the Germanic kings of western Europe, became Roman. But it was several centuries before they were fully assimilated. Meanwhile, just as a remnant of the Roman Empire survived around Constantinople, so a Chinese state survived to preserve the old traditions in the Yangtze Valley in South China. There were similar parallels in religious developments. In Europe, Christianity spread most rapidly after the fall of the Roman Empire and during the rise of the early Germanic kingdoms. In China, Buddhism spread most rapidly after the collapse of the Han Empire and during the period of confusion and division that followed. But Buddhism was never as strong and pervasive in China as Christianity became in Europe.

THE ATTACKS OF THE HUNS   Fourth century

Though it was favored by many rulers, other religions were tolerated, and Buddhism never became part of the political structure of Chinese states.

This was a crucial period in Chinese history. There were many forces working for Chinese unity—the relative isolation of the people, the fact that they all spoke dialects of a common language, the existence of a form of writing that represented ideas rather than sounds and hence could be understood whatever the dialect of the speaker, and most of all, a tremendous contempt for the outer barbarian. But the strength of these forces had not been fully tested until the collapse of the Han Empire. The three centuries of barbarian rule of the north might have led to a permanent division of China. The fact that China was finally reunited proclaimed the enduring strength of the Chinese tradition. Never again did China go through such a long period of fragmentation.

Suggestions for Further Reading

Note: Asterisk denotes a book available in paperback edition.

India There are a number of valuable works on the early history of India. P. Masson-Dursel, *Ancient India and Indian Civilization* (1934), in the *History of Civilization* series, treats all facets of early Indian history and culture and is a good starting point for study. Another fine survey is that of the great Indian authority R. C. Majumdar, *Ancient India* (1952), which devotes considerable space to religion and culture and has bibliographic material. A. L. Basham, *The Wonder That Was India** (1954), is particularly good on early Indian art and literature. Majumdar, *An Advanced History of India* (1946), is a more scholarly work with special attention to political history. The same author's *The Military System in Ancient India* (1955) traces the evolution of the military system up through the Moslem conquest of Hindustan. M. Wheeler, *Early India and Pakistan* (1959), is a very readable study based largely on archeological evidence. For an essentially political account, H. Raychaudhuri, *Political History of Ancient India* (1952), is interesting but technical, and P. Mookerjee, *Local Government in Ancient India* (1919), stresses that India's elaborate system of local government preserved the independence and integrity of Hindu culture. H. G. Rawlinson, *India and the Western World* (1916), studies the relations between India and the West up through the fall of the Roman Empire.

China Probably the best introduction to the early history of China is H. G. Creel, *The Birth of China** (1937), which deals with the political, social, and cultural life of China in early times. L. C. Goodrich, *A Short History of the Chinese People** (1943), has very good material on the political history of China through 600 A.D., and W. Eberhard, *A History of China* (1955), is an excellent account of Chinese history with concentration on sociological development. Eberhard includes a good critical bibliography. C. P. Fitzgerald, *China: A Short Cultural History** (1938), a standard work on the subject, stresses the vitality of Chinese culture throughout its history. R. Grousset, *The Rise and Splendour of the Chinese Empire** (1952), is impressionistic but stimulating.

For the economic history of China, see the valuable monograph of E. S. Kirby, *Introduction to the Economic History of China* (1954), which has material on the period before 600 A.D. Liu Wu-chi, *A Short History of Confucian Philosophy** (1955), is a good starting point for the study of Chinese philosophy and the Chinese moral system, and H. G. Creel, *Confucius: The Man and the Myth* (1949), is valuable on the influence of Confucius. Both Wu-chi and Creel are great authorities.

For bibliography on Chinese history, L. C. Goodrich, *A Syllabus of the History of Chinese Civilization and Culture* (1941), is invaluable.

7

The Germanic Kingdoms in the West

The great empires of the Eurasian continent had all been destroyed by internal struggles and foreign invasions during the third, fourth, and fifth centuries. They had all suffered a decline in economic and cultural activity. Everywhere men faced the problems of adapting the remains of an old civilization to new conditions, of rebuilding political organization and stimulating economic growth. The people of western

Europe had perhaps the most difficult task of all, for disintegration and barbarization had gone further there than in most other areas. The period during which western Europe slowly rebuilt its civilization is known as the "Middle Ages," and it is to the early centuries of the medieval period that we now turn.

During the fifth century all the Roman territories of the West fell under the control of Germanic peoples. The Vandals ruled North Africa; the Visigoths held the Iberian Peninsula; Italy itself was occupied by the Ostrogoths. Gaul was split among the Visigoths in the southwest, the Burgundians and Ostrogoths in the southeast, and the Franks in the north and center. The Angles and Saxons gradually took over most of Britain, although the Celts preserved fiercely independent kingdoms in Scotland and Wales.

THE NORTHERN AND SOUTHERN KINGDOMS

The Germanic kingdoms that emerged from this welter of migration and conquest had very different fates. The Mediterranean group—the Vandals, Visigoths, Ostrogoths, and Burgundians —absorbed Roman civilization readily and preserved much of the Roman way of life. But though they seemed to be more advanced than the northerners, the Germanic kingdoms of the Mediterranean had no staying power. During the sixth century the Vandals and Ostrogoths were crushed by the Eastern Roman Empire, and the Burgundians were conquered by the Franks. The Visigoths weakened and finally, in the eighth century, came under the rule of Moslem invaders. In contrast, the northern invaders—the Franks and the Anglo-Sax-

Wood relief from lid of a Frankish casket, probably *ca.* seventh century, showing a battle scene.

Religious carving from Niederdollendorf, probably depicting the symbols of Thor.

ons—learned much less from the Romans and at first had a lower level of civilization. But their kingdoms endured and became the strongest states of medieval Europe.

This difference in the history of the northern and southern kingdoms can be explained largely by geographic and demographic factors. The Germanic groups that reached the Mediterranean were entirely cut off from their old homes and could not be reinforced by new migrants. They found themselves in the most densely populated and most thoroughly Latinized area of the Empire, and they were vulnerable to attack from the strong states of the eastern Mediterranean—first the Eastern Roman Empire and then the Moslem caliphate. The Goths, Vandals, and Burgundians also suffered from having been converted to the heretical Arian form of Christianity. This made it extremely difficult for their rulers to win the loyalty of the orthodox Roman population. Thus the Germanic kingdoms that had the greatest need for strength were actually the weakest. The number of their fighting men dwindled, and the apathetic Roman population gave little support to the new rulers.

The northern invaders, on the other hand, remained in constant contact with their homelands, and for several generations their ranks were strengthened by new bands of migrants. In the sparsely settled lands they entered, they had an opportunity to preserve their old customs and to maintain effective armies. Since they were eventually converted to orthodox Christianity, they gained the support of the Church. The Eastern Roman Empire never touched Gaul, and the Moslems, even at the height of their power, could only send raiding parties toward the Loire. Thus the northern invaders had time to develop new institutions strong enough to enable them to survive during the troubled centuries of the early Middle Ages.

A glance at a modern map will illustrate this difference between the northern and southern Germanic kingdoms. Italy and Spain have retained their old Roman names; they did not become East Gothia and West Gothia. But the Franks imposed their name on Gaul, which became France, just as the Angles imposed

Gold coin of Theodoric, Ostrogothic king of Italy in the early sixth century.

theirs on the largest part of Britain, which became known as England.

And yet the southern kingdoms, even though they were politically short-lived, aided the difficult transition to a new age by making a conscious effort to adapt Roman culture to the needs of a simpler, semibarbaric society. Latin literature and Roman law survived in the South, but not in the North. The Burgundian and Visigothic kings, for example, issued brief codes of Roman law for the use of their Roman subjects. These codes would have seemed crude and incomplete to the great lawyers of the Roman Empire, but they covered most of the cases that were likely to arise and they preserved some of the basic principles of Roman law. Moreover, the existence of Roman law codes encouraged Germanic kings to put some of their own legal customs in writing.

The Ostrogothic Kingdom of Italy

The most important work in assimilating Roman culture was done in Ostrogothic Italy. Theodoric, king of the Ostrogoths, had been closely associated with the court at Constantinople and understood Roman ways very well. During his reign in Italy (493–526) he safeguarded the elements of Roman civilization and ensured the continuation of the Roman administrative system. The fact that the Ostrogothic army had its own law meant no more to the ordinary citizen than does the existence of military law in a modern society. Theodoric also named eminent Roman scholars to the highest official posts. Two of these men, Boethius and Cassiodorus, eager to preserve the learning of the past, made a deliberate effort to put it into a form that could be used by future generations.

Boethius (ca. 480–524) was especially disturbed by the gap that had opened between Greek and Latin learning. Since the fourth century few inhabitants of the West had studied Greek, and even so eminent a writer as St. Augustine was not able to read it easily. This ignorance of Greek was particularly serious in mathematics, science, logic, and philosophy, where Latin scholars had done little original work and where all the advanced texts were in Greek. Boethius hoped to preserve this precious heritage by writing elementary treatises on mathematics and translating the major works of Aristotle and Plato. Unfortunately, Boethius did not live to complete his ambitious project, and some of the translations he did make were neglected by later scholars. But his basic mathematical texts and his translations of two of Aristotle's introductory treatises on logic were used throughout the Middle Ages. Until the twelfth century these treatises supplied medieval scholars with most of their philosophical vocabulary and ideas about logic. By showing, in his theological *Tractates,* how logic could be applied to problems of Christian theology, Boethius ensured the survival of logic as a branch of medieval learning.

Boethius' career was cut short when he fell into political difficulties. Theodoric, in spite of his admiration for Roman culture, was always a little un-easy about the loyalty of the upper-class Romans. The Arianism of the Ostrogoths offended the Catholic Romans, and the emperor at Constantinople, who still claimed authority over the West, encouraged intrigues against Theodoric. It is possible that Boethius entered into these plots against his king; at any rate he was accused of treason, jailed for a year, and then executed. While he was still in prison he wrote the work for which he is best remembered, the *Consolation of Philosophy,* a long dialogue, partly in prose and partly in verse, between the prisoner and Philosophy. Philosophy argues that all worldly honors and pleasures are vain and that external misfortunes are unimportant. The only thing worth striving for is the good of the soul, expressed in virtue and in reason. This idea was at least as old as Plato, but the conviction with which Boethius stated it made his work a real consolation to many troubled men in years to come.

Top: Bust of a young German warrior, of the type the Romans fought. The soldier wears a pagan necklace with magic power. Bottom: woolen clothes worn by warriors of the Migration period and recovered from graves.

Cassiodorus (ca. 490–580) was more skillful in riding out political storms. Though he had been secretary to Theodoric, he survived both court intrigues and the long wars between the Eastern Romans and the Goths and died peacefully at the age of ninety in his ancestral home in southern Italy. He was something of a pedant; the letters he wrote for Theodoric are tricked out with far-fetched allusions to classical literature and mythology. But he saw, perhaps more clearly than Boethius, that ancient learning could be saved only with the aid of the Church. In his last years he founded a monastery to preserve the secular learning that he felt was necessary for true understanding of Christian writings. Cassiodorus preserved as many classical texts as he could and, in his *Introduction to Divine and Secular Literature*, outlined the basic reading that was necessary for an educated clergyman.

Digests such as that of Cassiodorus, and elementary treatises such as those of Boethius, made up the basic educational materials of the early Middle Ages. Many classical works had been lost, and those that survived were seldom studied because they were too long or too difficult. The digests and handbooks were no real substitute for the originals, for they stressed what was obvious and omitted or oversimplified what was complicated. Nevertheless, they preserved useful knowledge. Even more important, they suggested that better sources might be available. A quotation from Vergil might make a reader eager to ferret out the whole *Aeneid*; a reference to Aristotle might encourage a scholar to seek the original work. It was a long time before any large-scale efforts were made to recover and study the basic works of the classical period, but at least the men of the early Middle Ages were aware that their knowledge was incomplete.

GERMANIC SOCIETY

The early Germanic kingdoms were not very successful in preserving the intellectual heritage of Rome. They were even less successful in preserving the Roman political and administrative system. Here they ran into a double difficulty: the native population was weary of the old imperial forms of government, and the Germans themselves had no concept of the state and no experience in administration. Consequently, there was a drastic simplification of political institutions in all the countries of the West.

Since the early Germans had lived in rather small groups given over to agriculture and cattle raising, they had felt no need to create elaborate political institutions. The family was their basic social unit—not the small family of father, mother, and children, but the large family that included grandparents, uncles, and cousins out to the second or third degree. The family protected the lives and property of its members, sometimes waging blood-feuds with other families. Above the family was the neighborhood, a group of family heads who cooperated in local defense, in settling disputes, and in performing difficult agricultural tasks. The folk, or people, which was made up of many neighborhoods, was supposedly a blood-group descended from a few common ancestors. It had almost no function except to make war on or defend itself against neighboring peoples.

Early Germanic society was not democratic; it was very conscious of differences in class and rank. Certain families, which claimed descent from the gods, had great wealth and supplied leaders in time of war. But these leaders—the kings and the nobles—had little to do in time of peace. Their wealth and ancestry won them respect, and their bands of armed retainers commanded fear. Although their advice was often sought when trouble arose, they did not administer a state or govern a people. Most of the ordinary business of the people was conducted by the family and neighborhood groups.

Germanic Courts

The difference between Germanic and Roman political organization is seen most clearly in the administration of justice. A Roman who had a grievance against a neighbor went to a court established by imperial authority. His case was judged according to laws promulgated by the emperors, and the court's decision was enforced by local administrative officials.

A German who felt that he had been wronged, however, had to rely first and foremost on his own strength and that of his family. The most common remedy was reprisal, which easily developed into the blood-feud. Only if the injured family felt that reprisal and feud were unnecessary or dangerous would the case go to a court. The usual court was an assembly of neighbors that, lacking coercive power, relied largely on public opinion and religious sanctions. It had no power to force a defendant to come to court. If he did appear and denied his deed, the court had no means of establishing the facts in the case. A defendant with a bad reputation was usually sent to the ordeal. This meant that he was obliged to expose himself to a test and let the gods indicate whether or not he was lying. He might, for example, be thrown into a pond to see if he would float or sink. Floating was a sign of guilt, for it meant that the pure element of water had rejected the accused. A man of good reputation, however, could clear himself by compurgation—that is, he would swear that the charge against him was baseless and a fixed number of friends and relatives would swear that his oath was "clean." These oath-helpers were not giving testimony in behalf of the accused, for they might know nothing at all about the facts in the case. They were simply swearing that the accused was not a perjurer, and by so doing they automatically cleared him of the charges against him.

If the plaintiff won his case, he received compensation from the defendant, either in money or in kind. This was true even for crimes of violence, such as homicide or mayhem. There was no idea that crime was an offense to the community as a whole, and no attempt was made to inflict physical punishment on the wrongdoer. Tables of compensation made up the largest part of the laws of every Germanic people. It cost more to kill a man of high birth than an ordinary freeman, more to kill a woman of childbearing age than a grandmother. The

Artifacts of the Migration period. Top: a torc, or armlet, worn especially by Gauls and Britons, sixth to eighth centuries. Right: Ostrogothic gilt bronze buckle with jewels, sixth century. The style is Germanic.

penalties were substantial; the compensation for killing a man of high birth would ruin a poor family. However, no provision was made for collecting the penalties, other than the threats of the injured family and the pressure of public opinion.

These courts were probably more effective than we might think in dispensing a rough kind of justice. The most common offenses among the early Germans were acts of physical violence, of which no one was ashamed and which

Compurgation

When Chilperic I was assassinated, he left a young son who was to hold his father's share of the Frankish kingdom under the guardianship of his uncle, King Guntram. There were doubts about the boy's legitimacy, doubts which Guntram apparently shared.

After this King Guntram went to Paris [in 585] and openly addressed all the people, saying, "My brother Chilperic on his death is said to have left a son . . . but the boy is concealed, he is not shown to me. Therefore I feel certain that matters are not as they have been represented, but that the child is, as I believe, the son of one of our nobles. For if it had been of our blood, it would have been brought to me. Know therefore, that I will not acknowledge it until I receive satisfactory proofs of its paternity." When Queen Fredegonda [the mother of the boy] heard this she summoned the chief men of her kingdom, namely three bishops and three hundred nobles, and with them made oath that Chilperic was the father of the child. By this means suspicion was removed from the king's mind.

From Gregory of Tours, *History of the Franks,* trans. by Arthur C. Howland, *Translations and Reprints* (Philadelphia: University of Pennsylvania Press, 1897), Vol. IV, No. 4, p. 3.

Archbishop Hincmar
on the Ordeal by Cold Water
Ninth century

Now the one about to be tested is bound by a rope and cast into the water, because, as it is written, each one shall be holden with the cords of his iniquity. And it is evident that he is bound for two reasons; to wit, that he may not be able to practice any fraud in connection with the judgment, and that he may be drawn out at the right time if the water should receive him as innocent, so that he perish not. . . . And in this ordeal of cold water whoever, after the invocation of God, who is the Truth, seeks to hide the truth by a lie, cannot be submerged in the waters above which the voice of the Lord God has thundered; for the pure nature of the water recognizes as impure and therefore rejects . . . such human nature as has once been regenerated by the waters of baptism and is again infected by falsehood.

From Archbishop Hincmar, trans. by Arthur C. Howland, *Translations and Reprints* (Philadelphia: University of Pennsylvania Press, 1897), Vol. IV, No. 4, p. 11.

no one sought to conceal. To quarrel, fight, wound, and kill was the natural behavior of a self-respecting man. Thus in many cases the facts were not denied and the sole function of the court was to prevent a feud by determining the compensation to be offered to the injured party. When the facts were in dispute, ordeal and compurgation, though they might not reveal the truth, at least provided quarreling families with an excuse not to launch a feud. Once the gods had spoken, it was unnecessary to prove one's manhood by fighting. Like many other legal systems, the system dictated by Germanic custom was more concerned with stopping fights than with administering abstract justice. Any solution, so long as it was peaceful, was better than a grievous outbreak of blood-feuds.

Nevertheless, this Germanic legal system had serious defects, and no civilized life was possible until they had been remedied. It gave no place to public authority and set loyalty to the family far above loyalty to any larger group. It accepted as natural a state of violence in which no man's life was secure. Effective only in dealing with open wrongdoing, it could not easily be applied to commercial transactions. From the fifth to the twelfth century western European rulers struggled to create effective courts of justice; only when they had succeeded in this difficult task could the people they ruled advance beyond the stage of small, self-sufficient agricultural communities.

Germanic Kingship

The loyalties of a German were personal. He was loyal first of all to his family—and understandably so, for he could scarcely hope to exist without family backing. Men who had no families or whose families were weak had to become dependents or even slaves of some strong man. Next, the German showed loyalty to the leaders of the local community. Finally, he might show some loyalty to the king, if that king was known and respected for his prowess in war. But the king could not count on the unanimous support of his people; his real strength lay in his bands of armed retainers. These retainers lived with the king, were bound to him by personal oaths of loyalty, shared in the spoils of conquest, and were usually faithful to him unto death. A king seldom had more than a few hundred of these devoted retainers. The rest of his subjects were not ready to die to protect him from usurpers or outside enemies. So long as there was a king to lead them in times of emergency, they cared little who he was.

It was difficult enough for kings to exercise authority when they ruled small groups in limited territories and when they were personally acquainted with most of the fighting men of the folk. The task became far more difficult when they tried to rule large populations, composed of different races, scattered over wide areas of the old Empire. The king could not be present in all parts of his realm, nor could he know more than a few of the leading men in each district. He could neither preserve the old Roman administrative system nor create a new Germanic one. The idea of a civil service was foreign to Germanic custom, and the Germans did not know how to delegate authority. Either they ignored the king's delegate and tried to deal directly with the king, or else they transferred their

A German king (top) and his bishop. From an early manuscript copy of Alaric's code of law.

loyalty to the delegate himself and enabled him to become an almost independent ruler in his administrative district. Until kings were able to delegate authority without losing control—and it took them centuries to find out how—European kingdoms remained loose federations of local communities.

Given the primitive state of the Germanic economy and the structure of Germanic society, the local community was almost self-sufficient. The ordinary German might like to hear stories of adventures in distant lands, but otherwise he was not particularly interested in anything that happened more than a day's journey from his home. He drew almost everything he required from his own land and he produced nothing to sell in distant markets. He relied on the great men of his community for local defense and followed them to war without worrying about causes or objectives. Thus the establishment of a large kingdom did little to aid the ordinary German, nor did the division of a large kingdom into little principalities hurt or shock him.

Although settlement in the Western Empire posed puzzling new problems for the Germanic kings, it also gave them some help in solving those problems. Royal authority was always greatest in time of war, and the period of migration was a period of almost constant war. And, though they did not fully understand the Roman concept of the state and of public authority, they learned enough from contact with Romans to make them eager to be more than mere tribal war leaders. Most important, the Church, which had taken over many of the Roman traditions of government, sooner or later gained great influence in all the Germanic kingdoms. Not all churchmen were good administrators or enlightened statesmen; in fact, many were only one degree less barbarous than the flocks they tended. But most of them realized that Christianity could not flourish in an area broken up into isolated small communities and that, bad as the kings might be, there was more to be hoped for from them than from the even more unenlightened lords of petty provinces. Many bishops served as advisers to the kings and helped to create a rudimentary cen-

tral government. Others preserved a certain degree of unity by meeting together in local church councils. Prominent laymen frequently attended these church councils, which often dealt with such secular matters as the suppression of violence or declarations of loyalty to a king.

THE CHURCH IN THE GERMANIC KINGDOMS

Though the Church had a privileged place, it suffered severely during the chaotic years following the Germanic ascendancy. The old Roman population was far from being completely Christian in the fifth century, and the new Germanic population was either pagan or Arian. Even when they had been converted to Catholic Christianity, the Germans often tried to use the Church for their own purposes. A good many bishops of doubtful character, for example, were foisted on the Church by kings anxious to reward their friends and supporters.

The Church at this time was not yet the self-sufficient, highly organized Church it was to become in later centuries. Formerly it had relied on the imperial government for support and protection, and it had not yet perfected its own administrative system or established clear lines of authority. Theoretically, the kingdoms should have been divided into dioceses, each administered by a single bishop. North of the Alps this division was far from complete; many bishops had dioceses that were too large or whose boundaries had not been defined. The division of the dioceses into parishes had gone even less far. This meant that there were no churches at all in many rural areas and that many nominal Christians had little opportunity to attend Christian services. Finally, while the pope's authority to determine questions of faith and morals was generally acknowledged, his power to remove inefficient or corrupt bishops was not yet fully established. Thus the influence of the Church varied from diocese to diocese with the character of the bishop and the amount of aid he could get from his king.

Fortunately for the Church, the growth of monastic communities provided a new, disciplined force at a time when it was badly needed. In the Late Empire many Christians, feeling that they could not live a truly religious life while absorbed in secular activities, had withdrawn from the world to wilderness or desert and had passed their lives in contemplation and prayer. But it was not easy for the hermit to endure the rigors of an isolated existence; his devotion might falter or he might be unable to provide himself with food and clothing. Thus there was a tendency for hermits to come together in communities in order to obtain spiritual and physical assistance from their fellows. By the end of the third century, some of these communities had become formally organized as monasteries under the headship of abbots.

Monasteries and monastic rules had existed in the East for several generations and were spreading to the West at the time of the Germanic migrations. But the eastern rules were not entirely suitable for western conditions; they were both too harsh and too soft. They were too harsh in physical matters, for the scanty food and clothing that would support life in the Egyptian desert were completely inadequate in the colder northern countries. They were too soft in matters of authority, for many eastern monks were completely undisciplined and wandered about from place to place as they saw fit. Yet the monastic life was becoming steadily more attractive to men in the West; it offered both spiritual and physical security in an age of increasing violence and instability. Many abbots in Italy and Gaul tried to develop rules suited to western conditions, but none had more than local influence.

St. Benedict and Monasticism

It was St. Benedict of Nursia (480–543) who was most successful in adapting monasticism to the needs of the Western Church. He was born of a well-to-do Roman family, but like many other men of his time he had fled in disgust from a world that seemed hopelessly corrupt. At first he lived as a hermit in the hills near Rome. As his reputation for holiness attracted others to him he found himself forced to organize a regular monastic community. He built a monastery on the commanding height of Monte Cassino,* near the main route from Naples to Rome, and established a rule that gradually became the basic constitution for all western monks.

The great strength of the Benedictine Rule lay in its combination of firmness and reasonableness. The abbot's authority was absolute. Monks were not to leave their monastery or transfer to another monastery without permission. They were to keep themselves occupied all day. Their first and most important duty was to do the "work of God"—that

---

St. Benedict on the Authority of the Abbot

This excerpt illustrates the firm yet reasonable discipline that St. Benedict sought to instill in western monasteries.

Whenever any weighty matters have to be transacted in the monastery let the abbot call together all the community and himself propose the matter for discussion. After hearing the advice of the brethren let him consider it in his own mind, and then do what he shall judge most expedient. We ordain that all must be called to council, because the Lord often reveals to a younger member what is best. And let the brethren give their advice with all humble subjection, and presume not stiffly to defend their own opinion. Let them rather leave the matter to the abbot's discretion, so that all submit to what he shall deem best. As it becometh disciples to obey their master, so doth it behove the master to dispose of all things with forethought and justice.

In all things, therefore, every one shall follow the Rule as their master, and let no one rashly depart from it. In the monastery no one is to be led by the desires of his own heart, neither shall any one within or without the monastery presume to argue wantonly with his abbot. If he presume to do so let him be subjected to punishment according to the Rule.

From the *Rule of St. Benedict*, trans. by Cardinal Gasquet (London: Chatto and Windus, 1925), pp. 15–16.

---

*A great battle of the Second World War was fought for the strategic position of Monte Cassino. The mountain had been continuously occupied by a Benedictine monastery ever since the time of St. Benedict, though the buildings destroyed in the battle were not the original ones.

Page from a Gothic Bible, *ca.* 500. This translation, by the Arian bishop Ulfila, helps explain the success of the Aryans in converting the Germans. Orthodox Catholics did not translate religious works into German until much later. Ulfila's bible is one of the earliest specimens of a Germanic dialect and is the basis of most scholarly work on early German. Notice that some new letters, not in the Latin alphabet, had to be devised to accommodate unusual sounds in the Gothic language.

A Benedictine monastery in a Germanic kingdom exerted a powerful influence. It offered pure Christian doctrine to people who were pagans, heretics, or at most only nominal Catholics. Very early the monasteries became centers of missionary activity and reform. At the same time the Benedictine emphasis on obedience to higher authority helped to hold the Church together during a period when any sort of centralization was hard to achieve. The Benedictines emphasized papal authority and a well-organized Church; they opposed local autonomy and lack of discipline. Finally, in many parts of Europe the Benedictines introduced valuable new techniques, such as building in stone and organizing agriculture around the large estate. Benedictine monasteries often served as nuclei for the growth of towns, for they were almost always more prosperous than the neighboring countryside.

In view of these benefits, many kings and wealthy landowners decided that founding a monastery was a good investment. The founder and his family gained both spiritual and material rewards. It was obviously good for the donor's soul to have holy men praying for him; it was

St. Benedict giving his Rule to his monks. This eighth-century drawing is the oldest known representation of St. Benedict.

is, to take part in religious services that filled many hours of the day. But they were also to perform any manual labor that was necessary for the welfare of the house, including such activities as copying manuscripts. The primary purpose of the Rule, however, was not to make the monastery an intellectual center but to keep the monks from extremes of idleness or asceticism. Most monks were neither writers nor scholars, and most monasteries never distinguished themselves by their literary productions. They did, however, distinguish themselves as centers of prayer and worship, as dramatic examples of the Christian way of life. Most monasteries also performed certain social services, such as extending hospitality to travelers or giving food to the poor, and a few operated important schools.

In the illustration:
FLUUIUS APE ILE NA SESTINU RIUS
SCS MARTINUS

A self-sufficient monastery. Its produce included fish bred in the *vivarium* shown in the foreground.

and much of the cultivated area sank back into wilderness. Christianity survived among the natives who were being driven back into Wales; from Wales it spread into Ireland. But the conquering Anglo-Saxons were slow to accept the religion of their enemies, and in any case the Christians of Wales and Ireland, cut off from the rest of the western world, were developing peculiar ideas and usages. They celebrated Easter at a different time; they gave abbots authority over bishops; they did not follow the Roman ritual. In short, in Anglo-Saxon England the basic ingredients that were to produce early medieval civilization—the Latin, Germanic, and Christian traditions—had not yet begun to fuse.

The picture began to change during the pontificate of Gregory the Great (590–604). Gregory had been a monk and then an abbot; in fact, he had been most unwilling to leave his monastic life to

also good to know that the monastery might furnish grain in time of famine and lend its gold and silver ornaments when its benefactor ran short of money. By attracting settlers to waste lands, it might increase productivity and enhance the ruler's authority in remote areas. Thus monasteries spread rapidly throughout most of the Germanic kingdoms, often more rapidly than organized dioceses and parishes.

The Conversion of the Anglo-Saxons

England offers a good example of the importance of monasteries under the Germanic kingdoms. The Anglo-Saxon conquest of Britain was slow, piecemeal, and bloody. The Britons put up a stiffer resistance than any other group in the western part of the Empire, and during this long resistance they abandoned many of their Roman ways. Faced with a stubborn enemy, the Angles and Saxons had to be more destructive than, for example, the Franks were in the Seine Valley. Very little of Latin civilization remained in Britain: the language was abandoned, the towns were deserted,

THE ANGLO-SAXON KINGDOMS OF ENGLAND   Seventh century

take on the responsibility of governing the Church. He realized more fully than his predecessors the value of the monks as a disciplined force obedient to the orders of Rome. Gregory also realized how hard it was to maintain unity and decent conduct among the clergy of the Western Church. His correspondence shows how diligently he worked at this task and how difficult it was to make any impression on bishops and priests protected by Germanic kings. Gregory kept some measure of control in Italy, but beyond the Alps he could do little more than register his complaints. And beyond the Frankish area, where at least a form of Christianity existed, though corrupt and unsatisfactory, stretched a great expanse of heathen territory, from the North Cape down to the middle Danube, from England across Frisia and North Germany into the limitless lands of the Slavs.

Gregory probably prepared no master plan for the reform and conversion of the West. But he was quite ready to take advantage of special opportunities and he turned to the monks for help. Britain seemed to be a promising field for conversion, since the king of Kent, in southern England, had married a Christian Frankish princess. So in 597 Gregory sent a group of monks to Kent, led by an abbot named Augustine.*

Augustine converted the king of Kent without much difficulty and established the first English bishopric, at Canterbury. But after this promising start the Roman version of Christianity spread only slowly through the island, partly because Augustine was not a very good organizer, partly because Irish missionaries were influential in the North, and partly because the Anglo-Saxons were divided and quarrelsome. It was only late in the seventh century that these obstacles were overcome. Most of the North abandoned Irish forms, and in 669 a great organizer, Theodore of Tarsus, became Archbishop of Canterbury. Theodore gave the Anglo-Saxon Church a firm institutional base by dividing the country into regular

*This Augustine also became a saint, but he should not be confused with the great theologian St. Augustine of Hippo, who died more than a century and a half before the mission to England (see p. 119).

A Northumbrian cross, *ca.* 700.

The helmet of a seventh-century Anglian king. From the Sutton Hoo treasure, one of the great archeological discoveries of this century, found under the untouched funeral mound of an early Anglian king.

dioceses and made the Church an integral part of Anglo-Saxon society.

From this time on the Anglo-Saxons were loyal and energetic supporters of the Roman Church. The most successful missionaries of the eighth century were Anglo-Saxon monks, who not only converted the remaining pockets of heathen Germans on the Continent but even succeeded in reforming and making obedient to the pope the corrupt and anarchical churches of the Frankish kingdom. Gregory's decision to support monasticism and missionary activities produced remarkable results, for the missionary monks both increased the number of Christians and greatly strengthened the pope's authority in western Europe.

THE RISE OF THE FRANKS

During this period of missionary activity, the Franks were rising to political dominance in western Europe. They occupied a favored position. They had penetrated deep enough into the Empire to profit from its wealth but not deep enough to jeopardize the sources of their military power. They held northern Gaul, which

Roman Gaul	Merovingian Dynasty	Carolingian Dynasty	Capetian Dynasty

Childeric, father of Clovis and an early king of the Franks, from a signet ring found in his tomb. His long hair and his spear are signs of royal authority.

was Roman, but they also held the solidly Germanic regions of the middle and lower Rhine. Their first great king, Clovis, a member of the Merovingian* family, came to power in about 480. He was king of only one group of Franks, and at first he held only a small corner of Gaul. But Clovis was both a good fighter and a skillful intriguer: he rapidly increased the size of his realm by assassinating or defeating his rivals. Clovis had married a Catholic Burgundian princess, and through her he gained the idea that the Christian God could be a powerful help in war. He put this idea to the test in a battle with the Alamanni in 506 and gained a hard-fought victory. Convinced by this demonstration, Clovis sought baptism from the Catholic bishop of Reims.

* This family was named for an early and almost unknown Frankish king, Meroweg.

The Morals and Faith of the Early Franks

Ragnachar was then king at Cambrai, a man so unrestrained in his wantonness that he scarcely had mercy for his own near relatives. . . . Clovis came and made war on him, and he saw that his army was beaten and prepared to slip away in flight, but was seized by his army, and with his hands tied behind his back, he was taken with Ricchar his brother before Clovis. And Clovis said to him: "Why have you humiliated our family in permitting yourself to be bound? It would have been better for you to die." And raising his ax he dashed it against his head, and he turned to the brother and said: "If you had aided your brother he would not have been bound." And in the same way he smote him with his ax and killed him. . . . These kings were kinsmen of Clovis, and their brother, Rignomer by name, was slain by Clovis's order at the city of Mans. When they were dead Clovis received all their kingdom and treasures. And having killed many other kings and his nearest relatives, of whom he was jealous lest they take the kingdom away from him, he extended his rule over all the Gauls. . . . For God was laying low his enemies every day under his hand, and was increasing his kingdom, because he walked with an upright heart before Him, and did what was pleasing to His eyes.

From Gregory of Tours, *History of the Franks*, ca. 575, trans. and annot. by E. Brehaut (New York: Columbia University Press, 1916), pp. 48–50.

The conversion of Clovis, even more than that of Constantine, which it resembled so closely, was based on expediency. Clovis remained a bloody and treacherous barbarian; all he wanted was to exploit the power of the Christian God and gain the support of Catholic bishops and the old Roman population against Arian Germans. He used his newly acquired orthodoxy as an excuse to attack the Visigoths, who still held southwestern Gaul as well as Spain. Proclaiming that he could not endure the presence of heretics in Gaul, Clovis drove the Visigoths back across the Pyrenees and annexed their territories on the French side of the mountains. This victory almost completed the task of unifying Gaul. Only the Burgundian kingdom in the Rhone Valley escaped Clovis' domination, thanks to the aid it received from the Ostrogoths of Italy.

The Frankish kingdom remained strong for a century after Clovis' death in 511. His sons finally succeeded in conquering the Burgundians and added their territories to the Frankish realm. They also began to extend their authority over the Bavarians and other Germanic peoples east of the Rhine. Although the Frankish kings quarreled bitterly among themselves, the Franks still had the best army in the West, and none of their neighbors could profit from their disunity.

The Frankish kings also profited from the fact that their orthodoxy was seldom questioned, whatever might be said of their morals. Orthodoxy gained them the steady support of the bishops, most of whom came from old aristocratic families and had great influence with both Frankish warriors and Gallo-Roman land holders. Bishops could be very useful to kings, especially as they did not insist on impossibly high standards of conduct. Thus Bishop Gregory of Tours (538–94), who wrote a famous *History of the Franks*, was rather gentle in his judgment of the

Frankish kings. Gregory admits that Clovis was treacherous and that on one occasion Clovis bewailed his lack of relatives "not because he grieved at their death but with the cunning thought that he might perhaps find one still alive whom he could kill." But Gregory could still sum up Clovis' career by saying: "The Lord cast his enemies under his power day after day, and increased his kingdom because he walked with a right heart before Him and did that which was pleasing in His sight." Gregory was equally favorable to King Guntram (561–93), of whom the best that could be said was that he murdered somewhat fewer people than his rivals did. "One would have taken him," says Gregory, "not only for a king, but for a priest of the Lord."

Nevertheless, the bishops did make an effort to mitigate the cruelty and selfishness of their rulers. They protected men unjustly accused; they did their best to prevent civil wars among members of the royal family. They were aided by the monasteries, which were just beginning to appear in the Frankish realm. Monks who had already abandoned the world were not easily terrified by the threats of kings. St. Columban, the founder of Luxeuil, denounced King Thierry (595–613) to his face as a sinner and predicted that his sons would never be kings. The saint was exiled, but he soon returned and saw Thierry's family wiped out in a civil war. Yet in spite of all the efforts of bishops and monks the Franks were Christians only in externals; it took a long time for the faith to sink into their hearts.

The Collapse of the Gothic Kingdoms

While the Franks were gaining control of Gaul and western Germany, their only possible rivals were being eliminated. After Theodoric's death, Justinian, the Roman emperor at Constantinople (see pp. 160–61), was determined to conquer the Ostrogothic kingdom in Italy. It took years of hard fighting, but by 552 the desperate resistance of the Ostrogoths had been snuffed out and a devastated Italy was restored to imperial

control. But Italians did not have any great loyalty to an empire that had ruined them, and they were too weak to defend themselves. As a result, when a new Germanic people, the Lombards, began to push into Italy from the Danube in the latter part of the sixth century, a large part of the peninsula lay open to conquest. The imperial forces held onto the South and some outposts in the North, such as Ravenna and Venice; the Lombards took the rest. They extended their conquest somewhat during the next century, but they never subdued the whole peninsula; in fact, no one was able to unite Italy again until 1870. The Lombard kingdom, weak, divided, and far less influenced by Roman civilization than the Ostrogothic kingdom had been, posed no threat to the Franks, who conquered it in the eighth century.

The Visigothic kingdom of Spain lasted a little longer than the Ostrogothic. The Visigothic kings strengthened themselves by abandoning their Arian heresy and accepting Catholic Christianity. Justinian struck them only a glancing blow; he regained some of the southeast coast of Spain but never had enough resources to reconquer the whole peninsula. But for more than 150 years the Visigoths suffered all the usual troubles of Germanic kingdoms—disputed successions, weak control by the central government, and the rise of semi-independent local magnates. Thus when a Moslem army crossed the Straits of Gibraltar in 711 (see p. 175) there was no effective resistance, and the Visigothic kingdom collapsed at once. A few Christians took refuge in the northern hills of Galicia and established a petty kingdom there. The rest of the peninsula was drawn into an Arab empire and remained under Moslem control for centuries.

The Decline of the Merovingian Kings

After the sixth century only one power was left in western Europe—the Frankish kingdom. The Anglo-Saxons were divided into petty kingdoms; the Scandinavian monarchies were just beginning to take form; the Germans of the north and east, such as the Frisians and

Two Ostrogothic brooches. The one at top is made of gold inlaid with emerald and garnet and marks the zenith of the Ostrogothic style; the one on the bottom, made after the defeats of 552–53, is poor in quality and crudely decorated.

the Old Saxons, had almost no organization; and the Visigoths and the Lombards were weak and divided. But the apparent strength and solidity of the Frankish kingdom were deceptive. The Franks soon began to suffer from the same political ills as the other Germanic peoples; their kingdom survived only because it was not seriously threatened by outside enemies. In Frankland, as elsewhere, the kings had found it difficult to establish any sort of central control, and political power was passing rapidly into the hands of the great noble families.

In addition to holding large amounts of land, these families were the local representatives of royal authority. The Frankish kingdom was divided into counties, each ruled by a count who collected the revenues, presided over the courts, and controlled the military forces of his district. The king supposedly could name counts as he saw fit, and in the sixth century men of poor families sometimes achieved the position. But this was always distasteful to the great families, and as the kings weakened the nobles gained a virtual monopoly of all important offices. By the eighth century counts could be selected only from a small group of aristocrats. Many countships were, if not strictly hereditary, usually held within the same family.

Frequent outbreaks of civil war strengthened aristocratic control over local government. The Frankish kings treated their state as private property and regularly divided the kingdom among their sons. Just as regularly, one or more of the rival kings tried to eliminate his brothers and cousins and acquire their territories and treasuries. To gain support, he rewarded his own men and bribed the retainers of his rivals with grants of land and concessions of governmental power. These grants further weakened royal authority. Whatever central power remained passed more and more into the hands of an official known as the mayor of the palace.

The Mayors of the Palace

Originally the mayor was merely the head of the royal household, the man who managed the king's private affairs. But the Germans made little distinction between public and private affairs and used any official for any business. Thus the mayor of the palace, who was always at court, gradually became a viceroy who acted for the king in all important matters. The mayor was usually a member of one of the great Frankish families, supported by a coalition of local magnates. In order to keep his place, he had to grant favors to these magnates just as the king had done.

To make things worse, by 700 the Frankish lands had been split into an eastern, largely Germanic kingdom called Austrasia, a western, more Latinized kingdom named Neustria, and a much weaker southern kingdom of Burgundy. Southwest Gaul (Aquitaine) and southeast Germany (Bavaria) were practically autonomous. In each of the major kingdoms there was a mayor of the palace who was constantly threatened by rebellion among his own supporters and who constantly threatened his rival mayors with direct attacks and underhanded intrigues. Wars among the mayors were as bad as wars among the kings, and there seemed to be little hope that the Frankish kingdom could survive this turmoil.

Yet by 700 a remarkable family had appeared that was to reunite the Frankish kingdom and strengthen it so that within its shelter a new western European civilization could begin to take shape. This family—called Carolingian, from its most famous member, Charlemagne, or Charles the Great (Carolus Magnus)—came from the eastern Frankish kingdom of Austrasia. It gave strong support to the Church and especially to missionary and reform activities. It also showed remarkable skill in gaining and keeping the loyalty of the counts and great landowners. With their support the head of the family, Pippin, made himself mayor of the palace in both Neustria and Austrasia late in the seventh century. When Pippin died there was a rebellion, but his illegitimate son, Charles Martel (714–41), was eventually accepted as mayor of all the Frankish kingdoms. With Charles Martel all power in the Frankish kingdoms was caught up by the Carolingian family. Although the Merovingian kings kept their empty title a few more years, they had no further influence on the course of events.

Suggestions for Further Reading

Note: Asterisk denotes a book available in paperback edition.

Theodoric, Boethius, and Cassiodorus

The life of one of the striking figures of the early Middle Ages is portrayed by T. Hodgkin, *Theodoric the Goth* (1891). Hodgkin writes in the "grand manner" of the nineteenth-century historian, and the book is still fresh. His *The Letters of Cassiodorus* (1886) contains the extensive correspondence of Cassiodorus and good biographical sketches of Cassiodorus and Boethius. A superior study of Cassiodorus and his monastic writings is *Introduction to Divine and Human Readings,* trans. by L. W. Jones (1946). Boethius' works are available in numerous translations. The most scholarly is in the *Loeb Classical Library,* trans. by E. K. Rand and H. F. Stewart (1918), but the Modern Library edition of Boethius' most famous work, *The Consolation of Philosophy,** trans. by W. V. Cooper (1942), is more readable. Both E. M. Rand, *Founders of the Middle Ages** (1928), and H. O. Taylor, *The Emergence of Christian Culture in the West** (1901), discuss Cassiodorus and Boethius as "transmitters" of the Greco-Roman legacy. M. L. W. Laistner, *Thought and Letters in Western Europe, 500–900** (1931), combines fine scholarship with good style. Paul the Deacon's *History of the Langobards,* trans. by D. Foulke (1907), is our chief source for the Lombard kingdom of northern Italy.

St. Benedict and the Monasteries

The cornerstone of monasticism in the West is the short *Rule of St. Benedict,* trans. by J. McCann (1952). The best scholarly study of the Rule is P. Delatte, *Commentary on the Rule of St. Benedict* (1908), but the more recent study by H. van Zeller, *The Holy Rule* (1958), is more interesting and more understandable to the modern student. C. Butler, *Benedictine Monachism* (1923), is valuable for an understanding of the spirit and meaning of the monastic life, and J. McCann, *St. Benedict** (1952), gives a good account of St. Benedict and Benedictines through the centuries. A fascinating and provocative picture of monastic life today, in the form of a diary, is T. Merton, *The Sign of Jonas** (1956). The classic work of William James, *Varieties of Religious Experience** (1902), does a great deal to explain the "phenomenon" of monasticism in the perspective of modern civilization.

The Franks—— Gregory of Tours

A shockingly vivid picture of the chaotic society of sixth-century Gaul is presented by the contemporary Gregory of Tours, *History of the Franks,** trans. by E. Brehaut (1916); or, in a fuller version, by O. M. Dalton (1927). This is our best evidence for the political and social condition of Merovingian Gaul. There is an excellent study of Gregory's language and its reflection of the decline of learning in the West in E. Auerbach, *Mimesis** (1946). *The Life of St. Columban,* trans. by D. C. Munro (1921), reinforces Gregory of Tours' picture of moral decadence. F. Lot, *The End of the Ancient World** (1951), contains a scholarly study of Gaul under the Merovingians, with emphasis on political conditions. The older work of S. Dill, *Roman Society in Gaul in the Merovingian Age* (1926), emphasizes economic and social aspects. A good overall survey is J. M. Wallace-Hadrill, *The Barbarian West: 400–1000** (1966); see also this excellent book on the Franks, *The Long-Haired Kings* (1962).

The Conversion of the Anglo-Saxons

The Venerable Bede of Jarrow's *The Ecclesiastical History of the English Nation** is incomparably the greatest authority we have for the early centuries of the English settlements. The best study of the life and works of Bede is the scholarly collection of essays edited by A. H. Thompson, *Bede: His Life, Times, and Writings* (1935). The classic poem *Beowulf,** trans. by D. Wright (1957), is a mine of information about Anglo-Saxon society in the seventh and eighth centuries. D. Whitelock, *The Beginnings of English Society** (1952), is a very good introductory treatment of the period, and G. O. Sayles, *The Medieval Foundations of England,** Chapter 1–3 (1948), is a "history of ideas in action" with an excellent and detailed critical bibliography. See also S. J. Crawford, *Anglo-Saxon Influence on Western Christendom* (1933).

Gregory the Great

F. H. Dudden, *Gregory the Great,* 2 vols. (1905), the standard study of Gregory's pontificate, gives a good account of conditions in Italy at the time. Dudden pays special attention to the conversion of England. The increasing activities of the papacy under Gregory are shown in his letters in *Library of Nicene and Post Nicene Fathers,* Vols. XII and XIII (1895). *The Dialogues of St. Gregory the Great,* trans. by E. G. Gardner (1911), illustrates the religious and intellectual climate of the times. *The Dialogues* is our chief source for the life of St. Benedict.

Mosaic portraits of Justinian and his wife Theodora, Ravenna, *ca.* 574.

8 Byzantium and Islam

The East was the first region of the Empire to be threatened by the barbarian inroads of the fourth and fifth centuries. Before moving west, the Visigoths and the Ostrogoths had held the Balkans for a time. But their presence, which was to alter profoundly the political and social pattern of the West, was only a passing episode in the history of the East. By 500 the Roman Empire in the West had vanished, whereas the Empire in the East was beginning a revival that was once more to give it a strong government, a highly developed economy, and an active intellectual and artistic life.

THE EASTERN ROMAN EMPIRE

This contrast shows once more that internal weaknesses rather than external attacks were the real cause of the collapse of the Roman Empire. In the West, where the internal weaknesses were more serious and more pervasive, nothing could be done to save the Empire. But in the East there were strengths as well as weaknesses. There the cities were economic assets rather than parasites, as they were in the West. Christianity was both more widespread and more deeply felt in the East than in the West, and it served as a substitute for patriotism. The excellent defensive positions of the East, especially Constantinople, made it impossible for the Germans to touch the richest cities and provinces. Moreover, the eastern emperors and their advisers were somewhat more skillful—or at least more successful—politicians than their colleagues in the West. They prevented the Goths from making any permanent settlement in the Balkan Peninsula, and they freed themselves from dependence on Germanic soldiers by recruiting troops in Asia Minor. Because they retained control of the great trading cities of Constantinople, Antioch, and Alexandria, the eastern emperors could always collect enough taxes to support their administration and their army. With the departure of the Ostrogoths for Italy and the weakening of the Huns, the Eastern Empire was freed from immediate danger. During the sixth century it was able to start the difficult task of recovery.

Justinian

The leader of this first revival of the Eastern Empire was the emperor Justinian (527–65), a man of ambition, energy, and imagination. In spite of his abilities, however, his stubborn determination in pursuing mistaken policies led him to waste resources, miss opportunities, and plunge the Empire into useless wars. He was successful in most of his projects, but a less successful ruler might have done less harm. Every success encouraged him to extend his commitments, so that by the time of his death both the loyalty and the resources of his subjects had been nearly exhausted.

Justinian was not the sort of ruler one would expect to find in a state composed largely of Greeks, Syrians, and Egyptians. His family came from the extreme west of what was left of the Empire, from a district near the Adriatic, where Latin was still spoken. This Latin background may explain some of Justinian's policies. Fascinated by the idea of recovering the West, he was willing to sacrifice the people of the East in order to regain the old heart of the Empire. In a sense, Justinian was the last of the Roman emperors. After his death the Latin tradition died out, Greek became the official language of the Empire, and the ties between East and West slackened.

Justinian was lucky in his immediate predecessors, for they had rebuilt the army, set the Empire's finances in order, and repaired its administrative system. He was even luckier in what seemed at first a disastrous marriage. While he was still a young man, he had fallen in love with a woman named Theodora, who had been the sixth-century equivalent of a stripteaser. She had had many lovers and to marry her seemed socially impossible and politically unwise. But Justinian insisted on marrying his mistress, and he never had cause to regret it. Theodora was a courageous woman who kept Justinian from fleeing early in his reign when he was threatened by a rebellion of the people of Constantinople. She also understood the people of the East far better than her husband did; after her death he found it hard to retain their loyalty. Theodora secured important positions for many of her friends; through these supporters and through her own personal influence she was able to modify and even to reverse imperial policy, especially in the field of religion.

Nevertheless, the basic objectives of the reign were set by Justinian. He was determined to restore the Empire, to regain its lost territories, and to rebuild its cities. He always aimed high, reaching for the utmost in power and magnificence. Unfortunately, his resources were inadequate and his plans were often contradictory.

Byzantine gold wedding ring, *ca.* fifth century.

Justinian's determination to reconquer the West was strengthened by the weakness of the Germanic kingdoms on the Mediterranean. His first campaigns were encouragingly successful. The Vandal kingdom of Africa fell after a short war in 533. The Ostrogoths in Italy, left without a capable leader after the death of Theodoric, at first offered little resistance to the imperial army. In the end, the tide of reconquest even reached far-off Spain, where Justinian seized a strip of the southeastern coast with very little difficulty.

But it was easier to gain provinces in the West than to keep them. The Roman population of Italy, Spain, and Africa experienced no patriotic thrill on being reunited with the Empire. In fact, the reintroduction of the imperial tax system made many people long for the easier rule of the barbarians. Justinian tried to gain their loyalty by accepting Roman religious dogmas and rejecting the views of a large part of the clergy of Syria and Egypt. But he succeeded only in alienating many of his eastern subjects without

gaining solid support in Italy. Soon the West lapsed into its old apathy. Justinian's rule was based on a small group of soldiers and bureaucrats; the bulk of the population was passive, taking part in neither politics nor war.

The barbarians were quick to take advantage of the situation. The Vandals had been thoroughly crushed, but the Berbers, fierce tribesmen living on the fringes of the civilized area, took up the fight for Roman Africa. After many years of conflict, the Berbers were pushed back from the coastal towns, but they continued to hold most of what is now Morocco and western Algeria.

Justinian had even more trouble in Italy. There the Ostrogoths, who had been defeated but not broken, elected a new king who nearly drove the imperial forces from the peninsula. Justinian never gave his Italian commanders enough troops, partly because so many other demands were being made on his resources and partly because he feared, like many a Roman emperor before him, that a too successful general might seek the throne for himself. As a result, the war dragged on for eighteen years, from 535 to 553. In the end the Goths were almost exterminated, but Italy had been devastated. Although Justinian retained Italy for the rest of his reign, it contributed nothing to the strength or wealth of the Empire.

In the long run Justinian's policy of reconquest was a failure. None of the western provinces he regained was secure, either in a political or a military sense; most of them were lost within a generation or two after his death. The Lombards, who had migrated from the North into what is now Austria, pushed through the mountain passes and settled in the Po Valley, to which they gave their name, Lombardy. Then they drove down past Rome, and in the end all that was left of Justinian's Italian conquest was a large part of the South and the districts of Venice, Ravenna, and Rome. The Spanish reconquest proved just as ephemeral; by 624 the Visigoths had regained all the coastal territories they had lost. North Africa stayed with the Empire a little longer but fell to the Moslems at the end of the seventh century.

Though Justinian waged an offensive campaign in the West, he was kept on the defensive in the East. The Persian kingdom, the ancient enemy of Rome, was once more growing in strength and pressing hard on the eastern frontiers. On several occasions the Persians broke through the Roman defenses and plundered much of Syria and Asia Minor. With a large part of his army tied up in the West, Justinian was never able to defeat the Persians decisively, but through force of arms, diplomacy, and bribery he did manage to retain Syria and western Asia Minor. In the Balkans, Hunnic groups, aided by Slavic allies, staged raids that at times came very close to Constantinople. Justinian held on to most of the Balkan Peninsula, but he had to allow some of the Slavs to settle there. This was the beginning of Slavic predominance in the Balkans.

Justinian's policy in the East was not only cautious, which may have been sensible; it was also expensive. Diplomacy, bribes, and occasional payments of tribute to exceptionally dangerous enemies cost huge sums of money, but they did not end the necessity for maintaining an army and building fortifications. At the same time, many eastern provinces that were devastated by raids and invasions failed to pay their share of taxes.

Burdened though he was by wars of conquest in the West and by wars of defense in the East, Justinian did not spend the Empire's entire income on military operations. Restoration of the Empire meant more to him than territorial expansion; he was determined to re-create the magnificence of Rome at the height of its power. The New Rome of Constantinople was to be even more splendid than Old Rome, and provincial capitals were to reflect this splendor. Justinian put as much energy into this program as he did into his wars, and the results were somewhat more lasting.

They were more lasting because he accepted eastern standards instead of trying to impose his own western, Latin prejudices. Classical Roman art and architecture had simply decayed in the West, but in the East they had been transformed under the joint impact of Christianity and the revival of Oriental cultures. A new style was already emerging when Justinian gained the throne, and he gave it a chance to express itself through his great building program. All through the Empire, from Mount Sinai in the Egyptian desert to Ravenna in reconquered Italy, magnificent churches rose, rich with mosaics, goldsmiths' work, and many-colored marble.

The architects of these churches, so far as we know their names, came from the Asiatic provinces, and the decoration was largely inspired by Oriental examples. The new churches emphasized the interior, which blazed with light and color, rather than the exterior, which was often left rough and unadorned. In the famous church of St. Sophia in Constantinople, Justinian's architects built a great dome pierced with many windows high over the central part of the building. By solving the problem of setting a circular dome firmly atop a rectangular opening, they made the dome a far more effective element than it had been before, both esthetically and as a source of light.

Earlier Roman architects had bolstered their domes with high walls that concealed them from view and blocked out the light. Even when Justinian's architects did not use the dome, they raised the walls of their churches and enlarged the window spaces in order to admit more light. And everywhere there were brilliant mosaics, gold and silver ornaments, richly woven textiles, polished stones of every hue. The decoration was stylized, symbolic, and not at all realistic; for this very reason it had a greater impact on the beholder. The endless ranks of saints and angels along the walls were clearly not human beings; rigid, solemn, and intense, these figures were unmistakably inhabitants of another world. And with the saints and angels appeared the figures of Justinian and Theodora, humble before their God, but haloed like saints and immeasurably superior to all other human beings. One of the emperor's most cherished titles was "Equal of the Apostles," and his churches gave visible support to this claim.

Religious Disputes

Justinian was certainly a sincere and pious Christian. But he was also something of a scholar with a dangerous taste for theology, and he ruled over subjects who would fight for religious dogmas when they would fight for nothing else. There had already been serious quarrels over basic articles of the faith before Justinian became emperor; he probably could not have avoided interfering in religious matters even if he had so desired. But he did not so desire. Instead, he wanted to use religion to unify the restored Empire. His efforts failed, although he bullied popes, deposed patriarchs, and imprisoned monks and priests. At his death the Empire was still badly divided in its religious beliefs.

The basis of the controversy was the old argument about the union of the human and the divine in Jesus Christ. If Jesus was not fully divine, then the Redemption was impossible; if Christ was not fully human, then he did not suffer

Opposite: View of the interior of St. Sophia in Constantinople.

Procession of Saints and Martyrs, Saint Apollinare Nuove, Ravenna, *ca.* 574.

for us, and so the Crucifixion lost its meaning. Few people any longer took the extreme positions of "fully divine" or "fully human," but in trying to describe the way in which divine and human were joined together it was easy to overstress one or the other and thus fall into heresy.

When Justinian took over the imperial government the most dangerous heresy was that of the Monophysites, a group that recognized the existence of a human nature in Christ but subordinated it to the divine nature to such an extent that it became meaningless. Those who supported and those who opposed the Monophysites were stirred by something more than a desire for precise theological definitions. Monophysitism had become the national religion of Egypt, and in Syria it probably had more adherents than any other sect. It gave the inhabitants of these lands a chance to voice their long-suppressed desire for cultural and spiritual independence. It was anti-Greek, anti-Roman, antipapal, and anti-West.

Justinian's own beliefs were opposed to Monophysitism, and his political aims intensified his opposition. As we have seen, he wanted to recover the West, and the West, led by the pope, was almost unanimous in its rejection of Monophysite doctrine. Early in his reign, therefore, Justinian persecuted the Monophysites and tried to suppress their teachings.

But in religion as in war, Justinian found that he could not concentrate exclusively on the West. Theodora, always far more understanding of eastern viewpoints than her husband, realized that his flat opposition to Monophysitism was endangering imperial control of Egypt and Syria. She probably had some personal inclinations toward the doctrine as well. Under her influence, Justinian became somewhat more tolerant and finally settled for an interpretation that was technically orthodox but that leaned toward the Monophysite position.

No one was pleased with this solution. Pope Vigilius, who had come to Constantinople against his better judgment to confer with the emperor, refused at first to accept the compromise formula. He yielded only after a long period of house arrest and threats. The orthodox clergy of Constantinople were equally indignant, though easier to deal with; Justinian simply dismissed them from their posts. The Monophysites themselves, whom Justinian was trying to conciliate, found the new orthodox doctrine just as unacceptable as the old. Almost all Egyptians, and many Syrians, seceded from the official Church and formed their own religious organizations, which were bitterly hostile to the government and to the orthodox, Greek-speaking clergy. This sharp division in religion helps explain the ease with which the Arabs took over most of the East in the next century (see p. 173). Syrians and Egyptians preferred the rule of tolerant Moslems to the rule of intolerant and orthodox Greeks.

Justinian's Summary of Roman Law

Justinian's love of precise definition, which led him into dangerous religious policies, found happier expression in the field of law. Perhaps his only two completely successful achievements were the building of St. Sophia and the codification of Roman law. The most impressive intellectual achievement of the Romans had been in law, and the keenest minds

Gold coin portraying Justinian on horseback. The coin was struck to commemorate the defeat of the Vandals in 535.

164

of the Empire had worked on legal problems. But this was the very reason that codification was needed; Roman law had developed over so many centuries that its basic rules had to be sought in the voluminous works of generations of lawyers and officials. There had been earlier attempts to codify and digest Roman law, but no one had had the energy or the determination to survey the entire mass of legal literature and reduce it to manageable proportions.

Justinian attacked the problem of codifying the law with the same energy and ruthlessness with which he planned the reconquest of the West. At the very beginning of his reign he picked a group of capable men, led by the great jurist Tribonian, and gave them a free hand to produce a statement of the law that would be brief, clear, and consistent. He must have put heavy pressure on them, for they completed the task with incredible speed. The essential work was done between 528 and 534, and little was added after 546, the year of Tribonian's death.

The books produced by this effort came to be known collectively as the *Corpus Juris.* The first and most important unit was the *Digest,* a collection of extracts from the works of leading Roman lawyers, especially those of the second century, the golden age of Roman law. These extracts dealt with such basic problems of jurisprudence as the nature of law and justice, and the relation between law and custom. But they also included brief statements on the guiding principles of Roman law in, for example, such matters as property, contract, and inheritance. The next book of the *Corpus Juris* was the *Code,* a restatement and simplification of statute law. These two major works were followed by the *Institutes,* a textbook of Roman law for students, and the *Novels,* laws promulgated after 534 to amend or supplement the *Code.*

The speed with which the *Corpus Juris* was compiled led to some unfortunate results. Important material was omitted, while insignificant and even contradictory statements were included. Moreover, because the *Corpus Juris* was the only authorized version of Roman law,

earlier works on the subject were neglected and lost. Almost none of the thousands of volumes on Roman law written under the Empire have survived. On the other hand, judging by what happened to Latin literary works, most of the legal writings would have been lost in any case, and the *Digest* did at least preserve quotations from the ablest Roman lawyers.

Curiously, although the *Corpus Juris* was never applied as actual law in the West, it had a far greater effect on western countries than it did on the East. In the East the emperors continued to revise the laws, treating Justinian's work not as a final summary of legal thinking but only as a foundation for their own efforts. In the West the *Corpus Juris* was regarded as the final and perfect expression of Roman law. For many generations the *Corpus Juris* was neglected in the West, but when the revival of medieval civilization began in the late eleventh century (see Chapter 10), Justinian's work seemed a treasure beyond price. It gave men who were struggling with primitive and confused notions of social relationships the precise concepts of a highly developed legal system. It had a tremendous impact on both the state and the Church, on both private and public institutions. The *Corpus Juris* became an essential part of the western intellectual tradition and affected the law of every western European country. Justinian's real reconquest of the West came many centuries after his death, not through his armies but through his law.

From Eastern Roman to Byzantine Empire

It is well to remember this ultimate triumph of Justinian, for the immediate results of his reign were disastrous. His successors ranged from mediocre to despicable, but even able emperors would have found it difficult to cope with the legacy of bankruptcy, internal discontent, and external enmity that Justinian had left. Repeated rebellions made it impossible to guard the frontiers. The western conquests were lost, while in the East the Persians again attacked the Asian provinces of the Empire. And a

Greek Fire, a mixture of quick-lime, petroleum, and sulphur that ignited when it came in contact with water, was introduced into the Byzantine navy after 675. It was a very effective weapon against the Arabs. (From a fourteenth-century manuscript.)

new danger arose in the North: the Avars, a nomad people akin to the Huns, pillaged the Balkan provinces and threatened Constantinople itself. The Slavs again assisted the invaders and occupied large areas of the Balkans.

Early in the seventh century the plight of the Eastern Empire seemed hopeless. The Persians had taken Syria and Egypt, and the Avars had set up permanent camps close to Constantinople. But the Eastern Empire clung to life with amazing tenacity and showed marvelous powers of recuperation. Beneath the appearance of luxury and decadence, behind the intrigues and the factional quarrels, was a very hard core of administrative competence, diplomatic skill, military capacity, and a passionate loyalty among the people of Constantinople to their state and their religion. In the seventh century, as it would again and again in the future, the Empire rallied and beat off its enemies.

Heraclius, who became emperor in 610, slowly worked out a policy of avoiding conflict with the Avars through bribes and diplomacy, while throwing the bulk of his army against the Persians. He had little success at first, but he finally ended the war with a raid deep into Persian territory that forced the Persians to make peace in 628.

The half-century of civil and foreign war that followed the death of Justinian wrought profound changes in the character of the Eastern Roman Empire. In the first place, the Latin element in the Empire, which had long been weakening, almost vanished. Early in his reign Justinian had used Latin for the *Corpus Juris,* but by the time of his death Greek was the only language that could be used for administrative and legal purposes. In the second place, religious dissent grew in Syria and Egypt, and the long period of Persian occupation and raiding did nothing to strengthen loyalty to Constantinople. The heart of the Empire was now the Greek-speaking, religiously orthodox region centering around Constantinople. The city itself supplied the wealth, the educated classes supplied the administrative personnel, and the poorer part of the population supplied the politico-religious fervor that kept the Empire going. Only one more thing was needed—an army—and the best recruiting ground for soldiers was Asia Minor. Therefore a successful emperor had to hold Constantinople and enough of Asia Minor to maintain his military strength.

If he could keep this core area, the Empire would stand virtually unbeatable. Heraclius seems to have had some understanding of this principle; at least he made little effort to hold the northern and western Balkans and postponed the reconquest of Syria until he had gained access to the old recruiting grounds in eastern Asia Minor.

But an empire based on Constantinople and Asia Minor was no longer a Roman Empire, even though the name continued in official use. To mark the change, most historians have called the continuation of the Roman Empire in the East the Byzantine Empire. This term, derived from the old Greek name for Constantinople (Byzantium), emphasizes the importance of the capital city and the Greek-speaking element in the Empire. It should not be used, therefore, for the sixth-century Empire, which was still Mediterranean in outlook and largely non-Greek in population. It becomes increasingly appropriate during the seventh century, however, when Syria, Egypt, and North Africa were lost, and when the Empire was restricted to the eastern Balkans, Asia Minor, and a few districts in Italy.

The Byzantine Empire gradually developed patterns of behavior and organization that made it very different from western Europe. In religion, for example, slight differences in creed, organization, and ritual between the Christians of the West and those of Constantinople were magnified by quarreling theologians, ambitious rulers, and subjects who feared everything foreign. The Roman Catholic Church and the Greek Orthodox Church slowly drifted apart, a divergence that encouraged divergences in other fields.

But religion alone does not account for all the profound differences between the Byzantine Empire and its neighbors. More than any other state, it preserved the cultural traditions of Greece and the political techniques of the old Roman Empire. Not that the Byzantine Empire was a stagnant society. It showed marvelous skill and flexibility in adapting itself to new conditions, and this is precisely why it was able to preserve so much of its heritage. The Byzantine Empire never had to make an entirely fresh start, for it was always able to modify and thus retain its old ideas and institutions. It always possessed a highly trained bureaucracy, skillful diplomats, and a professional army. Economic activity and church administration were manipulated for the benefit of the government. Art, literature, and scholarship were encouraged, so that there was no break in the Greek literary and artistic tradition.

In short, the Byzantine Empire stood forth as a highly centralized and autocratic state at a time when the very concept of the state had been almost forgotten in western Europe. This state had a great urban center, an active commercial life, and a sophisticated literary and artistic tradition in contrast to the agricultural and largely illiterate society of western Europe. Both Augustus and Louis XIV would have understood and sympathized with many of the ideas and practices of the Byzantine Empire, but few western Europeans between 700 and 1400 could fathom the Byzantine way of life.

The differences between the Byzantines and the Arabs, who conquered Syria, Egypt, Armenia, and Palestine in the seventh century, were not so great as those between Byzantines and western Europeans. The Arabs took over much of the administrative system and many of the intellectual traditions of the old Eastern Empire. But religious hostility hampered intellectual contacts, since the Arabs had accepted the new religion of Mohammed. Moreover, Arabic scholars were more interested in Aristotle and the Greek scientific tradition, while Byzantine scholars emphasized Plato and the Greek literary tradition. There were interesting similarities between the Arab Empire and the Byzantine Empire, but these similarities became less apparent when the Arab Empire broke up into warring and short-lived states. No Moslem state endured as long as Byzantium or created such a permanent bureaucracy. Thus the Byzantine Empire gradually became unique, and it soon began to glory in its uniqueness. The Greeks of Constantinople, like their remote ancestors of the fifth century B.C., believed that they were the only civilized

A Byzantine lady of rank, late fifth or early sixth century. Note her elegantly draped mantle and the snood-like bonnet of the imperial type.

Early Byzantine jewelry continued Hellenistic and Roman features. The clasp of this late sixth-century necklace, for example, is of a Hellenistic type, while the cylindrical slides between pendants represent a late Roman feature.

people and that their neighbors—especially their European neighbors—were barbarians. Caught between the barbarous West and the infidel East, the Byzantines clung with increasing tenacity to their government, their culture, and their religion.

MOHAMMED AND THE RISE OF THE ARAB EMPIRE

A few years after the death of Justinian in 565, a child was born in Arabia who was to found a religion that spread more rapidly than Christianity and an empire that was larger than that of Rome at the height of its power. Few men have had more impact on history than Mohammed. His religion split the old Mediterranean world and transformed the civilization of the Middle East; his influence is felt today in a broad belt of territory stretching from West Africa to the East Indies. Islam was the last of the three great world religions to emerge, and for many centuries it was more vigorous than either of its rivals—Christianity in the West and Buddhism in the East.

The Early Arabs

Arabia had played no important role in history before the time of Mohammed. The huge peninsula, about one-third the size of the United States, was like an arid wedge driven into the fertile lands of the Middle East. Most Arabs were nomads, driving their herds from one scanty patch of vegetation to another. A much smaller, but very influential, group was made up of traders who dealt in products from the southern part of the peninsula, notably frankincense, and in goods imported from India and the Far East. Overland trade through Arabia was not extensive, but there was enough to support a few small towns along the southern and western sides of the peninsula.

The early Arabs were thus in touch with all the civilizations of the East and had learned something from all of them. Semites themselves, they had been most influenced by the Semitic peoples who lived in the fertile crescent north of the peninsula. The Arabs had a system of writing related, at least indirectly, to the Phoenician alphabet. They had the usual Semitic interest in religion, though it was expressed in almost indiscriminate polytheism. They had hundreds of gods; they knew something of the Jewish and the Christian scriptures. They honored poets, and the ideal Arab leader was as ready to make verses as he was to make war. They knew a good deal about astronomy, for knowledge of the stars is as helpful in crossing the desert as it is in navigating the seas. At their best, the Arabs were imaginative and eager to absorb new knowledge. They were far more ready to profit from Greco-Roman civilization than the Germans were when they entered the Empire.

And yet there were grave defects in the social and political organization of the early Arabs. The nature of the country forced them to live in small, scattered tribes, and each tribe was almost constantly at war with its neighbors. The leading families within each tribe were often jealous of one another, so that blood-feuds were frequent and persistent. Weaker members of each tribe, and indeed of each family, were harshly treated by their stronger relatives. Sickly children were often killed, and orphans had little hope of receiving their parents' property. Women had almost no rights; their fathers or their husbands controlled their lives and their property. Men who could afford it had many wives and could divorce any of them whenever they wished. The divorced woman was usually left without any property or regular income.

In spite of all this disunity, certain strong ties bound the Arabs together. They were great genealogists; the leaders of many tribes could trace their ancestry back to the same ancient families—families that were known and respected throughout Arabia. Most of the tribes accepted a few common religious observances. There was a sacred period in each year, for example, when fighting was suspended and when many Arabs made a pilgrimage to the religious center of Mecca, a trading town near the west coast. In Mecca was the Kaaba, an ancient building full of images, including

The holy Kaaba in modern Mecca, the most sacred of Islamic shrines.

one of Christ. Here almost every god known to the Arabs could be worshiped. Here, too, was the sacred Black Stone that had come from heaven, the most venerated object in the Arab world. This habit of worshiping together at Mecca was the strongest unifying force in Arabia and one that was carefully preserved by Mohammed.

Mohammed's Teaching

Mohammed was born about 570 in Mecca. We know little about his early years, except that he was a poor orphan. When he reached adolescence he began to work for his cousin, a rich widow named Khadija. In her service he made many caravan trips, during which he may have accumulated his information about the Jewish and Christian religions and his knowledge of the legends and traditions of other Arab tribes. He eventually married his employer, though she was considerably older, and the marriage gave him the wealth and leisure to meditate on religious problems.

Like many other Arabs, Mohammed had a sensitive mind, a deep appreciation of the wonders of nature, and a strong interest in religion. These qualities were enhanced by mysterious seizures, to

An Early Revelation to Mohammed

By the brightness of the morning, and by the night when it groweth dark, thy Lord hath not forsaken thee, neither does he hate thee. Verily, the life to come shall be better for thee than this present life, and thy Lord shall give thee a reward wherewith thou shalt be well pleased. Did he not find thee an orphan, and hath he not sheltered thee? Did he not find thee in error and hath he not guided thee to the truth? And did he not find thee needy and hath he not enriched thee? Wherefore, oppress not the orphan nor repulse the beggar, but declare the goodness of thy Lord.

From *The Koran*, Ch. 93, trans. by G. Sale (Philadelphia: Lippincott, 1874).

which he had been subject since childhood. During these attacks he seemed to be struggling to express ideas that were not yet fully formed in his own mind. He gradually came to believe that this was God's way of trying to communicate with him, but until he was about forty he had no clear idea of what he was meant to do. Then he had his first revelation: a vision of the angel Gabriel, who commanded him to speak "in the name of the Lord, the Creator . . . the Lord who taught man what he did not know."

Mohammed was still doubtful about his mission, but as revelation succeeded revelation he became filled with the vision of the one, eternal God, the Lord of the world. He began to appeal to his fellow citizens of Mecca to abandon their host of false deities and to worship the one, true God. These early revelations bear some resemblance to the Psalms, both in their poetic quality and in their appeal to the wonders of nature as proofs of God's greatness and mercy. The stars in the heavens, sunshine and rain, the fruits of the earth—"all are signs of God's power if you would only understand."

By now Mohammed was convinced that he was a prophet, the last and greatest in the succession of prophets whom God had sent to enlighten and save mankind. He never claimed to be more than a prophet and even denied that he could work miracles, although he admitted that some of his predecessors had had this gift. He also admitted the divine mission

of the Jewish prophets and of Jesus, but he claimed that their teachings had been distorted or misinterpreted. He was quite certain that the revelations he received superseded everything that had come before. The earlier prophets had had glimpses of the true religion, but he alone had received the full message. Their teachings were to be accepted only when they agreed with the final word of God, which had been revealed to him.

Mohammed at first made little progress in converting his countrymen. His wife, Khadija, believed in him and comforted him when he was despondent, and his cousin Ali was one of his first converts. But most Meccans of good family were hostile; most of his early followers were poor men or slaves. Mohammed's attacks on idols angered those who believed that the prosperity of Mecca depended on its being the center of worship of all the known gods. Mohammed's followers were persecuted and his own life was threatened. Finally he fled with his supporters to the city of Yathrib, some distance north of Mecca. The Mohammedan era begins with this flight, or Hegira, which took place in 622 A.D.*

Mohammed was welcomed in Yathrib, which was renamed Medinet-en-Nabi (Medina), the City of the Prophet. Jewish influence was strong there, and the Arabs of Medina found nothing strange in the doctrine of a single, all-powerful God. Mohammed soon gained many converts among the pagan and half-Jewish Arabs and became virtually the ruler of the community. He now became involved in political problems, and the revelations he received during this period dealt largely with law and government. For example, it was at Medina that the rules about marriage, inheritance, and the punishment of criminals were laid down.

During the stay at Medina, Mohammed's reputation and power increased steadily. A desultory war between Medina and Mecca gradually became more serious, and by 630 Mohammed had gained so many supporters that he was

---

*This does not mean that dates of the Moslem era can be converted to our reckoning simply by adding 622 years. The Moslem year is based on a lunar calendar, and so does not coincide with ours. The year 1972 A.D. was 1392 A.H.

able to capture Mecca with little difficulty. He immediately destroyed the idols in the Kaaba, except for the Black Stone, and made the temple the center of his religion. He had long asserted that the Kaaba had been built by Abraham and that Abraham had placed the heavenly Stone there as a sign of God's power. Thus he was able to preserve Mecca as the religious center of Arabia.

The fall of Mecca convinced many Arabs that Mohammed really was a prophet or at least that he was too strong to oppose. During his last years, most of the tribes of the peninsula acknowledged his spiritual and political leadership. Nevertheless, when Mohammed died in 632 Arabia was far from being a unified state, and many Arabs had only vague ideas about the religion they had accepted.

The Koran

Mohammed, however, had left behind the Koran, a collection of his revelations. He had taught that the Koran was God's guide for the human race, that it had always existed in heaven, but that no one had been worthy of receiving it before his own appearance on earth. Although he had received the Koran piece by piece, as circumstances made its teachings applicable, it formed a consistent and coherent whole. It contained all that man needed to know, and it was to be followed without question. Mohammed said: "Let the Koran always be your guide. Do what it commands or permits; shun what it forbids."

From the very start of Mohammed's mission, his followers had carefully written down his revelations on parchment, palm leaves, or whatever else was available. The task of sorting out and arranging this mass of sayings was begun soon after Mohammed's death by Abu-Bekr, but his version was not universally accepted. Othman, who ruled the Arab Empire from 644 to 656, ended the disputes that arose by compiling an authoritative version and banning all other collections. Othman's version has remained almost unchanged down to the present.

In no other major religion was there such early agreement on the official version of the founder's teachings. In fact, the Koran was put together so hurriedly that it seems somewhat confused and illogical to a non-Moslem. The first revelation, in which Mohammed was ordered to begin his mission, comes in Chapter 96, after many of the long, prosaic Medina passages. Seemingly repetitious and even contradictory statements were never harmonized. But these faults are not admitted by orthodox Moslems, who consider the Koran a

Leaf from a manuscript of the Koran, Egypt, eighth or ninth century.

masterpiece of Arabic literature as well as the ultimate word of God to man.

The religion taught in the Koran was easy to understand and easy to follow. The basic creed was simple: "There is no God but Allah and Mohammed is his prophet." The faithful must also believe in the resurrection and the day of judgment, when every man will be rewarded according to his merits. The Mohammedan hell is very like the Christian one, but the Mohammedan paradise is unmistakably Arabian—a green garden full of running water and fruit trees with beautiful damsels to wait on the souls in bliss. Finally, the Koran emphasizes predestination: "Every man's fate have We bound around his neck"—that is, all human events have been determined, once and for all, by the will of God. Mohammed's own name for his religion was Islam—"submission to the will of God"—and his followers were called Moslems—"those who submit."

The principal religious practices of Islam were as simple as its theology. Every Moslem was to pray five times a day and to fast during the daylight hours of the month of Ramadan. Alms giving was a religious duty. Finally, every believer was to make a pilgrimage, if possible, to Mecca. But "only he shall visit the Mosque of God who believes in God and the Last Day, and is constant in prayer, and gives alms and fears God alone."

The Koran forbade wine drinking and gambling, and a dietary law, somewhat like that of the Jews, banned certain foods, especially pork. There was also a rudimentary code of law designed to check the selfishness and violence that had prevailed among the Arabs. Arbitration was to take the place of the blood-feud, infanticide was condemned, and elaborate rules of inheritance safeguarded the rights of orphans and widows. Mohammed also made an effort to improve the position of women by ruling that no man might have more than four wives. Divorce was still easy, but the divorced wife could no longer be sent away penniless. These and other provisions were enough to furnish a framework for a judicial system.

There were obvious resemblances between Islam and Christianity, espe-

cially between Islam and the Christian heresies that denied or minimized the divinity of Christ. Since Mohammed admitted that Jesus was a major prophet, many heretics could accept Islam without feeling that they had greatly changed their beliefs. Other unorthodox Christians in Asia and Africa were so angered by their persecution by the Greek Church that they turned to Islam as a lesser evil. And in the competition for the loyalty of groups with little knowledge of either religion, Islam had a great advantage. It needed no organized church, for it had neither a priesthood nor a sacramental system. Each individual had to assure his salvation by his own right belief and good conduct. Every essential act of the religion could be accomplished by a man living quite by himself. It was customary for the faithful to meet together for prayers, especially on Friday, and from the earliest period certain men devoted themselves to explaining the Koran. But none of this was essential; anyone could accept Islam without waiting for the organization of a religious community, and any believer could make converts without waiting for an ordained priest to come and validate his action. Simple and uncomplicated monotheism was easier to explain than the doctrine of the Trinity.

These advantages often gave Islam the victory in competition with Christianity. On several occasions in the Middle Ages the Moslems were able to move in and convert a pagan people while the Christians were still trying to recruit a troop of missionary priests. And even today Islam is spreading more rapidly among the peoples of Asia and Africa than is Christianity.

The Caliphate

Mohammed left no very clear instructions about how his successor should be chosen. At his death there was confusion in the ranks of his followers and rebellion on the part of recently converted tribes. The faithful finally decided to choose a caliph, or successor to the prophet, who would act as both spiritual and political leader of Islam. The first caliph was Abu-Bekr, one of the

An Islamic coin (698–99), the first silver coinage struck of purely Islamic type. The inscription in the center of the coin is: "There is no God but God alone; no one is associated with him." The insistence on God's oneness and the lack of an associate to him is directed against the Christians and their doctrine of the Trinity.

Islamic door with ivory panel, eighth century.

earliest and most pious of Mohammed's converts. Though he ruled only two years (632–34), he succeeded in suppressing the revolts and in completing the unification of Arabia. Under his successor, Omar (634–44), the great conquests began. The Arabs had long been in the habit of raiding their wealthier neighbors to the north. Now they found themselves united for the first time, while both the Byzantine and the Persian states had been weakened by disastrous wars. In their first probing attacks, the Arabs met such slight resistance that they soon turned to wars of conquest. Their defeat of a Byzantine army at the Yarmuk River in 636 determined the fate of all the eastern provinces. Some fortified towns held out for a few years, but by 649 the Arabs had conquered Syria, Armenia, Palestine, and Egypt. Persia gave even less trouble and was completely in Arab hands by 642. Only the outbreak of civil war in Arabia slowed this first wave of conquest.

The civil war was caused by bad feeling between the early converts and some

of the leading Arab families who had accepted Islam only after Mohammed's triumph was assured. The trouble began under the caliph Othman (644–56), who was an early convert himself but who was not so fanatically opposed to the latecomers as were some of the prophet's other companions. He was accused of favoring recent converts and of pushing forward his kinsmen, the Ommiads, who had at one time led the Meccan opposition to Mohammed. The accusation was largely true, but it is hard to see what else Othman could have done. He now had an empire to govern, and he needed the help of every man who displayed qualities of leadership, whatever his past religious behavior had been.

Quarrels between the two factions led to the assassination of Othman in 656. He was succeeded by an old believer, Ali, the son-in-law and adopted son of Mohammed. But since Ali was suspected of complicity in Othman's murder, the Ommiads soon revolted and secured the nomination of one of their family as caliph. Ali held Persia and Mesopotamia for a while but was assassinated in 661 by a member of a small, fanatical sect that believed the office of caliph was unnecessary. After Ali's death the Ommiad caliph, who had taken no part in the assassination, was accepted as ruler by the entire Moslem world.

The Ommiad Dynasty

The first Ommiad caliph transferred the capital of the Arab Empire from Mecca to Damascus. This act was typical of the family, which put far more emphasis on politics than on religion. Damascus was not the prophet's city, but it had public buildings, a large group of educated and experienced civil servants, and a central location. It was far more satisfactory as a capital than Mecca, and it had the additional advantage of containing few of the prophet's early companions. The Ommiads bestowed key positions on members of the Arab aristocracy rather than on the early converts, and they filled the government bureaus with Christian Syrians and Egyptians. Thus the Arab Empire began to change from a loosely organized theocracy into a centralized state employing many Byzantine administrative techniques. Finally, the office of caliph ceased to be elective and was made hereditary in the Ommiad family.

The policy of the Ommiads toward conquered peoples was also based on purely political considerations. The Arabs had never paid taxes, and they had no intention of doing so now that they were lords of a large part of the civilized world. The government was financed by tribute exacted from unbelievers, which meant that mass conversions would be a threat to its financial stability. So, instead of forcing Islam on their subjects, the Ommiad caliphs discouraged conversion. New converts had to pay a heavy land tax from which Arabs were exempt, and they were seldom given responsible positions in the government.

This policy caused little trouble in Syria, where the Arab aristocracy was satisfied with its special privileges and where Christians were numerous. But in both Persia and Mesopotamia, where Ommiad control was less secure, most of the population became converted to Islam. The new converts resented their inferior position and often revolted against the rule of Ommiad officials. They were encouraged in their resistance by the more pious Arabs, who felt that the Ommiads were far too worldly, and by survivors of the faction that had supported Ali.

In spite of hidden weaknesses in their state, the Ommiad caliphs profited more from the late Roman civilization they had taken over than did the Germanic kings of the West. Syria, the heart of the Ommiad state, had always been more advanced intellectually and economically than Gaul, the heart of the strongest Germanic kingdom. The Ommiads began to draw on their heritage from the older civilization almost as soon as they gained power. They organized their administrative services on Roman and Persian models. They welcomed scholars of all nationalities to their court and urged them to undertake the task of translating philosophical, scientific, and medical works into Arabic. They built impressive mosques at Damascus and Jerusalem, adapting Syrian architecture to the needs of the Mohammedan religion. A new civilization began to grow up around the Ommiad court, a civilization based on Greek, Syrian, Egyptian, and Persian traditions and yet with a style and a spirit of its own. This new civilization reached its peak only after the Ommiads had lost the throne and the capital had been moved from Damascus to Baghdad. Much of the work of the Ommiads was either absorbed in or surpassed by the accomplishments of their successors. But the Ommiads laid the foundations, and they did so at a time when western kings had almost no administrative services, when western scholars had almost no books but compendia and epitomes, and when western architects showed almost no skill in designing large buildings.

New Conquests

The stability and prosperity assured by the early Ommiads soon made it possible for the Arabs to undertake further conquests. In the East the Ommiads took Khiva, Bokhara, and Samarkand, thus gaining control of one of the oldest and most important trade routes in Eurasia—the silk road from China. These conquests in turn opened the way to the occupation of Afghanistan and the valley of the Indus. The strong Moslem position on the northwest frontier was a permanent threat to India, as the invasions of the next thousand years were to demonstrate.

In the West the Arabs advanced steadily along the southern shore of the Mediterranean. North Africa was their first objective, and here, as often before, the invaders profited from the fact that the native population hated Byzantine government. Justinian's reconquest of the Vandal kingdom had been followed by heavy taxation and persecution of heretics. Many of the Romanized Africans had fled the country; the Berbers, who remained, were neither Romanized nor obedient to the orders of Byzantine officials. When the Arab attack came, both the Roman cities and the Berber countryside resisted bravely, but there was little cooperation between them. The Arabs quickly defeated their divided enemies, taking Carthage in 697 and winning control of the entire North African coast by 708.

Although the Berbers had fought fiercely to preserve their independence, they felt no particular antipathy to Islam. Many of them became converts and joined the victorious army in the hope of sharing in the spoils of the next conquest. This addition to their strength enabled the Arabs to pass over into Spain. The Visigothic rulers of Spain had been weakened by internal quarrels and had little control over their powerful nobles. A single victory in 711 was enough to open the whole country to Tarik, who commanded the invading

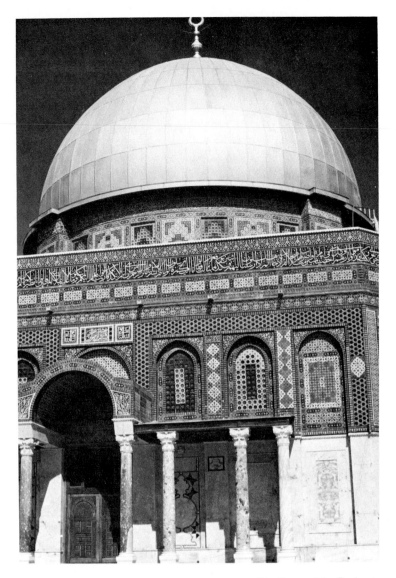

The Dome of the Rock, at Jerusalem. This mosque was built on the spot from which Mohammed was believed to have ascended to heaven. The Wailing Wall, sacred to Jews, is back of the mosque. That juxtaposition has caused many quarrels between Jews and Moslems.

forces, and from whom Gibraltar takes its name.* The largest part of his army was probably composed of recently converted Berbers, and now many Visigothic nobles joined the victors—an illustration of the Arabs' ability to gain the cooperation of conquered peoples in a remarkably short time. Only the support of thousands of non-Arabs made possible Islam's rapid conquests.

The Moslem army quickly overran the entire Iberian Peninsula except for the extreme northwest, where a few Christians maintained their independence. The Moslems then pushed on across the Pyrenees into the Frankish

*Gebel Tarik—Tarik's hill.

kingdom, which was not quite so helpless as Spain. The Franks could not defend the south, but when the raiders pushed north the Frankish leader, Charles Martel, assembled an effective army that checked the invasion. Charles' victory at Poitiers in 732 was not very decisive, for the Moslems withdrew in good order and held towns in southern Gaul for another thirty years. But they made no more raids on the north.

During the early years of the eighth century the Ommiads reached the height of their power. They had created the largest Moslem state that ever existed, and in less than a hundred years they had built an empire larger than that of Rome. But they had reached their limit; their setback at Poitiers in 732 had its counterpart in an earlier failure to take Constantinople in a great siege in 716–17. Although the Byzantine Empire had lost almost all of its outlying provinces, it had preserved the most important part of its territories. Like the Frankish kingdom, Byzantium grew stronger after the early eighth century, and the Moslems were long unable to make any headway against these two bulwarks of Europe.

The Rise of the Abbasids

The Ommiad state had also begun to weaken internally. It was difficult to rule a vast empire that stretched from Spain to India and that embraced dozens of different peoples. Moreover, many Moslems continued to distrust and oppose the Ommiads. There was still a party that honored the memory of Ali and considered the Ommiads usurpers; there were also puritanical Moslems who loathed Ommiad luxury and worldliness; and there were recent converts, especially in Mesopotamia and Persia, who resented the domination of the Arab aristocracy.

All these groups were united by Abu'l Abbas, who was to found the Abbasid dynasty. By claiming one of Mohammed's uncles as an ancestor, he satisfied most of the legitimists; by making himself appear more devout than the Ommiads, he gained the support of most of the inhabitants of Mesopotamia and Persia. By 750 Abu'l Abbas was strong enough to risk rebellion. He decisively defeated the Ommiad caliph and almost

exterminated the family. One Ommiad escaped to Spain, where he founded an independent state in 756, but the rest of the Moslem world accepted Abu'l Abbas as caliph.

Since the Abbasid caliph's primary strength was in Mesopotamia and Persia, he moved his capital to Baghdad, a new city built on the banks of the Tigris. This move symbolized a turning point in the history of civilization. The old unity of the Mediterranean world, shaken by earlier events, was now forever destroyed. The Ommiad caliphs at Damascus had drawn heavily on Greco-Roman civilization, but the Abbasids at Baghdad were increasingly influenced by the ancient traditions of Mesopotamia and Persia. The Moslem world on the southern and eastern shores of the Mediterranean became more and more unlike the Christian world on the northern shores. At the same time, Moslem pressure was forcing Byzantium in on itself and accentuating the peculiarities of the Byzantine way of life.

A citizen of the Roman Empire had been equally at home in Rome and Constantinople, in Alexandria and Antioch. Now these centers of civilization were drifting apart and becoming more and more strange to one another. By the tenth century a westerner, merely by crossing the Mediterranean, entered a completely different world. Egypt was as strange as China, and even Christian Byzantium seemed remote and Oriental.

Thus the world of the Romans had broken into three fragments of unequal size and wealth. The largest and richest area was held by the Moslems, who also controlled the key trade routes to India and China and all but one of the great cities of the Middle East. Next came the Byzantine Empire, anchored on impregnable Constantinople, rich from its own industry and from the trade that flowed through its lands to the West. Far behind was western Europe, poverty-stricken and ill-governed, no match for the great civilizations centered in Constantinople and Baghdad. For centuries western Europe had depended on the East in trade and industry, in art and religion. It remained to be seen what the Europeans could do now that they were on their own.

Suggestions for Further Reading

Note: Asterisk denotes a book available in paperback edition.

The Age of Justinian P. N. Ure, *Justinian and His Age** (1951), is lively reading. The contemporary accounts by Procopius, *History of the Wars,* trans. by H. B. Dewing (1935) and *Secret History,** trans. by G. A. Williamson (1969), are also lively, but not entirely trustworthy. For this and the next section, A. H. M. Jones, *The Late Roman Empire,* 3 vols. (1964), is extremely valuable.

Byzantium A wealth of literature is available on the life and thought of Byzantine civilization. P. N. Ure, *Justinian and His Age** (1951), which discusses many facets of Byzantine history and civilization, is a good starting point. S. Runciman, *Byzantine Civilization** (1933), combines deep knowledge of the subject with a superb prose style in a very sympathetic treatment. The old theory that the Byzantine Empire was perpetually moribund is severely attacked in N. H. Baynes, *The Byzantine Empire* (1926), which stresses the vitality of the Empire's history. N. H. Baynes and H. L. B. Moss, *Byzantium** (1948), is a collection of essays on Byzantine history and culture written by leading scholars in the field. The most thorough and scholarly treatment of Byzantine history is G. Ostrogorsky, *History of the Byzantine State,* trans. by J. M. Hussey (1956). The older work of A. A. Vasiliev, *History of the Byzantine Empire,* 2 vols. (1928), is more readable than Ostrogorsky but lacks recent bibliographic material. Two works by the French scholar C. Diehl, *History of the Byzantine Empire* (1901) and *Byzantium: Greatness and Decline** (1957), are valuable for the facts but are considerably dated in historical interpretation.

The beauty of Byzantine art has fascinated many who have come in contact with it. C. R. Morey, *Early Christian Art* (1942), which has good plates, describes the influence of Byzantine iconography on western art in the early Middle Ages. But for the magnificence of its reproductions and the general excellence of its text, no survey of Byzantine art can compare with the fine Skira edition, *Byzantine Painting,* ed. by A. Grabar (1953). The brief study of D. T. Rice, *Byzantine Art** (1935), is worthwhile and perhaps more accessible.

Islam The best introduction to the world of Islam is the Koran,* of which there are many translations. Perhaps the best is that of G. Lamsa, *The Koran* (1949). H. A. R. Gibb, *Mohammedanism** (1949), is a good historical survey of the Moslem religion, while B. Lewis, *The Arabs in History** (1950), emphasizes the political and social aspects of Moslem history. Both books have good critical bibliographies. The foremost American historian of Islam, P. K. Hitti, has written a number of fine studies. His *The Arabs** (many editions) is a scholarly treatment of the rise and spread of Mohammedanism; his translation of *The Origins of the Islamic State* (1916) traces the growth of Islam and is excellent for an understanding of the Moslem world-view. The now classic study by H. Pirenne, *Mohammed and Charlemagne** (1936), advances a significant theory about the impact of Islam on western Europe in the early Middle Ages. H. A. R. Gibb and H. Bowen, *Islamic Society and the West,* 2 vols. (1950), explores the impact of the West on Islam in later times. G. von Grunebaum, *Medieval Islam** (1946), traces the temper and flavor of the Moslem Middle Ages and gives a fine account of the Moslem influence on western Europe in the Middle Ages. Both R. P. A. Dozy, *Spanish Islam* (1913), and S. Lane-Poole, *The Story of the Moors in Spain* (1886), give exciting accounts of the Arabs in Spain. Washington Irving's *The Alhambra** gives a vivid and unforgettable picture of Moslem culture in Spain. There is interesting material on the Ommiads in W. Muir, *The Caliphate: Its Rise, Decline and Fall* (1915), and in T. W. Arnold, *The Caliphate* (1912), but neither is so thorough in historical interpretation as is the research of Hitti. D. S. Richards, *Islam and the Trade of Asia* (1971), shows the shift in interest toward the East under the Abbasids.

H. A. R. Gibb, *Arabic Literature* (1926), is a brief survey of Arabic literature with an appendix of Arabic works in English and other modern languages. T. W. Arnold, *Painting in Islam** (1928), is a readable study of the place of art in Moslem culture, with very good reproductions. T. W. Arnold and A. Guillaume, *The Legacy of Islam* (1931), an account of the elements in European culture which are derived from the Islamic world, is the best one-volume study of Moslem culture and thought.

9 The Emergence of a Western European Civilization

Not all contacts were lost when the Mediterranean world broke into three distinct cultural units—a German-Latin bloc in the West, a Greek-Slavic bloc in the East, and an Arab-Syrian-Persian bloc in the South. Merchants still traveled back and forth across the Mediterranean; ideas and artistic techniques passed from the Byzantine Empire and the Moslem Caliphate to Italy, France, and Germany. And yet contacts among the West, the East, and the South of the Mediterranean world were less frequent and less intimate than they once had been. This was due in part to the endless wars between Byzantium and Islam, which discouraged Mediterranean commerce. It was due even more to the poverty and backwardness of western Europe, whose stocks of precious metals had been seriously depleted, making it difficult for westerners to purchase eastern goods. The western commodities most useful to the Greeks and Arabs were timber, iron, and slaves—all of which could be considered contraband of war in times of conflict. As a result, the West could not earn enough foreign exchange to trade extensively with either Byzantines or Arabs. Nor did the West have adequate intellectual capital for a rewarding exchange of ideas with Greek or Arab scholars. There were relatively few educated men in western Europe, and most of them were painfully at work trying to understand the writings of the Latin Church Fathers and fragments of the Latin classics. Until the West had fully assimilated its Latin heritage, it was to have little interest in the learning of the East.

Thus the people of western Europe were more dependent on their own resources than they had been for centuries. They had to create their own civilization. Several favorable factors allowed them to do so. Although western Europe seemed poor and backward in comparison with the East, it actually possessed great potential for growth. It had plenty of good agricultural land and virtually untouched resources of raw materials. Trade in the Mediterranean had fallen off, but trade in the northern seas was flourishing. The Scandinavians, who traded with the western kingdoms, were also beginning to import eastern goods through the Russian river system. The Church had preserved the rudiments of an educational system and some ideas about political and social organization. Finally, the new line of Frankish rulers that had emerged in the eighth century brought political stability and laid the foundations for a new civilization.

KING PIPPIN
AND THE CHURCH

This new line of rulers descended from Pippin and Charles Martel, the mayors of the palace who had put an end to the disorders of the seventh century. These men had been content with the title of mayor, but the son of Charles Martel, another Pippin, decided in 751 to seek the kingship itself. He won over most of the nobles, and to overcome the scruples of those who were still attached to the old dynasty Pippin asked the pope for an opinion on the legitimacy of his bid. Pope Zacharias declared that the man who bore the responsibilities of the king deserved the title; his successor actually journeyed to France and anointed Pippin in the manner in which the Old Testament kings had been anointed. This was probably the first use of this ritual in the West, and it is hard for us to realize the impression it must have made on public opinion. As God's anointed, Pippin became a semisacred personage, far above all ordinary lay dignitaries. It was God's will that he and his family should rule the Franks.

Charlemagne presents a model of his church at Aix-la-Chapelle to the Virgin. Scene from a panel of the shrine at Aix.

An Iconoclast whitewashing an image in a Byzantine church (from a ninth-century psalter). In 730 Leo III issued an edict forbidding the veneration of images. For a hundred years thereafter, icons, mosaics, and frescoes in churches were destroyed or whitewashed.

These acts of the papacy had serious consequences for future European kings. The pope had not initiated the change of dynasty, but the very fact that he had been consulted enabled later pontiffs to claim that Zacharias had deposed an unworthy king and had chosen a suitable successor. Therefore the Church could remove other unworthy rulers. Equally significant was Pippin's consecration, for it was soon believed that a king did not enjoy full authority until he had been anointed by the Church. It could then be claimed that church officials were superior to lay rulers, since no layman could consecrate a bishop but a bishop could consecrate a king. The obvious conclusion was that royal power, in some fashion, was dependent on the sanction of the Church.

The Alliance of the Papacy with the Franks

Probably none of this had been foreseen by either Pippin or Zacharias. Their cooperation was based on the realization that each could gain some practical advantage by supporting the other. The pope, who received little support from the Byzantine emperor, was constantly harassed in Italy by Lombard attacks. He was also distressed by the condition of the Church in the Frankish realm. Many of the Frankish clergy were ill educated and corrupt, and the Church had little influence on a large part of the population. A strong Frankish king might be willing to protect the pope against the Lombards and aid in the administrative and moral reform of the Church.

As for Pippin, he had inherited a family tradition of cooperating with the Church. One of his ancestors had been a bishop and a saint, and his father, Charles Martel, had had the support of the Church in his struggle with the Frankish aristocracy. In return, Charles had supported the work of missionaries and reformers in the Frankish kingdoms. The family was undoubtedly pious, but it also had political reasons for aiding church reform. Educated and reformed bishops were likely to support strong government and resist aristocratic factionalism, and they would make useful advisers and administrative agents for the king. Moreover, a reformed Church that emphasized the principles of Christian morality could assist the king in his task of preserving public order.

The alliance between Pippin and the pope changed the political fate of western Europe. First, and perhaps most important of all, it removed Italy from the Byzantine sphere of influence and attached it to the Germanic North. The popes had long found the Byzantine emperors unsatisfactory suzerains. It was bad enough when they failed to push back the Lombards; it was even worse when they stirred up an unnecessary theological controversy by forbidding images of sacred personages in churches. It is true that eastern Christians had begun to pay extravagant respect to sacred images and that certain monasteries had gained enormous political influence by possessing images that were especially revered. But excessive devotion to images had not been particularly troublesome in the West, and the popes felt that the drastic remedy of iconoclasm (the destruction of images) was unnecessary. The largely illiterate western population needed images as illustrations of Christian doctrine, and the popes had no intention of abandoning them.

Dislike of iconoclasm, combined with concern over the Lombard threat, prompted the pope to look to the Franks for support. Charles Martel had refused to intervene in Italy, but Pippin was more willing to aid the papacy. In 753 he invaded Italy and forced the Lombards to withdraw from the environs of Rome. The campaign closed with two significant acts: Pippin gave Pope Stephen II a large strip of territory in central Italy which had formerly been held by the Byzantine Empire. The pope gave Pippin the title of *patricius Romanorum,* which had formerly been held by the chief Byzantine representative in Italy.

To ignore Byzantium's centuries-old claim to Italy was a bold act. It needed justification, which may be why an unknown churchman (probably a Frank) forged the famous *Donation of Constantine* at about this time. According to the forger, Constantine, as an act of gratitude after his conversion, had given all Italy and the western part of the Empire to the pope. After withdrawing to the East, the emperor was supposed to have left the pope as the supreme authority in the West. This was a clumsy falsehood, but no one disproved its authenticity for 700 years. Meanwhile it supported papal claims to lordship over a large part of central Italy and vaguer rights of intervention in the political affairs in the West.

North of the Alps, Pippin and the pope helped each other to gain control over peoples who were only nominally their subjects. Pippin had little authority in such outlying districts as Bavaria and Aquitaine; the backing of the Church aided him in gaining some measure of obedience from the rulers of these provinces. The Church had little influence over the people of Gaul and Germany; Pippin gave full support to the work of one of the greatest missionaries and organizers the Church has ever known, an Anglo-Saxon monk named Boniface.

St. Boniface

Boniface came to Frankland as a young man hoping to convert the still-heathen Germans of Frisia and Saxony. He soon realized that an even graver problem was posed by the state of Christianity among the Frankish people, many of whom were called Christians only because they had no other faith. They seldom saw an orthodox priest, and the visits of wandering Irish monks did little to strengthen their belief. Boniface realized that thorough reform and reorganization of the Frankish Church were essential, and he spent most of his life at this task. In 748 he was made archbishop with full powers over the German clergy. He used this authority to create the basic structure of the German church. In Gaul he summoned local councils to improve the morality of Frankish churchmen and to make them more obedient to the pope. As the years passed, the Church north of the Alps became an effective force in the lives of the people, and its increased centralization and improved administration gave the Church strength enough to influence the ruling classes. At the end of his life Boniface returned to missionary work and found the martyrdom he had long desired. He was killed by heathen Frisians in 754.

The Donation of Constantine

Constantine tells how Pope Sylvester I cured him of leprosy. In gratitude Constantine accepts baptism and decrees

that the sacred see of blessed Peter shall be gloriously exalted above our empire and earthly throne. . . . And the pontiff who presides over the most holy Roman Church shall be the highest and chief of all priests . . . and according to his decision shall all matters be settled . . . for the worship of God or the confirmation of the faith.

We convey to the most blessed pontiff, our father Silvester, universal pope, both our palace [the Lateran] and likewise all provinces, places and districts of the City of Rome and Italy and of the regions of the West, . . . bequeathing them to the power and sway of him and his successors.

Wherefore we have perceived that our empire and the power of our government should be transferred to the regions of the East . . . for it is not right that an earthly emperor should have authority . . . where the head of the Christian religion has been established by the Emperor of heaven.

From the Donation of Constantine, as quoted in *Select Documents of European History,* ed. by R. G. D. Laffan (London: Methuen, 1930), Vol. I, pp. 4–5.

The Establishment of Parishes and Tithes

Boniface's work was made more effective by the development of rural parishes in the Frankish kingdom—a development that had begun earlier but that received its greatest impetus from the descendants of Charles Martel. So long as churches existed only in the cities, as they did at first, country-dwellers found it impossible to maintain regular contact with the clergy and hence Christianity had little influence on them. A rural parish with a resident priest was the obvious solution to this problem, but priests were not likely to stay resident until their churches had an adequate income. North of the Alps the landlords and counts were the only men wealthy enough to build and endow rural churches. They began to do so on a large scale only in the eighth century, prompted by Boniface's reforms and by the example and persuasion of the ruling family.

The ultimate step in giving parish churches an adequate income was taken when Pippin's son Charles made tithing compulsory. The clergy had long taught that the faithful should give 10 percent of their income to the Church, but they had permitted tithing to remain a purely voluntary act. By ruling that all Christians had to pay the tithe, the king assured the Church sufficient income to support an extensive network of rural parishes. Not all tithes went to parish priests; in fact, their share tended to diminish as time went on. Nevertheless, they always received enough so that the rural churches could function.

These were revolutionary changes. For the first time the ordinary inhabitant of the Frankish realm was in regular and frequent contact with Christian priests. The rapid growth of the parish system gave the Church more opportunities to impress Christian doctrine and morality on the people. There had always been sincere believers, but in the Merovingian period many men had acted as if Christianity were only a superior form of magic. Although they venerated relics that were alleged to bring good luck, they had no strong convictions about either faith or morals. Now Christianity began to be a

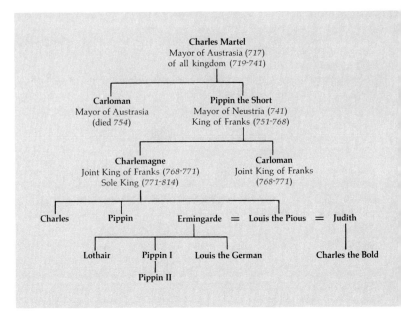

The Carolingian family tree.

matter of internal concern rather than one of exterior behavior. The eighth century is the first period in which one can be sure that all western Europe was hearing and beginning to understand the Christian message.

This improvement in the position of the Church had begun before Pippin's time and continued under his descendants. But Pippin's reign was the crucial period. He accelerated the pace of the reform movement, and he made the binding alliance with the papacy that ensured the cooperation of religious and secular authorities in building a new civilization. Pippin's work was overshadowed by that of his son Charles, but Charles built on the solid foundation left by his father.

CHARLEMAGNE

Pippin died in 768 and was succeeded by his two sons, Charles and Carloman. Fate saved the Franks from the dangerous consequences of divided authority, however, for Carloman died after three years and Charles assumed sole control of the government.

Charles' reign was so successful that even in his own lifetime he was known as Charlemagne, or Charles the Great. To his contemporaries he was great first and foremost because he was a persistent and victorious warrior. He solved the Lombard problem by defeating the Lombard king and annexing the Lombard lands in northern and central Italy. He eased the Moslem threat by crossing the Pyrenees and annexing a small strip of Spanish territory to the Frankish kingdom. When the nomadic Avars, who had established themselves on the middle Danube, became troublesome, he almost annihilated them in a single campaign. His longest and hardest war was with the Saxons of northeastern Germany, the last large group of German heathens. The Saxons resisted Frankish domination and Christianity with equal bitterness, and only after thirty years did Charlemagne finally manage to conquer and convert them.

Charlemagne's Educational Reforms

Charlemagne was more than a successful general, as many of his contemporaries realized. He wanted a strong kingdom, but he also wanted it to be a Christian kingdom, and his efforts to make it so left an indelible impression on western civilization. Even more than his father, Charlemagne realized that an uneducated clergy was an unorganized and uninfluential clergy. Both by decree and by his own example he tried to raise the level of learning in the Frankish realm. He imported scholars from every country of western Europe and either kept them with him in his Palace Academy or gave them high positions in the Frankish Church. The most famous of these scholars was the Anglo-Saxon Alcuin, abbot of St. Martin's of Tours, but there were also Franks, Lombards, and even Saxons among them.

The work of these scholars was not very original or imaginative, but originality and imagination were not the chief needs of the eighth century. What was needed were men who could preserve and assimilate the intellectual heritage left by Rome and the early Church. Even preservation was no easy task, for much of Latin literature had already been lost and there were few copies of the works that had survived. The Scriptures and the works of the Church Fathers were in less danger of being lost, but Charlemagne complained that copies of the Bible were full of serious errors. By encouraging the making of new and accurate copies of ancient texts, Charlemagne saved many classical works from oblivion; we have few manuscripts of Latin authors from before his time. The acceleration of manuscript production in turn led to a reform in handwriting, a reform in which Alcuin and his monastery at Tours played a leading role. The scribes of Tours developed a beautiful, clear script that was a notable improvement on earlier handwriting. The Romans had used only capital letters, which were hard to read when they filled a solid line, especially since the Romans did not separate words. Later writers separated words and developed small letters, but the letters were badly shaped and easily confused. It was the Carolingians who gave small letters almost the form they have today.

Charlemagne's educational revival gave Europe a common cultural tradition. As we have seen, scholars of all nations mingled at the Frankish court and

The elegant Carolingian handwriting was characterized by small letters and bold, rounded design. It is the basis of modern type. (Detail from a ninth-century manuscript.)

in patria pax inuiolata inregno. & dignitaf gloriofa regalif palatii-maxi mo fplendore regiae poteftatif- oculif omnium luce clariffima corufcare atqp fplendefcere · qua fplendidiffi mi fulgorif maximo pfufa lumine worked with the same materials—the Bible, the Church Fathers, the encyclopedias of the Late Empire, and some of the Latin classics. When they became bishops or abbots, they carried this common stock of learning to various regions and taught it to their own students. All students used Latin, whatever their native tongue, so there was no problem of translation. Thus scholars everywhere were reading the same books and commenting on them in the same language, and western Europe developed a common stock of ideas and a common vocabulary in which to express them. If western Europe has any unity at all today, that unity lies in its ideas, in its way of looking at the world, and for this unity it owes much to the work of Charles the Great.

CHARLEMAGNE'S CONQUESTS AND EMPIRE 814

Revival of the Empire in the West

By wiping out the Lombard kingdom, Charlemagne had made himself directly responsible for the security of the pope and the government of Rome. He also felt it his personal duty to make Christianity a more effective force in his kingdom. His laws dealt as often with ecclesiastical matters as with secular affairs. He laid down rules of proper conduct for monks and priests; he ordered schools to be established for the training of the clergy; he intervened in theological disputes; and, as we have seen, he gave the Church a solid financial basis by making the payment of tithes compulsory. He was the head of a Christian people, and he expected clergy as well as laity to follow his leadership.

This close relationship between king and Church reached its climax in the year 800. Pope Leo III, driven from Rome by his enemies in the city, had appealed to Charlemagne for aid. Charlemagne reinstated the pope and stayed on in Rome to make sure there would be no further trouble. On Christmas Day, 800, the pope placed the imperial crown on Charlemagne's head and hailed him as Augustus. The West once more had an emperor.

In one sense, the coronation merely symbolized existing facts. As ruler of France, Germany, and most of Italy, Charlemagne already had more power than the last western Roman emperors. The emperor had been the traditional protector of the Church, and Charles was clearly performing this function. There seems to be no doubt that Charlemagne wanted to be emperor, for the pope was in no position to impose undesired titles on his powerful protector.

Nevertheless, a man who knew Charlemagne well said that the king grumbled that he never would have gone to church that Christmas Day had he known what the pope had in mind. If the report has any substance it may reflect Charlemagne's misgivings about receiving his title from the pope, misgivings that proved well founded. Later popes claimed that Leo III, by his own authority, had transferred imperial power from the Greeks to the Franks, and that Charlemagne's coronation was one more proof of the superiority of ecclesiastical rulers over secular rulers. But whatever his doubts, Charlemagne accepted the situation. He referred to himself as emperor in public documents, and, before his death, he was careful to see that his son was crowned emperor. The pope took no part in this coronation, which suggests again that Charlemagne did not want to admit that the pope could make an emperor.

Charlemagne's Government

The essential unit of government under Charlemagne, as under his Merovingian predecessors, was the county. Each county was headed by a count, who was almost always a member of a noble and wealthy family. The count had to share his power with various subordinates; he had to respect the position of the other noble families of his county and of the neighboring bishops and abbots. Nevertheless, an energetic count could build up a strong position in his county. He presided over the local courts and kept a third of the fines that were collected there. He led the freemen of his district to war; he collected tolls; he built and garrisoned forts. Clearly, the king's chief problem was to keep his counts under control.

Charlemagne tried to meet this problem by two devices. First, in order to keep the counts from abusing their judicial power, he created independent groups of local judges to decide cases. Second, he sent out royal envoys—called *missi dominici*—to see that the counts obeyed his orders and observed reasonable standards of justice and honesty. The *missi* were chosen from men of the highest standing at court and had the full support of the emperor. Their admonitions and reports helped immeasurably to improve the conduct of local govern-

Ninth-century statue of Charlemagne on horseback. He wears a crown and carries an orb, symbol of royal power.

ment. Nevertheless, even the *missi* did not give the emperor full control over his counts. Abuses of power continued, and there were cases of flat disobedience to Charlemagne's orders.

The Coronation of Charlemagne

Now when the king upon the most holy day of the Lord's birth was rising to the mass after praying before the tomb of the blessed Peter the Apostle, Leo the Pope, with the consent of all the bishops and priests and of the senate of the Franks and likewise of the Romans, set a golden crown upon his head, the Roman people also shouting aloud. And when the people had made an end of chanting praises, he was adored by the pope after the manner of the emperors of old. For this was also done by the will of God. For while the said Emperor abode at Rome certain men were brought to him who said that the name of Emperor had ceased among the Greeks, and that there the Empire was held by a woman called Irene, who had by guile laid hold on her son the Emperor and put out his eyes and taken the Empire to herself. . . . Which when Leo the Pope and all the assembly of the bishops and priests and abbots heard, and the senate of the Franks and all the elders of the Romans, they took counsel with the rest of the Christian people, that they should name Charles king of the Franks to be Emperor, seeing that he held Rome the mother of empire where the Caesars and Emperors always used to sit.

From *Chronicle of Moissac*, trans. by J. Bryce, *The Holy Roman Empire* (New York: Macmillan and St. Martin's Press, 1911), p. 54.

Gold coin bearing the likeness of Irene, empress in Constantinople when Charlemagne was crowned (797–802). She was the first woman to assume sole rule over the Empire (and she took the title of Emperor, not Empress). Her rule provided the pope with an excuse to crown Charlemagne to fill the allegedly vacant throne.

one capitulary contained rules for the education of the clergy, and another regulations about the powers and behavior of the counts. Charlemagne seldom attempted to make law, since he, like most men of his time, believed that law consisted of eternal and unchanging principles. Nevertheless, some capitularies interpreted, and thus changed, the law. And by laying down rules that were applicable to all subjects, Charlemagne did a good deal to wipe out earlier distinctions between Roman and German, or Frank and Burgundian. There was never complete uniformity of law among his subjects, but the differences that remained were regional rather than racial and were never so great that regions with differing laws could not cooperate.

Charlemagne, working against great obstacles, had united the West and given it common ideals and common institutions. But he had succeeded only because he was a man of boundless energy, unusual perseverance, and strong person-

The central government was not well enough organized to direct and coordinate the work of local authorities. The secretarial staff was very small—barely able to handle correspondence and keep records. It is worth noting that under Charlemagne these men were all members of the clergy,* whereas the Merovingians had had no difficulty in finding laymen capable of keeping records and writing letters. This change demonstrates the decline of education among laymen and the political as well as the religious importance of an educated clergy. In addition to the secretaries there were a few lay judges to hear the rare cases that were brought to the emperor's court, and a large and undifferentiated group of household officials and counselors. Any of these men could be used for any task, but no one had permanent responsibility for overseeing local courts or centralizing local revenues.

In directing and controlling local officials Charlemagne issued many capitularies (ordinances made up of various *capitula*, or chapters). Most of these were administrative directives that told the local officials what to do. For example,

Louis the Pious, son of Charlemagne. The words in the poem written across the portrait can also be read as a crossword puzzle, so that the letters in the cross and halo also form verses (*ca.* 840).

*This is reflected in the similarity of our English words *clerk* and *cleric*. From the time of Charlemagne to the end of the Middle Ages all "clerks" were members of the clergy.

186

THE DIVISION OF CHARLEMAGNE'S EMPIRE

ality, who had impressed himself on his contemporaries. It was too much to expect his descendants to be men of equal stature, and the Carolingian Empire was too large, too loosely administered, and too imperfectly unified for lesser men to hold it together. There were few economic ties among the far-flung regions. Bavarians, for example, had no reason to care about what happened in Aquitaine. Western Europeans could satisfy their common ideals simply by sharing in the life of the Church. Their common institutions, which were most effective at the county level, seemed to work equally well whether there was one empire or many kingdoms. Charlemagne himself apparently was not particularly concerned about preserving the unity of the Empire, for he followed the old Frankish tradition and divided his holdings among his sons. It was only the premature death of two of his heirs that gave an undivided realm to his son Louis.

THE COLLAPSE OF THE CAROLINGIAN EMPIRE

Louis had increasing difficulty in holding the Frankish state together. He was a well-meaning but weak man, easily swayed by his family and friends. In order to gain the aid of the Church, the only institution that was really concerned with western unity, he humbled himself as Charles never would have done. Thus Louis allowed himself to be crowned emperor a second time by ecclesiastical authority and did public penance for mutilating a nephew who had rebelled against him. The greatest danger to the Empire sprang from the jealousies among his three sons, Lothair, the younger Louis, and Charles. Louis drew up several plans for partitioning the Empire, but none of them satisfied all his heirs. They fought with him and they fought with one another. When Louis died in 840, he left the Empire in a state of civil war.

Louis' sons finally settled their quarrels by dividing the Empire (and the imperial estates) in the Treaty of Verdun (843)—a division that had a lasting effect on European history. Charles received the western part of the Empire, a kingdom that corresponded roughly to modern France. Louis took eastern Frankland, including Saxony, Bavaria, and the counties along the Rhine. The eldest son, Lothair, became emperor and received the largest part of the family estates. This gave him a long, narrow strip of territory between the eastern and western kingdoms embracing the Low Countries, Alsace-Lorraine, Switzerland, Savoy, Provence, and North Italy. Lothair's kingdom turned out to be a buffer state, and like

Section from the Strasburg Oaths, earliest examples of the dialects that became French and German. The oath was taken by Louis the German and Charles the Bald in 842, when they agreed to oppose their brother Lothair. The first paragraph gives the oath in French, taken by Louis, the second the same oath in German, taken by Charles.

The oath of Louis: "For the love of God and the salvation of the Christian people and our common salvation, from this day forward, in so far as God gives me knowledge and power, I will succour this my brother Charles in aid and in everything, as one ought by right to succour one's brother, provided that he does likewise by me, and I will never undertake any engagement with Lothair which, by my consent, may be of harm to this my brother Charles."

Pro dõ amur & p xpian poblo & nro comun
saluament · dist di en auant · in quantdr
saur & podir me dunat · si saluarai eo ·
cist meon fradre Karlo · & in ad iudha ·
& in cad huna cosa · sicu om p dreit son
fradra saluar dist · In o quid il mi altre
si faz& · Et ab ludher nul plaid nnqua
prindrai qui meon uol cist · meon fradre
Karle in damno fit | Quod cu lodhuuic
oplesse& · karolus teudisca lingua sic'oc
eade uerba testatus est.

In godes minna ind urthes xpanes folches ·
ind unser bedhero gealnissi · fon these
mo da ge frammor desso framso mirgot
gewuzci ind imadh fur gibit sohal dihtes
du mnan bruodher soso manmit rehtu
sinan bruher scal mthi irtha zermig soso
madno · ind dimit lubheren in nohein miu
hing nege ganga · zhe minan uuillon imo
ces cadhen uuerhen ·

many buffers it was ground to pieces in conflicts between its neighbors. After Lothair's death in 855 the kings of West Frankland and East Frankland began to contend for possession of parts of the Middle Kingdom. In the end the Treaty of Mersen (870) gave the king of East Frankland the provinces that lay north of the Alps, but the dispute continued even to our own day. In 1870, 1914, and 1939, France and Germany were still fighting for Alsace and Lorraine, fragments of the old kingdom of Lothair.*

The New Invasions: The Northmen

The Frankish state, gravely weakened by civil wars, now was threatened by a series of new invasions with which the later Carolingians simply could not cope. Attacks from the north, east, and south strained the resources of the central governments and threw the burden of defense on local leaders.

* Lorraine is simply a French form of Lotharingia— Lothair's kingdom. The German Lothringen shows the connection even more clearly.

The most dangerous and persistent of these new invaders were the Scandinavians of the north. Though related to the Germans, and just as fond of fighting, the Scandinavians had taken no part in the early migrations and conquests. By the ninth century, however, many of them had begun to venture overseas. They were expert seamen and traders, and they had perfected a type of long, shallow-draft ship that was very effective for raiding. These vessels used a sail when the wind was astern, but they were usually propelled by oars. Equipped with such craft, the Scandinavians could swoop down from the sea and loot a whole river valley before the local troops, moving slowly over bad roads, could be mobilized to repel them.

No one knows why the Scandinavians became so aggressive during the ninth century. It may be that improved metallurgical techniques enabled them to construct better weapons, such as their famous war axes. It may be that frequent civil wars forced defeated bands of warriors to flee the country. It may be that some families had a surplus of younger sons who sought adventure abroad. In any case, the political weakness of Europe would have tempted anyone. The Frankish Empire was disintegrating; the British Isles were split up into small, warring kingdoms; and the Slavs who now held eastern Europe were politically disorganized. The Continent lay open to any group of determined men bent on marauding, on looting, and even, perhaps, on founding a new state.

Although the Scandinavian raiders called themselves vikings, the rest of Europe usually referred to them as Northmen. In their first serious raids against Ireland early in the ninth century they rapidly occupied the east coast. They met somewhat stiffer resistance from the Anglo-Saxons in England, but by 870 they had subdued all the Anglo-Saxon kingdoms except the southern state of Wessex. They had already begun to attack the Frankish lands. Year after year the Northmen pushed their long ships up the Rhine, the Seine, and the Loire to collect tribute and loot from towns and monasteries. Finally, an especially strong band of raiders forced the

West Frankish king to cede them the land at the mouth of the Seine. This outpost, founded about 911, became the nucleus of Normandy, the most famous of the viking states.

In a show of bravado, the Northmen even sailed their ships into the Mediterranean and plundered a few coastal cities in Spain, southern France, and Italy. Their move west across the Atlantic had more permanent results, for they had settled Iceland by the year 1000, and from Iceland a few adventurous leaders moved on to Greenland. Along the west coast of the island they established colonies that endured to the fourteenth century. And from Greenland some ships

reached the North American continent, although it is still not known just where the Northmen landed or how long they stayed.

The viking raids and settlements in the West were largely the work of Danes and Norwegians. In the East the Swedes began to push down the Russian river valleys toward Constantinople. They had known this route for a long time; eastern goods and eastern coins had been common in Scandinavia long before the great raids began. In the late ninth and tenth centuries, however, the Swedes began to settle in Russia and to bring the scattered Slavic population under their control. The fortified trading posts where the

INVASIONS OF THE NORTHMEN, THE MOSLEMS, AND THE MAGYARS
Eighth to tenth centuries

A rune stone (*ca.* ninth century) found in Scandinavia. The carving is distinctly viking: within an elaborate border are two panels, one showing a chieftain on a horse and the other, a viking ship on a voyage.

Swedish drinking horn, *ca.* eighth century.

vikings settled soon burgeoned into towns; the most famous of them was Kiev, which became the capital of a large principality. Once they had gained a footing in Russia, the vikings, with typical boldness, turned their eyes south to Constantinople. Their attacks on the imperial city were unsuccessful, but they did manage to wrest a favorable commercial treaty from the emperor. These early viking princes and warriors gave the eastern Slavs their first effective political organization; in fact, the word *Russia* itself probably comes from *Rus,* the name of a Swedish tribe.

The New Invasions: The Moslems and the Magyars

Compared to the Northmen, who settled from Greenland to the Ukraine and raided from Northumberland to North Italy, the other invaders of the ninth and tenth centuries seem almost provincial. But they covered enough ground to cause suffering in many parts of southern and central Europe. The Moslems, coming up from the south, seized Sicily and the other islands of the western Mediterranean, thus endangering navigation in that part of the sea. They also established fortified outposts near Rome and on the coastal road from France to Italy, from which they molested land travelers as well.

Even worse were the Hungarians, or Magyars, who belonged to the nomadic stock of central Asia that had launched earlier raids against the coastal civilizations of China, India, and Europe. The Magyars were as great horsemen as the vikings were seamen, and their skill gave them the same advantages of surprise and mobility. They drove into the Danube Valley in the ninth century and established headquarters in what is now Hungary. From this base they raided Germany and Italy regularly and eastern France occasionally. The Magyar occupation of the middle Danube basin split the western Slavs into two groups. The Slavs were politically backward in any case, but this division made it even harder for them to form kingdoms strong enough to resist subjugation. And the weakness of the states of the western

Slavs has in its turn tempted their neighbors to fight with and dominate them, as the history of Czechoslovakia demonstrates.

The End of the New Invasions

The people of western Europe suffered grievously at the hands of the new invaders. Large areas were depopulated and impoverished, and the plundering of monasteries dissipated many of the benefits of the Carolingian reforms. Yet western Europe resisted the new invasions far more successfully than Rome had resisted the earlier invasions of the Germans and Huns. Instead of a whole continent, only a few small territories, such as Normandy and Hungary, were permanently relinquished to the invaders. The Northmen and Magyars were converted to Christianity and accepted western traditions fairly quickly; the Moslems were pushed back from their advanced positions.

How was it that western Europe managed to weather these disastrous new invasions? There were several reasons. First, the new invaders were probably not so numerous as the Germanic and Hunnic groups that had overrun Europe at the end of the Roman Empire. Second, the Church took an active role in opposing the invaders. Finally, and most important, there was effective local resistance. The people of the Roman Empire had depended almost entirely on the imperial government for protection; when its armies failed they had accepted barbarian rule without protest. But when the Carolingian kings failed to defend Europe during the ninth-century invasions, local leaders appeared who had enough military power to defend their territories.

This growth of new leadership was especially noticeable in England, Germany, and France. In England the collapse of all the other Anglo-Saxon kingdoms had left Wessex alone to face the Danish invaders. The king of Wessex, Alfred the Great (870–99), proved to be a brave and stubborn fighter. Though he was defeated again and again, he never gave up. He eventually forced the Danes to accept a peace that gave him control of about half of England. His son and grandson carried on the fight until they had seized the rest of the Danish-occupied territories. By 950 all England was united under the Wessex dynasty. In Germany, the new Saxon dynasty that replaced the Carolingians first checked and then, in 955, thoroughly defeated the Magyars.

France is the most instructive example of the development of new leadership. So long as the Carolingian kings were able to raise armies to fight the Northmen, they kept the loyalty of most of the country. But when, at the end of the ninth century, they failed completely in their efforts to defend northern France, local leaders took over most of the responsibility for defense. Eventually, in 987, Hugh Capet, the descendant of one of these local leaders, seized the throne from the helpless Carolingians.

In short, the inhabitants of western Europe showed a will to resist that had been lacking in the fourth and fifth centuries. The resistance was strongest at the local level, among the counts who governed local districts and among the professional fighting men whom they controlled. When the kings proved that they could defend their countries, as they did in England and eventually in Germany, the local nobles supported them and a certain degree of unity was preserved. But when the kings failed, as they did in France, the counts became virtually independent rulers and gained the loyalty of most of the people in their districts.

FEUDALISM

Out of the ninth-century invasions emerged a new type of government, which we call feudalism. The invasions were only a contributing factor to this development, however, for the civil wars among the last Carolingians and the lack of strong economic ties between districts also played a part. Nevertheless, the fact that feudalism first appeared in northern France and only gradually spread to other countries suggests that the invasions gave the final push toward the development of this new form of political

The Ceremony of Becoming a Vassal, 1127

This description comes from the period when feudalism was fully developed. It is very full, because the leading men of Flanders had just accepted a new count, after a disputed succession. Homage (the specific obligation of the vassal) is carefully distinguished from the more general obligation of fidelity. By this time it is assumed that most vassals have fiefs.

On Thursday, homages were done to the count. First, they did homage in this way. The count asked [the vassal] if he wished to become his man without reserve, and the latter answered: "I do." Then, joining his hands together, he placed them in the hands of the count, and they bound themselves to each other by a kiss. Then the man who had just done homage pledged fidelity . . . to the count in these words: "I promise on my faith to be faithful from now on to count William and to observe [the obligations of] my homage completely, in good faith, and without deceit." This he swore on the relics of the saints. . . . Finally, with a little stick that he held in his hand, the count gave investiture of fiefs to all those who had . . . promised security, done homage, and taken the oath.

From Galbert of Bruges, *De Multro Karoli comitis Flandriarum*, ed. by H. Pirenne (Paris, 1891), p. 89.

organization. France had suffered more severely from the invasions than any other country, and its kings had been less successful than other monarchs in coping with the danger.

The Ingredients of Feudalism

Feudalism may be defined by three characteristics: fragmentation of political authority, public power in private hands, and the lord-vassal relationship. The typical feudal state was a county, or a fraction of a county, and the typical feudal lord was a count, or a custodian of a castle, who had turned his office into a private, hereditary possession that he exploited for his own benefit. Rights of government were treated just as if they were rights to land; they could be given away, exchanged, or divided among heirs. The lord kept control over his district through his vassals, or retainers, many of whom lived with him in his fortified dwelling. Other vassals lived on their own estates, which the lord had granted them as a reward for faithful service. The lands and rights held by a

Twelfth-century seal depicting a vassal giving homage to his lord.

vassal from a lord were at first called benefices; later, fiefs.* All vassals were bound to help their lord in war and government. Though their chief duty was to fight for their lord, older and wealthier vassals might also be asked to attend law courts or to administer small areas within the county. This was feudalism in its simplest form: a small area ruled by a lord with the aid of a band of military retainers.

Some of the ingredients of feudalism had come into existence during the last years of the Merovingian kingdom, but it was almost two centuries before these ingredients were combined into a consistent pattern. The lord-vassal relationship, for example, first emerged clearly in the eighth century, probably because of a change in military tech-

*Our word *feudalism* comes from the medieval Latin *feudum*, which meant fief. No medieval writer ever spoke of "feudalism"; he was more likely to say "vassalage," which stressed the personal relationship between lord and retainer.

niques. During the wars with the Moslem invaders Charles Martel and Pippin discovered that heavy-armed cavalrymen gave them increased striking power. They wanted large numbers of these soldiers, but ordinary freemen, with at best a small farm, could not afford to provide themselves with specially bred horses, mail shirts, and swords and spears. No ordinary horse could carry a fully armed soldier, nor could an ordinary village blacksmith make armor or forge a sword. Only the king or wealthy lords could afford to provide this equipment, and they naturally expected the men who received it to accord them special loyalty in return. The new type of fighting men became vassals of the king or the lords and before long were the most effective element in the army.

The Frankish kings soon sensed that the bond between lord and retainer was far more compelling than the loose tie between king and subject. So they began to use vassalage to strengthen their political authority as well as their military position. Pippin, Charlemagne, and Louis all encouraged fighting men to become vassals of lords, and lords to become vassals of the king. They began the practice of granting public offices, such as countships, as benefices to lords, just as the lords granted estates as benefices to some of their soldiers. But there was a great difference between an ordinary mounted soldier who was completely dependent on his lord for his livelihood and a powerful count who needed no help from the king. The lesser vassals were almost always obedient to their lords and gave them good service. But the great vassals of the king became more and more disobedient during the ninth century and gave him service only when they chose to. The king received a certain amount of deference and exercised some influence over the lords with whom he had contact. But by the end of the tenth century the real rulers of France were the lords who had succeeded in building little principalities out of the fragments of the old Frankish kingdom.

Feudalism was primarily a political device for assuring a minimum of security to each section of a badly fragmented

The Church and Feudalism

At the height of feudalism, churches needed protection against raiders but feared that they would lose much of their wealth to their protectors. This charter is an attempt to avoid both dangers.

I, Baldwin, by the grace of God count of Flanders, acknowledge and testify before all my barons that the abbey of Marchiennes was always free from obligations to an advocate. . . . However, because of the present evil state of the world, it needs an advocate for its defense. That I may be the faithful advocate and defender of the church, the abbot gave me two mills and two ploughlands in the town of Nesle. I, however, have given the mills and the land with the consent of the abbot to Hugh Havet of Aubigny, so that he may be a ready defender of the church in all things.

And this is what he receives in the abbey's lordship. He shall have one-third of all fines in cases where the church has asked his assistance and has gained something by his justice. If he is not called in he shall have nothing. In time of war he shall have from each plough-team two shillings, from half a team one, and from each laborer three pennies. He shall not give orders to the men of the abbey, nor hold courts of his own, nor take money from peasants. He is not permitted to buy lands of the abbey, or to give its serfs in fiefs to his knights, nor to extort anything from them by violence. . . . Done at Arras in the year of our Lord 1038.

From *Polyptyque de l'Abbé Irminion,* ed. by B. Guerard (Paris, 1844), Vol. II, pp. 356–57.

country. But counts, lords of castles, and their vassals had to have adequate incomes, and the scanty public revenues that remained—mainly tolls, market dues, and fines from courts—were inadequate to meet the needs of the governing class. In the end everyone in authority (including bishops and abbots as well as laymen) was dependent on dues squeezed out of the peasants, who constituted the vast majority of the population.

The burden on the peasants varied greatly, according to the region in which they lived and the degree of freedom that they enjoyed. In some areas (for example, Normandy) most peasants were free and owed relatively little to their superiors—a few pennies or small amounts of grain per acre for the use and protection of their land, presents (which soon became compulsory) of hens and eggs at Christmas and Easter, three or four days' work a year on the lord's land at harvest time. At the other extreme were the unfree serfs (numerous in eastern France) who owed heavy payments, worked several days a week for the lord, and could not even marry a subject of another lord without buying permission. Economic considerations, however, cut across these lines. A serf with a large holding might be better off than a freeman who had only four or five acres; a man who had oxen was far more prosperous than a man who had no draft animals. But everywhere crop yields per acre were low, and even in a good year the average peasant did not rise far above a subsistence level of living.

From the point of view of the governing classes, the neatest arrangement was to possess a village in which all the peasants were under one lord and in which the lord's land, intermingled with that of the peasants, could be cultivated by the village as a whole. Such villages were relatively easy to exploit and usually produced a fairly regular income. But many villages were divided among several lords, and not all peasants lived in well-organized villages. Dues from scattered holdings and hamlets were difficult to keep track of and to collect.

It is easy to see why the greater lords eventually granted some of their estates,

FEUDAL FRANCE Late eleventh century

especially their smaller and more remote lands, to their vassals. The vassal had to be supported in any case; by giving him an estate the lord lost little income and saved himself the trouble of collecting peasant dues. The vassal who received and lived on a small estate might exploit it more efficiently than a distant lord. Thus in the long run large numbers of peasants became tenants, or serfs, of lesser vassals.

This did not mean, especially in the ninth and tenth centuries, that the knight or other minor vassal had much political power over the peasants whose dues he received. He had to be given enough authority to force peasants to pay what they owed, and eventually most knights acquired a sort of police-court jurisdiction. They could judge cases of disorderly conduct; they could settle minor squabbles among peasants over the boundaries of fields and the division of family holdings. But they could not judge serious criminal cases or disputes over the possession of fiefs; such matters were reserved to counts and other great lords.

of the Count of Flanders and the Duke of Normandy, who added many counties to their original holdings and kept them under fairly effective control. Other lords in France, West Germany, and North Italy were almost as successful, and their wars and alliances determined the political history of the area for two centuries. Second, since these new states were too large to be governed through the informal and personal decisions of their rulers, various new legal and financial institutions were created, which produced a body of feudal law. Third, the benefice, or fief, became more important. In the early years many vassals had been primarily household retainers; they had no fiefs and spent most of their time with their lord or in garrisoning his forts. But, as we have seen, lords gradually found it more convenient to assign estates to their vassals, and by 1100 it was customary to give fiefs even to lesser vassals. It also became customary for the vassal to spend most of his time on his fief and to serve his lord only on special occasions or in time of war. Moreover, the fief, which originally had been only a loan to the vassal, gradually became hereditary, to be held by the vassal and his heirs as long as they gave service.

In short, the relationship between vassal and lord was changing, with the vassal becoming more of a country gentleman and less of an armed retainer. He began to begrudge the time spent in his lord's service and tried to reduce it as much as he could. The lord countered by defining the service owed by vassals more and more precisely and by developing legal procedures for confiscating the fiefs of defaulting vassals. What had at first been a close personal relationship began to assume the form of a contractual obligation.

Feudalism was an inadequate and limited form of government; it did little for the mass of the people except to protect them against external and internal enemies. Even this protection was not always effective. In the endemic wars between neighboring lords, a favorite tactic was to ravage the peasants' fields and drive off their animals. Lords held local courts from time to time, but they were more interested in pocketing fines

The life of a feudal knight—accompanying a traveling king, feasting, and carrying a standard into battle.

In short, the fragmentation of political authority never went down to the lowest level of the feudal hierarchy. The smallest effective political unit was the area ruled by the lord of a castle, not the estate held by a knight.

A Changing Institution

During the centuries when feudalism was at its height—from about 900 to about 1100—the institution underwent several striking changes. First, some lords succeeded in subduing their neighbors and building up relatively large and powerful states. This was especially true than in administering justice. They made little effort to maintain roads and other public facilities. At its best, feudal government was inefficient paternalism; at its worst, it was pure exploitation of the peasants.

Yet with all its disadvantages, feudalism had vitality and real capability for growth. It spread from France throughout most of western Europe, and the countries that were most thoroughly feudalized, France and England, were the first medieval states to develop effective political institutions. Moreover, feudal rulers managed to gain the loyalty of their subjects, something that neither the late Roman emperors nor the Germanic kings had achieved. There was personal devotion to the ruling dynasty; there was also a feeling that each man had an interest in preserving the customs and institutions of his little state. With this loyalty it was possible to build stronger states and to give more protection and better justice to the people.

Feudalism was almost perfectly adapted to conditions in early medieval Europe. The working political unit, the area dependent on a castle, matched the working economic unit, the local neighborhood. The struggle to base a large political organization on what was essentially a local economy—a struggle that had weakened both the Roman and the Carolingian empires—was abandoned. The exploitation of the peasants by an aristocracy was nothing new, and at least the feudal aristocracy had duties as well as privileges. Lords had to defend and govern their lands in person—no one else would do it for them—and if they did their job badly they would lose their lands to more efficient neighbors.

Even the fact that feudal government was rudimentary was an advantage. Europe at this time could not support a complex government; it had to concentrate on essentials. And precisely because early feudalism was highly informal and personal, change was easy and experimentation common. In the end the ablest feudal lords devised more effective forms of government than Europe had had for many centuries, and their methods were copied by their less imaginative colleagues.

GERMANY

It took several centuries for feudalism to reveal all its possibilities. At first it seemed to do as much harm in encouraging local wars as it did good in warding off outside raiders. Feudal France was weak and divided. Germany and England, still unfeudalized and united under their kings, were far stronger. Germany, in fact, was the dominant country in Europe from the early tenth century down to the end of the eleventh century.

In the period after the breakup of the Carolingian Empire, Germany had remained more united than France. It had suffered less from invasion and civil war, which meant that the lords had had fewer opportunities to usurp power. Even the transition to a new ruling family was made more easily in Germany than in France. The last able German Carolingian died in 899; by 919 King Henry I had established the new Saxon dynasty firmly on the throne.

In spite of these advantages, however, the German king had lost much of his authority by 919. During the troubles of the ninth century most of the country had come under the control of five great lords, the dukes of Saxony, Franconia, Swabia, Bavaria, and, after its final annexation to Germany in 925, Lorraine. Each of these dukes ruled a wider territory than that of any French feudal lord, and each exercised reasonably effective control over the counts and other nobles of his duchy. The dukes were willing to have a king as a sort of president of their club, but they expected to be virtually independent within their own duchies. Henry I, for example, was strong only in his own duchy of Saxony; elsewhere he had to negotiate with the other dukes to carry out his policies. Sons had begun to succeed their fathers as a matter of course in both duchies and counties.

Nevertheless, Germany was not yet feudalized, although feudal ideas were creeping in through Lorraine, the duchy that lay closest to France. Counts and dukes were not completely independent of the king; they were public officers who could be removed if they failed to show obedience. Lords had not yet gained a monopoly of power; ordinary freemen

Papal Coronation of
Otto the Great
962

Death of
Frederick II
1250

Napoleonic Reorgar
of the Germanies
18

H O L Y   R O M A N   E M P I R E

had a voice in the courts and still served in the armies. Strong regional loyalties, especially in Saxony and Bavaria, held the duchies together. In short, Germany had not fragmented as France had, and the king still had a chance to establish his authority throughout the realm.

Otto the Great
and the German-Roman Empire

Otto the Great (936–73) made the most of this opportunity. He held Saxony in his own right, and he gradually brought the other duchies under control by forcing out disobedient dukes and bestowing their offices on members of his own family. This policy was not wholly successful, for Otto's own sons rebelled against him. But there was still the Church, which had great wealth and cherished the idea of unity. Most of the bishops and abbots owed their positions to Otto; they supplied him with money and troops from their estates and they provided him with administrative offi-

cers. The support of the Church made Otto supreme in central Europe; he was able to put down all rebellions and inflict a crushing defeat on the Magyars in 955.

Otto's position was so strong that he was able to intervene in Italian affairs and eventually to annex northern Italy. He has often been blamed for this action, since in the long run involvement in Italian politics weakened the German monarchy. But, given the situation in the tenth century, it would have been difficult for Otto to avoid involvement. The Italian kingdom was small—it included only the northern half of the peninsula—and its kings were weak. Tempted by this weakness, French feudal lords had already tried to establish themselves as kings of Italy, and the Duke of Bavaria also had thoughts of crossing the Alps. Otto, anxious to preserve his position as the strongest ruler in western Europe, could hardly allow Italy to pass to a potential rival, much less to one of his own subjects.

Otto's close relations with the Church in Germany also impelled him to intervene in Italy. He was not a mere exploiter of the Church; he felt, as Charlemagne had, that it was his duty to preserve and strengthen ecclesiastical institutions. The papacy was in miserable condition; deprived of the support of the Carolingians, it had fallen under the control of corrupt and self-seeking Roman nobles. So little authority and prestige did it enjoy that a tenth-century German archbishop actually refused to become pope. Otto may have hoped that intervention in Italy would free the papacy from domination by Roman nobles and that he could ensure his continued use of church resources by gaining a voice in papal elections.

Otto at least had a romantic excuse for his invasion of Italy. Adelaide, widow of an Italian king, was being annoyed by her husband's successor. Otto came to the rescue of the queen, married her, and

GERMANY AND ITALY AT THE TIME OF OTTO THE GREAT   962

then claimed the Italian throne. A ruler backed by the German Church and in control of northern Italy could hardly be ignored by the pope, who recognized Otto's position by crowning him emperor in 962.

Since there had been no emperor with real power since Louis, Charlemagne's son, and not even a nominal emperor since 924, Otto's coronation constituted a refounding of the medieval Empire. After Otto there was no break; the imperial title and the German kingship were to remain indissolubly united for the rest of the Middle Ages. This Roman Empire of the German Nation, as it was called by some contemporaries, was the strongest state in Europe until about 1100 and an important force in European politics for 200 years after that. Especially significant were the relations between the German-Roman Empire and the popes. Otto, as successor to Charlemagne, thought of himself as leader of the Christian West and protector of the papacy. He took this second responsibility so seriously that by the end of his life he dominated papal elections. The Church eventually reacted violently against imperial control, but for almost a hundred years the emperors named and deposed popes. And on the whole they strengthened the Church; popes

Otto the Great, offering a model of Magdeburg Cathedral to Christ (Ivory, second half of tenth century).

chosen by the emperors were abler and better men than those selected by Roman nobles.

Gerbert

Having revived the Carolingian tradition of an alliance between emperor and Church, an alliance in which the emperor was unquestionably the dominant partner, Otto proceeded to revive the Carolingian interest in scholarship. One of the most famous of the scholars he encouraged was Gerbert, who was born in

Ivory panel showing Otto II, his wife, and their child, the future Otto III, in adoration (ca. 980).

The four provinces of Slavinia, Germania, Gallia, and Roma (left) paying homage to Otto III (right), from the Reichenau Gospels, tenth century. Note that Otto wears a Roman imperial costume, not a Germanic one.

southwestern France about the middle of the tenth century but who spent much of his life in the service of Otto's son and grandson. Gerbert had studied in Spain, where contact with the Moslems had revived interest in mathematics and astronomy. He learned what he could of these subjects—very little by later standards but enough to give him a reputation for profound, even magical, knowledge in his own day. He also tried to teach elementary ideas about astronomy and devised some simple apparatus to demonstrate his points.

Although few westerners had paid much attention to mathematics or astronomy during the ninth and tenth centuries, these scientific interests were not unprecedented. What made them significant was the fact that Gerbert was more than a secluded scholar; he was one of the most influential churchmen of his time. The emperors he served made him first the abbot of a great monastery, then Archbishop of Reims, and eventually pope. As Pope Sylvester II (999–1003) he was the chief adviser of the emperor Otto III (983–1002), whose tutor he had been. The two men dreamed of an empire that would be much more like the old Roman Empire than Charlemagne's had been, an empire in which emperor and pope would act as the joint heads of a unified western state.

This was a hopeless dream, though

both pope and emperor died before they realized quite how hopeless it was. But the fact that they could conceive of such a plan shows how strong Roman ideas were in the Ottonian court. And Gerbert might be excused for overestimating imperial power. After all, his spectacular career had been largely due to the emperor's support.

Gerbert's political program was a failure, but his scholarly work marked a turning point in European intellectual history. The fact that such an influential man was interested in mathematics and science attracted younger students who carried on his work. Other scholars took the road to Spain and prepared the way for the intellectual revival of the twelfth century, a revival in which western Europeans, for the first time, took a real interest in science.

Gerbert had also become absorbed in the study of logic, partly because logic and science were closely related in the Greek scientific tradition he was trying to revive, partly because he felt that he needed this tool in order to comprehend the new knowledge he had acquired. Logic, like Latin, was essential in assimilating ancient knowledge, and Gerbert's use of logic, simple as it was, greatly impressed his contemporaries. Here again his example was not forgotten. The study of logic continued throughout the eleventh century and was one of the most important forces in the intellectual revival which came at the end of that century.

The direct line of Otto I ended in 1002 with the death of Otto III, but collateral branches of the family retained the throne and kept the Ottonian system of government going. Compared with France, which was splitting up into feudal states, Germany seemed to be flourishing. The German emperors stood unchallenged in their realm. They had wealth and prestige, and the greatest scholars of Europe came flocking to their courts. But the German state had serious weaknesses that had been masked by the remarkable ability of the emperors and the relatively slow development of feudal elements in German society. Imperial power depended on the support of the Church, and it was by no means certain that the Church would always be willing to remain subordinate to a secular ruler. The power of the local lord was growing in Germany as it had earlier in France, and there was no assurance that local lords would not some day seek independence. The emperor had to rely on churchmen and nobles to carry out his plans, for he had no bureaucracy. In short, the Ottonian Empire was little more than a slightly modified Carolingian Empire, an empire that had long been out of date. The emperor's position rested on a precarious balance of forces—clergy versus laymen, one group of lords versus another group—and the crises that arose in the last half of the eleventh century were to show just how precarious that balance was.

ANGLO-SAXON ENGLAND

England, like Germany and unlike France, was not feudalized in the tenth century. Like Germany again, it developed a relatively strong monarchy and an active intellectual life during that century. As the descendants of Alfred drove back the Danes, they had to develop new institutions with which to hold and govern the territories they reconquered. These institutions were especially effective at the local level—so effective that they survived the Anglo-Saxon monar-

chy for centuries and even formed the basic pattern of local government in the United States.

New Institutions

The Anglo-Saxon kings of the tenth century divided the country into shires, or counties, and then subdivided the shires into smaller units called hundreds. Shires and hundreds were judicial as well as administrative units; there was a shire court that met twice a year and a hundred court that met about once a month. Fortified towns, which were both military and trading centers, were called boroughs; the borough also had a court of its own.

This system was not unlike that of the Carolingian Empire and the states that succeeded it. But there was one

ENGLAND AFTER THE NORMAN CONQUEST
Late eleventh century

striking difference: in England the nobles never gained control of shire, hundred, and borough government, whereas in France the count was the ultimate authority within his county. In England the highest royal official was the alderman, later called the earl. The alderman was usually responsible for many shires, and he could not handle all problems of local administration. An official was needed in each shire to collect revenue, muster troops, and preside over the courts. After a long period of experimentation the Anglo-Saxon kings eventually developed a very effective local official, the shire-reeve, or sheriff.

At first the shire-reeve was only one of a group of reeves, or agents, who managed the king's estates. It was logical to ask one of these men in each shire to supervise the others and to see that all the king's revenue in that district was brought together in one place. Eventually the chief reeve became the king's representative in all affairs, with wide administrative and executive powers. Just as the sheriff of a western county in the United States in the nineteenth century was the key official in his district, so the Anglo-Saxon sheriff by the eleventh century was the most important official in his shire.

Powerful as the sheriff was, he never became independent of the king. He ranked beneath the really great men, the aldermen, or earls, and he could always be replaced if he failed to do his job loyally and efficiently. With a few exceptions, the office of sheriff never became hereditary. From 1000 on, the king of England always had a local official in every part of his realm who would carry out his orders with reasonable efficiency and collect his revenues with reasonable honesty. Kings on the Continent grew weak and poor because they had lost control of local government and revenues. But the king of England gained power and wealth, even though his country was small and thinly populated, because he could use the resources of all his counties.

Law and Literature

The Anglo-Saxon kings of the tenth and eleventh centuries also improved internal security by discouraging blood-feuds and by insisting that certain serious crimes, such as murder, arson, and rape, were offenses against the king. Since he received a substantial fine when a defendant was convicted of such crimes, the king had an added incentive to strengthen and support the courts in which these cases were tried. Much of the legislation of the Anglo-Saxon kings deals with the arrest and punishment of criminals. And it is a sign of their power that they could issue general laws; the great period of Anglo-Saxon legislation was between 950 and 1050, a time when the king of France could hardly make rules even for his own private estates.

Like the German kings, the Anglo-Saxon rulers encouraged ecclesiastical reform and sponsored literature and scholarship. But they were interested in writings in the vernacular as well as in Latin. Alfred the Great had translated Latin works into Anglo-Saxon, and under his successors Anglo-Saxon literature reached its peak. The epic of *Beowulf* was put into its final form about 1000; the two great battle poems *Maldon* and *Brunanbuhr* came about the same time. Even more important for the historian is the *Anglo-Saxon Chronicle,* which was probably begun in the days of Alfred and was continued into the twelfth century. It is mainly a history of kings and bishops, of wars and rebellions, but it tells us much about Anglo-Saxon customs and beliefs.

Page from the earliest manuscript of *Beowulf,* tenth century.

Military Weakness

With all its achievements, the Anglo-Saxon monarchy was not exempt from the difficulties that had weakened the continental kingdoms. Most of the peasants had put themselves under the protection of lords, and most of the lesser landlords had placed themselves under the patronage of the king or an earl. Everywhere the bond between lord and follower was becoming stronger than the old ties of kinship and community. But, though the followers of the king and the great men had honorable status and were entrusted with important missions, they were not primarily a class of specially trained military retainers. Thus there were weaknesses in England's military posture. As the lords interposed themselves between people and king, the folk-army became less effective, and no one was developing the bands of heavy-armed cavalrymen that were proving so effective on the Continent. King and lords depended largely on their household retainers—good fighters, but probably not as well armed nor as versatile as French vassals.

This military weakness became evident soon after 1000 when the Danes renewed their attacks on England. King Ethelred the Ill-Counseled, after failing to defeat the Danes in battle, resorted to the hopeless expedient of buying them off with the proceeds of a national tax, the Danegeld. This gesture only encouraged the Danes, and by 1016 their king Canute (or Knut) had completed the conquest of England.

England did not suffer greatly under Danish rule (1016–42) although some Anglo-Saxon lords lost their lands and official positions to Danes. Canute preserved, and even strengthened, Anglo-Saxon institutions; in fact, the last Anglo-Saxon laws were promulgated during his reign. But he did not entirely solve England's military problem. He increased the body of royal house-carls, or retainers, to several thousand; however, they were warriors of the old Germanic type, not mounted knights. A heavy-armed cavalry was essential; England still could not match the new type of force that was developing in France.

Edward the Confessor

When Canute's sons died without leaving direct heirs, the Anglo-Saxons had no trouble in restoring the old line of kings descended from the House of Wessex. But Edward the Confessor (1042–66) was strong only in his piety; in all other things he was easily swayed by his relatives and advisers. Having spent long years of exile in Normandy, he wanted to bring Norman ways into England and give Normans high positions in both ecclesiastical and secular administration. At the same time he was influenced by the earl Godwin, who was half Danish and wholly anti-French. Edward married Godwin's daughter and gave earldoms to Godwin's sons. Other Anglo-Saxon earls were naturally jealous of Godwin, and quarrels among the various factions at times reached the level of civil war.

Edward's situation was not unlike that of the last French Carolingians. Like them, he strove to preserve a precarious balance among aristocratic factions. Like them, he had to accept a notable transfer of political power into private hands. Bishops, abbots, and great lay lords assumed control of the courts of many hundreds, and even lesser lords acquired police-court jurisdiction over their men. Moreover, many of the powerful lords built up bodyguards large enough to constitute private armies.

Here we have some of the ingredients of feudalism, and it is possible that even without the Norman Conquest England might have developed its own kind of feudalism. The Anglo-Saxons, however, had not gone very far in this direction. The followers of the lords did not have the special military training of French vassals. Many of them were not even permanently bound to their lord; as the records say, they "could go with their land" to any lord they chose. This meant in turn that there were no fiefs, that the followers of a lord did not hold land and offices in return for service. And this was even truer of the earls than it was of ordinary retainers. They were not vassals of the king, and they owed him no service for the lands they possessed. They expected, of course, to be consulted by the king, and they also expected to receive the chief offices of government, such as the earldoms. On his side, the king expected the earls and their relatives to assist him in the work of governing and defending the realm. But there were no permanent and binding obligations on either king or lord. The king could take an earldom from one lord and give it to another, and a lord who failed to serve the king in an emergency did not thereby forfeit his land.

England, in fact, was facing the same problem that Germany was facing in the eleventh century. In both countries the king still acted on the theory that the great men were his obedient subjects, that he could use them as public officials and dismiss them at will. But in both countries this theory was becoming unrealistic; the great men had acquired independent strength and it was increasingly difficult for the king to control them. But while in Germany the tendency toward disintegration proved irreversible, in England it was checked at the end of the eleventh century. A disputed succession and quarrels among the earls exposed the Anglo-Saxon kingdom to conquest by a French feudal army. The leader of this army, William the Conqueror, introduced into England the most rigorous type of feudalism that Europe had yet seen. He imposed heavy and precise obligations on the lords and seized their lands if they failed to fulfill them. Thus William corrected the chief weakness of the old Anglo-Saxon state. At the same time, he preserved all the really effective Anglo-Saxon institutions, especially the remarkable Anglo-Saxon system of local government. The work of the Anglo-Saxon kings had not been wasted; the combination of their institutions with Norman feudalism was to make England for many generations the strongest state in Europe.

Suggestions for Further Reading

Note: Asterisk denotes a book available in paperback edition.

Pippin and St. Boniface

"The evolution of monarchical institutions and the idea of kingship during the Dark Ages from 400 to 1000 provides one of the most instructive examples of the complex process by which different social and religious elements became interwoven in a culture," writes C. Dawson in *Religion and the Rise of Western Culture* * (1950), a very good introduction to this period. C. H. Talbot, *Anglo-Saxon Missionaries in Germany* (1954), gives the correspondence of Pippin and St. Boniface and provides a cross section of the religious life of the eighth century difficult to parallel elsewhere.

Charlemagne and the Revival of the Empire

The best biography that we have of the man who was at the center of this epoch is the contemporary Einhard's *Life of Charlemagne*,* foreword by S. Painter (1960). J. H. Robinson, ed., *Readings in European History*, Vol. I (1904), has excellent source material on the administration of the Carolingian Empire. There are several good studies of the man and the age: H. Kleinclausz, *Charlemagne* (1934), is a scholarly work which concentrates on political conditions, while the recent and very readable study by H. Fichtenau, *The Carolingian Empire* * (1957), gives greater attention to social conditions. F. L. Ganshof, *The Imperial Coronation of Charlemagne* (1949), focuses on a problem which has interested many historians. Ganshof's collection of essays, *Frankish Institutions under Charlemagne* (1968), is also useful. The best study of the rise and decline of the Carolingian Empire is L. Halphen, *Charlemagne et l'Empire Carolingien* (1949). Halphen, however, is not such interesting reading as Fichtenau.

| The Carolingian Renaissance | Most of the general works cited above have material on the Carolingian Renaissance. M. L. W. Laistner, *Thought and Letters in Western Europe, 500–900* (1951), devotes considerable attention to the prose and poetry of the period. E. S. Duckett, *Alcuin, Friend of Charlemagne* (1951), gives a somewhat romantic picture of the Frankish court and the palace school. The influence of political and social factors on Carolingian art is brought out in A. Hauser, *Social History of Art,* Vol. I (1957). W. Levison, *England and the Continent in the Eighth Century* (1948), combines great knowledge of the literature of the age with a fine prose style. J. Boussard, *The Civilization of Charlemagne* (1969), is very helpful. |

The Carolingian Renaissance

Most of the general works cited above have material on the Carolingian Renaissance. M. L. W. Laistner, *Thought and Letters in Western Europe, 500–900** (1951), devotes considerable attention to the prose and poetry of the period. E. S. Duckett, *Alcuin, Friend of Charlemagne* (1951), gives a somewhat romantic picture of the Frankish court and the palace school. The influence of political and social factors on Carolingian art is brought out in A. Hauser, *Social History of Art,* Vol. I (1957). W. Levison, *England and the Continent in the Eighth Century* (1948), combines great knowledge of the literature of the age with a fine prose style. J. Boussard, *The Civilization of Charlemagne* (1969), is very helpful.

Collapse of the Empire and the New Invasions

For an overall view of this period drawn from the sources, see R. S. Lopez, *The Tenth Century* (1959). P. Sawyer, *The Age of the Vikings,* 2nd ed. (1971), gives a good description of the Northmen. J. Brønsted, *The Vikings** (1960), presents a fascinating account of viking art and civilization. T. D. Kendrick, *A History of the Vikings* (1930), shows the impact of the viking invasions on Britain, western Europe, Russia, and even America. A. Olrik, *Viking Civilization* (1930), and G. Turville-Petre, *The Heroic Age of Scandinavia* (1951), interpret the age of the vikings from the legends and sagas of individual Norsemen; of the two, Turville-Petre is the more readable. The great poem *Beowulf,** trans. by D. Wright (1957), provides information about viking civilization which has been documented by archeological findings. C. A. Macartney, *The Magyars in the Ninth Century* (1930), is a scholarly study of the origins and wanderings of the Magyars.

Feudalism

Both *Raoul de Cambrai,* trans. by J. Crosland (1926), and *The Song of Roland,** trans. by D. L. Sayers (1957), present excellent pictures of the ideals and attitudes of the feudal caste in the first age of western feudalism. F. L. Ganshof, *Feudalism** (1952), shows the development of "classical feudalism" from its Carolingian origins. M. Bloch, *Feudal Society** (1961), is an outstanding study from a more social and economic point of view, while J. R. Strayer, *Feudalism** (1965), gives a brief account emphasizing political factors. A. Boutrouche, *Seigneurie et féodalité* (1959), studies the first age of the feudal and manorial systems and compares European feudalism with eastern forms. Boutrouche has a thorough recent bibliography. F. Kern, *Kingship and Law in the Middle Ages* (1939), is a historical essay which is invaluable for an understanding of the nature and development of the idea of kingship in early medieval Europe.

Otto I and the Saxon Dynasty

Medieval Germany, Vol. I, trans. by G. Barraclough (1938), has as its theme the internal development of the German state in the obscure period from the tenth to the thirteenth century. There is information on Otto I and the Saxon dynasty in H. A. L. Fisher, *The Medieval Empire,* Vol. I (1898), but G. Barraclough's chapters in *Origins of Modern Germany* (1949) are more up-to-date. Luitprand of Cremona, *Chronicle of the Reign of Otto I, Embassy to Constantinople,* trans. by F. A. Wright (1930), presents a picture of Church-state cooperation under the Saxons and an insight into the western attitude toward Byzantium in the eleventh century.

The Anglo-Saxon Monarchy to 1066; Anglo-Saxon Art

The Anglo-Saxon Chronicle (Everyman's Library) is the indispensable framework for developments in England before 1066. There is interesting source material in *Six Old English Chronicles,* trans. by J. Giles (1875) and *English Historical Documents,* Vol. I, *500–1042,* ed. by D. Whitelock (1955); Vol. II, *1042–1189,* ed. by D. C. Douglas and G. W. Greenway (1953–55). F. Barlow, *The Feudal Kingdom of England, 1042–1216* (1953), has a good account of the reign of Edward the Confessor. The best scholarly treatment of the entire period is F. M. Stenton, *Anglo-Saxon England* (1943), but G. O. Sayles, *Medieval Foundations of England,** Chapters 5–16 (1948), is much more readable and has a good critical bibliography. D. Whitelock, *The Beginnings of English Society** (1952), is a good brief account.

Most of the works cited above have information on the artistic achievements of the period. T. D. Kendrick, *Anglo-Saxon Art* (1938), is a good survey. D. Talbot-Rice, *English Art, 950–1100* (1952), traces the development of architecture, sculpture, and manuscript illumination. It has good plates and an excellent bibliography. A. W. Clapham, *English Architecture before the Norman Conquest* (1930), is a first-rate introduction to early Anglo-Saxon architecture.

10

Revival and Reform in Western Europe

Battered and torn by invasions and civil wars during the tenth century, western Europe began to recover after 1000. The worst of the invasions were over; France was achieving some degree of stability under its feudal lords; England and Germany were relatively peaceful under their kings. Italy was more turbulent, and Spain was still being devastated by Christian-Moslem wars. But the heart of western Europe, the great stretch of land running from Rome to London and from Bremen to Venice, had survived its worst difficulties.

Although the increase in security in the eleventh century was slight, western Europe had the resources and the vitality to profit from even slight improvement. Beginning in the last half of the eleventh century and continuing throughout the twelfth, there was a surge forward in all forms of human activity. Production and trade increased; political, legal, and religious institutions grew stronger; religious feeling became deeper and more meaningful. Along with these advances, remarkable work was done both in art and in scholarship.

THE ECONOMIC REVIVAL

The first and most obvious result of increased stability was a rise in population. The evidence for this rise—indirect, but convincing—is simply that during the late eleventh and twelfth centuries men could always be found to undertake new occupations and activities. There were enough men to clear forests and drain swamps, to enlarge old towns and build new ones, to establish new farms and villages in the half-deserted Slavic lands beyond the Elbe. There were enough men for conquests and crusades, for William's seizure of England, for the expansion of Christian holdings in Spain, for expeditions overseas to regain the Holy Land. And there were enough men, too, to furnish a striking increase in the number of students and teachers, of writers and artists, of clergymen, lawyers, and doctors.

Agriculture

The increase in population would have been a burden on society, rather than a stimulus, if production had not increased at the same time. The most important, and most difficult, increase to achieve was in the production of food. Clearing new land helped, since soil that had lain uncultivated for centuries was often very fertile. But new land came into production slowly, not nearly fast enough to keep up with the growing population. Production from old land had to be increased by better organization of labor and by better farming techniques.

Where soil and terrain permitted, the peasants developed a tightly integrated village community whose resources they used with considerable efficiency. The arable land was divided into large fields, each of which was in turn divided into long, narrow strips. Each peasant held strips in each field, and some strips were cultivated for the benefit of the lord. All the heavy work was done in common; the peasants pooled their work animals to form plow teams, and all joined together to harvest the big fields when the grain was ripe. Since farm animals were few and scrawny and tools were dull-edged and heavy, this was the best way to handle a hard job in a reasonable length of time.

One of the most bothersome problems was to find enough feed for the work animals. The yield of grain was low, not more than four times the amount of seed sown, and almost all of it had to be saved for human consumption. Since grass grew only in small meadows along the streams, few villages produced enough hay to feed their animals during the winter months. To solve this problem, the peasants reserved the poorer lands exclusively for pasture and allowed the animals to graze on the cultivated fields after the crops had been harvested. Here again, through community organization the peasants saved themselves trouble and time, for a few herdsmen could take care of all the animals of the village.

Finally, the village had to have a common woodland. Wood was needed for fuel, for the frames of peasant huts, and for tools, which were made with as much wood and as little iron as possible. Forests were also used for pasturing large herds of half-wild pigs. These pigs supplied the peasants with most of their meat, since other animals were too scarce to serve as a regular source of food. The wild game of the forests was reserved for the lords, though there was a good deal of poaching.

The Labors of the Months (for example: November, pig butchering) a twelfth-century bas relief on the tympanum of the old church of St. Ursin at Bourges.

Illustration from an eleventh-century calendar depicting the work of January, plowing.

The agricultural system had obvious advantages and equally obvious drawbacks. It left little room for individual initiative: everyone had to follow customary routines of planting and harvesting, and the work pace was set by the slowest oxen driven by the most stupid villager. Moreover, it provided no chance to improve the breed of animals or the stock of seed, since the animals ran together in common pastures and the seed on one strip was inevitably mixed with that of neighboring strips.

The medieval village, however, was less hostile to innovation than is sometimes believed. In the obscure years between the breakup of the Carolingian Empire and the end of the eleventh century, improved agricultural techniques spread widely throughout much of Europe. The heavy wheeled plow with a moldboard to turn the soil had been used in a few Germanic regions even before the collapse of the Roman Empire. It was far more effective than the light Mediterranean plow in cultivating the heavy, wet clay soils of northern Europe, but it required a large team to draw it. The ordinary peasant had at most one or two oxen, but those who lived in integrated villages could pool their animals to form a plow-team. By 1100 the heavy plow had been adopted in Germany, northern France, and southern and central England. Its use increased food production, for the peasants could now cultivate lands the Romans had never touched.

Another innovation, also closely connected with the integrated village, was the three-field system. Since artificial fertilizers were unknown and manure was scarce, the usual method of preserving the fertility of the soil was to let half the land lie fallow each year. In northern Europe farmers discovered that they could get equally good results by dividing the land into three large blocks (hence the term three-field system) and rotating their crops. During the first year of the cycle, they planted one block in winter wheat, which they harvested in July; then they let the winter-wheat field rest until the following spring, when they sowed it with spring grains. This crop they harvested in the fall, and then let the land rest once more until the following fall, when it was sown with winter wheat. Thus in any year, one-third of the land produced winter wheat, one-third produced spring grain, and one-third was left uncultivated. And yet, over the three-year cycle, each field could lie fallow for at least a year and a half. This system could not be used in the Mediterranean basin, where there is not enough summer rain for spring grain to mature. And it was hard to use in regions where there were no well-organized villages. But where it was used, it increased production by a third.

Only about half of western Europe was organized in integrated villages. Where the soil was thin or the rainfall scant there were only small, loosely organized hamlets and individual farms, as in northern England, Brittany, and Mediterranean France. Except for wine-growing areas, these districts produced less per acre and per man than the integrated villages, though they were normally self-sufficient in food. Overall, western Europe had a food surplus by the middle of the twelfth century. Nevertheless, bad roads, a shortage of draft animals, and local wars and brigandage meant that there might be severe local famines even in a year of general surplus.

Commerce and Industry

During this same period, the towns of western Europe were experiencing a striking growth in size and number. They absorbed some of the surplus population and furnished a steadily growing market for agricultural products. They also intensified trade among all parts of Europe and increased the production of textiles and metalware. The growth of towns was especially conspicuous throughout Italy and Flanders.

The Italian towns depended almost entirely on international trade, particularly in Oriental goods such as silk and spices. During the eleventh century, Italian shipping in the Mediterranean increased steadily. With the Byzantine Empire weakening and the Moslem Caliphate breaking up, the Italian merchants had little competition. As if to aid the Italians in their new-found prosperity, nomadic invaders were strangling the alternate trade route from the East along the Russian rivers to the Baltic. Thus the Italians almost monopolized the trade in Oriental goods for western markets. And these markets were becoming steadily more profitable, thanks to the general increase in prosperity and security throughout the West. The great seaports of Venice, Pisa, and Genoa flourished most brilliantly, but the towns of the Po Valley, especially Milan, were not far behind. As the Italian merchants carried their wares north through France and Germany, they stimulated the growth of other trading centers along the routes they traveled.

The towns of Flanders found their nourishment in industry rather than trade. The flat, marshy lands along the sea seemed to be good only for sheep raising, so that Flanders had a surplus of wool from a very early date. Moreover, since Flanders was one of the first feudal states to achieve a relatively high level of stability and internal security, there was soon a surplus population that could be used to process the surplus wool. Wool was the basic clothing material in western Europe, for cotton was scarce (it had to be imported) and both linen and silk were terribly expensive. But to transform raw wool into good cloth took a great deal of time and energy. The wool had to be cleaned and carded, spun into thread, woven, smoothed by shearing off the knots and rough places, and finally dyed. All these tasks could be performed after a fashion by village workers, but the rough cloth they turned out was neither comfortable nor attractive. Anyone who had an income above the subsistence level wanted better cloth produced by skilled craftsmen. For many people, a good suit of clothes was the only luxury they possessed. This is why, from the early Middle Ages into the nineteenth century, the textile industry was the most important industry in western Europe.

Perhaps as early as the time of Charlemagne, and certainly by the eleventh century, Flanders had become the textile center of Europe. It had the wool, it had the labor, and soon Flemish cloth was famous near and far. It was bought by well-to-do people throughout Europe and even found markets in the Middle East. The first European manufactured product with much appeal for non-Europeans, it helped to balance European trade with the Orient. By the twelfth century the Flemish textile towns of Ghent, Bruges, and Ypres rivaled the flourishing seaports of Italy in wealth and population.

Weaving became an important industry in the eleventh and twelfth centuries. Top: detail of a miniature painting from *Rabanus Maurus,* an eleventh-century encyclopedia. Note that the upright loom was used instead of the horizontal loom. Below: drawing from a twelfth-century manuscript; the woman at left is spinning wool.

A peddler offering silver beakers, from a twelfth-century manuscript.

Outside Italy and Flanders the towns were smaller and the growth of commerce and industry was less spectacular. But everywhere old towns were expanding and new towns were springing up. Some served as distribution centers along the trade routes; others specialized in manufacturing goods for local consumption. Thus western Europe began to enjoy a more rational division of labor and a better use of human resources. Peasants and landlords began to specialize in producing food for the market, while skilled craftsmen in the towns concentrated on manufacturing. This development may seem so elementary that it is hardly worth mentioning. But it was precisely this division of labor between town and country that had been lacking in the late Roman Empire and the early Germanic kingdoms.

The growth of towns stimulated the economy of Europe, but it put serious strains on the social and economic system. The ruling classes, feudal lords and churchmen, knew how to control and exploit peasants, but they were not so sure of themselves in dealing with merchants and artisans. Obviously, townspeople needed personal freedom and some local self-government. A serf could not function as a merchant, and feudal courts were poorly equipped to deal with lawsuits among businessmen. But if the townsmen became too free they might escape completely from the control of the ruling classes. The more intelligent lords granted the towns enough freedom to become prosperous but retained enough control to share in that prosperity, through taxes, tolls, and payments for market rights. It was not always easy to strike this balance, however, and all through the eleventh and twelfth centuries lords and towns haggled over the terms of their relationship. The Church had an especially difficult time. Like all landlords, it hated to surrender any of its rights, and it had little sympathy with the businessman's way of life. In eastern France there were bloody conflicts between bishops and their towns, and Rome itself staged frequent rebellions against the pope throughout the twelfth century.

In the end, the towns gained personal freedom for their people and a separate system of municipal government. But the extent of self-government varied with the strength of the country's kings and nobles. In England and in the feudal states of France, for example, the towns never became independent. Towns in Spain enjoyed considerable liberty at first, but it was gradually whittled away as the kings became stronger. In Germany the process went the other way: so long as the emperors were strong, the towns had little independence; but after the collapse of the Empire in the thirteenth century many, though not all, of the cities became free. In Italy no medieval ruler managed to control the towns for any length of time, and most of them became independent city-states. These differences in the autonomy of towns from one country to another were to have a significant effect on the political structure of Europe. Rulers who could not tap the

An Early Medieval Merchant

When the boy had passed his childish years quietly at home [in Norfolk, England], he began to follow more prudent ways of life, and to learn carefully and persistently the teachings of worldly forethought. He chose not to follow the life of a husbandman but . . . aspiring to the merchant's trade, he began to follow the peddler's way of life, first learning how to gain in small bargains and things of insignificant price and thence . . . to buy and sell and gain from things of greater expense. For in his beginnings he was wont to wander with small wares around the villages and farmsteads of his own neighborhood, but in process of time he gradually associated himself by compact with city merchants. . . . At first he lived for four years as a peddler in Lincolnshire, going on foot and carrying the cheapest wares; then he traveled abroad, first to St. Andrews in Scotland and then to Rome. On his return . . . he began to launch on bolder courses and to coast frequently by sea to the foreign lands that lay about him. . . . At length his great labors and cares bore much fruit of worldly gain. For he labored not only as a merchant but also as a shipman . . . to Denmark and Flanders and Scotland; in all which lands he found certain rare wares, which he carried to other parts wherein he knew them to be less familiar and coveted by the inhabitants. . . . Hence he made great profit in all his bargains, and gathered much wealth in the sweat of his brow, for he sold dear in one place the wares which he had bought elsewhere at a small price.

Life of St. Godric of Finchale (eleventh century), trans. by G. G. Coulton, *Social Life in Britain from the Conquest to the Reformation* (Cambridge University Press, 1925), pp. 415–17.

wealth of their towns found it difficult to build strong centralized states; this is one reason why Italy and Germany remained disunited for so long. Conversely, rulers who could draw on the resources of their towns were able to build powerful administrative and military organizations; this is one reason why France and England had centralized governments at such an early date.

THE POLITICAL REVIVAL

The economic revival of Europe was accompanied by a political revival, which was most noticeable in northern France and in England. In northern France the Count of Flanders and the Duke of Normandy had built up relatively well-governed states. The counts of Flanders were fortunate in having neither dangerous neighbors nor powerful vassals. They enlarged the boundaries of their original holdings without ever losing personal control over the county. They named their own men to occupy the fortified castles; they suppressed private wars; and they kept the higher law courts firmly in their own hands. Warfare often broke out along the borders, but the heart of Flanders was relatively peaceful and Flemish industry grew apace.

The vikings had received Normandy in 911, but it took some time for the wild sea rovers to settle down on the land. Only after 950 could the dukes of Normandy begin to organize their government. Given the environment, this had to be a feudal government, but the dukes stressed those elements in the feudal relationship that kept them strong and minimized those that reduced their power. They avoided the fragmentation of political authority that occurred elsewhere and kept full control over barons and lesser vassals. The Duke of Normandy could raise a larger army in proportion to the size of his holdings than could any other French feudal lord. At the same time, to ensure that no vassal became too powerful, he discouraged private war, ordered that no new castle could be built except by special license, and reserved to himself justice over serious crimes throughout Normandy. His

The Duke of Normandy and the Norman Church

This document comes from the twelfth century (1172) but it repeats obligations laid on the Norman Church in the times of William the Conqueror.

The bishop of Avranches owes 5 knights, and another five from the fief of St. Philibert.

The bishop of Contances, 5 knights
The bishop of Bayeux, 20 knights
The bishop of Sées, 6 knights
The bishop of Lisieux, the service of 20 knights
The abbot of Fécamp, the service of 10 knights
The abbot of Mont St. Michel, the service of 6 knights in the Avranchin and Cotentin and 1 knight in the Bessin
The abbot of St. Ouen of Rouen, the service of 6 knights (other abbots owe a total of 25 knights).

From Charles H. Haskins, *Norman Institutions* (Cambridge, Mass.: Harvard University Press, 1925), p. 8.

firm control over most of the towns assured him a good income from their growing commerce. And, since he named all the bishops and most of the abbots, he dominated the Norman Church. In order to keep their lands, churchmen had to supply the duke with a large part of his army and much of his administrative staff. Normandy, like Flanders, was a relatively peaceful and prosperous state, and its population soon began to expand.

The energies of Normandy and Flanders were directed into different channels, however. The Flemings concentrated on industry and agriculture. Many of them settled in the towns and became textile workers; others began the centuries-long struggle to reclaim from the sea the flooded land of the coast. They became so skillful in the arts of diking and draining that they were sought by rulers of other provinces. In the twelfth century thousands of Flemish peasants moved across Germany to clear and drain the lands that German lords had won from the Slavs. In Normandy, on the other hand, though some new land was cleared, there was none of the intensive agricultural and industrial activity that marked Flanders. Instead, the Normans turned toward military and political expansion.

THE NORMAN CONQUEST
OF SOUTHERN ITALY   1130

The first Norman conquest was in southern Italy than there were in England, and their first leaders had little authority. But in Italy, as in Normandy earlier and in England later, the Normans showed an uncanny ability to build a strong government out of whatever institutions they found ready at hand. They introduced Norman feudalism in order to guarantee the ruler a strong army, but they preserved much of the Byzantine and Moslem bureaucratic apparatus. The Norman kingdom of Sicily, when it finally took shape in the twelfth century, was one of the wonders of the medieval world. Norman barons and knights, Greek secretaries, and Moslem financial experts all worked together to make the king strong. He had full control over justice and administration; he regulated the commerce of the entire kingdom; he enjoyed a steady income collected by a centralized financial bureau. Only the king of England could rival him in these matters, and during most of the twelfth century even the king of England probably had less authority.

The Normans in Italy

The first Norman conquest was in southern Italy, where only the wreckage of earlier political systems survived. The Byzantine Empire held the mainland coasts; the interior was divided among Lombard princes; and the island of Sicily was ruled by rapidly shifting Moslem dynasties. The first Normans came to Italy in the early eleventh century as mercenary soldiers, but soon they were fighting for themselves instead of for their employers. Under Robert Guiscard the Normans had conquered almost all of the mainland by 1071. Meanwhile Robert's younger brother Roger had launched the conquest of Sicily. In this slow and bloody operation, the Moslem strongholds had to be reduced one by one, but by 1091 Sicily was firmly in Roger's possession. His son, Roger II, eventually inherited the mainland conquests as well and in 1130 took the title of King of Sicily.

This conquest of southern Italy and Sicily was in many ways a more remarkable feat than the Norman conquest of England. There were fewer Normans

Norman archers, detail from the Bayeux tapestry. Notice that the longbow was not yet in use.

The Norman Conquest of England

In the long run, however, it was the Norman conquest of England that had the more important consequences. The brilliant Sicilian state fell on evil days in the thirteenth century when it was conquered by a French prince. Only in England did the Norman genius for government have an opportunity to produce lasting results.

As we have seen, in the years just before 1066, Anglo-Saxon England was torn by dissension. King Edward the Confessor could not control his quarreling earls, and he had no direct heir. At one time he had thought of naming his mother's cousin William, Duke of Normandy, to succeed him. But William was not descended from the Anglo-Saxon kings and the English disliked the Normans. Later Earl Godwin and his son, Earl Harold, became so strong that William's claims were set aside. Harold gained the dominant voice in the government, and when Edward finally died in 1066 Harold was unanimously chosen king by the leading men of the country.

But William was determined not to lose the inheritance to which he thought himself entitled. As Duke of Normandy he already had a powerful army, and he reinforced it by recruiting soldiers from all the neighboring feudal states. The pope, who was annoyed with the Anglo-Saxons because they had driven out a French Archbishop of Canterbury during one of their anti-Norman demonstrations, gave his blessing to William's enterprise. By the summer of 1066 William had assembled an army of over 5,000 men.

Harold, aware that the attack was coming, massed his forces in southern England. But just as William was ready to sail, Harold was called north to face the last great invasion of the Northmen. Harold defeated the invaders in a hard battle and hurried back to the south in time to take up a strong position on a hill near Hastings. He might have been better advised to stay back of the Thames and let William's army waste away, as invading armies usually did in the Middle Ages. Forced marches had exhausted the Anglo-Saxon army, and heavy battle casualties had thinned its ranks; moreover, expected support from the northern earls failed to materialize. Harold made a heroic defensive stand, but in the end he was killed and the English shield-wall broke. William marched on London and was accepted as king.

William's victory owed much to chance, but his subsequent consolidation of power in England demonstrated his real ability as a ruler. He had to deal with a bewildered and disoriented native population and with an unreliable group

Norman troops on horseback engaging Anglo-Saxon foot troops in battle. From the Bayeux tapestry, late eleventh century.

of conquerors, more than half of whom were not Normans. There were some Anglo-Saxon risings; there were even more cases of disobedience and rebellion on the part of his French barons. But he rode them all down: "The rich complained and the poor murmured," says the *Anglo-Saxon Chronicle,* "but he was so sturdy that he recked naught of them; they must will all that the king willed, if they would live or would keep their lands."

William's power rested on two basic principles. First, he insisted that he was the lawful heir of Edward the Confessor and so had inherited all the rights of the Anglo-Saxon kings. The Anglo-Saxon aristocracy, by opposing their rightful ruler, had forfeited their lands and rights. This led to the second principle: the new Norman aristocracy now held all lands and rights as fiefs of the king. No lord *owned* anything; he merely had a right to hold it so long as he obeyed and rendered service to the king. This arrangement overcame the chief weakness of the Anglo-Saxon monarchy—namely, its failure to control or discipline the earls and great landlords. A Norman baron who resisted the king knew that he would lose part or all of his land.

William gave his barons and knights extensive powers in local government. He transferred most of the hundred courts to private hands and named Norman barons as sheriffs. This put the peasants at the mercy of the new aristocracy, and many freemen became serfs. But men above the peasant level were protected by the king. The county courts were still the king's courts, and any baronial sheriff who showed signs of trying to build up independent power could be summarily removed. The king kept the peace so well that, to quote the *Chronicle* again, "a man might travel through the kingdom unmolested with a bosomful of gold."

Norman Government in England

The most striking results of the Norman conquest was a steady growth in the power of the king's central court. This court had a solid core of household officials and clerks, and a fluctuating population of bishops and barons who happened to be with the king at any given moment. The court assisted the king in any business he laid before it; it could advise on policy, audit accounts, or try cases involving the barons. William kept it very busy, and he himself traveled incessantly up and down England settling local quarrels. When he could not be present himself, he sometimes sent a delegation from his court to represent him. These delegations, with the full authority of the king, could try suits involving land disputes among the king's

Left: The death of Harold, as portrayed in the Bayeux tapestry. Above: Silver penny bearing the likeness of William the Conqueror.

vassals. They often used a new and very effective procedure that William had imported from Normandy: trial by inquest. In an inquest, neighbors of the litigants were sworn to give true answers to questions concerning the matters in dispute. Procedure by inquest was a much better way of getting at the facts than trial by battle (the procedure favored by the Norman barons), and it enabled the king to settle disputes peacefully and to protect both his own rights and those of his vassals.

The most famous example of the inquest was the Domesday Survey. Faced with the confusion caused by the rapid redistribution of land after the conquest, William wanted to know what each district owed him and what estates were held by his vassals; he probably also wanted to settle a number of boundary disputes among his barons. In 1086 he sent delegations from his court to every county in England with orders to swear in a group of men to make an inquest in each village. The village inquests told the king's men how much land there was in the village, how many men, who had held the land before the conquest, who held it now, and what it owed the king. The results of all these inquests were summarized by the king's clerks in Domesday Book, a nearly complete survey (London and the northern counties are missing) of the kingdom of England. This amazing feat shows both William's power and his administrative skill. No other eleventh-century king could have done it; no later medieval king had vision enough to attempt it. Domesday stands alone between the tax surveys of the Roman Empire and the censuses of the modern period.

William died in 1087 and was followed by his sons William Rufus (1087-1100) and Henry I (1100-35). Rufus exploited his rights over bishops and barons until he brought them to the point of rebellion, but he made no permanent innovations in government. Henry, on the other hand, made the central government much more efficient. Following earlier precedents, he segregated the financial work of the court in a separate department, the Exchequer, to which the sheriffs had to give an accounting twice a year for every penny of income and expenditure. All these reports were copied out each year in a long document called a Pipe Roll. By consulting earlier Pipe Rolls the Exchequer could make sure that the sheriffs had not overlooked or embezzled royal revenues and that they were paying their arrears. Though England was still thinly inhabited—Domesday figures suggest a population of not much over one million—Henry's efficient administration gave him an income larger than that of the king of France, who nominally ruled a much larger country.

Henry also improved the administration of justice. He sent out delegates

The Domesday Survey
1086

The monks of Ely added this note to their copy of Domesday returns for their lands.

Here is written down the inquest of the lands [of Ely] as the king's barons inquired about them: namely, by the oaths of the sheriff of the shire and of all the barons and their French soldiers, and of the whole hundred [court], and of the priest, the reeve and six villeins of each vill. Then, how the manor is called, who held it in the time of King Edward [the Confessor] and who holds it now, how many hides,* how many plows on the demesne, how many men, how many villeins, how many serfs, how much woods, how much meadow, how much pasture, how many mills . . . how much it was worth altogether and how much now. . . . All this three times over, once for the time of King Edward, once for the time when King William gave it out, and once as it now is—and whether more can be had from it than is now being given.

Trans. from W. Stubbs, *Select Charters* (Oxford: Clarendon Press, 1921), p. 101.

*hide: 120 acres.

from his court so often that they came to be more like circuit judges than special commissioners. Few important cases were any longer heard by the sheriffs—a precaution which, added to the strict financial accounting imposed on them, removed any danger of their becoming too independent. Henry also used inquests frequently and kept the peace as his father had done. At his death in 1135 England was a unified kingdom, far more peaceful than most of western Europe, far more powerful than its size and population seemed to warrant.

THE RELIGIOUS REVIVAL

The perfecting of the parish system and the elimination of paganism west of the Elbe during the Carolingian period meant that for generations everyone in western Europe had been exposed to Christianity. By the eleventh century the cumulative effects of this exposure began to make themselves felt. True, the strength of Christian ideals was diluted by the corruption or ignorance of many members of the clergy, but the ideals were powerful enough to survive. Slowly Christianity became less and less a matter of external observance, more and more a matter of strong internal conviction. A great wave of popular piety swept through Europe in the eleventh and twelfth centuries, changing the whole character of European society.

The Peace Movement

The Peace Movement was one of the earliest manifestations of the growing influence of Christian ideals. Feudal warfare was waged largely at the expense of noncombatants; the usual tactic was a raid on enemy lands in which crops were destroyed, cattle driven off, and churches plundered. During the late tenth century, bishops in central France tried to protect their people from the horrors of war. Under their leadership peace associations were formed in which each member swore not to attack peasants, merchants, or churchmen. The associations raised armies to punish violators and often levied an annual assessment to support their operations. The movement to protect noncombatants was known as the Peace of God. Leaders of the Peace Movement also tried to forbid fighting on certain holy days, such as Sunday and the Christmas and Easter seasons. This attempt, known as the Truce of God, was far less effective than the Peace of God and did little to curb feudal warfare.

So long as the Peace of God depended on diocesan armies led by churchmen, it had only limited success. But in the eleventh century the idea was taken up by powerful lords in northern France and western Germany as a means of restraining unruly vassals. With no hope of plunder, feudal war seemed less enticing; and with no chance to make war on his neighbors, a minor lord could seldom become strong enough to challenge his lord. The Count of Flanders and the Duke of Normandy, along with many other rulers, enforced the Peace of God in their lands. Thus the Peace Movement gave added security to peasants and merchants and helped increase agricultural production and trade.

Monastic Reform

Another sign of the growing strength of Christian ideals was the movement toward monastic reform. The older monasteries, rich in endowments and resigned to the demands of kings and nobles, were no longer centers of piety or learning. Reform was clearly necessary; the movement began in Germany and France in the tenth century and reached its peak in the eleventh. Reforming abbots, after they had improved the discipline and the administration of their own monastery, were often asked to help reorganize neighboring establishments. Thus groups of monasteries, inspired by the same ideals and governed by the same methods, were formed. The most famous of these groups was the one headed by Cluny, a monastery in eastern France, and the abbot of Cluny was often as influential as the pope.

Many people were attracted by the opportunity to enter one of the reformed monasteries, so that by the end of the eleventh century there were more monasteries and more monks than ever before.

And, without exactly intending it, the reformed monks stirred up such enthusiasm for strict adherence to Christian ideals that it spilled over into other areas and caused drastic changes in the Church.

The Problem of Secular Control

The most dramatic manifestation of popular piety and the desire for reform was a struggle, in the late eleventh century, to free the Church from secular control and to make it the final authority in western society. The early monastic reformers had worried little about this problem. So long as kings and lords let them restore discipline within their orders they were quite willing to give service to the ruler and even to accept his candidates as abbots. What happened outside the monastery was the king's business, not theirs. But so long as laymen controlled the appointment of bishops and abbots, there was no hope of creating a truly Christian society outside the monasteries. At best, kings and great lords appointed good administrators who spent most of their time on secular affairs. At worst, they sold abbacies and bishoprics or gave them as a sort of pension to incompetent relatives. In either case prelates appointed in this way were likely to be poor spiritual leaders. Some reformers were reluctant to break entirely with the kings, who after all were semisacred personages, but as the eleventh century went on, more and more of them came to believe that the Church could not accomplish its mission until it was independent of lay authority.

They also came to believe that the only way to gain independence and authority for the Church was to strengthen the position of the pope. An isolated bishop or group of clergymen could not resist the pressure of secular rulers. But if the Church were tightly organized under the pope's leadership, then the moral influence of the entire Church could be brought to bear on all the problems of European society. By 1050 the reformers began to proclaim that the pope should be completely independent of all laymen, even the emperor, and that he should have complete administrative

Bronze figure of a monk writing on the tail of a monster, on which he is seated. From a cross or candlestick base, North German or English, *ca.* 1150.

jurisdiction over all churchmen, even those who were officials and vassals of kings.

The man who did most to formulate and execute this program was the monk Hildebrand, who later became Pope Gregory VII. He had served in the papal court since the 1040s, and in 1059 he inspired a famous decree that placed the election of the pope in the hands of the cardinals. The cardinals were the leading clergymen of the Roman region—priests of the major Roman churches and bishops of the dioceses around the city. This decree, designed to eliminate the influence of both the Roman nobility and the emperor, proved remarkably successful; after 1059 no pope owed his position to direct lay appointment.

The Investiture Conflict

Hildebrand soon became pope. As Gregory VII (1073–85) he tried to gain the same independence for the Church as a whole that he had already won for the papacy. He concentrated his attack on the appointment of bishops by laymen. Eventually, this controversy became focused on lay investiture, the practice by which a secular ruler bestowed the symbols of spiritual authority, such as the

Detail of a manuscript illustration of Gregory VII.

ring and the staff, on the bishops he had appointed. The target was well chosen. A king might legitimately claim that he should have some influence in the choice of bishops, since they had secular as well as religious duties. But he could hardly justify a ceremony that suggested that he was bestowing spiritual authority on officials of the Church. Gregory, however, was seeking more than the abolition of an obnoxious ceremony. He was trying to end all forms of lay control over ecclesiastical appointments and so free the Church to exert its influence directly on all people in western Europe.

The attack on lay interference with ecclesiastical appointments plunged Gregory into a bitter struggle with the emperor Henry IV (1056–1106). Henry had had a difficult time asserting his authority in Germany; he had succeeded only because he controlled the resources of most of the bishoprics and abbeys of the country. Thus Gregory, by forbidding lay investiture, was in effect depriving Henry of the only means he had to preserve the unity and strengthen the central government of Germany.

Henry's reaction was violent and ill advised. He had just defeated a dangerous group of rebels in Saxony and was feeling both belligerent and overconfident. He denounced Gregory as an illegally elected pope and summoned a council of German bishops to depose him from the papal see. In a bitter letter announcing this decision to Gregory, Henry ended with the curse: "Down, down, to be damned through all the ages!" Gregory countered by excommunicating Henry and freeing his subjects from their oath of allegiance to him. "It is right," said Gregory, "that he who attempts to diminish the honor of the Church, shall himself lose the honor which he seems to have."

The issue was fairly joined. Now everything depended on the reaction of the bishops and princes of the Empire. Many of the German princes were delighted to have an excuse to resist Henry; the bishops, who owed their jobs to the king, were more loyal. The religious issue, in the end, brought the waverers over to Gregory's side, and an assembly of bishops and princes at Oppenheim in 1076 decided to depose Henry unless he was absolved by the pope.

Henry, headstrong but no fool, saw that he must make his peace with the pope. In wintry weather, he journeyed to Italy and came to Gregory at the castle of Canossa in 1077. He stood as a penitent outside the castle for three days while Gregory wrestled with the conflict between his political aims and his spiritual duties. If he absolved Henry he would wreck the coalition supporting his German policies, but the head of the Church could scarcely reject a repentant sinner. In the end Gregory admitted Henry, accepted his promise to obey papal orders, and then granted him absolution.

In the short run Henry gained a political victory by his act of submission. As both he and Gregory had foreseen, the German princes felt that the pope had failed them; they could no longer oppose a king who had been reconciled

---

Principles of Gregory VII   ca. 1075

This document was certainly drawn up in Gregory's circle, and probably by the pope himself. It expresses the views of those who were trying to increase papal power in both Church and state.

1. That the Roman church was founded by the Lord alone.
2. That only the Roman pontiff is rightly called universal.
3. That he alone can depose or reestablish bishops.
4. That his legate, even if of inferior rank, is above all bishops in council; and he can give sentence of deposition against them. . . .
12. That it is permitted to him to depose emperors. . . .
18. That his decision ought to be reviewed by no one, and that he alone can review the decisions of everyone.
19. That he ought to be judged by no one.
20. That no one may dare condemn a man who is appealing to the apostolic see.
21. That the greater cases of every church ought to be referred to him.
22. That the Roman church has never erred nor will ever err, as the Scripture bears witness.
23. That the Roman pontiff, if he has been canonically ordained, is indubitably made holy by the merits of the blessed Peter. . . .
24. That by his precept and license subjects are permitted to accuse their lords. . . .
27. That he can absolve the subjects of the unjust from their fealty.

From *Dictatus Papae Gregorii VII*, trans. by E. Lewis, *Medieval Political Ideas* (New York: Knopf, 1954), Vol. II, pp. 380–81.

with the Church. Henry regained much of his authority; he even became strong enough to invade Italy and force Gregory to take refuge with the Normans in the South. But in the long run the victory went to the papacy. The pope had demonstrated that he could force the most powerful ruler in the West to yield and that he could stir up rebellion against an anointed king. The lesson was not lost on western rulers; for two hundred years after Canossa few of them were willing to risk prolonged defiance of the pope.

The struggle over lay investiture persisted for a generation after Gregory's death in 1085. Henry was plagued by rebellion for the rest of his reign and trouble continued under his son, Henry V (1106–25). At last a compromise was reached at the Concordat of Worms (1122) by which lay investiture in the strict sense was abandoned. The emperor could still nominate bishops, but the pope could refuse approval to men who were clearly unqualified, and he could suspend or even remove bishops who proved unworthy. In practice, this meant that the German bishops had to show a certain amount of obedience to the pope if they wanted to keep their jobs. The German ruler, deprived of full control over the Church in his own country, lost his chief source of power. The independence of the German princes increased accordingly.

Similar but less acute struggles took place in France and England. In neither country was the king as dependent on control over the Church as the German emperor had been, so it was easier to reach a settlement. The outcome was about the same: the pope admitted royal influence over appointments, but he remained the final judge of the qualifications of bishops. No one who offended the pope could hope to become or remain a bishop. Assured of administrative control of the Church, the pope could now insist that his policies be accepted throughout Europe. Acceptance was slow and grudging in some places, but it could never be entirely denied. The Church, far stronger and more independent than it had ever been before, had an unprecedented opportunity to guide and control European society.

The First Crusade

During the Investiture Conflict many barons and knights had supported the pope. The influence of the Church over the military class was further demonstrated by the First Crusade. A crusade was a military expedition organized by the pope to attack enemies of the Church. Earlier expeditions against the western Moslems had been encouraged by the pope, but these campaigns included only small groups of knights and were not fully under the control of the Church. By the end of the eleventh century, however, the papacy was stronger and the military class was eager to prove its devotion to the faith.

The First Crusade was proclaimed by Pope Urban II at the Council of Clermont in 1095. He had many reasons for his action, and it is impossible to decide which was dominant. Urban had just

Henry IV before Canossa, a miniature from an early twelfth-century manuscript of the life of Countess Matilda of Tuscany. Henry, kneeling, asks Abbot Hugh of Cluny and Countess Matilda to intercede for him with Pope Gregory VII.

Urban's Speech at Clermont

I exhort you . . . to strive to expel that wicked race [the Turks] from our Christian lands. . . . Christ commands it. Remission of sins will be granted for those going thither. . . . Let those who are accustomed to wage private war wastefully even against believers go forth against the infidels. . . . Let those who have lived by plundering be soldiers of Christ; let those who formerly contended against brothers and relations rightly fight barbarians; let those who were recently hired for a few pieces of silver win their eternal reward. . . . The sorrowful here will be glad there, the poor here will be rich there, and the enemies of the Lord here will be His friends there. Let no delay postpone the journey . . . when winter has ended and spring has come . . . enter the highways courageously with the Lord going on before.

Adapted from Fulcher of Chartres, *History of Jerusalem,* trans. by M. E. McGinty (Philadelphia: University of Pennsylvania Press, 1941), p. 16. Fulcher was at Clermont and went on the crusade.

reaffirmed the principles of the Peace of God, and he certainly believed that Europe would be more tranquil if the military classes turned their weapons against an outside foe instead of fighting one another. Moreover, the investiture struggle was still going on; if the pope could enlist large numbers of fighting men under his banner, it would demonstrate that he and not the emperor was the real leader of the West. Finally, the situation in the Near East seemed ripe for intervention. The Turks, who had come into Mesopotamia as mercenary soldiers of the caliphs, had crushed the Byzantine army at Manzikert (1071) and had occupied most of Asia Minor. The Byzantine Empire, in mortal peril, turned to the West for aid. At the same time Jerusalem had fallen to a fanatical Moslem dynasty that ruled from Cairo. Pilgrimage to the Holy City was now more difficult than it had been when Jerusalem was held by the tolerant Abbasid caliphs. A western army could strengthen Byzantium, and gratitude for its assistance might close the breach that had opened up between the Roman and Greek Churches since the controversy over iconoclasm. The capture of Jerusalem would make it easier for Christians to accomplish the most salutary of all pilgrimages, the visit to the Holy Sepulchre.

Urban's appeal for an army to fight the Turks and regain Jerusalem met with an astonishing response. The Count of Toulouse was the first to take the Cross, and he was soon joined by the Duke of Lorraine, four great lords from northern France, two Norman princes from southern Italy, and thousands of lesser men. The largest number of crusaders came from France and the German provinces near France, but all the countries of western Europe were represented in the undertaking. Nothing shows more clearly the strength of religious conviction and the effectiveness of the leadership of the Church. Some of the greater nobles may have thought of the crusade as an opportunity to acquire new lands; some knights may merely have been seeking adventure. But the majority of crusaders had purely religious motives. Urban had promised them full absolution for their sins and immediate entrance to Heaven if they died fighting the infidels. So numerous were the volunteers that it took a year to organize the main armies; meanwhile thousands of noncombatant pilgrims, escorted by a few knights, set off for the East. Most of them were massacred by the Turks; only a few survived to join the armies that followed.

The crusaders' slogan was "God wills it!" Certainly it was a near miracle that they succeeded. Almost everything was against them: they knew nothing of the geography or politics of the East; they had little money and no supply services; they had no single commanding officer, and bitter feuds broke out among their leaders even before they entered Moslem lands. The Byzantine emperor, as soon as he found that he could not use them as mercenaries, grew suspicious of them; he wanted to reconquer Asia Minor, not go off on a harebrained raid on Jerusalem. That the crusaders overcame all these obstacles was due partly to their enthusiasm, and partly to the fact that the Turks were divided into many small principalities and were disliked by other Moslems. Moreover, the heavy-armed western cavalry was one of the best fighting forces on the Eurasian continent. The crusaders suffered severely from disease and starvation; they were battered in two hard-fought battles; they were weakened by continuing dissension among their leaders. But somehow they kept going. In 1099 they took Jerusalem and set up a series of crusading states stretching from Antioch in the north down through Tripoli and Jerusalem to the Dead Sea.

The dramatic success of the First Crusade reinforced the influence of the Church and strengthened the self-confidence of the peoples of western Europe. The many chronicles that describe the great campaign, though ascribing victory to God's protection, nevertheless show obvious pride in the crusaders' heroic deeds. But it would be a mistake to overemphasize the effects of the crusade; it was a result, not a cause, of the great medieval revival.

THE "RENAISSANCE OF THE TWELFTH CENTURY"

That revival continued without break into the twelfth century. Few periods in the history of the West have shown as

Pilgrims, in a scene of the Last Judgment, Cathedral of Autun, early twelfth century.

much energy and originality. The men of the twelfth century not only continued the reform of ecclesiastical and secular government but also laid the foundations for a new architecture, a new literature, and a new system of education. All these activities drew on the Church for intellectual inspiration and material support, and in many of them churchmen played a leading role.

St. Bernard

The most powerful churchman of the early twelfth century was St. Bernard of Clairvaux (1090–1153). He was the first outstanding leader produced by the Cistercian Order, one of the very strict monastic groups founded toward the end of the eleventh century. Earlier reformers, such as the monks of Cluny, had aimed only at honest observance of the Benedictine Rule, but this was not enough for the new generation of religious leaders. The strong religious feeling that made possible the First Crusade also found expression in more ascetic forms of monastic life. The Cistercians refused to own serfs or revenue-producing properties and insisted on living in the wilderness by the labor of their own hands. In the end this uncompromising attitude gained them considerable wealth, for they had to develop new agricultural techniques, such as large-scale sheep-raising, to make up for their lack of serfs. But in the early, heroic days the Cistercians attracted many able and zealous men by the example of their rigorous life.

St. Bernard, who entered the Cistercian Order as a young man, was soon sent to found a new monastery at Clairvaux. Under his direction Clairvaux became a center of piety and asceticism. St. Bernard sought only to be a worthy abbot of this model monastery, but while he had no ambitions for himself, he had great zeal for the Church. Whenever he saw its unity threatened by schism or heresy, or its ideals menaced by worldly pressures and interests, he could not rest. Therefore this abbot, who wanted only a narrow cell in a secluded monastery, spent most of his life in public business, advising popes, giving lectures to kings, preaching to crowds, and writing letters to every prominent man in Europe.

From 1125 to the year of his death in 1153, St. Bernard dominated the West through his eloquence, his piety, and his boundless energy. His support saved causes that were tottering to failure; his opposition damned men who seemed born for success. In a disputed papal election in 1130, St. Bernard convinced the rulers of Europe that Innocent II should be recognized as the rightful pope, even though he had received fewer votes in the College of Cardinals than an opposing candidate. Innocent II was naturally influenced by St. Bernard, as was Pope Eugenius III (1145–53), who had been a Cistercian monk himself. When Eugenius inaugurated the Second Crusade in 1147 to regain some lost territories in Syria, he returned to St. Bernard for help in recruiting leaders for the campaign. St. Bernard did not disappoint the pope; he persuaded both the king of France and the emperor of Germany to take the Cross. When the Second Crusade failed, St. Bernard wrote the official apology ascribing the debacle to the sins of the Christians.

St. Bernard was in many ways a conservative man. He disliked the new architecture of the twelfth century; costly churches seemed to him unnecessary for the worship of God and a waste of money that might better be given to the poor. He disliked the new learning, which exalted human reason and led men to think that they could approach God through logic rather than through faith. He worried about the growing bureaucracy at the papal court, even though he realized it was essential to the unity of the Church and the authority of the pope.

But although he was a conservative in worldly matters, St. Bernard was an innovator in religion. He was a leader of the new piety, the movement to humanize Christianity and Christianize human life. He emphasized devotion to the Virgin and dwelt on the life of Jesus on earth among men. As Dante was to point out, the central theme in St. Bernard's teaching was love, the love of God for man and the love that man should have for God. He talked more of the joys of Paradise than of the pains of Hell. He was saddened and angered by those who rejected the love and mercy of God, but he always hoped to save the sinners he denounced. In all this he gave a lead to his contemporaries. The number of churches dedicated to the Virgin increased sharply, more emphasis was placed on the Nativity and the childhood of Jesus, and hope of salvation began to outweigh fear of damnation. In many ways the twelfth century was an age of optimism, an optimism that was reflected in its religion as well as in its secular activities.

Cistercian monks shown living by their own labor. Detail from a manuscript of St. Gregory's *Moralia in Job*, written at the motherhouse of Cîteaux in the twelfth century.

St. Bernard on Love

First, then, a man loves his own self for self's sake, since he is flesh, and he cannot have any taste except for things in relation with him; but when he sees that he is not able to subsist by himself, that God is, as it were, necessary to him, he begins to inquire and to love God by faith. Thus he loves God in the second place, but because of his own interest, and not for the sake of God Himself. But when, on account of his own necessity, he has begun to worship Him and to approach Him by meditation, by reading, by prayer, by obedience, he comes little by little to know God with a certain familiarity, and in consequence to find Him sweet and kind; and thus having tasted how sweet the Lord is, he passes to the third stage, and thus loves God no longer on account of his own interest, but for the sake of God himself. Once arrived there, he remains stationary, and I know not if in this life man is truly able to rise to the fourth degree, which is, no longer to love himself except for the sake of God. . . .

From S. J. Eales, tr., *Some Letters of Saint Bernard* (London: J. Hodges, 1904), pp. 202–03.

Abbot Suger and Gothic Architecture

Another great abbot, second only to St. Bernard in influence, was Suger of St. Denis (*ca.* 1091–1152). The son of poor peasants, he had been given to the monastery by his parents when only a child. Sheer ability carried him to the position of abbot, an outstanding example of the opportunities the Church offered to men of low birth. St. Denis was one of the wealthiest monasteries in France as well as the burial place of the French kings. Suger was thus closely associated with the royal house, and his administrative ability made him a close adviser of two kings, Louis VI and Louis VII. During the absence of Louis VII on the Second Cru-

Left: Barrel vault, church of St. Savin, eleventh century. Although no light could be admitted in the upper part of the nave, the vault could be covered with fine Romanesque painting. Middle: Groin vault, formed by the intersection of two barrel vaults, Mont-Saint-Michel, twelfth century. The walls could now be pierced with windows. Right: Rib vault, Mont-Saint-Michel, late Romanesque. Ribs reinforce the groin vault, but the effect is still heavy.

sade, Suger acted as regent of France; he was remarkably successful in preserving both the stability and the solvency of the realm.

Suger was more than a successful administrator, however. He wrote several books, including an interesting biography of Louis VI. But his overwhelming interest was the rebuilding of the church of St. Denis, which he was determined to make the most beautiful church in France, the "crown of the kingdom." St. Bernard was suspicious of this desire for magnificence, as he was of Suger's involvement in worldly business, but the abbot of St. Denis had tact as well as energy. By giving his full support to the Cistercian's reform policy, he conciliated St. Bernard and gained a free hand for his own activities.

Suger wanted his church to be full of light and color. He had enough money to do as he wished and a remarkable willingness to experiment with new ideas. Workmen flocked to St. Denis from all over France, bringing with them solutions to problems of church architecture that had been worked out in the last half-century. The result was a church that, for the first time, incorporated all the essential elements of the Gothic style.

From 1000 on there had been a great wave of church building in western Europe. The basic plan was still that of the old basilica, a long nave with lower

side aisles and a transept crossing the nave before the altar. At first the churches were low and dark, with strong emphasis on horizontal lines. Then experiments were made in raising the walls and enlarging the windows. For example, architects discovered that a pointed arch over a window increased the area that could be glazed. There had also been some use of stained glass.

But the most important innovations had to do with the vaulting of the interior roof of churches. The flat wooden roofs of the early Roman churches were not very satisfactory in the wet, cold climate of the North. A stone vault covered by a steep-sloped roof would be far more satisfactory in keeping out the weather and reducing the danger of fire. But it took generations for architects to devise the best way of covering the great open spaces of a church with a stone vault. The first and easiest solution was the barrel vault, a continuous semicircular arch extending the entire length of the church. But this scheme was not particularly safe when used for very wide areas. Moreover, because the barrel vault put an equal strain on every part of the side walls, it made the use of large windows impossible, since any substantial cutting into the walls would weaken the whole structure. Then architects hit on the idea of designing a roof as if it were the intersection of two barrel vaults, in that way

Left: Early Gothic rib vault, Mont-Saint-Michel. Greater height and light are now being exploited. Right: Rib vaulting on a grand scale, the nave of Chartes Cathedral, 1194–1220. Great height and light have been achieved; the upper (clerestory) windows are larger and more useful than those at floor level.

concentrating the downward and outward thrust of the roof at a few points along the wall, which in turn could be strengthened by pillars, or piers, and buttresses. Now the walls could be pierced with large, high windows, flooding the church with light. The final refinement was to mark the lines of the intersecting vaults with stone ribs, thus both strengthening and improving the appearance of the roof.

The churches of the eleventh and early twelfth centuries were larger and more beautiful than any that had been built before in the North, but no one of them embodied all these innovations. They still adhered more or less to the old, or Romanesque, style. But the massive Romanesque churches, impressive and beautiful as they were, did not satisfy many churchmen of the twelfth century. They wanted a style that reflected

their new aspirations, something less practical and earthbound, something that symbolized the mystery and splendor of heaven.

Suger felt these longings with particular keenness, and it was under his direction in the church of St. Denis that the decisive step was taken in the evolution of the new style. Suger used almost all the new ideas: pointed arches, rib vaults, larger and higher windows, and stained glass. He described the result in one of his verses: "Bright is the noble building which is pervaded by the new light." Churches were built near Paris along the same principles, and the new Gothic style soon became the standard for church architecture. Southern France, Germany, and Italy clung for some time to Romanesque, but by the early years of the thirteenth century Gothic was triumphing in those areas as well.

Abelard

A third great figure of the early twelfth-century revival, Abelard (*ca.* 1079–1142), was also an abbot, but an unwilling and unhappy one. The son of a minor vassal in Brittany, he had, like many other men of the twelfth century, become inflamed with the love of learning. About 1100, he renounced his inheritance and went to study at Paris.

Paris was full of famous teachers, though there was as yet no formal curriculum. The growing horde of students had overflowed the old cathedral school on the Île de la Cité and lectures were already being given on the Left Bank in what was to become the Latin Quarter. This new enthusiasm for learning resembled in some ways the new piety; men were examining old texts that had been known for centuries and were discovering in them fresh meanings and personal applications. The learning of the Moslem-Byzantine world had not yet entered Europe, but students were finding a new excitement in the old books.

Abelard's first love, like that of many of his contemporaries, was logic. He mastered all the available material in a remarkably short time and immediately set himself up as a teacher, much to the annoyance of some of his former professors. Abelard thoroughly enjoyed teaching logic, but, again like many of his contemporaries, he saw in it more than a formal intellectual exercise. He was convinced that it was a universal tool (somewhat like mathematics today) that could be used to solve old problems and acquire new knowledge. To a man of his time, the most important problems were theological, so he decided to become a master of theology as well as logic. Again he completed his studies in record time and began to steal students from, and contradict, his old teachers.

Abelard was a great teacher and scholar; he was also a very brash young man. For example, he produced an exercise book for his students called *Sic et Non* (*Yes and No*), in which he marshaled opinions from the Bible and the Church Fathers on both sides of controversial questions. It took considerable ingenuity to find support for some of his state-ments—for example, that God is three-fold and the contrary; that sin is pleasing to God and the contrary—and his cleverness added to the suspicions of his contemporaries. The prologue to the book made it seem even more dangerous, for here Abelard announced: "The first key to wisdom is this—constant and frequent questioning. . . . For by doubting we are led to question and by questioning we arrive at the truth." Abelard also wrote a treatise on the Trinity in which he tried to define the attributes of each Person by a rigorous use of logic. This meddling with the central mystery of the faith annoyed St. Bernard, who in one of his angriest letters denounced Abelard as a writer who sought to "place degrees in the Trinity, modes in the Majesty, numbers in the Eternity." St. Bernard felt that God was too great to be defined by the human mind and that all the virtue went out of faith when it was made to seem too rational.

Abelard's personal life increased his reputation for vanity and presumption. His downfall began when he seduced Héloïse, the niece of a canon of the cathedral of Paris. The affair could not be hushed up, for his love poems had been circulated throughout the city, and Héloïse had a child. So Abelard felt it was his duty to marry the girl, an action that blocked his chances for advancement in the Church. Héloïse was ready to dissolve the marriage by taking refuge in a nunnery, but her self-sacrifice only irritated her uncle the more. Fearing that Abelard was seeking to repudiate his niece, he hired a gang of thugs to castrate the scholar. The scandal was so enormous that Abelard temporarily retired from teaching and took refuge as a monk in St. Denis.

Abelard, finding neither intellectual nor religious stimulation in St. Denis (this was just before Suger became abbot), tried to stir things up by criticizing some of the legends about the monastery's patron saint. He was right, as he often was, but the monks became so hostile that Abelard was obliged to flee. When Suger became abbot, he gave Abelard official permission to live elsewhere. This, however, merely led to new trouble. First Abelard was chosen as abbot of a remote Breton monastery, but he found the monks there brutal and ignorant and soon abandoned the post. Then he returned to the neighborhood of Paris and began teaching once more with great success. His return proved unendurable to his enemies. Led by St. Bernard, they succeeded in having his work on the Trinity condemned by a council of bishops. Abelard was forced to renounce his errors and then retired to Cluny, where he lived out the rest of his life in peace.

Abelard's real fault was vanity, not impiety; he had sought to make Christian doctrine more precise, but not to contradict it. He was only the most conspicuous of many scholars who were trying to combine logic, philosophy, and theology in an effort to give Christian doctrine a more rigorous intellectual structure. St. Bernard, who was a mystic rather than a scholar, was perhaps right in feeling that excessive rationalism would weaken the appeal of religion. But he was fighting a losing battle; the future belonged to men who followed Abelard's methods. For the rest of the Middle Ages theology was studied according to the rules of formal logic, and authorities were cited on both sides of every question in order to reach a final, and orthodox, answer. The most popular theological book of the twelfth century, Peter Lombard's *Sentences*, resembled Abelard's work far more than it did that of St. Bernard. The system used by Abelard, Peter Lombard, and others eventually became known as "scholasticism," and scholastic methods dominated European thought for the next three centuries.

The Beginnings of Universities

Exciting as theology was, it did not monopolize the attention of twelfth-century scholars. A revival of interest in the Latin classics, especially noticeable in the cathedral school of Chartres, led to a marked improvement in Latin style. John of Salisbury (d. 1180), who wrote one of the first medieval treatises on political theory, had had some connection with the scholars at Chartres. A growing interest in medicine, centered at Salerno in southern Italy, prompted the study of old Roman textbooks and the new observations of Arab doctors. But theology's real rival was law, and in the long run students of law became far more numerous than students of theology.

Although Roman law had not been completely forgotten during the early Middle Ages, it had been little studied, and most of the copies of Justinian's *Corpus Juris* had disappeared. At the end of the eleventh century there was a revival of interest in Roman law, especially in Italy and southern France. The first great teacher, Irnerius, attracted so many students to his school at Bologna that the city became, and remained for centuries, the chief center of legal studies in Europe. Roman law appealed to students for many reasons: it was a fine example of logical and precise reasoning; it was part of the intellectual legacy of Rome; it gave intelligent answers to problems of human relations that the unsophisticated customary law of medieval Europe had scarcely considered. The Romans had been the most legal-minded people of antiquity, and western Europe had inherited their fondness for law. The *Corpus Juris*, which summed up the work of

MEDIEVAL SCHOOLS AND UNIVERSITIES   1100–1250

- ● University
- ○ School
- + Well-known monastery

ATLANTIC OCEAN

Cambridge · + Bury St.Edmunds
Oxford ● + St. Albans
○ Cologne
+ Bec
Laon
Chartres ○ ○ Reims + Fulda
Orléans ● Paris
Hirsau
+ Clairvaux + Lorch
Vézelay + + Cîteaux + St. Gall
+ Cluny
La Grande Chartreuse
Toulouse
Pavia ○ Padua ●
Montpellier ● + Bobbio
Bologna
Salamanca
Coimbra
Lisbon
+ Monte Cassino
Naples ●
Salerno

MILES 0 — 300

MEDITERRANEAN SEA

generations of Roman lawyers in fairly compact form, could be mastered by students within a reasonable length of time. And a young man soundly trained in Roman law could look forward to a brilliant career; by the middle of the century legal training had become the surest route to promotion in the service of popes and kings. The number of law students who flocked to Bologna from the most distant parts of the Continent increased steadily during the twelfth century.

A special branch of legal studies was canon law, the law of the Church. The Church, of course, had relied heavily on Roman law in formulating its basic rules and procedures, but it had to cope with many problems that Roman law had never touched—for example, the forms to be followed in choosing a bishop, or the requirements for a valid Christian marriage. In deciding these questions the Church relied on the writings of the Fathers, decrees of councils, and administrative and judicial rulings of the popes. Some collections of this scattered material had been made, but none of them enjoyed unquestioned authority. Then about 1140 the monk Gratian produced his *Decretum*, or *Concordance of Discordant Canons*, which was rapidly accepted as the definitive treatise on canon law. Gratian, following the pattern already set by Abelard and other theologians, quoted the authorities on both sides of each question, and then gave what seemed to him the approved solution. Since Gratian taught at Bologna, students came there to study canon law as well as Roman law, and soon there was a large group of experts in the subject. Canon law, even more than Roman law, opened the road to high office, in this case high office in the Church. Many bishops and almost all the popes from 1159 to the end of the fourteenth century were students of canon law.

These groupings of students and teachers at centers like Paris and Bologna eventually coalesced into universities, one of the most significant institutional legacies of the Middle Ages. The best of the cathedral schools, such as Paris, had some degree of organization before 1150, but not all schools were cathedral

The Revival of Roman Law

Three times has Rome given her laws to the world, three times has she bound different peoples together: first, by the unity of the state, when the Roman people stood at the height of their strength, second, by the unity of the Church after the Empire had fallen, and third, by the unity of law when Roman Law was accepted during the Middle Ages. The first victory was won by force of arms, but the other two by the power of the mind. . . . Roman Law, like Christianity, has become an essential element of modern civilization.

From Rudolph von Jhering, *Geist des römischen Rechts* (Leipzig: Breitkopf und Härtel, 1907), Vol. I, p. 1.

schools, and even the cathedral schools needed a stronger structure and more powers of regulation. The many foreign students at Bologna, for example, felt that they were being cheated by the Italian boardinghouse keepers, and sometimes by their professors as well. They formed a union to keep down the price of food and lodging and to make sure that teachers covered an adequate amount of material in their lecture courses. At Paris the chief problem, illustrated by Abelard's career, was to determine at what point a student was entitled to set himself up as a teacher. The bishops, or their chancellors, who were supposed to license teachers, had neither the knowledge nor the time to deal with the growing number of applicants. So in Paris the teachers themselves formed a union, to which they admitted only students who had passed a rigorous examination. It was out of these unions of students and teachers that the university was to emerge.

The intellectual interests that created the first universities were the most striking manifestations of the new vigor of western European society. The people of western Europe had not yet equaled the Romans in the arts of government, and they perhaps had done no more than equal the Romans in total economic production. But they had an intellectual curiosity, an urge to acquire new ideas, that the Romans of the Empire had never possessed. And in the long run this curiosity and drive were to lead to the revival of science and the transformation of European society.

Suggestions for Further Reading

Note: Asterisk denotes a book available in paperback edition.

Economic Revival The first three volumes of the *Cambridge Economic History of Europe,* ed. by M. M. Postan (1952–66) contain excellent articles on medieval agriculture, commerce, and industry. (Be sure to get the second, much improved, edition of Volume I.) There is good source material on the revival of medieval trade in R. S. Lopez and I. W. Raymond, *Medieval Trade in the Mediterranean World* (1955). A useful short survey is R. Latouche, *The Birth of Western Economy* (1961). For England, see R. Lennard, *Rural England* (1959). The effect of the Moslem control of the Mediterranean on European economy is discussed by H. Pirenne, *Economic and Social History of Medieval Europe** (1937), with special attention on the economic activity of Italy and the Low Countries. H. F. Brown, *Venice: An Historical Sketch of the Republic* (1895), is the best one-volume study in English of that important commercial center. Georges Duby, *Rural Economy and Country Life in the Medieval West* (1968), is the best overall study of rural life. E. Power, *Medieval People** (1954), gives a vivid picture of social and manorial life from the point of view of individuals.

H. Pirenne, *Medieval Cities** (1925), is a fine general study of the beginnings of urban civilization and the part played by the middle class in the development of a modern economic system and modern culture. Both C. Stephenson, *Borough and Town* (1933), and J. Tait, *The Medieval English Borough* (1936), are scholarly studies of town development in England with opposing interpretations on the origins of towns. For source material see J. H. Mundy and P. Rienberg, *The Medieval Town* (1958).

Political Revival There are many valuable works on the political history of this period. C. Petit-Dutaillis, *Feudal Monarchy in France and England** (1936), discusses the preservation and development of the monarchy in France and England from the tenth to the thirteenth century. An excellent brief study of the growth of royal power in France is R. Fawtier, *The Capetian Kings of France,** trans. by L. Butler (1960). The older study of E. Lavisse, *Histoire de France,* Vol. II, Part II (1901), which reviews economic, social, and cultural phenomena as well as political, has not been surpassed for comprehensiveness.

Medieval Germany, Vol. I, trans. by G. Barraclough (1938), has good material on Germany in this period, and G. Barraclough, *The Origins of Modern Germany* (1952), analyzes the reasons why Germany lagged behind the rest of Europe in the development of political institutions.

We have interesting evidence on England at this time in the contemporary Ordericus Vitalis, *History of England and Normandy,* 3 vols., trans. by T. Forester (1854), which concentrates on religious events, and in William of Malmesbury, *Chronicle,* trans. by J. A. Giles (1847), which gives attention to both political and religious developments. Both histories go up to 1154. F. W. Maitland, *Domesday Book and Beyond** (1897), is a monument in historical prose writing. The best scholarly treatment of the establishment of Norman feudalism in England is F. M. Stenton, *First Century of English Feudalism* (1932). D. C. Douglas, *William the Conqueror* (1964), is an excellent biography.

C. H. Haskins, *The Normans in European History** (1915), shows the Normans as founders and organizers of states. Political developments in Italy are discussed by P. Villari, *Medieval Italy from Charlemagne to Henry VII* (1910), a broad, readable survey. C. Cahen, *Le Régime féodal de l'Italie normande* (1940), is a critical study of Norman institutions in Italy. An older but still useful book is E. Curtis, *Roger of Sicily and the Normans in Italy* (1912).

Religious Revival Since the impetus for the religious revival of the eleventh century was the monastery at Cluny, J. Evans, *Monastic Life at Cluny* (1931), is a good starting point for study. L. M. Smith, *Cluny in the Eleventh and Twelfth Centuries* (1930), is a valuable if somewhat disjointed study of the influence of Cluny on the religious life of Europe, while D. Knowles, *The Monastic Order in England* (1951), is a thorough and readable study of almost every facet of English monastic life from 900 to 1215.

There is interesting source material on the Investiture Controversy in B. F. Tierney, *The Crisis of Church and State* (1964), and in K. Morrison, *The Investiture Controversey* (1971). A. J. Macdonald, *Hildebrand: A Life of Gregory VII* (1932), is a good brief biography, and the *Correspondence of Gregory VII*, trans. by E. Emerton (1932), contains information not only on the problem of investiture but on the increase in papal activities under Gregory. The excellent book by G. Tellenbach, *Church, State, and Christian Society at the Time of the Investiture Controversy* (1940), shows the conflict as a papal attempt to revalue Christian society in the light of canon law. The consequences for the Church and the state are carefully analyzed by N. F. Cantor, *Church, Kingship and Lay Investiture in England, 1089–1135* (1959), a very scholarly study. W. Ullmann, *Growth of Papal Power in the Middle Ages* (1955), treats the effect of the controversy on the growth of the papal government.

The First Crusade

A. C. Krey, *The First Crusade* (1921), gives a very good picture of the crusade from the accounts of eyewitnesses and participants. One of the best chronicles of the crusade is Fulcher of Chartres' *History of the Expedition to Jerusalem,** ed. by H. S. Fink (1973). *The Alexiad of Anna Comnena,* trans. by E. A. S. Dawes (1928) contains the Byzantine attitude toward the crusade, and Usāmah ibn Murshid, *An Arab-Syrian Gentleman and Warrior in the Period of the Crusades,* trans. by P. K. Hitti (1929), gives the Moslem point of view. The best recent book on the crusade is the fascinating account of S. Runciman, *A History of the Crusades,** Vol. I (1954). Runciman includes a thorough bibliography. M. L. W. Baldwin, ed., *The First Hundred Years* (1955) (Vol. I of *A History of the Crusades* ed. by K. M. Setton), is a collection of essays by leading historians of the crusades. The establishment of feudalism in the conquered East is treated by J. La Monte, *Feudal Monarchy in the Latin Kingdom of Jerusalem* (1932).

The Renaissance of the Twelfth Century

The best general study of the revival of learning in the West is C. H. Haskins, *The Renaissance of the Twelfth Century** (1927), which discusses scholarship, Roman law, and philosophy, and has a good critical bibliography. Another excellent book is C. Brooke, *The Twelfth Century Renaissance** (1969). H. O. Taylor, *The Medieval Mind,* Vol. I (1953), has good material on intellectual developments in the twelfth century, and R. W. Southern, *The Making of the Middle Ages** (1953), presents an excellent account of the influence of the new piety on cultural growth. There is a good cross section of the poetry of the period from 900 to 1160 in H. Waddell, *Medieval Latin Lyrics** (1929).

St. Bernard, Abelard, Suger

There is a wealth of material on these three men, who to a great extent dominated the intellectual life of the first half of the twelfth century. *St. Bernard of Clairvaux,* trans. by G. Webb and A. Walker (1960) is an interesting biography written by Bernard's friend, William of St. Thierry. Bernard's relations with political and intellectual leaders of his time are presented in *The Letters of St. Bernard,* trans. by S. J. Eales (1904). E. Gilson, *The Mystical Theology of St. Bernard* (1940), stresses Bernard's thought. B. S. James, *St. Bernard of Clairvaux* (1957), focuses attention on Bernard the man.

Suger on the Abbey of St. Denis, trans, by E. Panofsky (1946) is a mine of information about the beginnings of Gothic architecture and about monastic government and life. Panofsky's introduction has a good brief biography of Suger. K. J. Conant, *Carolingian and Romanesque Architecture** (1959), gives the background out of which the new architecture developed.

The best serious study of Abelard is E. Gilson, *Eloise and Abelard** (1948). H. Waddell's novel *Peter Abelard** gives a good picture of twelfth-century intellectual activity based on sound scholarship. *Abelard's Letters,* trans. by C. K. Scott-Moncrieff (1926) shows the influence of the man on the life of the times.

11 Medieval Civilization at Its Height

The rose window of Amiens
Cathedral, thirteenth century.

After 1150 western Europe began to cash in on the pioneer work of the tenth and eleventh centuries. The boom in population, production, and trade brought increasing prosperity. The peasants embarked on a great migration to new lands, comparable only to the nineteenth-century movement to the New World. Forests were cleared in England, France, and western Germany; marshes were drained and walled off from the sea in the Netherlands. In the biggest shift of all, migration toward the East, the Germans filled up the land between the Elbe and the Oder and settled large areas of western Poland, eastern Prussia, and Bohemia. This drive to the East almost doubled the size of medieval Germany. It also set the stage for the contending nationalisms of modern times, for the Slavs remained numerous in Bohemia and the lands beyond the Oder, which meant that many German settlements were surrounded by Slavic populations.

TOWNS AND TRADE

Atlantic and Baltic trade grew steadily during the twelfth century. German merchants, who dominated Baltic commerce, pushed their outposts to Riga and to Novgorod in Russia. They dealt in furs, timber, and other bulky commodities that returned only a small profit per ton. Atlantic trade, in wool from England and in salt and wine from ports in the Bay of Biscay, was also only moderately profitable. Most of these goods were carried by German and French vessels; the English had little shipping and could not even move their own wool overseas. This northern trade brought modest prosperity to such towns as Lübeck in Germany and Bordeaux in France.

The really profitable trade, however, was still the trade in Oriental goods. Italian towns, especially Venice, Genoa, and Pisa, had by far the largest share of this lucrative business. Their fleets made regular voyages each year to Constantinople, Alexandria, and Acre to bring back incense, spices, and silk. By the end of the twelfth century these fleets were large enough to move whole armies. Crusaders no longer had to take the long and dangerous overland route; they simply hired ships.

It was not until the second half of the thirteenth century that the Genoese and

GERMAN EXPANSION TO THE EAST   800–1400

the Venetians began to make regular voyages through the Strait of Gibraltar to England and the Netherlands. Even then, most of their goods were sent north across the Alps by pack-train. The steady stream of merchants along this route stimulated the growth of the towns of the Po Valley, southern France, and southern Germany. It also stimulated the development of the fairs of Champagne, which became the central market for all western Europe. Champagne lay across the river valleys leading south to the Mediterranean and north to Paris, the English Channel, and western Germany. The counts of Champagne were wise enough to encourage commerce and strong enough to protect the wandering merchants. At the fairs of Champagne, textiles and wool from the north were exchanged for Oriental goods from the south. Merchants gradually developed the practice of settling their yearly accounts when they met in Champagne, thus making the fairs the money market as well as the commodity market of the West.

By the end of the twelfth century no one could deny any longer that businessmen were entitled to special status. Personal freedom and some degree of local autonomy made the townsmen a privileged class—not so privileged as the clergy and nobles, but still well above the peasants. As a privileged class they began to be accorded a special name— *bürgers* in Germany, *burgesses* in England, and *bourgeois* in France, whence the collective term, *bourgeoisie.** Most townsmen were satisfied with this special status; only in the greatest cities could they dream of full independence, and only in Italy did they have much hope of getting it. But the old hostilities still ran deep. The bourgeoisie still distrusted the nobility and criticized the clergy, who in turn still suspected the bourgeoisie of harboring dangerous ideas about religion and the social order. A twelfth-century clergyman could still speak of free towns as *tumor plebis, timor regis*—a cancer of the people, a threat to the king.

*All these terms are derived from the German word *burg,* which meant first a fort and then a walled town. Walls were the symbol of a town's autonomy.

Money-changers are portrayed in this stained-glass window at Le Mans Cathedral, thirteenth century.

Bankers and Moneylenders

The growth of banking and moneylending strengthened this hostility. The great international merchants, and the moneychangers who served them, had become expert at transferring funds from one region to another and had also accumulated surplus capital. They gradually began to act as bankers who received deposits, paid out money on order, and made loans. Kings and popes called on them when, for example, they wanted to transfer money to the East to pay for crusades. And bishops and abbots, lords and knights, all borrowed money from the bankers to pay for their steadily rising living standards. But as a result of all these transactions the bourgeoisie seemed to be profiting at the expense of the clergy and the nobility. Even kings had to pay a high rate of interest on loans—8 to 10 percent for a ruler with as good a reputation as Saint Louis of

France—and lesser folk paid more. When the day of reckoning came, the borrowers often had a hard time repaying their loans: kings had to impose new taxes on their subjects; barons had to sell their lands; churches had to melt down their altar vessels. Bankers were generally unpopular, for they seemed to be thriving on the misfortunes of their fellow Christians.

Artisans, Gilds, and the Proletariat

Most townsmen were not bankers or international merchants but small shopkeepers with purely local trade. Butchers, bakers, and the like profited little from the growth of international commerce. The same was true of many artisans in the metal industries. And even artisans who produced goods for a wider market had to rely on international merchants who kept most of the profits in return for their services. Many workers in the textile industry were only subcontractors, dependent on merchants for raw materials and for markets. A Flemish weaver in Ghent, for example, could not import his raw wool directly from England; he had to obtain it from a merchant. When his cloth was finished, he could not carry it to the fairs of Champagne or the ports of Italy; he had to sell it at a low price to a merchant who knew the markets and the trade routes and who was willing to assume the risks of distribution. The position of such workers was precarious and they often suffered prolonged unemployment. For the first time since the fall of the Roman Empire an urban proletariat began to appear in the countries of western Europe.

It was during the twelfth century that townsmen began to organize themselves into occupational groups. The men within each trade or craft naturally saw a good deal of one another and felt that they had common interests to defend against outsiders. They often had a code prescribing standards of good workmanship, and they were determined to see that these standards were maintained. And so they formed associations, called gilds in England, to pursue their common objectives. The gild contributed to the local church that honored its patron saint, and it acted as a mutual benefit society for the families of its members. It also tried to enforce regulations barring strangers and untrained men from the craft and forbidding careless or dishonest production. The gild was usually dominated by its most experienced members, the master workmen, who owned their own shops and equipment. Under them were the journeymen, who worked for daily wages, and under them the apprentices, who were boys learning the trade. In the thirteenth century, when most journeymen could hope to become masters themselves one day, there was little friction among these groups.

There was considerably more friction among the gilds themselves, including all the jurisdictional disputes that we find among trade unions today. For example, the harness of a horse contains both metal and leather: should it be made by leather workers, metal workers, or both? There was also a good deal of jockeying for political advantage. Strong gilds tended to take over the control of town governments, and often the larger gilds would line up against the smaller ones, or the wealthy gilds against the poor.

To escape such controversies and to protect themselves from the excessive power of the gilds, many lords refused to allow gilds to be established in their towns. But the advantages of some sort of trade organization were so obvious that the lords usually created similar, but looser, associations under their own control. In the nongild towns as well as the gild towns, there were the same regulations on production and the same division of workers into the three groups of masters, journeymen, and apprentices.

In the long run, the division between the urban rich and the urban poor sharpened into political conflict and even armed rebellion. But during the first part of the thirteenth century the people of most towns remained fairly well united. Still rather insecure in a society that originally had had no place for them, they feared outside oppressors more than internal exploiters. Only when the bourgeoisie began to feel reasonably secure did internal differences break out into open feuds.

LITERATURE AND ART

The general prosperity of the period was reflected in a burst of artistic and literary activity. Wealth does not necessarily produce great art, but it certainly increases the opportunities open to artists. Vast sums of money were needed to build a Gothic cathedral, and more cathedrals were built in the late twelfth and thirteenth centuries than at any other time in European history. This money did not all come from the Church; kings and feudal lords made large contributions, as did the people of cathedral cities. In fact, there seems to have been a good deal of civic rivalry: if one town erected a handsome new cathedral, its neighbors strove to surpass it. The classic example is Beauvais, whose residents decided that they would build the loftiest cathedral in France. The technical difficulties were great—the vaults collapsed twice—and by the time they were overcome, money and enthusiasm were running out. So the cathedral of Beauvais stands today still unfinished, with almost no nave. But it does have the greatest interior height of any church built during the period.

Gothic Art

As the example of Beauvais shows, the architects of the day were trying to exploit all the possibilities of the new Gothic style. They strove for greater height and more light by emphasizing vertical lines and making their windows larger and larger. In a small church like the Sainte-Chapelle in Paris they were able to build the walls almost entirely of

Two representations of the Visitation: Romanesque (left; façade of the abbey church of St. Pierre at Moissac, twelfth century) and Gothic (right; façade of Reims Cathedral, late thirteenth century). The Romanesque work is linear and heavily stylized, like a manuscript drawing. The Gothic sculpture is more naturalistic.

magnificent stained glass, supported by a few slender pillars. Even in the larger churches there was far more glass than stone at the upper (clerestory) level.

The portals of Gothic churches were filled with hundreds of statues of Christ, the Virgin, the apostles, and the saints. The windows all had a story to tell or a moral to point. There was a strong tendency toward allegory and symbolism; thus at Chartres the continuity between the Old and New Testaments is illustrated by windows in which a prophet carries an evangelist on his shoulders. But there was also a tendency toward realism in Gothic art, a tendency that appears even in the twelfth century in some of the floral decorations. This tendency grew stronger during the thirteenth century, preparing the way for the very realistic art of northern Europe in the fifteenth century.

Technically, Amiens is perhaps the most perfect Gothic cathedral of all—the cathedral in which all problems were solved successfully. But many critics prefer the massive solidity of Notre Dame of Paris or the less uniform but more interesting cathedral of Chartres, with its glorious stained glass. As the Gothic style spread to England, Germany, and other countries, it produced remarkable buildings, not entirely like the French, but beautiful in their own right. Only in Italy was Gothic a relative failure. The commercially minded Italians were less willing to spend money on their churches, and they were so imbued with Roman traditions that they never really understood the basic principles of the Gothic style.

Histories and Vernacular Literature

The great period of cathedral building was also a period of intense literary activity. We shall return to the work of scholars writing in Latin and mention only one of their activities here—the writing of history. Western Europeans had always been interested in historical narratives, partly because they had inherited this tradition from Rome, partly because the Christian religion puts strong emphasis on the way in which

Medieval English minstrels, as depicted in marginal drawings in *The Luttrell Psalter,* *ca.* 1340.

God's plans are worked out through history. There had always been chronicles, but never before had they been as numerous or as well written as they were after 1150. Kings began to patronize writers who would glorify their deeds and justify their policies—writers like Otto of Freising in Germany, Guillaume le Breton in France, and the St. Albans group of historians in England. Counts and bishops also sought to have their acts recorded in local histories. Western Europeans were proud of their recent achievements and wanted them to be remembered.

An even more striking change was the rapid development of vernacular literature. Minstrels had been composing songs and epic poems long before 1100, but very few of their compositions had been written down. During the twelfth century the practice arose of recording their poems in more or less permanent form, and by the early years of the thirteenth century there was a respectable body of literature in French, German, and Provençal (a southern French dialect). Italy lagged somewhat, perhaps because the Italian dialects were still so close to Latin that they were scarcely recognized as separate languages. England was even further behind because of the Norman conquest. The upper classes in England spoke French and patronized French poets well into the thirteenth century, and without their support the Anglo-Saxon literary tradition could not survive. Left to the peasants, Anglo-Saxon gradually became what we call Middle English; it was only toward the end of the thirteenth century that the ruling classes began to use this language and that English came to be a literary language.

Most works in the vernacular were written for the aristocracy. The *chansons de geste*, for example, are long narrative poems celebrating the courage and fortitude of feudal warriors. The most famous, the *Song of Roland*, tells of the heroic death of a handful of Charlemagne's knights ambushed by a Moslem army; others describe conflicts between unreasonable lords and long-suffering vassals. Lays, based on Celtic legends about King Arthur and his court, appear a little later. They introduce an element of the marvelous—Merlin and his magic—and also the theme of romantic love. Finally came the short lyric poems, which seem to have originated in southern France but quickly spread to Germany and Italy. Some of these lyrics describe the joys of battle, others are political satires, but many of them are love poems. They show a high degree of skill in versification; the sonnet, for example, was to develop out of this type of poem.

The rise of vernacular literature is significant for three reasons. First, it introduced themes, such as the story of Tristan and Isolde, that are still common in our literature, and in expressing these themes the poets of the day developed most of our traditional poetic forms. Second, it helped to weaken Latin as the universal language. Not all early vernacular literature was written for amusement; portions of the Bible were translated into French in the twelfth century, and several histories had been written in French by the early thirteenth century. If French could be used for these purposes, it could also be used for official documents, and during the thirteenth century an increasing number of royal letters and government records were written in French. This same pattern developed in other countries. The growing use of the vernacular language was one, though only one, of the forces that gave each kingdom a sense of its own identity and contributed to the rise of nationalism.

Finally, the new literature was one of the forces that helped soften the manners of the upper classes. Even the poems about warfare were often a substitute for violence. The lords and knights who listened to the *Song of Roland* were likely to be less belligerent than the heroes they admired. Love poems and religious works were even farther removed from the old tradition of violence. The new ideas of courtesy and chivalry were expressed in many romances. It is easy to exaggerate this development; many members of the feudal class were still ignorant and brutal. But in some circles and at some levels ignorance and brutality were being softened by the desire for a little learning and for rudimentary good

The Death of Roland

This passage comes from the *Song of Roland.* Roland, commander of the rear guard of Charlemagne's army, has been cut off by a greatly superior Moslem force. He beats off their attacks repeatedly, but finally all his men are killed and he himself is mortally wounded. He hears the horns of Charlemagne's army as it advances to avenge him, and prepares for death.

Then Roland feels that death is seizing him;
Down from the head upon the heart it falls.
Beneath a pine he staggers, lays him down
On the green grass, and hides beneath his heart
His famous sword and his great ivory horn.
He turns his face toward the infidel
For greatly he desires that Charles should say,
With all his men: "Roland, the noble count,
Roland the brave has died a conqueror."

Then Roland feels that his last hour has come.
Facing toward Spain he lies upon the hill. . . .
And many memories flood into his mind
Of all the conquests he, the brave, had made.
Of gentle France, of heroes of his House,
Of Charlemagne, his lord, who fostered him. . . .

He cries his Culpe, he prays to God for grace:
"O God the Father who has never lied,
Who called the holy Lazarus back to life,
And Daniel from the lions' jaws preserved,
Protect my soul, and pardon all my sins!"

His right-hand glove he proffered unto God;
Saint Gabriel took it from his faltering hand. . . .
God sent to him his angel cherubim
And the count's soul they bore to Paradise.

Translated from *La Chanson de Roland,* ed. by T. A. Jenkins (Boston: Heath, 1924), lines 2355-95.

manners. Vernacular literature both reflected and helped to spread this new pattern of courtly life.

THE WESTERN MONARCHIES

It is in this context of a more prosperous and more peaceful western Europe that political developments must be placed. There was a general desire for more government and better government to help preserve the gains of the last hundred years—a desire that eased the task of the leaders who were reorganizing secular government during the late twelfth and early thirteenth centuries. The greatest progress was made in England and France, but everywhere there was a tendency to create new institutions and to make laws that were more exact and more inclusive.

England under Henry II

Royal government in England had been weakened by a dispute over the successor to Henry I. But in 1154 Henry II, the grandson of Henry I, came to the throne with a clear title. He was already lord of all western France, for he had inherited Anjou and Normandy from his parents and had acquired Aquitaine by marrying Eleanor, the only child of the last duke. Henry spent more than two-thirds of his reign in France—naturally enough, since he held more land there than the French king. Nevertheless, he made a greater impression on England than many kings who spent their entire lives there. He needed a strong government in England both to keep the country quiet while he was abroad and to obtain men and money to protect his French possessions against jealous neighbors. In his attempts to strengthen the English government, he enlarged the activities of the royal courts and created the English common law.

Henry invented no new procedures; he simply used old devices, such as the circuit judge and the jury, more intensively. But by making regular and habitual procedures that his predecessors had employed only on exceptional occasions Henry changed the whole nature of royal government. Whereas William the Conqueror had used inquests or juries on a large scale only once in his reign (to obtain the information recorded in Domesday Book), Henry's circuit judges summoned juries in county after county, year after year. These juries were somewhat like our grand juries today, but they not only indicted criminals; they also had to answer questions about the state of the royal domain and the behavior of local officials. Again, William the Conqueror and Henry I had occasionally allowed prelates or barons to use juries to determine disputes over the possession of land and rights annexed to land. Henry II made this procedure available to every free man and threw open his courts to all cases involving land.

The early jury was by no means an ideal instrument of justice, for it based its decisions on common knowledge and

Henry II, King of England. From *The Pastyme of People*, printed in London in 1529.

neighborhood gossip rather than on the carefully tested evidence of sworn witnesses. But imperfect as it was, it was far better than trial by ordeal or combat. Litigants began to flock to the king's courts, and by the end of Henry's reign all disputes over land were being settled by juries in royal courts. By the middle of the thirteenth century all cases of any importance, both criminal and civil, were decided by juries.

This great increase in the amount of work done by the king's courts naturally strengthened the royal government and weakened the control of feudal lords over their vassals. Important cases no longer came to the courts of the lords, and if the lords tried to resort to extra-legal means their vassals could always turn to the king's courts for protection. The circuit judges rode regularly through the counties, and a permanent court at Westminster heard cases that came up when circuit judges were not available. Everyone in the country was subject to the king's justice, and most men, sooner or later, appeared in royal courts as jurors or litigants.

This constant exposure to royal justice enhanced the people's respect for royal power and indoctrinated generation after generation in the principles of English law. By applying the same rules in all parts of the country, the king's judges gradually created a common law for the whole realm. The first textbook on the English common law was written at the end of Henry's reign, and others followed in the thirteenth and fourteenth centuries. A powerful unifying force, the common law eventually became a symbol of English nationalism. Englishmen were proud of it, regarding it as a guarantee of their liberties rather than as a manifestation of royal power. And this pride is one reason that English common law survived when all the other countries of Europe were abandoning their medieval legal systems in favor of codes based on Roman law.

Henry II also increased royal revenue. Following a precedent of his grandfather, he regularly accepted money from his vassals in lieu of the military service they owed him. He also imposed a general tax on the country in 1188 in order to pay

for a crusade he had promised to join. A tax of this sort was not easy to make stick, for medieval opinion was strongly set against taxation, even for a worthy cause. But, while the king of France had to abandon his efforts to impose a tax for the same crusade, Henry's tax was collected and set a precedent for additional taxes in the years ahead.

Although the English barons offered no effective opposition to Henry's reforms, Henry did have one dangerous

ENGLAND AND FRANCE AT THE TIME OF HENRY II
1154–89

opponent: Thomas Becket, Archbishop of Canterbury, who resisted Henry's efforts to subject clergymen accused of crimes to the jurisdiction of royal courts. The quarrel grew bitter, and at last the archbishop was murdered in his own cathedral by four of Henry's knights, who thought they would please their king by ridding him of a troublesome foe. Henry swore, probably quite truthfully, that he had not planned the assassination, but he abandoned his attempts to bring clergymen under the jurisdiction of royal courts.

Magna Carta

Henry's sons, Richard (1189–99) and John (1199–1216), lacked his political ability. Richard was a good general and nothing more; he spent his entire reign either on the Third Crusade or in fighting Philip Augustus of France. Richard was feared for his strength and admired for his bravery, but he gave little attention to the government of England. He spent less than ten months during a reign of ten years in his island kingdom; all he wanted from England was men and money. It says much for Henry II's political institutions that the government continued to function despite Richard's neglect and his repeated demands for taxes to pay for his wars.

John was not even a good general. Richard had been winning the war with the king of France, but John lost it. Intelligent but neurotic, he suspected his most loyal supporters of treason and thus forced them into neutrality or opposition. William Marshal, Earl of Pembroke, was famous throughout Europe as a model of knightly behavior; John exiled him to Ireland because he did not trust him. This kind of behavior explains why, in the long war with Philip Augustus of France, John's vassals either deserted or fought with little enthusiasm. As a result, John lost Normandy, Anjou, and the northern part of Aquitaine to the French king. He also suffered a serious defeat by the Church; after resisting for five years, John finally was forced to accept an Archbishop of Canterbury he did not want but who had been chosen by the pope.

The murder of Archbishop Thomas Becket in his cathedral at Canterbury in 1170. This representation was made shortly before 1200.

John had taken large sums of money from his vassals for his wars in France; he had also punished without trial many of the men he distrusted. These actions might have been tolerated if he had been successful, but his repeated failures made him vulnerable. The barons of England were outraged by the loss of Normandy, where they or their relatives had had extensive holdings. Many of them had been unjustly punished by heavy fines or confiscation of their lands. In 1215 a large group of barons revolted. The Archbishop of Canterbury advised them and the merchants of London supported them. This coalition was too powerful for John to resist; on June 15 at Runnymede he put his seal to a charter that embodied the barons' demands for reform.

This document, which soon became known as "Magna Carta"—the Great Charter of Liberties—was reasonable and workable. It shows how well John's

We [John] have conceded to all free men of our kingdom, for us and our heirs forever, all the liberties written below, to be held by them and their heirs from us and our heirs: . . .

12. No scutage [redemption of military service] or aid [grant to the king] shall be taken in our kingdom except by the common counsel of our kingdom. . . .

14. And for obtaining the common counsel of the kingdom, for assessing an aid . . . or a scutage, we will cause to be summoned by our sealed letters the archbishops, bishops, abbots, earls and greater barons, moreover we will cause to be summoned generally by the sheriffs . . . all those who hold of us in chief [the other vassals] for a certain day . . . and place . . . and once the summons has been made the business shall proceed on the assigned day according to the advice of those who are present, even if all those summoned have not come. . . .

39. No free man may be seized, or imprisoned, or dispossessed, or outlawed, or exiled . . . nor will we go against him or send against him except by the legal judgment of his peers and by the law of the land.

40. To no one will we sell, to no one will we deny or delay right and justice.

Trans. from W. Stubbs, *Select Charters* (Oxford: Clarendon Press, 1921), pp. 294 ff.

predecessors had accomplished their task of unifying England and instilling a respect for law even among the feudal lords. The barons made no attempt to break England into autonomous feudal states or to preserve local laws and institutions. They accepted the new legal system and the institutions of central government created by Henry II almost without question. The barons simply wanted to restrain the abuses of the central government, not to destroy it. They insisted that the king, like everyone else, was bound by law and that he was not to tax them without their consent. They demanded that he observe due process of law and forgo punishing an alleged offender before he had been convicted in the king's courts. If the king broke these promises, the barons warned, his subjects were free to rebel against him.

The purpose of Magna Carta was to protect the rights of the barons, not to establish constitutional government. But the English barons were more advanced politically than the feudal lords of other countries, for powerful kings had forced them to work together and to think in terms of laws that affected the whole kingdom. Consequently, they stated the liberties they claimed for themselves in such a way that those liberties could easily be extended to other classes. Thus, before the end of the century the right to consent to taxes, originally restricted to the barons, was gained by lesser landholders and merchants and the right to a fair trial was appropriated even by unpropertied classes. Magna Carta symbolized the supremacy of law, the conviction that even the king was bound by law and must respect the limits it set on his power. Since it was invoked again and again in protests against the arbitrary use of royal power, it served as a foundation stone in the English system of constitutional government.

The Growth of Royal Power in France

In England, which had achieved unity at a very early date, the chief political problem was how to restrain an overpowerful sovereign. In France, which had been divided into autonomous feudal states since the tenth century, the chief political problem was how to build larger and more effective units of government. The first solutions to this problem had been reached in the feudal states themselves, and by the end of the twelfth century such provinces as Normandy, Flanders, and Champagne had well-developed legal, financial, and administrative systems. There were as yet no similar institutions for the kingdom as a whole, however. Even in the region stretching from Paris to Orléans, which the king ruled directly, political institutions were less advanced and less specialized than in some of the great feudal states.

As the king of France gained power and prestige during the twelfth century, however, he gradually became master of his own domain; no longer could petty lords defy him from castles only a few miles from Paris. A series of legends grew up about the king that transformed him into a semisacred personage far above any ordinary feudal lord—in the

Engraving of Philip Augustus, King of France.

Richard, King of England, spent much of his reign fighting in the Crusades or against Philip Augustus. Detail from the effigy on his tomb, 1199.

end, far above any other European king. At his coronation he was anointed with holy oil that had miraculously descended from heaven; he healed the sick; he carried the sword and banner of Charlemagne. This increased prestige was reinforced by the growing desire for law and order that appeared everywhere in the twelfth century. More men sought the judgment of the royal law courts, and the king was occasionally able to impose his decisions even on lords outside his own domains. In short, a real opportunity existed for a great expansion of royal power. And at the end of the twelfth century a king appeared who made the most of that opportunity.

This king was Philip Augustus (1180–1223), the first really able ruler of the Capetian dynasty. Because Philip could not be strong so long as the kings of England held all of western France, he spent much of his reign trying to pull them down. Richard withstood his attacks, but John was more vulnerable. John had made himself even more unpopular in France than in England by murdering one of his nephews, who was heir to the county of Brittany. He exposed himself even more by marrying an heiress who was engaged to one of his own most powerful vassals in Aquitaine. This was a clear breach of feudal law. John had dishonored his vassal, and the aggrieved man promptly appealed to the king of France, from whom John held all his French lands. Philip Augustus seized on this excuse joyfully. He was already planning to attack John; now he could do so in a way that would give him the support of many feudal lords. Philip summoned John to his court, and John, by failing to appear, again put himself in the wrong. Philip ordered all John's French fiefs confiscated for default and carried out the sentence by force of arms. John's English vassals fought badly, and many of his French vassals refused to fight at all. So Philip annexed Normandy, Anjou, and Poitou with little difficulty.

By this conquest of northwestern France Philip more than tripled the royal domain. For the first time in centuries the king of France was stronger than any of his vassals. And in order to hold and exploit the territory he had gained, Philip

went on to devise new institutions that set a pattern for all his successors. Because he created a territorial base from which the king could dominate the rest of the country and provided an institutional base with which to control the enlarged domain, Philip was the real founder of the French monarchy.

He seems to have been guided by two principles. One was to use local institutions whenever he could, thus preserving the earlier work of the feudal lords and at the same time conciliating his new subjects. The other was to divide the new provinces into small administrative districts and to give full powers in each district to men sent out from his own court. Thus Normandy, for example, retained its Norman law and its Norman court system and was never subjected to the law and customs of Paris. But it was divided into thirteen districts, in each of which a bailiff appointed by the king presided over the courts, collected the king's revenues, and commanded the castles and the military forces. No Norman was named as bailiff until much later in the century, and even then most of the bailiffs still came from the old royal domain around Paris.

Philip's principles of government served him well. His respect for local institutions and customs induced the conquered provinces to accept his control with little protest. The bailiffs, who depended on him for their high office, were loyal and reasonably efficient. Philip made sure that his bailiffs were always strangers to the district they ruled, and he moved them frequently from one district to another to keep them from forming local attachments. He paid them well and made it clear that they could expect better jobs if they gave him faithful service. Some of them were unnecessarily harsh and some were dishonest. But on the whole their behavior convinced Philip's new subjects that royal government was, for the most part, better than the government of the feudal lords had been.

All Philip's successors followed his practice of permitting local diversity within a centralized bureaucratic framework. They enlarged the administrative districts, reducing the thirteen original districts in Normandy to five, for example, and they sent out more and more officials to help the bailiffs in their work. But they did not alter Philip's basic system. In the end, France became a very different sort of country from England. With no common law, most Frenchmen remained attached to their local rights and customs. This meant, in turn, that local leaders were uninterested in the problems of the central government; their loyalties were primarily to their provinces. France was held together by the king and his officials; it was a much more bureaucratic state than England.

THE EXPANSION OF THE ROYAL DOMAIN IN FRANCE
1180–1314

Moreover, as France grew into the most powerful state in Europe, its example was followed by others. The bureaucracies of the continental countries today are all descended from the model set by Philip Augustus.

Germany and Italy under the Hohenstaufen

Germany and Italy, meanwhile, were still nominally united under the emperor. But the emperor's power, which was based on his control of the Church, had been seriously weakened by the struggle over lay investiture. The German princes, profiting from the emperor's predicament, had seized local rights for themselves and had begun to insist on their right to elect the emperor. The towns in Italy were becoming almost as independent as the German princes. Thus the old institutions of the Empire were falling into decline, and there were no new institutions to replace them.

In spite of these difficulties, Frederick Barbarossa (1152–90) of the new Hohenstaufen dynasty* made a heroic and almost successful effort to unify the Empire once again. Apparently impressed by the achievements of the kings of France and England, he modeled much of his program on their example. Imitating the king of France, he tried to build a secure royal domain in the Hohenstaufen lands in the southwest corner of Germany. Imitating the king of England, he tried to make all vassals take an oath of allegiance directly to the king, no matter who their immediate lord was. Most important, however, was his attempt to transform German feudalism into a coherent and all-embracing system of government. Many of the most powerful men in Germany owed him no allegiance, and many of those who did

*The Hohenstaufen descended, in the female line, from Henry V. They took their name from their ancestral castle in Swabia.

240

held part of their lands as private property exempt from feudal obligations. Frederick seems to have hoped that by bringing all men and all lands into a feudal system he could check the disintegration of the Empire. Thus by making the leading churchmen vassals of the king, as they were in England, he could regain his control over the resources of the Church; and by making the princes of the Empire his vassals, he could curtail their growing independence and punish them for disobedience by confiscating their fiefs.

Frederick had some success in these attempts, but his own version of feudalism proved inadequate. Both points are illustrated by his conflict with Henry the Lion, Duke of Saxony and Bavaria. Henry was the head of the Welf family, which had long had hopes of gaining the imperial throne, and his two duchies made him the most powerful man in Germany. When Henry failed to give Frederick the military support he owed during an imperial war, Frederick decided to eliminate this dangerous enemy once and for all. He had Henry condemned by a feudal court in 1180, just as Philip Augustus of France was to have John of England condemned by a feudal court some twenty years later. But while Philip was able to seize John's lands and incorporate them into the royal domain, Frederick was immediately obliged to grant Henry's duchies to other princes. Frederick seems to have been seduced by the idea of a perfect feudal pyramid, in which all lesser lords held their lands and powers from the princes, who in turn held them from the emperor. Thus when one prince was dispossessed, his place had to be filled by another, or else the pyramid would lose its symmetry. For obvious reasons the princes were delighted with this rule, and for reasons of his own the emperor seems to have accepted it as well. In the long run this peculiar form of feudalism tended to build up the power of the princes rather than that of the emperor.

Frederick also tried to reassert his imperial rights in Italy, for he knew that if he could gain control of the Italian towns he would be the richest ruler in western Europe. The incessant quarrels

Late twelfth-century gilded reliquary bearing the features of Frederick Barbarossa.

among the Italian towns enabled him to establish himself in the Lombard plain and take control of many of its cities. But the Italians, frightened by his success, quickly called a halt to their feuds and formed a coalition—the Lombard League—to oppose him. Pope Alexander III, who feared that any increase in imperial power in Italy would threaten his independence, supported the League. Frederick tried to overcome this opposition by supporting an antipope and by destroying Milan, the chief Lombard town. But the hostile coalition proved too strong for him. The towns of the Lombard League defeated Frederick at Legnano in 1176 and with the pope's backing forced him to accept a peace that assured them virtual independence.

Frederick, still hoping to make something of his Italian claims, moved his base of operations farther south to Tuscany, where the towns were weaker and less hostile. Though he had some success in Tuscany, his advance there created new problems for himself and his successors. Tuscany was closer to Rome than Lombardy; the imperial base there frightened the pope and involved Frederick more and more deeply in Italian affairs.

The involvement became deeper when Frederick's son married the heiress of the Norman kingdom of Sicily. When Frederick was drowned in 1190 while leading a crusading army through Asia Minor, his son, Henry VI (1190–97), was accepted as emperor by the German princes. But Henry spent almost all his time in Italy, first making good his claim to Sicily and then opening a corridor along the east coast of Italy to connect his south Italian kingdom with Germany. Henry secured his corridor by taking lands claimed by the papacy by virtue of the donations of Pippin and Charlemagne. With Rome now encircled by lands held by the emperor, the popes' old fears of imperial domination were revived.

THE CHURCH AT THE HEIGHT OF ITS POWER

The late twelfth century was a bad time in which to alarm popes, for they were at the height of their power. They had full administrative control of the Church, and in a fervently Christian Europe this meant that they could control public opinion. While kings, lords, or local clergy might nominate bishops, the pope had to approve all appointments and could quash those he felt to be irregular. In the event of a dispute over the choice of a bishop, the pope frequently set aside both candidates and imposed a man of his own choice, as he did at Canterbury in 1207. At the same time he kept close watch over the bishops by sending out legates to enforce papal orders and by encouraging appeals from bishops to the papal court. The bishops in turn strengthened their control over the clergy of their dioceses by making frequent tours of inspection and appointing men trained in canon law to preside over the ecclesiastical courts. Thus the Church

Contemporary mosaic portrait of Innocent III, from the old basilica of St. Peter.

became a highly centralized organization, with the bishops responsible to the pope and with all lesser clergy responsible in turn to the bishops.

This centralization created new problems. As the popes and bishops spent more and more of their time on administrative and judicial details, they ran the danger of abdicating their role as spiritual leaders. St. Bernard had worried about this problem in the middle of the twelfth century, and later reformers shared his concern. Moreover, papal and episcopal courts had to demand heavy fees from those who did business with them. But these fees were not enough to cover extraordinary expenses, and in

1199 Pope Innocent III imposed an income tax on the clergy, an example that was followed by all his successors. The higher clergy shifted these expenses to the parish priests, who in turn began to exact fixed fees for such services as marriage and burial. Soon the complaint arose that the Church was selling its spiritual benefits.

Innocent III

The Church reached the height of its power at the end of the twelfth century, during the pontificate of Innocent III (1198–1216). Innocent, who felt responsible for the moral and spiritual welfare of all western Europe, once said, "Nothing in the world should escape the attention and control of the Sovereign Pontiff." The Vicar of Christ, "less than God but more than man," could reprove and punish kings who broke the divine law. A man of remarkable energy (he was only thirty-seven years old when he became pope), he came very close to making the papal court a supreme court for all of Europe. He kept the clergy under tight control and intervened repeatedly in secular affairs whenever he felt a moral issue was involved. Thus he threatened to support a French invasion of England in order to make John accept his own choice as Archbishop of Canterbury. But when John yielded, Innocent granted him papal protection and forbade the French to carry out their planned attack.

Innocent III and the Empire

Innocent's most striking intervention, however, was in the affairs of the Empire. The premature death of Henry VI in 1197 created a complicated problem of succession. Henry's heir, Frederick II, was only three years old, and, though Frederick's claim to Sicily was undeniable, the princes of the Empire had never accepted the rule of hereditary succession. They split into two factions, one supporting Philip of Hohenstaufen, the brother of Henry VI, the other supporting Otto, the son of Henry the Lion and head of the Welf family. Innocent took advantage of this dissension by driving the German troops and governors out of central Italy and resuming control of all the Papal States, including the territory on the east coast. Alleging that since the pope crowned the emperor he had a right to reject unworthy candidates, he postponed the solution of the German problem for ten years. Finally, in 1208, after Philip had been assassinated, Innocent recognized Otto as emperor on condition that Otto renounce all claims to the lands in central Italy that had been seized by Frederick Barbarossa and Henry VI. When Otto broke his agreement, Innocent turned against him and persuaded the German princes to accept Frederick II as their ruler. By 1215 the young Frederick was in full control of Germany, and Innocent felt that he had an emperor who would be a dutiful subordinate of the Church instead of a dangerous rival.

Actually, Innocent had made a series of disastrous mistakes. By prolonging the dispute over the succession in Germany, he had given the German princes a chance to increase their power at home; after 1215 the position of the emperor north of the Alps was very shaky indeed. Frederick II, soon deciding that he could make nothing of Germany, turned his eyes toward Italy, thus reviving the danger of encirclement that Innocent thought he had ended by putting Frederick on the German throne. Instead of showing gratitude for the pope's support, Frederick renewed the old attempt to annex a corridor along the east coast and to assert imperial power in Tuscany and Lombardy. But Innocent had committed the papacy to the propositions that the Papal States must stretch from coast to coast and that the emperor must not gain control of central and northern Italy. The result was a long struggle that badly damaged the prestige of the Church. It also destroyed the last chance of unifying Germany, or of bringing Italy under a single government, leaving two dangerous problems for the nineteenth century.

Innocent III and Heresy

Innocent also found that, for the first time in centuries, the Church was seriously threatened by heresy. Dangerous ideas were creeping in from the East

Ciama ne ceffef quafi tuba ẽralta uocem tuam . annũna poplo meo ſẽelera eo̅ ꝯ 7 domui Jacob peccata eo̅ꝯ . Vnde aplꝰ inquid epheſiꝭ . Mu̅de ſunt man̅ mee a ſanguine omium um̅ . no̅ eñ ſubⁱfug̅ quominuſ annũnare uob om̅e conſilium dei . Mu̅dus ergo a ſanguine ipo̅ꝝ no̅ eẽt . ſi eiſ annũnare dei uidꝰ cum noluiſſet . q̅ cum increpare ſlingm̅ſ noluerit . eoſ ꝓ culdubio tacendo paſ tor occidit . Cum itaꝗ in tremendi die uidiñi de uñſ . et ſubdiɫoꝝ uⁱⁱoꝝ aculiꝰ debeant reddere ronem . qᷓenam ꝗ de om̅i uerbo onoſo quodcu̅ꝗ locuᷤ fuerᷛnᷤ .

Detail from a page of Innocent's Register showing two wolves, one in Friar's clothing, probably assisting in an heretical mass. The page deals with the Church's power to punish sinners.

along the busy trade routes; others were being formulated by the leaders of towns in Italy and southern France. Many people charged that priests were ignorant, prelates greedy and immoral. Some of these critics remained Christian but felt that they were as capable as the clergy of interpreting the Bible. Laymen organized themselves into groups to read the Scriptures together and to try to apply Christian standards in their daily life. The Waldensians, who still exist, were typical of these groups; they had adherents throughout the Rhone Valley and in many northern Italian towns. Other groups accepted a new and only partly Christian faith that had originated in the Balkan provinces of the Byzantine Empire. Based on very early Christian heresies, it taught that all material things had been created by an evil god, who was engaged in a constant struggle with the God of good. It rejected the Old Testament as the work of the evil god and thought of Jesus as simply an emanation of the good God and so denied His humanity. The believers in this doctrine called themselves "Cathari" (the purified) because they had rejected the evil world. They organized a church of their own, with a very simple ritual and with leaders who were admired even by Catholics for their piety and goodness. Because they were especially numerous in the region of Albi in southern France, they were often called Albigensians.

By 1200 the heretics had the support of thousands of people and dominated whole communities. Innocent tried at first to convert them by peaceful means, but he soon became convinced that he would have to use force. He proclaimed a crusade against the Albigensians in 1207 and enlisted an army of knights from northern France to invade the South. The conflict was as much a civil war as a religious war; since the northerners aimed at the conquest of the South, many Catholic nobles of the region aided the Albigensians. An old legend reports that at the sack of Béziers the exasperated northerners cried: "Kill them all, God will know his own!" In spite of stubborn resistance, the southerners were crushed and the lords of northern France now ruled the entire land.

The victory over heresy was still not complete. Repeated revolts against northern domination could be suppressed only by a new crusade led by the king of France himself. He took over all the conquests of the northern lords; thus one unforeseen result of the Albigensian

Thirteenth-Century Arguments about the Crusade

Should the Crusade never be preached against schismatics and the disobedient and rebels? This is not expressly stated in the law and therefore certain people in Germany have doubts about it, saying that it does not seem right or honest to take up the cross against Christians. . . . However, the Son of God did not come into the world, nor did He die on the cross to gain land, but to call sinners to penitence. There is greater danger in permitting sin than in losing land because the soul is more precious than material things. Thus if we consider the degree of the offense, no one can doubt that disobedient and schismatic Christians are greater offenders than the Saracens. . . . And although the overseas Crusade may seem more desirable to the simple, the Crusade against disobedient Christians will seem more just and reasonable to anyone who considers the problem intelligently. . . .

Rome should not, I think, if one of her sons has fallen into error . . . send upon him an elder brother to destroy him. Rather should she summon, talk gently, and admonish him than waste his country. When the French go against the people of Toulouse, whom they consider heretics, and when a papal legate leads and guides them, that is not at all right in my opinion.

The first quotation is from Hostiensis (a cardinal and a famous canon lawyer), *Summa aurea* III, 34 (de voto), 19 (in quo casu). The second is from Guillaume le Clerc (a French poet), as cited by Palmer A. Throop, *Criticism of the Crusade* (Amsterdam, 1940), p. 43.

war was a marked increase in the power of the French king. The king's victory ended open manifestations of heresy, but many heretics continued to practice their rites in secret. In order to unearth them the Church had to develop a new court, the Inquisition. Any contact with heretics was ground for suspicion. The court accepted neighborhood rumors as a basis for accusations and used torture to secure confessions. The Church justified this procedure on the grounds that the heretic, who caused the loss of an immortal soul, was far worse than the murderer, who merely killed the body. In the end the Inquisition wiped out the Albigensian heresy, but it had an evil effect on European society. It often corrupted communities by encouraging fanatics and talebearers, and it provided a regrettable example for secular courts to follow. The only major areas to escape the Inquisition were England and Scandinavia, where there were not enough heretics to bother about.

The Revival of Science

By the middle of the twelfth century the scholars of the West had absorbed the Latin classics and the Roman law. Searching about for new materials, they seized on the rich store of learning in the East that had never been translated into Latin. Though Aristotelian logic had greatly stimulated the revival of scholarship, the West had only Aristotle's introductory treatises on logic. Scholars were deeply interested in astronomy and astrology, but they had only a few brief texts on these subjects, while the Greeks and Arabs had scores of volumes. The same problem existed in medicine and biology, in mathematics and physics. All the really advanced works were in the eastern languages; in Latin there were only elementary textbooks.

To correct this deficiency, the scholars of the West began the task of translating into Latin the works of Aristotle and the scientific writings of the Greeks and Arabs. The difficulties were formidable—there were no grammars, no lexicons, none of the scholarly apparatus we take for granted in learning foreign languages. The Romans had never been particularly interested in science and had never developed a scientific vocabulary; consequently, even when a translator knew the meaning of a Greek or Arabic word he had trouble finding a Latin equivalent. Moreover, many of the important texts had been corrupted by repeated translation.

Nevertheless, western scholars completed the task they had set for themselves. By the middle of the thirteenth century they had translated into Latin almost all the works of Aristotle and a great mass of other material. The West had acquired the philosophy and the

Illustration from twelfth-century English manuscript showing a surgical operation (top) and the process of heating the instruments (bottom).

science of the East—and just in the nick of time, for during the thirteenth century both Byzantium and the Arab world were shattered by civil wars and foreign invasions. Though they made a partial recovery later on, they were never again the intellectual centers they had been in the early Middle Ages. The scientific tradition that the Greeks had originated and the Arabs had preserved might have vanished had it not been for the efforts of the translators of the twelfth and thirteenth centuries.

Medieval science was not the science of our own day. It was based on authority rather than direct observation; it developed its ideas through formal logic rather than through experimentation; and it was contaminated by the wishful thinking of philosophers and magicians.

But at least it was an attempt to explain the physical world, to find ways of summing up seemingly unrelated phenomena in general laws. The important thing was not the accuracy of the results, but the fact that meaningful questions were asked about the nature of the universe. The questioning, once it began in the twelfth century, never stopped, and from that questioning our modern science has developed.

Understandably, the Church was suspicious of this new learning, which had been derived from pagan Greeks and handed on by Moslems and Jews. It carried with it many dangerous ideas—remnants of old religions disguised as magic, and philosophical doctrines that denied basic articles of faith. For example, some of the Arabic commentators on

A university lecture, as portrayed in a fourteenth-century Italian miniature. Attention to the lecturer was not undivided; several students are talking and one is certainly asleep.

Aristotle had advanced the idea that the world was eternal and by so doing denied the Creation and the Last Judgment. By 1200 western scholars were teaching these ideas to eager young students, especially in the great center of learning at Paris.

The First
Organized Universities

The Church wanted to control the new learning, and it found a means of doing so in the universities. As we have seen, twelfth-century professors and students had formed associations to protect their respective interests. Both groups found it to their advantage to insist on prescribed courses of study and examinations as prerequisites to obtaining a license to teach, or, as we would say, a degree. This system enabled the students to know what their obligations were and permitted teachers to bar unqualified men from their profession. It was not unlike the system that prevailed in the gilds, where a journeyman had to demonstrate his knowledge of his craft to a board of masters before he could become a master himself. In fact, the word "university" originally meant an association of any sort and not just an organization of accredited teachers and their students.

But any corporate group had to be recognized by some higher authority, and the natural authority for scholars was the Church. The Church saw obvious advantages in patronizing associations of scholars: it could more easily control the new learning, and it could use the professors as experts to examine suspect doctrines. The University of Paris, for example, began to denounce dangerous ideas derived from Aristotle and the Arabs almost as soon as it received official recognition from the pope.

Innocent III, who had been a student at both Paris and Bologna, favored university organization and bestowed valuable privileges on both his old schools. His patronage was matched by secular rulers, who needed educated men to staff their rapidly growing bureaucracies. By the end of the thirteenth century there were universities at Oxford and Cambridge in England, at Paris, Montpellier,

Toulouse, and Orléans in France, at Coïmbra and Salamanca in the Iberian Peninsula, and at Bologna and Padua in Italy. There was no university in Germany until the fourteenth century. Paris remained the unquestioned leader in theology and liberal arts, and Bologna in law, but many men studied at more than one university. The famous scholars of the thirteenth century were university professors, and university graduates filled high offices in the Church and important positions in secular governments. In short, during the thirteenth century the universities took over the intellectual leadership of western Europe.

The idea of the university was one of the most important medieval contributions to modern civilization. Most civilized peoples have had schools of one

Church Regulation
of the University of Paris

1215

Robert [de Courçon] by the divine mercy cardinal priest . . . and legate of the apostolic see, to all the masters and scholars at Paris, eternal safety in the Lord.

Let all know, that having been especially commanded by the lord pope . . . to better the condition of the students at Paris, and wishing . . . to provide for the tranquility of the students in the future, we have prescribed the following rules:

No one is to lecture at Paris in arts before he is twenty years old. He is to study in arts at least six years before he begins to lecture. . . . He must not be smirched with any infamy. When he is ready to lecture, each one is to be examined according to the form contained in the letter of the bishop of Paris. . . .

The treatises of Aristotle on logic, both the old and the new, are to be read in the schools in the regular and not in the extraordinary courses. The two Priscians [on grammar] . . . are also to be read in the schools in the regular courses. On the feastdays [there were nearly one hundred of these] nothing is to be read except philosophy, rhetoric, books on the *quadrivium* (arithmetic, geometry, music, and astronomy), the Ethics [of Aristotle] and the fourth book of the Topics [of Boethius on logic]. The book of Aristotle on Metaphysics or Natural Philosophy, or the abridgements of these works, are not to be read, nor the doctrines of [certain contemporary teachers accused of heresy].

From Robert de Courçon, *Statutes*, trans. by D. C. Munro, *Translations and Reprints* (Philadelphia: University of Pennsylvania Press, 1899), Vol. II, No. 3, p. 12.

kind or another, but they have usually concerned themselves with the private instruction of novices by priests, or the private tutoring of wealthy young men by individual teachers. True, the Roman Empire established professorships for scholars to lecture to anyone who cared to listen, but it never developed the university or an examination system. China, during the European Middle Ages, had a prescribed course of study, with an examination system and something very like our system of scholarly degrees, but it lacked an autonomous, self-perpetuating faculty. Only in medieval Europe does one find all the elements that make a modern university—a faculty constituting an organized and privileged community of scholars, a regular course of study, and final examinations leading to the degree as a certificate of scholarly competence. This type of educational organization has its disadvantages—it tends to become overly conservative and tradition-bound—but by and large it has proved the most successful form of higher education ever devised, and it has spread throughout the world.

The Mendicant Orders: Franciscans and Dominicans

The heresies mentioned above were only the most obvious manifestations of a threatened decline in the Church's influence over the population of western Europe. Even those who were not heretics criticized the character of the clergy and the administrative system of the Church. They felt that the Church was not doing its job, that it was failing to meet the challenge of changing times. They feared that it was yielding to the temptations created by a more prosperous and better-organized society—the love of wealth and the love of power—instead of finding ways to combat them. A society that had been oriented toward the future life was now finding far too much satisfaction in the pleasures of this world.

It was in response to these criticisms that the medieval Church, with the establishment of the Franciscan and Dominican Orders, embarked on its last great wave of reform. St. Francis (ca. 1182–1226), the son of a well-to-do Italian merchant, was particularly sensitive to the problem of wealth. His own conversion began with his renunciation of all claim to his family's property, and throughout his career he insisted on absolute poverty for himself and his followers. He also demanded literal and unquestioning observance of the precepts given in the Gospels to the disciples of Christ. Probably no other group of Christians has ever come closer to imitating the life of Jesus and the Apostles than did St. Francis and the early Franciscans. Their example of holy living impressed laymen who had become weary of routine religious services and encouraged them to make a new effort to apply Christian principles in their daily life.

The other leader of the new religious movement was St. Dominic (ca. 1170–

St. Francis Gives a Lesson in Poverty

Once when the blessed Francis had visited the Cardinal of Ostia [who was afterward Pope Gregory IX] at the hour of dinner he went as if by stealth from door to door begging food. And when he had returned, the Cardinal had already sat down at table, with many knights and nobles. But blessed Francis placed those alms which he had received on the table beside him. . . . And the Cardinal was a little ashamed . . . but he said nothing. . . . And when blessed Francis had eaten a little he took of his alms and sent a little to each of his knights and chaplains of the Cardinal on behalf of the Lord God. And they all received them with great joy and devotion. . . . [The Cardinal later rebuked him gently, but Francis answered:] "I will not be ashamed to beg alms, nay, I hold this a very great nobility and royal dignity before God and a means of honoring Him Who, when He was Lord of all, wished for our sakes to become servant of all, and when He was rich and glorious in His majesty became poor and despised in our humility."

From "The Mirror of Perfection," *The Little Flowers of St. Francis* (New York and London: Everyman, 1910), Ch. 23, p. 203.

1221), a Spanish priest who had begun his career by trying to convert the heretics of southern France. He was primarily concerned with the instruction of the faithful through preaching and teaching. Like St. Francis, he emphasized the ideal of absolute poverty, not only as good in itself but also because the leaders of the heretics he was combating had gained great influence by renouncing all worldly goods. Even more than St. Francis, he wanted his order to be an order of preachers. Realizing that perfunctory sermons and routine services were scorned by the more sophisticated groups of western Europe, he spent his life training men who would be subject to the rigorous discipline of a religious order but who would also be well enough educated to hold their own in arguments with scholars, townsmen, and secular officials. The Dominicans established excellent schools to train members of the order, and the graduates of these schools soon dominated the faculties of theology of European universities.

Both the Franciscan and the Dominican Orders met with immediate success. Thousands of men joined their ranks during the thirteenth century, and these friars, as they were called, became the most influential group among the clergy. Unlike the monks, who secluded themselves in their cloisters, the friars wandered about as missionaries, preaching and talking to laymen. They brought religion to the very centers of thirteenth-century society—to the courts, the universities, and the towns. At first there was some tendency for the Franciscans to appeal more to emotion and the Dominicans to reason, but by the middle of the century this difference had almost vanished. Each order produced a famous teacher of theology—the Dominicans, St. Thomas Aquinas; the Franciscans, St. Bonaventura. And each order carried on revivals among the people of the towns. The fact that the Church managed to preserve its leadership throughout most of the thirteenth century, in spite of the growing prosperity and worldliness of society, was due largely to the work of the friars.

Suggestions for Further Reading

Note: Asterisk denotes a book available in paperback edition.

Towns and Trade

The articles in the *Cambridge Economic History* remain the best guide for this period. Older and still useful works are W. Cunningham, *The Growth of English Industry and Commerce* (1910), and P. Boissonade, *Life and Work in Medieval Europe** (1929). R. de Roover, *Money, Banking and Credit in Medieval Bruges* (1948), is a readable study of the operations of the Italian merchant-bankers in Flanders. Lynn White, *Medieval Technology and Social Change* (1962), is a good introduction to the fascinating subject of medieval technology.

Gothic Art

There are many beautiful and exciting books on Gothic art. A. Temko, *Notre-Dame of Paris** (1955), is a charming study of this cathedral written as a biography. A. E. M. Katzenellenbogen, *The Sculptural Program of Chartres Cathedral** (1959), is a detailed study of Chartres, with the latest and most plausible historical interpretation. The best treatment of Gothic art in the High Middle Ages is P. Frankl, *Gothic Architecture** (1963), which traces the development of this architecture in all regions of Europe and stresses the slow perfection of the art. Frankl includes the most up-to-date bibliography. O. von Simson, *The Gothic Cathedral* (1956), is another first-rate book. The old work of T. J. Jackson, *Gothic Architecture* (1915), is sound and still valuable. Every student of medieval history should become familiar with one of the great monuments of American scholarship, Henry Adams' *Mont-Saint-Michel and Chartres** (1905). This is a great appreciation not only of the art but of the entirety of medieval civilization. In the same way, E. Mâle, *Religious Art in France in the Thirteenth Century* (1913) (published in paperback as *The Gothic Image**), is a study of the thought of the thirteenth century as expressed in art.

Vernacular Literature

Both C. C. Abbott, *Early Medieval French Lyrics* (1932), and J. A. Symonds, *Wine, Women and Song* (1899), have selections of typical lyric poetry of the twelfth century; the translation of Symonds, although somewhat more romantic, is superior. *French Medieval Romances*, trans. by E. Mason (1911) is a collection of short novels probably dating from the reign of Henry II. The best critical study of the vernacular literature of the twelfth and thirteenth centuries is E. Curtius, *European Literature and the Latin Middle Ages** (1963), which has excellent bibliographic materials.

Scholarship and the Rise of the Universities

Perhaps the central figure of the Christian humanism of the twelfth century was John of Salisbury, most of whose works have now been translated. *The Statesman's Book*, trans. by J. Dickinson (1927), a work of political theory, had a great influence on the development of twelfth-century humanism. John of Salisbury's *Historia Pontificalis*, trans. by M. Chibnall (1956) describes western Europe during and after the Second Crusade as seen through the eyes of an Englishman in the papal Curia. An excellent penetration into John's thought and personality and his close association with Canterbury and Rome is given in *Letters* of John of Salisbury, 2 vols., ed. by W. J. Millor and H. E. Butler (1955). C. J. Webb, *John of Salisbury* (1932), presents him as a great medieval churchman and plays down his role as scholar and humanist.

There is very good source material on university life in L. Thorndike, *University Records and Life in the Middle Ages* (1944). L. Thorndike, *History of Magic and Experimental Science*, Vol. II (1923), traces the origins of modern science in the medieval universities. C. H. Haskins, *The Rise of the Universities** (1923), is a good general survey of the beginnings of the universities. Another useful short account is by H. Wieruszowski, *The Medieval University** (1966). The standard scholarly study is H. Rashdall, *The Universities of Europe in the Middle Ages*, 3 vols., rev. and ed. by F. M. Powicke and A. B. Emden (1936). H. Waddell, *The Wandering Scholars* (1927), gives an amusing picture of student life.

Henry II, Richard, and John

The English practice of preserving records has provided us with a vast amount of evidence for this period. Both Roger of Hoveden, *The Annals*, 2 vols., trans. by H. T. Riley (1853), and Roger of Wendover, *Chronicle*, 2 vols, trans. by J. A. Giles (1849), are interesting contemporary histories. There is valuable material in *English Historical Documents*, Vols. II and III, ed. by D. C. Douglas and G. W. Greenaway (1953–55). For the study of the growth of English law there are representative documents in C. Stephenson and F. G. Marcham, *Sources of English Constitutional History* (1937). J. E. A. Jolliffe's *Constitutional History of Medieval England** (1937) is a readable and scholarly study with a good critical bibliography, and F. Pollock and F. W. Maitland, *History of English Law*, Vol. I (1923), is fundamental. J. E. A. Jolliffe's *Angevin Kingship* (1955) traces the character and growth of royal power and the development of the organs of government through the twelfth century. S. Painter, *The Reign of King John** (1949), gives an excellent account of the political and administrative history of this reign. Painter's *William Marshal: Knight-Errant, Baron, and Regent of England** (1933) is an exciting biography that presents a vivid picture of the thoughts and attitudes of the English feudal class. The most thorough treatment of Magna Carta is that of W. S. Mc-Kechnie, *Magna Carta* (1914), a chapter-by-chapter analysis. See also J. C. Holt, *Magna Carta* (1965). A. L. Poole, *Domesday Book to Magna Carta* (1951), is the most comprehensive one-volume history of this period; although it is sometimes dull reading (on a fascinating period), there is an excellent critical bibliography.

Philip Augustus

Both J. Evans, *Life in Medieval France* (1925), and A. Tilley, *Medieval France* (1922), are very good surveys arranged in topical fashion. There is a good account of French society in A. Luchaire, *Social France at the Time of Philip Augustus,** trans. by E. B. Krehbiel (1912). The works by Petit-Dutaillis, Fawtier, and Lavisse listed under Chapter 10, in the second section, also contain material on this subject.

Innocent III

The best study of this important pope is that of the great French historian, A. Luchaire, *Innocent III*, 6 vols. (1904–08). *Selected Letters of Innocent III Concerning England*, ed. by C. R. Cheney and W. H. Semple (1953) provides us with considerable information on English-papal relations in the stormy period from 1198 to 1216. There is a very readable interpretation of Innocent's remarkable ascendancy in S. R. Packard, *Europe and the Church under Innocent III* (1927).

Heresy and the Friars

H. C. Lea, *A History of the Inquisition of the Middle Ages*, 3 vols. (1888), has considerable material on the Albigensian heresy, but the reader would do well to take Lea's judgments with some reservations and to read in conjunction with it E. Vacandard, *The Inquisition* (1908), which sees this terrible institution more in the light of its time. S. Runciman, *The Medieval Manichee* (1947), follows the history of the Dualist tradition in Christianity. This is a sound and urbane book.

The best one-volume collection of the lives and writings of St. Francis is in *The Little Flowers of St. Francis** (Everyman's Library). P. Sabatier, *The Life of St. Francis of Assisi* (1894), is a scholarly book with good bibliographic material, but J. Jorgensen, *St. Francis,** trans. by T. O. Sloane (1955), is more interesting. B. Jarrett's *Life of St. Dominic** (1924) gives a good, if adulatory, picture of the man, and P. Mandonnet, *St. Dominic and His Work* (1944), emphasizes the spirit and work of the Order.

12

The Rise of the Secular State

T he popes and the mendicant orders had combined to check the spread of heresy in the thirteenth century. By organizing the Albigensian Crusades and the Inquisition the popes ended the threat of popular heresy. A remarkable group of theologians (mostly Dominicans and Franciscans) succeeded in reconciling the new Greco-Arabic learning with the Christian faith and thus reduced the danger of intellectual heresy. By the middle of the thirteenth century there was little open dissent from orthodox doctrine in western Europe. Most people were honestly and sincerely Catholic in belief; the few who were not found it expedient to pretend that they were.

THE IMPACT OF ECONOMIC CHANGE

Yet the position of the Church was less secure than it seemed. The Church could deal with the heretic, who was an open enemy; dealing with the lukewarm friend was a more difficult problem. Men had to make a living and obey their rulers. But at what point did a normal desire to make a decent living turn into an immoderate lust for wealth? At what point did obedience to authority turn into a loyalty that subordinated the interests of the Church to those of the state? It was easier to sense this gradual growth of

worldliness than to do anything about it, and the Church itself was infected by the ills it sought to cure. Some clergymen sought to accumulate offices in order to augment their income. Even more of them entered the service of secular rulers. The first group exposed the Church to criticism; the second often failed to defend its interests.

It has always been hard for a religion to deal with the problem of prosperity. Wealth creates pride and self-assurance, neither of which is entirely compatible with devoutness. The thirteenth-century Church strove, with some success, to give the wealthy a sense of social responsibility. It condemned flagrant profiteering and callous neglect of the poor. It accepted the idea that a man who invested in a commercial enterprise was entitled to interest on the money he risked, but it denounced the small moneylenders who charged high rates for personal loans. Many of these loansharks in the end left large sums to charities to atone for their profits from usury. But while the Church could mitigate some of the consequences, it could not alter the fact that western Europe was shifting to an economic system in which money was becoming more important than inherited status. Concern over money made it hard for men to follow the teachings of the Church or to put the interests of the Church ahead of their own.

Representatives of the three estates—a clergyman, a knight, and a laborer—from a late thirteenth-century manuscript. The chapter heading over the picture says: "Of the three sorts of people whom the philosophers place in the world."

E ē cē qui or lan en eſt
d e lacitē de parıſ neſt
p luſ q̃ de nule antr̄e cıtē
C ele en a la nobılıtē
d eſ · uj · manıereſ de genſ que
l ı phıloſoſe poſerent au mōde

fleıgie
regne
ore a
parıſ
Enſı q̃
ele fu
ıa dıſ
a athe
neſ q̄
ſıet en
grece

b ne cıtē de grꝰ noblēce
a phıloſoſe q̄ loez furent
Cr leſ autreſ enſegñ dır̄ent

Medieval coins. Top to bottom: Gold florin (Florence, thirteenth-century); gold ducat (Venice, thirteenth-century); obverse and reverse of silver penny of Henry III of England (thirteenth-century); gold agnel of Philip VI of France (fourteenth-century). The gold coins were used for large-scale transactions, silver for household purchases and wages.

The growth of a money economy involved the landed classes, including most churchmen, in an economic squeeze. Increasing demand caused a steady rise in prices, while income from land lagged behind. Ancient custom or fixed agreements determined what peasants paid. On many estates lords had commuted labor services and payments in kind for rents of a few pennies an acre. It was not easy to change customary payments or contractual agreements, for peasants who were pushed too hard could flee to the towns or to the new lands that were still being cleared in the East. Thus the real income of landlords tended to decrease during the thirteenth century.

Some landlords saved themselves by leasing their domain lands for short times. This gave them an income related to the market value of their produce rather than an income tied to a customary rent. In some regions landlords turned as much land as they could into pasture, since wool brought in more profit than grain. But these devices could not satisfy the financial needs of kings and princes, of popes and bishops, who had to govern as well as live comfortably. Sooner or later they had to supplement their ordinary income by taxes and fees. When they did, however, they stirred up bitter resentment among their subjects and conflicts among themselves over who had the right to tax.

The Church was especially vulnerable to criticism of its financial policies. The income tax on the clergy, first imposed by Innocent III, was levied more and more frequently, and at higher rates—10 percent or even 20 percent. Fees were imposed or increased for papal letters, legal documents, and confirmation of appointments to high offices in the Church. Both taxes and fees were derived, in the last analysis, from payments by laymen. As a result the Church was criticized for being too eager to raise money, too ready to give spiritual benefits in return for cash payments. The more zealous wing of the Franciscans urged that clergymen abandon all their property and lead lives of apostolic poverty, but this solution was hardly realistic. The Franciscan Order itself was ac-

quiring property, even though it tried to disguise the fact by vesting title in trustees. When reformers—Franciscans and others—became bishops and popes, they found that in the existing economic situation they could make no important changes in the Church's financial system. Since not even the most zealous reformers could find inoffensive ways of raising money, there was a loss of respect for the Church as an organization, even among men who were completely orthodox in doctrine.

THE FRENCH AND ENGLISH MONARCHIES

At the very time that respect for the Church was declining, the prestige of secular governments was rising. These governments were not hostile to the Church, but they were consciously or unconsciously competing with the Church for the loyalty of the people. And just as the Church was becoming more worldly and more like a secular government, so secular governments were beginning to surround themselves with an aura of sanctity and to take on responsibilities hitherto reserved for the Church. Kings claimed to be protectors of the common welfare, agents of divine justice, defenders of the faith. None of the great thirteenth-century popes became a saint, but several kings were canonized. And one of these saintly kings, Louis IX of France, probably exercised greater moral authority over the Europe of his day than did any churchman.

St. Louis

Louis IX (1226–70) was the grandson of Philip Augustus, the first really strong French king. Philip had conquered the northwestern part of France in his war with John, and Philip's son, Louis VIII, had acquired large holdings in the South by his timely participation in the crusade against the Albigensians. As a result, Louis IX was far more powerful than any combination of hostile French lords. He put down a few halfhearted rebellions early in his reign, and for the rest of his life his authority was never challenged.

No one could oppose Louis' claim to rights or land. An arrogant man might have abused this power, but Louis was determined to follow the ideals of a Christian ruler. He settled the long-standing dispute with England by a generous treaty that gave the English king many border districts in Aquitaine. He kept faith with all men, even with Moslems. In France he submitted all disputed questions to the decisions of his courts and did his best to restrain the zeal of his administrative agents, who tended to exaggerate the extent of royal rights. No other medieval king had such a reputation for honesty and fair dealing.

Louis was pious and generous, but he was not soft. His loyalty to the faith did not keep him from exercising independent judgment about the policies of the Church. He refused to join Pope Innocent IV in the attack on the emperor Frederick II; he rejected demands of the French bishops that he punish all men who remained excommunicated for more than a year. He felt that, as a Christian king, he knew better than anyone else how to provide for the spiritual and material welfare of his people.

Louis' concern for law and justice led, naturally enough, to a strengthening of the royal judicial system. During his reign one of the great institutions of the French monarchy was created—the Parlement of Paris. This was the king's own court, staffed with his closest advisers. It heard appeals from the decisions of his local administrative agents and, even more important, it heard appeals from the courts of the great feudal lords. By reviewing, and often reversing, the decisions of feudal courts, it established a legal basis for royal claims to supremacy over all subjects.

The king's local courts, headed by bailiffs and other administrative agents, were even more zealous than the Parlement in upholding royal rights. Since earlier kings had been too weak to enforce their theoretical claims, no exact boundary between the privileges of local lords and the rights of the monarch had ever been drawn. Thus on issues for which there were no clear precedents it was only natural that the bailiffs should rule in favor of the king. Louis did not

Statue of Louis IX, in the church of Mainville in Normandy.

St. Louis as Described by Joinville

Jean de Joinville, a noble of Champagne, was a friend of St. Louis and went with him on his crusade of 1248.

This holy man loved God with all his heart, and imitated his works. For example, just as God died because he loved his people, so the king risked his life many times for the love of his people. . . . He said once to his eldest son: . . . "I beg you that you make yourself loved by the people of your realm, for truly, I would rather that a Scot came from Scotland and governed the people of the kingdom justly and well than that you should govern them badly. . . ." The holy king loved the truth so much that he kept his promises even to the Saracens.

A friar told the king . . . that he had never read that a kingdom was destroyed or changed rulers except through lack of justice. . . . The king did not forget this lesson but governed his land justly and well, according to the will of God. . . . Often in summer he went to sit down under an oak-tree in the wood of Vincennes, after hearing mass, and made us sit around him. And all those who had suits to bring him came up, without being hindered by ushers or other people. And he would ask them: "Does anyone here have a suit?" And those who had requests would get up. . . . And then he would call Lord Pierre de Fontaines and Lord Geoffroi de Villette [two of his legal experts] and say to one of them: "Settle this affair for me." And if he saw anything to correct in what they said on his behalf, he would do so.

From Jean de Joinville, *Histoire de Saint Louis,* ed. by N. de Wailly (Paris: Firmin Didot, 1874), pp. 11, 34.

take undue advantage of this situation; in fact, he and his Parlement often modified the more extreme claims of the bailiffs. But the net result was an increase in royal power, an increase that was cheerfully accepted by most of the people in the country. After all, Louis had suppressed disorder, and his courts, though not perfect, dispensed a better brand of justice than those of most feudal lords.

A just and powerful king, Louis was also a zealous crusader. Jerusalem had been lost to the Moslems in 1187, and three efforts to recover it had failed. These successive failures had somewhat dampened enthusiasm for overseas expeditions, but Louis felt that his responsibilities as a Christian ruler extended beyond the limits of his realm. In 1248 and again in 1270 he led crusades to recover Jerusalem. The earlier expedition had some chance of success, but after a first victory Louis' army was cut off from its supplies and was forced to surrender. The second expedition was hopeless from the beginning, for Louis let himself be talked into attacking the outlying Moslem state of Tunis. Even if he had conquered the country, it would have done his cause little good; as it was, he and many of his followers died of fever soon after landing.

Louis IX was made a saint within a generation after his death. His canonization was more than a personal tribute to a pious crusader; it completed the work of sanctifying the French monarchy. Louis' long search for justice and order had created an almost inexhaustible reservoir of support for his dynasty. Some of his successors were evil and some were weak, but for centuries loyalty to the king was the strongest political force in France. The king stood as the symbol of unity and good government; he alone could override provincial differences and selfish local ambitions. France remained Catholic, but loyalty to the Church now took second place to loyalty to the state.

Henry III of England

France was united only through its king and his bureaucracy. The provinces retained their own customs and privileges; no one could have spoken of a French common law or the "rights of Frenchmen." But in England the monarchy, in its long years of ascendancy, had created a common law and common institutions. The propertied classes in England had become attached to the laws and institutions that protected their rights. Thus the growing loyalty to the English state was loyalty to a system of government as much as it was loyalty to a dynasty. The king could not claim that

King Henry III of England (1216–1272) discusses the progress of a building (perhaps Westminster Abbey) with his architects. The workmen are raising materials to the masons with a windlass.

he alone was working for the common welfare, for his opponents could assert that they too were seeking the good of the "community of the realm." Thus in England even bitter struggles between king and aristocracy could not destroy the unity of the country.

This unusual political situation in England explains certain apparent contradictions in the reign of Henry III (1216–72). On the one hand, royal officials strengthened the administrative and judicial institutions of the country. They created new types of general taxation and devised new writs for bringing more cases into royal courts. Most important of all, trial by jury, already used to settle most land disputes, became the normal procedure in criminal cases. All lawsuits of any significance were now tried by royal judges, and private courts began to die out. These developments were summed up in a remarkable treatise on English law written about 1250 by Henry de Bracton, a royal judge. Bracton gave a clear, logical, and thorough explanation of the common law, citing precedents and stating general principles. He made the common law so coherent and self-sufficient that it was invulnerable to all outside influences for many centuries, and his book became the basic text for the training of English lawyers.

On the other hand, during Henry's reign there was constant friction between the king and his barons. The barons were not trying to destroy the central government; they were trying to use it to protect their status and their views of what English policy should be. And they often found it expedient to claim that they were defending the realm against a foolish and spendthrift monarch.

When Henry came of age in 1225, the barons persuaded him to confirm Magna Carta by granting him a tax. There was no rebellion, as there had been in 1215, but a fair bargain. Henry III gave his consent without coercion, and the 1225 version of the Charter was accepted by everyone as the law of the land. What is more, the king made his officials enforce it, thereby satisfying the barons for some time. But by the 1240s they were once more in open opposition to the king. They could not hate him as they had John—Henry was a likable, honest man, almost as pious as St. Louis—but they did dislike his policies. He wasted money in vain attempts to reconquer lost territories in France. He filled bishoprics and secular offices with his French relatives and friends. Moreover, he allowed the pope to draw large sums of money from England for the papal war against the Hohenstaufen rulers of Italy. Modern nationalism did not exist in the thirteenth century, but we can see the beginnings of nationalism in the attitude of the barons: they were not interested in Henry's French lands; they resented his French friends; they saw no reason for England to help the pope. They wanted English jobs to be filled by Englishmen, and they wanted English money to be spent in England. The barons' opposition to foreign intruders and foreign entanglements was supported by most lesser landholders and by a surprising number of English clergymen.

Henry III's chronic shortage of money enhanced the power of the barons. Ordinary income from the royal domain was barely adequate for peacetime needs, and Magna Carta made it difficult to gain new revenues without the consent of the barons. If Henry wanted to wage war he had to levy taxes. But after 1240 the barons steadily refused to grant any taxes. Henry nevertheless went ahead with an ambitious project to help the pope conquer Sicily. The English clergy, under papal pressure, gave him some money but not enough. By 1258 Henry was hopelessly in debt, and his foreign policy was a complete failure. In desperation, he appointed a committee of barons to reform the government.

The baronial committee soon forgot reform and concentrated on making policy and appointing high officials. Naturally, it soon split into factions. The barons had found it easy to agree in their opposition to Henry's policies; they found it more difficult to agree on a positive policy of their own. Though the barons clearly needed someone to act as leader, they felt that they were all equal, and they were jealous of the ablest man in their group, Simon de Montfort. In the end, Simon gained control of the government, but he lost most of his baronial support in doing so. Henry's eldest son, Edward, managed to raise an army with which he defeated and killed Simon in 1265, and Henry's authority was fully restored.

This episode is significant for two reasons. First, it set a pattern that was to be repeated in England many times during the next two centuries. Again and again the barons, annoyed by royal policy, took over the central government; and again and again factionalism and jealousy kept them from maintaining their position. Second, the struggle between Henry and the barons for control of the central government speeded up the development of a representative assembly in England. The two sides were so evenly matched that they both sought support from men of lesser rank—the knights and other free landholders in the rural areas and the burgesses of the towns. The easiest way to win the support of these men was to invite them to send representatives to the full meetings of the king's court, which, from the 1240s on, were beginning to be given the name Parliaments.

The shield of Simon de Montfort (1208?–1265).

Early Parliaments

A Parliament, in the middle years of the thirteenth century, was a meeting of the king with his chief officials, his bishops, and his barons. *Parliament* was a slang term at first; it meant *talk-fest* and could be used for any sort of discussion. Gradually it came to mean a meeting at which difficult cases were heard that could not be decided by ordinary law courts. The English Parliament, like the French *parlement,* was a high court of justice. Even today the House of Lords is the highest court in England, though cases are actually heard only by specially appointed "law lords." But the English Parliament was also a Great Council that advised the king on matters of policy and granted taxes. It was in Parliament, for example, that the English barons criticized Henry III's plans and refused to give him money. A meeting of Parliament, with all the great men of the realm assembled to deliberate and make important decisions, was truly an impressive occasion.

Representatives from the countryside and the towns who were summoned before Parliament were naturally influenced by its authority and prestige, and they in turn influenced their constituents when they went back home to report what had taken place. It was useful to impress these people because local government in England was still largely controlled by local notables. The king of England, unlike the king of France, had never had to establish a provincial bureaucracy. With no conquered provinces to hold down and no strong loyalty to provincial institutions to fear, it was perfectly safe, and much cheaper, for the central government to pass on its orders to local notables, who served without pay. Thus in the counties the sheriffs, the tax collectors, and the custodians of royal property were usually knights of the shire—that is, country gentlemen resident in the district they governed. In the towns the mayors and aldermen were well-to-do businessmen. These local officials proved reasonably loyal, but they found their government jobs burdensome and annoyingly unprofitable. When they did not like government orders they could drag their feet with no fear of reprisal. It was no great punishment to be removed from office, and those removed had to be replaced with men of the same sort. Thus, when the king or his barons wanted to introduce any innovation in government, such as a new law or a new tax, it was clearly advisable to gain the goodwill of the knights and burgesses. And a good way of doing so was to invite them to send representatives to Parliament, where they could hear and discuss the reasons for the shift in policy.

Both Henry III and the baronial leader, Simon de Montfort, had tried to justify their policies by asking the counties to send knights to Parliament. In 1265 Simon de Montfort, in an effort to compensate for his loss of baronial support, took the additional step of asking the towns to send representatives. These precedents were not forgotten. In 1268 Henry III summoned both knights and burgesses to Parliament, and Edward I called the same groups to the first great assembly of his reign in 1275. These early representatives had little power and always accepted the propositions laid before them by king and barons, but the very fact that they were being summoned at frequent intervals was to be significant in the future.

Parliament was not the first or the only representative assembly. During the Middle Ages most governments found it expedient to summon local leaders to hear explanations of policy. Innocent III, for example, had called representatives of the towns when he was establishing his government in the Papal States, and the Spanish kings held similar assemblies during the reconquest of the peninsula from the Moslems. In the end, the English Parliament was to prove unique, but there was nothing unusual in the experiments conducted by Simon de Montfort and Henry III.

THE PAPAL-HOHENSTAUFEN FEUD

In Germany and Italy the central government was far weaker than in England and France—a situation that Frederick II,

Portrait of Emperor Frederick II, from a manuscript of his treatise, *The Art of Hunting with Falcons*.

whom Innocent III had made emperor, spent his life trying to correct. Though he failed in this effort, he came close enough to success in Italy to precipitate the last great struggle between Empire and papacy.

Frederick II was by birth and education an Italian, although he was descended from the Hohenstaufen of Germany. He spent a few years in Germany after becoming emperor, but he never felt at home there and never had much power over the Germans. Apparently deciding that he could do nothing with Germany, at least until he had brought Italy fully under control, he abandoned almost all authority to the princes of the Empire. All he expected from Germany was a supply of soldiers for his Italian wars.

In Italy he followed exactly the opposite course. First he eliminated all opposition in his hereditary kingdom of Sicily, transforming it into a nearly absolute monarchy, and then he began to revive the old imperial claims to central and northern Italy. Thanks to the factional quarrels within and among the Italian

GERMANY AND ITALY AT THE TIME OF FREDERICK II
ca. 1250

towns, he was able to make substantial acquisitions of territory. Some of the northern Italians became so frightened that they revived the Lombard League, but Frederick crushed them at Cortenuova in 1237. For the moment he seemed to be in control of the entire Italian peninsula.

The papacy, however, was still determined to keep Italy from falling into the hands of one master. The independence of the Church seemed bound up with the independence of the Papal States, and Frederick's victories were threatening that independence. No pope could believe that an emperor who ruled all Italy except the region around Rome would long respect Rome itself. Innocent III had kept the Empire in turmoil for years

rather than risk this danger; the precedents he laid down were hard to forget.

Moreover, Frederick II's orthodoxy was somewhat doubtful. No one was ever sure what this brilliant and inquisitive man really believed. He exchanged friendly letters with Moslem rulers; he dabbled in science and magic; he was accused of writing a book called *The Three Impostors: Moses, Jesus, and Mohammed.* This charge was completely false, but the fact that it could be made tells something of Frederick's reputation. He tried hard to convince people that he was an orthodox ruler, even going on a crusade and persecuting heretics, but these actions raised more doubts than they settled. He succeeded in regaining Jerusalem for a few years, not by fighting the Moslems but by making a treaty with the sultan of Egypt, and his persecution of heretics seemed prompted only by a desire to improve his political position.

When it became apparent that Frederick was going to insist on full control of both northern and southern Italy, the pope decided that drastic measures were necessary. Pope Gregory IX tried to hold a council in Rome to discuss the problem, but Frederick intercepted the fleet bearing many of the prelates and captured or drowned most of them. This direct attack on the Church did not improve Frederick's reputation. The next pope, Innocent IV, just as determined and almost as able as his great namesake, Innocent III, called a council at Lyons in 1245. The council declared that Frederick had forfeited all his possessions, and that neither he nor any member of his family should ever be allowed to rule in Germany or Italy. Innocent IV proclaimed a crusade against Frederick and imposed a tax on the clergy to pay for armies to carry it out.

The papal attack destroyed the last remnants of imperial power in Germany. Turning the conflict to their own advantage, the princes refused to obey either Frederick or an opposition line of rulers elected by a propapal faction. Germany became a loose confederation of states under the control of princes who were free to accept or reject the policies suggested by the nominal ruler. No German emperor after Frederick exercised any real authority except in his own family possessions.

In Italy the issue was not decided so quickly. Frederick held on to most of the territory he had gained, but he never managed to build up a strong government in the North. After his death in 1250 the towns of northern and central Italy became independent, though the Kingdom of Sicily remained loyal to his sons. The papacy might have been satisfied with this state of affairs—after all, the danger of encirclement had been dispelled forever—but it had been too badly frightened by Frederick to take any chances. So the popes carried on the war against the "viper brood" of the Hohenstaufens, refusing to rest until the hated family had been ejected from Sicily and Naples. They preached crusades, collected taxes from the clergy to cover their expenses, and sent cardinals out with armies to do battle with Frederick's heirs. And when all these efforts proved in-

effectual, they turned for help to England and France. The attempt to involve England led only to the rebellion of the English barons against Henry III, but the approach to France met with greater success. St. Louis reluctantly permitted his brother, Charles of Anjou, to attempt the conquest of the Kingdom of Sicily. Charles, aided by crusade privileges (including remission of sins for his soldiers) and crusade taxes, defeated the last Hohenstaufen ruler of Sicily in a lightning campaign in 1266. A grandson of Frederick II made a desperate attempt to regain the kingdom, but his forces were crushed in 1268 and the young Hohenstaufen was executed in cold blood. The papacy, aided by the French, had won a complete victory over its enemies.

Loss of Prestige by the Church

But in winning this political victory, the papacy had lost moral prestige. There

In 1241 Frederick's fleet captured (or drowned) two cardinals and a hundred bishops who were on their way to a Council summoned by Gregory IX to depose the Emperor. This manuscript illustration shows Frederick in the ship on the left, though actually he was not present. On the right, his soldiers attack the prelates in the ship bearing the papal ensign of the keys of St. Peter.

had been some doubts about the deposition of Frederick II—St. Louis had preserved a careful neutrality in this struggle—although the Church clearly had a case against him. Frederick was threatening the independence of the Papal States, and he was certainly unconventional and possibly unorthodox in his ideas. But Frederick's heirs were much less powerful and much less dangerous to the Church; it seemed pure vindictiveness to harry them for two decades. The Church was using its spiritual authority to gain a political end. The pope was acting very much like a secular prince, assembling armies, making alliances, carrying on political intrigues. The distinction between ecclesiastical government and secular government was no longer clear. One could argue that if it was proper for the pope to tax the clergy for a war in Italy, it was equally proper for a king to tax the clergy to defend his kingdom. This claim was to cause the next great conflict between the papacy and secular rulers.

Moreover, the popes had won their victory over the Hohenstaufen only by creating political instability in both Germany and Italy, and this instability in the long run weakened the Church. No one in Germany was strong enough to protect the bishops, so they had to fight and intrigue to protect themselves. No one in Germany was strong enough to wipe out the heresies that erupted in the fifteenth century and laid a foundation for Luther's revolt. In Italy the absence of any central government encouraged the growth of factionalism and local wars. These disorders spilled over into the Papal States and made the pope's position there almost untenable. He could either flee Italy and lose the prestige that was associated with Rome or stay and play the petty politics of a minor prince. Neither course would strengthen the papacy.

SCHOLARSHIP AND THE ARTS

It took a generation for the Church to feel the full consequences of the new political situation; meanwhile it enjoyed its last years of unquestioned leadership in Europe. The kings of the West were at peace with one another and obedient to the pope. Both the education and the behavior of the clergy had steadily improved. This last period of Church leadership (1250–75) saw the building of the most perfect Gothic cathedrals and the culmination of medieval Christian philosophy in the work of Thomas Aquinas (1225–74).

It was probably no accident that these two forms of expression reached their peak at about the same time. There was a strong logical element in the perfected Gothic cathedral, just as there was a strong architectonic quality in Thomas Aquinas' thought. In both, the basic structural plan is clearly revealed, uncluttered by architectural or literary embellishment. Just as the cross section of a pillar of a Gothic church shows exactly what the superstructure will be, so the first paragraph of a chapter by

St. Thomas Aquinas, detail from the Crucifixion, by Fra Angelico (1387–1455). Although this representation was made two centuries after Thomas lived, it seems accurately to depict his large head and bearlike appearance.

Thomas Aquinas reveals exactly how his argument will proceed. But while we still appreciate the qualities of Gothic architecture—the emphasis on height and light, the clean expression of the function of each architectural member—we are less at home with the methods and ideas of medieval scholastic philosophy.

St. Thomas Aquinas

Thomas Aquinas, unlike some other Christian thinkers, feared neither the world nor the new knowledge about the world that scholars had acquired from the Greeks and the Arabs. God had put man in the world not to punish him but to enlighten his feeble understanding through concrete examples. Man could rely on his reason, which was the gift of God; the truths discovered by the ancient philosophers were perfectly valid truths, though they might be incomplete. Thus a pagan philosopher could give an acceptable proof of the existence of God even though he knew nothing of the doctrine of the Trinity. Reason needed to be enlightened by faith, but there was no conflict between the two.

In the same way, there should be no conflict between the Church and secular governments. Secular government was necessary and good in itself, for it gave men an opportunity to manifest social virtues. Even among the pagans, secular governments were divinely established and should be obeyed. Thomas admitted that it was proper to resist a king who was openly violating the law of God, but he felt that resistance to a secular ruler should be resorted to only after everything else had failed.

As for the new wealth, here again there was no danger if men used their reason properly. God had given man dominion over the world, and it was part of the divine plan to make full use of the world's natural resources. Land did not fulfill its function unless it was cultivated; a tree was of no use unless it was used for construction. Men should remember their Christian duty to the poor, and they should never allow their desire for wealth to become immoderate. But there was nothing wrong in an honest effort to earn a decent living.

The Reconciliation of Christian and Classical Philosophy

This extract from the *Summa Contra Gentiles* by St. Thomas Aquinas shows how a thirteenth-century scholar was able to use the ideas of Aristotle.

We have now shown that the effort to demonstrate the existence of God is not a vain one. We shall therefore proceed to set forth the arguments by which both philosophers and Catholic teachers have proved that God exists.

We shall first set forth the arguments by which Aristotle proceeds to prove that God exists. The aim of Aristotle is to do this in two ways, beginning with motion.

Of these ways the first is as follows. Everything that is moved is moved by another. That some things are in motion—for example, the sun—is evident from sense. Therefore, it is moved by something else that moves it. This mover is itself either moved or not moved. If it is not, we have reached our conclusion—namely, that we must posit some unmoved mover. This we call God. If it is moved, it is moved by another mover. We must, consequently, either proceed to infinity, or we must arrive at some unmoved mover. Now, it is not possible to proceed to infinity. Hence we must posit some prime unmoved mover.

From *On the Truth of the Catholic Faith. Summa Contra Gentiles,* trans. by A. C. Pegis (New York: Doubleday, 1955), p. 85.

Thomas Aquinas believed that in the light of true reason everything made sense, that the world was a harmonious whole. Wisdom was the greatest earthly good, and the felicity of the afterlife consisted in the contemplation of the eternal Wisdom which is God. It was this serene conviction of the unity and rationality of all experience that made Thomas Aquinas' work so persuasive, that led to his early canonization and to his present reputation as the leading philosopher of Catholicism.

Even in his own day, not all scholars shared the views of Thomas Aquinas. Doubtless there was some professional jealousy involved; Aquinas was a Dominican, and scholars in other orders resented the influence the Dominicans had acquired in theological studies. But there was also honest concern, both about the extreme rationalism of his approach and about the reliance he placed

Dante's Divine Comedy

THE INSCRIPTION ON THE ENTRANCE TO HELL

Through me you pass into the woeful city
Through me you pass into eternal pain
Through me you go amid those lost forever.
Justice it was that moved my Great Creator;
Power divine and highest wisdom made me
Together with God's own primeval love.
Before me there was nothing save those things
Eternal, and eternal I endure.
All hope abandon, ye who enter here.

THE ATTACK AT ANAGNI

Dante disliked Boniface VIII, whom he consigned to Hell, but still
felt the attack at Anagni, which he describes below through the lips
of Hugh Capet, was an outrage.

O avarice, what worse canst thou now do
Since thou dost so completely rule my race
That they care nothing for their flesh and blood?
Past wrongs and future they will now compound.
Into Anagni storms the lilied flag;
Christ is a captive in his Vicar's form,
And the old mockery again renewed
With vinegar and gall. I see him bleed
Amid the living robbers; Pilate too,
I see, so cruel that even this dreadful deed,
Is not enough.

THE FINAL VISION

O grace abundant, through which I presumed
To fix my gaze on the eternal light
Which near consumes who dares to look thereon.
And in those depths I saw, bound up by love
Into one volume, all the universe. . . .
Here vigor failed the lofty vision, but
The will moved ever onward, like a wheel
In even motion, by the love impelled
Which moves the sun in heaven and all the stars.

From Dante, *Inferno*, canto 3; *Purgatory*, canto 20; *Paradise*, canto 33, trans. by
H. F. Cary (London: G. Bell, 1877).

phenomena. In correcting these mistakes they helped start a new trend in physics, which, advanced by obscure scholars of the fourteenth and fifteenth centuries, culminated in the work of Galileo. Roger Bacon was a member of this Oxford group, but he has received more credit than he deserves; his vague predictions about automotive vehicles and the like had no scientific basis. The real leader of the Oxford school was Bacon's teacher, Robert Grosseteste.

More important than these scholarly disputes was the fact that Thomas' arguments were too rational to have much influence on laymen. He might see no conflict between reason and faith, no opposition between secular interests and those of the Church, but for most people these contradictions did exist and could not be exorcised by words. They were faced with hard choices between the teachings of the Church and the demands of secular life, and they did not always choose the side of the Church.

Dante

The greatest medieval poet—one of the greatest poets of all time—was Dante Alighieri (1265–1321). One of the first men to write in the vernacular in Italy, he helped establish the Tuscan dialect as the standard form of the Italian language. He wrote graceful lyrics in Italian and two notable treatises in Latin, one defending his use of the vernacular, the other a strong plea for strengthening and preserving the Empire. But the work for which Dante will always be remembered is the *Divine Comedy*, a vision of Hell, Purgatory, and Heaven written in magnificent Italian verse.

Dante had a troubled and unhappy life. Deeply involved in Florentine politics, he was permanently exiled from the city he loved in 1302. In spite of these troubles Dante, like Thomas Aquinas, remained convinced of the unity and meaningfulness of all human experience. Unlike many of his contemporaries, he did not sink into pessimism or seek out partial truths. He was almost the last representative of the confident, optimistic, all-embracing spirit of the great period of medieval civilization.

on Aristotle and other Greek philosophers. The most eminent Franciscan theologian, St. Bonaventura, emphasized will rather than reason. And a group of Franciscan scholars at Oxford undermined the philosophy of Aquinas by proving that his chief authority, Aristotle, had made certain mistakes about natural

Dante was well-read in both secular and religious literature. His guide through Hell and Purgatory was the Roman poet Vergil and this part of his poem is full of allusions to classical mythology. But he also knew scholastic philosophy; the *Paradise* in many places reads like a verse translation of Thomas Aquinas. Like Thomas Aquinas, Dante saw no contradiction between the truths worked out by human reason and the truths revealed to the Church; all knowledge led to God if it was rightly used.

But to Dante knowledge was not enough; even good conduct was not enough. Faith in God and love of God and of one's fellow man were the essentials. In Hell the most lightly punished sins were those against oneself, such as gluttony. The lower depths were reserved for those who hurt others, and the worst sinners of all were Judas who betrayed Christ and Brutus and Cassius who betrayed Caesar. In Purgatory sins were purged through suffering, and angels sang Beatitudes at each step of the ascent. In Paradise Dante came closer and closer to the eternal Light until he finally had his great vision of God—"the love which moves the sun and all the stars."

The *Divine Comedy* was recognized as a classic almost as soon as it was written,

but admiration for the poem did not mean wide acceptance of its point of view. Few of Dante's contemporaries had his serenity or his breadth of vision; few could accept any longer his dream of a harmonious world in which men could seek both happiness on earth and eternal rewards in heaven. By the end of the thirteenth century secular and religious goals were coming into conflict, and more and more attention was being given to the secular.

Secularism in Art and Literature

The gradual growth of secular interests may be seen clearly in art and literature. For example, after 1270 there is a striking change in statues of the Virgin. In early Gothic sculpture she is the Queen of Heaven, majestic and dignified. In late Gothic sculpture she is girlish and human, with none of the semidivine characteristics of the earlier period. In literature the break is shown by the difference between the two parts of a famous poem, the *Romance of the Rose*. The first part, written by Guillaume de Lorris

Dante and his guide, Vergil, visiting the circle of hell to which usurers have been relegated. Illustration from a fourteenth-century Italian manuscript.

in the 1230s, is an allegory of courtly love; the second part, written forty years later by Jean de Meung, is a satiric encyclopedia. The first part respects the ethics and conventions of upper-class society; the second part attacks the fickleness of women and the greed of the clergy and gives brief summaries of the knowledge that every educated man was supposed to possess. The discrepancy between the two parts is obvious today, but apparently it was not obvious to men of the late thirteenth century. No other poem was so popular during the later Middle Ages. It was copied and recopied in hundreds of manuscripts, and at the end of the fourteenth century Chaucer began an English translation of it. Nothing illustrates better the rise of a class of educated laymen, eager for worldly knowledge, suspicious of the clergy, and a little cynical about ideals of any kind. Such men could no longer be counted on to support the policies of the Church if those policies interfered with their interests, or even with their convenience.

ENGLAND, FRANCE, AND THE PAPACY

In England and France the central government grew stronger than ever in the last quarter of the thirteenth century. Edward I of England (1272–1307) was determined to increase his power but clever enough to retain the support of most members of the propertied classes. He seems to have had two main objectives; first, to restore royal authority after the weak reign of his father, Henry III, and second, to make himself supreme ruler of the British Isles. He achieved his first goal through sheer force of personality, hard work, and intelligent selection of officials. Edward's royal rages were terrifying—the dean of St. Paul's dropped dead of fright during a dispute with him—and few men dared to contradict him openly. There was less reason to contradict him than there had been to oppose his father. Edward's policies were on the whole successful, especially during the first part of his reign. His avoidance of continental entanglements and his concentration on the conquest of Wales and Scotland harmonized with the desires of the aristocracy. As a result, Edward controlled his administration and, unlike his father, was not dominated by a baronial council.

He was less successful in attaining his second objective. He did complete the conquest of Wales, which had been begun long ago by the barons of William the Conqueror. He replaced the last native prince of Wales with his own infant son, thereby creating a precedent that has endured to the present day. But Scotland proved more troublesome. Edward first tried to install a puppet king, but when his candidate proved less subservient than he had hoped he deposed him and tried to rule the country directly. But Edward could not keep a big enough army in Scotland to suppress all

The Courtly Lover

But be thou careful to possess
Thy soul in gentleness and grace
Kindly of heart and bright of face
Towards all men, be they great or small. . . .
Watch well thy lips, that they may be
Ne'er stained with ill-timed ribaldry. . . .

Have special care
To honor dames as thou dost fare
Thy worldly ways, and shouldst thou hear
Calumnious speech of them, no fear
Have thou to bid men hold their peace. . . .
Above all else beware of pride. . . .
Let him who would in love succeed
To courteous word wed noble deed.

And next remember that, above
All else, gay heart inspireth love.
If thou shouldst know some cheerful play
Or game to wile dull hours away
My counsel is, neglect it not. . . .
And much with ladies 'twill advance
Thy suit, if well thou break a lance
For who in arms his own doth hold
Winneth acceptance manifold.
And if a voice strong, sweet and clear
Thou hast, and dames desire to hear
Thee sing, seek not to make excuse.

From Guillaume de Lorris, *Romance of the Rose,* Part I, *ca.* 1237, trans. by F. S. Ellis (London: Dant. 1900), Vol. I. 2184–291.

Scene from a manuscript of *Romance of the Rose.* The lover enters the garden in which he will catch his first glimpse of the Rose.

dissent, and the Scots rebelled, first under William Wallace and then under Robert Bruce. The rebellion was still raging when Edward died, and the Scots won their independence at Bannockburn in 1314.

Edward I and Parliament

Outside his own island, Edward had to resist an attempt by the king of France to take over the duchy of Aquitaine, the last French holding of the English royal family. Edward's wars cost huge sums of money and kept him very busy—two reasons why he made greater use of Parliament than any of his predecessors. With all the important men in the kingdom present at meetings of Parliament, Edward could get their advice on policy, settle difficult legal cases, make statutes, and obtain grants of taxes. He could probably have done all this outside Parliament, but it was more efficient to take care of everything at one time and in one place. Moreover, Parliament had great prestige; it was the highest court in the kingdom and it spoke for the community of the realm. England, unlike other countries, was so thoroughly united that decisions made in a single central assembly were accepted as binding on all men. Thus it was clearly advantageous to obtain the sanction of Parliament for as many decisions as possible. Edward lost nothing by following this policy, for he controlled Parliament as effectively as he did every other branch of government.

King Edward I of England
(1272–1307) on his throne.
From a fourteenth-century
manuscript.

He could not have foreseen that he was building up a powerful institution that might some day develop a will of its own.

Representatives of counties and towns came before the king in 1275, but for the next twenty years Edward summoned such representatives only sporadically. The essential element in Parliament was still the Council, composed of high officials, bishops, and barons. But in 1295 Edward summoned representatives to a very full meeting (the "Model Parliament"), and from that time on they were frequently present. Again, Edward's decision seems to have been prompted by the desire to save time and trouble. Legally, baronial approval was probably enough to validate his new laws and new taxes, but in practice it was necessary to win the support of the knights and burgesses as well. They were the men who, as sheriffs and mayors, would have to enforce the new laws, and they were the men from whose ranks tax collectors would have to be appointed. There were obvious advantages in bringing representatives of all the counties and towns together at a meeting of Parliament where they could listen to the great men of the realm discuss the king's needs.

These representatives had not yet joined together in an organized body, and their role seems to have been largely passive: "to hear and to obey," as some of the early summonses put it. Such opposition as there was in Parliament came from the barons. On one notable occasion in 1297, when Edward had pushed a new tax through at a very small meeting of the Council, the barons protested and forced the king to promise that in the future he would levy taxes only "with the common assent of the whole kingdom." This was not quite an admission that only Parliament could grant taxes, but it certainly implied that the assent of a large number of people was needed; and clearly the easiest way to obtain such assent was in Parliament. The barons hesitated to grant taxes on their own responsibility and were usually anxious to get the endorsement of at least the county representatives. And when, in the last years of the reign, the barons sent petitions to Edward asking for government reform, they invited the repre-

sentatives of both counties and towns to join them. In these ways the representatives gradually became caught up in the work of Parliament, though their position was still much inferior to that of the barons.

France under Philip the Fair

In France, which was less unified politically than England, the growth of royal power followed a different course. The French barons were still struggling to preserve their local rights of government and their exemptions from the authority of royal officials. Not particularly interested in controlling the central government in Paris, they simply wanted to keep it from interfering with their lands and their subjects. The chief problem of the French king was not to keep the barons from dominating his council but to see that his orders were enforced in their lands.

This problem came to a head in the reign of Philip the Fair (Philip IV, 1285–1314), the grandson of St. Louis. Like his grandfather, Philip was pious, upright in his private life, and imbued with a sense of the divine mission of the French monarchy. But he was narrowminded where St. Louis had been magnanimous, and grasping where St. Louis had been merely firm. The number of bureaucrats grew enormously during his reign, and Philip encouraged them in their efforts to expand royal authority. He was willing to condone any expedient to break the power of a local ruler who tried to retain a semi-independent status. Lesser vassals could not resist, but the more powerful men were indignant. It is not surprising that Philip spent a large part of his reign warring with his greatest vassals, including the king of England (as Duke of Aquitaine) and the Count of Flanders. He gained some land from both, but he never took the rich textile cities of Bruges and Ghent from Flanders, or the flourishing port of Bordeaux from Aquitaine.

Philip the Fair had a harder time than Edward I in raising money to pay for his wars. The French had never been subjected to a general tax, whereas the English had been afflicted with national taxes since the end of the twelfth century. Moreover, France was so divided that no central assembly like the English Parliament could impose a uniform tax on the whole country. Instead, royal agents had to negotiate with each region, and often with each lord or each town within each region. This cumbersome system consumed a great deal of time and reduced the yield. France was at least four times larger than England in both area and population, but it is doubtful whether Philip enjoyed any larger tax revenue than did Edward I.

These difficulties in collecting taxes explain some of the military weakness of France during the next hundred years. They also explain why the French representative assembly, the Estates General, never became as powerful as the English Parliament. Philip, as we shall see, was the first French king to call representatives to meetings at Paris. But he never asked them for a grant of taxes, for he knew that the country at large would pay little attention to the decision of a central assembly. This lack of any real power over taxation remained one of the chief weaknesses of the Estates General. Conversely, tax negotiations with local leaders and assemblies, though tedious, in the long run gave the ruler a free hand in imposing levies. It was easy to play one region off against another, or to threaten isolated areas that could not count on outside support. The royal bureaucracy was so persistent and skillful in conducting these negotiations that sooner or later it succeeded in breaking down most of the regional resistance to taxation.

Thus England was a strongly united country in which the king and the propertied classes cooperated in carrying out policies that they both approved. France was united more by the royal bureaucracy than by common interests, but the propertied classes in France were on the whole ready to trust the king on policy matters. And in both England and France some of the ideas that distinguish the modern sovereign state were beginning to appear: the welfare of the state was the greatest good; the defense of the realm was the greatest necessity; opposition to duly constituted authority was the

greatest evil. As one of Philip's lawyers put it: "All men, clergy and laity alike, are bound to contribute to the defense of the realm." People who were beginning to think in these terms were not likely to be impressed by papal appeals and exhortations.

The Struggle with Boniface VIII

The pope at this time was Boniface VIII (1294–1303), an able canon lawyer and a veteran of the political conflicts endemic to Italy. Sensing that the new type of secular authority developing in the West would be more dangerous to the Church than the medieval Empire had ever been, he tried to reassert the superiority of ecclesiastical interests and the independence of the Church. He made no claim that had not already been made by his predecessors, but the climate of opinion had changed since the days of Gregory VII and Innocent III. With the shift in basic loyalties from the Church to the state, many people now believed that their chief duty was to support their king rather than to obey the pope. As a result, Boniface was defeated in a head-on clash with the kings of England and France—a blow from which the medieval Church never recovered.

The issue was clear-cut: were the clergy to be treated as ordinary subjects of secular rulers, or were they responsible only to the pope? Specifically, could they be taxed for defense of the realm without the pope's consent? As we have seen, thirteenth-century rulers could not run their governments without taxes, and it was always a temptation to tap the resources of the Church. By imposing taxes on the Church for political crusades, the popes had suggested that the clergy might also be taxed for purely secular conflicts. And so, when Edward I and Philip the Fair drifted into a war over Aquitaine in 1294, they both asked their clergy for a grant of taxes. They were outraged when Boniface prohibited these grants in 1296. Both Edward and Philip succeeded in stirring up public opinion against the clergy as disloyal members of the community. Both kings seized ecclesiastical property and forbade the transfer of money to Rome. Edward went further and virtually outlawed the English clergy. In the end, the harassed churchmen of both countries begged the pope to reconsider and remove his ban. Boniface did so, grudgingly but effectively, in 1298.

This was bad enough, but worse was to follow. In 1301 Philip the Fair imprisoned a French bishop on a flimsy charge of treason and refused to obey a papal order to free him. When Boniface threatened to punish the king and his agents, Philip countered by calling a great assembly at Paris in 1302. This assembly contained representatives of the three Estates, or classes, of clergy, nobility, and bourgeoisie; it was the prototype of the French Estates General. The assembly gave its full support to the king and emphatically rejected any papal authority over France. When the dispute continued, Philip, through his minister, Guillaume de Nogaret, accused Boniface of immorality and heresy and appealed to a general council to condemn him. Local assemblies throughout France endorsed Philip's plan—the nobility and townsmen enthusiastically, the clergy reluctantly but almost unanimously. Philip undoubtedly resorted to pressure to ensure this response, but he clearly had the backing of his people, as subsequent events were to show. The people may not have believed all the accusations, but they felt that a worldly Church was probably corrupt and that the pope should not interfere with French internal affairs.

Assured of support at home, Philip now launched a very risky venture. In 1303 he sent Nogaret to Italy with a small force to join some of the pope's Italian enemies. Together they staged a surprise attack on Boniface's summer home at Anagni and succeeded in capturing the pope. They probably hoped to take him back to France as a prisoner to await trial by a church council, but they had no chance to put their plan into effect. The Italians had no great love for the pope, but they cared even less for the French. A counterattack by the people of Anagni and neighboring regions freed Boniface from his captors. He took refuge in Rome and began to prepare bulls of excommunication against the French. But Boniface was an elderly man, and the shock of capture had proved too much for him. He died before he could act.

Force had been used against earlier popes, but for the last two centuries the Church had always been able to retaliate and put the aggressor in a worse position than before. After the assault at Anagni, however, the Church did not dare to react strongly. No one, either inside or outside France, seemed disturbed by what had happened, and Nogaret remained one of Philip's favored ministers. Boniface's successor was not a strong man, and when he died within a year the cardinals surrendered completely. They elected a French archbishop as pope, a man who was not even a member of their group and a man who was clearly agreeable to Philip, if not suggested by him. This new pope, Clement V, yielded at every turn to the king of France. He absolved Nogaret and declared that Philip had been prompted by laudable motives in his attack on Boniface. By failing to defend itself—indeed, by

The Issue between State and Church

Boniface VIII says in the Bull Unam Sanctam (1302):

**Both the spiritual sword and the material sword are in the power of the Church. But the latter is to be used for the Church, the former by her; the former by the priest, the latter by kings and captains, but by the assent and permission of the priest. The one sword, then, should be under the other, and temporal authority subject to spiritual power....
If, therefore, the earthly power err, it shall be judged by the spiritual power. . . . Finally, we declare, state, define and pronounce that it is altogether necessary to salvation for every human creature to be subject to the Roman pontiff.**

One of Philip's ministers, speaking for the king, says (1302):

The pope pretends that we are subject to him in the temporal government of our states and that we hold the crown from the Apostolic See. Yes, this kingdom of France which, with the help of God, our ancestors . . . created—this kingdom which they have until now so wisely governed—it appears that it is not from God alone, as everyone has always believed, that we hold it, but from the pope!

From *Select Documents of European History*, ed. by R. G. D. Laffan (London: Methuen, 1930), p. 117, C. V. Langlois, *St. Louis, Philippe le Bel, et les derniers Capetiens directs* (Paris: Hachette, 1911), pp. 149–50.

praising the aggressor—the papacy revealed that it had surrendered its leadership and its control over public opinion. From this time on the papacy could influence and advise, but it could no longer command as Innocent III had done.

The Popes at Avignon

The pliability of Clement V soon led him to an even more momentous decision. After he was elected pope, he set off for Rome, but, dismayed by the disorder in Italy, he paused in the Rhône Valley. The papacy was now paying for its stubborn opposition to the establishment of a strong Italian kingdom; the warring city-states had made even the Papal States unsafe. Somehow Clement never got started again. France was

pleasant and Italy was dangerous; moreover, the French king and the French cardinals were urging him to stay on. And so Clement settled down at Avignon on the Rhône, where he and his successors were to reside for over seventy years.

This long period of exile in France (1305–78) is known in church history as the Babylonian Captivity.* The papacy did not lose its independence, for Avignon was papal territory and the surrounding country was technically part of the Empire and not of France. No subsequent Avignonese pope was as subservient to the French king as Clement

*This is an allusion to the exile of the Jews to Babylon under Nebuchadnezzar in the sixth century B.C. The original Babylonian Captivity lasted only fifty years.

Pope Boniface VIII receives St. Louis of Toulouse, a great-nephew of St. Louis of France and son of King Charles II of Naples. The representation of the pope corresponds to other pictures of him. Fresco by Ambrogio Lorenzetti, Siena, ca. 1330.

V had been; most of them were able, even forceful, administrators of the affairs of the Church. And yet, though the papacy did not lose its independence, it lost its reputation. Many people, especially the English, were convinced that the pope was a servant of the French king, in spite of evidence to the contrary. Many more believed that no true successor of Peter would abandon Rome for the "sinful city of Avignon." A spiritual leader was not supposed to be swayed by motives of expediency or fear of discomfort. Charges of worldliness and corruption leveled against the Church seemed more justified than ever.

Actually, although the Avignonese popes were not especially corrupt, they were primarily administrators rather than religious leaders. Their chief accomplishments were to perfect the Church's legal system and its financial organization. To men who were already critical, this very success looked like a proliferation of red tape and a perfection of methods of extortion. No one could obtain anything from the papacy without engaging in long and expensive lawsuits or paying heavy fees to everyone from doorkeeper to cardinal. So drastically did the prestige of the pope sink that he was forced to pay tribute to leaders of mercenary troops. Leadership in Europe had clearly passed from the papacy to secular rulers; what they would do with it remained to be seen.

Rome without a pope is pictured as a widow mourning her past glory. From a eulogy to Rome written before the return of the papacy.

Suggestions for Further Reading

Note: Asterisk denotes a book available in paperback edition.

St. Louis The royal councilor Joinville's *Life of St. Louis** (Everyman's and other editions) is one of our chief sources for the life of King Louis IX of France and for an understanding of the spirit of the thirteenth century. There is excellent material on the growth of monarchical power and the development of institutions under St. Louis in C. Petit-Dutaillis, *Feudal Monarchy in France and England** (1936), and in E. Lavisse, ed., *Histoire de France*, Vol. III, Part 2 (1911). J. R. Strayer, *The Administration of Normandy under St. Louis* (1932), is a study of one of the most important provinces of the French monarchy and the Norman influence on that monarchy.

Henry III and England There is a vast amount of significant detail in the contemporary Matthew of Paris, *Chronicle*, trans. by J. A. Giles (1852), a valuable framework for events in the period from 1235 to 1273. F. M. Powicke, *King Henry III and the Lord Edward*, 2 vols. (1947), is an excellent study of the political and social history of England at the time and the best biography of a medieval king. There is documentary material on early representative assemblies in C. Stephenson and F. M. Marcham, *Sources in English Constitutional History* (1937); the best commentary is F. Pollock and F. W. Maitland, *History of English Law,* Vol. II (1923). R. F. Treharne, *The Baronial Plan of Reform, 1258–1263* (1932), has a good account of the aristocratic reaction to royal rule presented as a great constitutional revolution. F. M. Powicke, *The Thirteenth Century* (1953), is a fine study of the period, with a critical bibliography.

The Papal-Hohenstaufen War

Philippe of Novara's *The Wars of Frederick II Against the Ibelins,* trans. by J. L. La Monte (1936), has primary material on the career and imperialism of Frederick II and presents a vivid picture of the life and ideas of the thirteenth-century knights who settled in the Latin Orient. E. Kantorowicz, *Frederick II* (1931), encompassing the broad and complex field of papal-Hohenstaufen relations, is a classic study in historical biography. There is a broad survey of politics, religion, literature, and art in H. D. Sedgwick, *Italy in the Thirteenth Century,* 2 vols. (1912). W. F. Butler, *The Lombard Communes* (1906), has information on the Lombard Communes in the Hohenstaufen wars. T. C. Van Cleve, *The Emperor Frederick II* (1972), can also be highly recommended.

Scholasticism: St. Thomas Aquinas

The most useful edition of St. Thomas' writings is *Basic Writings of St. Thomas Aquinas,* ed. by A. C. Pegis (1944), which contains a good selection of the most significant and widely read treatises. F. C. Copleston, *Aquinas** (1955), is a very good introduction to Aquinas' ideas, and G. Leff, *Medieval Thought** (1958), shows the influence of Aquinas' thought on the thirteenth century. M. De Wulf, *Philosophy and Civilization in the Middle Ages** (1922), describes how the thought of the period was intimately connected with the whole of medieval civilization. The best scholarly treatment of scholastic philosophy is in E. Gilson, *History of Christian Philosophy in the Middle Ages* (1954), which has valuable bibliographic material. E. Panofsky brilliantly shows the parallel development of art and philosophy in the thirteenth century in *Gothic Architecture and Scholasticism** (1954).

Edward I and Parliament

T. F. Tout, *Edward the First* (1893), is an old but sound biography of Edward with a good account of the beginnings of legislation and the English Parliament. A good introduction to the development of Parliament is G. L. Haskins, *Growth of English Representative Government** (1948). D. Pasquet, *Essay on the Origins of the House of Commons* (1925), is an excellent study of the evolution of Parliament from the king's court. There is much useful material on Parliament in B. Wilkinson, *Constitutional History of Medieval England,* Vol. III (1958). See also the titles by Stephenson and Marcham, and Pollock and Maitland mentioned above.

Philip the Fair and Boniface VIII

There is valuable material on the reign of Philip the Fair in E. Lavisse, ed., *Histoire de France,* Vol. III, Part 2 (1911). J. R. Strayer and C. H. Taylor, *Studies in Early French Taxation* (1939), explore the relationship between finances and early representative assemblies under Philip the Fair and Philip V. There is material on the reign of Philip the Fair in the books by Fawtier and Petit-Dutaillis cited above.

H. K. Mann, *Lives of the Popes in the Middle Ages,* Vol. XVIII (1932), is a lengthy study of Boniface VIII and his pontificate from a Catholic point of view. A. C. Flick, *The Decline of the Medieval Church,* Vol. I (1930), has material on Boniface from a Protestant point of view. Though interesting reading, both are rather provincial in interpretation. The best study of this pope is T. S. R. Boase, *Boniface VIII* (1933), which is a sympathetic but far more critical treatment.

Clement V and the Babylonian Captivity

W. E. Lunt, *Papal Revenues in the Middle Ages,* 2 vols. (1930), contains considerable source material on the bureaucracy and finances of the papal Curia. An amusing if infuriating study of the period of the Babylonian Captivity is L. E. Binns, *The Decline and Fall of the Medieval Papacy* (1934), which was written as a supplement to the great history of E. Gibbon. See also G. Mollat, *The Popes at Avignon** (1965). A serious introduction to this period, M. Creighton, *A History of the Papacy,* Vol. I (1904), traces the reasons for the decline of papal power. Geoffrey Barraclough, *The Medieval Papacy** (1968), explores the historical background of the papacy.

13

The End of the Middle Ages

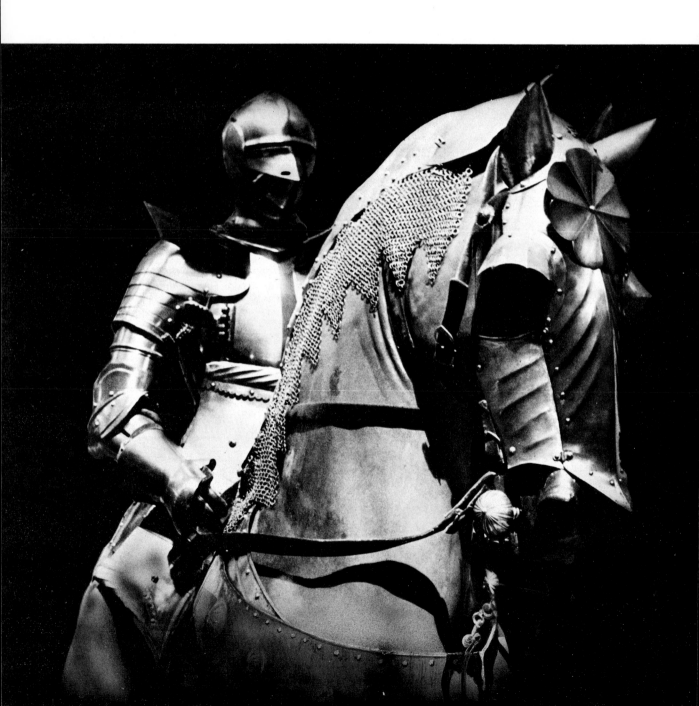

The fourteenth and early fifteenth centuries were a time of confusion and chaos in the West. Decade after decade everything seemed to go wrong: economic depression, war, rebellion, and plague harried the people, and neither ecclesiastical nor secular governments seemed capable of easing their distress. At times the whole structure of European society seemed to be crumbling, as it had at the end of the Roman Empire. Yet the Europe that emerged from this time of troubles went on to conquer the world. The science and technology, the navies and the armies, the governments and the business organizations that were to give Europe unquestioned supremacy for four centuries—all were taking shape in the fourteenth and fifteenth centuries. The dire stretch of history marked by the Hundred Years' War, the Black Death, and the Great Schism seems an unlikely seedbed for these great accomplishments. We are struck by the decay of the medieval way of life rather than by the almost imperceptible emergence of new ideas and new forms of organization. But we should not forget that the new ideas were there, that the people of western Europe never quite lost faith in their destiny, never quite gave up striving for a more orderly and prosperous society. There was confusion and uncertainty, but not the complete disintegration that had followed the collapse of the Roman Empire.

ECONOMIC WEAKNESS AND POLITICAL FAILURE

The most obvious cause of the troubles of the last medieval centuries was economic depression. Given the techniques then prevalent, by 1300 western Europe had about reached the limit of its capacity to produce food and manufactured goods, and, consequently, its ability to increase its trade. There were no more reserves of fertile land to bring into cultivation; in fact, a good deal of the land that was already being cultivated was marginal or submarginal in quality. For many years there was no significant increase in industrial output; production

might shift from one center to another, but the total output remained about the same. Population ceased to grow; most towns barely held their own and some, especially in southern France, declined sharply. The Italian towns fared better; they increased their share of Mediterranean trade and of the production of luxury textiles. But even Italy had economic difficulties during the middle years of the fourteenth century when northern rulers, like Edward III of England, repudiated the debts they owed Italian bankers. In short, until Europe found new sources of wealth and new markets both governments and individuals were constantly on the verge of bankruptcy.

Economic stagnation created a climate of opinion hostile to innovation and efforts to cooperate for the common welfare. Each individual, each community, each class was eager to preserve the monopolies and privileges that guaranteed it some share of the limited wealth available. It was during these years that the towns and gilds adopted their most restrictive regulations. Ordinary laborers found it difficult to become master workmen; master workmen were discouraged from devising new methods of production. Fortunately the attempt to preserve the *status quo* was thwarted by the weakness of government and by the ingenuity of enterprising businessmen. Some new techniques were introduced and some new industries were established. But capital was limited and it took many years before new techniques or new products had much impact on the economy.

Economic weakness helps explain the weakness of most governments. Rulers were always short of money, for the old taxes brought in less and less revenue and it was very difficult to impose new taxes. Salaries of government officials were insufficient, because of continuing inflation, and were often years in arrears. Most officials supported themselves by taking fees, gifts, and bribes from private citizens; they began to think of their offices as private possessions. Men with this attitude could keep up the routine, which was an important element of stability in a troubled society. But they showed much less zeal in perfecting their

Armor of the high Middle Ages, for horse and rider.

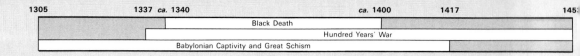
administrative techniques than had their thirteenth-century predecessors.

Financial difficulties were not the only cause of weakness in government. The assertion of sovereignty by secular rulers at the end of the thirteenth century had been somewhat premature. They had neither the ability to make realistic plans for the welfare of their people nor the authority to impose such remedies as they did devise. Most secular rulers could think only of increasing their revenues by conquering new lands. Such a policy solved no problems; it merely postponed them for the victor and aggravated them for the vanquished. With governments discredited by futile and costly wars, many men lost faith in their political leaders and turned to rebellion and civil war.

The leaders of revolt, however, showed no more ability than the kings and princes against whom they were rebelling. Many of the leaders were members of the landed nobility who still had wealth and influence even though they had lost their old rights of feudal government. But while they found it easy enough to gain power, they did not know how to exercise the power that they gained. Their main purpose was to preserve their own privileges or to direct government revenues to their own pockets—again, policies that solved no basic problems. Impatient with the routine tasks of administration, the aristocracy usually split into quarreling factions. The upper classes sometimes used parliamentary forms to justify their acts, but this only made representative assemblies appear to be vehicles of factionalism and disorder. When the desire for stronger government finally arose once again, the kings found it easy to abolish or suspend assemblies; only in England did representative assemblies retain any vitality.

Other classes performed no better than the nobles. The bourgeoisie thought in terms of local or, at most, regional interests, and they were inept in running their own municipal governments. The townsmen split into factions—old families against new families, international traders against local merchants, rich against poor—and the faction in power tried to ruin its opponents by unequal taxation or discriminatory economic legislation. The result was that local self-government collapsed in town after town. Venice remained powerful and in-

Lawlessness in Fifteenth-century England

John Paston was son of a royal judge and a well-to-do landowner in Norfolk. His father had bought the manor of Gresham but in 1448 Lord Molyns claimed it, though he had no right to it. John Paston tried to settle the claim peacefully, but Molyns' men occupied the manor house and John moved to another "mansion." While he was seeking help from his friends, his wife was left to defend his rights. She wrote her husband this letter late in 1448:

Right worshipful husband, I recommend me to you and pray you to get some cross-bows and windlasses to wind them with and arrows, for your house here is so low that no one could shoot out of it with a long-bow, even if we had great need. I suppose you could get these things from Sir John Falstoff [a friend of the Pastons]. And also I would like you to get two or three short pole-axes to guard the doors and as many jacks [padded leather jackets] as you can.

Partridge [leader of Molyns' men] and his fellows are sore afraid that you will attack them again, and they have made great preparations, as I am told. They have made bars to bar the doors cross-wise, and they have made loop-holes on every side of the house to shoot out of both with bows and with hand-guns. The holes made for hand-guns are scarcely knee-high from the floor and no one can shoot out of them with a hand bow.

[Margaret Paston apparently took all this as a matter of course; she then turned to an ordinary shopping list.] I pray you to buy me a pound of almonds and a pound of sugar and some cloth to make clothes for your children and a yard of black broad-cloth for a hood for me.

The Trinity have you in His keeping and send you Godspeed in all your affairs.

Put into modern English from Norman Davis, ed., *Paston Letters* (Oxford: Clarendon Press, 1958), pp. 9–10.

dependent under a merchant oligarchy, as did some of the German trading towns. But more often a tyrant seized power, as in certain towns in Italy, or else the officials of a king or a powerful noble took over control of the towns.

As for the peasants, they were far more restive and unhappy than they had been in the thirteenth century. With no new lands to clear and no new jobs to be had in the towns, they had little hope of improving their lot. Some of them managed to ease the burden of taxes and of payments to landlords by renegotiating their leases or by moving from one estate to another, but for most of them this road to advancement was too tedious and uncertain. The peasants rebelled in country after country, killing landlords, burning records, and demanding that payments for their land be lowered or abolished altogether. These rebellions were hopeless; untrained and poorly armed peasants were no match for an aristocracy with a strong military tradition. But the fact that the peasants did rebel reveals the despair and the tendency to violence that marked the end of the Middle Ages.

THE TROUBLES OF THE CHURCH

The failure of secular government would not have been so serious had the Church been able to regain its old leadership. The people of western Europe were still Christians, and they knew that they were not living up to the precepts of their faith. They multiplied religious ceremonies and appeals for the intercession of the saints; they flocked to revival meetings to repent their sins with tears and trembling. But the Church failed to remedy the disorders of western society; in fact, the Church was infected with the same evils that beset secular government. Repentant sinners returned to their careers of violence and fraud because no one could show them any other way to survive.

The Great Schism

The leadership of the Church was further impaired by the Great Schism that followed the Babylonian Captivity. The popes at Avignon, realizing that their exile was impairing their authority,

Miniature paintings of a fourteenth-century pewterer turning a jug on a lathe (left), and a locksmith (right), from the Guild Book of the Twelve Brothers' Foundation in Nuremburg.

had made several halfhearted efforts to return to Rome. Finally, in 1377, Gregory XI actually moved back to Italy, but he was appalled by the disorder in Rome and the Papal States. He was about to return to Avignon when he died, in 1378. The Romans, with the papacy once more within their grasp, had no intention of again losing the income from pilgrims and visitors to the papal court. When the cardinals met to elect Gregory's successor, they were besieged by a howling mob demanding that they choose a Roman, or at least an Italian, pope. It is hard to estimate how effective this pressure was; certainly it had some influence. In the end the cardinals elected an Italian archbishop who took the title of Urban VI.

The cardinals may have hoped that Urban would be a pliant and cooperative pope; instead he bullied them, rejected their advice, and denounced their behavior. The majority of the cardinals were French, but even the non-French were outraged by Urban's behavior. The whole group soon fled from Rome and declared that Urban's election was void because it had taken place under duress. They proceeded to choose a new pope, a French-speaking cardinal of the family of the counts of Geneva. He took the title of Clement VII, set up his court at Avignon, and denounced Urban as a usurper.

Emperors such as Henry IV and Frederick Barbarossa had tried to set up antipopes, but they had never deceived secular and religious leaders. Everyone knew who the true pope was, even if the emperors supported an opponent. But this time there was no such consensus, and most of Europe was honestly bewildered. Both popes had been elected by a majority of duly appointed cardinals; if Urban had the advantage of being the first named, he also had the disadvantage of being repudiated by the very men who had elected him. Rulers could decide which pope to follow only on the basis of political expediency. France, and its ally Scotland, naturally accepted the Avignonese pope; England just as naturally supported Urban at Rome. The Spanish kingdoms backed Clement, while most of Germany and Italy held to the Roman pontiff. Both popes intrigued

to gain support in hostile areas, and both created new cardinals. When Urban and Clement died, in 1389 and 1394, respectively, the rival groups of cardinals each elected a new pope, thus prolonging the Great Schism into the next century.

Though the people of western Europe were deeply distressed by the schism, they could see no way out of their troubles. Who could be sure which was the false pope and which the true one? This uncertainty weakened both the organization and the moral influence of the Church. The popes of the Captivity had at least been good administrators, but the schism made effective administration impossible. Reform in the Church's financial system was desperately needed, but a pope who controlled only half the Church could hardly afford to lose revenues or alienate supporters by abolishing profitable abuses. A divided and unreformed Church had little hope of guiding European society.

A manuscript illumination showing an antipope receiving his crown from the devil and in turn crowning an emperor as a pledge of mutual support against the true head of the Church.

THE GREAT SCHISM   1378–1417

0 MILES 300

ATLANTIC OCEAN

SCOTLAND

IRELAND

ENGLAND

NORTH SEA

NORWAY

SWEDEN

DENMARK

BALTIC SEA

HOLY ROMAN EMPIRE

POLAND-LITHUANIA

FRANCE

Avignon

HUNGARY

PORTUGAL

CASTILE & LEÓN

NAVARRE

ARAGON

CORSICA

Rome

SARDINIA

KINGDOM OF NAPLES

ADRIATIC SEA

MEDITERRANEAN SEA

SICILY

▨ Land giving allegiance to Rome

☐ Land giving allegiance to Avignon

▤ Shifting and divided

Reformers and Heretics

The state of the Church during the Captivity and the Great Schism seemed so hopeless that many men began to seek salvation through their own efforts. The mildest, and probably the most numerous, group of reformers did not break openly with the Church; they simply ceased to rely on it. They formed little associations, such as the Brethren of the Common Life, to encourage one another to lead devout Christian lives and to seek direct contact with God through mystical experiences. These groups, which were especially numerous in the Rhineland and the Low Countries, produced some remarkable works of devotion, such as the *Theologia Germanica,* which influenced later reformers. They also founded schools that were to play a great role in the educational revival of the fifteenth and sixteenth centuries; Erasmus (see pp. 376–77) was educated in such a school. These mystical and contemplative reformers were looked on with some suspicion by conservative churchmen, but most of them remained within the bounds of orthodoxy.

A more radical element was not content simply to withdraw into devout groups. These men wanted a thorough-going reform of the Church, and many of them felt that only laymen could do the job. An early example of this attitude can be seen in the *Defensor pacis,* written by Marsilius of Padua about 1324. Marsilius, who like many Italians had a completely secular point of view, believed that the state should control the Church just as it controlled other organizations. If the state could regulate the behavior of doctors, it could also regulate the behavior of priests. Marsilius' book was condemned, but his ideas inspired criticism of the Church throughout the fourteenth and fifteenth centuries.

Another dangerous critic of the Church was an Oxford professor, John Wiclif (*ca.* 1320–84). At first concerned mainly with the problem of private property, including the property of the Church, Wiclif decided that the Church was being corrupted by wealth and that it would be better for everyone if church lands were taken over by kings and nobles. This position naturally pleased influential laymen and may explain why Wiclif was never punished for his unorthodox doctrines. Wiclif went on to cast doubt on the Catholic doctrine that the bread and wine in the communion service are transformed into the Body and Blood of Christ. He wound up by attacking the whole administrative structure of the Church as corrupt and largely unauthorized by the Bible. He taught that the pope could err, that the hierarchy had no absolute authority, and that kings should protect and guide the Church in their own realms.

Though Wiclif had no intention of launching a popular movement, his ideas spread rapidly beyond the scholarly circles for which he had written. By emphasizing scriptural authority, he had encouraged his followers to produce an English translation of the Bible that could be used by wandering preachers. These preachers, taking advantage of social discontent, popularized Wiclif's most radical views and gained a considerable following among the lower and middle classes in England. Some of them became social as well as religious reformers: if uzadan a dit au meſſage en ſecroi

The burning of infected clothes during the Black Death (detail from a comtemporary manuscript illumination.).

cals—or Lollards, as they were called—after 1400. But the suppression was not wholly effective; the Wiclifite translation of the Bible and memories of Lollard doctrines survived until the time of the English Reformation. And the writings of John Wiclif reached as far as Bohemia, where they influenced John Hus, the great fifteenth-century opponent of the Church (see p. 361).

THE BLACK DEATH

The effects of economic depression, political confusion, and religious uncertainty were intensified by terrible outbursts of plague in the middle years of the fourteenth century. The Black Death (probably bubonic plague) first appeared in Italy in the 1340s and swept through Europe during the next two decades. The worst was over by 1360, but repeated, though less severe, outbreaks throughout the next half-century kept the population from reaching its preplague numbers. Although no accurate estimate can be made of the mortality, it was especially severe in thickly populated areas. Some towns lost more than two-fifths of their inhabitants, and some monasteries almost ceased to function. Since doctors were helpless, the only way to avoid the plague was to take refuge in isolated country districts.

The panic caused by the Black Death drove the sorely tried peoples of western Europe into emotional instability. It is no accident that the bloodiest peasant rebellions and the most senseless civil wars took place after the plague, and that the witchcraft delusion, unknown in the early Middle Ages, then reached its height. This was a double delusion. Innocent men and women were falsely accused of practicing black magic, but there were people, including men of high position, who genuinely believed that they could gain their desires by making a compact with the devil. More than anything else, the witchcraft delusion demonstrated the state of shock in which western Europe found itself at the end of the fourteenth century. The rationalism and confidence in the future that had been so apparent at the height of medieval civilization had vanished.

the Church had no right to property because it misused it, did the barons and knights have any more right? Such ideas may have helped to touch off the English Peasants' Rebellion of 1381. Fear of economic radicalism may have induced the English upper classes to join with the king in suppressing the religious radi-

The Black Death in England

Then that most grievous pestilence penetrated the coastal regions by way of Southampton and came to Bristol, and people died as if the whole strength of the city were seized by sudden death. For there were few who lay in their beds more than three days or two and a half days; then that savage death snatched them about the second day. In Leicester, in the little parish of St. Leonard, more than three hundred and eighty died; in the parish of the Holy Cross, more than four hundred, and in the parish of St. Margaret, more than seven hundred. . . .

And the price of everything was cheap, because of the fear of death, there were very few who took any care for their wealth, or for anything else. For a man could buy a horse for half a mark [about 7 shillings] which before was worth forty shillings, a large fat ox for four shillings, a cow for twelve pence, a heifer for sixpence, a large fat sheep for four pence. . . . And the sheep and cattle wandered about through the fields and among the crops, and there was no one to go after them or collect them. They perished in countless numbers everywhere, for lack of watching . . . since there was such a lack of serfs and servants, that no one knew what he should do. For there is no memory of a mortality so severe and so savage. . . . In the following autumn, one could not hire a reaper for less than eight pence [per day] with food, or a mower at less than twelve pence with food.

From Henry Knighton, *Chronicle*, in *The Portable Medieval Reader*, ed. by J. B. Ross and M. M. McLaughlin (New York: Viking, 1949), pp. 218–19.

ENGLAND IN THE LATER MIDDLE AGES

Even France and England, the two strongest states in the West, were shaken by the events of the fourteenth century. They had enough momentum and solid enough administrative structures to survive as political units, but there were times when neither country had a government capable of preserving law and order. While the bureaucrats were able to keep the machinery of government running, they could not hold back the rising tide of lawlessness. Under these circumstances, the nobles regained much of the power they had lost in the thirteenth century. They tried to control policy and direct revenues to their own pockets; in England they even deposed their kings.

The expansionist policies of Edward I (see pp. 266–67) had severely strained English resources. A reaction would have taken place in any case; it was made more acute by the character of Edward II (1307–27). So incompetent that no one respected him, Edward turned over the business of government to a series of favorites who were hated by the great lords. The barons tried the old expedient of setting up a committee to control the government, but it worked no better than it had under Henry III. Finally Edward's own wife and her lover Mortimer, one of the lords of the turbulent lands of the Welsh frontier, led a rebellion against him. Edward was deposed in 1327 and quietly murdered a few weeks later; his young son, Edward III (1327–77), became king.

The Hundred Years' War: The First Phase

Edward III shared his barons' fondness for courtly magnificence and chivalric warfare. More popular with the aristocracy than his father had been, he was also more susceptible to their influence. Never quite willing to risk his popularity by forcing a showdown with the barons, he allowed them to retain a strong position in Parliament and in the Council. This is probably why he drifted into the Hundred Years' War with France. War was a policy on which he and his barons could agree, and so long as the war was successful he could avoid domestic controversies.

There were, of course, other reasons for the war. France was still trying to annex the English holdings in Aquitaine and gain full control of Flanders, which was the best market for English wool. France was aiding Scotland, which had regained its independence in the battle of Bannockburn (1314) and was in a state of almost permanent hostility with England. French and English sailors were intermittently plundering each other's ships. These frictions were enough to cause a war, but they do not quite explain why the war lasted for generations. The king persisted because he gained new and valuable territories; the barons, because they acquired booty and profitable military commands.

After a bad start, caused largely by financial difficulties, Edward came up with an amazing string of victories. He

The Later Middle Ages

So violent and motley was life, that it bore the mixed smell of blood and of roses. The men of that time always oscillated between the fear of hell and the most naïve joy, between cruelty and tenderness, between harsh asceticism and insane attachment to the delights of this world . . . always running to extremes. . . .

Bad government, the cupidity and violence of the great, wars and brigandage, scarcity, misery, and pestilence—to this is contemporary history nearly reduced in the eyes of the people. The feeling of general insecurity . . . was further aggravated by the fear of hell, of sorcerers and of devils. Everywhere the flames of hatred arise and injustice reigns. Satan covers a gloomy earth with his sombre wings.

From J. Huizinga, *The Waning of the Middle Ages* (London: Arnold, 1929), pp. 18, 21.

gained control of the Channel in a naval battle at Sluys and nearly annihilated the French army at Crécy (1346). Then he went on to take Calais, which remained a port of entry for English armies for two centuries. Ten years later, Edward's son, the Black Prince, crushed another French army at Poitiers and took the French king prisoner. In the treaty that followed this victory the French agreed to pay a huge ransom for their king and to cede about two-fifths of their country to the English.

Edward had succeeded because his country was more united than France and gave him more consistent financial support, and also because he had developed new tactics for his army. He mixed companies of archers, armed with the famous English longbow, with companies of dismounted cavalry in heavy armor. A charge, by either mounted or foot soldiers, would be thrown into confusion by showers of arrows. The few men who broke through to the main line could be easily dealt with by the troops in heavy armor. The only weakness in Edward's formation was that it was essentially defensive; it could not be used for a charge. Only when portable firearms were invented at the end of the fifteenth century was it possible to use missile weapons for an attack.

Like many other generals, Edward found it easier to win victories than to profit from them. The French, with no intention of fulfilling the terms of the treaty they had signed, launched a war of attrition that gradually exhausted their enemies. England simply did not have enough men or enough resources to garrison territories larger than Edward's whole kingdom. The French learned to avoid headlong rushes at large English armies and concentrated instead on picking off isolated garrisons and small detachments. As a result, the English had lost a large part of their conquests by the time of Edward III's death in 1377.

Rebellion and Revolution

Military misfortunes abroad led to bickering at home. There was a complete failure of leadership during Edward's last years. The king was sinking into senility and the Black Prince, crippled by disease,

died a year before his father. One of Edward's younger sons, John of Gaunt, Duke of Lancaster, had more authority than anyone else, but he was disliked and distrusted by many members of the aristocracy. He was accused, with some justice, of associating with a group of corrupt officeholders and, with less justice, of coveting the throne. The duke's taste in art and literature was excellent —he gave a government job and a pension to Geoffrey Chaucer—but interest in the arts has seldom added to the stature of a politician in English public opinion.

The new king, Richard II (1377–99), the son of the Black Prince, was only a child when he inherited the throne. During the first part of his reign England was governed by successive groups of barons. These men did nothing to distinguish

THE HUNDRED YEARS' WAR *ca.* 1358–1453

Contested territory
English attacks
French attacks

0   MILES   100

MEDITERRANEAN SEA

282

themselves; their inefficiency and bad judgment led directly to the Peasants' Rebellion of 1381. The war in France was still costing large sums of money, even though the English were now almost entirely on the defensive. Casting about for a new source of revenue, the government hit on the idea of a poll tax, a levy of a few pennies on each English subject. This brought to a peak all the smoldering resentment of the peasants and the poorer inhabitants of the towns. They were already suffering from economic stagnation; now they felt that they were being asked to carry an unfair share of the tax burden. All southern England exploded in rebellion. Peasants and artisans burned tax rolls and manorial records, killed unpopular officials and landlords, and finally marched on London. The barons, taken off guard, scurried about trying to raise an army. Meanwhile Richard had to stand by and watch the rebels occupy London, burn the palace of the Duke of Lancaster, and murder the chancellor and the treasurer of England. Forced into humiliating negotiations with the rebel leaders, he was obliged to promise complete forgiveness for all past offenses, the abolition of serfdom, and the remission of almost all manorial dues.

The rebellion was suppressed as soon as the barons could get their troops together, for the poorly armed peasants and townsmen were no match for professional soldiers. The king repudiated his promises and apparently all was as before. Actually, the rebellion had two important results. First, serfdom declined steadily after 1381, and by 1500 there were almost no serfs left in England. Second, Richard had seen a convincing demonstration of the inefficiency and clumsiness of baronial government. It is not surprising that when he came of age in 1386 he tried to increase royal authority and to concentrate all power in his own hands.

Richard showed considerable skill in his efforts to strengthen the monarchy, but he made two fatal mistakes. The barons might have tolerated the loss of political power, but Richard threatened their economic position as well by confiscating the property of those he distrusted. Moreover, Richard failed to

Richard II, from the portrait by Beauneven of Valenciennes (1398) in Westminster Abbey.

A battle (Formigny) at the end of the Hundred Years' War. Notice that the English (right) are on foot and are flanked by bowmen, while the French are delivering a cavalry charge. Usually the English won in such circumstances, but this time they were defeated.

build up a powerful army under his own control. Most of the armed forces in the country were private companies paid by the king but recruited and commanded by barons and knights. This system had developed during the Hundred Years' War, when it had seemed easier to allow members of the aristocracy to raise troops than for the government to deal with the tedious problem of recruiting. Any lord with a taste for fighting could maintain his own little army at government expense, a situation that encouraged disorder and rebellion. The king's personal bodyguard was no match for the combined forces of several great barons. As a result, Richard was helpless

when Henry of Lancaster, son of John of Gaunt and cousin of the king, rebelled in 1399. Henry himself had been driven into exile and stripped of his lands, and he was supported by many members of the aristocracy who feared the same fate. Richard was deposed and died in prison, and Henry of Lancaster mounted the throne as Henry IV (1399–1413).

The Hundred Years' War: The Second Phase

The Lancastrian kings, who ruled from 1399 to 1461, never quite lived down the violence by which they had come to power. Their title was faulty—

there were other descendants of Edward III with a better claim—and they seldom had the unanimous support of the great lords. Henry IV had difficulty suppressing two serious rebellions, and Henry V (1413–22) tried to unite the country by the dangerous expedient of reviving the Hundred Years' War. He was a brilliant general, as he revealed in his victory at Agincourt (1415); he was the first commander of a European army to use siege artillery on a large scale. By securing the alliance of the Duke of Burgundy, a disgruntled French prince, he was able to force the French king, Charles VI, to accept a treaty in which Charles disinherited his son, married his daughter to Henry, and agreed that any son born of this union was to be king of France. The next year both Charles and Henry died, and a one-year-old baby, Henry VI, became king of England and France.

Henry V, with all his ability, would have found it hard to control two kingdoms; Henry VI never had a chance. His long minority was disastrous. In England his uncles and cousins, supported by baronial factions, quarreled bitterly. In France, the disinherited son of Charles VI claimed the throne as Charles VII and carried on the war from the unconquered country south of the Loire. The English pressed him hard, but just as his cause seemed hopeless he was saved by the appearance of Joan of Arc. To the English, Joan was "a limb of the devil." But she stirred the French to drive the English back from the Loire and to win an important victory at Patay (1429). After these successes it hardly mattered that Joan fell into English hands and was burned as a witch, for the courage and enthusiasm with which she had inspired the French survived her. The Burgundians abandoned the English alliance, and the English position in France deteriorated steadily. Forts and provinces fell one by one until by 1453 only Calais was left. And so after twelve decades of fighting and plundering, the war at last came to an end.

The Wars of the Roses

When the English could no longer blame Joan of Arc for their defeats, they began to blame one another. Commanders were accused of treason and incompetence; some were executed and others exiled. Henry VI, even when he came of age, could do nothing to stop the feuds among the great lords. Humble in spirit and weak in mind, he was dominated by a French wife whom most of the aristocracy disliked. The English barons had acquired the habit of violence, and a decade after the end of the Hundred Years' War they plunged England into the series of civil conflicts known as the Wars of the Roses. The ostensible reason for these wars was an attempt by some of the barons to replace the Lancastrian king with the Duke of York, who represented the oldest line of descent from Edward III. The attempt succeeded, but the Yorkist kings, who ruled from 1461 to 1485, had almost as much trouble with the barons as their Lancastrian predecessors. In fact, the Wars of the Roses were the last uprising of the barons, the last attempt of a small clique to take over the central government and use it for their own purpose. The wars destroyed everyone who took part in them—the House of Lancaster, the House of York, and many of the great noble families. It was left for the half-alien Tudors, indirect and illegitimate descendants of John of Gaunt, to restore order in England.

England made some economic gains toward the end of this period in spite of the failure of political leadership. The kings of the fourteenth and fifteenth centuries were no economists, but they were able to grasp one simple fact—that so long as England produced only raw materials, she would never grow very rich. From Edward III on, they encouraged the migration of textile workers to England and protected the growing English textile industry. They also encouraged the development of English shipping. The results should not be exaggerated, for even at the end of the fifteenth century England could not rival Flanders in textiles or Italy in shipping. But a good start had been made; England had come a long way from being a country whose chief economic function was to raise raw wool to be carried in foreign ships to Flemish looms.

The only known contemporary portrait of Joan of Arc.

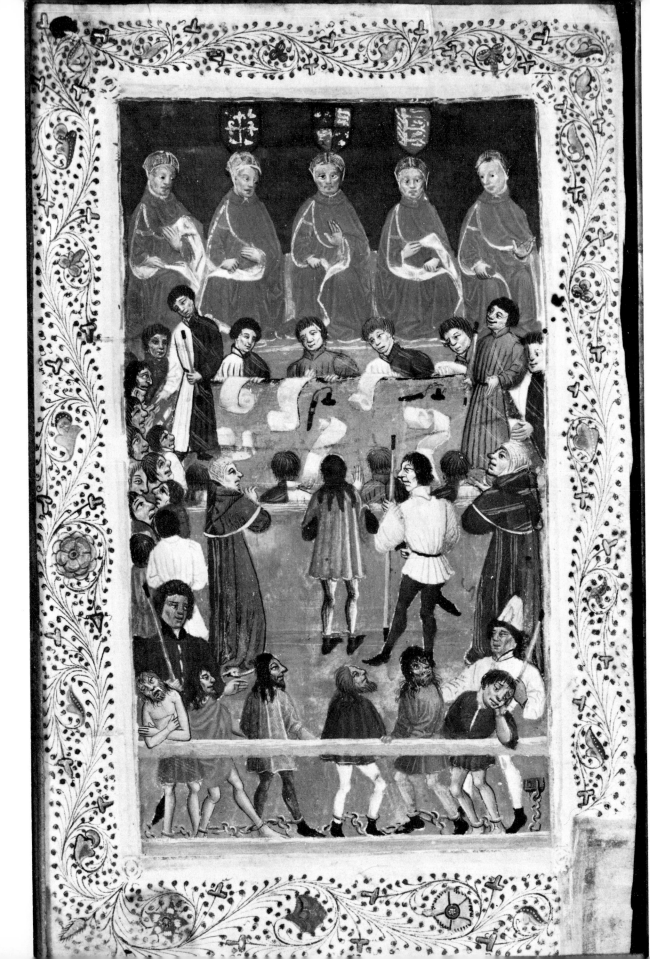

The Development of Parliament

There were also two important institutional developments: the rise of the justices of the peace and the continuing growth of Parliament. The justices of the peace were created by Edward III in the fourteenth century to take over some of the work of local law enforcement that had formerly been the duty of sheriffs and feudal lords. The justices were men of position and leisure, not great lords but well-to-do local landholders of the class that had long carried heavy responsibilities in local government. Like the sheriffs and the tax collectors, they served without pay; their reward was leadership in their own community. By the middle of the fifteenth century their powers had grown to a point where they controlled local government. They arrested criminals and tried minor offenses (major cases were reserved for the circuit judges). They were responsible for enforcing economic regulations and orders of the central government. They collected information for the Council and were supposed to inform it of plots against the government. In practice, the justices of the peace were often the creatures of the most powerful baron of their region. But when the Tudors reestablished royal authority, the justices of the peace, with their wide local knowledge and influence, became the key agents of the crown in the counties.

The century and a half of political instability, stretching from Edward II through Henry VI, gave Parliament a chance to make itself an indispensable part of the government. Weak rulers sought the appearance of public support, and usurpers sought the appearance of legitimacy. Both were eager for parliamentary ratification of important acts, since Parliament represented all the propertied classes of the country. Thus Edward III and Henry IV, after successful revolutions, asked Parliament to accept statements justifying the deposition of their predecessors. Similarly, all taxes and most legislative acts were submitted to Parliament for approval.

Equally important was the union (about 1340) of the county representatives (knights) and the town representatives (burgesses). These groups, which had acted separately under Edward I, now formed the House of Commons and made Parliament a far more effective assembly. Now there were only two houses (Lords and Commons) instead of three, or, as in some countries, even four. And the lower house included an element, the knights, which would have been considered noble in any other country. The knights were landlords, just as the barons were; they could intermarry with baronial families and some of them became barons themselves. Their presence gave the House of Commons much more influence than a mere assembly of burgesses (such as the French Third Estate) could have. Through the leadership of the knights, cooperation with the lords could be assured. This situation sometimes enabled Parliament to effect significant changes in government, for when both houses attacked a minister of the king they could usually force him out of office.

By the fifteenth century Parliament had become an integral part of the machinery of government, and no important act was valid until it had received parliamentary approval. So well established had Parliament become that it survived even the period of strong kingship that began under the Tudors in 1485. But Parliament only gave legal validity to acts of government; it did not make policy, which was the province of the king or the great lords. For example, Edward II and Richard II were not deposed by the initiative of Parliament; Parliament was merely asked to ratify the results of a revolution engineered by a few great barons. Not until the seventeenth century did Parliament begin to formulate policies of its own.

FRANCE IN THE LATER MIDDLE AGES

The monarchy in France also had its troubles during the fourteenth and fifteenth centuries. The sons of Philip the Fair (see pp. 268–70) died in rapid succession, leaving only daughters to succeed them. The barons, afraid that one of their number might gain excessive power by marrying a reigning queen, invented a rule barring women from the succession. In 1328 they placed Philip of Valois, a cousin of the last king and a nephew of Philip the Fair, on the throne. But since Philip owed his position to the barons, he had to spend most of his reign bestowing favors on his supporters and keeping peace among factions of nobles. The widespread loyalty to the king that had marked the late thirteenth century weakened, and rebellions and acts of treason plagued the country. These internal disorders help to account for the French defeats in the first few decades of the Hundred Years' War.

Philip's son, John (1350–64), had no better fortune. His capture by the English at Poitiers, with the subsequent loss of territory and the heavy taxes needed to raise his ransom, caused widespread dissatisfaction. In 1358 the peasants rose in a revolt that was no more successful than the English rebellion but much more bloody and destructive. In the same year the Estates General, led by the Paris bourgeoisie, tried to take over the government. The attempt failed, both because the Estates had had little experience in government and because their leaders had no support among the great nobles. John's son, Charles V (1364–80), regained much of the lost ground by suppressing his opponents at home and by driving the English from one stronghold after another. If his successor had been a more capable ruler, the French might have escaped another century of troubles.

Unfortunately, most of the brains and determination in the French royal family went to uncles and cousins of the new king rather than to the king himself. Charles VI (1380–1422) was never strong either in mind or in character, and after 1390 he suffered intermittent spells of insanity. The government was conducted largely by princes of the blood royal who quarreled bitterly among themselves over offices, pensions, and gifts of land.

When the Duke of Burgundy was assassinated in 1419 by the followers of the Duke of Orléans, the quarrels turned into a civil war and the new Duke of Burgundy allied himself with the English. Since, in addition to Burgundy, he had acquired Flanders and other provinces of the Low Countries, he was the most powerful prince in France and his defection proved disastrous. It was during this period of civil war that Henry V made his rapid conquests and forced Charles VI to recognize Henry's son as heir to the French throne.

The Defeat of England

Charles VII (1422–61) faced an almost hopeless situation when his father died. He had been officially disinherited; the English and their Burgundian allies held the largest and richest part of France. Charles had little military strength, and he was not using what he did have very effectively. It was at this moment that Joan of Arc, a peasant girl from the extreme eastern frontier, appeared at court and announced that heavenly voices had ordered her to drive the English out of the country. Joan, self-confident and persuasive, shook Charles from his lethargy and talked him into the counteroffensive that turned the tide of the war. Joan's execution by the English scarcely checked the reconquest, for Charles soon had another stroke of good fortune. England under Henry VI was as torn by factional strife as France had been under Charles VI, and the leader of one faction, an uncle of the English king, mortally offended the Duke of Burgundy. The duke's return to the French cause in 1435 greatly weakened the English and facilitated Charles' recovery of northern France.

Joan of Arc was not unique in having visions, for in those troubled years many men and women were convinced that they had had divine revelations. But in the content of her visions we can see how

A fifteenth-century Swiss halberd.

deep were the roots that the religion of the French monarchy had struck among the people. Joan was convinced that Charles VII was the only rightful king of France and that it was her religious duty to restore him to his throne. She also believed that "to make war on the holy kingdom of France was to make war on the Lord Jesus." Her beliefs were shared by people of all classes. In spite of the misgovernment of the last century there was still a deep reservoir of loyalty to the French monarchy. And in spite of treachery and factionalism there was at least a beginning of national feeling among the French people. Under all the confusion and disorder of the early fifteenth century they clung to two basic beliefs: faith in the French monarchy and faith in the Christian religion. When the two beliefs were united as they were in Joan of Arc, they were irresistible. Joan foreshadowed that union of religion and monarchy on which the absolute states of the early modern period were to be built.

Restoration of Royal Power

France suffered more severely than England during the Hundred Years' War, since all the fighting took place on French soil. Wide areas were devastated by raiding armies and wandering companies of mercenary soldiers who found plundering more profitable than loyal service. But precisely because the French predicament was so much graver than the English, royal power was restored more rapidly and more completely in France. A king who showed any promise of putting an end to disorder could override most limitations on his power to levy taxes. Charles V began the work of freeing the monarchy from these restraints, and Charles VII finished the job. As soon as he had the English on the run he began to levy taxes at will, without asking consent from the Estates. His task was made easier by the fact that provincial feeling was so strong in France that a central parliamentary assembly was seldom called, and when it was called it had little authority. Real influence lay with the provincial and regional assemblies, with the local Estates of Normandy or of Languedoc rather than with the Estates

General. And it was relatively easy for Charles to overcome the fragmented opposition of these local assemblies.

The same overwhelming interest in provincial affairs kept the great French nobles from entrenching themselves in the central government, which remained the preserve of the king and his bureaucrats. Thus in the long run the Hundred Years' War reinforced tendencies that had been apparent in France prior to the end of the thirteenth century—tendencies toward a bureaucratic state in which the king was strong and all other political forces were weak and divided. This French pattern became a model for the rest of Europe during the early modern period.

GERMANY IN THE LATER MIDDLE AGES

The political history of the rest of western Europe during the later Middle Ages resembled that of France and England. Everywhere there were rebellions, civil wars, and attempts to conquer neighboring territories. But all this furor produced surprisingly little change. A political map of Europe in 1450 looks very like a map of 1300, and the basic characteristics of most of the governments were similarly unchanged.

Certain developments in Germany deserve attention, however. First, during the fifteenth century the dukes of Burgundy gradually gained control over all the provinces of the Low Countries, roughly the equivalent of modern Belgium and the Netherlands. This was one of the richest and most productive regions of Europe. The union of the Low Countries under the House of Burgundy separated their fate from that of the rest of Germany and gradually gave them a distinct national identity. At the same time their wealth made them the object of a long series of European wars that began in the fifteenth century and have continued to our own day.

Second, during the fourteenth century the peasants and townsmen of Switzerland gradually gained their independence from the Habsburg family, which had dominated this part of Germany. In defeating the Habsburgs the

Swiss developed well-disciplined infantry formations, armed with long pikes, that could beat off a charge of heavy cavalry. By the fifteenth century companies of Swiss infantry had acquired such a reputation that they were being hired by French kings and Italian princes. The Swiss were also demonstrating the possibility of republican government to a Europe that had had little recent experience with this system. Each district, or canton, of the very loosely knit Swiss Confederation had its own institutions, and no canton was under a feudal lord. The towns were ruled by the wealthier burgesses, but the peasant cantons, where the movement for independence had begun, were almost pure democracies.

The third important development in Germany was the rise of a new power center on the middle Danube as a result of the peculiar electoral habits of the German princes. By the fourteenth century the number of princes taking part in imperial elections had been reduced to seven. These great men feared giving the title to any powerful prince, so for some time they regularly chose as emperors counts with small holdings. Though the title gave no real power, it did confer enough social prestige to enable such counts to marry well-endowed heiresses. Thus the Habsburgs, petty princes in West Germany who had served briefly as emperors around 1300, managed to acquire the duchy of Austria and nearby counties. A little later, the Count of Luxemburg, an equally undistinguished prince, became emperor and arranged a marriage through which his son received the kingdom of Bohemia. Later Luxemburg emperors acquired Silesia and eventually Hungary. When the last male Luxemburg leader died in 1438, his nearest heir was the Habsburg Duke of Austria. The union of the two sets of holdings marked the beginning of the vast Habsburg Empire, which for five centuries was to be one of the great powers of Europe.

ART, LITERATURE, AND SCIENCE

At first glance the art and literature, the scholarship and technology, of western Europe during this period seem almost as futile as the politics. There was a great deal of sterile imitation and elaboration of familiar themes. At times, exaggeration of earlier ideas gave good effects. For example, striking results were achieved in Gothic architecture by making windows higher and wider and by emphasizing perpendicular lines. On the other hand, many late Gothic churches were either cold and uninspired copies of earlier work, or gigantic wedding cakes in which spikes and gables, traceries and canopies, concealed the basic lines of the structure. It is no accident that one late Gothic style is known as the Flamboyant. In literature there was the same technical perfection that, too often, could not conceal lack of content. The old narrative poems became fantastic romances; the lyrics became society verse. In scholarship there were a few original thinkers, and pedants who thrashed old straw without producing much new intellectual grain. These were the aspects of late medieval culture that were to disgust the Italians of the Renaissance and lead them to damn most medieval work as "gothic" and barbarous.

Literature

But there was still fire beneath the ashes of imitation and fussiness, and some men managed to breathe new life

A fifteenth-century representation of Chaucer from the Ellesmere manuscript of *Canterbury Tales*.

into the old forms. Thus the French prince Charles of Orléans composed lyrics that expressed genuine feeling rather than conventional sentiments. A better-known example is Geoffrey Chaucer (*ca.* 1340–1400), who began as a mere translator and adapter of French works and developed into one of England's greatest poets. His most famous work, the Prologue to the *Canterbury Tales,* reveals his skill in describing individual characters and his wit in depicting human foibles. His people range from the "perfect, gentle Knight" and the poor parson, who taught Christ's lore, "but first he followed it himself," through the earthy Wife of Bath, who had buried five husbands, down to scoundrels like the Miller and the Summoner. Perhaps his knowledge of all levels of English society was due to the fact that Chaucer worked for years in the customs service in the busy port of London. But his subtle por-

trayal of human behavior, shown also in *Troilus and Criseyde,* came only from his own genius. Chaucer was something of a psychologist as well as a poet, but while he saw through pretense and sham he never became bitter. He rose fast in English society under the patronage of John of Gaunt; he accepted the world as he found it and rather liked what he found.

François Villon (b. 1431) was less fortunate. A friend of the thieves and prostitutes of Paris, and a convicted criminal himself, he shows how close French society came to breaking down under the strains of the early fifteenth century. He used the old poetic forms to describe with gusto life in taverns and thieves' dens. But his poems also express his bitterness over his wasted life and portray the hopes and fears of the poor and the outcast—the simple piety of an old woman, the last thoughts of men condemned to hang. The tendency toward realism, already evident in Chaucer, became even stronger in Villon.

Devotional works written for laymen were far more numerous after 1300 than they had ever been before. There was a tremendous desire among all classes for more intense and personal religious experience to supplement the conventional observances. The fourteenth and fifteenth centuries produced innumerable meditations, visions, and moral tracts. Some of the finest religious writings of any period were composed at this time, especially the *Imitation of Christ,* ascribed to Thomas à Kempis. In England there was *The Vision of Piers Plowman* by William Langland, one of the first important works written in English after the long eclipse following the Norman Conquest. We know little of Langland, except that he lived in the middle years of the fourteenth century and that he came of peasant stock. The English of Piers Plowman is archaic, but it is recognizably English and not, as Anglo-Saxon was, an early German dialect.

Piers Plowman also illustrates the widespread desire to transform religion into a strong social force. The poet criticizes every class for its worldliness and selfishness; only by a return to the pure principles of the Gospel can the world

Villon: Ballad of the Hanged Men

This is Algernon Swinburne's translation. Villon wrote this ballad when he and some of his accomplices had been condemned to death for burglary. His sentence was later commuted to exile.

If we call on you, brothers, to forgive,
Ye should not hold our prayer in scorn, though we
Were slain by law; ye know that all alive
Have not wit always to walk righteously,
Make therefore intercession heartily
With him that of a virgin's womb was bred,
That his grace be not as a dry well-head
For us, nor let hell's thunder on us fall.
We are dead, let no man harry or vex us dead,
But pray to God that he forgive us all.

The rain has washed and laundered us all five,
And the sun dried and blackened; yea, perdie,
Ravens and pies with beaks that rend and rive
Have dug our eyes out, and plucked off for fee
Our beards and eyebrows, never are we free
Not once, to rest, but here and there still sped,
Driven at its wild will by the wind's change led,
More pecked of birds than fruits on garden-wall;
Men, for God's love, let no gibe here be said,
But pray to God that he forgive us all.

From François Villon, *Poems,* ed. by John Payne (New York: Modern Library, n.d.), p. 246.

be saved. There was nothing anti-Catholic in Langland's program, but it did bear testimony to the continuing inability of ecclesiastical authorities to adequately satisfy the aspirations expressed in the poem and in many similar works.

Painting and Sculpture

The same tendency toward realism that we have noted in Chaucer and Villon is also evident in much of the sculpture and painting of the period. This tendency, which had already appeared in some of the details of thirteenth-century works, now began to be expressed in the principal figures. It sometimes took a macabre form: skeletons and corpses were depicted with loving care on funeral monuments and in the Dance of Death, a favorite subject of artists. But we also find at this time the first real portraits painted in western Europe and the first attempts to depict a landscape that is more than a conventional background. There were capable artists everywhere—English, French, and German sculptors, French and German painters. But the most interesting group were those who worked for the dukes of Burgundy. The Flemish school of painting, which developed in the late fourteenth and early fifteenth centuries, was a worthy rival of the Italians of the early Renaissance. In some techniques these painters were ahead of the Italians—the first painting in oils, for example, was done in Flanders. The best-known Flemish painters, such as the van Eycks, van der Weyden, and Memling, combined meticulous attention to detail with genuine religious feeling. And there is nothing in Italy that quite equals the Flemish portraits of this period, such as Jan van Eyck's picture of the Arnolfinis, or his *Léal Souvenir*.

Science

The scholarly work of the period is less well known, and a few years ago it would have been dismissed as unoriginal and unimportant. But even when it was unoriginal it was useful to men with ideas of their own. For example, Colum-

Death was a favorite subject for illustration in the late Middle Ages. Shown here is the Dance of Death from a manuscript of about 1400. Death, playing a trumpet decked with the papal banner of the keys of St. Peter, summons the pope.

bus drew most of his ideas about geography from books written in the fourteenth and early fifteenth centuries. And not all the work was unoriginal. In philosophy there was a sharp attack on the system of Thomas Aquinas that freed scholars, to some extent, from their adherence to the Aristotelian ideas that had been incorporated into Thomas' theology. Once Aristotle's ideas had been challenged, there could be wider speculation on scientific questions, especially on explanations of motion and acceleration. The problems through which Galileo revolutionized the science of physics had already been raised by fourteenth-century scholars.

More important than any specific achievement was the very fact that interest in scientific problems persisted. Up to the end of the Middle Ages, western scholars, relying largely on the work of the Greeks and Moslems, had made no outstanding contributions to scientific knowledge. But they were remarkably persistent and kept working on scientific problems after other peoples had given up. The Greeks and Moslems eventually lost interest in science, as did the Chinese, who had had their own independent scientific tradition. But from the twelfth century on, there were always some scholars in the West who were interested in science, and this long devotion led, in the end, to the great discoveries of the early modern period. Men like Copernicus and Galileo were trained in universities that used the methods and the books of the later Middle Ages.

No one has ever given a completely satisfactory explanation of this continuing interest in science. Certainly westerners were paying more attention to the things of this world during the later Middle Ages and less attention to the aims of the Church. But Chinese society was far more secular, and the Chinese, in the long run, fell behind the Europeans. Perhaps more important was the western tendency to be dissatisfied with the *status quo*, a tendency that was especially evident in the crucial years between 1300 and 1600. In China, a philosopher like Thomas Aquinas would have become an unchallenged authority; in Europe his system was questioned within a generation after his death. Europeans respected authority, but they always felt that authoritative treatises needed to be reinterpreted. Finally, there was a curious patience with details, a willingness and an enthusiasm to work very hard for very small gains.

Technology

These qualities also explain some of the advances in technology that were made in the last medieval centuries. Perhaps the most important was the development of firearms. Here, as in many other cases, the Europeans capitalized on a technique known to other peoples. The Chinese, for example, were probably the first to discover gunpowder, and they had cannon about as early as the Europeans. But Chinese guns were never very efficient, and the Chinese never developed an army that was primarily dependent on firearms. The Europeans carried their experiments with cannon much further than the Chinese. Although the first European guns were not very good—they were as apt to kill the men who fired them as those at whom they were aimed—they had become fairly reliable by the end of the fifteenth century. The military significance of this development

An early gun, lighter and more portable than the first cannon. The gun is placed on a forked stand and is braced against the ground by its long tail. From a German manuscript, *ca.* 1405.

is obvious. It reduced the power of local lords by making their castles untenable; conversely, it increased the power of kings and great princes like the Duke of Burgundy, for they were the only ones who could afford the expensive new weapons.

The development of firearms caused a rapid growth in other branches of technology. In order to make gun barrels that would not burst under the shock of an explosion, much had to be learned about metallurgy. And in order to make gun barrels that were truly round and hence could deliver the full effect of the charge, better metalworking tools and more precise measuring instruments had to be developed. Better techniques in using metals led to greater demands for metals, and this in turn stimulated the mining industry. The miners of Germany (including Bohemia and Austria), who were the chief suppliers of metals for Europe, learned to push their shafts deeper and to devise ways of draining off underground water. Increased use of metals and greater skill in mining in the long run transformed European industry. To take the most famous example, pumps operated by a piston traveling in a cylinder were developed in order to remove water from mines; it was this kind of pump that eventually furnished the model for the first steam engine.

The invention of printing in the fifteenth century (see p. 364) also owed much to developments in metallurgy. The essential element in printing was the use of movable type, and good type in turn depended on the availability of a metal that would take the exact shape of the mold into which it was poured. Thanks to their knowledge of metallurgy, the Germans succeeded in developing an alloy that expanded as it cooled, so that it fitted the mold exactly. Type faces molded from this alloy produced sharp, clear impressions.

Another technical advance of western Europe in the later Middle Ages was in ocean shipping. Here there was at first more patient experimentation than striking discoveries. By the end of the thirteenth century the sailors of western countries had ships that could tack against the wind and were seaworthy enough to survive the storms of the Atlantic. The navigators of the period could find their latitude, though not their longitude, by star and sun sights; they knew that the earth was round, and that the distance to the rich countries of the East was not impossibly great. Very little more was needed for the great voyages of discovery except practice, and during the fourteenth and fifteenth centuries daring men were mastering the art of oceanic navigation. French and Spanish seamen had reached the Canary islands at least by the early fourteenth century, and the Portuguese by 1400 had pushed down to the bend in the African coast, claiming Madeira and the Cape Verde Islands along the way.

These voyages illustrate the point that was made earlier: Europeans were no more skillful or intelligent than other peoples; they were simply more persistent or more aggressive. During the same years in which the Europeans were making their first sorties into the Atlantic, the Chinese were sending expeditions into the Indian Ocean. There they found rich kingdoms, ancient civilizations, and profitable sources of trade. In contrast, the Europeans discovered only barren islands and the fever-stricken coast of Africa. Yet the Chinese abandoned their explorations because they, or at least their rulers, were satisfied with what they had at home. The Europeans persisted, though it was almost two centuries before they reached the thriving trading centers of the East or the treasures of Mexico and Peru.

Not as striking as the early voyages, but almost as significant, was the invention of the mechanical clock. The first clocks, which appeared in the fourteenth century, were not very accurate, but they were soon improved by the discovery of the principle of escapement—that is, the system by which the train of gears moves only a precise distance before it is checked and then released to move the same distance again. Crude as the first clocks were, they modified, in the long run, the mental outlook of the western peoples. For several centuries one of the sharpest differences between the West and the rest of the world lay in attitudes toward precise measurement, especially the precise measurement of time. Western civilization has come to be dominated by the clock and the timetable, and westerners have had little sympathy with people who have managed to escape this domination.

Mechanical clock made in 1410. Only one hand moved around the clock at that time.

Suggestions for Further Reading

* Note: asterisk denotes a book available in paperback edition.

Economic Weakness H. A. Miskimin, *The Economy of Early Renaissance Europe, 1300–1460** (1969), is a good brief survey of the problem. J. W. Thompson's *Economic and Social History of Europe in the Later Middle Ages* (1931), which has excellent material on almost all aspects of European economic life in this period, is a good starting point for further study. There is a very thorough treatment of the methods for the enforcement of early economic legislation in England in B. H. Putnam, *The Enforcement of the Statutes of Labourers* (1908). B. N. Nelson, *The Idea of Usury* (1949), studies the development of a universal morality conducive to systematic capitalist enterprise. The second edition of Vol. I of the *Cambridge Economic History* is especially good on this period. See also E. E. Power and M. Postan, *Studies in English Trade in the Fifteenth Century* (1933), and S. L. Thrupp, *The Merchant Class of Medieval London* (1948).

Attacks on the Church: Marsilius, Wiclif, and Hus

There is a wealth of material available in English on these men who revolutionized the political and religious thinking of western Europe. A. Gewirth, *Marsilius of Padua*, Vol. I (1951), is a scholarly and readable treatment of the political philosophy of Marsilius. The great treatise of Marsilius, the *Defensor Pacis*, trans. by A. Gewirth (1956), brings out the premises by which Marsilius overthrew the doctrines of the papal plenitude of power and the Gelasian theory of the parallelism between the spiritual and temporal powers.

A good introduction to the political, social, and religious climate on which the thought of Wiclif fell is G. M. Trevelyan, *England in the Age of Wycliff** (1899). Trevelyan was one of the great social historians of his century and a very good writer. H. B. Workman, *John Wyclif*, 2 vols. (1926), is a study of the impact of Wiclif's thought on his times and on the English church. D. S. Schaff, *John Huss* (1915), is an interesting biography of this Czech nationalist and precursor of reformation. The short monograph of M. Spinka, *John Huss and the Czech Reform* (1941), is a study of the influence of Wiclif on the thought of Hus. There is valuable material on the influence of Marsilius and Wiclif on the evolution of political thought in C. H. McIlwain, *Growth of Political Thought in the West* (1932). For an excellent account of the Hussite movement, see F. G. Heymann, *John Ziska and the Hussite Revolution* (1955), and *George of Bohemia* (1965).

The Great Schism

The best background for understanding the Great Schism of the West is W. Ullmann, *Origins of the Great Schism* (1948). W. E. Lunt, *Papal Revenues in the Middle Ages*, 2 vols. (1934), has source material on the finances of the papacy at this time. There is a full account of the Great Schism in M. Creighton, *A History of the Papacy*, Vols. I and II (1905), and in L. Pastor, *History of the Popes*, Vol. I (1891), but the interpretation of Creighton is more balanced.

The Black Death

F. A. Gasquet, *The Black Death* (1893), is a good study of this terrible epidemic, with detailed material on the consequences of the plague for the social and economic life of England in the later Middle Ages. The more recent work of A. E. Levett, *The Black Death on the Estates of the See of Winchester* (1916), rejects the older view that the Black Death seriously disrupted the economic development of England. Differing points of view on this problem are presented by W. M. Bowsky, ed., in *The Black Death* (1971). There is material on the Black Death in all political and economic histories of this period.

England from 1307 to 1485

A. R. Myers, *England in the Later Middle Ages** (1952), a broad survey of this entire period, is a good introduction. There is valuable source material on the reign of Edward II in *The Life of Edward II*, trans. by N. Denholm-Young (1957), which goes into considerable detail on the revival of baronial powers and the civil wars under Edward. T. F. Tout, *The Place of the Reign of Edward II in History* (1936), sees this reign as the period of marked transition between court administration and national administration.

J. Froissart, *Chronicles** (many translations), presents a vivid picture of the life and spirit of fourteenth-century England. Froissart is an invaluable source for the reign of Edward III. There is a wealth of primary information on the reigns of Henry VI, Edward IV, and Richard III in *The Paston Letters*, 3 vols., ed. by J. Gairdner (1895). H. L. Gray, *The Influence of the Commons on Early Legislation* (1932), is a scholarly study of the development of the House of Commons and its power in the fourteenth and fifteenth centuries. S. Armitage-Smith, *John of Gaunt* (1904); A. Steel, *Richard II* (1941); and P. M. Kendall, *Richard the Third** (1955), are all interesting reading and based on sound scholarship.

For material on the development of the English constitution, see B. Wilkinson, *Constitutional History of England*, Vols. II and III (1958).

E. Perroy, *The Hundred Years' War*, trans. by W. B. Wells (1952), is an excellent account of the military history of this period, with a discussion of the implications of the war on the constitutional growth of England, R. B. Mowat, *The Wars of the Roses* (1914), is an interesting, if somewhat romantic, treatment of this confusing struggle.

France from 1314 to 1461

H. Pirenne and others, *La fin du moyen age* (1931), is a thorough study of this period by outstanding French historians. The broad scholarly work of E. Lavisse, ed., *Histoire de France*, Vol. IV, Part II (1902), is invaluable for the political, economic, military, and cultural history of France in this period.

There is a full documentary account of the trials of Joan of Arc in *Jeanne d'Arc*, ed. by T. D. Murray (1920), a very readable translation. L. Fabre, *Joan of Arc*, trans. by G. Hopkins (1954), is a fine biography of Joan and presents a fascinating picture of France in the period of the Hundred Years' War. R. Vaughn in *Philip the Bold* (1962), *John the Fearless* (1966), and *Philip the Good* (1970), gives a good picture of the growth of Burgundian power.

There are two very readable studies of the last Duke of Burgundy: J. F. Kirk, *Charles the Bold, Duke of Burgundy*, 3 vols. (1864–68), is a study of the man in relation to his times; R. Putnam, *Charles the Bold* (1908), concentrates on Charles the man. A good picture of the brilliant life of the Burgundian court is given in O. Cartellieri, *The Court of Burgundy* (1929). The outstanding achievement of J. Huizinga, *The Waning of the Middle Ages** (1929), is a study of the forms of life and thought in France and the Netherlands in the last days of the brilliant court of Burgundy.

Germany in the Later Middle Ages

Both J. Bryce, *The Holy Roman Empire* (many editions), and G. Barraclough, *Origins of Modern Germany** (1946), contain information on Germany in the later Middle Ages. Barraclough presents a fresher historical interpretation. The old study of H. Zimmer, *The Hansa Towns* (1889), is still valuable.

The origins and development of Switzerland are carefully treated in W. D. McCracken, *Rise of the Swiss Republic* (1901).

The titles by Pirenne and Lavisse in the sixth section above contain information on the rise of the Habsburg dynasty and the Burgundian takeover of the Low Countries.

Art, Literature, Science, and Scholarship in the Later Middle Ages

E. Panofsky, *Early Netherlandish Painting* (1953), is a beautiful study of art in northern Europe at this time, and M. Meiss, *Painting in Florence and Siena after the Black Death** (1951), describes the impact the Black Death had on the art of southern Europe. Both volumes are by outstanding art historians and have good reproductions.

Some of the greatest literature of the western world was produced in the later Middle Ages. Chaucer's *Canterbury Tales** (many editions), Villon's *Poems*, trans. by H. D. Stacpoole (1926), and Dante's *Divine Comedy,** trans. by D. L. Sayers (1949–58) are all masterpieces. Each was written in the vernacular, each reflects the changing world-view, and each gives a superb picture of the spirit and thought of the times. The great English poem of Langland, *Piers the Ploughman,** trans. by J. E. Goodridge (1959), is a fourteenth-century inquiry into the good life as judged by contemporary criteria. G. Lagarde, *Naissance de l'esprit laïque*, 2 vols. (1956–58), a brilliant treatment of late medieval thought and scholarship, traces the development in western Europe of a distinctly secular spirit. There is interesting material on late medieval science in H. Butterfield, *Origins of Modern Science** (1949), a broad survey. A. C. Crombie, *Medieval and Early Modern Science,** 2 vols. (1959), gives considerable attention to methods in physics in the late Middle Ages and stresses the continuity of the western scientific tradition from Greek times to the present. Crombie includes a good up-to-date bibliography. The thought of the fourteenth century is lucidly presented in G. Leff, *Medieval Thought** (1958), which discusses Occam, science, and political theories. E. Gilson, *History of Christian Philosophy in the Middle Ages* (1954), has information on Occam and the later Schoolmen. There is a wealth of material on the intellectual and spiritual life of the period from 1216 to 1485 in D. Knowles, *Religious Orders in England*, 2 vols. (1954–55).

14 Western Europe's Neighbors During the Middle Ages

This medieval reliquary captures the essence of Byzantine architecture—rounded line and sumptuous material.

At a time when the governments of western Europe were weak, its cities almost nonexistent, and its scholars limited to the study of encyclopedias and digests, both Byzantium and Islam had well-organized bureaucratic states, large commercial cities, and eminent scholars. Understandably, western Europeans felt awkward in dealing with their more fortunate neighbors, and their sense of inferiority often led them into suspicion and hostility. But neighbors they were, and contacts of some sort were inevitable.

THE BYZANTINE EMPIRE

The Byzantine Empire recovered only slowly from the external shock of the Arab conquests and the internal shock of the long religious controversy over the veneration of images. The Moslems remained a constant threat from the south, and the Bulgars, an Asiatic people who gradually mixed with the southern Slavs, menaced Constantinople from the north. But the Empire still had its wealth, its diplomatic skill, and its professional army, and with them it managed to limp through the eighth and early ninth centuries.

With the accession of Basil I (867–86), who founded the Macedonian dynasty, the Byzantine Empire began one of its marvelous recoveries. For a century and a half most of the emperors were first-rate generals. They took advantage of dissensions among their enemies to drive back the Moslems in the south and the Bulgars in the north. They recovered all of Asia Minor and gained control of the eastern Mediterranean, making possible the reconquest of Crete and Cyprus. The Byzantine Empire was never richer or more powerful than it was about the year 1000.

Byzantine Art and Literature

An intellectual and artistic revival accompanied and outlasted the political revival. The schools at Constantinople reached the peak of their activity soon after 1000, when a faculty of philosophy and a school of law were established.

This was not quite a university of the western type, since standardized courses and degrees were lacking, but professors were paid regular salaries and often held high positions at the imperial court. Byzantine scholars spent much of their energy copying and commenting on ancient texts, useful though not original work which preserved many books that otherwise would have been lost. Especially important was the Byzantine interest in Plato. The other great group of scholars of this period—those who wrote in Arabic—were much more concerned with Aristotle, and western Europe had inherited only a few fragments of Plato in Latin translation. When the Italians of the fifteenth century became interested in Plato, they had to obtain their texts, and scholars to expound them, from Constantinople.

Not all Byzantine writing, however, was based on ancient materials. The Byzantines produced some notable histories—works that were not impartial, since they were usually written to justify the actions of a ruler or a faction, but that were far superior to contemporary western chronicles. Another interesting genre that flourished during this period was the popular epic. Stories of heroic deeds performed against the enemies of the Empire were written in the language used by the people, and for this reason they were far more widely known than scholarly works written in correct classical Greek. The most famous of these poems, the epic of Digenis Akritas, was still remembered at the time of the Cypriote rebellion of 1957–58.

Under the Macedonian emperors and their immediate successors, Byzantine art entered into its golden age. As in scholarship, so in art there was a revival of classical influence. Byzantine artists were far less imitative, however, than were Byzantine writers. While deriving a certain dignity and sobriety from ancient works, they retained the Byzantine love of color and ornamentation. Unlike the scholars, they had something to say to the people; they portrayed the truths of the Christian faith and the events of recent history. Every church and many private homes had their icons (paintings of sacred personages); every important

Byzantine art exhibited Christian influence and a love of ornamentation. Top: a tenth-century clasp bearing the image of a saint; bottom: a reliquary cross, probably twelfth-century.

manuscript was illustrated with miniatures. With hundreds of artists at work, it is not surprising that many of them were competent and a few great.

Byzantium and the West

Byzantine influence was felt throughout western Europe. Italian merchants came regularly to Constantinople and after 1100 took over most of the carrying trade of the Empire. Byzantine influence remained strong in southern Italy, even after the Norman conquest, and in Venice, which had once been a Byzantine protectorate. Popes and German kings exchanged embassies with the emperor at Constantinople, and thousands of western pilgrims passed through the city on their way to the Holy Land. Easy access to the markets of Constantinople speeded up the growth of Italian cities and the Italian cities in tur_ led the economic revival of the West. The use of Byzantine artists by Italians—as in the designing of the Venetian Cathedral of St. Mark's—left its mark on Italian art. The first native Italian painters were clearly influenced by Byzantine models.

Western scholars were not greatly interested in the theology or philosophy of the Byzantines. But after 1100 a few westerners journeyed to Constantinople to discover and translate ancient manuscripts. Their work was less appreciated than that of their contemporaries who were working on translations from the Arabic, and sometimes books that had passed from Greek to Syriac to Arabic to Latin were preferred to direct translations from the Greek. Because western translators were primarily interested in Aristotle, they overlooked the opportunity to increase the stock of Platonic works available in Latin. Nevertheless, some important texts, such as the advanced works of Euclid, would have been unknown to western medieval scholars had it not been for the efforts of the translators at Constantinople.

During the eleventh century the Latin and Greek Churches gradually drifted apart. There had long been friction between them, since the patriarch at Constantinople rejected the pope's claims to universal authority and the pope re-

sented the patriarch's claim to independence. There were theological disputes, such as the one over sacred images, and the question raised by Charlemagne about the relationship between the Holy Ghost and the other two Persons of the Trinity. But the basic reason for the split was that the West and Byzantium were becoming so different in institutions and culture that each was suspicious of the other's motives. Finally, in 1054, pope and patriarch excommunicated each other and the two Churches broke off relations. The break was not taken too seriously at first; such splits had happened before and had always been repaired. But this time, in spite of repeated efforts, the breach could not be healed. Each Church went its own way and cooperation between them became more and more difficult.

Byzantium and the Slavs

Byzantium's greatest influence was on the peoples of the Balkans and Russia. In spite of frequent wars and rebellions, there were long periods in which the Serbs and the Bulgars were either subject to, or allied with, the Eastern Empire. Byzantine princesses were frequently married to Slavic rulers in order to gain influence in neighboring courts. These ladies brought with them missionaries and teachers, artists and scholars, thus helping to spread the Greek Orthodox religion and Byzantine culture throughout the regions inhabited by the eastern Slavs. The conversion of the Bulgars began in the ninth century and that of the Russians in the tenth; both peoples were soon thoroughly Christianized. For a long time the leading clergymen in Bulgaria and Russia were appointed by the patriarch of Constantinople. Even with a growing tendency toward autonomy in the Slavic churches, Byzantine influence remained strong. Down to the fifteenth century all but two or three of the metropolitans (heads) of the Russian Church were Greeks.

The fact that the eastern Slavs received their religion and culture from Constantinople had lasting consequences for the history of modern Europe. Byzantine civilization and western Euro-

Byzantine masons at work; miniature from a psalter, 1066.

pean civilization had a common origin, but, as we have seen, they drifted apart during the Middle Ages. Byzantium remembered much that the West forgot, and it was always more strongly influenced by eastern ideas and customs. The West went through experiences, such as the Investiture Conflict, and developed institutions, such as feudalism, that scarcely touched Constantinople. Misunderstandings were inevitable, and they were especially bitter because each region expected better things of a related Christian civilization and because each felt that the other was betraying a common heritage. The eastern Slavs, especially the Russians, shared these tensions. The West both attracted and repulsed them, and the current Russian attitude toward the West is a new and intensified form of an old suspicion.

THE MOSLEM CALIPHATE

The Abbasid Caliphate, established in 750, achieved its golden age before the tenth-century revival set in at Constantinople. It reached its peak of power and wealth under Harun-al-Rashid (786–809). Harun, who exchanged letters and gifts with Charlemagne, ruled a far larger empire than his western contemporary. The lands of the caliph stretched from Morocco to the Indus River, from the steppes of central Asia to the Sudan. After 900, although the Caliphate began to break up into separate states, the Moslem world remained an economic and cultural unit. In this vast territory, which was traversed by all the important East-West trade routes, there were dozens of populous and prosperous cities, but Baghdad was the largest and richest.

Arabic Scholarship

The city of Baghdad attracted books and scholars just as it did merchandise and traders. The Abbasids did even more than the Ommiads to transform their empire into a center of scholarship. Hundreds of Greek works, especially on philosophy, science, and mathematics, were translated into Arabic, and much was learned from Persian and Jewish sources. Chinese scholarship had little influence, but the Abbasids borrowed many ideas from the Indians, notably the system of arithmetic notation that we call Arabic figures. By the ninth century Moslem scholars had assimilated the work of their predecessors and were beginning to make original contributions of their own. From 900 to 1200 the most important work done anywhere in the world in mathematics, astronomy, physics, medicine, and geography was done in Moslem countries.

Much Arabic scholarship merely added details to support established scientific theories—for example, accurate observations of star positions or clinical descriptions of certain diseases. More was done in geography because the Arabs knew more about the world than had the ancient writers. But their most remarkable contribution was in physics and mathematics. In physics they performed interesting experiments in reflection and refraction. In mathematics, besides greatly simplifying arithmetical operations through the use of the new Arabic figures, they carried trigonometry far beyond the Greek accomplishment. And their work in algebra was even more impressive, for they fashioned a whole mathematical discipline out of the few hints provided by their predecessors. Their contribution is recorded in the very word algebra, which is Arabic.

Two notable Moslem mathematicians were al-Khwarizmi (d. *ca.* 840) and the poet Omar Khayyám (d. *ca.* 1120). Al-Khwarizmi recognized, more clearly than many of his contemporaries, the value of the new Hindu-Arabic figures, especially the zero. Use of the zero made it possible to reckon by position and simplified all work in arithmetic. Al-Khwarizmi did much to popularize this new arithmetic; he also wrote a text on algebra that was used in both Moslem and Christian countries for centuries. Omar Khayyám calculated the length of a solar year with great accuracy and devised methods of solving algebraic equations that had been too complicated for his predecessors.

Arabic Influence on the West

Moslem interest in mathematics and the natural sciences had a decisive influence on the course of western civilization. The Byzantines tended to neglect these subjects, and little was known about them in western Europe. The Chinese had great technical skill—for example, they discovered the principle of the compass very early—but they developed few general theories. And the Indians, after a promising start, lost their interest in mathematical and scientific problems. Thus the Moslem world was the only region that was both actively interested in science and close enough to western Europe to touch off a revival of scientific interest there. Western European scholars made their first attempts to recover ancient scientific texts by going to the Moslems of Spain and Sicily; only after the revival was well under way did they begin to seek manuscripts in Constantinople. Certainly the West would not have developed a scientific tradition of its own as rapidly as it did without the assistance of Moslem scholarship, and quite possibly it never would have developed the tradition at all.

It is somewhat anachronistic, however, to separate science so sharply from other studies. For Moslem scholars, as for medieval Christians, science was merely one aspect of philosophy. Aristotle, the great authority on science for both peoples, was thought of primarily as a philosopher, and one of the chief intellectual problems of the Middle Ages was to reconcile his philosophy with the revealed truths of religion. Here again, Moslem scholars led the way. Avicenna (ibn-Sina, 980–1037), who wrote a famous book in Arabic on medicine, also prepared commentaries on Aristotle that influenced western scholars during the twelfth and thirteenth centuries. Even more important was the Spanish Moslem Averroës (ibn-Rushd, 1126–98), some of whose assertions shocked both Islam and Christendom—for example, that the world is eternal, and that there is no personal immortality. But Averroës was no freethinker; one of his strongest convictions was that there can be no real conflict between the truths of philosophy and the truths of revealed religion. This doctrine, which was taken over by Christian scholars in the thirteenth century, made it easier for them to justify the assimilation of Greco-Arabic philosophy into the Christian tradition. Maimonides (Moses ben Maimon, 1135–1204), a Spanish Jew living under Moslem rule, was thoroughly familiar with the Arabic versions of Aristotelian philosophy and tried to reconcile them

A Moslem pharmacist concocting a medicinal wine, from a thirteenth-century manuscript of Dioscorides' *Materia Medica*. The text reads: "The making of a drink (*shirab*) for catarrhs, coughs, swelling of the belly, and loosening of the stomach." The recipe calls for wine mixed with myrrh, roots of *sussan,* and white pepper.

with the Jewish faith. His proofs of the existence of God are very like those advanced a half-century later by Thomas Aquinas.

Until the Moslems broke away from the Koran's strict ban on representing living beings, they could do nothing with sculpture and painting. They were, however, great builders and created a distinctive style out of such old forms as the dome, the arcade, and the tower. Moslem architectural styles made a deep impression on every country in which they appeared; their influence may still be seen in Spain and India. Moslem buildings were lavishly decorated with colored tiles and intricate geometric carvings—ideas that were imitated by neighboring countries.

THE DECLINE OF BYZANTIUM AND THE CALIPHATE

The Byzantine Empire and the countries controlled by the Abbasid Caliphate remained important centers of commerce and intellectual and artistic activity throughout the European Middle Ages. But after the tenth century they began to decline as political units. Some problems were common to both states—for example, the lack of a fixed rule of succession to the throne. Neither the emperor nor the caliph was necessarily the eldest son of his predecessor; he might be anyone connected with the ruling family who had been able to win the support of the bureaucracy and the army. Theoretically this practice might have assured the selection of the ablest man; actually it encouraged palace intrigues and civil wars. The western European tendency to insist on the rule of primogeniture was not an ideal way of picking a ruler, but in practice it gave greater stability and continuity to political institutions. Another problem common to both the Byzantine Empire and the Arab Caliphate was that of raising an army. It was easier to hire soldiers from among the neighboring barbarians than to disrupt civilian life by forcing city workers and peasant farmers into the army. But mercenaries were never entirely reliable, and the better they were as fighting men the greater the danger that they might try to take over the government.

Each state also had problems of its own. In Byzantium there was a growing hostility between the bureaucracy of the capital city and the great landlords of the rural districts. The bureaucrats, quite rightly, felt that the landlords were trying to reduce the peasants to a state of serfdom and to make themselves independent rulers in the outlying provinces. The landlords felt, quite rightly in turn, that the bureaucracy was a nest of intrigue and corruption. Attempts to weaken the landlords or reform the bureaucrats merely intensified the bad feelings between the two groups. These disruptive tendencies were held in check during the tenth century, but after the death of the last great Macedonian emperor, Basil II, in 1025, they grew more virulent.

The problems peculiar to the Caliphate sprang from its size and from the peculiar nature of Moslem law, which emphasized ethical and religious duties, but left enforcement to the whims of the ruler. It was almost impossible to establish a centralized administrative system for such widely separated regions, each with its own traditions. Regional viceroys had to be given extensive powers and there was always the danger that one of them would set himself up as an independent ruler. Moreover, though the caliphs had built up a bureaucracy on Roman and Persian models, and though they had developed a comprehensive legal system, Moslem government was always rather arbitrary and unpredictable. No one wanted to be bound by rules, least of all the caliph and his officials. Since everything depended on the whim of the man in power, it was better to catch his ear than it was to try to win a case at law. This lack of respect for legal principles encouraged intrigue and disobedience. Instability was increased by religious divisions among the Moslems. Minority groups that questioned the Abbasid ruler's claim to be the orthodox successor of Mohammed naturally felt very little respect for his government.

The first crack in the Caliphate showed itself in 756, when a member of the deposed Ommiad dynasty established an independent state in Spain. The loss of this outlying territory did little damage, but the next secessions were more serious, for they cost the Caliphate all of North Africa. In the tenth century much of this area was seized by the new Fatimid dynasty. This family claimed descent from Fatima, the daughter of Mohammed, a claim that gave it the support of the Shi-ites, the largest group of dissenters in Islam. The Shi-ites believed that Islam must always be led by a lineal descendant of Mohammed; they had rejected the Ommiad caliphs and were now ready to turn against the Abbasids. By taking the title of caliph in 909, the founder of the new dynasty directly challenged the claim of the Abbasid ruler to be leader of all the Moslems. In 969 the Fatimids conquered Egypt, thereby gaining one of the wealthiest Moslem provinces; they established their capital in the newly built city of Cairo in 973. The Fatimid domains now stretched from Morocco to the Red Sea and even included Jerusalem. At the height of their power the Fatimid caliphs of Cairo were far stronger than the Abbasid caliphs of Baghdad.

The Coming of the Turks

By the end of the eleventh century the Fatimid Caliphate was beginning to weaken. The Abbasids, however, profited little from the decline of their rivals. In an effort to hold on to their remaining provinces, they had come to rely more and more on mercenary soldiers, especially the Seljuk Turks. A branch of the nomadic stock of central Asia, the Turks had all the toughness, bravery, and love of conquest of their eastern relatives. They became devout Moslems and fought well for their new religion, but they also fought for themselves. Having become the dominant military power in the lands of the Abbasid Caliphate, they soon began to seek political power as well. By the eleventh century the Turkish sultans (kings) had become the real rulers of most of Syria and Mesopotamia. They preserved the caliph as a religious leader, but they did not allow him any real power in government.

The rise of the Turks had serious consequences for the Byzantine emperors as well. Disputes over the succession to the imperial throne and quarrels between the bureaucrats of Constantinople and the great landlords had seriously weakened the Eastern Empire. Suspecting that they would meet with little resistance, the Turks began to push into Asia Minor; when the emperor Romanus IV tried to drive them out he was defeated and captured at the battle of Manzikert in 1071.

The Byzantine Empire never fully recovered from this defeat. After Manzikert the Turks overran almost all of Asia Minor; they even took Nicaea, only fifty miles from Constantinople. Through heroic efforts a new Byzantine dynasty, the Comneni, regained some of the lost territory, but it could never eject the Turks from central and eastern Asia Minor. This was a serious loss to the

A knight of the later Crusades, manuscript illustration.

Empire, for the provinces seized by the Turks had furnished large numbers of fighting men and had protected the wealthy coastal regions. Skillful diplomacy and the wise use of limited resources enabled Byzantium to survive, but the Eastern Empire under the Comneni never had the vigor it had displayed under the Macedonians.

Fortunately for the Byzantines, the first Turkish Empire began to disintegrate almost as soon as it was established. As might have been expected in this part of the world, the lack of a fixed rule of succession did most of the damage. Each sultan established little principalities for junior members of the family, and military commanders began to turn their governorships into independent states. Each ruler fought and intrigued with his neighbors in order to gain more land. In the end the old Abbasid Caliphate dissolved into a welter of petty states, only loosely associated by their theoretical allegiance to caliph and sultan.

The Early Crusades

It was this confusion in the Middle East that made possible the success of the First Crusade and the establishment of the crusader Kingdom of Jerusalem in 1099. The Moslems were too divided to cooperate against the common enemy, and some of them even encouraged the Christians to attack their rivals. Only a part of the Turkish forces could be assembled to fight the crusaders at Antioch; once Antioch had been lost to the Christians, few of the Syrian Moslems cared about the fate of Jerusalem. Jerusalem, after all, was held by the Fatimid heretics, who were little better than the Christian infidels. The Fatimids, on their part, regarded Jerusalem as an outlying possession of little military or political value and made no great effort to regain the Holy City. A dynasty of Christian kings, descended from the crusader Baldwin of Lorraine, held Jerusalem and most of Palestine from 1099 to 1187.

The emperor Alexius Comnenus (1081–1118) must have looked on the First Crusade as a very successful piece of Byzantine diplomacy. He had shown remarkable skill in whisking unruly western armies through his lands with a minimum of friction and looting, and he had used the crusading forces to screen his reoccupation of much of western Asia Minor. The establishment in 1099 of the Kingdom of Jerusalem and the northern crusading states of Tripoli, Antioch, and Edessa drove a wedge into the Moslem states of the Middle East and made cooperation among them more difficult than before. Moreover, by posing a threat to Islam, the crusading states also distracted Moslem attention from Byzantine expansion in Asia Minor.

The crusade was not all profit for the Byzantines, however, for it reinforced

Turkish miniature depicting the Asiatic bowman. Unencumbered by armor, he could move swiftly on his small, strong horse.

CRUSADE ROUTES 1096–1270

Political boundaries are those of the middle of the twelfth century

- – · – 1 – First Crusade, 1096–99
- – · · – 2 – Second Crusade, 1147–49
- – · · · – 3 – Third Crusade, 1189–92
- – – 4 – Fourth Crusade, 1202–04
- – L – First Crusade of Louis IX, 1248–54
- – LL – Second Crusade of Louis IX, 1270

MILES
0 — — — — — 300

western suspicions of Byzantine morals and motives. The leaders of the crusade were sure that Alexius' failure to aid them in the siege of Antioch showed that he was more interested in recovering his lost provinces than in freeing the holy places from the Moslems. Western hostility to Byzantium was strengthened by the events of the Second and Third Crusades. The Byzantines were not really interested in fostering these movements; in fact, they twice withdrew into neutrality in return for advantageous treaties with the Turks. The westerners, dismayed by this subtle diplomacy, soon began to think that the Byzantines were almost as great a threat to Christendom as the Moslems. The sack of Constantinople by a crusading army in 1204 was the price Byzantium paid for arousing these suspicions.

The Moslems recovered only slowly from the shock of the Christian conquest of Jerusalem. Gradually a series of able army commanders began to reunite the scattered Moslem states. The first of these generals, Zangi, took the outlying Christian county of Edessa in 1144 and held it against the badly mismanaged Second Crusade. Even more decisive was the work of Zangi's son, Nureddin (Nūr-al-Dīn), who put an end to the decaying Fatimid Caliphate of Egypt in 1171. Nureddin was already master of most of Syria; by adding Egypt to his domain he became far stronger than the Christian kings of Jerusalem. He was succeeded by his ablest general, Saladin (Salāh-al-Dīn), who overran the Kingdom of Jerusalem and seized the Holy City itself in 1187. The Christians were left with only a few seacoast towns.

The loss of Jerusalem sent a shock of horror throughout Latin Christendom. The three greatest kings of the West—Frederick Barbarossa of Germany, Philip Augustus of France, and Richard Lionheart of England—agreed to unite their forces in an attack on Saladin. But this Third Crusade was only partially successful. Frederick was drowned while crossing Asia Minor with his army, and

Philip Augustus, after helping to recapture Acre, rushed back to France to look after the affairs of his kingdom. Richard hung on, fighting so bravely that he became a legend among the Moslems, but he never had a large enough army to risk an attack on Jerusalem. He did reconquer a long strip of coastal territory, thus prolonging the life of the Kingdom of Jerusalem for a century. But the revived kingdom was never strong; it played a far less important role in the thirteenth century that it had in the twelfth.

The Later Crusades

Saladin's empire began to dissolve soon after his death in 1193. As so often happened in the Moslem world, his states were divided among members of his family, who promptly began intriguing against one another. The Christians could once more hope to regain Jerusalem, and they staged three major and several minor expeditions to the Middle East in the first half of the thirteenth century. None of these crusades was successful; when Frederick II briefly regained Jerusalem he did it through a treaty with the sultan of Egypt. On the other hand, the thirteenth-century crusades, by weakening both Saladin's dynasty and the Byzantine Empire, aided the rise of new powers in the Middle East.

The Byzantine Empire in 1200 was neither as rich nor as powerful as it once had been. Most of its commerce was in the hands of Italian merchants; the Byzantine navy had almost ceased to exist; and the army, composed largely of mercenaries, was too weak to guard all the frontiers. The Turks were threatening Asia Minor and a revived Bulgarian kingdom was attacking Thrace. Internal dissension had reached a dangerous point, with many of the great families lined up against the emperor. More or less by accident, the first people to take advantage of this inviting situation were a group of crusaders.

The Fourth Crusade started in 1202 as a routine expedition against the Moslems of the East. But the army was heavily in debt to the Venetians, who had supplied ships to carry it to the East. The Venetians, who cared little about crusades but a great deal about profit, made the army work off part of its debt by capturing Zara, a rival trading town across the Adriatic. Then a pretender to the Byzantine throne turned up with a very tempting proposition: he would pay all the army's debts and augment its forces if the crusaders would make him emperor. The Venetians saw a chance to acquire a monopoly of trade with Byzantium, and under their urging most, though not all, of the crusaders agreed to attack Constantinople. Aided by Byzantine weakness and disunity, the small western force—probably not more than 20,000 fighting men—managed to seize one of the most strongly fortified positions in the world (1203).

They soon quarreled with their puppet emperor and took over the city for themselves (1204), sacking churches and stealing relics. Then they elected one of their own leaders, Baldwin, Count of Flanders, as emperor, and divided most of Greece and Thrace among the Venetians and western feudal lords. This Latin Empire of Constantinople lasted only a half-century (1204–61), but feudal principalities held by western lords survived in Greece to the end of the fourteenth century, and Venice held some of the Greek islands and ports in the Peloponnesus until the seventeenth century.

A Byzantine View of the Crusaders

Anna Comnena, the author of this piece, was the daughter of the Emperor Alexius I.

Now he [the emperor] dreaded the arrival of the Crusaders, for he knew their irresistible manner of attack, their unstable and mobile character, and all the peculiar . . . characteristics which the Frank retains throughout; and he also knew that they were always agape for money, and seemed to disregard their truces readily for any reason that cropped up. . . . The simpler-minded Franks were urged on by the real desire of worshipping at our Lord's Sepulchre, but the more astute, especially men like Bohemund . . . had another secret reason, namely the hope that . . . they might by some means be able to seize the capital itself. . . . For the Frankish race . . . is always very hotheaded and eager, but when it has once espoused a cause, it is uncontrollable.

From Anna Comnena, *The Alexiad,* trans. by E. A. S. Dawes (London: Kegan Paul, 1928), pp. 248, 250.

A Crusader's View of Byzantium

Odo of Deuil, the author of this piece, was a historian of the Second Crusade.

And then the Greeks degenerated entirely into women; putting aside all manly vigor, both of words and of spirit, they lightly swore whatever they thought would please us, but they neither kept faith with us nor maintained respect for themselves. In general they really have the opinion that anything which is done for the holy empire cannot be considered perjury. . . . When the Greeks are afraid they become despicable in their excessive abasement, and when they have the upper hand they are arrogant. . . .

Constantinople itself is squalid and fetid. . . . People live lawlessly in this city, which has as many lords as rich men and almost as many thieves as poor men. . . . In every respect she exceeds moderation, for just as she surpasses other cities in wealth, so too does she surpass them in vice. . . .

[The bishop of Langres] added that Constantinople is Christian only in name and not in fact . . . and that her emperor had ventured a few years ago to attack the [Crusader] prince of Antioch. . . . "Though it was his [the emperor's] duty to ward off the near-by infidels by uniting the Christian forces, with the aid of the infidels he strove to destroy the Christians."

From Odo of Deuil, *De profectione Ludovici VII in orientem,* trans. by V. G. Berry (New York: Columbia University Press, 1948), pp. 57, 65, 69.

Innocent III, who was pope at this time, at first severely condemned the diversion of the Fourth Crusade. After 1204, however, he was seduced by the prospect of ending the schism with the Greek Church and gave full support to the Latin Empire. His first reaction was the sounder one; the capture of Constantinople was a disaster for western Christendom. Instead of healing the breach between the two Churches, it intensified Byzantine hatred of the Latins and convinced the Greeks that the independence of their Church was synonymous with national survival. Even when they were about to be conquered by the Turks, the Greeks refused to consider union with Rome. As one of them said: "Better the turban of the sultan than the tiara of the pope." Nor did the capture of Constantinople help the Kingdom of Jerusalem; instead, it meant that western money and fighting men had to be diverted to support the Latin Empire and the feudal principalities of Greece. By ruining the Byzantine Empire the crusaders exposed all southeastern Europe to Turkish conquest. Even though the Latins were driven out of Constantinople in 1261, the revived Byzantine Empire was only a shadow of what it had been. It held only a fragment of the Balkans and a small strip of Asia Minor; it could not check the Turkish advance into Europe in the fourteenth century.

Saladin's dynasty would have lost power in any case, but the thirteenth-century crusades speeded up the process. Louis IX of France precipitated a crisis by leading an army against Egypt in 1248. The sultan of Egypt by this time was almost entirely dependent on his household slaves, who formed the core of his army and held many high administrative posts. There were many able men among these slaves, or Mamelukes, as they were called, and they were weary of fighting to keep a decaying dynasty in power. The early successes of the crusading army led them to assassinate the sultan and to replace him with one of their own commanders. For centuries Egypt was to be ruled by Mameluke generals who rose from the ranks of a slave army. Only tough and brutal men could reach the top, and when one of them showed signs of softening he was apt to be replaced by a younger and more vigorous fighter. But in spite of their internal quarrels, the Mamelukes were a first-rate military power. They were determined to drive the westerners out of the Middle East, and they rapidly accomplished their purpose. By 1271 they had occupied the entire area except for a few coastal towns, and in 1291 Acre, the last stronghold of the crusaders, was taken by the Mameluke sultan.

The fall of Acre did not end the crusades; there were some large-scale expeditions against the Turks in the fourteenth century, and popes talked of crusades as late as 1464. But none of the later crusades gained a permanent foothold in the East or did much to halt the Turkish advance. Whatever influence the crusades had on western civilization had been exerted by the end of the thirteenth century. And that influence was considerable: the crusades had helped to stimulate the growth of the Italian naval power that was to make the Mediterranean a Christian lake for three centuries. The fact that thousands of westerners lived in, or visited, Syria and Palestine encouraged the demand for eastern luxuries and thus changed western standards of living, although there would have been some increase in demand in any case.

On the other hand, the crusaders showed little evidence of intellectual or cultural interests. Armies of occupation are more likely to bring home material objects than ideas. Western scholars learned more from peaceful contacts with the Moors of Spain and the Greeks of Constantinople than they did from the inhabitants of the Kingdom of Jerusalem. In short, the significance of the crusades in East-West relationships was primarily political and economic. The crusades

marked the first attempt of western Europe to expand into non-European areas, and they added to the difficulties of both the Byzantine Empire and the Moslem Caliphates. They did little to promote understanding or intellectual contacts among the three civilizations that bordered the shores of the Mediterranean Sea.

THE MONGOL EMPIRE

Far more important than the later crusades was the advance of the Mongols into Russia and the Middle East. The Mongols were another of those nomadic peoples of central Asia who from time to time developed great military power and burst into the lands of their civilized neighbors. The pattern was a familiar one: an able leader would organize his own tribe into an effective striking force

THE MONGOL EMPIRE AND ITS SUCCESSOR STATES   Thirteenth century and then subjugate other tribes belonging to the same racial stock. Once he had established himself as the predominant power in the vast steppes of central Asia, other nomadic peoples would join him either out of fear or in the hope of sharing in the loot. Finally, the united forces would become strong enough to strike out at China, India, or Europe. This had been the story of the Huns, and it was to be the story of the Mongols.

A small group originally, the Mongols became the dominant element in a great federation of nomadic tribes. But while the Mongols followed the old pattern, they expanded more widely and held their conquests longer than any of their predecessors. The leader who began the expansion of Mongol power, Genghis Khan (*ca.* 1160–1227), was the ablest of all the nomad rulers, and his immediate descendants were almost as competent. The Mongol khans were not only first-rate generals; they also knew how to organize and administer an empire. As a result, the Mongols became the dominant power in Asia and eastern Europe for a century and a half, and they remained a formidable force well into the fifteenth century.

The Mongols first concentrated their forces against China; they took Peking in 1215 and had occupied most of northern China by the death of Genghis in 1227. The Sung dynasty in the South held out longer, and the Mongols were not able to gain control of the whole country until the 1270s. Meanwhile they found easier conquests to the west. A strong army, under one of the ablest Mongol generals, set out against Persia and Mesopotamia. The Mongols overran Persia quickly and in 1258 they took Baghdad, plundered the city, and put the caliph to death. This attack ended the Abbasid Caliphate, the last symbol of Moslem unity.

For a time it looked as if the Mongols were going to conquer all the Middle East. But when they attempted to take Syria, they were completely defeated by the Mameluke sultan of Egypt (1260). Since no one else from the Mediterranean to the Yellow Sea could claim to have defeated a Mongol army, this victory gave the Mamelukes great prestige. The Mongols made little effort to advance further, and the Mamelukes in Egypt and the Turks in Asia Minor remained independent.

Russia and the Mongols

Meanwhile another Mongol horde had attacked Russia, the chief outpost of Byzantine culture. The viking leaders, who had invaded Russia in the ninth century, had built a strong state around Kiev. This state controlled the trade route between the Black Sea and the Baltic, a route that in the early Middle Ages probably carried as many Oriental wares as the route across the Mediterranean. The princes of Kiev grew rich from their trade and were powerful enough to attack Constantinople itself on several oc-

RUSSIA ABOUT 1200

Genghis Khan, detail from a manuscript illustration, ca. 1310.

Iron and silver helmet found at the site of a battle between the sons of a Russian prince, 1216. The helmet bears the figure of Archangel Michael.

casions. But after the conversion of the Russians to Greek Orthodox Christianity at the end of the tenth century, relations between Kiev and Byzantium were generally friendly. The Russians accepted the civilization of the Eastern Empire along with its religion; they built their churches in the Byzantine style and their scholars translated Byzantine texts into Russian. Although the Russians added ideas of their own, Kiev at the height of its power in the early eleventh century must have resembled Constantinople in many ways. It was certainly larger, wealthier, and more of an intellectual center than either the Paris of the first Capetian kings or the London of William the Conqueror.

In the twelfth century Kiev began to decline. It lost some of its trade to the Italians, who exploited the Mediterranean route and sent their ships into the Black Sea. It suffered even more from the Pechenegs, a nomadic people who pushed through the gap between the Urals and the Caspian and cut the trade route between Constantinople and Kiev. Meanwhile other centers of power were developing in the upper Volga basin. The princes of Kiev had given outlying towns to younger members of their family to be ruled as dependent principalities. This practice worked well enough at first, but as Kiev declined and family ties weakened, the junior princes became greedy for power. They sacked Kiev itself in 1168, and this disaster, combined with commercial difficulties, put an end to the unity and prosperity of early Russia. The strongest ruler was now the prince of Suzdal, a region that included the newly founded town of Moscow, but his territories were poor and backward compared to Kiev in its great days. Once a land of cities and merchants, Russia was now becoming a land of peasants scratching out a bare living from the thin soils of the North. Declining prosperity, however, did not put an end to feuding among the princes, who found it almost impossible to take combined action against a common enemy such as the Mongols.

It is not surprising, then, that the Mongols conquered Russia so easily. Their first serious attack came in 1237;

by 1241 they had overcome all resistance and were pushing across the Carpathians into Hungary. Hungarians resisted no more successfully than Russians—their armies were slaughtered near Budapest—but the death of the Great Khan ended the Mongol threat to central Europe. The commander of the Mongol army rushed home to influence the choice of a new ruler, and he never resumed his attack. The Mongols were at last satiated. They had every right to be, for they had created one of the largest empires the world has ever known.

The Mongols used terror as a means of conquest, wrecking cities and executing entire populations in order to convince their foes of the dangers of resistance. But once they had established their empire they were willing to profit from the knowledge and skills of their subjects. In China and Persia, where they came in contact with relatively advanced civilizations, they soon became assimilated and carried on the old administrative and cultural traditions. In Russia, where they had less to learn, they held themselves apart and retained more of their own characteristics. They occupied only the steppes north of the Caspian, a region in which there never had been very many Slavs.

Western Europe and the Mongols

The coming of the Mongols might have changed the history of all Europe if western Europeans had been more alert. For several decades the most dangerous opponents of the Mongols were Mamelukes and Turks, and the Mongols repeatedly suggested to Christian rulers that they form an alliance against the common Moslem enemy. None of these suggestions was ever followed up very seriously, however, and an alliance may well have been impossible. Nevertheless, an alliance between Mongols and Christians might have checked the rising power of the Turks.

Europe also missed the opportunity to convert the Mongols. They were not greatly attached to their own primitive beliefs and at times they seemed attracted to Christianity. The first Mongol

Kublai Khan (1259–94), a descendant of Genghis Khan and ruler of China at the time of Marco Polo's visit.

viceroy of Persia had a Christian wife and favored her coreligionists, and the Mongol khan of China, Kublai, asked the pope several times to send him missionaries. Unfortunately, the thirteenth-century popes were occupied with matters nearer at hand, such as their feud with the Hohenstaufens and their efforts to preserve the crusading states. They sent a few envoys, but no solid corps of permanent missionaries. The popes of the early fourteenth century made a greater effort, but by that time it was too late. The western Mongols had already been converted to Islam, one more example of the advantage the simpler Moslem faith enjoyed in missionary competition. The Mongols of China were becoming submerged in the sea of Chinese culture and were soon to lose their power. The few missionaries who were sent from the West made thousands of converts, and a Catholic archbishop sat in Peking for a few years. But the whole effort was swept away when the Mongols were overthrown in 1368 and the strongly antiforeign Ming dynasty came to power.

Some Italian merchants took advantage of the opening of the overland route to China. The most famous of them was Marco Polo, who went to China in 1275 and spent many years in the country, part of the time as an official of the Mongol government. After he returned to Italy, Marco wrote a long and fairly accurate account of his travels, and his description of the wealth and splendor of the Far East did much to encourage the great explorations of the fifteenth century. But Marco had less influence on the people of his own time. He was accused of wild exaggeration and nicknamed "Marco Millions"; few other merchants followed in his footsteps. Here was another lost opportunity. At the end of the thirteenth century the European economy was grinding toward stagnation; it desperately needed the stimulus of new markets. But fourteenth-century Europe lacked the capital, the energy, and the technical skill needed to open direct trade with the Far East. It was not until the late fifteenth century that western merchants could again dream of reaching China.

RUSSIA: ISOLATION AND AUTOCRACY

During the Mongol occupation, the Russians were allowed to live under their own princes and had little direct contact with the Mongols. So long as the princes paid tribute and sought confirmation of their authority from the khan, they could have whatever laws and religion they pleased.

Loss of Contact with the West

Nevertheless, the period of Mongol domination was a difficult one for Russia. Contacts with the West were sharply reduced, for both in commerce and in diplomacy the Russians had to deal primarily with the Mongols. The Russians were also blocked off from the West by the growing power of Poland and Lithuania.

Poland had received its religion and much of its civilization from the West. It had been converted at the end of the tenth century by Roman Catholic missionaries, and for a long time it was a vassal state of the German Empire. Often weak and divided, the Poles gradually began to grow stronger in the fourteenth century, as the German Empire fell apart. Their trade was largely with the West; their official language, for government as well as for religious affairs, was Latin; and they were rather inclined to look down on the Russians as a backward people.

The Lithuanians were a very ancient people, of the Indo-European language group, who had struggled for centuries to maintain their independence in their home on the south Baltic coast. Both Russians and Germans had tried to convert them, but the bulk of the population remained pagan until well into the fourteenth century. Just as the Poles profited from German weakness, so the Lithuanians gained by the collapse of Kievan Russia. They expanded south and east, acquiring some of the most fertile Russian lands.

In 1386 the Poles and the Lithuanians united. The Poles accepted the Lithuanian grand duke as their king; in return the Lithuanians were supposed to become Latin Christians. Poland-Lithuania was oriented to the West and was usually hostile to the Russians. Down to the sixteenth century, Poland-Lithuania was larger and stronger than all the Russian principalities put together. It intervened again and again in Russian politics, and it acquired so much Russian land that Moscow, at times, was almost a frontier city. Russia was cut off from the Baltic and had few dealings with any western state.

Russia's loss of contact with the West was at first compensated for by increased contacts with the East. As long as the Mongols remained relatively united, the long land route across the Eurasian plain to China was heavily traveled—more heavily than it was to be again until the nineteenth century. But the subordinate khans who governed outlying regions of the Mongol Empire gradually became independent of the Great Khan, who had his headquarters in Mongolia. Thus the Russians had little to do with the relatively civilized Mongols of China and Persia. They dealt primarily with the so-called Golden Horde, the Mongols of the lower Volga region, who were the least advanced of all the Mongol groups.

Thrown back on themselves, the Russians took refuge in their religion. Their faith differentiated them from the Mongols, but it separated them almost as sharply from the West. They became fiercely orthodox and even less willing than the Greeks to compromise with the Roman Church. This stubbornness, added to their fear of the Catholic Poles, made them suspicious of westerners and western influences that might change their way of life and endanger their faith.

The Rise of the Autocratic Russian State

Isolation, poverty, and constant wars were not ideal conditions for the growth of Russian society. Opportunities dimin- ished for all classes, especially for the peasants. The most the peasants could hope for was to keep their freedom and a little piece of land, and often they found even these modest desires thwarted. Almost the only productive group in the country, the peasants had to support the Mongols, the princes, the nobles, and the Church. The easiest way for their overlords to make sure that they would meet all these obligations was to bind them to the soil; thus serfdom grew

The Church of the Savior at Novgorod, twelfth century. This is an early example of what became a typical style of ecclesiastical architecture in Russia.

in Russia at the very time it was declining in the West. In order to escape serfdom, some peasants moved off into the desolate forest regions of the northeast, but even there the princes caught up with them and assigned them as serfs to monasteries and nobles.

The government of the princes became increasingly arbitrary, though its arbitrariness was always tempered by administrative inefficiency. Economic pressure forced the princes into absolutism; their states were small and the burdens of Mongol tribute and war ex-

penses were great. The princes had inherited a tradition of autocracy from Byzantium, and Mongol demands encouraged the growth of absolutism. A prince who could not collect his tribute was sure to be in trouble; it did him no good to explain that he could not raise the money without violating the rights of his nobles and peasants.

During the fourteenth century the principality of Moscow became the strongest state in Russia. Its rise was due partly to chance; for several generations only one heir to the principality survived

THE GROWTH OF THE GRAND PRINCIPALITY OF MOSCOW   1300–1584

Grand Principality of Moscow ca. 1300

Acquisitions to 1462

Acquisitions to the death of Ivan III, 1505

Acquisitions to the death of Ivan IV, 1584

and thus it was not weakened by constant divisions. Moreover, the metropolitan of Russia moved his seat to Moscow, thus bestowing on the Muscovite princes the support of the highest religious authority in the country. Many of the Muscovite princes were men of superior ability, both in diplomacy and in war. They managed to keep on relatively good terms with the Mongols and were given the title of Grand Prince, which meant that they were the chief tribute-collectors for the entire country. This position gave them an excuse to intervene in the incessant quarrels of other principalities and an opportunity to annex surrounding territory. As the Mongols weakened, the Grand Princes of Moscow became bolder; one of them actually defeated a Mongol army in 1378. Their assertion of independence was premature, however, for the Mongols still had a strong enough army to defeat the Grand Prince and burn Moscow a few years later. Mongol suzerainty was reestablished and continued into the fifteenth century. Nevertheless, the Grand Prince had established himself as leader of the Russians, and his victory over the Mongols was better remembered than his subsequent submission.

During the fifteenth century a civil war broke out in Moscow, but it served to strengthen the principality. The legitimate heir won the final victory and established the principle that Moscow was not to be divided as other Russian states had been. From this point on, the growth of the Muscovite state was phenomenal. It quickly absorbed neighboring principalities and, under Ivan the Great (Ivan III, 1462–1505), annexed the Republic of Novgorod, which held all northern Russia to the White Sea and the Arctic. Ivan also rejected, once and for all, Mongol suzerainty, and the Russians soon began to annex Mongol lands along the lower Volga. By the end of the sixteenth century the Muscovite state had expanded into a Russian Empire, with territories stretching from the White Sea to the Caspian and from the Lithuanian frontier well into western Siberia. The original principality of Moscow had covered only about 500 square miles; the Russian Empire of the sixteenth century was the largest state in Europe.

Russia, the Heir of the Byzantine Empire

Letter of Abbot Philotheus of Pskov to Tsar Vasily III in 1511.

The Church of ancient Rome fell because of the Apollinarian heresy; as for the second Rome, the Church of Constantinople, it has been cut down by the axes of the Hagarenes [Turks]. But in the third, new Rome, the Universal Apostolic Church under thy [Tsar Vasily III] mighty rule sends out the Orthodox Christian faith to the ends of the earth and shines more brightly than the sun. And may thy lordship realize, pious Tsar, that all Christian kingdoms have come together under thy sole empire; thou alone in all the earth art Tsar to the Christians. . . . Two Romes have fallen, but the third stands, and there will be no fourth.

Adapted from Thornton Anderson, *Russian Political Thought* (Ithaca: Cornell University Press, 1967), p. 72.

Absolutism grew with the growth of the Muscovite state. The peasants had lost their rights long before; now it was the turn of the nobles. They were not as independent as the nobles of the West. Most of them had become servants of the princes and held their estates only so long as they performed services for the ruler. They had no permanent power base, such as a duke of Lancaster or a duke of Burgundy had in the West. Soon their very life and property depended on the whim of the prince. By the sixteenth century the greatest men in the land could be put to death on the mere suspicion of disloyalty, and bishops and metropolitans who contradicted the wishes of the sovereign were sent into exile. The old title of Grand Prince no longer seemed sufficient to express this concentration of power. Ivan the Great, who married a niece of the last Byzantine emperor, soon began to think of himself as successor to the Caesars. Moscow was to be the "Third Rome" that would endure forever, and Ivan began to call himself Autocrat and Sovereign of All Russia. He also occasionally used the title of tsar (a Russian form of Caesar), but this did not become official until the reign of Ivan the Dread (Ivan IV, 1533–84). Ivan the Dread was a great conqueror and one of the bloodiest tyrants in history. He massacred nobles and townsmen with little reason and killed his own son in a fit of rage.

Part of the dowry of the marriage of Byzantine Princess Zoe to Ivan the Great (1462–1505) was the right to adopt the Byzantine two-headed eagle as the tsar's royal coat of arms.

In spite of its size and the authority of its ruler, sixteenth-century Muscovy was not yet a powerful state. Still cut off from the main trade routes, its only outlet to the ocean was in the far north, on the White Sea. It was thinly settled; probably there were more people in France than in all the territories of the tsar. It was poor; it had almost no industry, and agriculture was backward. It was still militarily weak, open to attack by Poles on the west and Turks and Tatars in the southeast. The bulk of the peasants were still farming the poor soils of the North by primitive methods, and there were few settlers in the rich black-earth districts of the South. It was far behind its neighbors in all intellectual activities, in science and technology as well as in scholarship and literature. Only after 1600 did the Russians begin to overcome these great handicaps.

THE ADVANCE OF THE TURKS

The problem for much of Europe was not the Mongols but the Turks. As we have seen, the Mongol advance left the Turks of Asia Minor relatively unharmed, and the Byzantine Empire had been fragmented by the Fourth Crusade. The Serbs and Bulgars dominated the back country, western feudal lords ruled most of Greece, and Venice held the islands. The Byzantine Empire, as revived in 1261, possessed only Constantinople and a narrow strip of land on each side of the Straits. The new Turkish dynasty of the Ottomans, founded in 1299, rapidly exploited the weakness of the Christians. As good at war as their predecessors the Seljuks, the Ottomans showed far more ability in building a permanent state with a strong administrative system. After conquering most of western Asia Minor they began, in the 1350s, to make permanent settlements on the European side of the Straits. The Christians offered no concerted resistance and by 1365 the

Turks had established their capital in Adrianople, not far from Constantinople. In 1389 they broke the power of the Serbs, who had the strongest state in the Balkans, at the battle of Kossovo. This victory brought the Turks to the borders of Hungary, and the West at last began to take alarm. The pope proclaimed a crusade, and a large army—mostly German and Hungarian with some French knights—advanced against the Turks. But bad generalship and poor discipline ruined whatever chance of success it had, and the crusaders were thoroughly defeated at the battle of Nicopolis in 1396.

The battle almost destroyed Christian power in the Balkans, but before the Turks could fully exploit their victory they were attacked from the east. Timur the Lame (Tamerlane), who claimed to be a descendant of Genghis Khan, had created a nomad army worthy of his supposed ancestor. The Mongols were once more on the march, and this time the Ottoman Turks were one of their chief enemies. In 1402 the two armies met at Ankara, where Timur won a complete victory. The Mongols captured the Turkish sultan and occupied most of his lands in Asia Minor.

Timur died soon after his victory, and his successors made little effort to hold the remote regions he had taken from the Turks. Nevertheless, the defeat at Ankara, followed by a generation of civil war, was a severe test of the Ottoman political system. The fact that the state was pulled together once again showed that the early sultans had done their work well. They had created a corps of disciplined and capable administrators, and it was with their assistance that one of the Ottoman princes was able to re-establish himself as sole ruler. By the 1440s the Turks were once more advancing in the Balkans. Their chief opponents this time were the Hungarians, commanded by John Hunyadi. Though a first-rate general, Hunyadi lost two major battles to the Turks.

The End
of the Byzantine Empire

Now the road lay open to Constantinople. The last Byzantine emperor, Constantine XI, made a desperate appeal to the West for aid. Over the strong opposition of his subjects, he agreed to reunite the Greek and Latin Churches in return for western aid. But the union was never effective and the popes of the fifteenth century lacked the prestige needed to rouse the West. Constantine received no real help and was left to fight the final battles alone. In 1453 the Turks made an all-out attack on the imperial city. The emperor was killed defending a breach in the walls and the Turks poured into Constantinople. This was the end of the Byzantine Empire and of the emperors who claimed to be heirs of Caesar and Augustus. For many years there had been nothing Roman about them except their titles, but they were not unworthy of those titles in their last struggle.

Turkish advances in Europe continued after the fall of Constantinople, largely at the expense of Hungary. The Hungarians fought valiantly but were pushed back little by little until the Turks reached their high-water mark of conquest at the unsuccessful siege of Vienna in 1529.

As the Turkish advance slowed down in Europe, it speeded up in Asia and Africa. During the sixteenth century Syria, Mesopotamia, and Arabia were added to the Turkish Empire in Asia, and Egypt, Tunisia, and Algeria in North Africa. With this Turkish conquest of the southern and eastern coasts of the Mediterranean, Moslem naval power began to revive. The Turks never closed the Mediterranean to Christian shipping, but they and the semipiratical fleets of their subjects did interfere seriously with commerce from time to time. It was not until the 1800s that the Mediterranean became as safe for western merchants as it had been in the thirteenth century.

The Decline
of Moslem Civilization

The rise of the Turks coincided with a decline in Moslem intellectual activity. Both the Turks and the Mongols have often been blamed for this decline, but neither people seems to have been entirely responsible. It is true that both Turks and Mongols were originally rough warriors from the steppes with little interest in intellectual matters, but both of them absorbed Moslem civilization with great rapidity. Art and literature flourished under the Mongol rulers of Persia, while the Turks did some remarkable work in architecture and developed a highly literate corps of administrators. Moreover, one of the most eloquent laments over the decline of Moslem learning came from the historian ibn-Khaldun (1332-1406), who spent most of his life in North Africa, a region that was never touched by the Mongols and that fell under Turkish control only in the sixteenth century. There must have been more deep-seated causes, prevalent throughout the Moslem world, of the decline of Moslem civilization.

Ibn-Khaldun, probably the greatest of all Moslem historians, tried to work out

Mohammed II, ruler of the Turks when they took Constantinople in 1453.

a historical theory to explain the decline. His basic idea was that there had always been antagonism between the educated, open-minded, prosperous city-dwellers and the ignorant, narrow-minded, poverty-stricken inhabitants of the desert and the steppes. When the city people became soft and decadent, as they had in his time, power passed to the crude but warlike tribes of the open country. This political shift in turn caused a shift in the climate of opinion. Rigid orthodoxy was favored and science and philosophy were looked on with contempt and suspicion.

There is some truth in ibn-Khaldun's explanation. The dominant dynasties of the Moslem world in the fourteenth century were all nomad in origin, and some of them did emphasize strict Moslem orthodoxy. But this is only part of the story. Earlier nomadic conquerors, beginning with the Arabs themselves, had absorbed the intellectual heritage of the ancient world without difficulty, and fourteenth-century orthodoxy did not prevent the rise of mysticism in the Moslem world. Some leaders of the mystical movement, who had large followings, advanced ideas that went far beyond the early teachings of Islam, so that we cannot say that a sort of Islamic fundamentalism blocked all forms of speculation. It seems rather that Moslem science and philosophy had reached a dead end, and that the educated classes had become uninterested in them.

Perhaps Moslem learning had reached its peak too early and too rapidly. Few new ideas entered the world of Islam after the tenth century, and all the changes on the old themes had been rung by the thirteenth century. With nothing new to be done, there was naturally a loss of interest in academic subjects. In comparison, western scholarship, which was far inferior to that of the Moslem world in the tenth century, received a fresh stimulus every time it was about to reach a dead end. There were the translations from the Arabic in the twelfth century, the revival of Greek studies in the fifteenth, and the great scientific discoveries of the early modern period. Moreover, theology, philosophy, and science were so closely associated in Christian thought that activity in one field prompted activity in the others. Extraordinary interest in theology in the fourteenth century stimulated activity in philosophy and science. The theology of Islam, on the other hand, was much less complicated. Some Moslems took it for granted; others simply memorized the Koran, paying no attention to philosophy. Thus religious education in Moslem countries did not require corresponding activity in philosophy or science. Finally, as we have seen, western scholars were not quite so bound to authoritative, scholarly interpretations; more innovation was possible in fourteenth-century Paris than in fourteenth-century Cairo.

Whatever the value of these explanations, one basic fact is clear: for the first time in history, western Europe was to take the lead in certain types of scholarly investigation. Byzantine scholarship, never very original, was blighted by the Turkish conquest. Moslem scholarship was rapidly decaying in the fourteenth and fifteenth centuries. Of all the peoples who had inherited the great Greek tradition of philosophical and scientific inquiry, only the scholars of western Europe were still active. And their activity was to give the West an incalculable advantage in the next four centuries.

Suggestions for Further Reading

Note: Asterisk denotes a book available in paperback edition.

Byzantium, 750–1453   S. Runciman, *Byzantine Civilization** (1933), gives a good general picture of Byzantine institutions and culture and is the best introduction. The most thorough and scholarly study is G. Ostrogorsky, *History of the Byzantine State*, trans. by J. Hussey (1956). The older work of A. A. Vasiliev, *History of the Byzantine Empire*, 2 vols. (1928), is more readable than Ostrogorsky but not as thorough nor as fresh in historical interpretation. There is valuable material on the commercial activities of the Italian city-states within the Byzantine Empire in E. H. Byrne, *Genoese Shipping in the Twelfth and Thirteenth Centuries* (1930), and in C. Diehl, *Une République patricienne: Venise* (1916). G. Every, *The Byzantine Patriarchate* (1947), compares the liturgical and doctrinal differences between the Eastern and Western Churches; and J. M. Hussey, *Church and Learning in the Byzantine Empire* (1937), is useful for understanding Byzantine intellectual activity. See also the titles by Baynes, Diehl, Grabar, and Talbot-Rice mentioned after Chapter 8. An interesting survey of Byzantine civilization and its influence on the West is S. Vryonis, *Byzantium and Europe** (1967).

The Caliphate, 750–1258

B. Lewis, *The Arabs in History** (1956), a broad, quick survey, is a good starting point for study. B. Spuler, *The Muslim World,* Vol. I, trans. by F. R. C. Bagley (1960), is an authoritative survey of the entire period and a useful handbook. The old account of T. W. Arnold, *The Caliphate* (1934), is still valuable for the theory and development of the Caliphate. There is considerable material in P. K. Hitti, *A History of the Arabs** (1956), the standard treatment of the subject, invaluable for the facts of the period but quite controversial in historical interpretation. For the Caliphate as an institution, see E. Tyan, *Le Califut* (1954), and E. I. J. Rosenthal, *Political Thought in Medieval Islam* (1958). The growth of Turkish power is well treated by P. Wittek, *The Rise of the Ottoman Empire* (1958).

The Crusades

There are several accounts of the later crusades which give us real insight into the spirit and motivation of the crusaders. Both Geoffrey de Villhardouin, *The Conquest of Constantinople** (Everyman's Library), and Robert of Clari, *The Conquest of Constantinople,* trans. by E. H. McNeal (1936), are fascinating eyewitness accounts of the Fourth Crusade. Philippe of Novara, *The Wars of Frederick II Against the Ibelins,* trans. by J. L. La Monte (1936), contributes a great deal to our knowledge of Frederick II and his crusades. The counselor Joinville's *Life of St. Louis** (Everyman's Library) has exciting material on St. Louis' expeditions to Egypt and Tunis on the Sixth and Seventh Crusades.

E. Barker, *The Crusades* (1923), is old but still valuable. The best recent study is the beautifully written and highly urbane account by S. Runciman, *A History of the Crusades,** 3 vols. (1951–54). Runciman includes a thorough bibliography. There is good material on the crusades in the books by Setton, Hitti, and La Monte listed after Chapter 10, in the fourth section. For crusading efforts after 1300, see A. S. Atiya, *The Crusade in the Later Middle Ages* (1938).

The Mongols in the Arab World and Russia

B. Spuler, *The Muslim World,* Vol. II: *The Mongol Period,* trans. by F. R. C. Bagley (1960), is excellent. G. Le Strange, *The Lands of the Eastern Caliphate* (1905), a study of the historical geography of the Near East and central Asia in the Middle Ages, is an old treatment but very good reading. Juvaynī 'Alā' al-Din 'utā Malik, *The History of the World Conqueror,* trans. by J. A. Bayle (1952), is an important study, while V. V. Barthold, *Four Studies on the History of Central Asia* (1955), contains the authoritative history of central Asia and the Mongols. Probably the best treatment of the Mongol rule of Russia is G. Vernadsky, *The Monguls and Russia* (1953), a scholarly and readable work by a leading authority on Russian history.

Russia, 1100–1600

There are several very good studies of this period of Russian history. M. T. Florinsky, *Russia: A History and Interpretation,* Vol. I (1955), has valuable material on this formative period of the Russian state. The old work of V. O. Kluchevsky, *A History of Russia,* 2 vols. (1912), is very interesting reading and still important. Undoubtedly the best treatment of Russia from 1100 to 1600 is G. Vernadsky, *Russia at the Dawn of the Modern Age* (1959). Vernadsky includes excellent maps and genealogical tables and up-to-date bibliographic material. *A History of the U.S.S.R.,* ed. by A. M. Pankratova (1947), is a modern Marxist interpretation of the evolution of the Russian state.

The Decline of Arabic Learning

Most of the titles mentioned in the second section above contain information on Arabic learning. R. Landau, *Islam and the Arabs* (1958), devotes considerable attention to Moslem culture. T. Arnold and A. Guillaume, *The Legacy of Islam* (1947), provide a good summary that traces those elements in European culture that have roots in the Islamic world.

15

India, China, and Japan 500–1600 A.D.

The fifth-century invasions of the Huns and related tribes were a disaster from which northern India never fully recovered. Its political system was shattered, and not until the establishment of the Moslem sultanate of Delhi in 1206 did a single state manage to dominate northern India again. The Ganges Valley was divided into small warring kingdoms that were briefly united by the rajah Harsha (606–47). Northern India was fairly prosperous during his reign, and both scholarship and literature flourished. But Harsha was unable to conquer central India, and only his personal ability kept the Ganges Valley united. After his death his kingdom collapsed. During the next two and a half centuries northern India was dominated by the Rajputs, many of whom were descendants of warriors from central Asia who had entered India during the chaotic years following the Hunnic invasion. The Rajputs intermarried with Hindus and adopted Hindu religious beliefs and social practices with great enthusiasm. After a time they began to claim that they were members of the Hindu warrior caste—next to the Brahmans, the highest group in Hindu society—and therefore the rightful lords of the common people.

INDIAN KINGDOMS

The Rajputs created a way of life not unlike that of the nobles of western Europe in the thirteenth and fourteenth century. They loved combat and developed a chivalric code that valued fair fighting and mercy to the weak and helpless. They showed more respect to women than was customary in other parts of India; their court poets recited epics commemorating the heroes of the past. The Rajput aristocrats led a brilliant and exciting life, but they showed little political capacity. They used up their qualities of courage, honor, and loyalty in endless internecine wars and left northern India so weak that it was easily overrun by Moslem invaders after the tenth century.

Japanese Buddha, Kamakura period, 1253.

Siva, god of destruction and creation, as Lord of the Dance; Indian, twelfth or thirteenth century.

The dynasties established farther south had a somewhat longer life. South-central India, the Deccan, was united for two centuries under the Chalukya kings (*ca.* 550–*ca.* 750), who were strong enough to repel Harsha and other invaders from the north. Even after the fall of the Chalukyas, the Deccan was less fragmented than the northern region. It broke up into a few fairly large states, which preserved their independence until the fourteenth century. In the extreme South were the Tamils, remnants of the original Dravidian inhabitants of India. They too created large kingdoms, first Chola, which lasted from the tenth to the end of the thirteenth century, and then Vijayanagar, which fell to the Moslems only in 1585. At its height Vijayanagar held the whole southern third of the peninsula, carried on an active foreign commerce, and was fabulously wealthy.

The Spread of Indian Culture

The most important events of these centuries were not the rise and fall of dynasties, but the consolidation of Hindu culture and the spread of Indian influence overseas. As we have seen, Buddhism was declining in India during the Gupta period, and it lost even more ground during the invasions and wars that followed the downfall of the Gupta dynasty. By the end of the tenth century Buddhism was almost extinct in India and the entire population followed some form of the old Hindu beliefs. There were many variants of this religion; each part of the country had its own special rituals and favorite gods. But each sect was usually tolerant of the others, since all divinities were considered manifestations of the same underlying spiritual forces. And the basic elements of the Hindu way of life—the power of the Brahman priesthood, the caste system, and the intellectual and religious tradition—permeated the whole peninsula.

The real strength of Hindu civilization was in its social rather than its political structure. The great majority of the people lived in small agricultural villages that were administered by a council of elders and were advised—often dominated—by a Brahman priest. These villages showed little interest in the changes of dynasties and the rise and fall of kingdoms; they paid tribute to the ruler of the moment and preserved their traditional way of life through all the storms of war and rebellion. Under the caste system every man's place in society and his occupation were clearly marked out, and it took more than a change of rulers to upset such well-established patterns. At a higher level the Brahmans, who served as intellectual and religious leaders, preserved the continuity of tradition. Some kings were more influenced by the Brahmans than others, but between the collapse of Buddhism and the Moslem conquest of northern India there was no rival religious or intellectual leadership. In the long run the ideas of the Brahmans influenced all governments and all classes and gave a basic unity to Indian life in spite of extreme local diversity.

During the centuries of the European Middle Ages the Indians were barred from the West by the growing power of Islam, but they found that the backward and unorganized peoples of Southeast Asia were easily influenced by their civilization. It is still not clear whether Indian emigrants conquered neighboring lands or whether they secured a dominant position by peaceful penetration. Certainly

The Rajput Code

A widow speaks to the page who witnessed her husband's death:

"Boy, tell me, ere I go, how bore himself my lord?"

"As a reaper of the harvest of battle. I followed his steps as a humble gleaner of his sword. On the bed of honor he spread a carpet of the slain, whereon, a barbarian his pillow, he sleeps ringed by his foes."

"Yet once again, boy, tell me how my lord bore himself?"

"Oh mother, who can tell his deeds? He left no foe to dread or to admire him."

She smiled farewell to the boy, and adding, "My lord will chide my delay," sprang into the flames.

As quoted in H. G. Rawlinson, *India: A Short Cultural History* (New York: Appleton-Century, 1938), p. 202.

many of the ruling families of the kingdoms to the east of India bore Hindu names, and the art and literature of these countries show strong Indian influence. Imposing Buddhist and Hindu shrines were built, of which the most striking is the enormous temple of Angkor Wat in Cambodia. With its five great towers and its long walls covered with scenes from Hindu epics, Angkor Wat is one of the largest religious centers ever created by man. The complex of buildings covered more ground than most medieval European cities, and the individual structures were larger and more richly ornamented than most cathedrals.

Indian influence was strongest and most lasting in Burma, western Siam, and the Malay Peninsula. In Indochina it had to compete with Chinese influence from the north. Tongking and part of Annam (North Vietnam) were always closely connected with China, while South Vietnam, Cambodia, and Laos were more like India—a fact that may help to explain the present political situation in this region. Indonesia received Buddhism and much of its culture from India, and the Sailendra dynasty, which ruled the archipelago from the eighth to the eleventh century, built some of the most magnificent Buddhist shrines the world has ever seen. The Sailendra kings were followed by Hindu rulers, who held the islands until the Moslem conquest of the sixteenth century. Java, the most populous of the islands, became thoroughly Mohammedanized at this time, but the smaller island of Bali to the east preserved a basically Hindu culture.

The Political Weakness of India

During this eastern expansion India was at its best—full of energy, imagination, and understanding in dealing with strange peoples. But by the end of the tenth century the period of expansion was over and the qualities that had made it possible seem largely to have vanished. This decline was due partly to the Indians' failure to create permanent and stable governments. Every society needs constant rebuilding if it is not to stagnate or disintegrate, and rebuilding is very difficult in the absence of effective political institutions. Individual Indian rulers often had excellent ideas, but their plans died with them and India failed to adapt itself to new conditions.

There was little economic development. Trade remained at its old levels; industry was decentralized, with as many artisans in the countryside as in the towns, and the magnificent royal cities consumed more than they produced. The Indian peasant still carried most of society on his back. He was happiest when there were not too many middlemen (landlords and petty officers) between

A view of the temple of Angkor Wat, built in the twelfth century by the king of Cambodia.

him and the court that was the ultimate consumer of his taxes, but such good fortune was rare during periods of weak government.

In addition, the prevailing Hindu way of life became more and more conservative, while the leaders of Hindu thought became complacent and self-satisfied. They had little to do with the Moslems to the west, and their contacts with China decreased. The people they knew best were those of Southeast Asia, but they considered these people inferior. As a result, there was a tendency for Indian civilization to freeze in a rigid pattern—to fall back on its past accomplishments rather than to advance to new ground. The caste system became both more complicated and more unchangeable; little new work was done in science. Thinkers such as the great Indian philosopher Sankara, who tried to see one eternal being behind the multiplicity of gods, had little influence. Even the art of war fell into a set pattern in which armies were maneuvered according to the teachings of ancient writers rather than according to the needs of a particular campaign.

THE MOSLEM CONQUEST

All these weaknesses became critical when Moslem pressure on the northwest frontier increased. In the eighth century, during their first wave of expansion, the Moslems had taken over the southern Indus Valley, but this annexation neither influenced Indian culture nor caused much ill will between the Islamic and Hindu religious communities. The situation changed sharply, as it did in so many other regions, with the coming of the Turks in the tenth century. The Turks renewed the conquering tradition of Islam and showed themselves far less tolerant of alien religions than the Arabs. It is true that Hinduism, with its images, its hundreds of gods, and its elaborate ceremonies, contradicted everything for which Mohammed had stood, and that it was far easier for Moslems to be tolerant of Christianity, with which they had some common traditions, than of Hinduism, which was completely alien to them.

Brahma, Hindu deity personifying the supreme creator; Indian, tenth or eleventh century.

THE MOSLEM CONQUEST OF INDIA
1192–1320

Nevertheless, the Arab rulers of the lower Indus Valley had not been implacably hostile to the Hindus; it was the Turks who transformed the two religious communities into bitter and persistent enemies.

The Turks and related peoples first established themselves in Afghanistan in the tenth century and immediately began to nibble away at the holdings of the Rajput princes in northwest India. This process was completed by Mahmud of Ghazni, who held most of the northwest by 1022 and pushed his daring raids deep into Hindu territory. Intermittent raiding and fighting continued for a century and a half, until the next great Moslem conqueror appeared. This was Mohammed Ghori, who pushed east toward the Ganges Valley and defeated the allied Hindu kings of the North in a decisive battle at Panipat in 1192. This victory opened the entire region north of the Deccan to the Moslems. Mohammed Ghori was assassinated in 1206, but in the same year his chief minister made himself sultan of Delhi. The Delhi sultanate rapidly became the dominant state in India. It controlled all of the North by 1236 and had taken over most of the Deccan by 1320. Only Vijayanagar in the extreme South remained an independent kingdom in which the Hindu tradition and culture could flourish without Moslem interference.

The Moslem Impact on India

The Delhi sultanate lasted nominally until 1526, but it lost most of its power after 1398. Even with its decline the Hindus found no relief, however, for the Sultan's provincial governors set themselves up as independent kings and continued to dominate the native population. The Delhi sultanate failed to create stable political institutions and never established a fixed rule of succession. Most sultans acquired the throne by murdering their predecessor, and the art of government consisted largely in collecting taxes from the Hindu peasants. Heavy taxation was not only a means of supporting the government; it was also designed to keep the Hindus weak and powerless. Many of the sultans and their

Moslem and Hindu in the Fourteenth Century

Ala-ud-Din [sultan of Delhi, 1296–1316] was a king who had no acquaintance with learning and never associated with the learned. He considered that policy and government were one thing and law another. "I am an unlettered man," he said, "but I have seen a great deal. Be assured that the Hindus will never become submissive and obedient until they are reduced to poverty. I have therefore given orders that just enough shall be left them of grain, milk, and curds from year to year, but that they must not accumulate hoards and property."

From the Moslem historian Barani, as quoted by H. G. Rawlinson, *India: A Short Cultural History* (New York: Appleton-Century, 1938), p. 228.

agents were fanatical Moslems who delighted in killing Hindus or in forcing them to accept Islam at the point of a sword. This policy of forced conversion succeeded in making the northwest and the extreme northeast (Bangladesh) largely Moslem. Even in the Deccan some 10 to 15 percent of the population was persuaded to adopt the faith of the conquerors. But in the regions where conversions were most numerous, hostility between Moslem and Hindu was strongest, and it endured to our own day. When India gained its independence in 1947 the country had to be split into two states, Moslem Pakistan (northwest India and east Bengal, now Bangladesh) and Hindu India.

The Moslem conquerors—mostly Turks and Afghans—were the first invaders of India who did not merge fully with the Hindu population. But though they remained a separate community, they had some influence on Hindu civilization. Some of the most bloodthirsty sultans were also the patrons of scholars, writers, and artists. They introduced ideas from Persian and Arabic literature and elements of Moslem architecture, such as the minaret and dome. The conquerors even developed a new language, Urdu,* based on Hindu rules of grammar

* Urdu, which means "camp language," or "army language," comes from the Turkish word for a camp of armed tribesmen. In English the word has become *horde*.

but with a vocabulary that was largely Persian. This language is still spoken in Pakistan and also in parts of north-western India. Even in their most intolerant moods, Moslem rulers had to employ some Hindu officials, simply because there were not enough Moslems who knew much about local conditions. In this way, the Moslems had some influence on Indian art, literature, and social customs. For example, the practice of keeping women in seclusion and discouraging them from appearing in public was due largely to the example of the Mohammedan ruling class.

The Delhi sultanate was almost annihilated by an invasion by Tamerlane in 1398—the same Tamerlane who checked the advance of the Ottoman Turks in the West. Tamerlane, who wanted only booty from India, looted the northwest, sacked Delhi, and killed tens of thousands of noncombatants and prisoners. But he did not found a government in northern India, and the Delhi sultanate was eventually restored, though with only a fraction of its former territory. Independent Moslem rulers controlled the rest of the country, except for some Rajput strongholds in the North and Vijayanagar in the South. It was during this period that firearms and heavy artillery began to be used in India.

The Moguls

India finally gained some degree of unity and orderly government under the Mogul dynasty in the sixteenth century. The Moguls, who, like so many earlier conquerors, came from central Asia, had both Turkish and Mongol ancestry; the first strong Mogul ruler, Babur, claimed descent from both Genghis Khan and Tamerlane. He entered India in 1524 and defeated the sultan of Delhi on the old battlefield of Panipat in 1526, thus winning control of most of the North. Babur secured his position in 1527 by defeating a coalition of Rajput leaders who were

trying to establish an independent Hindu state in the northwest.

There was some dissension among the conquerors after Babur's death, but eventually his grandson, Akbar, gained the throne, and under him the Mogul Empire reached the height of its power. Akbar had completed the conquest of the North by 1576 and then turned to the Deccan, which he brought largely under control by 1600. A few more or less independent states survived in the South, but none of them had any importance. Vijayanagar had been destroyed by the Moslem kings of the Deccan shortly before Akbar's conquest, so that for all practical purposes Akbar was master of India.

THE MOGUL EMPIRE   1605

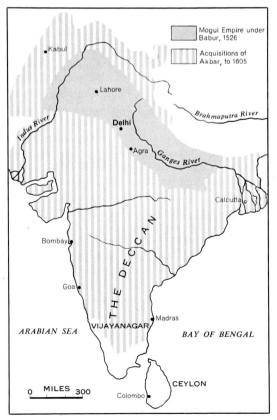

Akbar

Akbar was a Moslem in religion and a Turko-Mongol in race, but he had far more regard for his Indian subjects than most earlier conquerors with this background. He set up an efficient administrative hierarchy and tried to keep his officials reasonably honest by paying them regular salaries and punishing them severely for accepting bribes. He was determined to see that justice was done and often acted as a judge himself. His more efficient and honest government made it possible to keep taxation at a moderate level. In fact, the assessment of the land tax under the Moguls was equitable enough to be used as the basis for later assessments under British rule.

Akbar realized that religious intolerance and racial quarrels were a threat to the permanence of his empire. He tried to conciliate the Rajputs, who were still resisting at the beginning of his reign, by honoring their bravery and by marrying three Rajput princesses. He appointed Hindus to high government positions, though Moslems still held most of the important posts. Even more significant was his insistence on complete religious toleration. Scholars of all faiths were welcome at his court; he even extended hospitality to a Jesuit mission and allowed them to build a chapel. Toward the end of his life he became convinced that there was some merit in every religion and that claims to exclusive possession of the truth were unjustified. There were earlier precedents for this belief. During the long centuries of conflict, enlightened Hindus and Moslems had suggested that there was only one divine power, which was worshiped under many names. The Hindu poet Kabir (1440–1518) had been especially eloquent on this subject. But none of these earlier religious leaders had the power of an Akbar. He tried to create a universal religion that would include all that was good in earlier faiths and that would end religious controversy in India. But artificial universal religions, like artificial universal languages, have little appeal to most people. While Akbar lived he was able to win some support for his new faith, but on his death India fell back into its old religious disputes.

Akbar inspecting building operations at a royal city in the Ganges Valley. From the Akbar-nama manuscript, ca. 1590.

Akbar's Religious Beliefs

O God, in every temple I see those who seek thee.
And in every tongue that is spoken Thou art praised.
Polytheism and Islam grope after Thee.
Each religion says, "Thou art One, without equal."
Be it mosque, men murmur holy prayers; or church,
The bells ring for the love of Thee.
Awhile I frequent the Christian cloister, anon the mosque,
But Thee only I seek from fane to fane.
Thine elect know naught of heresy or orthodoxy, whereof
Neither stands behind the screen of Thy truth.

From a poem by Akbar's secretary, Abul Fazl, as quoted in H. G. Rawlinson, *India: A Short Cultural History* (New York: Appleton-Century, 1938), p. 310.

Tree of Life and Knowledge, South India, seventeenth century.

Akbar's court was a center of art and learning. He collected a large library and was eager to have his books illustrated by the best artists of the country. One of the most brilliant schools of manuscript illumination that has ever existed developed at his court. Akbar was also a great builder, and some of the finest Indian architecture comes from his period. Both manuscript illumination and architecture showed strong Persian influence, but the Hindu tradition continued and many works of art show an intermingling of the two styles.

The Collapse of the Mogul Empire

In spite of his ability, Akbar did not succeed in ending the evils of misgovernment and religious controversy that had plagued India for so many centuries. Under his successors, who were less competent and less broadminded than he, Islam was reestablished as the official religion of the governing class, and discrimination against Hindus again became common. Civil wars among members of

the ruling dynasty weakened the government, and provincial viceroys gradually became independent rulers. Hindu leaders began to organize resistance groups to throw off Mogul domination. India, as it had done so often in the past, was dissolving into a welter of conflicting states.

This time, however, there was a new force to be reckoned with—the merchants and soldiers of western Europe. The first European settlements in India had been made by the Portuguese just before the founding of the Mogul Empire. The Portuguese never held more than a few seacoast towns, but they were followed by French and English merchants who were more ambitious and had more powerful governments to back them. The growing disunion of India gave these adventurers from overseas easy opportunities to establish themselves in key positions throughout the country. The battles that determined the fate of modern India were directed by French and English generals and were fought for the profit of their respective nations. The heirs of the Moguls were to be not the Hindu rajahs who struggled so hard to regain their independence, nor the Moslem viceroys who tried to hold together fragments of the old empire, but the directors of the British East India Company.

CHINA UNDER THE T'ANG DYNASTY

The old center of Chinese civilization, the valley of the Yellow River, fell to the nomads of the steppe only about a century before the western nomads (the Huns) helped to destroy the Western Roman Empire. For almost three centuries, from about 317 to about 589, northern China was ruled by Huns or other nomadic people. There was little political stability; few dynasties lasted for as long as a century, and most of the time China was divided into several warring states.

Yet with all these political difficulties, Chinese civilization made a quicker recovery from the shock of conquest than did the civilization of the Roman West.

In the North, the Chinese slowly assimilated the barbarians. In the South, the Chinese remained for the most part independent, and the fertile valley of the Yangtze was fully exploited, for the first time, by refugees from the North. These settlers in the Yangtze Valley preserved and developed all the essential elements of Chinese civilization and began to impress their ideas on the still barbarous peoples who lived even farther south. Contact with all these strange peoples had a stimulating effect on the Chinese; they were more open to foreign influence at this time than they were to be again for centuries. It was during this period that Buddhism made its greatest gains in China. It was also during this period that Chinese Buddhists made frequent pilgrimages to India and other countries in Southeast Asia. They brought back information about the history and geography of Asian lands, and some very useful mathematical and scientific lore from India. Thus, instead of decaying, Chinese civilization spread beyond its original limits and was enriched by new ideas from abroad.

Nevertheless, these years of disunity and foreign invasion were hard for the masses, who suffered from war, famine, and exploitation by selfish rulers. There was a great burst of energy and optimism when the country was at last reunited under Chinese rulers. The Sui dynasty (581–617), which accomplished this feat, "ruled without benevolence," as one Chinese writer put it, but at least its harshness had some purpose. The country was reunified. The Sui emperors built huge granaries to help avert famine; even more important, they built roads and a canal system that united North and South and made it easier to move grain from surplus to deficit regions. But these useful tasks could be accomplished only by impressing thousands of laborers, who were harshly treated. Resentment grew, and defeats by the Turks brought open rebellion at home. The Sui dynasty was overthrown and replaced by the T'ang.

The T'ang period (618–906) was one of the most brilliant in Chinese history. The first emperor of the dynasty, an able general, drove the Turks and other nomads from the frontiers and eventually attacked the heart of Turkish power in central Asia. Most of the Turkish leaders acknowledged the suzerainty of the Chinese emperor and paid him tribute. This victory extended Chinese power into Turkestan and ended, for over a century, the threat of invasion from the northwest. Succeeding emperors made Korea a protectorate and, at the southern extremity of the empire, established their authority in northern Indochina. Not until the time of the Manchus in the seventeenth century was China again to control such a vast territory.

Chinese Government and Society Under the T'ang

Early T'ang government was efficient and, on the whole, benevolent. It clearly separated military from civilian offices and revived the professional civil service,

The Chinese of the T'ang and Sung periods were open to contact with foreigners. This silk painting shows barbarian royalty worshiping the serene Chinese Buddha. Note the caricature in the depiction of the dress and expression of the foreigners.

Seated court lady, sculpture of T'ang period (618–906).

going far beyond the rather undeveloped system that had existed in the Han period. By recruiting most civil servants through a system of competitive examinations, it followed the precedent of the Han period, although the Han examinations had been neither as regular nor as uniform as those of the T'ang era. Under the T'ang emperors young men were examined at regular intervals on a fixed body of materials, mainly the classics of Chinese literature and philosophy. There were various levels of difficulty, ranging from the preliminary examination, which admitted a man to an official career, to the highest examination, which qualified him for the top posts in the imperial court. Theoretically the examinations were open to all subjects, regardless of birth and wealth. In practice, few men could take them unless they belonged to the family of an official or a landlord, and recommendations from powerful men still carried much weight. Even if there was no favoritism, it took years of study to qualify for even the preliminary examination, and more years to reach the highest level. No peasant could afford such expensive training for his son.

This flaw in the examination system illustrates one of the enduring characteristics of Chinese society. From at least the T'ang period until the twentieth century, the most influential class in China was the one that has been called the scholar-gentry. This was a landlord class, which owned and leased to the peasants most of the land in the country. It was also the class that furnished most of the officials to the government at both the local and higher levels. And since official position depended on education, it was the class of scholars. Thus a single family might own most of the land in a district, hold most of the government jobs there, and have one or two representatives in high positions at court.

These scholar-gentry families were almost indestructible. If they lost favor at court, they retired to their estates and waited until the ruler or the dynasty changed. If the central government collapsed, they kept local government going until central authority could be reestablished. If nomad invaders conquered the country, they preserved classical learning and Confucian philosophy and taught them to the conquerors. More than any other group, they were responsible for the continuity of the Chinese way of life.

At the same time, the scholar-gentry class was responsible for some of China's social problems. It was supported by the peasants and it often exploited them. If the central government made unreasonable demands, the gentry sometimes passed them on to the peasants, thus increasing their burden. If the central government was weak, the gentry sometimes used its official position to increase its land holdings and to take illegal payments from peasants and artisans. No government could exist without using the services of the gentry, but it was often difficult to make them behave according to the Confucian principles they professed. And oppression by the gentry often led to peasant rebellions.

Most Chinese dynasties, when they were strong, tried to protect the peasants against the landlords, and the early T'ang rulers were no exception. They broke up some of the large estates and remitted taxes in years of crop failure. They were able to reduce the burden on the peasants because commerce was flourishing, and therefore taxes on merchants and government monopolies on sales of salt and iron more than made up for a decrease in peasant payments.

China seems to have been generally prosperous during the early T'ang period. There was a wide market for silk and porcelain, which were exported to Japan on the east, to India and Indochina on the south, and to the Arab Empire on the west. The population increased notably, an indication that the peasants and artisans were thriving. It was also during the T'ang period that tea became the national drink of China. Formerly tea had been a luxury, but now it could be purchased by all classes. Since it had to be shipped from the South, the only region where it could be grown, its use throughout the country suggests that transportation facilities were good and that even the poorest people had risen a little above a bare subsistence level.

Religion under the T'ang

The T'ang dynasty's revival of a national government and its emphasis on knowledge of the Chinese classics for admission to the civil service eventually strengthened Confucianism and weakened other faiths. Confucianism, which was the basis for the Chinese political and social system, was highly rational and secular in spirit. A good many T'ang officials were Buddhists, but others looked with suspicion on Buddhism, which, in some of its variants, led to emotional excesses and antisocial behavior. They were also worried by what seemed to them an excessive number of Buddhist priests, monks, and nuns. They used the same arguments against them that European politicians used against Christian monks in the sixteenth century: they were idle and unproductive; they held too much of the wealth of the country; they encouraged superstition. On several occasions the government seized Buddhist temples and monasteries and compelled the monks and nuns to return to secular life. These attacks were intermittent, and Buddhism continued to influence many inhabitants of China. But Buddhism was gradually weakened by official disfavor and its influence on Chinese life slowly declined.

A considerable number of middle- and lower-class Chinese had no very clear idea of religious differences. Any manifestation of divine inspiration was to be respected; they gave equal honor to Confucius, the Buddha, and Taoist teachers. Even the upper classes, though officially Confucianist, admitted that other philosophies had some merit. In this lukewarm religious atmosphere, Buddhism had no real power.

T'ang Scholarship

The T'ang period was an age of scholarship during which encyclopedias were compiled, a national academy was established, and dictionaries of foreign languages were prepared. The government established the practice of employing large groups of scholars to write histories of earlier dynasties, a practice that was faithfully followed by later rulers. As a result, China has hundreds of volumes of official histories covering almost its entire past, though the histories are concerned mainly with the affairs of the court and the bureaucracy.

The Buddhist monks, despite their troubles, made important contributions to T'ang scholarship. One spur to their scholarly work was their desire to translate large numbers of Sanskrit texts into Chinese. Since the two languages are very different, the monks came to pay careful attention to problems of syntax, grammar, and vocabulary. Some of the first books to bridge the language gap were the work of Buddhist monks. Hsuan-tsâng, a famous traveler who made a pilgrimage to India in 629–44, was one of the leaders in this work. He wrote a notable account of his travels and translated some of the complexities of Buddhist thought into Chinese.

An example of Chinese calligraphy. This stone rubbing was made from an inscription in the Regular Style by Ou-Yang Hsün, a scholar and calligrapher of the T'ang dynasty.

First portion of the oldest printed book, *The Diamond Sutra,* 868. It was printed on a scroll from wooden blocks. This page gives discourses of Buddha and shows him teaching.

Chinese Printing

The Buddhists were also probably responsible for the invention of block printing. They wanted to make many copies of their sacred writings, both because the act of multiplying prayers and sacred texts was meritorious in itself, and because they could reach more people by reproducing key passages of their scriptures. They had an ideal material on which to print, for paper had been invented in China in the first century A.D. The Chinese had probably already developed the custom of brushing engraved seals with ink and stamping them on paper, and block printing carried this idea one step further. The text of an entire page was carved out of a single block of wood; the wood was inked; and then a sheet of paper was pressed on it. The first block prints come from the eighth century, and the first printed book (only six sheets of text) was published in 868.

Although preparing these printing blocks required a tremendous amount of labor, once they were ready it was easy to make many copies of a text. Later, Chinese scholars began to experiment with individual, movable type, but this idea was never accepted by Chinese printers. Since there are thousands of Chinese characters, preparing and setting movable type seemed to offer little saving in time and expense. Korea, however, used individual, movable type with great success early in the fifteenth century.

The history of the diffusion of paper and printing shows how isolated China was, in spite of superficial commercial contacts, and how slowly ideas and techniques spread from East to West. Paper, invented in China a little before 100 A.D., began to be used in Arab countries only in the eighth and ninth centuries. Western Europeans learned about it from the Arabs, but it was seldom used in Europe until the thirteenth century and did not become common until the fifteenth. Thus it took over a thousand years for a fairly simple and obviously useful technique to travel to Europe from China.

The history of printing is even more curious. Block printing spread rapidly throughout the Chinese cultural area and was used in Japan almost as soon at it was invented in China. But the Moslems, who sat in the middle of every trade route between China and the West, took no interest in block printing and, except for a few early experiments, never used the invention. Eventually Europe obtained a few samples of Chinese printed work, such as playing cards and paper money, and these may have stimulated some early European experiments with block printing. But there is no evidence that Europeans knew that the Chinese had occasionally used movable type. The typical European method of printing with individual pieces of movable type, locked in a form and mounted in a press, seems to have been an independent invention. It is an amazing coincidence that men at the two extremities of the Eurasian continent—Korea and Germany—discovered almost simultaneously how to put movable type to practical use.

T'ang Poetry

The T'ang period was an age of poets as well as an age of scholars. The Chinese believe that this was their greatest period of lyric poetry and have preserved thousands of poems of the T'ang era. In the West, Li Po (*ca.* 700–62) is probably the best known of the T'ang poets, but some Chinese critics would place Tu Fu (712–70) higher. Chinese poetry tries to recreate a mood, brief flashes of intense feeling caused by the sight of a mountain valley, a sudden rainstorm, an empty road, or piercing moments of clarity in which the unity of nature or the impermanence of worldly beauty is realized. It is often indirect and allusive, and always highly subjective. At its best it is very great poetry, and it has been increasingly appreciated by the rest of the world.

There is a gentle melancholy in much of this poetry; rain, loneliness, and autumnal scenes are favorite topics. One of Tu Fu's poems ends:

A few last leaves are falling, blown by the breeze;
The sun sets behind the curving hill.
How late the solitary crane returns!
In the twilight the rooks are already flocking to the forest.

The same note of sadness appears in many of Li Po's verses:

Before my bed a patch of moonlight shone;
I thought there must be frost upon the ground,
And raised my head and stared at the moon so bright,
Sank back again and longed for my native land.

And at times T'ang poetry becomes sardonic, as in this poem of Li Po:

Life is a journey, death is a return to the earth.
The universe is like an inn, the passing years are like dust.
We complain when we think of the past.
We would complain more if we thought of the future!

In criticism of the T'ang wars of conquest, Tu Fu wrote:

Snow is falling, the army makes its way through the high mountains;
The track is dangerous; for fear of slipping they cling from rock to rock,
Their frozen fingers slip on ice. . . .

There they are far distant from the land of Han [China].
When will men be satisfied with building a wall against the barbarians?
When will the soldiers return to their native land?*

The Fall of the T'ang Empire

The T'ang period was one in which China strongly influenced its eastern neighbors. Both Korea and Japan adopted some of the basic elements of Chinese civilization at this time—the Chinese system of writing, Chinese literary and artistic techniques, Chinese ideas about philosophy and religion. Buddhism came to Japan from China and

*All these excerpts are quoted from René Grousset, *The Rise and Splendour of the Chinese Empire* (London: Geoffrey Bles, 1952; Berkeley: University of California Press, 1953), pp. 155, 152, 163.

	580	618		906		1127	1234	1328		164

Sui Dynasty	T'ang Dynasty	Disunity	Sung Dynasty	Chin Empire	Mongol Empire	Ming Dynasty

960   1279

struck even deeper roots in the islands than it had on the continent. Japanese students read the Chinese classics; in fact, the curriculum in Japanese schools was almost the same as that in Chinese schools. Even in government Korean kings and Japanese emperors borrowed many techniques from their Chinese contemporaries.

The T'ang dynasty flourished for over a century. It then began to suffer from internal weakness and external attacks. As more money was spent on the army, army officers became more influential. Provincial governors gradually gained a considerable degree of autonomy and they tended to be drawn more from the military than from the civilian group of officials. Under these circumstances, the quality of government declined. Intrigue weakened both central and local institutions, while inefficiency and corruption stirred up unrest among the people. On the frontiers, the subject peoples regained their independence and the nomads again threatened the northern frontiers. The Turks inflicted a decisive defeat on a Chinese army in 751 and weakened the T'ang position in central Asia. During the ninth century, the T'ang emperors struggled valiantly against popular rebellions and nomad raids, but their position grew steadily weaker. By 900 they had lost control over many provinces either to their own officials or to outside invaders. In 906 the T'ang dynasty came to an end.

THE SUNG DYNASTY AND THE MONGOLS

The fall of the T'ang was followed, as usual, by a period of disunity and internal war. But this time there was no long gap between dynasties. Order was soon restored by the Sung dynasty, which began to reign in the North in 960 and had gained control of the independent southern states by 979. The Sung were never as strong militarily as the T'ang, and they were always threatened by nomads in the North, who held Peking and northeast China, including Manchuria. The dominant group was the Khitan tribe from whom we get the old English name for China, "Cathay." The Khitan in turn were overcome by the Jurchen nomads. By 1126 the Jurchen had conquered all the lands north of the Yangtze. They established the Chin dynasty that ruled northern China until the Mongol invasion. South China remained under the Sung until the last decades of the thirteenth century.

In spite of military weakness the Sung period saw some notable advances in Chinese civilization. Block printing was much more extensively used than under the T'ang, and the basic religious and scholarly texts were more widely distributed. A history of China from 400 B.C. to the advent of the Sung was written by Ssu-ma Kuang. Confucianism was reinterpreted and strengthened by the addition of religious and philosophical ideas—many of them borrowed from Buddhism and Taoism. Thus the idea that there was a common moral law governing the entire universe became prominent at this time. There was also a strong belief that human reason, pushed to its limits, could grasp the basic principles behind the workings of the universe. These ideas were brilliantly expressed by Chu Hsi in the twelfth century, and this modernized version of Confucianism gradually became the dominant force in Chinese philosophy and religion.

Two important inventions were made in the Sung period. The exact date of the origin of the compass is uncertain, but it was certainly in use by the end of the eleventh century. It is still not clear whether the compass came to Europe from China, or whether it was independently invented in the West. Gunpowder had long been known to the Chinese but had been used only for fireworks. In the twelfth century it began to be used in warfare in the form of bombs and grenades. It is not certain when cannon were invented, but they were certainly used by the Mongols in the fourteenth century and it is likely that the Mongols got the idea from the Chinese. However, as we have seen, gunpowder was not very useful until metallurgical techniques had reached a high level of development. Europeans learned of gunpowder later than the Chinese, but they soon surpassed them in the art of making firearms.

Sung Culture and Government

If the T'ang period was the great age of Chinese poetry, the Sung was the great age of Chinese art. Like T'ang poetry, Sung painting tried to recreate a mood—the beauty and vastness, the harmony and inner meaning, of nature. Like poetry again, the paintings are reduced to bare essentials; a few lines suggest the whole. The landscapes of the Sung painters are especially famous; perhaps no other people ever painted so many landscapes or painted them so well.

The Sung period was also a time of rapid growth of population, industry, and trade. A larger percentage of the people lived in cities than ever before, and this massive urbanization had strong repercussions on agriculture. The production of grain—especially rice—had to be increased, and provision had to be made for shipping food over long distances. China became more of an economic unit than before; merchants and moneylenders became more important.

Such changes put a strain on any society. The strain was especially great in Sung China because this was a period of revival of the Confucian tradition. This tradition was hostile to direct intervention by the government; it stressed ethical principles, not imperial legislation. Moreover, the Chinese of the Sung period were under heavy pressure from the hostile nomads who had occupied lands on the northern frontiers, and the government could not both fight wars and

THE SUNG AND CHIN EMPIRES
Eleventh century

remodel society. Some men, such as the statesman Wang An-shih (1021–86), realized the need for extensive reforms—protection of the poorer farmers by regulating and refinancing loans on small holdings, reform of the examination system by putting more emphasis on practical knowledge—but their efforts had

Civil Service Examinations under the Sung Dynasty

The candidates had to get up in the middle of the night and come to the palace at dawn, bringing their cold meals with them, for they would not be able to leave until the examinations were over. During the examinations they were shut up in cubicles under the supervision of palace guards. There was a rigorous system to prevent bribery or favoritism. The candidates' papers were recopied by official clerks before they were submitted to the examiners, to avoid recognition of their identity by their handwriting. In the recopied papers the writers' names were taken out and kept on file. While the candidates were let out after the examinations, the judges themselves were shut up within the palace, usually from late January till early March, until the papers were properly graded and submitted to the emperor. The candidates were examined first on questions of history or principles of government. There was a second examination on the classics, and finally, after the successful ones had been graded, there was one—under the direct supervision of the emperor—on lyrics, descriptive poetry, and again, essays on politics.

From Lin Yu-t'ang, *The Gay Genius* (New York: Day, 1947), p. 38.

Detail from *Clearing Autumn Skies over Mountains and Valleys,* Sung landscape scroll attributed to Kuo Hsi, *ca.* 1020–90.

only limited results. But in spite of war, the dislocations caused by economic growth, and the misery of marginal producers, Sung China was on the whole prosperous and contented. Especially in the earlier years of the dynasty, almost all government officials were drawn from the intellectual elite of the country through rigorous application of the examination system. The upper and middle classes probably had the most comfortable existence and the highest level of culture of any people in the Eurasian continent.

The Mongols in China

Despite internal strains and losses to the northern nomads, the Sung made a surprisingly strong resistance to the rising Mongol power. At the same time that Genghis Khan united the nomads of the steppes and sent his armies west into

Everyday life in the Sung dynasty. Top: pillow, Tz'u-Chou stoneware. Right: porcelain winepot. Far right: scroll painting of Buddhist monks laundering, by Lin T'ing-Kuei, twelfth century.

Russia, he attacked the Jurchen kingdom of northern China (a nomad state) and took its capital, Peking, in 1215. The successors of Genghis Khan rapidly completed the conquest of the North, but the Sung dynasty in the South held out for almost two more generations. It was only in 1279 that the last Sung ruler was killed—curiously enough, in an attempt to reach Formosa and set up a government-in-exile. China was now ruled by the Mongols, the first time a foreign dynasty had held the entire country.

The vast Mongol Empire was too large to remain unified, however. It was at first divided into subordinate khanates, ruled by members of the royal family under the suzerainty of the Great Khan. But in 1260 the Khan of China, Kublai, became practically independent, and he and his successors ruled China as a separate empire until 1368. Korea was also under the control of this Mongol dynasty, and Kublai annexed Yunnan (now the southernmost Chinese province) and established his suzerainty over part of Indochina. He failed, however, in his efforts to conquer Japan. The Mongols knew little of naval matters and their Chinese subjects were not enthusiastic about an attack on the islands. Kublai finally succeeded in sending a fleet against Japan, but it was destroyed by a typhoon. This was the "Divine Wind" (Kamikaze) that the Japanese invoked during their struggle with the United States during the Second World War.

The Mongols were at first greedy and brutal; they pillaged rather than governed the Chinese. They soon found that there were limits to the profits to be obtained by looting and tried to reestablish the old imperial system. But it was some time before they fully trusted the Chinese; Marco Polo, who knew Mongol but no Chinese, was made a district governor in preference to a native. By 1300, however, the Mongols had accepted many aspects of Chinese civilization and were using a good many Chinese officials in their bureaucracy. They soon restored the prosperity of the country. They built a network of roads, with relays of horses every twenty-five or thirty miles to carry official messages. They repaired and extended the canal system and built granaries to store food against famine. Trade by both land and sea increased, and for-

Marco Polo Describes Chinese Paper Money

ca. 1275

When ready for use, it [a specially prepared paper] is cut into pieces of money of different sizes, nearly square, but somewhat longer than they are wide. . . . The coinage of this paper money is authenticated with as much form and ceremony as if it were actually of pure gold or silver, for to each note a number of officers, specially appointed, not only subscribe their names, but affix their signets also; and when this has been done . . . the principal officer, deputed by his majesty, having dipped into vermilion the royal seal committed to his custody, stamps with it the piece of paper, so that the form of the seal remains impressed upon it, by which it receives full authenticity as current money, and the act of counterfeiting it is punished with death. When thus coined in large quantities, this paper currency is circulated in every part of the grand khan's domains, nor dares any person, at the peril of his life, refuse to accept it in payment. All his subjects receive it without hesitation, because, wherever their business may call them, they can dispose of it again in the purchase of merchandise they may have occasion for, such as pearls, jewels, gold, or silver.

From *The Travels of Marco Polo* (New York and London: Everyman's Library, 1950), p. 203.

eign travelers journeyed throughout the empire.

The Mongols and the West

In contrast to the Sung period, China was now in close contact with foreigners from many lands. While the Mongol supremacy lasted, it was easier to travel by land from Europe to China than it had ever been before or than it was ever to be again until the nineteenth century. Ambassadors from the pope and the King of France visited the Mongol court, and dozens of Europeans found employment there. Marco Polo's book shows how easy it was for a European to travel through the Mongol domains and to obtain office in their empire. His account, and those of other travelers, gave Europeans their first real information about China. Stories about the great wealth and strange customs of this distant land made a strong impression on Europe and did much to inspire the voyages of discovery of the fifteenth and sixteenth centuries.

The Mongol emperors were open-minded and ready to use good men and new ideas, whatever their origin. The Mongol court was full of officials of every race and religion—Persian Moslems, Russian Christians, Chinese Confucians. And with the men came the ideas, such as a new grain crop, sorghum, and a new instrument for handling problems in arithmetic, the abacus.

The Mongols had no very strong religious convictions and were willing to listen to missionaries of every faith. As we have seen, Kublai asked for Christian priests, but the Church had too many problems in Europe to comply with his request. When missionaries were finally sent in the fourteenth century, it was too late. Although there was a Catholic archbishop of Peking in the 1340s, and some thousands of Chinese converts, the small Chinese Christian organization was not strong enough to survive the downfall of the Mongol dynasty.

THE MING EMPIRE
Fourteenth to seventeenth centuries

THE MING DYNASTY

Like most other Chinese dynasties, the Mongol line of rulers degenerated after the first few generations. They allowed the people to be oppressed by corrupt officials and failed to maintain their military strength. Rebellion broke out in the South, and finally in 1368 an ex-Buddhist monk captured Peking. He founded the Ming dynasty, which ruled China until the coming of the Manchus in the 1700s.

The Ming dynasty has had a bad reputation because, in its efforts to wipe out the memory of Mongol domination, it encouraged a rather imitative culture based on the works of the T'ang and Sung periods. Thus the civil service examinations became more difficult and more formalized, demanding an encyclopedic knowledge of Confucian works. The restatement of Confucian doctrine by the Sung philosopher Chu Hsi became the official dogma for all candidates for government posts. In fact, one Ming writer remarked that Chu had discovered everything worth knowing and that no more scholarly books were necessary. In art and in poetry there was the same tendency to imitate or at most to add only a few minor refinements. It is perhaps significant that the most interesting literary works of the Ming period are novels, a form of writing that had not been greatly cultivated before and hence had fewer set standards to follow.

Ming Explorations and Commerce

The early Ming emperors, who were intensely interested in exploration by sea, sent out fleets that surveyed the Indian Ocean and even penetrated the Persian Gulf and the Red Sea. They forced distant rulers, including the king of Ceylon, to pay them tribute and brought back many novelties and luxuries. Chinese shipbuilding and navigation must have been flourishing to make these voyages possible. But they suddenly ceased after 1433, and an imperial edict restricted Chinese shipping to coastal voyages. This decision was probably the result of Ming suspicion of foreign influences and the jealousy that civil servants felt for military men who commanded the fleets. It was a turning point in world history, for it left the eastern seas open to the Portuguese invaders and their French and English successors.

The Ming dynasty was ruling China when the first Europeans reached the country by sea in the sixteenth century. This was unfortunate, for the Ming period, like several earlier periods, was marked by dislike of foreigners and strong belief in Chinese superiority. It is true that the first Portuguese traders were cruel and arrogant, but the Chinese were almost equally arrogant in their dealings with Europeans. They did not reject the obvious advantages of mutual trade, but they tried to minimize foreign influence on the Chinese way of life. They confined the traders to a few coastal towns and dealt with them through a handful of carefully selected officials. They were suspicious of European ideas and even of European technology. Thus the coming of the Europeans tended to reinforce Ming conservatism rather than to stimulate a reexamination and an enrichment of Chinese culture.

At the end of the dynasty the Ming emperors did begin to take an interest in European learning, thanks to the efforts of Jesuit missionaries such as Matteo Ricci. But by this time it was too late to shake off the effects of generations of hostility to foreign influences. China never assimilated European science and technology; after 1750 it became steadily weaker compared to European powers.

Porcelain jar of the Ming period.

Japanese tea ceremony,
painting by Kitagawa Utamaio,
eighteenth century.

JAPAN

The Japanese islands were inhabited at least as early as 3000 B.C., but very little is known about their early history. The first inhabitants were probably the Ainu, who still exist on the northernmost island, and who are very different physically from the Japanese. The Ainu were overrun by successive waves of Mongoloid invaders who entered the islands by way of the narrow Korean Straits. There is also evidence of invasions by Malay-like peoples coming up from the islands south of Japan. All these peoples except the Ainu gradually merged and formed one culture.

The Early Japanese

Chinese records begin to mention Japan after 25 A.D., but these early accounts describe it as a very backward and primitive country. Only in the fifth century A.D. did writing become common in Japan, and then the Chinese script was used. Since Chinese characters were not

well suited to Japanese word forms, the written language could not be very precise. Even today the Japanese use Chinese terms for all legal, political, and moral concepts.

Even more important than the beginning of writing was the introduction of Buddhism in 552 A.D. The old native religion, Shinto, was a rather undeveloped form of nature worship, and, though its supporters made some resistance, Buddhism spread rapidly throughout the islands. By this time there was some degree of political unity on the main island of Honshu, and Buddhism profited from the support of the imperial family. The first great Japanese scholar, Prince Shotoku (d. 621) was especially active in promoting Buddhism, as well as Chinese culture. Dozens of temples with enormous statues of the Buddha were erected, and Buddhist monasteries were founded in many parts of the country.

With Buddhism came a significant increase in Chinese influence. Priests and scholars came over from China, and Japanese Buddhists crossed to the mainland to study with the leaders of Chinese Buddhism. There was great and fully justified admiration in Japan for all aspects of Chinese culture. These close contacts began when China was at the height of the T'ang civilization, and the Japanese borrowed their administrative system, their court ceremonial, their fashions, their art, and their literature from the Chinese.

At the same time, Japan was not a mere imitation of China. It developed its own verse forms, its own drama, and its own style of painting. Tea drinking was learned from China, but the elaborate tea ceremony was a Japanese development. On the other hand, although there were some notable Japanese scholars, learning was never honored in Japan to the extent that it was in China.

Japanese Political Development

The most conspicuous difference between the two countries, however, was in their political development. China had its periods of weak government and civil war, but in general the country remained unified. The emperor and his officials ruled the country effectively and military men seldom had much power. When an imperial family produced a series of weak rulers power was transferred to a new imperial family, but not to the army. In Japan, on the other hand, the emperor was revered as a sacred personage, descended from the Sun Goddess. To remove the imperial family from the throne was unthinkable sacrilege, but most emperors were unable to control the warring Japanese clans. The solution was to retain the emperor as a symbol of unity and as a very remote and formal source of authority and to give real power to the military leaders. Civil wars between the heads of the great military families were frequent, especially in the period from 1200 to 1600. The most honored men in Japan were soldiers, not scholars. While China emphasized civilian virtues, Japan respected, above all else, the military virtues of bravery and loyalty.

During the sixth century A.D. there had been an attempt to make the Japanese emperor the counterpart of a T'ang ruler. The Taikwa reforms (645–650) asserted that he was all-powerful, owner of all the land, and direct ruler of all the people. In practice, however, he had to allow powerful nobles to accumulate great estates, and he tended to lose more and more control over actual government. The leading courtiers intrigued for power and often dominated the emperor by marrying to him ladies of their own families.

Finally, even the appearance of power was transferred from the imperial court. There had long been a custom of appointing an official, known as the shogun (generalissimo), to take full charge of the defense of the country in times of emergency. About the middle of the twelfth century the general Yoritomo succeeded in making the office permanent and the title hereditary in his family for several generations. He established a new government under his control, leaving the emperor and his court with only religious and ceremonial duties.

Japanese Feudalism

Under the permanent shogunate emerged a feudal system not unlike that of western Europe. Beneath the shogun were great lords, the daimyos, and beneath the daimyos were fighting men, or samurai. All these men were immeasurably superior to common peasants and artisans, who had to prostrate themselves whenever a member of the military caste passed by. The whole system was based on the labor of the peasants; a feudal lord was usually given a fief of so many measures of rice, which the peasants had to produce.

The Tokugawa Shogunate

Like feudalism in Europe, Japanese feudalism produced frequent wars. Some shoguns were overthrown and others had little authority. These shifts in power went on for centuries, and in the fifteenth century Japan seemed ready to disintegrate into a group of petty warring states. It was saved from this fate by two great soldiers of the sixteenth century, Hideyoshi and Iyeyasu. Hideyoshi united the country and brought most of the warring daimyos under his authority. When he died in 1598, Tokugawa Iyeyasu completed his work and reestablished the authority of the shogunate. The Tokugawa shoguns ruled Japan from this time until 1867. The civil wars came to an end and Japan remained at peace for almost three centuries.

Hideyoshi and Iyeyasu were also responsible for Japan's long isolation from the rest of the world. During the sixteenth century first the Portuguese and then the Dutch had begun to trade with Japan. With the traders came Jesuit missionaries, who converted thousands of Japanese. Hideyoshi felt that the new religion might cause renewed factional quarrels and feared that European soldiers and colonizers would follow the missionaries. Both he and his successor persecuted the Jesuits and the native Christians, and in 1614 Christianity was outlawed. The final step toward isolation was taken in 1639 when foreign ships were forbidden to come to Japan. The Dutch were allowed to keep a small trading post at Nagasaki, but otherwise Japan was closed to foreign contacts until Commodore Perry forced the shogun to accept a commercial treaty in 1853.

Drawing of Hideyoshi, with an inscription by his son, early seventeenth century.

Suggestions for Further Reading

Note: Asterisk denotes a book available in paperback edition.

The Rajputs
There is interesting source material on India in this period in *The History of India*, Vols. I and II, ed. by H. M. Elliott (1867). R. C. Majumdar, *Ancient India* (1946), is probably the best general treatment of political history to 1200 A.D. Majumdar, a leading authority on Indian history, includes a good critical bibliography. The older study of S. Lane-Poole, *Medieval India* (1903), is less scholarly than Majumdar but presents a more exciting account of India under Moslem rule. V. A. Smith, *The Oxford History of India* (1923), is an excellent reference work. There is considerable material on the medieval period in J. C. Powell-Price, *A History of India* (1955), and in I. Prasad, *History of Medieval India* (1928), which stresses military and administrative achievements.

The Spread of Indian Culture
H. G. Rawlinson, *India: A Short Cultural History** (1938), is a thorough account of India's contribution to world culture and a good starting point for study. R. C. Majumdar, *Ancient Indian Colonies in the Far East,* 2 vols. (1955), is a scholarly treatment of the expansion of Indian culture, and F. W. Thomas, *Indianism and Its Expansion* (1917), treats the same subject in a somewhat more lucid fashion. The best recent work is R. Mukerjee, *The Culture and Art of India* (1959), which gives excellent selections of Indian literature and beautiful illustrations of Indian art. Mukerjee includes a good up-to-date bibliography. A. A. MacDonell, *India's Past* (1927), a survey of India's literatures and religions, traces the growth and spread of its culture. For a valuable summary of India's achievement, see *The Legacy of India,* ed. by G. T. Garratt (1937).

The Moslem Conquest
Undoubtedly, the best account is given in the brief monograph of R. C. Majumdar, *The Arab Invasion of India* (1931). The impact of Moslem rule on the political, economic, and cultural life of India is carefully studied in *The Struggle for Empire,* ed. by R. C. Majumdar (1957), a collection of essays by leading scholars of Indian history.

See also the general works cited above for material on the Moslem period.

European Contacts in the Sixteenth Century
There is an exciting eyewitness account of India in early modern times in F. Bernier, *Travels in the Mogul Empire,* trans. by A. Constable (1891). P. Spear, *India, Pakistan, and the West** (1949), traces the relations between India and the West in a good survey. *The Travels of Peter Mundy in Europe and Asia,* ed. by R. Temple (1956–58), describes East-West relations in the sixteenth century.

China under the T'ang Dynasty
Most of the general works cited after Chapter 6, in the second section, touch upon the T'ang period. W. Bingham, *The Founding of the T'ang Dynasty* (1941), is probably the best study of the early history of the dynasty. *The Veritable Record of the T'ang Emperor Shun-Tsung,* trans. by B. Solomon (1955), is a fascinating picture of China in the early ninth century and gives valuable insight into the old Chinese world-view. E. O. Reischauer's *Ennin's Travels in T'ang China* (1953) is an absorbing summary of the travels of a ninth-century pilgrim. E. H. Shafer, *The Golden Peaches of Samarkand* (1963), is an excellent description of the material culture of the T'ang period. The standard study of Chinese history is K. S. Latourette, *The Chinese: Their History and Culture* (1946), a scholarly and readable work with excellent bibliographic material. Excellent translations of poems from the T'ang period may be found in A. Waley, *Translations from the Chinese* (1941). See also *China, India and Japan: The Middle Period,* ed. by W. H. McNeill and J. W. Sedlar (1971), which is useful for all three countries and especially good on China.

Buddhism in China
*The Buddhist Scriptures,** trans. by E. Conze (1959), contains a good selection of Buddhist writings drawn from the central tradition of Buddhism. C. Humphreys, *Buddhism** (1951), devotes considerable attention to Buddhism in China and is a very good introductory survey. There is material on the growth of Buddhism in China in both L. Wieger, *History of Religious Beliefs and of Philosophic Opinions in China,* trans. by E. T. C. Werner (1927), and J. Edkins,

Chinese Buddhism (1893). The most thorough treatment is that of E. Zürcher, *The Buddhist Conquest of China*, 2 vols. (1959). A good short survey is A. F. Wright, *Buddhism in Chinese History* (1959).

Printing and Scholarship

T. F. Carter and L. C. Goodrich, *The Invention of Printing in China and Its Spread Westward*, 2d ed. (1955), is very important. There is information on printing and scholarship in C. P. Fitzgerald, *China: A Short Cultural History** (1938), and in H. G. Creel, *Chinese Thought from Confucius to Mao Tsê-tung** (1953), a very interesting work by a leading American authority.

The Sung Dynasty

The first volume of the monumental study of K. A. Wittfogel and Fêng Chia-shêng, *History of Chinese Society, 907–1125* (1945), includes texts and translations from major Chinese sources on this period. Since the civil service system was the key feature of the Chinese state, E. A. Kracke, *The Civil Service in Early Sung China** (1953), is important for an understanding of the Chinese political system; this work also shows China as a classic example of the managerial state in practice. J. T. C. Liu, *Reform in Sung China* (1959), reveals the "modern" policies of an eleventh-century reformer.

The Mongols

Both R. Grousset's *L'Empire des Steppes* (1939) and his *Conqueror of the World: The Life of Chingis Khan*, trans. by D. Sinor and M. MacKellar (1967), are reliable accounts which give special attention to political history. The famous thirteenth-century Venetian's trip to the Mongol court is presented in H. Yule, *The Book of Ser Marco Polo*, 2 vols., rev. ed., H. Cordier (1921). L. Olschki, *Marco Polo's Asia* (1960), is a careful analysis of Polo's account. The best account of Christianity in China under the Mongols is A. C. Moule, *Christians in China Before the Year 1550* (1930).

The Ming Dynasty

The most trustworthy general treatment is in R. Grousset, *Histoire de l'extrême-orient*, 2 vols. (1929). There is material on the Ming period in two works of O. Lattimore, *China: A Short History* (1944) and *Inner Frontiers of Asia** (1940), which is more detailed but also more interesting. F. Michael, *The Origin of Manchu Rule* (1942), is excellent for the development of the Manchus.

China's First Contacts with Europe in the Sixteenth Century

The best picture that we have of Chinese-European intercourse is *China in the Sixteenth Century: The Journal of Matthew Ricci*, trans. by L. J. Gallager (1953), an account of missionary activity. C. R. Boxer edited three travelers' adventures in *South China in the Sixteenth Century* (1953). K. S. Latourette, *A History of Christian Missions in China* (1932), is a most comprehensive treatment, while C. Cary-Elwes, *China and the Cross* (1957), though not so scholarly, is more readable than Latourette.

Japan from the Beginnings to the Tokugawa Period

K. S. Latourette, *The History of Japan* (1947), is a quick survey of Japanese history and a good introduction. Latourette is mainly concerned with Japanese influence on China. Sir G. B. Sansom covers the period in more detail in *A History of Japan to 1334* and *A History of Japan, 1334–1615* (1958, 1960). There is excellent material on political and social history in F. Brinkley, *A History of the Japanese People* (1915), an invaluable handbook. The standard treatment of the intellectual achievement of Japan is G. B. Sansom, *Japan: A Short Cultural History* (1943). For economic development, see Y. Takekoshi, *The Economic Aspects of the History of the Civilization of Japan*, Vol. I (1930), a scholarly and readable study. A fascinating picture of Japanese civilization in the twelfth century is offered in M. Shinoda, *The Founding of the Kamakura Shogunate* (1960).

The titles by Latourette, Brinkley, and Takekoshi above have information on Japanese feudalism and religion. There is excellent material also in *Feudalism in History*, ed. by R. Coulborn (1956) and in R. Boutrouche, *Seigneurie et féodalité* (1959). For the Tokugawa period see J. W. Hall and M. B. Jansen, *Studies in the Institutional History of Early Modern Japan* (1968). Probably the best study of antiforeignism in Japan is in J. Murdoch, *A History of Japan*, Vol. II (1964). There is also an interesting study by C. R. Boxer, *The Christian Century in Japan, 1549–1650* (1951).

16 The Revival of Europe

During the course of the fourteenth century economic depression, plague, and war had weakened western Europe. Secular rulers, who in 1300 had seemed close to establishing absolute monarchies, had lost much of their power over the privileged classes and thus much of their ability to main-tain law and order. The prestige of the Church had declined during the Babylonian Captivity and the Great Schism. Most men believed in monarchy as the best form of government; almost all believed in the Church as the only source of salvation. But with both these traditional authorities functioning badly, there seemed to be little hope for religious reform or a revival of security and prosperity. Everyone desired peace, a healing of the schism in the Church, better government, and increased production and trade. But there was little agreement on where to begin, and none of the many projects for reform was very successful.

By the end of the fifteenth century, a startling change had taken place. The economic depression had ended; new industries at home and new trade routes overseas had opened up new opportunities and created new wealth. Kings and princes had clearly gained the upper hand over the privileged classes, especially in France, Spain, and England. The papal schism was ended, and Rome was once more the capital of Western Christendom. New forms of learning based on

The three states of human society: the beggar, the artisan, and the lord. Late fifteenth-century miniatures by Jean Bourdichon.

an intensive study of the classics were competing with or modifying older studies. New forms of art were challenging the late Gothic style. Most important, there was a note of optimism and confidence, of excitement and enjoyment. There was talk of a "new age" dawning, a "dark age" past, a rebirth of the best qualities of classical civilization. By 1500 the basic characteristics of our "modern" world were becoming visible: its dynamic economy and fluid society, its sovereign nation-states and international anarchy, its secular ideals, and its intellectual and moral values.

We can now see that the political and economic revival of Europe was led by the North, while intellectual, literary, and artistic innovations were largely the work of Italy. But this sharing of responsibilities was less obvious in the fifteenth century than it was later, and in the transition from the medieval to the modern world the Italians had the great advantage of being the first to realize that a transition was taking place. They were the ones who talked of a new age, of a break with the barbarous past; they were the ones who believed that a new civilization could be created that would be a worthy heir of Greece and Rome. As a result, in the two centuries between the death of Dante (1321) and the sack of Rome by mutinous imperial troops (1527), Italy exerted increasing influence over the rest of Europe. Italians set the style in architecture, sculpture, and painting; they dictated the literary taste that Europe was to follow for generations. By combining the old ideal of the chivalric, courtly knight with their own interest in learning, they developed a genuinely new social ideal, that of "the gentleman," and the educational ideal of a "liberal education." Italy was the school of Europe. Northerners flocked there by the thousands, and Italians, in turn, appeared in every northern court, even in remote Muscovy.

There were several reasons for Italy's leadership in the change from medieval to early modern ways of life. Italy had always been somewhat different from the rest of Europe during the Middle Ages. It was never completely feudalized, and it early rejected most feudal institutions.

A Renaissance prince and his wife: Giovanni Bentivoglio, lord of Bologna, and Ginevra Bentivoglio. From paintings by Ercole Roberti, *ca.* 1480.

It rejected a unified monarchy under the German emperor even more decisively. Scholasticism never dominated Italian thinking, nor did the Gothic style ever dominate Italian art. Since the medieval tradition in Italy was weak, it could easily be rejected. Moreover the Italian cities had great wealth, large populations, and complete independence. When they tried new experiments in art, literature, and politics, they became powerful instruments of social change.

THE CITY-STATES OF NORTHERN ITALY

The northern Italian cities were dominated by international trade. A third of the population of Florence lived by importing wool from agricultural countries and selling finished cloth all over Europe and the Levant. Almost all the population of Venice depended directly or indirectly on trade in Oriental goods such as silk and spices. In such communities, capitalists—the banker, the export merchant, the large-scale manufacturer—were the most important figures.

The Italian towns controlled the countryside around them as northern European towns did not. They had broken the power of the landed nobility and had absorbed the defeated class into their own communities. Peasant villages and small market-towns had been annexed by large urban centers. Thus city-states were created—that is, a strong city government controlled not only its own immediate area but hundreds of square miles of rural territory.

Class divisions were sharp in these city-states. At the top were the wealthy merchants and bankers—the *popolo grasso*, or "fat people," as they were called. Beneath them were the lesser bourgeoisie, the *popolo minuto*, or "little people"—craftsmen, shopkeepers, and petty businessmen. And beneath them was a growing proletariat of workers. Outside the town walls were the peasants, who had no political influence and little hope of improving their condition. Conflict was constant between the *popolo grasso* and the *popolo minuto*, and occasionally the workers themselves rose in brief, short-lived rebellions, as they did in Florence in 1378. Generally an oligarchy representing the big business interests managed to maintain political control. But the oligarchs did not always agree among themselves, nor did they always preserve internal security or financial stability. During the fourteenth century, quarrels among oligarchs and conflicts between classes became so frequent and so disturbing that town after town accepted the leadership of a strong man and gave him absolute power to restore law and order. These men set up military dictatorships and held on to their power through a combination of ruthlessness and shrewdness. They shed the blood of political opponents without hesitation or scruple, but they were generally careful to improve the city's public utilities, strengthen its defenses, devise an efficient system of taxation, provide

War and Diplomacy

police protection, and above all, foster business. Thus the rise of big business led to irreconcilable personal and class struggles, and these in turn to "the age of the despots."

War and Diplomacy

Oligarchs and despots, realizing that the merchants and shopkeepers disliked military service, replaced citizen militias with mercenary troops called *condottieri.* These troops were not very reliable; they were loyal to their generals rather than to their employers. The generals sought to preserve their military assets by winning wars through clever maneuvers and negotiations rather than by pitched battles. But while they did not fight very much, they did have a monopoly of military power and some generals displaced weak despots or divided city governments, and became despots themselves.

What distinguished northern Italy most sharply from the rest of Europe was the total independence of its city-states from any central government. From Venice, oldest and proudest of the city-

states, on down to towns of a few thousand inhabitants, city governments acted as if they were subject to no superior power. Motivated by economic and political self-interest, each city-state engaged in endless wars, making and breaking alliances, and jealously watching the most powerful state of the moment to make sure that it did not become strong enough to conquer the peninsula. Early in the fifteenth century the Italian city-states began to maintain resident ambassadors at the courts of foreign states to keep rulers in constant touch with governments that might one day become either useful allies or dangerous enemies. At about the same time a kind of "balance of power" began to operate among the five leading states in Italy— Venice, Milan, Florence, the Papal States, and the Kingdom of Naples—in response to an unwritten understanding that no one of the five must be allowed to gain enough power to threaten the others. When France and Spain intervened in Italy at the close of the fifteenth century, both these practices—the basic machinery of modern diplomacy and the balancing of power among a group of sovereign states—spread to the larger stage of Europe. By the mid-sixteenth century, resident ambassadors were common throughout central and western Europe, and a rough balance of power had been established between the ruling dynasties of the two most powerful states, France and Spain.

Milan, Venice, and Florence

Behind these generalizations lie the striking variety and individuality of the Italian cities of this era. Milan, the largest city of the Po Valley, was perhaps the most typical. It submitted early to a despot and about 1400 a Milanese ruler, Gian Galeazzo Visconti, came as close as any strong man of the time to eliminating his rivals and uniting northern Italy. He failed, but the fear he inspired persisted, and no other despot managed to come so close to dominating northern Italy.

Venice, the greatest commercial power of the peninsula, was absorbed in its widespread Mediterranean interests and was relatively isolated from Italian politics until it began to acquire territory on the mainland in the later fifteenth century. Its republican constitution was the oldest and its government the most stable in Italy. There was no despot in Venice—the doge, or duke, was a figurehead—but a tight-knit commercial aristocracy ran the city through a small and tough-minded executive committee, the Council of Ten. Perhaps because the energies of the whole population were so absorbed in commerce, there were no real revolutions and few conspiracies in Venetian history. The constitution of the "most serene republic" (the official title of Venice) stood as a model of republican stability to other Italians.

Florence, like Venice, was proud of being a republic among the welter of despotisms and was especially proud of having helped to frustrate Gian Galeazzo Visconti's attempt to snuff out republican liberties in Italy. But in every other respect Florence and Venice were unalike. Venice lived primarily by commerce; Florence primarily by banking and industry. The most astute bankers and the finest textiles in Europe were both to be found in Florence. The energies of Venetians were directed outward toward the sea; the energies of Florentines were focused on industry and politics within the city walls. Venetian society and Venetian government exhibited a high degree of stability, whereas nothing seemed stable in Florence. Revolution seemed to be the chief outdoor sport and constitution-making the chief indoor sport.

During the fourteenth and early fifteenth centuries the Florentines tried everything from dictatorship to radical democracy; they compromised on oligarchy and finally ended with boss rule. In 1434 a new-rich party within the oligarchy, led by one of the city's wealthiest and shrewdest bankers, Cosimo de' Medici, gained power. For almost sixty years Cosimo and his grandson, Lorenzo the Magnificent (d. 1492), ran the city by manipulating elections and tinkering with the republican constitution. Cosimo was a banker who had been forced to play politics in order to save his financial interests. Lorenzo was more of a politician, only incidentally concerned with the family banking business. But each devoted his energy, his money, and his taste to the job of protecting, expanding, and beautifying the city. The most glittering example of Italy's golden age was Florence under the Medici.

ITALIAN URBAN CIVILIZATION

In these busy, crowded cities of northern Italy a new sort of society and a new set of social ideals grew up, quite unlike feudal society and chivalric ideals. The handicaps of low birth and inferior status could be overcome fairly easily. The chivalric virtues of loyalty and honor seemed irrelevant. Here were urban communities built on advanced industrial methods and division of labor, and dependent on the continental market for their economic existence. Competition was keen at every level, from managing a shop or fashioning an altar piece to serving as banker to the pope or running a city government. Careers were open to talent everywhere, and talent, education, and determination counted as much as high birth or ownership of land. The

The rise of the Medici: Cosimo de' Medici has the look of the wily businessman, while his grandson Lorenzo appears every inch the prince. Above: Cosimo, detail from a fresco by Gozzoli. Below: Lorenzo, by an unknown artist.

man who ended his life as a famous painter, a widely read author, a wealthy banker, or an infamous despot may well have begun life as a poor peasant or a simple artisan. Self-reliance, rational calculation, ingenuity in adapting means to ends, imagination, and boldness—these were the qualities that carried men to the top. And there was always room at the top for creative and brilliant minds, if they had also the will to achieve fame. All these qualities were summed up in a word often on the lips of artists, writers, and statesmen: *virtù*. This was the quality that made a man a true man (Latin: *vir*). It did not mean "virtue" in the modern sense, but rather "virtuosity," that combination of genius, determination, and, when necessary, lack of scruples, that made for greatness in artistic creation, statesmanship, or big business.

Individualism

The first mark of this society, at its upper levels at least, was individualism. Few of the old authorities carried the weight they once had carried for the typical Italian city-dweller. He owed no allegiance to a feudal lord. His gild could not regulate his business practices so closely as it might have done two centuries earlier. The city government demanded strict obedience, it is true, but he had some say in how this government was run and could lay down limits that not even a despot could overstep without facing trouble. He recognized no worldly power of king or emperor or pope within the boundaries of his city-state. And although the city-dweller professed himself a good Christian and a hater of heresy, he generally despised the clergy and tended to accept their authority only when it was backed by strong ecclesiastical sanctions.

Thus in the fifteenth century there was a new emphasis on man as a private person, mainly concerned with himself, his family, his friends, and his own self-development. Such individualism sometimes went to extremes, as it did in the case of Benvenuto Cellini (1500–71), a sculptor who described his violent and colorful career in a famous *Autobiography*.

Cellini assumed that the ordinary laws of morality were made for ordinary people and that they neither could nor should be enforced in the case of geniuses like himself. He also assumed that autobiography, a literary form that had been very rare in the Middle Ages, was a natural form of expression and one that would find eager readers. He begins his book: "All men of whatsoever quality they be, who have done anything of excellence, . . . ought to describe their life with their own hand." Later he remarks, "I make no profession of writing history. It is enough for me to occupy myself with my own affairs." Cellini was obviously interesting to himself, and he was sure he was interesting to others.

Secularism

The second mark of this new society was its predominantly secular tone. This does not mean that it was pagan or anti-Christian. It means that the things of this world increasingly occupied the time and attention of the Italian townspeople—the

---

A Man of Virtú

Benvenuto Cellini, a Florentine goldsmith and sculptor, had struck medals and coins for Pope Clement VII (1523–34). He claimed that he had been insulted by a jeweler named Pompeo (who also worked for the Pope) and after several quarrels, Cellini stabbed Pompeo to death in a street brawl. Clement VII had just died; Cardinal Farnese was elected Pope on 13 October 1534 and took the name of Paul III.

After he had put affairs of greater consequence in order, the new Pope sent for me, saying that he did not wish any one else to strike his coins. To these words of his Holiness one of his gentlemen named Latino Juvinale [a Humanist] answered that I [Cellini] was in hiding for the murder of Pompeo of Milan, and set forth what could be argued for my justification in the most favorable terms. The Pope replied: "I know nothing of Pompeo's death but plenty of Benvenuto's provocation, so let a safe-conduct be at once made out for him." A great friend of Pompeo's was there; he was a Milanese called Ambrogio [Ambrogio Recalcati, a papal secretary]. This man said: "In the first days of your papacy it is not well to grant pardons of this kind." The Pope answered: "You know less about such matters than I do. Know then that men like Benvenuto, unique in their profession, stand above the law."

From *The Life of Benvenuto Cellini*, trans. by John Addington Symonds (New York: Charles Scribner's Sons, 1926), p. 144.

Minters making silver thalers (from which comes our word *dollar*). A heated metal disk has been placed on top of the die, another die has been placed on top of the disk, and the minter is striking the top die with an iron mallet. Detail from a painting by Hans Hesse, Church of St. Anne, Annaberg, Saxony.

next, without denying the ultimate importance of the next. There was a latent conflict between the older and the new ideals. This conflict troubled many writers and artists and led to outbreaks of revivalism in the most worldly cities, such as Florence. In fact, tension between worldly and otherworldly ideals was more typical of the period than was the frank and untroubled enjoyment of temporal pleasures.

Humanism

The third mark of Italian urban society was its enthusiasm for classical antiquity. This enthusiasm came to be called Humanism—from the Latin *humanitas,* as used by Cicero to describe the literary culture proper to a well-bred man. The Middle Ages had always lived in the shadow of Rome, and interest in classical literature was nothing new. John of Salisbury in the twelfth century had a first-rate knowledge of Latin literature, and the greatest medieval poet, Dante, made it his conscious concern to blend the best of both classical and Christian ideals throughout the *Divine Comedy.* However, Francesco Petrarca, or Petrarch (1304–74), is rightly called the father of a new Humanism. His enthusiasm for Cicero, his admiration for Rome (he said he wished he had been born in the ancient world instead of his own), and his feel for the style of classical Latin were contagious. He loved the classics for their own sake, not because they could be used to explain the language of the early Church Fathers. Within a generation or two after his death Petrarch's followers were busily discovering classical manuscripts in monastic libraries, writing letters to one another in impeccable Ciceronian Latin, pouring contempt on the Latin style of medieval scholastic philosophers, and, most important, getting jobs as secretaries at the papal Curia and the courts of the despots, or as teachers of the children of the ruling classes in the cities.

balance of profit and loss, well-built houses and fine clothes, rich food and drink, the enjoyment of leisure—and that the ascetic and otherworldly ideals of the medieval Church seemed more and more remote to them. Their tastes and attitudes are evident in the ribald stories of Boccaccio's popular *Decameron* (*ca.* 1350). The heroes and heroines are not exactly irreligious or critical of Christian ideals, but they despise the hypocrisy of priests and monks, and they rejoice in the triumph of clever people of the world over clerical busybodies.

The secularism of Italian society can thus be broken down into two components: preoccupation with worldly pursuits, and contempt for those who professed the ascetic ideal but did not live up to it. There were a few pagans or atheists. But most men simply thought more constantly of this world than of the

These professional Humanists were something new in European society. Generally they were laymen who made a living by their learning, not clerics or monks devoting spare time to classical study. They were self-made men who were peddling a new type of scholarship to their contemporaries—and who found the market very good. Enthusiasm for the classics was heightened after 1395, when refugee scholars from the Byzantine Empire began to teach Greek to eager students in Florence and elsewhere. And by the end of the fifteenth century a few Italians were even beginning to learn Hebrew and Arabic. Humanism was both a scholarly movement and a social fad. The Humanists revived the study of classical Latin, Greek, and Hebrew, and they got the ruling classes of the Italian cities excited about what they were doing.

The Humanists initiated a revolution in educational theory and practice. Formal education in the Middle Ages had been dominated by the clergy and directed mainly to the production of clerics. The nobility had their own program of training knights to hunt and fight and behave properly at court. But neither of these systems of education offered much to the sons of business and professional town-dwellers, and by the thirteenth century, if not earlier, there were town schools, primarily for laymen, that taught arithmetic and Latin grammar. The Humanists of the fifteenth century rediscovered what Greco-Roman writers had meant by the "liberal arts": the liberating effect on mind and imagination of the study of great literature and philosophy. To this they added the chivalric emphasis on outdoor activity and athletic skill and so formed a new pattern of education. The result was a program designed to produce well-rounded and well-read laymen, able to write classical Latin and perhaps Greek, well mannered and at home in polite society, physically strong and well groomed, skillful in the art of war. "We call those studies liberal," wrote one Humanist educator, "which are worthy of a free man . . . that education which calls forth, trains, and develops those highest gifts of body and of mind which ennoble men." In practice this education too often degenerated into a narrowly literary training, floundering in the grammatical details of dead languages. It was available only to a few and it was consciously aristocratic in its

Young student reading Cicero; detail from a painting by Vincenzo Foppa.

ideals. But at its best it passed on to later generations, including our own, the goal of turning out well-balanced human beings, devoted to both classical and Christian ideals, and able to become better businessmen or lawyers or statesmen because of their liberal education.

Petrarch on the Classics and Christianity

You are well aware that from early boyhood of all the writers of all ages and races the one whom I most admire and love is Cicero. You agree with me in this respect as well as in so many others. I am not afraid of being considered a poor Christian by declaring myself so much a Ciceronian. [This is an allusion to a famous vision of St. Jerome in which God told him: "You are a Ciceronian and therefore not a Christian."] To my knowledge, Cicero never wrote one word that would conflict with the principles proclaimed by Christ. If, perchance, his works contained anything contrary to Christ's doctrine, that one fact would be sufficient to destroy my belief in Cicero and in Aristotle and in Plato. . . .

Christ is my God; Cicero is the prince of the language I use. I grant you that these ideas are widely separated, but I deny that they are in conflict with each other. Christ is the Word, and the Virtue and the Wisdom of God the Father. Cicero has written much on the speech of men, on the virtues of men, and on the wisdom of men—statements that are true and therefore surely acceptable to the God of Truth.

Letter to Neri Morando, 1358, trans. by M. E. Cosenza, *Petrarch's Letters to Classical Authors* (Chicago: University of Chicago Press, 1910), pp. 18–19.

Historical Self-Consciousness

The fourth and final mark of this urban society was its historical self-consciousness. The historical sense of the Middle Ages was not highly developed. The crucial events of the Christian drama had already happened, and time now had only to run on and out to its conclusion in the Last Judgment. Caesar and Charlemagne wore the same costume in medieval drawings. Frederick Barbarossa thought it perfectly reasonable to insert his own edicts in the *Corpus Juris* of Justinian. There had been no essential change since the triumph of Christianity. There was no significant difference between Constantine and Otto III, or between St. Peter and Innocent III. The passage of time brought only minor variations in a persisting pattern.

Petrarch and his Humanist successors in the fifteenth century revolutionized this conception of the past. They became more interested in this world and its history. Their enthusiasm for classical antiquity enabled them for the first time to see the ancient world as a civilization that had run its course. It had been born, it had flourished, and it had died. They talked of the "Fall of Rome" and of a "Dark Age" that had followed. Above all, they talked of a "rebirth," or "revival," that was beginning in their own age. Rome had had its Golden Age and had fallen; darkness had succeeded, but now the light was beginning to dawn once more. The Humanists and their followers were highly conscious of their position in history and of their historical mission.

THE "RENAISSANCE"

While the Italian Humanists were sure that they lived in an age of rebirth, they were not nearly so sure of the profound implications of their work as were later historians. Chief of these was the Swiss Jacob Burckhardt, who wrote a brilliant book called *The Civilization of the Renaissance in Italy* (1860). Thanks to Burckhardt, western historians accepted the idea that there was a "Renaissance," or rebirth, after the Middle Ages, that it marked a sharp break with medieval ideals and practices, and that it was centered in Italy. There was much truth in Burckhardt's thesis, but he exaggerated both the sharpness of the breach with the medieval past and the uniqueness of Italy compared to the rest of Europe.

The term "Renaissance" is most useful when it is applied to the revolutionary change in the arts, in literature, and in the concept of man that took place in Italy in the fourteenth, fifteenth, and early sixteenth centuries. It is less useful when applied to political and ecclesiastical history because it is hard to say what "rebirth" means in these areas. And it is quite useless when applied to economic and social history, in which changes are always slow and in which the important developments began as far back as the eleventh century. Historians of art and literature are relatively sure of what "Renaissance" means; other historians are unsure in varying degrees to the point of total doubt. This does not mean that artistic and literary developments had no connection with economic and social change. It means simply that the word "Renaissance" is best used to describe the changes in artistic and literary taste and skill that occurred at the close of the Middle Ages.

Literature, Philosophy, and Scholarship

Wherever there were classical models to fall back on, the tendency at first was

"The Adimari Wedding," by an anonymous painter, mid-fifteenth century. The painting shows the parade of guests at the wedding reception, held under a canopy outside the church in Florence. Such paintings often adorned the bride's *cassone,* a wedding chest designed to hold her trousseau.

for both writers and artists to lose themselves in simple imitation, in the first flush of excited rediscovery. It was easy, for instance, for Humanists to imitate the letter writing, the orations, the moral essays, and even the poetry of the Romans—and they did, relentlessly, in the early fifteenth century. When it became possible for educated Florentines to read Plato in the original Greek, the Medici fostered an informal group of scholars who became known as the Platonic Academy. Their leading members, Marsilio Ficino (1433–99) and Pico della Mirandola (1463–94), tried to reconcile Platonism and Christianity, as Thomas Aquinas had tried to reconcile Aristotelianism and Christianity. It was the one serious attempt at philosophical synthesis during the Renaissance, and it was a failure. But enthusiasm for Plato and Platonism was infectious and had widespread influence on poets and painters throughout Europe in the next century. In fact, Plato dominated the imagination of the Renaissance as Aristotle had earlier dominated the thought of medieval scholars.

All was not mere imitation in Italian thought and writing, however. Modern critical scholarship, in the sense of careful linguistic and historical analysis of the literary remains of the past, dates from the Renaissance, and particularly from one of the keenest minds of the age, Lorenzo Valla (*ca.* 1405–57). Valla analyzed the language and the historical background of the so-called Donation of Constantine, one of the main bulwarks of the popes' claims to temporal power, and proved beyond a shadow of a doubt that the document was a clumsy forgery of the Dark Ages. He further compared several Greek manuscripts of the New Testament with the accepted Latin translation, the Vulgate, and showed that the translation was full of errors and distortions. The critical spirit and scholarly technique that he inaugurated influenced Erasmus, Pierre Bayle, and Voltaire and resulted in the "scientific" scholarship of the nineteenth century.

Social and Political Thought

Much of Renaissance thought about the relation of man to man simply paraphrased the ethics and political theories of the Greeks and Romans. But sometimes a man wrote freshly from his own experience and spoke directly to the members of his own society. For example, Leon Battista Alberti (1404–72) in his book *On the Family,* described the interests and ideals of the Florentine families he knew: prudence and thrift, strong family feeling and little concern for larger causes outside, appreciation of comfort, planning and foresight, and pride in owning a house in the city and an estate in the country to produce all the family's food. It is one of the earliest idealized portraits of what will later be called the bourgeois virtues.

A late sixteenth-century portrait of Niccolò Machiavelli by Santi di Tito. The artist has tried to suggest both the intellectual brilliance and the shrewdness of the man.

Machiavelli on Cruelty and Clemency

Is it better to be loved than feared or feared than loved? It may be answered that one should wish to be both, but it is much safer to be feared than loved when one of the two must be chosen. Men on the whole are ungrateful, fickle, false, cowards, covetous. As long as you succeed, they are yours entirely. They will offer you their blood, property, life, and children when the need is distant, but when it approaches they turn against you. And a prince who, relying entirely on their promises, has neglected other precautions, is ruined. . . . Men have fewer scruples in offending one who is beloved than one who is feared, for love is preserved by the link of obligation which, owing to the baseness of men, is broken at every opportunity for their advantage, but fear preserves you by a dread of punishment which never fails.

Nevertheless, a prince should inspire fear in such a way that if he does not win love, he avoids hatred; because he can endure very well being feared while he is not hated, and this will be true as long as he abstains from taking the property of his subjects or their women. But when it is necessary for him to take the life of someone, he must do it with proper justification and for manifest cause, and above everything he must keep his hands off the property of others, because men more quickly forget the death of their father than the loss of their heritage.

From *The Prince*, trans. W. K. Marriott (London: J. M. Dent, n.d.), pp. 134–35.

A social stratum just above that described by Alberti is sketched in Baldassare Castiglione's (1478–1529) *The Courtier*, based on his memories of the court of the Duke of Urbino. If Alberti painted the good householder for future generations, Castiglione painted the gentleman—graceful, attractive, courteous, liberally educated, noble in spirit if not necessarily in birth, at home either on the field of battle or among cultivated ladies. The concept of "the gentleman" owed much to chivalry and other traditional sources, but Castiglione presented it as a genuinely fresh ideal in the history of European civilization.

In the case of Niccolò Machiavelli (1469–1527), wide reading in the classics illuminated years of practical political experience. Machiavelli's career as ambassador and secretary of the Florentine government helped him to understand the political history of Rome as described by Livy, and Livy helped him to understand the power politics of his own age. Exiled by the Medici to his country home in 1512, he began to read widely and to reflect on what makes states expand and grow, what are the causes of political breakdown, how political leaders get and hold power, what can be learned from the past.

Machiavelli set down his reflections in a long, rambling book, *Discourses on Livy*, and in a briefer and more famous essay, *The Prince*. He made it clear that he was describing things as they were, not as they ought to be. Ideal states he left to others; in the world as it is, power is what counts. The Roman Republic, he thought, was the best example in history of successful state-building. Its constitution was a masterly blend of monarchy, aristocracy, and democracy; it had good laws and a good citizen army; its religion supported the civic virtues of justice, prudence, and courage, not those of patience and humility; its rulers knew that the good of the state came before the dictates of individual morality. And so Rome, unlike any Italian city-state of Machiavelli's day, had been able to unite the whole of Italy and to endure for centuries.

But Machiavelli realized that this ideal, real though it once had been, might be too difficult for a corrupt and divided group of Italian city-states to revive. Perhaps a prince of real *virtù,* with the courage of a lion and the cunning of a fox, might be able to learn the laws of politics from history and experience and use them to build a strong state in Italy. He would know that men in their collective relations with one another are bad, and therefore he would not be held back by any moral scruples. If others broke faith with him, as they certainly would, the prince must be prepared to break faith with them for the good of his state. Fortune might frustrate his work, but a man of *virtù* had at least an even chance of overcoming bad luck. If his generation had both the intelligence and the will, Machiavelli believed, something could be done about the helpless state of Italy, which was falling under the heels of France and Spain.

Machiavelli's *Prince* was to become a grammar of political and diplomatic practice to heads of state as remote as Mussolini and Hitler. In its origin it was a perfect example of the fruitful combination in Renaissance thought of classical "rebirth" and contemporary "new birth," of historical example and practical experience. Both his disillusioned analysis of things as they were and his passionate plea for reform were entirely characteristic of the age.

The Arts

The influence of classical examples was strong also in the visual arts, but here original elements were even more noticeable than in social and political thought. Roman buildings survived, of course, all over Italy, Brunelleschi (1377?–1446), the greatest architect of his generation, absorbed their spirit and designed new churches in semiclassical style after 1420, thus inaugurating a return to the classical from the Gothic style in architecture. The late Roman sculpture that was dug up (hardly any of the Greek works of the classical age were yet known) inspired sculptors to imitation. But there were no ancient paintings to look at (Pompeii was not unearthed until the eighteenth century), and so Italian painters had to depend on the inspiration

---

Machiavelli on the Policy of Princes

You must know, then, that there are two methods of fighting, the one by law, the other by force: the first method is that of men, the second of beasts; but as the first method is often insufficient, one must have recourse to the second. It is therefore necessary for a prince to know well how to use both the beast and the man.

A prince being thus obliged to know well how to act as a beast must imitate the fox and the lion, for the lion cannot protect himself from traps, and the fox cannot defend himself from wolves. One must therefore be a fox to recognise traps, and a lion to frighten wolves. Those that wish to be only lions do not understand this. Therefore, a prudent ruler ought not to keep faith when by so doing it would be against his interest, and when the reasons which made him bind himself no longer exist. If men were all good, this precept would not be a good one; but as they are bad, and would not observe their faith with you, so you are not bound to keep faith with them.

From Machiavelli, *The Prince,* in *The Prince and the Discourses,* ed. by Max Lerner (New York: Modern Library, 1940), Ch. 18, p. 64.

---

of their medieval predecessors and their own genius in elaborating their art.

Italian Renaissance painting, like that of France and Flanders, tended more and more toward realism. Giotto, the first Italian to develop the new style, was little influenced by northern art; later on some ideas were borrowed from the Low Countries (notably the use of oil paint). But north or south, the dominant interest of fourteenth-century writers, artists, and philosophers was in the concrete, individual thing as it actually existed, not in the general idea or eternal truth behind and in all things, which had been the typical concern of earlier medieval thinkers. Late medieval artists and writers tried to represent nature and man more and more realistically—to model a leaf as it actually appeared in nature, to chisel the features of a real man or woman, to sketch the character of a person in concrete detail, as both Boccaccio and Chaucer did with such success in their collections of tales. In fifteenth-century painting, particularly in the Netherlands, this effort resulted in the most astonishing skill in representing the smallest details of visual reality.

It was an Italian painter, however, who first realized that surface realism is not enough, that the artist must conceive the human figure as a whole, place it in three-dimensional perspective, and arrive at a more sophisticated realism that sacrifices minute details to organic unity. This painter was Masaccio (1401–*ca.* 1428), the founder of Renaissance painting and one of the great innovators in the history of the art.

Italian painting of the fifteenth and sixteenth centuries is far too rich in content and varied in technique for us to describe in detail. Some of its general characteristics may be suggested, however. The first thing that strikes the historical observer is the separation of painting and sculpture from architecture. It was as if the sculptured prophets and many-colored saints had stepped down from their niches and stained-glass windows in the great medieval cathedrals to be reincarnated in bronze statues in Italian public squares or painted portraits in Italian palaces. Painting and sculpture were no longer arts subordinate to architecture. Painters began to adorn the walls of monasteries and houses with frescoes. After they had learned from Flemish artists the technique of painting with oils, the Italians went on to develop the easel painting, meant to be hung in a palace or house and to be enjoyed for its own sake. Donatello (1368?–1466), in his *David,* was the first to model a free-standing nude figure, and from then on to the great works of Michelangelo (1475–1564) sculptors developed their art with no thought but of its own perfection.

The zest for solving fresh problems infected architects as well as painters and sculptors. Brunelleschi went far beyond classical or medieval models in designing and building his famous dome over the transept of the cathedral in Florence (1420–36). Architecture, sculpture, and painting each went its own way. An individual artist might turn his hand to all three, and a painter might borrow ideas from sculpture. But in each case the artist could create as he pleased without subjecting one art to another.

The second characteristic worth noting was the heightened individuality and social prestige of the artist. A famous passage in Cellini's *Autobiography* de-

Donatello's *David, ca.* 1440. Compare this with the David by Michelangelo on the opposite page.

scribes the unveiling of his bronze statue of Perseus in the central square of Florence in 1554. "Now it pleased God," he wrote, "that on the instant of its exposure to view, a shout of boundless enthusiasm went up in commendation of my work, which consoled me not a little." Such a shout might have greeted the proclamation of a crusade in the eleventh century or the triumphant conclusion of a world war in the twentieth. But the public appreciation of a work of art, the assumption that great art is the product of individual "genius," which is something to be nurtured—these were as characteristic of the Renaissance as they were atypical of ages before and after.

The artist was to the age of the Renaissance what the saint was to the Middle Ages and what the scientist was to be to the modern world. Italy's Golden Age was the golden age of the artist and the writer.

In seeking a higher realism, Italian painters studied the laws of spatial perspective about the same time that Humanists were restudying the temporal or historical perspective of their day. As a result the artists pictured real persons whom they knew, in recognizable space. Some of them spent their lives probing the psychological depths of human beings and trying to put on canvas what they found. The chief of these was the lonely scientific and artistic genius, Leonardo da Vinci (1452–1519), whose curiosity about the secrets of nature was as insatiable as his curiosity about the nature of man. In painting *The Last Supper* he chose not the moment when Christ breaks the bread and remarks, "This is my body . . . ," as a medieval artist might have done, but the more humanly dramatic and startling moment when He announces, "One of you will betray me." The resulting psychological crisis experienced by each disciple is carefully portrayed. The climactic episode of the Creation, as Michelangelo painted it on the ceiling of the Sistine Chapel in St. Peter's, was the creation of Adam—an almost superhuman man at the threshold of self-consciousness, languid, wondering, awakening—almost as if he were a symbol of the man of the Renaissance. According to some interpreters, Michelangelo chose to portray Moses at the moment when he has caught sight of his people's idolatrous Golden Calf and is struggling to control himself.

These few examples typify the Renaissance point of view. The central concern is man here in this world, troubled, striving, with unknown possibilities. Thus Renaissance art is humanistic in the broader, more philosophical meaning of the word. Not that the artists rejected God or ignored nature. God is still there, and Renaissance landscapes are charming. But God is seen through man, through man's heroism and his tragedy; and generally nature is of interest only as background or setting to the human

Michelangelo's *David*, 1501–04. Instead of representing David after his victory over Goliath, as Donatello did, Michaelangelo chose to represent him as watchful of the approaching foe, with muscles tensed in gathering strength.

drama. The most important question is what is to become of man. Pico della Mirandola, in a famous *Oration* on man's dignity (1486), pictured God as giving man something he had given to no other creature, the unique gift of freedom:

Thou, constrained by no limits, in accordance with thine own free will, in whose hands We have placed thee, shalt ordain for thyself the limits of thy nature. . . . We have made thee neither of heaven nor of earth, neither mortal nor immortal, so that with freedom of choice and with honor, as though the maker and molder of thyself, thou mayest fashion thyself in whatever shape thou shalt prefer.

Michelangelo, *Creation of Adam,* fresco from the Sistine ceiling of the Vatican, 1508–12.

Leonardo da Vinci, *Ginevra de Benci, ca.* 1481.

Raphael, detail from *Madonna with the Goldfinch,* 1505–06.

Every other creature had its pattern and its limits, but to Pico man's nature and destiny were in his own hands. The men of the Renaissance had not lost belief in God, but they were convinced, in a way their medieval ancestors would not have understood, that man was on his own.

The greatness of Italian art lay in the fact that it reflected all the tensions and contradictions in the prevailing attitudes toward man. There was no party line in Renaissance art; there were no premature solutions of sharp differences, no accepted syntheses. Some artists were realists, others idealists. Donatello modeled despots as he saw them, with hard and observant realism, while Raphael (1483–1520) a generation later idealized the peasant girls he knew as calm and self-possessed Madonnas of ethereal beauty. Some artists were scientists and psychologists like Leonardo, who tried to peer into the souls of men and women, while others were like the Venetian Titian (1477–1576), who was more interested in the external marks of character and the glorious play of color on the objects about him. Michelangelo, perhaps the most typical as well as the greatest artist of them all, gave his life to attempting the impossible: to reconciling the classical ideal of harmony, balance, and "nothing in excess," with the limitless goals and boundless love of Christian piety. This attempt to reconcile the Greco-Roman and Hebraic-Christian worlds was the central striving of the Renaissance. It failed, but the failure left an imperishable record in the arts.

Natural Science

The Renaissance contributed relatively little to the progress of natural science, but this little was important. The Humanists in general were more interested in man than in nature and more absorbed in literature than in mathematics and physics. Nevertheless, even at the height of the Renaissance, the Humanists never had full control of higher education. The old medieval curriculum, which included mathematics and physics, drew as many students as the new curriculum based on the classics. And on the practical side, the desire of the upper classes for greater comfort, and the striving of artists for greater realism, led to significant advances.

As craftsmen, mechanics, and engineers, the Italians were the best in Europe. In the science of perspective, their painters worked out the mathematical principles of representing figures in space. Their artists and doctors together advanced the knowledge of human anatomy beyond where it had been left by the Greeks. The *Notebooks* of Leonardo da Vinci, a landmark in the history of both art and science, show how closely the two interests were related in the fifteenth-century mind. His studies of anatomical detail, for instance, are of equal interest to painters and doctors. Furthermore, the medieval interest in science survived in the northern Italian universities, particularly Padua. There the study of mathematics flourished and the arguments over Aristotelian laws of motion, which had been begun at Paris and Oxford, continued. Padua eventually passed on to Galileo a theory of scientific method in something like its modern form.

THE COUNCILS AND THE PAPACY

Italian energy and enthusiasm did something to dissipate the pessimism of the late fourteenth century. But Europe was still profoundly Christian and could not be entirely satisfied until its religious problems were solved. Of the three difficulties that faced the Church in 1400—the schism, heresy, and administrative reform—only one was completely overcome. By the mid-fifteenth century there was only one pope in Rome, even if the prestige of his office had not regained its thirteenth-century height. The most dangerous heresies had been walled off or driven underground, but the religious atmosphere was still heavy with discontent and revolt. And the more men talked of religious and administrative reforms in the Church, the more impossible it seemed to effect them.

The Great Schism had imposed an almost intolerable psychological burden on Europe. In theory there could not possibly be two true Vicars of Christ, yet there was no way of being sure which of the two claimants was the real successor. Men felt as if they were in a sinking ship: "If we remain in it," a contemporary wrote, "we must perish with it, and if we stray outside, salvation escapes us, since outside the ship there is no salvation." Many Lollards and other heretics had strayed outside. Those who remained on board tried desperately to find some solution.

The stubborn behavior of the two lines of popes at Rome and Avignon, in refusing to resign or to submit to arbitration, had increased antipapal feeling among both clergy and laity throughout Europe. In 1395 the French became so exasperated with their own pope that the French clergy, under pressure from the government, withdrew their obedience from him for five years. This was the first appearance of a policy that was to have an ominous future: secession from papal jurisdiction by the clergy of a large nation under the pressure of the secular government. Even in the fifteenth century there were signs that Christendom might dissolve into independent national churches.

The Conciliar Movement

As early as 1379, the year after the schism developed, scholars at the University of Paris had suggested a more conservative and practical scheme than the withdrawal of obedience. They urged that a general council of the Church be called. The leading advocates of the idea

at the university worked out a revolutionary conception of the Church to support their proposal. The Church, they argued, was not centered in the papacy but was made up of the whole body of believers. Thus the final authority in the church was a council representing all the faithful, and the pope was only a limited monarch responsible to this representative assembly. The so-called fullness of power, which canon lawyers claimed for the pope, was a usurpation. Authority in the Church came from the bottom up, not from the top down. This conciliar theory of the constitution of the Church was to have strong appeal to secular rulers who were looking for a club to hold over the papacy. It was also to have a strong attraction for reformers during the next century.

In 1408 most of the cardinals of both sides deserted their popes and summoned a general council to meet at Pisa the next year. For a moment, a group of cardinals without a pope confronted two popes without any cardinals, but the result was simply the election of a third pope by the council. Unfortunately, neither the Roman nor the Avignonese pope resigned, as had been hoped. After five more years of confused negotiations, the German emperor Sigismund compelled the Pisan pope, John XXIII, to summon a genuinely representative assembly.

This great council, which met at Constance in Switzerland from 1414 to 1418, made a strong impression on the imagination of the age. It healed the schism by bullying John XXIII into resigning, persuading the Roman pope to resign

Mobile bakers, one of the various groups who provided for the delegates of the Council of Constance, 1414–18. Notice the "pretzels" in the upper right corner. From a manuscript version of Ulrich Richental's *Chronicle*, 1465.

after he had gone through the formality of resummoning and approving the council himself, and deposing the Avignonese pope, who by now had fled to Spain and was supported only by Aragon. In 1417 the council elected a new pope, Martin V, who soon commanded the allegiance of all western Christendom. The council was less successful in instituting reform. The English and German delegates worked in vain to have reform considered before the election of a new pope; the Latin nations were more anxious to heal the schism first and let reform come later. Once Martin V was elected, interest flagged in even the mild report of a committee to study abuses, and the council dispersed without ever really facing the complicated malpractices in the hierarchy. On the other hand, the council dealt energetically, though shortsightedly, with the problem of heresy.

John Hus

The danger spot in 1414 was Bohemia. Here during the preceding century the emperor Charles IV had helped to foster a national and cultural awakening among the Czechs. But Czech scholars ran into two obstacles: a corrupt and leaderless Church, and a steady influx of Germans into the cities and into the University of Prague. Since the Czechs tended to be reformers, while the Germans generally supported the *status quo* in the Church, the gifted group of Czech preachers and teachers who attacked ecclesiastical abuses soon found themselves leading a movement that was as much patriotic as it was religious. In 1402 a brilliant young leader appeared in John Hus (*ca.* 1369–1415). The burden of his preaching was that faith must be based on the Bible as the only source of authority, that Christ, not the pope, was the true Head of the Church, and that a man is saved by God through Christ, not by trusting in ceremonies and in a mediating priesthood that was thoroughly corrupt. Hus knew and used the ideas of Wiclif, whose books had been brought to Bohemia by Czech students returning from England, but he had developed his basic theories independently. By 1414 Hus had been excommunicated by the Roman

John Hus being burned at the stake in 1415. He wears a fool's cap with pictures of the devil and the word "heresiarch" (leader of heretics).

pope, but he was at liberty and his ideas were accepted by a majority of the Czech people.

Hus eagerly seized the opportunity to journey to Constance to present his case before the council. He was almost immediately imprisoned for heresy. The emperor, who had granted him a safe-conduct, withdrew his protection the moment the dreaded charge of heresy was made. The conciliar leaders would have preferred a public recantation that could have been publicized throughout Bohemia, but Hus stood firm. In the dramatic trial that followed, the essential issue was whether the Bible and a man's conscience are the ultimate religious authority, as Hus argued, or whether the Catholic Church represented by the clerical hierarchy is the sole authority, as the council declared. Hus was condemned and burned at the stake outside the walls of Constance in May 1415. His follower, Jerome of Prague, was burned on the same spot the following spring.

Before the council disbanded, civil and religious warfare had broken out in Bohemia. It lasted for almost twenty years. The upshot was an agreement in 1436 between the more conservative Hussites and the Church. This agreement recognized a national church in Bohemia with local control over ecclesiastical appointments and with its own liturgical practices, notably the right to offer the cup as well as the bread to the laity when giving communion. For the first time the Church had made an agreement on equal terms with condemned heretics after excommunicating them and solemnly preaching a crusade against them. Wiclif's Lollards had been driven underground in England, but the Hussite heresy had simply been walled off in Bohemia.

The Papacy's Triumph over the Conciliar Movement

The restored papacy, which owed its existence to the Council of Constance, was more successful in defeating the conciliar movement than it was in extirpating heresy. The fathers had decreed at Constance that general councils must be summoned every ten years. But the superior diplomacy and the more efficient administrative machinery of the Roman papacy soon made this provision a dead letter. Leading churchmen and secular rulers ceased to support the conciliar ideal, and by the time Nicholas V became pope (1447–55) the threat that the Church might be transformed into a limited monarchy was over. Never again was there a general council of the church that the pope could not control.

The popes' triumph over the councils left the papacy stronger in some respects but weaker in others. No one within the Church itself could challenge the papal "fullness of power," but the victory had been bought by making wide concessions to secular rulers. In opposing the reforming element in the councils, the popes had isolated themselves from clerical and lay leaders of opinion, particularly in the north of Europe. As a result, the popes depended on the support of lay rulers and could not resist their efforts to control the clergy within their own realms. In 1438 the king of France summoned an assembly of the French clergy and issued a solemn decree known as the Pragmatic Sanction of Bourges.

This decree strictly limited the pope's power of appointment and taxation in France and in effect set up a national, or "Gallican," Church, as it was called. In later years the popes were able to persuade the French monarchs to modify this one-sided action by "concordats," or agreements, between the papacy and the French crown. But in these agreements the monarchy always retained its control over appointments to the higher clergy. With some differences, the kings of England and Spain established similar limitations on papal power during the fourteenth and fifteenth centuries. In Germany, where there was no central government strong enough to stand up to the pope, papal rights of appointment, taxation, and jurisdiction were not limited as they were in the stronger monarchies. The popes had eliminated all their clerical rivals for power, only to be faced by much more greedy and formidable lay rivals—the monarchs.

The Renaissance Papacy

The eighty years between the accession of Nicholas V to the papacy (1447) and the sack of Rome (1527) are often called the period of the Renaissance Papacy. It was a brilliant but tragic era in the history of the Church. Some of the popes of the period were patrons of Humanism and the arts, notably Nicholas V, founder of the Vatican Library, and Julius II (1503–13), builder of St. Peter's. Pius II (1458–64) had been Aeneas Sylvius, a celebrated Humanist, before his election. Two were particularly noted for their wars: Sixtus IV (1471–84), who was rumored to have died of rage at the conclusion of a peace settlement; and Julius II, who was known to his generation as "the Warrior Pope." More than one was notorious for his nepotism, as favoritism to relatives, including bastard children, was called. Roderigo Borgia, Alexander VI (1492–1503), was by far the worst of the lot. His mistresses lived openly with

Cesare Borgia, anonymous copy of an authentic portrait.

Aerial view of St. Peter's in Rome. In 1505 Pope Julius II commissioned Bramante to construct a church that would mirror the classical-Christian aspirations of the sixteenth century. The plans were changed several times, and the building was not completed until 1626. Michaelangelo designed the dome; the colonnades were designed by Bernini in the 1600s.

him; his voracious Spanish relatives got whatever they asked for; and his illegitimate son, Cesare Borgia, made a bloody attempt to become the ruler of all central Italy with his father's help.

All the accumulated evils of many years seemed to become intensified in the papal court: simony, nepotism, immorality, involvement in secular politics and warfare. Two centuries before, Innocent III had been immersed in secular diplomacy, but it had been on a Europe-wide scale and the excuse had always been the advancement of the Church's cause. Now the scale of involvement was limited to the Italian peninsula, and the popes were generally motivated by selfish family interests. As time went on, the papacy became thoroughly Italianized, perhaps out of fear of another schism. (Since the end of the schism in 1417, only one non-Italian pope has been chosen, in 1522.) Most secular rulers came to assume that as ruler of the Papal States the pope would act like any Italian despot, at the dictates of his own personal and family interests—with the unfair competitive advantage, of course, that he was considered to be the Vicar of Christ. But even when the papacy seemed to be simply another Italian principality it was sustained by the basic belief that the office was greater than the man, that the moral character of the pope did not lessen his authority in spiritual matters.

The open corruption of the papal Curia during the fifteenth century had much to do with the Protestant revolt that began in 1517. As one historian has put it, the popes of the Renaissance tried to substitute splendor for reform. In the hands of an intelligent and devoted Humanist like Nicholas V this was not an unworthy ideal. To him it meant reconciling Christianity with the best in ancient civilization and rebuilding Rome as the capital of a revived Christendom. But this ideal did not satisfy the mystical and moral strivings of thousands of the faithful, particularly those outside Italy. Significantly, it was under a cultivated son of Lorenzo de' Medici, Pope Leo X (1513–21), that much of Germany rebelled against the papacy, and under an illegitimate son of Lorenzo's brother, Pope Clement VII (1523–34), that England set up a national Church.

ECONOMIC GROWTH IN THE NORTH

While Italy was building city-states on the wealth derived from its monopoly of Mediterranean trade, northern and western Europe was building nation-states based on new industries and new trade routes. The cumulative effects of technological change began to stimulate the transalpine economy during the fifteenth century. Thus gradual improvements in building and rigging sailing ships made possible the great voyages of Vasco da Gama and Columbus. Da Gama's voyages gave the Atlantic countries an increasing share of the lucrative trade in Oriental goods. Columbus gave the same countries a monopoly of the wealth of a New World. Even though Italian trade remained close to its old level, it was dwarfed by the much greater trade of Portugal and Spain, of France, England, and the Netherlands.

In Europe, new and profitable industries began to appear. For example, im-

An early printing press, as shown in an early sixteenth-century French print.

pended on advances in metallurgy. And that invention, in the middle of the fifteenth century, had even more revolutionary effects than the invention of the cannon. So long as books had to be laboriously copied by hand, only a few men could aspire to higher learning. But as printing presses spread rapidly from the Rhine Valley to Italy, the Netherlands, France, Spain, and England, Europeans had a flood of books available at prices that would have been unbelievable a century earlier. There were "standard editions" of the Bible, the Church Fathers, and the classical writers in both Greek and Latin, scientific works, devotional treatises, and popular manuals in the vernacular languages. Like all mechanical inventions, printing brought both good and evil in its train. The "standard editions" could multiply errors as well as corrections, and the pamphlets that were now so easy to print and circulate in large numbers could mislead as well as inform. But one thing was clear: learning would never again be the monopoly of a small upper class in European society. Anything human beings had written could now be multiplied and placed quickly and cheaply in the hands of anyone who could read.

Industry and Agriculture

New industries such as cannon founding and printing required large initial investment in plant and machinery. They were organized from the start as capitalistic enterprises—that is, enterprises in which accumulated wealth was deliberately used to produce more wealth. In addition to capital, these industries needed and attracted free laborers from town or country who could be employed for a wage and dismissed when business slacked off.

Even in rural areas capitalistic methods calculated to produce a profit were occasionally being applied to the land. Landlords had long realized that raising sheep for wool might be more profitable than accepting a customary rent. Legally or illegally, many of them, particularly in England, managed to fence off, or "enclose," lands formerly reserved for the common use of villagers, or to convert ploughed land to pasture.

proved techniques in metallurgy made it possible to take full advantage of the discovery of gunpowder and to make cannon for sieges and naval warfare. Since more metal was needed, mining methods had to be improved and blast furnaces had to be enlarged to enable metal workers to use the increased supply of ore. The Atlantic states were able to gain control of world sea lanes not only because their ships were slightly better than those of their rivals but because they were more powerfully armed with naval cannon. On land the use of siege cannon weakened the noblemen and strengthened the monarchs, and so increased security. The noble's castle was no longer a secure retreat, and no ordinary noble could afford the vast cost of heavy guns. If they were to maintain their military tradition, the nobles had to become officers in the armies of kings and princes who could afford to buy the new weapons. They were not always well-disciplined officers, but they were no longer independent war-lords.

As we have seen, the invention of printing from movable type also de-

Since tending sheep required far fewer man-hours than raising food on the same amount of land, many families were displaced from the soil. Occasionally "improving landlords" turned to more intensive cultivation of the soil in order to produce a larger cash crop of food for the growing urban markets, often riding roughshod over the preference of villagers for timeworn methods.

In short, capitalism was being applied to industry and agriculture wherever individual entrepreneurs saw profit to be made in producing books, weapons, clothing, or food for sale in the open market. For some peasants and workers this meant new opportunity. Many an ambitious peasant was able to better his position, as Martin Luther's father did by becoming a miner. But a great deal of misery and unemployment also resulted from the breaking down of customary economic relationships, the eviction of

THE FINANCIAL EMPIRE OF JAKOB FUGGER
ca. 1485–1525

Jakob Fugger with his bookkeeper. The cabinet in the rear lists the names of cities where Fugger had branch offices—Innsbruck, Nuremberg, Lisbon, among others. Painting by Matthaus Schwartz, 1516.

peasants from their holdings, and the movement of population to the new industrial centers. "Sturdy beggars" and "vagabonds" were a constant problem for sixteenth-century town governments.

Wealth derived from the new industries and commerce tended to concentrate in a few hands in a few places. For a brief period the most powerful banking house was that of the Fuggers of Augsburg in South Germany. Jakob Fugger (1459–1525) invested in Austrian mines and Spanish colonies and was banker to the pope. On the whole, however, from about 1476 to 1576 Antwerp was the Wall Street of northern Europe, with Lyons not far behind. Then, for a century after 1576, it was Amsterdam. The wealth that poured in from the Orient and the New World had a way of gravitating to the commercial centers of the Netherlands. Where the investment market was freest, where the largest and most aggressive firms transacted most of their business, here were the nerve centers of European finance. Italy was losing its old place as the banking center of Europe. Financial power was clearly shifting to the North.

POLITICAL CONSOLIDATION AND CENTRALIZATION

The most highly developed monarchies of western Europe—England and France—had undergone a severe crisis in the fourteenth century (see Chapter 13). The successors of Edward I and Philip the Fair allowed their political ambitions to outstrip their financial resources. The Hundred Years' War (1338–1453) exhausted both France and England, and plague and social revolt added their toll of misery to war. The monarchs were not equal to the strain. As the fifteenth century opened, France was ruled by a king who had periods of insanity (Charles VI), and England was ruled by a usurper who owed his throne to his fellow barons and to Parliament (Henry IV). The future did not seem very bright for the monarchies that had been so painfully built up in the twelfth and thirteenth centuries.

The later fifteenth century, however, saw a remarkable recovery of monarchical institutions in western Europe. As people grew more and more weary of war, violence, and anarchy, the forces striving to restore some semblance of law and order rallied to the support of the monarchs in France, the Spanish kingdoms, and England. Even weak rulers profited from the demand for peace and strong government. And economic growth made it easier to support stronger armies and more effective bureaucracies.

France

At times during the Hundred Years' War the authority of the French king had almost disappeared, but there had been considerable recovery before the war ended in 1453. Charles VII was not a great king, but he was clever enough to make use of the widespread enthusiasm aroused by Joan of Arc to expel the English and to restore law and order to the French countryside. In 1438, by the Pragmatic Sanction of Bourges, he asserted his authority over the French clergy at the expense of papal power. In the 1440s he solved the financial problem of the crown by obtaining consent from the Estates to a broad-based tax on land called the *taille;* he then continued to levy the tax on his own authority. He organized a small standing army (at most, 25,000 men) under direct royal control, gained the support of wealthy merchants who supplied him with a siege train of heavy artillery, and methodically ousted the English from all their strongholds on the Continent except Calais.

Louis XI (1461–83) carried on his father's work and left the monarchy stronger than it had been since Philip IV. Louis, a slovenly and superstitious man with a morbid fear of death, had none of the majesty of kingship. He was called "the Spider" because he preferred to trap his enemies in diplomatic webs than to fight them. Machiavelli admired him, with reason. The greatest threat to the French monarchy was the powerful state that the dukes of Burgundy had built up on France's eastern frontier, including the wealthy provinces of the Netherlands as well as Burgundy proper. Louis never actually defeated his rival, Charles the Bold, Duke of Burgundy (1467–77), but he shrewdly helped Charles defeat himself. Louis encouraged quarrels between Charles and his eastern neighbors and in the end the duke was killed in battle against the Swiss. The richest portion of his inheritance, the Netherlands, fell to the Emperor Maximilan (1493–1519) through his marriage with Mary, daughter of Charles the Bold; but the strategically located Duchy of Burgundy went to the king of France. At home, Louis encouraged trade and kept a firm rein on the nobles and higher clergy. His successor Charles VIII (1483–98) married the heiress of Brittany and so brought the last remaining feudal duchy under direct royal control.

With France fully under control, Charles felt strong enough to invade Italy (1494) in order to assert his claims to Naples as the remote heir of Charles of Anjou (see p. 261). Spain, which also had claims in Italy, quickly reacted, and foreign armies fought over the peninsula for half a century. The Italian city-states were helpless; even if they had been united they probably could not have resisted such powers as France and Spain. As it was, Spain gradually gained a dominant position in Italy, and with the loss of independence Italian life lost much of

| | | | | Aragon and Castille United | |
| 750 | 1085 | 1212 | | 1469 | 1504 |

| Moslem Rule in Spain | The "Reconquista" | Gradual Amalgamation of Kingdoms into Portugal, Aragon, and Castille | Joint Reign of Ferdinand and Isabella |

its vigor and excitement. On the other hand, France was not greatly weakened by its losses in the Italian wars, an indication of the monarchy's new strength.

Spain

The Iberian Peninsula had suffered almost as severely as France from war and anarchy in the early fifteenth century. From 1085 to 1252 the Christian kingdoms of northern Spain had fought heroically to reconquer the peninsula from the Moslems in a movement known in Spanish history as the Reconquista. By the fifteenth century these kingdoms had coagulated into three monarchies: Portugal in the West, Castile in the center, and Aragon on the Mediterranean coast. The Kingdom of Granada, a small strip in the South, was the last remnant of Moslem rule. In 1469 a momentous marriage took place between Ferdinand of Aragon (1479–1516) and Isabella of Castile (1474–1504). The marriage brought no organic fusion of the political institutions of the two states, but husband and wife followed a common foreign policy and their heir could properly be called king of "Spain." A new national monarchy had been born from a dynastic union.

Isabella reestablished the authority of the crown in Castile and with her husband led a successful "crusade" to expel the Moors (as the Moslems in Spain were called) from Granada in 1492. The victory touched off a wave of national patriotism and religious intolerance, which had been slowly gathering force during the later fifteenth century. In 1492 all Jews in both kingdoms were ordered either to become Christians or leave the land, and ten years later, in spite of promises of toleration when Granada fell, all Moors in Castile were offered the same choice. In 1478 some Dominicans had persuaded the pope to authorize Ferdinand and Isabella to set up the Spanish Inquisition. This dreaded in-strument became a powerful force toward royal absolutism when the monarchs directed it against "converted" Jews and Moors who were suspected of secretly adhering to their old beliefs. There was thus a note of religious fervor and racial hatred, which was lacking elsewhere, in the birth of Spain as a great power.

A second marriage was greatly to affect Spain's European destiny in the sixteenth century. The Emperor Maximilian and his wife, Mary of Burgundy, had a son, Philip, who was heir to Austria through his Habsburg father and to the Netherlands through his mother. Philip married Joanna, the daughter of Ferdinand and Isabella. Their son Charles, born in 1500, eventually became

Habsburg Emperor Maximilian I (left rear) and his wife, Mary of Burgundy, flank their son, Philip. Philip's marriage to Joanna, daughter of Ferdinand and Isabella of Spain, produced a son (front center) who became Charles V, Holy Roman Emperor and King of Spain.

king of Spain (1516–56) and ruler of the Netherlands, Austria, Milan, Naples, and the Spanish possessions in America. In 1519 the German princes elected him emperor as Charles V. Thus Spain was thrust out into the full stream of European politics and world empire by coming under the Habsburg dynasty in 1516.

Spain was not a wealthy country, nor were its two halves, Castile and Aragon, ever thoroughly amalgamated. Even today Catalonia is markedly different from Castile. But the Spanish armies soon proved themselves the best in Europe during campaigns in Italy and the Netherlands, and Columbus' discoveries brought in a stream of gold and silver from the New World that surpassed all European dreams of wealth. As a result, Spain was to become the leading power in Europe in the sixteenth century.

England

The Hundred Years' War had been a heavy burden on England. But its most severe trial followed the end of the war, when a restless nobility and professional soldiery returned from France to plunge into thirty more years of intermittent civil strife in the Wars of the Roses (1454–85). When it was all over, the first of the Tudors was on the throne as Henry VII (1485–1509), by right of conquest and a dubious hereditary claim. The bloodshed and violence of the wars had sickened the people, and plots and counterplots had killed off most of the leaders of the nobility. Taking advantage of the opportunity to restore the monarchy, Henry proved himself one of the ablest rulers in English history. He kept England out of foreign wars, encouraged trade, restored the sources of royal revenue, and eliminated all pretenders to the throne. His son, Henry VIII (1509–47), inherited a full treasury, a united nation, and (for its day) an efficient administration. Henry VIII soon wasted the

treasury surplus in war with France, but he and his overbearing minister, Cardinal Wolsey, did manage to concentrate power in their own hands. Henry VIII's England could compare well with either France or Spain in governmental efficiency and potential military strength, even though it had only about half Spain's population and a fourth that of France.

The Monarchs and the Nobility

Louis XI, Ferdinand and Isabella, and Henry VII all had common problems, which they met in strikingly similar ways. The chief obstacle in the path of rebuilding royal authority in the later fifteenth century was the military, political, and economic strength of the great nobles in each country (the kings were wise enough never to attack the social prestige of the nobility). The monarchs used various expedients in their cold war with overmighty subjects. The key to success was to make the royal Council an effective agency of central government. Councillors were selected from among nobles who were loyal to the king and from members of the upper middle class who sought power and promotion. Key councillors, often at their own expense, developed groups of agents who kept them informed about internal and external threats to the security of the state. At the same time the Council, or one of its committees, was given supreme judicial power so that it could act quickly in any emergency. Thus in England the Secretaries of State, who were the most influential members of the Council, were well aware of plots against the throne through their close contacts with local authorities, with English ambassadors abroad, and with a network of spies. The Star Chamber, the judicial arm of the Council, could be used to suppress any manifestations of aristocratic independence, and the ordinary courts almost never failed to convict men accused by the Council. In France and Spain the Council was equally well informed and had even greater judicial power.

The Monarchs and the Representative Assemblies

A second possible obstacle to royal absolutism was the representative assembly: the Estates General in France, the Cortes in the Spanish kingdoms, and Parliament in England. These assemblies had reached the peak of their influence in the fourteenth century. In the fifteenth century, they declined everywhere but in England. This was due more to the ineffectiveness of assemblies than to the hostility of monarchs. Except in England, provincial feeling was so strong that it was difficult to reach agreement on any issue. Assemblies were more ready to grumble than to act. In France, for example, the Estates General, in spite of repeated requests, neither supported nor proposed clear-cut alternatives to royal policies. It is also true that the kings had weakened the Estates by depriving them of their financial powers; old taxes were continued and new ones imposed by royal authority alone. Thus the Estates General of France were weak and useless and gradually ceased to meet. In Spain, the monarchs played off class against class by summoning only the representatives of the cities when they needed money, thus depriving the townsmen of the possible aid of the great nobles. Anxious to support royal authority, the town representatives usually consented readily to whatever taxes the king demanded. Deprived of any real power, the Cortes of Castile, like the Estates General of France, met less and less frequently after the end of the fifteenth century.

In England Henry VII apparently had little respect for Parliament and, after the first years of his reign, seldom summoned it. But, since the English Parliament could speak for all the privileged classes and all parts of the country, it was more difficult to ignore than the weak and divided assemblies of other countries. In England provincial rivalries scarcely existed; landowners and the bourgeoisie usually cooperated, and no general tax could be levied without Parliamentary consent. When Henry VIII got into trouble with the pope, he summoned Parliament to give him support. This use of Parliament as an accomplice had unanticipated results. By 1600, thanks to the frequent use Henry Tudor and his successors made of it, Parliament had become a more powerful force in English government than ever before. By that time the representative assemblies on the Continent, in states governed by absolute monarchs, had become hollow forms.

Effigies on the tombs of Ferdinand of Aragon and Isabella of Castile, the "Catholic Kings" who created a united Spain.

The Monarchs and the Church

The final obstacle to the development of monarchical power was the Church. Against this obstacle the kings moved cautiously. Louis XI was proud to be called "Most Christian King" of France, Ferdinand and Isabella were proud to be known as the "Catholic Kings," and Henry VIII was especially proud of his title "Defender of the Faith," which the pope granted him in 1521. But on the three crucial questions of appointment of the higher clergy, taxation of the clergy, and the appeal of ecclesiastical cases to Rome not one of the monarchs admitted the full papal claims. The kings of England and France had established their right to tax their own clergy by 1300. The French kings had asserted their right to control clerical appointments in the Pragmatic Sanction of Bourges, and the pope had granted Francis I the right to nominate the higher clergy and to settle the bulk of ecclesiastical disputes in France in the Concordat of Bologna in 1516. Even the "Catholic Kings" of Spain asserted and maintained their right to appoint, to tax, and to reform the clergy within their kingdoms, despite papal objections. Thus long before the Protestant Reformation there were "national churches" in Europe that looked to the authority of the secular ruler in matters of appointment, taxation, and even jurisdiction, although not in doctrine.

Consolidation and Centralization Elsewhere in Europe

These tendencies in western Europe toward the consolidation of territory and the centralization of political power also appeared in the kingdoms of Norway and Sweden. They appeared too in Russia, where Ivan the Dread (1534–84) ruthlessly broke the power of the aristocracy. In Italy, however, there was no central government to be strengthened (much to the despair of observers like Machiavelli). In the German Empire the central government was a sham. There was no imperial army, no system of imperial taxation, no imperial supreme court with overriding authority. An attempt at the close of the fifteenth century to give the Empire these advantages was almost a total failure. When Charles V became emperor in 1519, his real strength lay in the fact that he was duke of Austria, lord of the wealthy towns of the Netherlands, and king of Spain, with its well-equipped armies and overseas treasure. Becoming emperor added something to his prestige, much to his responsibilities, but little to his power. Many German princes expanded their territories at the expense of weaker neighbors and increased their authority within their principalities by methods very similar to those of the kings of western Europe. But in 1500 there was no central authority in Germany strong enough to resist papal exactions, foreign intervention, or the spread of heresy.

This lack of central authority was to be of crucial importance for the future. On the one hand, it meant that the Protestant Reformation, once it started, could not be brought under control. On the other, it meant that the emperor could rely only on his own hereditary domains in meeting a new threat that came from the East. The Turks had advanced steadily after the fall of Constantinople in 1453. The greatest of their sultans, Suleiman the Magnificent (1520–66), captured Belgrade, won most of Hungary in the battle of Mohacs (1526), and almost took Vienna in 1529. With a divided Germany behind him and a dangerous enemy facing him in the Danube Valley, the emperor could not play his old role of defender of Christendom until he had built a new state out of the old Habsburg territories.

Suggestions for Further Reading

Note: Asterisk denotes a book available in paperback edition.

General J. Burckhardt's great "essay," *The Civilization of the Renaissance in Italy** (1860), is still the starting point for study. J. A. Symonds, *The Renaissance in Italy,** 7 vols. (1875), is more readable but less scholarly than Burckhardt. W. K. Ferguson, *The Renaissance in Historical Thought* (1948), traces the development of the idea of "rebirth" from the Humanists themselves through Burckhardt to the present. The same author has also written a good brief survey, *The Renaissance** (1940). The introductory volume to the *Rise of Modern Europe* series, ed. by W. L. Langer, by E. P. Cheyney, *The Dawn of a New Era: 1250–1453** (1936), treats economic, political, and cultural phenomena which were to have significance for later centuries. The next volume in the series is M. P. Gilmore, *The World of Humanism: 1453–1517** (1952). Both make excellent use of recent monographic material and offer critical bibliographies. D. Hay, *The Italian Renaissance** (1962), is a new work of considerable value.

Italian Society and Politics	A. W. O. von Martin, *Sociology of the Renaissance** (1941), is a good example of the approach to the Renaissance of modern social historians. There is interesting material on Renaissance businessmen and bankers in M. Beard, *A History of the Business Man* (1938), and R. de Roover, *The Medici Bank* (1948). I. Origo, *The Merchant of Prato* (1957), is an enjoyable study of a small-town businessman. G. Mattingly, *Renaissance Diplomacy** (1955), traces the origins of modern diplomacy in Italy in a fascinating way. There are histories of all the major Italian states, but the most important for an understanding of the Renaissance are those on Florence. F. Schevill, *A History of Florence** (1936), is the best brief treatment in English. Based on this is the same author's briefer *The Medici** (1949). D. Herlihy, *Pisa in the Early Renaissance* (1958), and W. M. Bowsky, *The Finance of the Commune of Siena* (1970), provide the history of two other leading cities. H. Baron, *The Crisis of the Early Italian Renaissance,** 2 vols. (1955), is an important recent study of Florentine politics and culture in the early fifteenth century. Perhaps the best single volume on Machiavelli is F. Chabod, *Machiavelli and the Renaissance** (1958). D. Merejkowski's novel, *The Romance of Leonardo da Vinci** (1902), gives a vivid and unforgettable picture of Italian society based on sound historical scholarship. D. S. Chambers, *The Imperial Age of Venice: 1380–1580** (1970), examines Venice's power as a commercial enterprise.

Literature and Art	Most of the general works listed above contain discussion of the literary and artistic achievements of the age. The classic literary history, still well worth reading, is F. de Sanctis, *History of Italian Literature* (1870; trans. 1931). G. Highet, *The Classical Tradition** (1949), traces Greek and Roman influences on western literature. P. O. Kristeller, *Renaissance Thought** (2 vols., 1961, 1965), is a brief but penetrating analysis. The best introduction to the educational theories of the Humanists is W. H. Woodward, *Vittorino da Feltre and Other Humanist Educators** (1905). Of the many works on Italian Renaissance art, two by masters of their subjects may be mentioned: B. Berenson, *The Italian Painters of the Renaissance,** rev. ed. (1930), and E. Panofsky, *Renaissance and Renascences in Western Art,* 2 vols. (1965). An older handbook, still useful, is H. Wölfflin, *The Art of the Italian Renaissance** (1903; edited as *Classic Art,* 1952). A. C. Krey, *A City That Art Built* (1936), is an interesting brief attempt to relate cultural flowering to economic and political circumstances in Florence. See also A. Smart, *The Renaissance and Mannerism in Italy* (1971).

Contemporary Writings	It is easy to become acquainted with the thought of Renaissance writers because of the number of readily available translations. Two source collections are particularly good: *The Renaissance Philosophy of Man,** ed. by E. Cassirer (1948), which includes Pico's *Oration,* and *The Portable Renaissance Reader,** ed. by J. B. Ross and M. M. McLaughlin (1953), which includes a selection from Alberti's *On the Family.* There are many editions of Boccaccio's *Decameron,* Cellini's *Autobiography,* and Castiglione's *The Courtier.* N. Machiavelli, *The Prince and the Discourses** (trans. 1940; Modern Library), is the most convenient edition. C. B. Coleman has edited *The Treatise of Lorenzo Valla on the Donation of Constantine* (1922), and E. A. McCurdy has edited *The Notebooks of Leonardo da Vinci,* 2 vols. (1938). *The Vespasiano Memoirs** (trans. 1926) offer contemporary thumbnail sketches of Humanists, artists, and princes. B. Burroughs has recently edited Vasari's *Lives of the Artists** (1961).

The Church	There is a full account of the Councils of Constance and Basel and of the Renaissance popes in the five-volume work by an Anglican bishop, M. Creighton, *A History of the Papacy from the Great Schism to the Sack of Rome* (1882–94). The best account, however, based on the Vatican archives, is the still larger work of the Swiss Catholic, L. Pastor, *History of the Popes,* 40 vols. (trans. 1891–1953). On conciliar ideas, see B. Tierney, *Foundations of the Conciliar Theory* (1955), and E. F. Jacob, *Essays in the Conciliar Epoch* (1953).

Technological and Economic Growth in the North	L. Mumford, *Technics and Civilization** (1934), is always stimulating but often inaccurate in detail. On printing, see P. Butler, *The Origin of Printing in Europe* (1940); D. C. McMurtrie, *The Book: The Story of Printing and Bookmaking,* 3rd rev. ed. (1943); E. P. Goldschmidt, *The Printed Book of the Renaissance* (1950); and V. Scholderer, *Johann Gutenberg,* (1963). R. Ehrenberg, *Capital and Finance in the Age of the Renaissance* (trans. 1928), is a study of the Fuggers. The Fugger Newsletters of the later sixteenth century are available in *News and Rumor in Renaissance Europe.**

17

Reform and Revolution in Western Christendom

In this anonymous allegorical painting, Luther's protector, Frederick the Wise of Saxony (far right), dreams that Luther is posting his theses with a gigantic quill pen.

At the opening of the sixteenth century, the Roman Church was in greater danger than it had been at any time since the Great Schism. Suspicion of Church policy and contempt for the leadership of the Church were widespread. Even the peasants were annoyed by the financial demands of the clergy and bored by routine services; many of them were ready to respond to radical evangelical preachers. There had always been some tension between the Church and the bourgeoisie. The Church had never been able to incorporate business ethics into its system of values, and the bourgeoisie had never been happy about the Church's special financial privileges. The better educated the townsmen became, the more clearly they saw the weaknesses of the Church. The nobility either denounced the corruption of the Church or profited from it.

Most dangerous of all were the secular rulers who were limiting the papacy's powers of taxation, jurisdiction, and appointment. Caught in the maelstrom of Italian power politics, the popes of the fifteenth century found themselves threatened by leagues of Italian princes and thus forced to seek help from and make concessions to more distant and more powerful rulers. The popes had no military power of their own. Moreover, by 1500 they were regularly in debt, with little prospect of finding any easy way out of their financial straits.

THE NEED FOR REFORM IN THE WESTERN CHURCH

Even able and devoted Vicars of Christ might have had difficulty defending the independence of the papacy and raising its moral prestige. But this was the era of the Renaissance popes—at best, good administrators and patrons of artists and scholars; at worst, corrupt and immoral men with secular tastes and interests. Some, like Alexander VI, used the contributions of the faithful to carve out principalities for their illegitimate sons. Most of them, under financial pressure, sold justice in their courts and appointments to office in their councils.

Bishops and archbishops throughout Europe were generally of noble blood, and many of them had been nominated by monarchs or by the pope for loyal service rather than for their piety or administrative ability. Some held more than one bishopric, although this was contrary to canon law, and some rarely visited their sees (one bishop visited his only once, when he was buried there). Even conscientious bishops found that their power to appoint the clergy and to reform abuses within their dioceses had diminished. Many powers that properly belonged to the bishop had either fallen into the hands of local laymen or had been "reserved" by the pope. The ignorance and immorality of the parish clergy were bywords among contemporary writers. The parish priest in fact was no better or worse than he had been for centuries, but moral sensitivity to clerical misconduct had been rising. Furthermore, the tithes that the priest levied and the fees that he charged for baptisms, marriages, and burials were burdensome to peasants and small craftsmen. In earlier centuries monks and friars had made up for many of the deficiencies of the parish clergy, but by 1500 the religious orders had little influence on laymen. Monastic life no longer attracted the pious, as it had several centuries earlier, and monasteries now had to search out recruits to keep their numbers up.

The most widespread complaints were caused by practices that could be interpreted as the selling of spiritual benefits. The Church was rich in land but poor in the newer forms of wealth. It cost money to maintain such a large institution, and the clergy had a right to ask for a fair share of the growing wealth of Europe. But the methods used to raise money and the purposes for which the money was spent (such as waging war to regain territory claimed for the Papal States) outraged many believers. Papal demands for money were passed from the bishops to the parish clergy to the people. Thus some priests demanded the best garment of a deceased parishioner as a "mortuary fee" and had regular tables of charges for other religious rites. Even worse were the abuses that the pope allowed to creep into the sale of indulgences.

A pair of woodcuts by Cranach the Elder contrasting Jesus and the pope. In one, Jesus is driving the money-changers from the temple; in the other, the pope is taking money for indulgences.

Indulgences

Indulgences, in fact, were the raw nerve of the Church's whole financial system. An indulgence was a remission of the temporal penalty for sin (penances in this life and the pains of Purgatory after death) imposed by a priest in the sacrament of penance. It was granted on condition of true contrition for the sin and in consideration of some pious deed performed, such as going on a crusade or a pilgrimage. During the Middle Ages a money "contribution" became the normal consideration, and the necessity for contrition was often forgotten by the believer. In the fourteenth century the popes developed the doctrine that Christ and the saints had accumulated a "treasury of merits" from which Christ's Vicars could dispense benefits to the faithful through indulgences. In the fifteenth century Sixtus IV, on the strength of this doctrine, claimed the power to release the souls of the dead from the penance they were undergoing in Purgatory as the temporal penalty for their sins. This claim helped make the indulgence trade even more lucrative. It was hard to withhold a contribution that would release the soul of a dead parent from years of suffering in the next world. In theory, contrition was still necessary, and the money was a "contribution." But many laymen concluded that the Church was selling salvation at a price—and was then wasting the money on petty wars and luxurious living.

The Dangers of Criticism

Criticism of the Church was not new. Though the Church was divinely instituted, everyone knew that it was administered by fallible human beings—that is, by sinners. The moral state of the clergy was probably better in 1500 than in the year 1000. But the world of 1500 was far different from that of 1000, and it is well to review some of the main differences in order to understand why criticism now constituted a real danger to the Church.

The European world of 1500 was more secular in its interests and ideals, as we have seen. The artist, the despot, the sea captain, and the businessman were pursuing careers that seemed more exciting than sainthood, and the medieval interpretation of life in this world as a pilgrimage to life after death seemed unsatisfying, even though it was not yet openly rejected. Granted that salvation was the goal of mankind, some men began to ask: Was renunciation of the world the only, or even the surest, way to gain that goal?

While the fifteenth century was an age of increasing secular interests for

In the first of this pair of woodcuts Cranach shows Jesus kissing the feet of his disciples as he washes them. The other woodcut shows the pope offering his foot to be kissed by kings and nobles.

some, it was an age of heightened religious sensitivity and piety for others. Both the worldly-minded and the devout were becoming critical of the growing complexity of the Church's sacraments and ceremonies. Popular piety of the late Middle Ages had nurtured a luxuriant growth of religious practices that seemed to verge on superstition and idolatry. The cult of the saints and the veneration of relics became a kind of obsession. For almost every human ill there was a saint, who, if properly approached, could prevent or heal the affliction. And as the number of sacred symbols and ceremonies multiplied, their religious significance almost disappeared. A fifteenth-century French artist painted a sensual, photographic portrait of the French king's mistress as the Virgin Mary, apparently without being conscious of any blasphemy. As a modern historian has put it, the religious atmosphere of the later Middle Ages was "supersaturated," and the most observant church leaders of the fifteenth century grew worried. They saw that the Church was becoming dangerously vulnerable to radicals who might ask: What is the core of Christianity? Is it to venerate an image of St. Anthony, to avoid meat on Fridays, and to go on a pilgrimage? Or, rather, is it to love one's neighbor and to live a Christlike life?

A final reason why ecclesiastical abuses were so dangerous to the Church in 1500 was that there were now secular rulers strong enough to use the cry for reform for their own purposes. The monarchs of western Europe were already appointing and taxing the clergy. The upper classes all over Europe coveted the wealth of the Church. Many secular rulers, should they so decide, now had the power to confiscate the Church's lands, buildings, and revenues in the name of reform. Reform by royal command sometimes had good results. In Spain, Cardinal Jiménez de Cisneros, strongly backed by Ferdinand and Isabella, instituted many reforms in the Spanish clergy at the opening of the sixteenth century. But there was always the danger that reform by a secular power might result in state control of the Church and confiscation of its property.

Failure of Fifteenth-Century Reform Movements

Various schemes for reform had been advanced in the fifteenth century. In the Rhineland, the Brethren of the Common Life, a group of laymen who devoted themselves to communal living and biblical piety, emphasized direct, intimate communion with God in their communities and schools. In Florence between

1494 and 1498 one of the most remarkable preachers of the age, the Dominican monk Girolamo Savonarola, moved multitudes to repentance and for a time had the crowds making bonfires of their wigs, makeup, and other "vanities." These reformers still held to the medieval conception of reform. According to that conception, the Church itself was divinely constituted and so could not be "reformed," but the individuals who composed it could and should be regenerated. The leaders at the councils of Constance and Basel were reformers of a more modern sort. They meant to reform the institution itself by giving more power to representatives of the clergy, thus making the pope a limited monarch. Hus wanted to reform both the individual and the institution by returning to the Bible as the standard of Christian living and ecclesiastical practice.

Each of these differing conceptions of reform was to take root and bear seed in one way or another during the sixteenth century. But before 1500 the impetus of each movement was soon spent and the institutional abuses remained untouched. The councils failed to make permanent changes in the constitution of the Church, and both Hus and Savonarola were executed as heretics. Whenever attempts at reform threatened to undermine the status of the clergy as mediators between God and man, or the power of the pope as the Vicar of Christ, they were declared heretical and stamped out. It seemed that the strength of vested interest and the dead weight of authority were so strong that the Church would never be roused from its complacency.

Christian Humanism

A new and hopeful type of reform movement emerged in the sixteenth century—Christian Humanism. Under the inspiration of the classical revival in Italy, a number of scholars in northern Europe began to recommend a return to the best of both the classical and the Christian traditions through a study of the classics and the Bible. They argued that if men could appreciate the ethical perfection of Socrates and Jesus, of Plato and Paul, then the absurdities of theological hair-splitting and the irrelevance of many ecclesiastical practices would become evident. Reform would inevitably follow from a better understanding of the simplicity of primitive Christianity—and of the noble ideals of the Greeks and Romans, which they felt to be complementary rather than antagonistic to Christianity. Let the Church take for its guides the Bible and the early Fathers rather than the scholastic theologians of the Middle Ages. Abuses would disappear if laymen and clerics alike would recognize that Christianity was an attitude of mind and a way of life, not a complex set of dogmas and ceremonies.

This program was fundamentally conservative, designed to save the Church from itself. Its leaders were almost without exception loyal to Rome. It was obviously optimistic in its estimate of human nature. It rated the power of reason and education very high. It encouraged historical and literary studies in the hope that they would reveal earlier and purer practices. Cardinal Jiménez in Spain set scholars to producing a monumental edition of the Bible that presented the original Hebrew and Greek texts in parallel columns with the Latin. In Germany, Johann Reuchlin defended the

---

Erasmus' Preface to His Edition of the New Testament

I utterly dissent from those who are unwilling that the sacred Scriptures should be read by the unlearned translated into their vulgar tongue, as though Christ had taught such subtleties that they can scarcely be understood even by a few theologians, or, as though the strength of the Christian religion consisted in men's ignorance of it. The mysteries of kings it may be safer to conceal, but Christ wished his mysteries to be published as openly as possible. I wish that even the weakest woman should read the Gospel—should read the epistles of Paul. And I wish these were translated into all languages, so that they might be read and understood, not only by Scots and Irishmen, but also by Turks and Saracens. To make them understood is surely the first step. It may be that they might be ridiculed by many, but some would take them to heart. I long that the husbandman should sing portions of them to himself as he follows the plough, that the weaver should hum them to the tune of his shuttle, that the traveller should beguile with their stories the tedium of his journey.

From Erasmus, "Paraclesis," *Novum Instrumentum,* trans. by Frederic Seebohm, in *The Oxford Reformers* (New York: Dutton, 1914), p. 203.

study of Hebrew literature as a means of understanding the Old Testament, even though a group of Dominicans wished to destroy all Hebrew books. In France, Lefèvre d'Etaples studied the Epistles of Paul and translated the New Testament into French (1523) in an effort to enlighten his contemporaries and further the cause of reform. For Sir Thomas More in England, study and reform were also closely related. In his famous *Utopia*, More wrote a searching analysis of the most glaring social, political, and ecclesiastical evils of his day from the point of view of a scholar steeped in Humanism and the Gospels as well as in the monastic tradition of the Middle Ages.

Erasmus

The acknowledged leader of these Christian Humanists was Erasmus of Rotterdam (*ca.* 1466–1536). Erasmus' enthusiasm for the Greco-Roman classics matched his enthusiasm for the Bible and early Christian writings. He devoted his life to scholarship in the conviction that sound learning would help save the Church. He edited the New Testament in the original Greek (1516), with a preface urging that it be translated into all the vulgar tongues, and he published editions of the early Church Fathers. His hundreds of letters and his briefer books were even more influential. In them, with lively humor, underlying seriousness, and an unsurpassed command of the Latin language, he argued for what he called "the philosophy of Christ," the love of God and neighbor that he saw as the essence of Christianity. He feared that the Church of his day had obscured this essential truth with useless forms and ceremonies. In a typical passage he ridiculed monkish ideas of religion. When the final reckoning comes, one monk will point to his fastings and ceremonies for credit "another will boast that for sixty years he never touched money, except when his fingers were protected by two pairs of gloves." Christ will interrupt their boasts and say, "Whence comes this new race of Jews [i.e., Pharisees]? I promised the inheritance of my Father, not to cowls, prayers, or fasts, but to works of charity." This device of

Portrait of Erasmus by Dürer.

imagining how Christ himself would judge the world of the 1500s was characteristic of Christian Humanism.

Christian Humanism offered the last chance of peaceful reform. But it was a movement that needed time, patience, and understanding to have any impact on the upper classes, and it never had much appeal for the mass of the population. It influenced every effort, both Protestant and Catholic, to reform the Church, but as a practical program it was doomed to failure. It was too aristocratic and too intellectual. The times were revolutionary and the remedies that Europe was to adopt were both sterner and simpler than Erasmus' "philosophy of Christ."

LUTHER'S REVOLT FROM ROME

On October 31, 1517, an Augustinian friar serving as Professor of Bible in the little University of Wittenberg in Saxony prepared 95 theses, or propositions, for academic debate on the subject of indulgences. The author, Martin Luther (1483–1546), was outraged by the unscrupulous salesmanship of a Dominican friar named Tetzel who had been hawking indulgences in Magdeburg. "So soon as coin in coffer rings," Tetzel was re-

ỷ ir deutſchen meicket mich recht/
Des heiligen Vaters Pappſtes Knecht/
Bin ich/vnd br ing euch iſt allein/
Zehn tauſent vnd neun hundert care in/
Gnad vnd Ublaß von einer Sünd/
Vor euch/ewer Eltern/Weib vnd Kind/
Sol ein feder gewehret fein
So viel ihrleg e lns Räſtelein/
So bald der Gülden im Becken klingt/
Jm huy die Seel im Himel ſpringt/

Contemporary caricature of Johann Tetzel hawking indulgences. The last line of the jingle is: "So soon as coin in coffer rings, the soul from Purgatory springs."

ported as preaching, "the soul from Purgatory springs." The proceeds from this particular sale of indulgences were meant to go toward the building of St. Peter's church in Rome, though most of it actually ended up in the pockets of the Archbishop of Mainz and of the Fugger banking firm. Luther's theses were immediately printed and debated not only in Wittenberg but all over Germany. The sensation they caused marked the start of the Protestant Reformation.

Luther on Justification by Faith

For the word of God cannot be received and honored by any works, but by faith alone. Hence it is clear that, as the soul needs the word alone for life and justification, so it is justified by faith alone and not by any works. For if it could be justified by any other means, it would have no need of the word, nor consequently of faith. . . .

It is evident that by no outward work or labor can the inward man be at all justified, made free and saved, and that no works whatever have any relation to him. And so, on the other hand, it is solely by impiety and incredulity of heart that he becomes guilty and a slave of sin, deserving condemnation; not by any outward sin or work.

Therefore the first care of every Christian ought to be to lay aside all reliance on works, and strengthen his faith alone more and more, and by it grow in the knowledge, not of works, but of Christ Jesus, who has suffered and risen again for him.

Martin Luther, *On Christian Liberty*, trans. by H. Wace and C. A. Buchheim, in *First Principles of the Reformation* (London: Murray, 1883), pp. 107–08.

Luther's chief propositions were:

There is no divine authority for preaching that the soul flies out of purgatory immediately the money clinks in the bottom of the chest. . . . It is certainly possible that when the money clinks in the bottom of the chest, avarice and greed increase. . . . All those who believe themselves certain of their own salvation by means of letters of indulgence will be eternally damned, together with their teachers. . . . Any Christian whatsoever, who is truly repentant, enjoys plenary remission from penalty and guilt, and this is given him without letters of indulgence.

At the time, Martin Luther was a strong-willed, keen-minded, high-strung man in his early thirties. He was the son of a prosperous peasant turned miner, who had been able to give his boy a university education. The young Luther had experienced several severe emotional crises; the most acute one led him to become a friar. But in his convent he had become increasingly dissatisfied with the emphasis his teachers laid on good works. He had been a most conscientious friar; he had fasted and prayed and confessed without end. If good works could win a man salvation, surely they should win it for him, he thought. Yet performing the acts commanded by the Church gave him no inner sense of forgiveness, only a growing sense of guilt, despair, and deepening spiritual crisis. Peace came to him when he suddenly understood, as in a revelation, what St. Paul had meant when he said that a man is saved not by doing the works of the Jewish law but by his faith in Christ. The ceremonies and religious practices of the medieval Church seemed to Luther a new Jewish law. Man is too corrupted by sin to meet the demands of such a law by his own efforts, and so he must rely on his faith in God's mercy. It is unthinkable that a man can buy God's favor by doing a good deed or performing some sacramental act. In the matter of saving a man's soul, Luther concluded, God does everything, man can do nothing.

It took Luther some time to work out the revolutionary implications of this thought. If man is saved by faith alone, then ceremonies and sacraments, pilgrimages and indulgences, everything the medieval Church called "good works," are at best irrelevant and at worst dangerous. Indulgences were the first "good work" at which he struck. Within a short time after his attack their sales dropped off sharply in Germany. When the Dominicans, chief sellers of the indulgences, persuaded Pope Leo X to condemn his theses, Luther was gradually driven to deny the authority of the pope. Soon afterward, when he came to believe that John Hus had been right on certain matters in spite of his condemnation by the Council of Constance, he denied the authority of general councils as well. By April 1521 Luther was standing before the Emperor Charles V at an imperial diet at Worms and declaring that he was bound by the authority of the Scripture and his own conscience rather than by that of either pope or council. He could not recant any of his writings, he added, because his conscience was "captive to the Word of God" and because it was "neither safe nor right to go against conscience." The Bible and conscience—these were to be the two chief pillars of Protestant Christianity.

Luther was not burned at Worms, as Hus had been at Constance. His safe-conduct was respected and he was allowed to return to the protection of his ruler, Frederick, the Elector of Saxony. For twenty-five years, till his death in 1546, he taught, preached, and wrote at Wittenberg. Meanwhile the revolt against the papacy that he had started gathered momentum and spread over northern Europe. In the end, the unity of Western Christendom was permanently destroyed.

Lutheran Principles

In breaking with the papacy, Luther was guided by three main principles: salvation by faith, not by works; the ultimate authority of the Bible; and the priesthood of all believers. The three were closely related. It was through study of the Bible that Luther came to his belief in salvation by faith, and it was to the Bible that he always appealed against the authority of tradition or the

Portrait of Martin Luther by Cranach, 1533.

Luther on the Church

Thus it may come to pass that the Pope and his followers are wicked and not true Christians, and not being taught by God, have no true understanding, whereas a common man may have true understanding. Why should we then not follow him? Has not the Pope often erred? Who could help Christianity, in case the Pope errs, if we do not rather believe another who has the Scriptures for him? Therefore it is a wickedly devised fable—and they cannot quote a single letter to confirm it—that it is for the Pope alone to interpret the Scriptures or to confirm the interpretation of them. They have assumed the authority of their own selves. And though they say that this authority was given to St. Peter when the keys were given to him, it is plain enough that the keys were not given to St. Peter alone, but to the whole community. . . . Moreover, if the article of our faith is right, "I believe in the holy Christian Church," the Pope cannot alone be right; else we must say, "I believe in the Pope of Rome," and reduce the Christian Church to one man, which is a devilish and damnable heresy. Besides that, we are all priests, as I have said, and have all one faith, one Gospel, one Sacrament; how then should we not have the power of discerning and judging what is right or wrong in matters of faith?

From Martin Luther, "Address to the Christian Nobility of the German Nation," *Luther's Primary Works,* ed. by H. Wace and C. A. Buchheim (London: Hodder and Stoughton, 1896), pp. 170–71.

papacy. His greatest literary work was a German translation of the Bible (completed in 1532), which he wrote in order that God's Word might be put into the hands of every devout person in Germany who could read. There was no essential difference between a priest and a layman, he insisted. A dedicated layman reverently reading the Scripture was closer to divine truth than a worldly pope proclaiming dogma for the Church. Christ had meant every believer to be a priest to his neighbor; He had not intended a special few to act as mediators between man and God. A Christian can serve God as well by being an honest merchant or a faithful housewife as by becoming a monk or a nun. Thus Luther encouraged the dissolution of the monastic orders, and in order to dramatize his convictions he married a nun and became the happy father of six children.

Luther's original protest had been a purely religious matter, rooted in his own spiritual experience. But to gain support he had to appeal to the nationalistic and financial grievances of his fellow Germans. "What has brought us Germans to such a pass that we have to suffer this robbery and this destruction of our property by the Pope?" he asked in 1520. "If the kingdom of France has resisted it, why do we Germans suffer ourselves to be fooled and deceived?"Luther appealed to princes eager to confiscate church property, to businessmen restive under papal taxation, to German patriots resentful of the Italians who dominated the papacy and the College of Cardinals, and to devout laymen and conscientious priests who were shocked by the corruption in the Church. His principles of salvation by faith and of serving God in one's secular calling appealed especially to laymen, who found in them a way of reconciling Christian devotion with an active concern about worldly affairs. High-minded and low-minded motives were inextricably mixed in the minds of those who accepted Luther's arguments.

Luther had no intention of breaking away from the true Church of Christ or of setting up a rival organization. But after 1520 he was convinced that the Church founded by Christ and the Apostles had wandered from the true path somewhere in the Middle Ages, and that the bishop of Rome was not the Vicar of Christ, but rather the Anti-Christ. Much of the dogma and ritual of the Church of his day, Luther believed, was the work of men, not of God. Such accretions must be stripped away, leaving only the pure faith of the Apostles and the early Church Fathers. In his zeal for reform, Luther actually set up a new church under the protection and control of secular rulers in Germany. In this church there were two sacraments (Baptism and Holy Communion) in place of seven, a simplified ritual in German rather than Latin, and more emphasis on the congregation's participation in the service. But Luther never wavered in his belief that he was not setting up another "church" but that he was purifying *the* Church. There could be only one true Church Catholic, into which all men were received in Baptism. Either the pope was right when he excommunicated Luther as a heretic in 1520, or else Luther was right when he burned the bull of excommunication. At first there were not two churches, one "Catholic" and the other "Lutheran," but an irreconcilable argument over the nature of the one true Church.

The Spread of Lutheranism

Luther's ideas were spread by his students and by his books, which poured from the new printing presses in both German and Latin. Many priests and monks were among his first converts, and his views were particularly popular among the middle classes of the German cities and the princes of northern and central Germany. The Humanists at first greeted his attack on indulgences with joy, but as Luther became more vehement most of them retreated to the fold of the Roman Church. They wanted reform, not revolution, as Erasmus made clear when he finally and reluctantly broke with Luther in 1524. To Erasmus, Luther was a fanatic; to Luther, Erasmus was only half a Christian.

The peasants were excited by Luther's message at first, but he lost most of them after the Peasants' Rebellion of 1524–25. This was the largest and blood-

Title page of the first German translation of the Bible, by Martin Luther, printed in 1534 with the approval of the Elector of Saxony.

iest of the many peasant uprisings that resulted from complex economic and social causes during the later Middle Ages. The rebels' chief aim was to abolish serfdom and the burdens of the manorial system. "Therefore do we find in the Scripture that we are free," they argued, "and we will be free." Luther was close enough to his peasant origins to sympathize with their demands, but the freedom he was interested in was an inner religious freedom, freedom from an ecclesiastical system, not from social or political bondage. At last, the atrocities committed by the peasants turned him against them, and he wrote a bitter condemnation of the uprising. The rebellion itself was finally put down with atrocities that went beyond even those of the rebels. The peasants felt that Luther had betrayed them, but the middle and ruling classes welcomed his social conservatism. After 1525 he and his followers fought as hard against radicals on their left, who wanted to carry the religious revolt too far, as they did against the Roman Catholics on their right, who wished to wipe out Lutheranism.

There was at first no effective resistance in Germany to the spread of Luther's ideas. The emperor Charles V never wavered in his orthodoxy, but the task of holding together his scattered dominions proved so difficult that he was unable to bring political or military pressure to bear on cities and states that had turned Lutheran. From 1522 to 1559 Charles and his son Philip were caught up in a series of conflicts with France that absorbed much of their energy and income. Meanwhile Charles and his brother Ferdinand were also trying to stem the tide of Turkish conquest in the Mediterranean and the Danube Valley. The French in the West and the Turks in the East, sometimes in alliance with each other, allowed the emperor only a few intervals of peace in which to turn his attention to the religious division of Germany.

By the time of Luther's death in 1546, the German cities and principalities were about evenly divided between the two faiths. In 1547, during a peaceful interlude in his international struggles, Charles V finally found an opportunity

Engraving of 1524 depicting a noble lady and her son kneeling before peasant rebels to plea for their lives during the outburst of 1524–25.

to attack the Lutheran states. The confused war that followed proved that neither side could destroy the other, and in 1555 the emperor reluctantly allowed his brother Ferdinand, who was ruler of Austria and later emperor, to conclude

THE SPREAD OF PROTESTANTISM   Sixteenth century

the Religious Peace of Augsburg. This peace allowed the city-states and princes of the Empire to choose between Lutheranism and Catholicism and bound them to respect each other's rights. *Cuius regio, eius religio,* as someone later summed up the principle: The ruler determines the religion for the region. People who disliked the ruler's choice might migrate to another state. Lutherans were allowed to keep any church lands they had seized before 1552, but it was agreed that every Catholic bishop or abbot who turned Protestant in the future would have to resign his title and leave his lands in Catholic hands. This last clause was difficult to interpret and caused trouble later. The chief flaw in the settlement, however, was the exclusion of Calvinists, whose numbers were growing rapidly, from the benefits of the peace.

The Peace of Augsburg was the first official recognition, however grudging, that Western Christendom had been rent asunder and would have to continue as a house divided. It was not religious toleration, but it was a step along the way. In the end, northern Germany became mostly "Protestant" (as Lutherans had been called since 1529, when they presented a "protest" at an imperial diet); southern Germany remained mostly "Catholic." The division remains today about as it was in 1560. Outside Germany, Lutheran ideas spread widely but took root only in Scandinavia, where Denmark, Norway, and Sweden became Lutheran before mid-century. Perhaps because Luther spoke so forcefully in the German idiom to his fellow Germans, his teaching was not so well adapted to export as was the teaching of John Calvin.

CALVINISM

Luther's University of Wittenberg was not the only center from which reform ideas radiated. Other important centers were Zurich, Basel, Strasbourg, and especially Geneva. In these southern German and Swiss cities there developed a type of Protestantism closely related to Lutheranism but different in emphasis—more rational and systematic, more organized and disciplined, laying more stress on moral conduct and political action, less on the inner relation of man to God. The members of this second family of Protestant churches are generally called "Reformed" churches, in contrast with the "Lutheran."

Among the early Swiss and South German reformers were Ulrich Zwingli of Zurich (1484–1531) and Martin Bucer of Strasbourg (1491–1551). Neither man agreed entirely with Luther. Zwingli took a more radical position on the sacraments, arguing that Communion was essentially a memorial service commemorating the Last Supper. Bucer tried to reconcile various Protestant groups and was more tolerant than most of the other reformers.

More influential than either Zwingli or Bucer was John Calvin (1509–64). Calvin had been trained as a lawyer and a Humanist in his native France before he became converted to Protestantism and settled down as a pastor in Geneva. He learned much from Luther, as well as from Zwingli and Bucer. Through these influences and through his early training, he became the chief theologian and organizer of second-generation Protestantism. His *Institutes of the Christian Religion*

Calvin on Predestination

Predestination we call the eternal decree of God, by which he has determined in himself, what he would have to become of every individual of mankind. For they are not all created with a similar destiny; but eternal life is foreordained for some, and eternal damnation for others. . . .

In conformity, therefore, to the clear doctrine of the Scripture, we assert, that by an eternal and immutable counsel, God has once for all determined, both whom he would admit to salvation, and whom he would condemn to destruction. We affirm that this counsel, as far as concerns the elect, is founded on his gratuitous mercy, totally irrespective of human merit; but that to those whom he devotes to condemnation, the gate of life is closed by a just and irreprehensible, but incomprehensible, judgment. . . .

How exceedingly presumptuous it is only to inquire into the causes of the Divine will; which is in fact, and is justly entitled to be, the cause of everything that exists. . . . For the will of God is the highest rule of justice; so that what he wills must be considered just, for this very reason, because he wills it.

From John Calvin, *Institutes of the Christian Religion*, trans. by John Allen (Philadelphia: Westminster Press, 1930), Book III, Ch. 21, pars. 5, 7; Ch. 23, par. 2.

Sketch of Calvin drawn by a student, perhaps during a lecture.

The more rigid Protestants objected to all religious paintings and sculpture as leading to idolatry. In this engraving of 1579, Calvinists are pulling down statues of saints and destroying stained glass windows.

served as the basic handbook of Protestant principles for two centuries. It was a clear, well-organized, well-written book in both its Latin and its French versions, and its argument had all the logic a trained lawyer could bring to it. Calvin's two polar principles were the absolute sovereignty of God and the radical depravity of man. No acts of sinful man can merit salvation; God, through his inscrutable will, has chosen some to be saved and some to be damned. The effect of this doctrine on Calvin's followers was not to induce resignation and despair but to stimulate moral activity and strenuous effort as God's instruments. Good works could not save a Calvinist—but they might be evidence that God was working through him. Good works were a "sign" that a man was probably one of the Elect.

As time went on, Calvin's church in Geneva became the model for Presbyterian or Reformed churches in France, England, Scotland, the Netherlands, the Rhineland, Bohemia, and Hungary—later in North America and Dutch South Africa. Calvin advocated that each local congregation have a ruling body composed of both ministers and laymen (presbyters, or elders) who were to watch carefully over the moral conduct and beliefs of the faithful. These officials then

met in synods that linked up the Reformed congregations of a whole district or nation. Thus in place of the Roman Catholic hierarchy of bishops and priests under the pope, and in place of Luther's state-churches, Calvin devised a peculiarly tough and flexible system of church government that resisted control by the state, maintained strict discipline, and, in the lay elders, included a potentially democratic element. Unlike Lutheranism, Calvinism met the two conditions for successful export all over Europe: it possessed a systematic theology and it offered a practical substitute for medieval church organization.

By the 1550s Calvinism was spreading rapidly. Except in a few cities like Geneva, the nerve center of the movement, and in Scotland, Calvinists never became a majority. But the Calvinist minorities were stubborn, well organized, and widely distributed over Europe. Calvinism left a deep imprint on English society in the form of Puritanism, on France through the Huguenots, on Hungary, and on the Dutch Netherlands. Calvinist minorities formed a kind of revolutionary international society throughout Europe in the later sixteenth century. Like their chief rivals, the Jesuits, the Reformed ministers were often able to elicit a religious loyalty that transcended loyalty to secular rulers and nations. Calvinism was the militant, international form of Protestantism.

THE RADICALS

Some reformers wanted to move much further and faster along the road of religious revolution than Luther, Zwingli, or Calvin. Throughout Germany workers and peasants had been hard hit by the economic changes of the fourteenth and fifteenth centuries. Often their discontent took on a religious coloring, combining easily with what survived of earlier heresies—Waldensian, Lollard, and Hussite, for example. These uneducated men and women took most of Luther's ideas literally—the Bible as ultimate authority, the priesthood of all believers, the freedom of true Christians from manmade ecclesiastical laws and organizations. During the 1520s in Switzerland and in the upper Rhine Valley particularly, little groups of such people came together proclaiming that a true church of Christians was a voluntary association of converted believers, not an official or established institution like that of the Lutherans or Catholics. Most of them believed that until a man came of age and knew what he was doing, he should not be admitted to the church through baptism. Thus, since they had to rebaptize most of their converts, their enemies called them Anabaptists, or rebaptizers. Their ritual was simple, and generally they took the Bible literally. Most of them would not take an oath in a law court, accept public office, or serve as soldiers; some practiced communism of goods on the model described in the second chapter of Acts.

They were cruelly persecuted by Catholics and conservative Protestants alike as dangerous heretics and social radicals. A small but violent minority gave temporary excuse for such persecution by capturing the city of Münster and conducting a reign of terror there for over a year (1534–35). But generally they were pacifists and eager to suffer as their models, the Apostles, had done. After the 1530s the Anabaptists were to be found mainly in the Netherlands, Bohemia, Poland, and England, having been stamped out in southern Germany where they had originated.

In addition to such "evangelical" groups, which tried to return to the first-century Gospel even more literally than Luther, there were other religious radicals. Some, like the Quakers in the seventeenth century, continued the medieval mystical tradition by following an inner voice rather than the letter of the Scripture. Others were more rationalistic, anticipating the doctrine that the nineteenth century was to call Unitarianism, the belief that there is only one God, not a Holy Trinity, and that Jesus was not God but man at his best. No one in the

---

Radical Protestantism: The Teaching of Menno Simons

Menno Simons (1496–1561) was one of the ablest leaders of the radical wing of the Reformation. Simons' followers formed the Mennonite Church, which still exists. His ideas also contributed to the development of the Baptist Church. He never summed up his doctrine in a single document; it has to be put together from scattered pamphlets.

We do not find in Scripture a single word by which Christ has ordained the baptism of infants, or that his apostles taught and practiced it. We say that infant baptism is but a human invention. . . . To baptize before that which is required for baptism, namely faith, is to place the cart before the horse.

Never should any commandment be observed which is not contained in God's holy Word, either in letter or in spirit.

The regenerated do not go to war nor fight. . . . How can a Christian, according to Scripture, consistently retaliate, rebel, make war, murder, slay, torture, steal, rob, and burn cities and conquer countries?

Where have you read in the Scriptures, that Christ or the Apostles called upon the power of the magistracy against those who would not hear their doctrine or obey their words? . . . Faith is a gift of God, therefore it cannot be forced on anyone by worldly authorities or by the sword.

We must be born from above, must be changed and renewed in our hearts and thus be transplanted from the unrighteous and evil nature of Adam into the righteous and good nature of Christ, or we cannot be helped in eternity by any means, divine or human.

From "Selections from the Writings of Menno Simons," in *The Medieval World and its Transformations*, Vol. II, ed. by G. M. Straka (New York: McGraw-Hill, 1967), pp. 463, 466, 467, 468, 470.

sixteenth century went quite this far, but the Spanish physician Michael Servetus (1511–53) combined an emphasis on the humanity of Christ with mystical and rationalistic ideas. He was imprisoned by the Catholic Inquisition, escaped, and in 1553 was burned at the stake in Geneva as a result of Calvin's influence.

The ideas of these religious radicals, who went too far not only for Roman Catholics but also for Luther and Calvin, were of great importance in the religious history of the Anglo-Saxon peoples. It was in England during the seventeenth century and later in the English colonies in America that Anabaptist ideas were fully realized. There the doctrine that the church should be a voluntary association, "a free church in a free state," organizing itself and electing its pastor, was accepted without any restrictions. Modern Baptists (who believe in adult baptism only), Congregationalists (who emphasize the autonomy of local congregations of Christians), and Quakers (who rely on the "inner light" and tend toward pacifism) all look back to the religious radicals of the sixteenth century as their remote ancestors. American Protestant conceptions of the place of the church in society derive more from Anabaptism than from either Luther or Calvin.

ANGLICANISM

The peculiarity of the English Reformation is that it was initiated by a king for reasons that had almost nothing to do with religion. Henry VIII cut England off from the papacy much as the king of France had cut his realm off from the papal obedience in 1395. But in England the jurisdictional breach with Rome was followed by a decisive religious change.

In 1527, ten years after Luther had written his 95 theses, both England and its king seemed entirely orthodox. Parliament had restricted papal rights of appointment and jurisdiction in England, but England had not gone so far toward developing a national, or "Anglican," Church as France had in "Gallicanism." Lutheran ideas, strongly opposed by the king, had taken only shallow root in England among a few merchants, monks, and university scholars. There was some

anticlericalism and opposition to papal taxation among the people, and some talk of reform among the intellectuals, but no organized movement of revolt. Henry, however, found himself in a personal quandary that was to lead him into direct conflict with the pope, Clement VII. After eighteen years of married life, Henry's wife, Catherine of Aragon, had given him only one living child, a daughter. He knew that the lack of a male heir might well throw England into a new War of the Roses, and he knew that Catherine could bear him no more children. Furthermore, he was infatuated with a lady of the court named Anne Boleyn. Henry therefore asked the pope to annul his marriage with Catherine so that he might marry Anne. It was not hard to find technical grounds for the annulment. Catherine had been married to Henry's short-lived elder brother, and it was against Church law to marry the widow of one's brother. But it was hard to persuade the pope to grant the annulment because he was in the power of the

Title page of Daniel Featley's Description of 1645, known also as "The Dippers Dipt," a satirical view of the Anabaptists.

Sir Thomas More, after Hans Holbein, 1527.

emperor, Charles V, and Charles was the nephew of Catherine.

Henry, a strong-willed man convinced that he was right, was skillful in political manipulation. In 1529 he summoned Parliament, determined to make the nation his accomplice in whatever he

might have to do. He and his chief minister, Thomas Cromwell, deftly built up anticlerical sentiment in Parliament and forced the English clergy to acknowledge that the king was "Supreme Head of the Church in England." Then Henry threatened to withdraw all revenue and obedience from the pope. When Clement still refused to grant the annulment, Henry carried out his threat. He had the marriage annulled in England by Thomas Cranmer, whom he had just persuaded the pope to name as Archbishop of Canterbury, married Anne, and then, in 1533–34, had Parliament cut all ties between the Roman papacy and England by a series of statutes. Conscientious monks, priests, and laymen who resisted this separation were executed. The most prominent martyr was Sir Thomas More (1478–1535), author of *Utopia* and chancellor of England from 1529 to 1532, who was proclaimed a saint in the twentieth century. Henry was now a kind of pope of the Church in England, except that as a layman he never claimed the power to administer the sacraments. Between 1535 and 1539 he and his agents demonstrated the extent of his authority by dissolving all English monasteries, turning their inmates out into the world and confiscating their lands. Because Henry needed ready money to carry on a war with France, most of these lands were eventually sold to nobles, gentry, and merchants. The result, probably unforeseen, was to bind a whole new class of landowners to the English crown and to the new religious settlement.

In breaking with the papacy, Henry had no intention of breaking with orthodox Catholic belief and practice. He made it clear to his people that the breach with Rome meant no letting down of the bars against heresy, whether Lollard, Lutheran, or Anabaptist. It was impossible, however, to seal England off from the influx of Protestant tracts and ideas, and Henry himself approved the distribution to churches of an English translation of the Bible. By the time of his death in 1547, the Protestant wing of the English clergy led by Archbishop Cranmer was growing in power. During the brief reign of Henry's sickly son Edward VI (1547–53) the government moved rapidly toward building a church

A Catholic, Sir Thomas More, on the Church

The true Church of Christ is the common known church of all Christian people not gone out nor cast out. This whole body both of good and bad is the Catholic Church of Christ, which is in this world very sickly, and hath many sore members, as hath sometime the natural body of a man. . . . The Church was gathered, and the faith believed, before any part of the New Testament was put in writing. And which was or is the true scripture, neither Luther nor Tyndale [translator of the New Testament into English] knoweth but by the credence that they give to the Church. . . . The Church was before the gospel was written; and the faith was taught, and men were baptised and masses said, and the other sacraments ministered among Christian people, before any part of the New Testament was put in writing. . . . As the sea shall never surround and overwhelm the land, and yet it hath eaten many places in, and swallowed whole countries up, and made places now sea that sometime were well-inhabited lands, and hath lost part of his own possession in other parts again; so though the faith of Christ shall never be overflown with heresies, nor the gates of hell prevail against Christ's Church, yet in some places it winneth in a new people, so may there in some places by negligence be lost the old.

From *The Workes of Sir Thomas More* (1557), pp. 527, 852, 853, 921.

that was moderately Protestant in doctrine and ritual. Cranmer gathered together the most impressive parts of the ancient liturgies of the Catholic Church and translated them into majestic English in the Book of Common Prayer. This collection served as the rallying point of Anglicanism, as Luther's hymns did for Lutherans and Calvin's *Institutes* for Calvinists.

This new official Protestantism had no time to take root among the people. In 1553 Catherine of Aragon's daughter Mary, the most honest and least politic of all the Tudors, came to the throne. She tried to vindicate her mother and atone for her father's sins by turning the clock back to 1529, abolishing all antipapal legislation, and restoring England to the papal obedience. But she outraged her people's patriotism by marrying a foreigner, Philip II of Spain, son and heir presumptive of Charles V, and she shocked their humanity by allowing three hundred Protestants to be burned for heresy in about three years. The courage with which Cranmer and more obscure victims went to their deaths, together with the arrogance of Philip's courtiers, left an indelible impression on the English people. Patriotism and Protestantism became identified in the public mind.

When Anne Boleyn's daughter, Elizabeth I (1558–1603), came to the throne, there was little possibility that she would keep England in the Catholic camp. Elizabeth cautiously guided her Parliaments and her bishops into a compromise religious settlement. She accepted the title of "Supreme Governor" of the Church in England, but she saw to it that revised articles of the faith and the Book of Common Prayer could be accepted by both moderate Catholics and Protestants. For the rest, she refused "to make windows into men's souls," as she put it; that is, she persecuted only open opponents of her policies but not those who quietly dissented from them. After the pope excommunicated her in 1570 she was forced to treat zealous Catholics in England as traitors, but she was almost as annoyed with the "Puritans," who wished to go much further than she in purifying the Anglican Church of Catholic traditions. The Puritans were strong

Henry VIII, after Hans Holbein.

in Parliament, but when they became obstreperous Elizabeth clapped some of them into jail. The idea that patriotism required independence from Rome became dominant during her reign, and in the end England was the largest single state to secede permanently from the Roman obedience. The secession cost less in bloodshed than it did elsewhere, largely because of the firm control that Henry VIII and Elizabeth exercised over the pace of religious change in England.

Anglicanism was the most conservative form of Protestantism. In fact, many Anglicans today follow Henry VIII in insisting that their church is not "Protestant" at all. In Anglican theory it was the Roman papacy that in effect had "seceded" from the Catholic tradition during the Middle Ages, and it was Henry VIII and Cranmer who restored the true continuity between the Church of the Fathers and the Church of the sixteenth century. In England itself the Anglican position was a broad middle ground between a Catholic minority that wished to bring England back to Rome and a Puritan minority that wished to build a more radically Protestant church in England.

THE CATHOLIC REFORMATION

Luther, Calvin, Cranmer, and the radical reformers thought of what they were doing as a "reformation" of the Church, and to this day the movement is generally called the Protestant Reformation. To Roman Catholics, however, the movement was a "revolt" against the divine authority of the Vicar of Christ, a religious revolution. From this point of view the only true "reformation" was the successful effort finally made by the Roman Church to reform itself, partly in response to the Protestant attack, partly as a result of internal pressures. Historians call this movement the Catholic Reformation, or the Counter Reformation.

This movement was both a religious revival and a counterattack on Protestantism. Before Luther appeared on the scene, some distinguished members of the clergy founded the Oratory of Divine Love at Rome in the hope of beginning a spiritual revival among the clergy. They directed their efforts toward the monastic orders and the papal court itself. In the course of the sixteenth century they succeeded in transforming the atmosphere at the Vatican. The bloody sack of Rome in 1527 by undisciplined imperial troops practically ended papal hopes of becoming powerful Italian princes. As dreams of temporal power waned, better popes were chosen, who in turn appointed better cardinals. In the second half of the century, several of the popes were zealous, almost fanatical, men who would have seemed utterly out of place in the Renaissance papacy a century earlier. Politics still influenced religion and certain administrative abuses persisted, but the popes of the later sixteenth century were spiritual leaders, not Italian princes.

The driving forces behind the Catholic Reformation, especially the political forces, originated in Spain. Years of crusading against the Moors had given Spanish Catholicism a peculiarly intense quality lacking in the rest of Europe. King Philip II of Spain (1556-98), the son of Emperor Charles V, was a devoted Catholic who felt that it was Spain's destiny to stand as the bulwark of Roman Catholicism against the Protestants in Europe. He tended to give orders to the popes rather than to take orders from them, but during his reign Spanish armies and navies, Spanish diplomacy, and Spanish saints constituted the hard core of a revived and militant Catholicism all over Europe.

The most powerful single agency in restoring papal power, in rolling back the tide of Protestantism, and in carrying Catholic missions overseas was a new order founded by one of the most single-minded and influential saints in Christian history, a Spaniard of Basque descent named Ignatius of Loyola (1491-1556). While he was fighting the French in the service of his king, Ignatius' leg was fractured by a cannon ball. During a long and painful convalescence, he devoured the lives of the saints, which were the only reading matter at hand, and decided to enlist as a kind of Christian knight in the service of the Virgin Mary. During a lengthy period of trial and temptation he perfected the "spiritual exercises" which he later passed on to generations of followers. These exercises consisted in the believer's concentrating his imagination on the most vivid details of Hell and of the life and death of Christ in order to strengthen his will and to direct it toward salvation. While Ignatius was a student at the University of Paris (about the same time as Calvin), he enlisted ten friends who became the nucleus of a new order. This new order, which was approved by the pope in 1540, was the Society of Jesus. Its members became known as Jesuits.

The rules of the new order were designed to develop a flexible, disciplined, and efficient body of ecclesiastical shock troops for the papacy. The Jesuit wore no distinctive habit; he dressed as his job might require, as priest, teacher, missionary, or secret agent. He swore a special oath of obedience to the pope. He was carefully selected and trained for the most dangerous and difficult tasks the Church might require, from serving as confessor to a king, to venturing into Protestant countries where he might be executed as a traitor, to voyaging to foreign lands as remote as Brazil or India. The Jesuits were spectacularly successful. They strengthened the pope's control over the Church itself; they ran the best schools in Europe; and during the late sixteenth century they won back most of Bohemia, Poland, Hungary, and southern Germany from Protestantism.

Engraving showing the Council of Trent, 1562–63. An amphitheater was set up in the church of St. Maria Maggio.

printed books was instituted for the Church as a whole in 1559 and approved by the Council of Trent, which issued an "Index" of books that the faithful were forbidden to read.

The Roman Church had found a new religious vitality and had closed its ranks against the Protestant threat. By the second half of the sixteenth century a relatively monolithic Catholic Church, reorganized from within and backed by Spain, the strongest military power in Europe, faced the divided Protestants on somewhat better than even terms.

SIGNIFICANCE OF THE REFORMATIONS

It is not easy to sum up the significance of the Protestant and Catholic Reformations. They were religious movements, phrased in theological terms, rooted deep in the religious experience of men like Luther and Loyola, and resulting in a religious fragmentation of Western Christendom that has lasted to the present day. But Luther's angry protest against indulgences would not have had such far-reaching results had not the economic, social, and political conditions been just right. The religious upheaval was intermingled with the growth of capitalism, of secularism, of national sentiment, and of absolutism in government. It is very difficult to say precisely what was cause and what was effect. While German princes, for example, took advantage of purely religious protests to confiscate church property for their own interests, religious reformers also utilized purely secular events, like Henry VIII's desire to get rid of his wife, to advance the Protestant cause.

One thing is clear. The era of reform and revolution in the Church temporarily arrested the trend toward the secularization of culture that had begun in the last centuries of the Middle Ages. The century that followed Luther's death was a religious age; its most serious arguments were religious arguments; its wars were intensified by religious fanaticism; and most of its leading figures were either men of religion or men considerably affected by religion. Intensified interest

The Roman Church strengthened itself against the Protestant attack in other ways as well. A general council was held at Trent in three sessions between 1545 and 1563 to define Catholic dogma and to reform abuses. Since the papal representatives and the Jesuits controlled the deliberations from the beginning, there was no danger of a revolt against the papacy as there had been in the councils of a century before. In reply to the central doctrines of Protestantism, the council declared that salvation is by both faith and works and that final religious authority is in the Bible and tradition as interpreted by the Roman Church. The worst financial and administrative abuses in the ecclesiastical organization were reformed, and seminaries were set up for the training of priests. The council defined the Church's teachings much more sharply than they had ever been defined before and reestablished the absolute supremacy of the pope over the clerical hierarchy. Rome had lost much in the struggle with heresy, but the Catholic Church of 1563 was far better able to cope with future heresies than it had been in 1500. New forms of the Inquisition had been established in Spain (1480), the Netherlands (1523), and Italy (1542), and a system of censorship of

Luther tweaks the beard of Calvin as both of them pull the hair of the pope. This satirical engraving presents a Catholic view of the reformation controversy.

CALVIN   LE PAPE   LUTHER

argued and denied that Protestantism, with its emphasis on serving God in one's secular calling and with its appreciation of the bourgeois virtues of honesty, thrift, and self-discipline, provided the necessary religious sanction for the development of capitalism. It has been argued and denied that Lutheranism aided the growth of divine-right monarchy whereas Calvinism provided a spur toward the development of constitutionalism, and Anabaptism toward the development of modern socialism. It has been argued and denied that Protestantism wrecked the development of art by destroying religious sculpture and paintings and by rejecting most religious symbolism. And it has been argued and denied that by dissolving monasteries and thus destroying educational foundations Protestants set back elementary education many years. Both the good and the bad in modern capitalism, modern nationalism, and modern secularism have been attributed to Protestantism by one historian or another.

The historical data are far too complex for dogmatic judgments in such matters. The permanent schism of Western Christendom and the temporary intensification of religious motives in European politics can justly be attributed to the Protestant movement. Beyond this, all that can be said surely is that Protestantism allied itself with developments that had their origins far back, sometimes intensified them and accelerated their growth, occasionally blocked or countered their expansion. Capitalism, democracy, nationalism, and the secularization of culture appeared in Catholic as well as Protestant lands, and none of these phenomena can be explained by a simple chain of causes leading back to Luther and his revolt from Rome.

in religion introduced a new and intolerant "ideological" element into the familiar economic and political causes of conflict in European society. The hatred among Catholic, Lutheran, Calvinist, and Anabaptist was as profound in the sixteenth century as the hatred among fascist, communist, and democrat in the twentieth, and for somewhat the same reasons. No man could believe that he or his family or his society was safe so long as opposing religious groups were allowed to exist. Only in time did it become evident that differing religious beliefs did not necessarily lead to civil war and the collapse of the state. Religious toleration was an eventual result of the Reformation but not of the efforts of the reformers.

For over a century the long-run effects of the Protestant Reformation on the economic, political, and cultural development of Europe have been vigorously debated by historians. It has been

Suggestions for Further Reading

Note: Asterisk denotes a book available in paperback edition.

The Religious Upheaval

The best attempt at a synthetic treatment of social, political, and religious developments is still P. Smith, *The Age of the Reformation** (1920), a lively and opinionated book. H. J. Grimm, *The Reformation Era* (1954), does religious developments fuller justice than Smith and is abreast of recent scholarship, particularly on Luther. H. Holborn, *The Reformation* (1959) is excellent on Germany. There are briefer treatments of the period in general in R. H. Bainton, *The Reformation of the Sixteenth Century** (1952), G. L. Mosse, *The Reformation** (1953), and E. H. Harbison, *The Age of Reformation** (1955).

The mental and emotional climate of the fifteenth century is vividly described in J. Huizinga, *The Waning of the Middle Ages** (trans. 1924); the piety of the period is examined in A. Hyma, *The Christian Renaissance* (1924). There are perceptive biographies of Erasmus by P. Smith* (1923), J. Huizinga* (trans. 1952), and R. H. Bainton, *Erasmus of Christendom* (1969). Erasmus' best-known writings are available in modern editions: *The Praise of Folly*, ed. by H. H. Hudson (1941) and *Ten Colloquies of Erasmus,** ed. by C. R. Thompson (1957).

The best short biography of Luther in English is R. H. Bainton, *Here I Stand** (1950). Another excellent work is R. Friedenthal, *Luther* (1970). H. Boehmer, *Road to Reformation** (1946), is another good Protestant account of Luther's development to 1521. H. Grisar, *Martin Luther: His Life and Work* (1935), is the best brief Catholic biography. There is no better biography of Calvin in English than W. Walker, *John Calvin* (1906), but this older account may be brought up to date by using the fine, broader survey of J. T. McNeill, *The History and Character of Calvinism** (1954). Modern translations of the writings of Luther, Calvin, and other reformers are appearing fast—for instance, in the *Library of Christian Classics*. These are too numerous to list here. H. E. Fosdick's anthology, *Great Voices of the Reformation* (1952), is a useful selection of passages from the works of the reformers from Wiclif to Wesley.

For the radicals, see G. H. Williams, *The Radical Reformer* (1962). Good introductions to different aspects of the "left wing" of the Reformation are offered in F. H. Littell, *The Free Church* (1958), R. H. Bainton, *The Travail of Religious Liberty** (1951), and N. Cohn, *The Pursuit of the Millennium* (1957).

The best work on England is A. G. Dickens, *The English Reformation* (1964). See also the brief and authoritative accounts by F. M. Powicke, *The Reformation in England* (1941), and T. M. Parker, *The English Reformation to 1558** (1950). G. Mattingly, *Catherine of Aragon** (1941), is a very perceptive and readable biography. A good Catholic account is by P. Hughes, *The Reformation in England,* 3 vols. (1950–54).

An excellent discussion of the Catholic Reformation is H. Daniel-Rops, *The Catholic Reformation,** 2 vols. (1961). Another good treatment is P. Janelle, *The Catholic Reformation* (1949). The best biography of St. Ignatius is by the Jesuit, P. Dudon (1949). For a less favorable treatment, see R. Fülöp-Miller, *The Power and Secret of the Jesuits* (1930). H. Jedin is engaged in writing a definitive *History of the Council of Trent,* the first two volumes of which have appeared in translation (1957). See also A. G. Dickens, *The Counter Reformation** (1969).

Results of the Reformation

On the economic, political, and cultural consequences of the Reformation there are wide differences of opinion. A famous essay of M. Weber, *The Protestant Ethic and the Spirit of Capitalism** (1905), became the starting point of a long controversy about the economic significance of Protestantism, which still continues sporadically. *Protestantism and Capitalism: The Weber Thesis and Its Critics,** ed. by R. W. Green (1959), is a convenient collection of selections from the literature of this controversy. R. H. Tawney, *Religion and the Rise of Capitalism** (1926), is a stimulating essay in the Weber tradition; H. M. Robertson, *Aspects of the Rise of Economic Individualism* (1933), is severely critical of Weber. E. Troeltsch, *Social Teaching of the Christian Churches,** 2 vols. (1912), is difficult but rewarding reading on the economic, social, and political theories of Catholics, Lutherans, Calvinists, and "the sects." The same author's *Protestantism and Progress** (1906) maintains that the Reformation was still largely "medieval" and that the Enlightenment was the true beginning of "modern" times. K. Holl, *The Cultural Significance of the Reformation** (1911) is more inclined to view Luther as the prophet of modern Germany and of twentieth-century culture in general. For a readable and perceptive survey of the period, see A. G. Dickens, *Reformation and Society in Sixteenth-Century Europe** (1966).

A sixteenth-century sailing ship, with its navigator (left center) sighting the sun to determine his latitude. The foremast (right) is square-rigged for running with the wind. The mainmast and the mizzenmast astern (left) are lateen-rigged for better tacking against the wind.

18

The Age of Discovery and the Greatness of Spain

The Protestant Reformation struck a Europe that was already in the throes of a different sort of revolution. That revolution was launched by Portuguese voyages down the northwest coast of Africa; it quickened with the discovery of America and the sea route to India; and it continued unabated throughout the sixteenth century. For Europeans this was an age of discovery without parallel. For the first time they found themselves in direct contact with all the continents on the globe and with all the civilized peoples who inhabited them. That contact began to have a profoundly disturbing effect on the economy and the politics of Europe just as the Peace of Augsburg was bringing a respite from religious strife.

THE DEVELOPMENT OF OCEANIC COMMERCE

In 1400 Europeans knew scarcely more about the earth than the Romans had. The oceans around the Continent were still impenetrable barriers; the only long voyages ever taken by Europeans were the almost forgotten expeditions of the Northmen to Greenland and America.

Franciscan friars and the Polos of Venice had shown that China could be reached by land and that the steppes linked Europe and Asia. But after the collapse of the Mongol Empire in the fourteenth century the routes across the steppes were no longer safe for missionaries or merchants. Arab sailors now became the middlemen between the Orient and Europe. They brought the spices and textiles of India and the East Indies to Alexandria and Beirut, whence the Venetians distributed them to the rest of Europe. The Europeans themselves had no direct contact with the East.

By the end of the sixteenth century an almost incredible geographical revolution had taken place. Arnold J. Toynbee defines it as "the substitution of the Ocean for the Steppe as the principal medium of world-communication." Europeans had mastered both the technological and the psychological problems of making long voyages over the sea. Their ships had crossed and recrossed the Atlantic Ocean, rounded the southern tips of Africa and South America, pushed into the Indian Ocean, and crossed the Pacific. Before this time men had believed that there was far more land than water on the surface of the globe. Now explorers were discovering that there was far more water than land, and that the water could serve as a highway to any coast in the world for men who knew how to use its winds and ride its waves. The Mongol Empire had rested on mastery of the steppes. The empires of the future would rest on mastery of the oceans. When the first ship to circumnavigate the globe finished its voyage in 1522, Europe had begun to cast a web of communication and influence around the earth. During the next four centuries that web was to draw all the civilizations of the world under the influence of Europe.

Conditions for Maritime Discovery

By the year 1000, Norsemen from Iceland and Greenland had coasted North America in small, open boats. They were too few, however, to make any permanent settlement, and their dis-

coveries were unknown to the rest of Europe. Before Europeans could make a sustained drive to push out across the Atlantic they needed better ships, more reliable aids to navigation, and stronger motivation.

Better ships were long in coming. Oar-propelled galleys had already mastered the Mediterranean, and by the thirteenth century Genoese and Venetian galleys were venturing out into the Atlantic to Morocco and Flanders. But on the open seas mariners needed sails rather than oars and broad, round hulls

Top: Mediterranean war galley with lateen sail, *ca.* twelfth century; middle: lateen-rigged vessel, much like Columbus' *Niña*, early fifteenth century; bottom: Spanish galleon of sixteenth century, the typical long-distance ship for Spanish commerce.

rather than long, narrow galleys. By the fifteenth century the Portuguese had devised a craft capable of long ocean voyages: the squat, three-masted caravel, with two masts generally square-rigged and one mast lateen-rigged. The caravel preserved the advantages of both the northern European square-rig, which was better for running before the wind, and the Arab lateen-rig, which was better for sailing close to the wind. It was slower than the galley, but it had more space for cargo and for supplies on long voyages.

Galleys had generally stayed close to land, hugging the shoreline. Before ships could venture straight out to sea, shipmasters needed some way of determining their direction and their whereabouts. The compass gave them a sense of direction in dark weather; the astrolabe enabled them to determine their latitude with fair accuracy; and improved charts gave them confidence that they could recognize the approaches to most European ports. (No precise way of determining longitude was known until the eighteenth century.)

City-states were the original bases for long-range navigation. Venetian and Genoese merchants linked the Black Sea and Egypt with Italy and England, and the Germans of the Hanseatic League traded from Russian Novgorod to French Bordeaux. But transoceanic exploration, trade, and colonization required a broader base for support. The new monarchies of western Europe were better situated geographically than the Italian or German city-states to open up the Atlantic. They also had advantages in manpower, resources, and political centralization. After 1400 the larger monarchies gradually replaced the cities as the major centers of commercial enterprise.

It is not easy to determine the motives that prompted Europeans—rather than Chinese or Moslems—to "discover" the rest of the world by taking to the sea. The Moslems had been crossing the Indian Ocean for centuries, and the Chinese regularly sailed up and down the East Asian coast and into the Indian Ocean; but neither people tried to go farther. Certainly the crusade ideal influenced Portuguese and Spanish rulers. To convert the heathen and to weaken Islam by placing Christian allies in the Moslem rear was the goal of many explorers. Crusading zeal was not the main impetus of the great discoveries, but it could be used to inspire enthusiasm for dangerous ventures and to sanctify more worldly motives.

Of those more worldly motives, the need to find precious metals was the most compelling. In an age without refrigeration, the spices that helped preserve meats and make them more palatable—pepper from India, cinnamon from Ceylon, ginger from China, nutmeg and

An illustration from a sailing book, *Art de Naviguer,* 1583, demonstrating how to determine latitude by observing the sun's height.

cloves from the East Indies—were luxuries that were almost necessities. The long journey from India or the Moluccas and the Arab-Venetian trade monopoly made such spices expensive. But Europeans needed them (and other luxuries such as cotton and silk cloth) more keenly than Asians needed anything Europe had to offer except gold and silver; so there was a steady flow of precious metals from Europe eastward. This drain limited the supply of specie (hard coins) in Europe at a time when it was increasingly needed as currency. Before credit systems became widely used in the seventeenth and eighteenth centuries, the only practical way to provide the money needed by burgeoning commerce and industry was to increase the supply of bullion. European mines had never been very productive and were nearly exhausted by 1400. Fifteenth-century rulers were acutely aware of their need for gold. They knew that they had to have hard cash in their treasury to hire soldiers, equip navies, and maintain bureaucracies, and they knew that European supplies of precious metals were limited.

By the late fifteenth century a restless, energetic, and bold seafaring population was scattered along Europe's Atlantic coastline. Resourceful sailors, fishermen, and merchants had developed the techniques and the ships for making long voyages. They had religious and economic motives strong enough to overcome their superstitious fears of what lay beyond known waters, and their governments were often ready to back them. Europe needed direct contact with Asia, and some Europeans believed that it would not be too difficult to reach Asia by sea. Ptolemy in the second century had underestimated the size of the globe and had overestimated the span of Asia, and the geographers of the fifteenth century, accepting his miscalculations, were convinced that Japan and China lay only a few thousand miles west of Europe. The size of Africa was also underestimated so that an eastern route did not seem to be too difficult. Either an eastern or a western voyage seemed possible, and the material and psychological environment was favorable for an age of discovery.

Portuguese Exploration

Perhaps the most interesting figure of the whole age stands at its very beginning: Prince Henry the Navigator (1394–1460), the younger son of King John I of Portugal. Prince Henry was obsessed with the desire to learn more about Africa; he devoted his life to organizing, equipping, and sending out fleets that pushed farther and farther down the African west coast. In a remarkable observatory at Sagres on Cape St. Vincent, the southwestern tip of Portugal, he brought together the scientific and the seafaring knowledge of his day. He had vague notions of outflanking Islam by reaching lands that the Moslems had never touched, but his main objective was to find gold. When the Portuguese reached the Gold Coast of Africa in the 1450s this objective was achieved.

After Henry's death the impetus of exploration was lost for a time. But Henry's grandnephew, King John II (1481–95), speeded up the effort to find an all-water route to India that would short-circuit the Venetian-Arab monopoly. By 1488 Bartholomew Dias had discovered the Cape of Good Hope, and in

Toynbee on the Age of Discovery

Since A.D. 1500 the map of the civilized world has indeed been transformed out of all recognition. Down to that date it was composed of a belt of civilizations girdling the Old World from the Japanese Isles on the north-east to the British Isles on the north-west. . . . The main line of communication was provided by the chain of steppes and deserts that cut across the belt of civilizations from the Sahara to Mongolia. For human purposes, the Steppe was an inland sea. . . . This waterless sea had its dry-shod ships and its quayless ports. The steppe-galleons were camels, the steppe-galleys horses, and the steppe-ports "caravan cities." . . . The great revolution was a technological revolution by which the West made its fortune, got the better of all the other living civilizations, and forcibly united them into a single society of literally world-wide range. The revolutionary Western invention was the substitution of the Ocean for the Steppe as the principal medium of world-communication. This use of the Ocean, first by sailing ships and then by steamships, enabled the West to unify the whole inhabited and habitable world.

From Arnold J. Toynbee, *Civilization on Trial* (New York: Oxford University Press, 1948), pp. 67–70.

The Portuguese as others saw them. Top: detail from a seventeenth-century Japanese screen painting showing a Portuguese sailor playing a game of go with a Japanese friend in a native ship. Below: African bronze sculpture of Portuguese exploiter.

1497 Vasco da Gama rounded the cape with four ships, reached Calicut on the Malabar Coast of India in 1498, and was back in Lisbon with two of his ships in 1499. In 1500 a larger fleet, commanded by Cabral, touched the coast of Brazil and then headed for India in Da Gama's wake.

This first contact by sea with India was to have momentous consequences, but neither side was particularly impressed by the other on first meeting. The Hindus had only contempt for the bedraggled sailors who had spent months aboard Da Gama's ships, and the Europeans soon made it clear that they found nothing to respect in the civilization of India. When the Hindus asked Da Gama what he sought in India, he is said to have replied laconically, "Christians and spices."

During the sixteenth century the Portuguese strove to build a commercial empire in the Indian Ocean. Affonso de Albuquerque, the brutal but able Portuguese governor from 1509 to 1515 and the real founder of that empire, understood the relationship between trade, sea power, and strategic bases. He seized Goa on the western coast of India to serve as his headquarters, Malacca on the Strait of Malacca to control the trade between the Spice Islands and the Indian Ocean, and Ormuz to dominate the Persian Gulf. He failed to capture Aden, a base from which he could have strangled the Arab-Venetian trade through the Red Sea. He was as ruthless in disciplining his own men as he was in terrorizing Hindu princes and fighting Arab seamen. At Albuquerque's death in 1515 the Portugese had a large share of the spice trade (though not a monopoly) and controlled strategic bases all the way from Africa to the East Indies.

It was easy for the Portuguese and other Europeans to seize footholds in India because the Moslem and Hindu princes of the coastal districts were weak, and the Mogul Empire of the North had little power in the South. The Portuguese, however, established only trading posts, not colonies of settlement, in India, and even the trading posts soon ceased to be very profitable. The early voyages had made large profits for their backers. But the cost to the Portuguese government of equipping fleets and maintaining fighting forces soon ate up the profits. Portugal was a relatively small and poor country, with a small merchant class. Italian, German, and Flemish bankers soon dominated the Portuguese trade, and the spices that arrived at Lisbon were sent on directly to Antwerp, which proved to be a better point from which to distribute them to Europe. The burden of empire was already proving heavy when Portugal fell into the grip of Spain in 1580.

Columbus
and Spanish Exploration

In 1484, before the Portuguese had reached the Cape of Good Hope, a Genoese sailor named Christopher Columbus had tried in vain to persuade King John II of Portugal to back him in a voyage of exploration to the west. Columbus was convinced by all the evidence at hand

that it would be comparatively easy to reach Cipangu (Japan) by sailing due west. But for years he was unable to persuade any monarch to back him. At last the rulers of Spain, who had conquered the Moorish Kingdom of Granada in January 1492, were free to turn their attention elsewhere. And so it was under Castilian auspices that Columbus sailed on his famous voyage. It took the Portuguese almost a century of patiently organized effort to reach the Old World eastward, while the Spanish reached the New World westward in one brilliant voyage. There was a large element of luck in the founding of Spain's empire in the New World.

Columbus touched land in the Bahamas on October 12, 1492, thinking he had struck some small islands in the Japanese archipelago. Throughout four voyages and until his death in 1506, he remained convinced, even after touching the mainland, that it was the Old World of Japan and China that he had dis-

Christopher Columbus, the Genoese sailor who sailed west in search of Japan and found the New World. This portrait of Columbus is thought to be the closest existing likeness of him. It is a copy, made in about 1525, of an earlier painting that has been lost.

covered. And so, although it was Columbus who named the "Indians" he found on the shores of Haiti and Cuba, it was the Florentine Amerigo Vespucci who gave his name to the continents Columbus had discoverd. Amerigo, director of the Medici branch bank in Seville, sailed on both Spanish and Portuguese voyages and described what he saw in letters that were widely read throughout Europe. In one he referred to the great southern continent in the west as *Mundus Novus*, a New World. Later map makers labeled the two new continents "America," for the man who first realized that it was a new, not an old, world that was opening up to view.

The Treaty of Tordesillas, 1494

Since both Spain and Portugal were seeking the same lands, they soon had to appeal to the pope for an adjudication of their rival claims to unoccupied and heathen lands around the globe. The pope, Alexander VI, was a Spaniard, and the line of demarcation that he drew in 1493 a hundred leagues west of the Cape Verde Islands was favorable to Spain.

Portugal, however, gained a diplomatic victory through a treaty with Spain in 1494—the Treaty of Tordesillas. By this treaty a line was drawn from pole to pole 370 leagues west of the Cape Verde Islands, separating Portugal's claims to the east from Spain's to the west. The Portuguese assumed that the line applied only to the Atlantic (it gave them Brazil, though they did not know this in 1494). The Spanish preferred to believe that the line extended round the world, cutting it in half as a knife cuts an orange. They hoped that this interpretation might give them the Moluccas, the heart of the Spice Islands, but later (1527) Spain sold all its claims to these islands to Portugal.

Magellan

By 1512 the Portuguese were in the Moluccas, and in 1513 the Spaniard Balboa sighted the Pacific from the Isthmus of Darien in Central America. In the years to come, the Spanish, the English, and others tried again and again to discover a strait through the New World by which they might sail westward into the Pacific and reach the Spice Islands. The Portuguese navigator Magellan was convinced that he could do just that by rounding the southern tip of South America. He knew that Portugal would never back him in such an expedition because it would create a Spanish-dominated route to the islands, so in 1519 he sailed with Spanish backing. It was the third of the truly great voyages—along with those of Columbus and Da Gama. Magellan negotiated the straits that are named for him and got across the Pacific after incredible hardships, only to be killed by natives in the Philippines. His navigator, Sebastian del Cano, brought one of the five original ships back to Lisbon by way of the Cape of Good Hope in 1522, the first ship to sail round the world.

THE SPANISH EMPIRE IN THE WEST

From 1520 to 1550 the conquistadors of Spain carved out an empire in the West. As the Spaniards on the Caribbean

Above: Vasco da Gama. Below: Magellan plotting his position, detail from an allegorical portrait by De Bry.

islands began to hear exciting tales of wealthy, half-civilized empires, they turned from exploration to conquest. The most notable of the conquistadors were Hernando Cortes, who in 1519–21 conquered the formidable Aztec Empire in Mexico with 600 men, 16 horses, and a few cannon, and Francisco Pizarro, who in 1533–34 conquered the Inca Empire in Peru with even fewer followers. Their firearms, steel swords, and horses gave the Spaniards an advantage over the more primitively armed groups that faced them, but it was primarily their daring, their discipline, and their fanatical faith that accounted for their fantastic successes.

Within a generation Spanish soldiers, lawyers, and friars unexpectedly found themselves the undisputed rulers of vast stretches of territory and millions of human beings. Often the new ruling class simply stepped into the place of former conquerors like the Aztecs and Incas, living on the tribute from subject populations that had supported their predecessors. But the Spaniards needed labor to exploit the new lands fully, and the upland Indians could not survive in the rich, but unhealthy lowlands. Thus when sugar became an important crop, Negro slaves had to be imported from Africa to do the work. Until the seventeenth century, however, the industry most favored by the Spanish government was the mining of gold and silver. After the discovery of enormously rich silver mines in both Mexico and Peru in 1545, the extraction and shipment of silver became the main business of the Spanish Empire as a whole. Every spring after 1564 the plate fleet of twenty to sixty vessels gathered at Havana harbor to be convoyed by warships to Seville. And every year the Spanish government waited anxiously until the bullion, which everyone agreed was the key to national strength, was safely in harbor.

The empire that grew out of these exploits and these economic activities was a kind of compromise between what the Spanish settlers, the Christian friars, and the Spanish government at Madrid would each have liked to see develop in America. The settlers, many of them former conquistadors, would have liked to set themselves up as manorial lords living on the forced labor of the natives, unmolested by any political direction from Madrid. The Franciscans and other friars, particularly the great Dominican, Bartolomé de las Casas, would have liked to see the natives treated as fellow Christians and fellow subjects of the Spanish crown. Las Casas worked tirelessly to protect both the legal and the moral rights of the Indians in the face of relentless pressure from the settlers to exploit them. The government in Spain was determined to centralize all decision making in Seville or Madrid, and to protect the natives so far as possible, as the friars urged.

The theory of the Spanish Empire, as it had unfolded by the end of the sixteenth century, was remarkably sensible and humane by contemporary standards. The settlers were allowed to command the forced labor of the subject Indians, but this labor was regulated by public authority, not by private right. There

Las Casas on the American Indians in the Sixteenth Century

It has been written that these peoples of the Indies, lacking human governance and ordered nations, did not have the power of reason to govern themselves—which was inferred only from their having been found to be gentle, patient and humble. It has been implied that God became careless in creating so immense a number of rational souls and let human nature, which He so largely determined and provided for, go astray in the almost infinitesimal part of the human lineage which they comprise. From this it follows that they have all proven themselves unsocial and therefore monstrous, contrary to the natural bent of all peoples of the world.

. . . Not only have [the Indians] shown themselves to be very wise peoples and possessed of lively and marked understanding, prudently governing and providing for their nations (as much as they can be nations, without faith in or knowledge of the true God) and making them prosper in justice; but they have equalled many diverse nations of the world, past and present, that have been praised for their governance, politics and customs, and exceed by no small measure the wisest of all these, such as the Greeks and Romans, in adherence to the rules of natural reason.

From Bartolomé de las Casas, *Apologética historia de las Indias,* in *Introduction to Contemporary Civilization in the West,* 3rd ed. (New York: Columbia University Press, 1960), Vol. I, p. 539.

ycpolínhq mexica

were serious abuses, especially in Mexico, and the long arm of the home government was often awkward and exasperatingly slow in dealing with local problems. But as time went on the Spanish came close to accomplishing what the Portuguese failed to accomplish in the East and what the English never attempted in North America: the Christianization and Europeanization of a whole population. The Spaniards took seriously the papal bulls of 1493 which gave them the heathen peoples of the New World to convert and nuture in the Christian faith. In theory, the natives were considered Christians and subjects of the king (unlike the unfortunate Negroes, who were dismissed as the slaves of West African kings). The gulf between Span-

iard and native was never entirely closed, in either religion or culture. But Spanish and Portuguese in the end became the languages of all but the most isolated Indians, and Roman Catholicism the dominant religion. Intermarriage was so common that the mestizos, or descendants of mixed marriages, eventually became more numerous than the pure-bred of either race. The Spanish (and the Portuguese in Brazil) made a serious attempt to convert the New World to western civilization.

SPAIN UNDER PHILIP II

In the later sixteenth century Spain was the dominant power in Europe as well

Cortes accepting the surrender of Quauhtemoc, last king of the Aztecs. The artist was a Spanish-trained native from Tlaxcala, who chronicled Cortes' conquest of Mexico. Notice the mixture of European and Indian styles.

as in America. The accession of the Habsburg Charles to the throne of Spain in the early sixteenth century had thrust the Spanish into the full stream of European politics and diplomacy at a moment when the Protestant revolt was beginning to spread, the Turks were expanding up the Danube Valley, and the job of exploring and colonizing America was demanding a huge expenditure of energy. To roll back the threats of heretics and infidels while conquering a new world was a heavy task for a state so recently formed. But for a brief and brilliant time, the Spanish under the Emperor Charles V (1515–56) and his son, King Philip II (1556–98), were almost equal to the challenge. The sixteenth and early seventeenth centuries were the golden age of Spain.

In 1555–56 Charles V divided his family holdings between his brother Ferdinand and his son Philip. To Ferdi-

nand went the Habsburg possessions in Austria and the imperial crown (still elective in theory, but by now always bestowed on a Habsburg). To Philip went the crowns of Castile and Aragon, with Castile's possessions in the New World, the Kingdom of Naples and the Duchy of Milan (which meant control of Italy), and the Netherlands. Thus for a century and a half after 1556 there were "Austrian Habsburgs" and "Spanish Habsburgs," separate ruling houses but houses that cooperated closely in matters of dynastic policy. Except for the Netherlands, which might well have gone to Ferdinand because of the Netherlands' close cultural and geographical ties with the Empire, the possessions of Philip II formed a more tight-knit and centralized state than his father's holdings.

Philip II was thoroughly Spanish in speech, thought, and character. After the conclusion of peace with France in 1559, he returned from the Netherlands to Spain to remain until his death almost forty years later. He caught the imagination of his people as few of their rulers had done. To the Spanish he is still "Philip the Prudent," one of their greatest kings. Distrustful of his advisers, unable to delegate authority even in minor matters, slow in coming to a decision, strongly Catholic in religion (his enemies would have said "bigoted"), convinced of his divine right to govern Spain as an absolute ruler strictly accountable to God but to no one else, Philip devoted his country to the ideal of a restored Catholic Christendom with the Spanish monarchy as its leading power and defender. For centuries the Spanish had fought the Moors. To Philip, the crusade would continue against half-converted Jews and Moors at home and against Turks and Protestants abroad until the Christian Commonwealth of the Middle Ages had been restored. Meanwhile the Catholic faith would be carried to the New World. Since Spain was the divinely chosen agent of this mission, what was in the interest of Spain was naturally in the interest of Christendom as a whole. Or so it appeared to Philip and to most of the Spanish nobility.

If ever there was a monarchy and a ruling class with a sense of destiny, it was the Spanish of the sixteenth century. This spirit was evident in the Spanish Jesuits who guided the Council of Trent and helped to reconvert much of central Europe to Catholicism, in the Spanish friars who labored to convert the American Indians, in the conquistadors who toppled native empires in the New World, and in the tough Spanish infantry who for over a century defeated every foe they met in Europe. Philip II's Spain was the strongest miltary power on the Continent, the strongest naval power in the Atlantic, and the wealthiest state in Europe. Spain was the nerve center of the Catholic Reformation. No wonder the terror of the Spanish name lived on into the seventeenth century long after Spanish strength had begun to waste away.

Economic Policy

The economic basis of Spain's predominance was the gold and silver that flowed to Seville in a swelling stream from the New World. Early in the sixteenth century the bullion imported was almost entirely gold. But after the discovery in 1545 of the rich mines in Peru and Mexico, it was mostly silver. The value of the treasure that reached Spain rose enormously between 1500 and 1600. In very round figures the average yearly value of bullion imports at the beginning of the century was something under $300,000; by about 1550 the value had increased 15 times; and by 1600 over 40 times, to about $12,000,000. Then a steady decline set in, until about 1660 the average was down to around $1,200,000. The Spanish crown received about a quarter of the total as its share.

This influx of precious metals, combined with internal financial problems, led to a steep rise in prices. At first the rise was slow and generally stimulating to Spanish industry and commerce. But it had become precipitous by the middle of the century, amounting to a severe inflation that struck first Spain and then the rest of western and central Europe as the metal flowed out of the Iberian Peninsula (in spite of all government prohibitions). It has been estimated that prices quadrupled in Spain in the course of the

Philip II of Spain by Titian.

On Philip II of Spain

The pallor of his complexion was remarked on by all observers, and most of them drew the proper conclusion, namely, that it indicated a weak stomach and lack of exercise. Reddened eyes were a penalty of his excessive devotion to the written word both day and night. . . . Reading and writing occupied the major portion of Philip's day. . . . He had taken deeply to heart his father's injunction to direct everything himself, and never to give his full confidence even to the most faithful of his ministers, and the natural result was that his time was completely occupied with receiving and answering reports and letters. . . . Reports, reports, and even more reports; Philip was literally submerged with them in his later years, and moreover he did not stop at reading them; he annotated them, as he went along, with comments on matters as absurdly trifling as the spelling and style of the men who had written them—all in that strange, sprawling hand of his, one of the most illegible hands of an age more than usually replete with chirographical difficulties.

From R. B. Merriman, *The Rise of the Spanish Empire* (New York: Macmillan, 1934), Vol. IV, pp. 21–24.

century. Since prices rose faster than taxes could be increased, Philip II was forced to repudiate his government's debts three times, in 1557, 1575, and 1596. (His successors had to follow the same course in 1607, 1627, and 1647.) The effect of inflation on Spanish industry was eventually disastrous. Since prices always rose faster in Spain than elsewhere, it was relatively more expensive to manufacture goods in Spain than in other countries. This meant that Spanish producers could not sell their goods abroad and that cheaper foreign products captured the Spanish market.

In the short run, Spain's silver enabled it to maintain supremacy in Europe by paying its armies in cash and buying what goods it needed abroad. In the long run, this policy helped to ruin Spain's industry and commerce, and even to undermine its agriculture. There were other reasons for Spain's economic troubles in the seventeenth century, such as the expulsion of its best farmers, the Moriscoes, as the converted Moors were called. But the influx of precious metals was probably the major reason for both the rapid rise and the equally rapid decline of Spain as the leading power in Europe. Spain lived for a century on the windfall of American treasure, but when the supply of bullion dwindled in the seventeenth century Spain found that the real sinews of its national strength—native industry and agriculture—were ruined.

Religious Policy

Philip II's religious policy was the most narrowly intolerant of his time. He abhorred heresy and unbelief with a holy hatred and said he would rather be king in a desert than in a land of heretics. He feared Islam as the ancient enemy both of Christendom and of his people. In his eyes and in those of most of his countrymen, the Moors who had been forcibly Christianized after the conquest of Granada in 1492 were still Moslems at heart. Furthermore, they were more prosperous than most Spanish farmers, and they were reputedly in league with the Moslems of North Africa. In 1566 Philip ordered them to stop using the Arabic language and learn Castilian, to give up their

Moorish dress, and to stop taking hot baths, as was their custom. In 1569 the exasperated Moriscoes broke into a revolt, which was savagely suppressed. They were driven out of Andalusia and scattered over Spain. In the years after 1609 they were driven out of the country entirely. Their numbers and importance have sometimes been exaggerated, but there is no doubt that their loss helped to weaken the Spanish economy.

At the height of the revolt of the Moriscoes in 1570, the Turks captured Cyprus from the Venetians. Once again Europe trembled before the threat of Islamic expansion. Philip II immediately allied with the pope and the Venetians to counter the danger, and in October 1571 a Spanish and Venetian fleet won a famous victory over a large Turkish fleet at Lepanto in the Gulf of Corinth.

The baptism of Moslem women, from a Spanish relief of 1520.

Nothing decisive came of the battle because the Christian forces were unable to follow up their victory. But the event had considerable importance for European morale because it was the first time a Turkish fleet had been defeated.

The Apogee of Spanish Prestige

Philip's prestige probably never stood higher in Europe than in the years immediately following Lepanto. He was popular at home, and his defeat of the Turks gave him the undisputed political leadership of Catholic Europe. France, potentially the strongest monarchy in Europe, was torn by civil war during most of his reign and so was unable to contest his leadership. England seemed weak and divided by religious controversies, and its queen had been excommunicated by the pope in 1570. Meanwhile the Empire was safely in the hands of Philip's Habsburg cousins. It seemed as if his dream of a resurgent Catholic Christendom dominated by Spain was about to become a reality.

This dream was shattered during the last quarter of the sixteenth century by the revolt of the Netherlands, the rise of English sea power, and the accession of a former Protestant to the throne of France. In his struggle with the embattled forces of Protestantism in northern Europe, Philip overreached himself, exhausted his resources, and started his nation on its long decline.

THE REVOLT OF THE NETHERLANDS

The Netherlands were the wealthiest and most densely populated of Philip II's dominions. The 3 million people dwelling beside the mouths of the Rhine and the Meuse had lived by their industry and commerce since the early Middle Ages. The looms of the southern provinces turned out great quantities of linen and woolen cloth, while the fisheries and shipping of the northern provinces steadily increased in value. The comfortable houses of Bruges, Ghent, Antwerp, and Amsterdam were built with the profits of this flourishing industry and trade.

The seventeen provinces of the Netherlands had been united in a personal union by the dukes of Burgundy. But when Charles V inherited the territories in 1519 through his grandmother, Mary of Burgundy, there was little in the way of national feeling or common institutions to bind them together. Charles, who was brought up in Flanders and spoke Flemish as his native language, was the closest thing to a native ruler the united Netherlands had ever had, but he regularly sacrificed their interests to his broader imperial aims. During his reign the faint beginnings of a Netherlandish national consciousness appeared.

The provinces were a crossroads for ideas as well as for commerce. The Humanism of Erasmus as well as the teachings of Luther took early root in the Netherlands, to be followed by Anabaptist ideas. But in the 1550s a militant, disciplined Calvinism spread rapidly and soon became the dominant form of Protestantism. When Philip II took over the rule from his father in the fall of 1555, Calvinists constituted tight-knit minorities in most of the cities of the seventeen provinces.

Within ten years after his accession, Philip had alienated most of the nobility and bourgeoisie of the provinces. Native nobles were displaced in favor of Spaniards in the governing council, a policy that hurt the pride of the upper classes. A threat to enforce the laws against heresy with new efficiency and severity sent a chill of terror through the Calvinist merchants and ministers. Madrid was almost a thousand miles away from Brussels, and Philip's Spanish-Catholic mind was even more remote from the interests and concerns of his busy, prosperous Dutch and Flemish subjects, whether they were Calvinist or Catholic. The revolt that ensued was partly a provincial reaction against centralization, partly a patriotic movement directed against foreign rule, and partly a religious protest against an inquisitorial Catholicism.

In 1566 Calvinist mobs began to break images of the saints and smash stained-glass windows in Catholic

Contemporary map showing Spain as the head and crown of sixteenth-century Europe.

churches throughout the Netherlands. Philip decided to make a frightful example of the iconoclasts. He sent the Duke of Alva and about 10,000 Spanish regulars to the Netherlands with orders to bring the trouble-makers either to the block or to the stake. Alva set up what came to be called a "Council of Blood" and boasted (with some exaggeration) that within the six years of his residence in the Netherlands (1567–73) he had executed close to 18,000 people. In addition to spilling so much blood, Alva and his council confiscated large amounts of property and imposed a 10 percent sales tax that almost strangled the trade of the country during the year or two it was in force. The Netherlanders never forgot these six years. Instead of crushing the opposition to Philip, Alva's policy solidified their resistance, at least for a time.

William the Silent and Dutch Independence

By 1572 the resistance movement had found a leader in William the Silent, Prince of Orange, the wealthiest landowner in the provinces. William was no military genius—he lost almost every battle he fought against the Spanish—but he had political wisdom, integrity, and patience, a rugged kind of patriotism, and a deep hatred of religious fanaticism, whether Calvinist or Catholic. He tried his best to hold the Calvinists in check, keep all seventeen provinces united against the Spanish, and still find a solution that would leave Philip as titular ruler. For a few years it looked as if he might succeed. In 1576 Calvinist excesses provoked a frightful sack of Antwerp by Spanish troops known as the "Spanish Fury." This was enough to frighten all seventeen provinces into an agreement to stick together. The agreement was called the Pacification of Ghent.

Within three years, however, both Protestant and Catholic radicals had got out of hand, moderates had lost influence, and animosity between Catholics and Protestants had begun to undermine the universal hatred of Spain. The almost unanimous opposition to Alva gradually gave way to a savage civil war in which the Calvinists, the best-disciplined mi-nority, took over leadership of the opposition to Philip. Most of the Catholics rushed back into the arms of Spain for protection. The seventeen provinces split in two as Calvinists fled to the Dutch provinces in the north beyond the great rivers, where they were better able to defend themselves, and Catholics fled to the Walloon provinces in the south, where Spanish troops could be maintained and supplied from the upper Rhine. In 1579 the Dutch provinces in the north formed the Union of Utrecht. This union ultimately became the foundation of the United Provinces, or Dutch Netherlands, which formally declared their independence of Philip II in 1581. And so the unanticipated result of the revolt of 1566 was that the seven northern provinces broke away from Spanish rule while the ten southern provinces remained under Habsburg control and eventually (in 1830) became the kingdom of Belgium.

William the Silent by Anthony Moro.

The Rise of the United Provinces

The Dutch Netherlands had to fight for their independence for two generations after 1581. They got some help from French and English troops at various times, but the price that the French Duke of Anjou and the English Queen Elizabeth asked for their help was often dangerously high. In the long run it was dogged determination, geography, and the rivalry of their enemies that won the Dutch their independence. William the Silent was assassinated in 1584, but his descendants carried on his tradition of able and disinterested leadership as *stadtholders* (regents) of one or more of the seven provinces. The "United Provinces" never formed more than the loosest sort of political federation, but the Dutch fought with stubbornness when they had to. The Duke of Parma, who became Philip's representative in the Netherlands in 1578, was one of the best military commanders of his day, but he was unable to reconquer the provinces beyond the bend of the Rhine and Meuse, especially since he lacked control of the sea. The Dutch "Sea Beggars," or privateers, won as many battles against the Spanish on the water as William's armies lost on

Example of propaganda badge worn by Dutch "Sea Beggars." The insurgents' hatred of Catholicism is expressed in the inscription which reads "Better the Turks than the pope."

the land. When Philip's Invincible Armada was broken up in 1588 by the English and the weather, reconquest of the northern provinces became impossible. Finally, in 1648, the king of Spain recognized the independence of his former Dutch subjects.

By this time the new Dutch state had become one of the great powers of Europe. Most long wars exhaust even the victors, but the Dutch came out of this war the most powerful commercial nation in Europe. By the early seventeenth century they were building more ships each year than all other nations combined (2,000, it was said), and they were better ships than any others. During the first half of the seventeenth century the Dutch captured more and more of the carrying trade not only of Europe but of the world. Their rates were cheaper, their business methods more efficient, their handling of cargo more skillful. Antwerp (in the Spanish Netherlands) had been ruined by the Spanish soldiery and blocked off from the sea through the closing of the Scheldt River by the Dutch. Thus Amsterdam (in the United Provinces) took Antwerp's position as the commercial and financial center of Europe. Until their own vulnerability to attack by land became evident after 1660, the Dutch had no rivals who could contest their power.

The sheer geographical extent of Dutch commercial operations was remarkable. Dutch ships handled much of the grain trade of the Baltic and a large part of the carrying trade of England, France, Italy, and Portugal. When Philip II seized the crown of Portugal in 1580 and stopped the Dutch from visiting Lisbon (whence the Dutch were accustomed to distribute Portuguese spices to the rest of Europe), the Dutch with characteristic daring went out to the source of the spices themselves in the Moluccas. In 1602 the Dutch East India Company was formed and soon established its headquarters at Batavia on the island of Java.

By the middle of the century the Dutch had seized the richest part of Portugal's eastern empire—the Moluccas, Malacca, and Ceylon. For over a century the company paid very large dividends, mainly by ruthlessly monopolizing the production of spices and limiting it to keep up prices. In 1652 the Dutch founded a colony at the Cape of Good Hope. A few years earlier they had come close to ousting the Portuguese from Brazil. By 1614 they had a settlement on Manhattan Island named New Amsterdam that became the center for a large Dutch carrying trade in the New World. When the French and British embarked on overseas trade and colonization, they found not only the Spanish and the Portuguese but the Dutch ahead of them all over the world.

So it was an economic giant that Philip II conjured up when he set out to

THE DIVISION OF THE NETHERLANDS 1581

Amsterdam harbor, center of a worldwide trade, detail from an engraving by Pieter Bast, 1597.

Elizabeth I of England, and her signature. The silver medal commemorates the defeat of the Spanish Armada, 1588.

crush his rebellious subjects in the Netherlands. The revolt of the Netherlands may be considered as a kind of dress-rehearsal-in-miniature for those larger popular and patriotic revolts against absolute monarchy, beginning with the Puritan Rebellion in England and continuing through the American and French revolutions, that marked the next two centuries. There are many differences among these movements, but there are many similarities in the mixture of economic, patriotic, and religious grievances, the blindness of the absolute monarchs, and the ultimate triumph of "middle-class" interests.

ELIZABETHAN ENGLAND

Philip of Spain was almost as unfortunate in his dealings with England under Queen Elizabeth I as he was in his dealings with the Netherlands. England was crucial to his plans. If he could have added control of England to his control of Spain, Milan, and the Netherlands, France would have been encircled and the vital sea routes between Spain and the Netherlands would have been safer. For a few years (1554–58), while Philip was married to Queen Mary of England, it seemed as if the Emperor's dream would be realized: England had been brought within the Habsburg orbit and restored to Roman Catholicism. But

Elizabeth's accession to the throne in 1558 changed everything.

Queen Elizabeth I (1558–1603) is generally accounted the greatest of the Tudors and one of England's ablest rulers, though to some critics she was simply a stingy and narrow-minded woman. Whatever the judgment, England was immeasurably stronger at her death than at her accession, and she died beloved by the great majority of her people. At twenty-five, when she came to the throne, she had already lived through disgrace, humiliation, and even danger of execution during her sister Mary's reign. She had seen how Mary had lost the love of her people by marrying a foreigner and by burning heretics. These early experiences left her a strong-willed and shrewd young woman, aware of how precarious both her own situation and that of her nation were, determined to put politics before religion and to follow a purely national policy.

Her instinct was always to temporize and compromise. As the daughter of Henry VIII and Anne Boleyn, she could never allow England to submit to papal authority. But she wanted a religious settlement that would not alienate patriotic Catholics, and she hoped she could deceive the Catholic powers of Europe for a time into thinking that she could be won back to Rome. On the other hand, she resented the attempt of the Puritan minority to dictate a radical religious settlement and a risky, pro-Protestant foreign policy. However, she never completely broke with her patriotic Puritan subjects and never lost their loyalty, even when she punished them for advocating radical measures. Elizabeth's policy was nationalist first and Protestant second, but the long-term result was to encourage that fusion of patriotism and Protestantism that became a permanent characteristic of English public opinion.

She compromised and temporized in her foreign policy as well. Her instinct was to avoid clear-cut decisions, to keep a dozen intrigues afoot so that there were always avenues of escape from any policy, and to avoid war at almost any cost. The chief danger at her accession was from French influence on Scotland. The French had long been allies of the Scots, and Mary Stuart, Queen of Scots, was married in 1558 to the heir to the French crown. A year later John Knox, who had become a Calvinist, returned to his native Scotland from Geneva and began a religious revolution. Catholicism and French influence on the Scots were both undermined. Moreover, since Mary Stuart's husband was now king of France, it was clear that France would make every effort to defeat the Calvinists. For once Elizabeth made a rapid decision: to ally with the Calvinist party in Scotland and keep the French out. By 1560 Knox, the Kirk (Scottish Church), and the pro-English party were in control, and the French had lost all influence in Scotland. The way was paved for the union of the English and Scottish crowns in 1603.

Mary Queen of Scots

Mary Stuart returned to Scotland in 1561 after her husband's death. She was a far more charming and romantic figure than her cousin Elizabeth, but she was no stateswoman. A convinced Catholic, she soon ran head-on into the granitelike opposition of Knox and the Kirk. Her second marriage, to her cousin Lord Darnley, turned out badly and she became involved in a plot resulting in his murder. In 1567 she was forced to abdicate, and in the following year she fled from Scotland and sought protection in England from Elizabeth. No visitor could have been more unwelcome. Mary, as Henry VII's great-granddaughter, had the best hereditary claim to be Elizabeth's heir, but she was a Catholic and a foreigner. Elizabeth would never formally recognize her as her successor, nor would she marry in order to produce another heir, nor would she do anything to harm her fellow sovereign, except keep a close watch on her through her agents. This policy exasperated Elizabeth's Puritan advisers and left Mary free to become the center of almost every French or Spanish plot against Elizabeth's life during the next twenty years.

The Anglo-Spanish Conflict

Though there were many sources of friction between them, Elizabeth and Philip of Spain remained on relatively good terms for over twenty years. As time went on, however, it became increasingly difficult to keep the peace. England was a small country with less than half the population of Spain, but during the quarter-century of peace that Elizabeth's cautious temporizing gave her people, English industry, commerce, and shipping expanded considerably. For reasons we have already suggested, the Spanish were unable to produce the goods needed by their colonies. And Spanish shipping was incapable of supplying the insatiable colonial demand for African slaves. An aggressive merchant named Sir John Hawkins was the first Englishman to carry both goods and slaves direct to the Spanish settlements in 1562. It was profitable but dangerous work. In 1569 he and his cousin, Sir Francis Drake, were almost wiped out by a Spanish fleet. In revenge, Drake seized the annual silver shipment from Peru on its way across the Isthmus of Panama. In 1577–80 he followed Magellan's route around the world and demonstrated the vulnerability of the Spanish Empire. Meanwhile English sailors were boldly probing the coasts of North America in a vain search for a Northwest Passage that would short-circuit the Portuguese route to the Indies. Like their fellow Protestants, the Dutch, the English were contesting the Spanish-Portuguese monopoly of overseas trade.

It was the revolt of the Netherlands, however, that finally brought England and Spain to blows. For centuries the economic ties between England and the Low Countries had been close. The English people sympathized with Alva's victims, and English Sea Dogs cooperated informally with Dutch Sea Beggars to prey on Spanish shipping and to cut Spanish communications by sea with the

Mary Stuart, Queen of Scots, and her signature. Lead medal by Jacopo Primavera, *ca.* 1572.

The Spanish Armada in a fight off the Isle of Wight, July 25, 1588. Early seventeenth-century engraving by John Pine, from tapestries now destroyed.

The Armada

When the Spanish Armada challenged the ancient lords of the English on their own grounds, the impending conflict took on the aspect of a judicial duel in which as was expected in such duels, God would defend the right. . . . So when the two fleets approached their appointed battleground, all Europe watched. For the spectators of both parties, the outcome, reinforced, as everyone believed, by an extraordinary tempest, was indeed decisive. The Protestants of France and the Netherlands, Germany and Scandinavia saw with relief that God was, in truth, as they had always supposed, on their side. The Catholics of France and Italy and Germany saw with almost equal relief that Spain was not, after all, God's chosen champion. From that time forward, though Spain's preponderance was to last for more than another generation, the peak of her prestige had passed. . . . So, in spite of the long, indecisive war which followed, the defeat of the Spanish Armada really was decisive. It decided that religious unity was not to be reimposed by force on the heirs of medieval Christendom, and if, in doing so, it only validated what was already by far the most probable outcome, why, perhaps that is all that any of the battles we call decisive has ever done.

From Garrett Mattingly, *The Armada* (Boston: Houghton Mifflin, 1959), pp. 400–01.

Netherlands. Philip's ambassadors in England became deeply involved in one plot after another against Elizabeth's life, usually with the object of setting Mary Stuart on the throne. In 1587 Elizabeth reluctantly consented to Mary's execution when confronted with unmistakable evidence of her complicity in these plots. Philip immediately planned an attack on England. In 1588 he sent his "Invincible Armada" north to hold the Channel while Parma ferried his Spanish veterans across to conquer England for Spain.

The story of the defeat of the Armada has become an allegory of the triumph of a young, vigorous nation over an old and senile nation. The Spanish ships were large and slow, equipped with inferior cannon, and commanded by a landlubber. The fleet was conceived as a means of transporting troops, not of fighting battles at sea. The English ships that put out from Plymouth to harry the Spanish up the Channel were smaller and more maneuverable, trained to fire their cannon at longer range. When the Spanish reached Calais and anchored there, Parma had still not completed his

Civil
Wars

1328   1562 ⌒ 1593   1793

| House of Valois | | House of Bourbon |

1589

plans. The English sent in fire ships among the Spanish ships as they lay at anchor, drove them northward in panic, and attacked them fiercely off Gravelines. Stormy weather completed what the English had begun. Hardly half the galleons that had left Spain made their way back northward and westward around Scotland and Ireland. The victory gave a lift to the morale of Englishmen and of Protestants everywhere. It ended all further thought of Spanish conquest of England—or reconquest of the Netherlands, for that matter. It did not mean the end of Spanish sea power, which was still greater than that of any other country. But when peace was finally signed in 1604, the English, with the Dutch, stood close to the Spaniards as powers on the sea.

THE FRENCH WARS OF RELIGION

One obvious reason for Spain's ascendancy in the later sixteenth century was the fact that France, traditionally the chief obstacle to Habsburg expansion, was torn by a series of civil and religious wars that prostrated the monarchy and devastated large areas of the country between 1562 and 1593. Almost overnight France was transformed from an aggressive national monarchy into a victim of intervention by neighboring states.

Background of the Civil War

France, with a population about double that of Spain, was the largest nation in Christian Europe under a single government. But, impressive as the French monarchy was, it was far from having absolute power. There was still a powerful and turbulent aristocracy in France, and French provinces clung jealously to local customs and privileges. The country was imperfectly unified; there was no body that could speak for the whole realm, as Parliament could for England. Class differences were sharp and the bureaucracy was overworked, corrupt, and inefficient.

Into this half-established absolute monarchy the strong irritant of religious conflict was injected about the middle of the century in the form of militant Calvinism. The rational theology and disciplined organization of Reformed Christianity—not to mention the superb French style of Calvin's writings—appealed widely to many nobles and bourgeois throughout France. The French Calvinists were nicknamed Huguenots. On the eve of the civil wars they boasted about 2,500 churches. They probably never numbered more than a sixth of the population (some scholars say as low as a twelfth), but they were an aggressive and well-organized minority, sure of their faith, and confident of the support of a few men, such as Admiral Coligny, at the very top of the social hierarchy. Arrayed against them were strongly Catholic noble families, and, more important, the University of Paris and the Paris *parlement* (High Court). Most important of all was the fact that the Concordat of Bologna had given the kings of France full control over the appointment of the higher clergy as well as considerable indirect control of papal taxation and jurisdiction. In short, the king and his advisers could see no advantage in religious change, and consequently the Huguenots remained a permanent minority in France.

The Course of the Wars

The wars that broke out in France in 1562 were at once social, political, and religious. When Henry II died in 1559, the royal authority fell into the hands of the Queen Mother, Catherine de' Medici, during the reigns of her three weakling sons, Francis II (1559–60), Charles IX (1560–74), and Henry III (1574–89). Catherine was an astute woman who put politics before religion and did her best

Catherine de' Medici in 1561, by an unknown artist.

to keep the feuding factions at court and the religious fanatics throughout the country from flying at each other's throats. But she lacked formal authority and by now the animosities had become bitter. Calvinists allied themselves with discontented nobles and upholders of local autonomy. On the other side were Catholics, royal agents, and defenders of the *status quo*. Fanatics on both sides appealed for foreign aid, the Huguenots to the English, the Dutch, and the Germans, the Catholics to Spain. Both England and Spain sent troops, mostly at the beginning and again at the end of the wars.

Fighting was of the savage and bitter kind that characterizes civil wars. The Catholics won most of the pitched battles but were unable to wipe out the Huguenots. In 1572 Catherine was persuaded by the Catholic fanatics that one sharp blow might end all the trouble. At two o'clock on the morning of St. Bartholomew's Day, Catholic armed bands set upon the Huguenots in Paris, where many of their leaders were gathered for the wedding of the king's sister to the Protestant, Henry of Navarre. Coligny and many others were killed. The slaughter spread quickly to other French cities, and before it was over probably 10,000 Protestants had been massacred. This was the most spectacular of innumerable atrocities on both sides. It horrified Protestants throughout Europe and, according to one story, made Philip II laugh aloud. But it had little effect on the conflict in France.

Henry of Navarre

The wars dragged on for twenty more years, becoming more and more confused and purposeless until the Hugue-

Henry of Navarre in court dress, a seventeenth-century enamel.

not Henry of Navarre came to the throne in 1589 as Henry IV (1589–1610). Though he was the nearest male heir, he was only remotely related to the previous king. He had a difficult time making good his claim to the crown against a Catholic League that held Paris and against troops of Philip II that intervened from the Spanish Netherlands under Parma. In the end he found that the only way he could capture Paris was to renounce his faith and become a Catholic, which he did in 1593. He did not forget his former fellow Protestants, however. By the Edict of Nantes in 1598 the Huguenots were granted freedom of conscience, freedom of worship in specified places, equal civil rights, and control of some 200 fortified towns throughout France. In short, the edict simply recognized a religious stalemate, and zealots on both sides of the religious fence considered it only temporary. But it constituted the first formal recognition by a European national monarchy that two religions could be allowed to exist side by side without destroying the state, and growing numbers of Frenchmen who preferred civil peace at any price to the anarchy and fanaticism of the past forty years supported it. With the conclusion of peace with Spain and the publication of the Edict of Nantes in 1598, France was ready to resume building a strong monarchy.

THE GENERAL CHARACTER OF THE LATER SIXTEENTH CENTURY

The age of Philip II and of Elizabeth of England has been called the Age of Religious Warfare. It is true that religion was often the spark that set aflame the combustible materials of sixteenth-century society, but early nationalism, economic instability, and social unrest also played their part. A more precise description of the period might be the Age of Religious Politics. Until the Reformation, European politics and diplomacy had slowly grown less religious and more secular. Now for a century, thanks to the religious schism, politics and diplomacy became once more strongly motivated and embittered by religion. The monarchies were faced by religious ideologies that often commanded fiercer loyalties than could the

The Escorial, Philip II's monastery-palace near Madrid.

Religion and Patriotism

A Spanish ambassador reporting the words of a French Catholic in 1565:

Nowadays Catholic princes must not proceed as they once did. At one time friends and enemies were distinguished by the frontiers of provinces and kingdoms, and were called Italians, Germans, Frenchmen, Spaniards, Englishmen, and the like. Now we must say Catholics and heretics, and a Catholic prince must consider all Catholics of all countries as his friends, just as the heretics consider all heretics as friends and subjects whether they are their own vassals or not.

An English Protestant writing in 1589:

All dutiful subjects in this land desire with all their hearts the continuance of God's religion; the preservation of Queen Elizabeth; and the good success of the English navy. These particulars, I grant, are not expressed in flat in the Lord's Prayer; but they are contained within the compass of, and may be deduced from the petitions of that excellent prayer. Whosoever doubteth of this is void of learning.

As quoted in Erich Marks, *Die Zusammenkunft von Bayonne* (Strassburg: K. J. Trübner, 1889), p. 14; as quoted in Benjamin Hanbury, *Historical Memorials Relating to the Independents* (London: Congregational Union of England and Wales, 1839–44), Vol. I, p. 71.

dynasties themselves. A Jesuit might scheme and work and die for an ideal that obviously transcended all state boundaries. In the same way a Scottish Presbyterian, a Dutch Calvinist, and a French Huguenot might have more in common than subjects of the same king. Thus religious differences sometimes undermined the power of monarchs, as they did in France and the Netherlands. And sometimes religious zeal reinforced loyalty to the dynasty, as it did in Spain and among English Protestants. Perhaps the best symbol of this Age of Religious Politics was the Escorial, which Philip II built for his residence near Madrid. The building was half-palace, half-monastery; and the private chamber of the king was connected directly with the chapel of the monastery. A century later a palace would be built at Versailles that would express the spirit of a quite different age.

"Golden Ages"

In spite of internal and external conflicts, the late sixteenth and early seventeenth centuries witnessed a "golden age" of literature and the arts in three of the nations under consideration. Shakespeare's plays and Spenser's poetry in Elizabethan England, Cervantes' *Don Quixote* and Velasquez' paintings in Spain of the early seventeenth century, and Vondel's poetry and Rembrandt's portraits in Holland of the mid-seventeenth century represent a kind of summit of achievement in the history of the arts in these three nations. Shakespeare (*ca.* 1564–1616), Cervantes (1547–1616), and Vondel (1587–1679) are still the greatest figures in the literary history of their native countries, and, though England produced no great painter, Frans Hals (*ca.* 1580–1666) and Rembrandt van Rijn (1606–69) are the towering figures in Dutch painting, as El Greco (*ca.* 1548–1614) and Velasquez (1599–1660) are in Spanish.

In each case the artistic flowering accompanied or, as in Spain, immediately followed a period of heroic national struggle, effort, and achievement. It is tempting to say that ages of national expansion and excitement, times of heroism and "crusade," provide great artists with the stimulation and the receptive audiences they need. On a more mundane level, it is clear that "golden ages" depend on the existence of a class of people with enough education, wealth, and leisure to appreciate luxuries like books and paintings. The historian can record the existence of such classes and the occurrence of heroic national effort in England, Spain, and the Dutch Netherlands during these years. But he cannot account satisfactorily for Shakespeare's extraordinary appreciation of the complexities of human motivation, Cervantes' sympathy for all sorts and conditions of men, or Rembrandt's penetration of the depths of the religious soul. All these are manifestations of purely individual genius. Nor can he account for the appearance in France during a time of troubles of three writers who have profoundly influenced the French mind: Montaigne (1533–92), Descartes (1596–1650), and Pascal (1623–62). The historian can explain something about the conditions and characteristics of "golden ages." He cannot explain the appearance of genius.

Suggestions for Further Reading

Note: Asterisk denotes a book available in paperback edition.

Geographical Discovery   Two brief general studies provide a good introduction to the subject: J. H. Parry, *Europe and a Wider World, 1415–1715* (1949), and C. E. Nowell, *The Great Discoveries and the First Colonial Empires** (1954). J. H. Parry gives a more detailed account in *The Age of Reconnaisance* (1963). W. C. Abbott, *The Expansion of Europe*, 2 vols. (1918), is an older but still valuable general account, including consideration of the effect of the discoveries upon Europe. *The Great Age of Discovery*, ed. by A. P. Newton (1932) is a collection of reliable articles by various authors. Sir Percy Sykes, *A History of Exploration* (1934), surveys the whole subject from ancient times on; H. H. Hart, *Sea Road to the Indies* (1950), describes the Portuguese exploits; J. B. Brebner, *The Explorers of North America, 1492–1806** (1933), and A. P. Newton, *The European Nations in the West Indies, 1493–1688* (1933), treat exploration in particular areas. E. Sanceau has written a good modern biography of Henry the Navigator (1947). S. E. Morison, *Admiral of the Ocean Sea,** 2 vols. (1942), is the best account of Columbus. A shorter discussion by Morison is *Christopher Columbus, Mariner* (1955), and he gives an excellent overall view in *The European Discovery of America* (1971). C. M. Parr, *So Noble a Captain* (1953), is a reliable account of Magellan. E. Sanceau, *The Land of Prester John* (1944), traces Portuguese interest in Abyssinia. The best correctives for older Anglo-Saxon notions of Spanish colonizing are C.H. Haring, *The Spanish Empire in America* (1947), and L. Hanke, *The Spanish Struggle for Justice in the Conquest of America* (1949). R. L. Reynolds, *Europe Emerges** (1961), is a good analysis of European expansion in general.

Spain   R. B. Merriman, *Rise of the Spanish Empire in the Old World and in the New*, 4 vols. (1918–34), is a superbly written and scholarly account of Spain in Europe and overseas to the death of Philip II. J. H. Elliott, *Imperial Spain, 1469–1716** (1964), is a remarkable book. R. Trevor Davies, *The Golden Century of Spain, 1501–1621** (1937), and *Spain in Decline, 1621–1700** (1956), are well-informed, interesting, sometimes controversial accounts. J. H. Parry, *The Spanish Theory of Empire in the Sixteenth Century* (1940), studies the effect of empire upon the Spanish monarchy. E. J. Hamilton, *American Treasure and the Price Revolution in Spain, 1501–1650* (1934), is the starting point for study of sixteenth-century inflation.

The Netherlands   The most scholarly brief account of the Dutch rebellion and its consequences is in the two books of P. Geyl, *The Revolt of the Netherlands, 1555–1609** (1932), and *The Netherlands Divided, 1609–1648* (1936). There is a beautifully written popular biography of William the Silent by C. V. Wedgwood* (1944).

Elizabethan England   There is a wealth of well-written, scholarly books on the period. Sir John Neale, author of three brilliant volumes on the parliamentary history of the reign, has written the best biography of Elizabeth, *Queen Elizabeth I** (1952). E. Jenkins, *Elizabeth the Great** (1959), adds insight on the purely personal side. C. Read's thorough biographies, *Mr. Secretary Walsingham*, 3 vols. (1925), and *Mr. Secretary Cecil* (Lord Burghley), 2 vols. (1955, 1960), provide intimate knowledge of the politics of the period. A. L. Rowse has written with zest on Elizabethan society in *The England of Elizabeth** (1950) and *The Expansion of Elizabethan England** (1955). J. A. Williamson, *The Age of Drake,** 3rd ed. (1952), is by a master of naval history; and G. Mattingly, *The Armada** (1959), is one of those rare books, a definitive treatment of its subject which is at the same time magnificent reading. A good brief survey is S. I. Bindoff, *Tudor England** (1959).

France   It is more difficult to find good reading in English on France than on England in the sixteenth century. L. Batiffol, *The Century of the Renaissance* (trans. 1916), is an older general account of France in the sixteenth century. J. E. Neale, *The Age of Catharine de' Medici** (1943), is very useful, as is H. Pearson, *Henry of Navarre* (1963). There is a brief modern account of the period in F. C. Palm, *Calvinism and the Religious Wars* (1932). J. W. Thompson, *The Wars of Religion in France, 1559–1576* (1909), is older but still useful. A. J. Grant, *The Huguenots* (1934), is both scholarly and brief. W. F. Church, *Constitutional Thought in Sixteenth Century France* (1941), discusses with discernment the conflict of medieval and modern ideas of government during the civil wars.

19

Political and
Economic Crises of
the Seventeenth Century

The seventeenth century, much more than the fifteenth or sixteenth, is the century in which modern European civilization took on recognizable form. It was also a century that was afflicted by severe political, social, and economic crises, crises at least as dangerous as those that had shaken the medieval civilization of Europe in the fourteenth century. Everywhere the growing power of the state was challenged, and in the 1640s the three strongest European monarchies—Spain, France, and England—were weakened by outright rebellions. War was endemic—the last of the religious wars merged with wars to preserve the balance of power, and these in turn with the first commercial wars. The ravages of war were compounded by bad weather, famine, and plague. Population growth leveled off and in some areas, notably Germany, population declined. There was also a prolonged economic depression, running through the middle decades of the century. The flow of silver from the New World, which had stimulated the economy, dropped off sharply, and industrial production in Europe increased only slightly, if at all. Only gradually, after 1670, did growth in commerce and industry start spiraling upward again. Meanwhile, poverty exacerbated social unrest, and inadequate revenues limited the capabilities of governments.

Yet out of this unpromising environment a new Europe emerged. Governments, businessmen, and intellectual leaders were determined not to be deprived of the gains they had made in the last two centuries. Every challenge was met, at different dates and by different means in different countries. But the net result was that Europe was richer, controlled more of the world's commerce, and had more effective governments in 1700 than in 1600. And, as an unexpected bonus, there was an intellectual revolution, a sharp change in ways of thinking about man and the universe, that did more to change the nature of human life than any of the new ideas that had emerged during the Italian Renaissance (see Chapter 21).

Although seventeenth-century statesmen and writers recognized the impor-

tance of economic problems more clearly than had their predecessors, they still felt that political problems deserved primary consideration. They wanted to complete the process that had begun in the thirteenth century, the building of a sovereign territorial state. This process had been interrupted by the troubles of the fourteenth century and the religious conflicts of the sixteenth century; now it was to be pushed to a conclusion. From a theoretical point of view, this meant defining the concept of sovereignty ever more clearly. From a practical point of view, it meant concentrating supreme power in some organ of the state, either in the monarchy (as in France and most other states) or in the representative assembly (as in England).

FRANCE: IN SEARCH OF ORDER AND AUTHORITY 1598–1661

Seventeenth-century France still felt the effects of the anarchy and violence that had prevailed for almost half a century before the Edict of Nantes in 1598. Three weakling kings had tarnished the prestige of the monarchy, and the great nobles had become powerful and unruly. Merchants and manufacturers had been hard hit by the wars, and the peasants had suffered heavily from the ravages of undisciplined soldiers. The mass of the people were weary of disorder, eager for security, but still somewhat suspicious of any authority that might violate local privileges and increase the burden of taxation.

Jean Bodin, the most penetrating political thinker of the tragic years just past, had seen what was needed. In his book *The Republic,* which he published in 1576, Bodin argued that in any well-ordered state, supreme power or sovereignty must be clearly lodged somewhere in some organ of the state, preferably the monarchy. Sovereignty he defined as the power "to lay down the law to subjects in general without their consent." Bodin did not think of this power as arbitrary or capricious: the sovereign was still subject to the laws of God and of nature. But he insisted that sovereign power must

Jean Bodin on Sovereignty

Bodin was a sixteenth century French lawyer who was interested in political and economic problems. The *fact* of sovereignty had been recognized for some time, but Bodin was the first writer to express the *idea* in clear and uncompromising terms.

Sovereignty is supreme power over citizens and subjects unrestrained by laws. . . . A prince is bound by no law of his predecessor, and much less by his own laws. . . . He may repeal, modify, or replace a law made by himself and without the consent of his subjects. . . . The opinion of those who have written that the king is bound by the popular will must be disregarded; such doctrine furnishes seditious men with material for revolutionary plots. No reasonable ground can be found to claim that subjects should control princes or that power should be attributed to popular assemblies. . . . The highest privilege of sovereignty consists in giving laws to the people as a whole without their consent. . . . Under this supreme power of making and repealing laws it is clear that all other functions of sovereignty are included.

From Jean Bodin, *Six Books Concerning the Republic*, from the Latin version of 1586 [the earlier French version of 1576 is less coherent], trans. by F. W. Coker, in *Readings in Political Philosophy* (New York: Macmillan, 1938), pp. 374, 375, 376, 377, 380.

not be limited by any human agency—that is, it must be "absolute" to be effective. He insisted that it could not be divided—for instance, among king, Estates General, and *parlements*. It must be recognized as legitimately residing in one person or one political institution. No one had defined sovereignty so clearly before or argued so persuasively for it as the only remedy for insecurity and civil war. Bodin's prescription for France's ills was fulfilled in the French absolute monarchy that became the model and envy of most of Europe.

Henry IV and Sully

The first steps toward restoring the power of the monarchy and the prosperity of the land were taken by Henry IV and his minister, Sully. Henry, first of the Bourbon dynasty, was a popular king—courageous, vigorous, humorous, tolerant, and sound in his judgment of men. But he spent much of his time in hunting and lovemaking and left the routine business of government to Sully

"Triumphal Entry of Henry IV into Paris," large sketch by Rubens, *ca.* 1630.

and others. Sully was a puritanical Huguenot with a keen sense of economy and a hatred of dishonesty. He improved the financial condition of the monarchy, partly by avoiding expensive wars and partly by patching up the tax-collecting system. The French taxation system was inefficient, corrupt, and inequitable. Many taxes were "farmed"—that is, the right to collect them was granted to private collectors who paid the government a fixed sum and then collected all they could. The burden fell most heavily on the peasant, since the nobles and the upper bourgeoisie were exempt from major taxes. Sully could do nothing to make the system more just (nor could any French minister down to the Revolution), but he could make it work better by discharging dishonest and inefficient tax farmers. (It has been estimated that as a rule hardly half the taxes collected in France at this time reached the treasury.) Moreover, the reestablishment of internal peace and order, which allowed agriculture and commerce to recover, helped to increase the government's revenues, especially from customs duties. When Henry IV was assassinated by a Catholic fanatic in 1610 there was a sizable surplus in the treasury.

The Estates General of 1614

Within a few years the work of Henry and Sully was in ruins. Under the regency of Henry's widow, Marie de' Medici, the treasury surplus was sopped up by rapacious courtiers, and Spain began once more to intervene in French affairs, sometimes in a strange alliance with the Huguenots. In 1614 the Estates General were summoned to one of their rare meetings, but the deliberations soon turned into a struggle among the First and Second Estates (the clergy and the nobility) and the Third Estate (the bourgeoisie, who were represented largely by provincial royal officers). No group was willing to take responsibility; and no group had the power to demand reform. The assembly dissolved with a strong declaration that "the king is sovereign in France, and holds his crown from God only." It was not to meet again until 1789, on the eve of the Revolution.

Three studies of Richelieu by Philippe de Champaigne.

Richelieu

In 1614 Henry IV's son, Louis XIII, was still only fourteen years old. He was soon to be married to Anne of Austria, daughter of Philip III of Spain, as a symbol of Habsburg influence on France. There was not much to be hoped for from the monarch himself—except that he might choose and support some able first minister. The man was already in sight—a brilliant young bishop named Richelieu—but it took him several years to become a cardinal (in 1622) and head of the king's council (in 1624). From 1624 to his death in 1642 Richelieu was the real ruler of France. Richelieu, rather than any member of the Bourbon dynasty, founded absolute monarchy in France.

There is no mystery about Richelieu, as there is about many other great figures in history. He had the clearest and most penetrating mind of any statesman of his generation. And he made his purpose perfectly plain: to enhance the power and prestige of the French monarchy beyond any possibility of challenge. He came to his task with a marvelous grasp of political and diplomatic possibilities, an infallible memory, and an inflexible will unhampered by moral scruples. Richelieu admired Machiavelli's writings, and the heart of his political creed was *raison d'état*—the doctrine that the good of the state is the supreme good, and that any means may be used to attain it. He would coolly send an innocent man to his death in order to frighten other troublemakers, enhance the authority of the monarchy, and so save bloodshed in the end. "In judging crimes against the state," he argued, "it is essential to banish pity." He was not irreligious, but the workings of his mind were overwhelmingly this-worldly. "Man is immortal; his salvation is hereafter," he once argued against some conscientious scruples of the king, but "the state has no immortality, its salvation is now or never." While his cardinal's robes helped protect him against assassination, his policy was that of an astute secular statesman who put public order before religious zeal. His reputation for diabolical cleverness went even beyond the reality and helped him to bewilder his enemies and gain his ends.

Richelieu had three concrete objectives that had to be carried out more or less simultaneously. First, he meant to break the political and military power of the Huguenots. Second, he meant to crush the political influence of the great nobles. And finally, he meant to destroy the power of the Habsburgs to intervene in French internal affairs.

The Edict of Nantes had allowed the Huguenots to garrison about 200 towns, the chief of which was La Rochelle on the west coast. Richelieu persuaded Louis XIII that he would never be master in his own house until he had wiped out this "empire within an empire." Rumors that the government had decided to attack provoked the Huguenots to rebel, and Richelieu proceeded to besiege and capture La Rochelle. At the Peace of Alais in 1629, which settled the dispute, Richelieu was unexpectedly generous in his terms. He had no respect whatever for what he contemptuously called "the allegedly Reformed religion," but he allowed the Huguenots the right to worship as they pleased once he had attained his primary objective of eliminating their political and military autonomy. He did not wish to alienate Protestants abroad who could help him in a war with Spain and Austria, and he hoped he could make loyal and useful citizens out of the Huguenots. In this he was successful. The Huguenots served the crown in the war that followed against the Habsburgs and loyally supported the monarchy in the crisis of the Fronde.

Richelieu's attack on the political power of the nobility was less successful than his attack on the Huguenots, but it was just as determined. Until the very end of his career, he was constantly threatened by aristocratic intrigues. In response to this threat, he developed a network of spies, set up a special tribunal to try noble lawbreakers, and sternly forbade dueling, a privilege that marked the freedom of the aristocracy from ordinary restraints. He gradually weakened the power of the great nobles who were provincial governors and gave more local administrative responsibilities to direct representatives of the crown. These representatives, called *intendants*, were usually drawn from the *noblesse de la robe*, ennobled office-holders of middle-class ancestry. They were therefore more dependent on the monarchy than the older nobility. Richelieu did nothing to lessen the economic or social privileges of the French nobility, but he did curtail its political power.

Richelieu was no financier, nor did he have any interest in bettering the condition of the common people. He spent large sums on rebuilding the armed forces and even more in actual warfare against Spain. He left the government's finances and the nation's peasants in worse condition than he had found them.

But through his subtle diplomacy and his well-timed intervention in the Thirty Years' War, he made France, instead of Spain, the leading European power.

Mazarin and the Fronde

Richelieu's death in 1642 (Louis XIII died a few months later, in 1643) put his work to a severe test. Louis XIV was a child of five when his father died, and so his mother, Anne of Austria, was appointed regent. However, she left the business of government to the man whom Richelieu had picked and trained to succeed himself, an Italian cardinal named Mazarin. Mazarin had the subtlety and political skill of his master but not his inflexible will; he was both more adaptable and, as a foreigner, less popular than Richelieu. His two main objectives were to continue the war against Spain until the Habsburgs were defeated and to maintain the prestige of the monarchy at the level to which Richelieu had raised it. The nobility hated him as a

foreign upstart, however, and the bourgeoisie hated him for the high taxes he imposed to carry on the war. The result was the last serious rebellion to take place against the monarchy until the French Revolution—a complicated and uncoordinated movement of resistance known as the Fronde (1648–52).

The word "Fronde" referred to a game of slinging clods at passing coaches, which was played by the more unruly children of Paris. The rebellion was like the game; it was annoying, but in the end it did not keep the monarchy from driving along the road to absolutism. The leaders did not want to destroy the French monarchy nor did they wish to upset the established social order. They were composed of several groups—the judges of the High Courts and the chief financial officers, who were practically hereditary bureaucrats, and the nobles led by princes of the blood. Each group wanted to modify the structure of government so that it could have more influence. But no group could agree

tbursts during the Fronde
Paris, 1648.

with others on a joint program, with the exception of the purely negative policy of exiling Mazarin. Thus the *parlements*, which began the struggle, stood for the privileges of the corporations of bureaucrats who controlled the courts and the financial bureaus. They wanted the king to rule with their advice, rather than with that of councilors whom he could make or break as it pleased him. They insisted especially that no tax could be imposed without their consent. The nobles, who joined the rebellion later, had no intention of letting the *parlements* become dominant in government; they wanted to get rid of the *intendants* and regain their old powers as provincial governors. In the provinces, many men rebelled to protect or enlarge local privileges, but they often found it hard to decide whether they should support a *parlement* or a noble governor.

The result might have been different if anyone had dared draw on the deep-seated resentment of the lower classes—a resentment that had been expressed during the first half of the century in many local riots against taxation and misgovernment. But while a few theorists talked of liberty and democracy, no one was willing to take the chance of unleashing forces that might not be controllable. Unlike the contemporary English rebellion, in which the middle and lower classes accepted radical doctrines and defeated the king (see p. 426), the Fronde remained dominated by the nobility and the upper bourgeoisie. Each group approached the brink of making unlimited war on the king even at the risk of social revolution, and each drew back in horror. This innate conservatism, combined with lack of unity among the leaders, led to the disintegration of the rebellion. There was very little hard fighting; by the end of 1652, Mazarin, who had had to flee the country, was once more back in the saddle. Most Frenchmen concluded that a strong monarchy was preferable to futile civil war. The young king, Louis XIV, was to profit from this reaction when he came of age. Meanwhile, he remembered with loathing the violence and instability of the Fronde. He came to hate Paris, from which he had had to flee in 1648, despise the mob, and fear the nobles unless they were restrained by a firm royal hand.

In spite of the Fronde and the tax burden that continued to oppress the common people, Mazarin carried on the war with Spain until the Spaniards were forced to ask for terms in 1659. France gained two Pyrenees counties and Maria Theresa, daughter of Philip IV of Spain, was married to Louis XIV. Both the treaty and the marriage symbolized the humiliation of Spain and the triumph of France as the leading power in Europe. Mazarin died in 1661, and Louis XIV announced to his ministers that he would henceforth be his own prime minister. Now the work of Richelieu had come to full fruition. The French monarchy no longer had anything to fear from Huguenots and nobles at home or from Habsburgs abroad. It was an absolute monarchy, endowed with a fuller sovereignty than any other yet seen in European history.

ENGLAND: IN SEARCH OF CIVIL AND RELIGIOUS LIBERTY, 1603–60

While Richelieu and Mazarin were laying the foundations of absolute monarchy by divine right, leaders in England were slowly developing a constitutional, parliamentary monarchy. Richelieu could see clearly where he was going, but the goal was never clear to English leaders during their century of conflict with the crown. Englishmen groped their way toward a conception of sovereignty as something rooted in law rather than in personal authority, something to be lodged in the hands of an assembly that represented the community, or at least its more wealthy and influential members. England was not alone in its resistance to absolute monarchy, but the result in other countries, such as Poland, was anarchy and confusion. Only in England was a representative assembly able to increase its power without wrecking the state. When Queen Anne came to the throne in 1702 the English government was both a stronger and a more popular government than it had been in 1603 when James I succeeded Elizabeth I. The example of England, particularly as reflected in the writings of John Locke, was to have an enormous influence on western history throughout the following two centuries.

England, on the periphery of European civilization, had always been peculiar in its political development. For instance, although the strong monarchy of the Tudors (1485–1603) was part of a general European trend, the survival and strengthening of Parliament under such a monarchy was without parallel elsewhere. The Tudors continued to use Parliament in legislation and taxation whereas rulers on the Continent found representative assemblies either useless or obstructive. Parliament, particularly the House of Commons, slowly acquired a corporate feeling and a sense of being an integral part of the national government. The House of Commons, it will be remembered, represented both the mercantile classes in the towns and the gentry in the country. The knights and squires had been increasing in numbers, wealth, and political influence since the dissolution of the monasteries. They governed England at the local level as justices of the peace (the English monarchy had no paid bureaucrats like the French *intendants*), and they dominated the lower house of Parliament by sitting as representatives not only of the counties but of many boroughs as well. The House of Commons in which they sat had grown steadily in wealth and influence, until one member could boast in 1628 that the lower house could afford to buy the House of Lords three times over.

Thus the English Parliament in the early seventeenth century represented all the politically active classes of the nation in a way no other representative assembly in Europe did. There were no provincial estates or privileges in England as there were in France, and the class lines between peers, gentry, and wealthy burgesses were not so sharply drawn as the line between nobility and Third Estate on the Continent. English merchants were continually buying land and becoming gentlemen, and younger sons of the nobility often went into the professions. This meant that if the monarch should ever fall out with Parliament—and with

the social groups it represented—he would not be able to play class against class or district against district.

The Tudors

Queen Elizabeth had had arguments with her Parliaments, but the threat from abroad and the political good sense of both the queen and the opposition kept these arguments from becoming dangerous. It was generally recognized that only Parliament could make a law or impose a tax. It was also recognized that making policy, especially foreign policy, lay outside the competence of Parliament and within the sphere of what was called the royal prerogative.

The Tudors felt, however, that it was sometimes wise to confirm royal policy by parliamentary statute, particularly in the delicate field of religion. Henry VIII used Parliament to break with Rome; Mary had asked Parliament to restore England to the Roman obedience by statute; and Elizabeth had broken with the pope once more by statute. Elizabeth's Parliaments tried more than once

Formal meeting of Parliament in 1625. The Lords are seated; the Commons stand outside the bar.

to reform the Anglican Church in a Puritan direction and to nudge the queen on foreign policy—presumptuous acts for which Elizabeth scolded them sharply. But she was too popular for Parliament ever to make a real issue of the conflict and too astute ever to demand a clear definition of her prerogative. Tudor "despotism" was a popular despotism, and Tudor rulers found that they could exercise their sovereign power most effectively by seeking the cooperation of Parliament.

James I and Parliament

The Stuarts, who ruled from 1603 to 1714, either could not or would not cooperate with Parliament. James I (1603–25), the son of Mary Queen of Scots, was a well-meaning but pedantic intellectual who never understood the social structure or the political realities of the kingdom he inherited from Elizabeth. His aims were praiseworthy—peace with Spain, toleration of the Catholic minority in England, union of England and Scotland, and a strong but benevolent monarchy—but he did not inspire confidence as a political leader. Moreover, many of his ministers were incompetent. Unlike Elizabeth, who often concealed her imperious will in cloudy and ambiguous language, James liked to have things dangerously clear. He had written a book, *The True Law of Free Monarchies,* in which he insisted that kings owed their position to God alone, were responsible only to God, and in fact were themselves like gods on earth.

His belief in a monarchy "free" of restraints, free to do as it pleased for the common good, did not appeal to the classes represented in Parliament. Some of James's policies might have really helped the poor; others simply transferred wealth from one privileged group to another. In either case, opposition to the king could not endanger the country.

James I by D. Mytens, 1621.

The Tudors had long ago ended the threat of aristocratic violence, and peace with Spain in 1604 removed the danger of foreign conquest. Only their own king could now attack the beliefs or interfere with the property rights of the privileged classes. Parliament, fearing royal tyranny, began to criticize James's acts. James, fearing parliamentary intervention in policy matters, began to scold Parliament. The delicate Tudor balance was destroyed.

Friction rapidly developed over three related issues: religion, finance, and foreign policy. The Puritans and their sympathizers in the House of Commons wished to "purify" the Anglican Church of everything that savored of Catholic practice, from "popish" ritual to the authority of bishops. James was convinced that the Presbyterian system of church government, which he had known in his youth in Scotland, would not only destroy royal control of the church, but would threaten the monarchy itself. "No bishop, no king," he remarked within a year of his arrival in England. Parliament, annoyed by the extravagance of James's court and dubious about his policies, denied him enough money to meet the rising costs of government. James replied by raising money without parliamentary approval—for example, by increasing the customs duties on his own authority. When his right to take such actions was contested, the courts ruled in his favor—probably correctly, since the king controlled foreign trade as part of his control of foreign policy. But the seeming subservience of the courts to the royal will further disturbed Parliament.

Meanwhile James was following a foreign policy that exasperated the Puritan majority in Parliament. He was too friendly with Spain for the Puritan taste, he did little to defend Protestants abroad against the rising tide of Catholicism, and he tried in vain to marry his son Charles to the Spanish Infanta. When James chided the House of Commons in 1621 for even discussing his foreign policy, the House bristled and passed a unanimous Protestation defending its right to discuss "the arduous and urgent affairs concerning the King, State, and defence of the realm, and of the Church of England." This was revolutionary talk. James tore the resolution from the Commons' *Journal,* but he could not undo what had been done. The House of Commons, which Queen Elizabeth had kept under the control of her privy councilors, was now taking the initiative under leaders of its own. An aggressive and powerful element among James's subjects was demanding a voice in politics that he was utterly unwilling to grant.

Charles I
and the English Rebellion

The situation rapidly worsened during the first four years of the reign of Charles I (1625–29). Charles tried to please Parliament by attacking Catholic countries, but his incompetent favorite, the Duke of Buckingham, failed to capture Cadiz in Spain or to relieve the French Huguenots at La Rochelle. Parliament had urged war but had not granted adequate taxes, so the government tried to pay for the wars by levying a forced loan and by imprisoning those who objected to paying. Parliament in 1628 drew up a formal protest in the form of a Petition of Right, which they finally compelled Charles to approve. Its two main provisions were that no one should henceforth be compelled to pay any tax or loan "without common consent by Act of Parliament," and that no one should be imprisoned without cause shown.

Next year the House of Commons was roused to fury before Charles dissolved it. It declared that anyone who introduced anything savoring of Catholic practices in the Anglican Church was "a capital enemy to this kingdom and commonwealth," and that anyone who advised or submitted to the levying of taxes without parliamentary consent was "a betrayer of the liberties of England." The issue of "sovereignty" had finally been raised, and the word itself was being debated by lawyers and parliamentary

Charles I by D. Mytens, 1631.

orators. Where did the supreme power in England lie—in the king or in Parliament? The old answer, that it lay in the "king-in-Parliament," would no longer do. The royal prerogative and "the liberties of England" were not reconcilable any longer.

Charles I now took things into his own hands and ruled without Parliament for eleven years (1629–40). He was less intelligent and more stubborn than his father. James had always yielded before conflict became irreconcilable. Rather than yield, Charles was to resort to duplicity and falsehood in the crises ahead of him, and as a result he ended his life on the scaffold, trusted by almost no one. Trying to duplicate Richelieu's brilliant work across the Channel, he chose tough-minded advisers: Thomas Wentworth, Earl of Strafford, in political affairs, and William Laud, Archbishop of Canterbury, in ecclesiastical affairs. With them and others, Charles devised new methods of nonparliamentary taxation that provided enough money to run the government so long as it stayed out of war. Laud began a movement back toward more ritual and formality in the Anglican service, a movement the Puritans regarded as an attempt to restore Catholicism. All opposition, whether to arbitrary taxation or to innovations in worship, was sternly suppressed by the courts. Everything went well until Laud tried to force the Anglican Book of Common Prayer on stubbornly Presbyterian Scotland. Before long an angry and well-led Scottish army was encamped in northern England. Charles and Strafford, finding themselves unable to raise an army to fight the Scots, had to summon Parliament to get the money to buy them off.

The Long Parliament, which met in November 1640 and was not dissolved until 1653, became a workshop of revolution. It sent Strafford and Laud to the scaffold. It passed an act stating that a Parliament must be summoned at least every three years. It outlawed all nonparliamentary taxation and abolished the special royal courts (the Court of Star Chamber, which dealt with opposition to the government, and the Court of High Commission, for ecclesiastical affairs), which had been the chief instruments of the "Eleven Years' Tyranny." In other words, in less than a year (1640–41) Parliament had made absolute monarchy impossible in England. This much of its work won unwilling approval from Charles, since sentiment for it was virtually unanimous. But when the more radical Puritans in Parliament went on to abolish bishops in the Anglican Church and to seek control of the army, a party began to form around Charles in opposition to the parliamentary majority. And thus a civil war broke out in 1642 and lasted until 1649.

Enough has been said to suggest that the English Rebellion was primarily a war of ideas, not of classes or of districts or even of interests, although the interests of merchants and gentry who were outraged by nonparliamentary taxation were certainly involved. Generally the towns, the middle class, and the economically advanced southeastern counties of England supported Parliament, while many rural areas, aristocrats, and the backward northwest supported Charles. But nobles, squires, and artisans from all parts of England were to be found on both sides. Unlike the Fronde, in which narrow interest groups failed to work out programs with broad appeal, the English Rebellion offered a real alternative to the established order: parliamentary monarchy instead of benevolent absolutism, and a Presbyterian Church governed by elected "presbyters," or elders, instead of an Anglican Church governed by bishops appointed by the crown. Unlike the Fronde again, the English Rebellion was able to attract and to accept men with really radical ideas—men who wanted neither a monarchy, nor an established church, nor power in the hands of landlords.

As the civil war intensified, Parliament proved to be more successful than the king in raising money and in building a strong army. A brilliant cavalry officer named Oliver Cromwell formed a "New Model Army" largely from among his fellow Independents, or Congregationalists. These Independents were generally of lower economic status than either Anglicans or Presbyterians. They were unsophisticated, Bible-reading Puritans of strict morals who believed in independent congregations democratically organized, with little or no national organization. Cromwell and his army finally defeated the king's forces in 1645, only to fall out with the Presbyterians, who had dominated Parliament since the Anglicans withdrew in 1642 to join Charles. With Parliament and the army at loggerheads about what to do with the king and about what sort of government to set up in England (many in the army wanted a truly democratic regime), the king was able to escape and make one last bid for victory before being finally defeated by Cromwell in 1648. Cromwell and the Independents in the army were determined now to get at what they considered the root of the trouble. They "purged" Parliament of its Presbyterian members, executed King Charles I in 1649, abolished monarchy and the House of Lords, and set up a republic, or

Oliver Cromwell, painting from the original panel by Samuel Cooper.

ENGLAND DURING THE ENGLISH REBELLION   1642–46

"Commonwealth," with the "rump" of the Long Parliament as its government and Cromwell as its moving spirit.

Cromwell

Cromwell proved to be a revolutionary leader unlike almost any other in western history. He was a deeply religious man who tried in vain to avoid becoming a dictator. Yet he was ruthless and determined when he felt his policies were threatened. He massacred the Catholic Irish when they rebelled, defeated the Scots when they intervened in favor of the son of Charles I, fought a commercial war with the Dutch in 1652–54, and boldly dissolved what was left of the Long Parliament in 1653. In a few short years he had decisively won a civil war, united the British Isles under one government for the first time, made England again the terror of the seas, and apparently wiped the slate clean for any political experiment he wished to try. The rest of his career until his death in 1658, however, was a tragic search for answers to insoluble problems: how to guarantee religious toleration to all kinds of Protestants except determined Anglicans, and at the same time how to develop some constitutional basis for his government. Cromwell tried to rule through a written constitution (the first in the history of any major state) and with the assent of a Parliament. He took the title of Lord Protector instead of king, but he quarreled with his Parliaments as bitterly as the Stuarts had quarreled with theirs. At one point Cromwell had to set up an open military dictatorship to keep his Parliament from disbanding his army and persecuting his coreligionists. The plain fact was that most Englishmen were not ready for religious toleration, especially toleration of the radical religious minorities that made up Cromwell's army.

Furthermore, it became more and more evident that it was impossible in England to break utterly with history and to set up a new sort of government simply by writing a constitution. There was already a "constitution" deeply ingrained in the English political tradition, although it was nowhere written down.

Soon after Cromwell's death even his own supporters saw that the only possible alternative to military dictatorship was Parliament, and that the only way to restore Parliament was also to restore the monarchy. In 1660 the monarchy, Parliament, and the Anglican Church were all restored when a "Convention Parliament" invited Charles II to return from France and take up the crown.

The Restoration

At first glance nothing more remained in England after twenty years of civil war and revolutionary experiment than had remained in France after the defeat of the Fronde. To this day Englishmen refer to the events just described as the "Puritan Rebellion." They do not call it a revolution because it was suc-

The Dutch view of Cromwell. Detail from a print dated April 30, 1653.

Democratic Ideas in the English Revolution

After it was sure of victory, the Parliamentary Army began to worry about a proper government for England. A Council of the Army, including representatives of the ordinary soldiers, held a series of debates at Putney in 1647 on a constitution for the country. One of the basic issues was whether all men could vote.

Major Rainborough: I think that the poorest he that is in England hath a life to live, as the greatest he, and therefore truly, sir, I think it's clear, that every man that is to live under a government ought first by his own consent to put himself under that government, and I do think that the poorest man in England is not at all bound in a strict sense to that government that he hath not had a voice to put himself under.

[General Ireton argued that only those with property should vote.]

Sexby [a representative of the soldiers]: I see that though liberty were our end, there is a degeneration from it. We have ventured our lives to recover our birthrights and privileges as Englishmen, and by the arguments urged there is none. There are many thousands of us soldiers that have ventured our lives; we have had little property . . . yet we have had a birthright. But it seems now, except a man hath a fixed estate in this kingdom, he hath no right in this kingdom. I wonder we were so much deceived.

From *Puritanism and Liberty*, ed. by A. S. P. Woodhouse (Chicago: University of Chicago Press, 1951), pp. 53, 69.

ceeded by the "Restoration." But one thing at least had been decided: There was to be no absolute monarchy in England. All acts of the Long Parliament before the outbreak of civil war were still valid, and these acts put severe limitations on royal power, even if the balance of power between king and Parliament was still uncertain. Strafford and

Laud had tried to do for Charles I what Richelieu and Mazarin had done for Louis XIV, but all three Englishmen died on the scaffold while all three Frenchmen died in their beds. The turmoil of the first half of the seventeenth century left most Englishmen with certain half-expressed convictions whose effects can be traced in English history for generations. Among these convictions were a fear of allowing any one individual to acquire too much political power, a deepened respect for government by law rather than by personal command, a reverence for Parliament as the defender of individual rights against arbitrary despotism, and a distaste for standing armies.

The early seventeenth century was a brilliant age in the history of English literature, including Shakespeare's mature work, the Authorized, or King James, Version of the Bible (1611), and Milton's formative years. It was also a brilliant period in political thinking, as statesmen and pamphleteers argued for royalist, parliamentary, or radical principles of government.

Perhaps Thomas Hobbes' *Leviathan* (1651) best represented the political insights and fears, if not the greatest hopes, of these turbulent years. Writing in the midst of civil war, Hobbes pictured the life of man without government as "solitary, poor, nasty, brutish, and short." Without some authority to enforce law, there is no society, no order, only "a war of every man against every man." Men in general are inclined to "a perpetual and restless desire of power after power." So they set up a sovereign power by agreement or contract (it makes no difference whether the sovereign is a king or a Parliament), by which all men agree to obey the sovereign, but only so long as he is able to maintain order. The sovereign is not bound by anything in the contract. No clearer argument for might as the necessary basis of all right had ever been written. Hobbes took Bodin's argument for a legitimate sovereign authority and subtly transformed it into justification of sheer arbitrary power. His book could be used equally well to support Charles I or Cromwell. In a sense the main effort of Englishmen during the seventeenth cen-

The restoration of King Charles II: the crowning in Westminster Abbey. From a contemporary print.

tury was to find some way to refute Hobbes—to subject political power to the restraint of law and to increase its responsibility to the governed. They finally succeeded in 1688.

GERMANY: DISINTEGRATION AND DISASTER, 1618–48

While France was building the strongest monarchy in Europe and England was undergoing a constitutional crisis from which it was to emerge with new strength, the German-speaking peoples were caught up in one of the most futile and destructive wars in the history of Europe. The Thirty Years' War (1618–48) was really four successive wars that began in Bohemia, spread to the rest of the Empire, and finally involved most of the major powers on the Continent. It was a savage and demoralizing conflict that left "Germany" poorer and weaker than the western European states.

The Causes
of the Thirty Years' War

The war sprang out of a complicated mixture of religious and political grievances. Lutherans and Catholics had not fought each other since the Peace of Augsburg (1555), but the Catholics were disturbed by the fact that, in spite of the provisions of the peace, most of the Catholic bishoprics in northern Germany had fallen into Lutheran or secular hands. This gave some grounds for creating an ultra-Catholic movement headed by the Jesuits and the German Catholic princes, particularly Maximilian, Duke of Bavaria. The spread of Calvinism introduced a new source of friction because Calvinists had been excluded from the Peace of Augsburg. When Maximilian roughly disciplined the Protestant town of Donauwörth, Frederick V, the Calvinist ruler of the Palatinate, a small state on the middle Rhine, took the lead in forming a Protestant Union among the

German princes and cities in 1608. In reply, a Catholic League was organized the next year under the leadership of Maximilian. By 1609 two illegal military alliances faced each other within the Empire, each afraid of the other and each determined to keep the rival religion from making any further gains.

Revolt in Bohemia

As these examples show, each component of the Empire was a virtually independent state. The Habsburgs, who held the imperial title, realized that the only way to rebuild and expand imperial authority was to establish firm control over what had been their old family domains—Austria, Bohemia, and Hungary. Thus the Austrian Habsburg, Ferdinand of Styria, got himself elected King of Bohemia in 1617.

Bohemia was a flourishing kingdom in which two nationalities (Germans and Czechs) and several religions (Catholicism, Lutheranism, Calvinism, and remnants of the Hussite movement of two centuries earlier) lived fairly peaceably together under earlier Habsburg promises of toleration. Ferdinand, a zealous Catholic, began systematically to undermine this toleration and to re-Catholicize the country. This action provoked rebellion by the Bohemian Estates, which were dominated by a strong Protestant majority. In May 1618 two of Ferdinand's councilors were tossed from a castle window in Prague and civil war broke out between the Habsburg ruler and the Estates. The Estates raised an army, deposed Ferdinand, and offered the crown of Bohemia to Frederick V of the Palatinate. When Frederick unwisely accepted, the Protestant Union became involved in defending the Bohemian Estates while Maximilian of Bavaria brought the Catholic League to the support of Ferdinand. In 1619 Ferdinand was elected emperor. Thus a war that might have remained a local affair soon spread throughout the Empire.

The Bohemian phase of the war was soon ended. The forces of the emperor and the League won an overwhelming victory in 1620. Frederick fled, and the emperor proceeded to work his will on the prostrate Bohemians. Half the property in the country changed hands through confiscation. The Jesuits, with strong secular backing, set out to reconvert the country to Catholicism, and within ten years they had succeeded. The prosperity of the country was ruined, Protestantism was stamped out or driven underground, and Czech nationalism was crushed for two centuries to come. The Habsburgs and their Catholic allies had won the first round decisively.

Danish Intervention

The fall of Bohemia terrified German Protestants and elated the Catholics. The Spanish Habsburgs came to the aid of their fellow Catholics, and the armies of the League were everywhere triumphant. In spite of the common danger, the Protestants could not unite. The Lutherans had been more afraid of a Calvinist victory in Bohemia than of an imperial triumph, and so Lutheran Saxony had actually helped Ferdinand put down the revolt. Although Frederick V was the son-in-law of James I, Protestant England gave no help because James and Charles were too involved in difficulties at home.

In 1625 the Protestant king of Denmark intervened, partly to save the cause of his coreligionists but primarily to pick up some territory in northern Germany.

Within a year he was beaten in battle by a large army raised by the most inscrutable figure of the war, a wealthy war profiteer and professional soldier named Wallenstein, who had offered the emperor his services. Wallenstein had no religious convictions whatever, and his political aims have puzzled generations of historians. His immediate aim seems to have been to build an imperial Habsburg military machine of such strength that it could not only eliminate all Protestant opposition but could operate independently of all other forces in the Empire, including the Catholic League. Before long Wallenstein and the League were as much at loggerheads on one side as Calvinists and Lutherans were on the other. Religion slowly receded in significance as the war became a struggle for the hegemony of Europe.

The high-water mark of Habsburg triumph and Catholic reaction was reached in 1629. Denmark withdrew from the war, leaving Wallenstein's army supreme. The Catholic League and Jesuit advisers persuaded Ferdinand to issue the Edict of Restitution, which restored to Catholic hands all ecclesiastical lands lost to Protestantism since 1552. It was evident that this edict could not be carried out without more bloodshed, because it meant that Catholic bishops were to be restored throughout northern Germany. Such an act would destroy the rough balance between Catholicism and Protestantism in Germany and weaken the northern states for the benefit of Austria and Bavaria. This threat finally roused the Lutherans inside and outside Germany to a sense of their peril.

Swedish Intervention: Gustavus Adolphus

In 1631 growing Habsburg power was blocked by the intervention of Sweden, a country that had not appeared before on the stage of international politics. Gustavus II (Gustavus Adolphus) was the ablest ruler of his generation. His country was sparse in population and resources, but he had cultivated its iron and timber industries, united the nation behind him, and built the best army of the day. It was not large, but it was well

equipped (with the first uniforms and an improved musket), well disciplined, and inspired by high morale. Gustavus had already come close to making the Baltic a Swedish lake in wars with Denmark and Poland. He now stepped into the fray as the sincere champion of Lutheranism, hoping apparently to set up a federation of Protestant states in Germany under Swedish leadership.

The siege of Magdeburg in 1651 by Habsburg and Catholic forces. This siege resulted in one of the bloodiest massacres of the Thirty Years' War.

The Sack of Magdeburg   May 1631

Then was there naught but beating and burning, plundering, torture, and murder. Most especially was every one of the enemy bent on securing much booty. When a marauding party entered a house, if its master had anything to give he might thereby purchase respite and protection for himself and his family till the next man, who also wanted something, should come along. It was only when everything had been brought forth and there was nothing left to give that the real trouble commenced. Then, what with blows and threats of shooting, stabbing, and hanging, the poor people were so terrified that if they had had anything left they would have brought it forth if it had been buried in the earth or hidden away in a thousand castles. In this frenzied rage, the great and splendid city that had stood like a fair princess in the land was now, in its hour of direst need and unutterable distress and woe, given over to the flames, and thousands of innocent men, women, and children, in the midst of a horrible din of heartrending shrieks and cries, were tortured and put to death in so cruel and shameful a manner that no words would suffice to describe, nor no tears to bewail it.

From Otto von Guericke, in *Readings in European History*, ed., by James Harvey Robinson (Boston: Ginn, 1906), Vol. II, pp. 211–12.

Gustavus arrived too late to save Magdeburg from a terrible sack by the Habsburg Imperialists in May 1631, but in the fall of 1631 he overwhelmed the Imperialist armies at Breitenfeld in Saxony. He then marched triumphantly to the Rhine. Wallenstein, whom the emperor had dismissed under pressure from the Catholic League, was recalled, only to be beaten by Gustavus at Lützen in 1632. Gustavus himself was killed in the battle, however, and by 1634 his army had finally been outnumbered and beaten, Wallenstein had been murdered by one of his staff, and another phase of the war had come to an end. Swedish intervention had saved German Protestantism but had not gained a decision. The most powerful state of all had been watching the course of events closely and was now about to intervene with decisive results.

French Intervention: Richelieu

Since coming to power in 1624, Richelieu had kept in close touch with the progress of the war through his ambassadors and agents. But for ten years he did not feel that the French army was strong enough to intervene in Germany. His major purpose was to crush the Habsburgs, both Austrian and Spanish, and he was ready to ally with anyone, Protestant or Catholic, who was opposed to them. The Dutch, who went back to war with their old enemies the Spanish, were his first allies, and in 1631 he subsidized the invasion by Gustavus Adolphus. When the Swedes were finally defeated in 1634, Richelieu saw that he would have to intervene directly if he was to check Habsburg expansion in, and perhaps control of, Europe. And so in May 1635 he sent a French herald to Brussels to declare war on the king of Spain.

The Thirty Years' War had lasted for seventeen years with no decisive result, and it was to continue for thirteen more dreary years while French, Swedish, and Dutch armies fought against the Spanish and Austrian Habsburgs. Spain was weakened by the successful rebellion of Portugal and the almost successful rebellion of Catalonia (1640). In 1643 the French finally destroyed the legend of Spanish invincibility by crushing a Spanish army at Rocroi in the Netherlands. It was the first time in 150 years that a Spanish army had suffered a major defeat. The emperor's allies deserted him, and by 1648 the Swedes were threatening Vienna and storming Prague. The dream of Emperor Ferdinand II (who had died in 1637) of re-Catholicizing Germany and establishing a strong Habsburg monarchy in central Europe lay in ruins.

The Peace of Westphalia, 1648

A peace was finally worked out at the Congress of Westphalia (1643–48), Europe's first great peace conference and the first international gathering of importance since the Council of Constance (1414–18). But it was a far different gathering from that of two centuries earlier. The atmosphere and the business at hand were now entirely secular, and the communities represented were sovereign territorial states that recognized no earthly superior and only the most shadowy common interests. "Christendom" had dissolved, and the word "civilization" would not be coined till the next century to express in secular terms what "Christendom" had once meant to Europeans in religious terms.

Almost every act of the Congress emphasized the importance of the sovereign state. For example, it recognized the right of each German principality to make alliances and to declare war on its own. This constituted practical recognition of the disintegration of the Empire into over 300 separate sovereignties. Switzerland and the Dutch Netherlands were finally recognized as sovereign states, independent of all ties to the Empire. France acquired some very ambiguous rights to Alsace, Sweden acquired strips of German territory along the shores of the Baltic and the North Sea, and the two German states of Brandenburg and Bavaria ended up with increased territory and prestige. As for religion, the old principle of *cuius regio, eius religio* was reaffirmed. Calvinism was simply added to Catholicism and Lutheranism as one of the recognized faiths. The ownership

Austrian Habsburg lands
Spanish Habsburg lands

of church lands was settled as of 1624, meaning in general that northern Germany remained Protestant and southern Germany Catholic. France and Spain were unable to reach agreement, so their war continued until French victory was finally recognized in the Peace of the Pyrenees in 1659. France received some territory along the Pyrenees and in Flanders, and the Spanish princess, Maria Theresa, married Louis XIV. In general, the peace settlements of the middle of the century left France the strongest power in Europe, Spain prostrate, the Empire shattered, and a kind of power vacuum in the center of Europe.

The Social Results of the War

The Thirty Years' War was one of the most brutal and destructive wars of which we have record until the twentieth century. Armies robbed, raped, and murdered their way back and forth across Germany. The lack of any modern supply system meant that they had to live off the land. There are gruesome records of towns totally wiped out, cities reduced to a small fraction of their original population, and cultivated land reverting to waste. Starvation and disease killed more than the sword. It is impossible to be sure of the total decline in

population, but some historians believe that Germany lost almost a third of its inhabitants. Others insist that the destruction was not so great as contemporary sources would suggest, and that recovery in farming districts was rapid. The social and psychological effects, however, were certainly frightful. A whole generation grew up accepting violence and brutality as normal. Superstition and witchcraft increased in influence. The fragmentation of the Empire into practically independent states hampered economic recovery. Cultural and political provincialism were to go hand in hand for the next two centuries in German history. In fact, it is almost impossible to find any good result of the generation of aimless fighting in Germany known as the Thirty Years' War.

THE MERCANTILE ECONOMY OF EARLY MODERN EUROPE

Seventeenth-century kings and ministers were aware that political power depended on economic strength. They sought to increase the wealth of their own countries and to decrease the wealth of rival countries, or at least to prevent its growth. Agriculture, of course, was still the chief occupation in every part of Europe, but very little could be done either to increase home production or to decrease foreign production of food and fibers. Industry was more susceptible to state interference, but none of the major countries was very dependent on industry. On the other hand, the volume and value of European trade had increased enormously. Growth between 1500 and 1600 had been so spectacular that some historians have described it as a "Commercial Revolution." And the countries that were assuming political leadership in Europe were becoming the centers of trade. The main routes now led to Amsterdam, London, and Paris rather than to Venice, Lisbon, and Seville. In the Netherlands, England, and France, the merchant was far more important than the industrialist and far more influential than the farmer.

Therefore, a ruler who wanted to use economic controls as a political weapon thought primarily in terms of altering the patterns of international trade. This policy seemed so natural that no one bothered to give it a name. In 1776, however, Adam Smith, looking at the process with some disapproval, coined the phrase "the mercantile system." This phrase, or its equivalent "mercantilism," has been used ever since.

Problems of Economic Organization

By the end of the sixteenth century it was evident that old forms of economic organization were not able to deal with the vast increase in the volume of trade. The gilds, which controlled production in many towns, could not supply the growing demands of merchants and governments. Most gilds were geared only to local markets and insisted on following traditional, and often inefficient, methods of work. Many governments tried to regulate gilds in order to get uniform, nationwide standards of production, but except for a few luxury articles, this policy proved a failure. It was easier to let the merchants deal with the problem of industrial organization.

One method, already used by the end of the Middle Ages, was called the putting-out system. For example, in the textile industry an entrepreneur would buy wool, pass it out to peasants to be spun into thread, carry the thread to others to be woven into cloth, take the cloth to the dyers, and finally sell the finished product. This system had the double advantage of bypassing the gild restrictions in the towns and of tapping new sources of cheap labor in the countryside. Underemployed peasants with only a few acres were glad to have any extra income; in England they took almost all the work away from the old textile towns. In the same way, English merchants bought Swedish iron, gave it out to Sheffield tool-makers, and sold the product abroad. (The English were the best precision-tool-makers in Europe.) The putting-out system dominated the textile industry from the sixteenth to the eighteenth centuries.

Another type of organization was the gathering-in system (the factory system).

In industries like printing, cannon founding, mining, and shipbuilding, for example, and even in some textile processes such as silk weaving and calico printing, it was more efficient to gather workers together at some central place where their work could be directly supervised and coordinated. There was not much division of labor; each man made a finished or semifinished article. But transportation costs were cut and quality could be controlled. In both the putting-out and the gathering-in systems, it was almost invariably the merchant, not the manufacturer or the technician, who did the organizing.

Joint Stock Companies

In commerce an important innovation was the joint stock company. The small partnerships of the Middle Ages (and even the Medici Bank was small by seventeenth-century standards) could not raise the capital needed for large-scale, overseas voyages. So merchants formed associations—the "regulated companies." Governments gave such groups a monopoly on trade to a given area, but each member of the group, while he helped meet common expenses, traded on his own account. They were associations of men, not of capital. What was needed, however, was a type of association that would attract the investments of men who had neither the desire nor the ability to qualify as active traders in a regulated company. The answer was the joint stock company, an amazingly flexible institution that was to be the parent of many other economic and political institutions on both sides of the Atlantic.

The joint stock company began as an association of investors, not of traders. Individuals bought shares in a venture, such as a trading voyage, and shared in the profits in proportion to their investment. When the association continued beyond a single venture, it became a joint stock company. This device had two advantages: It enabled anyone from a modestly wealthy man to Queen Elizabeth to invest in a business enterprise like Drake's voyages, and it associated businessmen with courtiers and statesmen at a time when both business sense

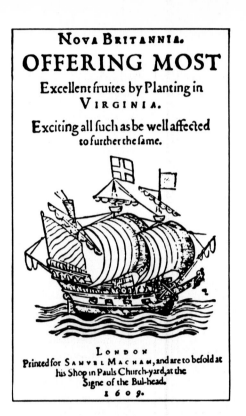

NOVA BRITANNIA.
OFFERING MOST
Excellent fruites by Planting in
VIRGINIA.

Exciting all such as be well affected
to further the same.

LONDON
Printed for SAMVEL MACHAM, and are to be sold at
his Shop in Pauls Church-yard, at the
Signe of the Bul-head.
1 6 0 9.

Page from a pamphlet put out by the London Company in 1609 to persuade investors to support its enterprise in Virginia.

and influence at court were necessary to the success of commercial ventures. The joint stock idea originated in southern Europe, but it was first applied to large-scale overseas enterprise in England in the Russia Company of 1553. The English East India Company, the companies that founded Virginia and Massachusetts, and the Bank of England were all joint stock companies. As these examples show, the first joint stock companies were dependent on government support (usually in the form of a trade monopoly) and were not concerned with industry. The joint stock company rapidly became the dominant form of commercial organization; it developed more slowly in industrial production.

The cumulative effect of these changes was to make the king, not the town, the chief regulator of economic activity. The unit of economic activity in the Middle Ages, apart from agriculture, was the town or the city-state. As stronger monarchs appeared at the end of the Middle Ages, urban economy was steadily absorbed into the national economy throughout much of Europe, except in Italy and Germany. The monarch stepped into the shoes of medieval town officials and regulated trade and production much as municipal governments had done, but on a larger scale.

Mercantilism

The aim of this regulation was to advance the common good, not to increase the wealth of individuals. But a king's definition of the common good was the strength and security of his realm, not a general rise in consumption or standards of living. During the seventeenth century monarchs began to believe that their goals could be attained by following the economic doctrine called mercantilism. This doctrine, as applied in the seventeenth century, assumed that there is only a certain stock of wealth in the world at any given time, and if one country gains wealth another loses it. (This is a fairly typical assumption in a period of depression; it had already emerged in the fourteenth century and is not unknown today.) To prevent loss, home industries and shipping should be encouraged and colonies founded to provide raw materials that would otherwise have to be bought from foreigners. By regulating trade in these ways a country's stock of precious metals might be increased and surely would not decrease. This was not an unreasonable precaution in an age when credit devices were in their infancy and when, in case of war, a country had to have a reserve of gold and silver to pay its suppliers and soldiers.

The obvious way to build such a reserve—short of discovering new mines or capturing a Spanish plate fleet—was for a nation to export more than it imported. Foreign buyers would have to settle their balances in precious metals. At the very least there should be a balance of trade, so that more money would not leave the country than stayed in it. And so mercantilism called for tariffs to discourage imports and various benefits to encourage export industries. But some exports—gold and silver, scare raw materials, and skilled workmen, for example—weaken a state and should therefore be forbidden. Logically, mercantilist theory called for the abolition of all internal tariffs and all internal barriers to trade in order to build up the home market, though it was impossible to accomplish this except in England. At the core of mercantilism was the conviction that trade is the most important of all economic activities, that the regulation of trade is the government's most important economic concern, and that regulation should result in self-sufficiency and readiness for war.

As we shall see (p. 439), when new colonial policies were developed during the seventeenth century, mercantilists favored tropical colonies that enhanced the strength of the mother country by furnishing products such as sugar and tea and by buying home manufactures. They had no use for colonies that raised crops or produced manufactured goods that competed with the home country's products, nor for colonies that traded directly with other nations. The integration of colonies into the home economy was a cardinal mercantilist principle.

An Englishman on the Importance of Trade
ca. 1630

Although a kingdom may be enriched by gifts received, or by purchase taken from some other nations, yet these are things uncertain and of small consideration when they happen. The ordinary means therefore to encrease our wealth and treasure is by foreign trade, wherein we must ever observe this rule; to sell more to strangers yearly than we consume of theirs in value. For suppose that when this kingdom is plentifully served with the cloth, lead, tin, iron, fish and other native commodities, we do yearly export the overplus to foreign countries to the value of twenty-two hundred thousand pounds; by which means we are enabled beyond the seas to buy and bring in foreign wares for our use and consumptions, to the value of twenty hundred thousand pounds; by this order duly kept in our trading, we may rest assured that the kingdom shall be enriched yearly two hundred thousand pounds, which must be brought to us in so much treasure; because that part of our stock which is not returned to us in wares must necessarily be brought home in treasure. . . .

Behold then the true form and worth of foreign trade, which is, the great revenue of the king, the honour of the kingdom, the noble profession of the merchant, the school of our arts, the supply of our wants, the employment of our poor, the improvements of our lands, the nursery of our mariners, the walls of the kingdoms, the means of our treasure, the sinews of our wars, the terror of our enemies.

From Thomas Mun, *England's Treasure by Foreign Trade* (New York: Oxford University Press, 1933), p. 5.

Arms granted by Elizabeth to the East India Company.

Mercantilism has necessarily been made to seem more clear-cut and consistent than it actually was in practice. It differed from one country to another, in response to the interests of the ruling group. In France the system was often called *Étatisme,* or state-ism. The hand of the government was very heavy in France: government intervention in commercial enterprise was direct and positive, regulation was intense, and relatively little initiative was left to individual enterprise. In England mercantilism also meant regulation of the economy in the government's interest. But even before 1688, and especially afterward, the English government was more responsive to the pressures of businessmen than was the French. It is often very difficult to tell whether English economic policy represented the interest of the state as a whole or the interests of individual entrepreneurs. In the United Provinces, where the federal government was in effect a government of businessmen, the interest of the state and the interests of the business community practically coincided. Dutch mercantilism was not so much the regulation of trade by the state as it was the control of economic policy by organized business. In the rest of Europe, how-

ever—in Spain, Portugal, Austria, Prussia, and Sweden—mercantilism represented primarily the interest of the monarchy and so followed the French model more than the Dutch.

Financial Problems

The rise in prices that had marked the sixteenth century slowed down in the seventeenth, and may even have been reversed for a while. It has been estimated that while prices more than doubled between 1500 and 1600, they rose no more than 20 percent during the next hundred years, and most of that gain came during the first two or the last two decades of the century. The problems of inflation had been hard enough to handle. With prices rising faster than government income bankruptcy was always just around the corner. In Spain, with its heavy military commitments, the government had had to repudiate its debts at frequent intervals (see p. 404). But the problems of deflation were even more serious. Taxes brought in less while government expenditures continued to increase. The optimism that comes with inflation, at least to the classes able to profit from it, decreased. The classes that had profited from the inflation of the sixteenth century—merchants, bankers, men who invested in land (like the English gentry)—found the financial atmosphere of the seventeenth century rather chilling. This is one reason why taxation seemed so oppressive after 1600.

Spain never managed to solve its problems and continued to hang on the edge of bankruptcy until late in the century. France did better, partly because its taxes fell most heavily on the peasants, and agricultural prices remained at a higher level than prices of other commodities, thus giving the peasants enough of a surplus to pay for the extravagances of the court and the waste of war. But the French taxation system was antiquated and trouble was simply postponed to the eighteenth century. In England the Stuarts were never able to build a sound system of government finance because they lost the confidence of Parliament, which controlled the major part of the royal revenue. But after

1688 a government that had gained the confidence of Parliament as well as the business community was able to construct an exceptionally strong system of public finance that included parliamentary taxation, a national bank, and a permanent public debt. In large measure this system was modeled on Dutch governmental finance, the most successful of the age. Since the rulers of the United Provinces were representatives of the business community, they had little difficulty, at least for a century, in raising the money and credit they needed for their overseas empire building and their wars. In an age dominated by trade, a state that had a flourishing commerce and could command the confidence of its merchants could weather any financial storm. A state that had little commerce, or in which commerce was growing slowly while merchants were discouraged, was likely to find itself in financial difficulties.

EUROPEAN COLONIES IN THE SEVENTEENTH CENTURY

European expansion overseas was checked briefly in the seventeenth century, and picked up again only after some fundamental changes were made in patterns of colonial settlement. The earliest and easiest type of colony was a fortified trading post, to which the natives brought readily salable commodities, such as gold, spices, and slaves. This was the Portuguese pattern, and, as the Dutch gradually ousted the Portuguese from the East Indies, it was the pattern which the Dutch tried to follow. But even the Dutch eventually found that they had to go inland and take over responsibility for governing large numbers of people in order to maintain the flow of commodities, and no other colonizing power found it possible to avoid administrative responsibilities for more than a brief period. The Spaniards, for example, could not exploit the wealth of America without taking over the Aztec and the Inca Empires.

Moreover, it became harder and harder to get riches without effort. There was an apparently inexhaustible supply of slaves in Africa, which is why European colonies there could remain at the trading post level. But the market for spices was soon glutted, and, once the pillaging of the American Indians ended, gold and silver could be acquired only by laborious and expensive mining operations. A new type of colony was needed, a colony that produced goods desired by Europeans with its own labor. The first such colonies were the sugar islands of the Caribbean; later came the tobacco, tea, and coffee colonies.

The East

At first the Dutch, the English, and the French tried to cut in on the Portuguese trade in India, Ceylon, and the East Indies. The English East India Company was founded in 1600, the Dutch in 1602, the French in 1664. The Dutch discouraged English trade with the Spice Islands—they killed ten English merchants in 1623—so the English withdrew to India. There they set up "factories," or trading posts, on the Portuguese model. Until the breakup of the Mogul Empire in central India early in the eighteenth century, it was never possible for Europeans to penetrate very far into the subcontinent of India. Their footholds on the coast depended entirely on sea power for support; and as Portuguese sea power declined in the seventeenth century and as the Dutch busied themselves farther east, the English were able to establish themselves at Bombay, Madras, and Calcutta. Meanwhile, the French at Pondicherry had become their most important potential rivals. The stage was set for a struggle in the next century between the British and the French East India companies over India's commerce and riches.

The Caribbean

In the Caribbean the Dutch, the English, and the French were all searching for footholds around the periphery of the Spanish settlements. After an unsuccessful attempt to take Brazil from the Portuguese, the Dutch seized Curaçao as a base from which to raid Spanish commerce. The English settled Barbados in

Miniature by an Indian artist of a foreigner, possibly a merchant of the East India Company, ca. 1600.

The Javanese port of Batavia, from a Dutch engraving of 1682. Notice the Dutch architecture, entirely inappropriate for the climate.

1624 and acquired Jamaica in 1655. Meanwhile, the French settled Guadaloupe and Martinique. These acquisitions were made just as the new colonial model—the colony as a producer of tropical goods—became popular. All the West Indian islands rapidly became rich sugar-producing areas, thanks to slave labor. So the English and the French, who came to the Caribbean to trade and buccaneer in the Dutch manner, stayed on to become plantation owners in the Spanish manner. The English and French sugar islands were the darlings of mercantilists at home. The planters cultivated a crop that could not be grown in Europe; they developed no industries to compete with home industries; and they were entirely dependent on their mother countries for shipping. Not surprisingly, the sugar islands were the center of attention among financiers and diplomats for over a century.

The chronic dearth of manufactured goods and slaves in the Spanish colonies meant that foreign smugglers who could slip by the Spanish navy were always welcome. As Portuguese control of the slaving stations on the western coast of Africa relaxed, the Dutch and English stepped in to supply the Spanish West Indies with the slaves needed on their sugar plantations. The brutality of this trade has become a byword, but it aroused no protest whatever in any European nation during the seventeenth and early eighteenth centuries.

North America

In North America a new wave of colonial expansion was beginning that was to have more far-reaching results than West Indian sugar planting, though it was long overshadowed by the economic success of the tropical islands. There were many reasons why the Dutch, the English, and the French became interested in North America at the opening of the seventeenth century. For some time their sailors had been searching for a northwest passage to the Indies. Their ships were already engaged in cod fishing on the Newfoundland Banks. It was evident that North America could supply vast quantities of furs and timber. There might be precious metals, and it might turn out that sugar could be grown farther north than the Caribbean. Permanent settlements could support all these economic activities and at the same time help turn the flank of the Spanish in the New World.

Sir Walter Raleigh's unsuccessful attempt to found a colony in Virginia during the 1580s, however, had revealed some of the difficulties of settling the land the Spanish had left unoccupied.

Colder climate, poorer soil, and hostile natives discouraged a plantation type of economy. To plant a permanent colony in North America a whole labor force would have to be transported and supported, perhaps for years, until the settlement became self-sufficient. This called for a large investment of capital and a large number of settlers. Furthermore, it called for strong belief and determination.

The Dutch, the French, and the English

It was the English and, to a lesser degree, the French, not the Dutch, whose determination proved strongest. The Dutch explored the Hudson in 1609 and settled New Amsterdam on Manhattan Island in 1621, but their colony of New Netherland never became more than a center for maritime trade and the export of furs. Unsupported by the company that founded it, it fell to the English in 1664. The French were more successful. From Cartier, who discovered the St. Lawrence in 1535, to La Salle, who coursed the Mississippi in 1682, their explorers were more adventurous, their fur traders better able to adapt to the country, and their Jesuit missionaries more determined, than the representatives of any other European nation in the New World. In 1605 there were French settlers in Acadia and in 1608 Champlain founded Quebec. By 1640 there were perhaps 3,000 Frenchmen in Canada; by the end of the century about 10,000.

The growth was slow for several reasons. The settlement of French Canada

The Indian village of Pomeiock in "Virginia" (actually North Carolina), watercolor by John White, an artist who took part in Raleigh's attempt to establish a colony at Roanoke in 1585. In his text White notes that mats and the bark of trees were used to cover the dwellings; the town was encompassed with poles instead of a wall.

was marked by paternalism and relatively little individual initiative. Only when the French government actively encouraged Frenchmen to emigrate, as it did under Colbert in the 1660s and 1670s, did the colony grow appreciably. Since land was granted in large blocks, or *seigneuries,* to a few proprietors under semifeudal conditions, there was little inducement for peasants to emigrate. The government strictly prohibited the Huguenots, who wanted to emigrate, from going to Canada (they went to the English colonies instead). A fairly solid block of settlements grew up in the St. Lawrence Valley, but the slow-growing colony of *seigneurs* and *habitants* (as the peasants were called) was soon far outdistanced by the English settlements to the south.

The founding of the English colonies in North America was the result of a peculiarly favorable set of historical circumstances in the mother country. The idea that colonization meant wealth had been skillfully sold to ordinary Englishmen by enthusiasts and businessmen before Queen Elizabeth's death. London and Bristol merchants were ready for colonizing ventures and able to organize such ventures by means of joint stock companies. The constitutional and religious conflicts that troubled England through most of the seventeenth century provided many people with both material and idealistic motives for wishing to emigrate. Finally the English government, whether it was that of the Stuarts or of their revolutionary opponents, encouraged but did not interfere with colonizing projects. In particular, it put no bar in the way of religious minorities that wished to emigrate.

The first successful colony, planted at Jamestown by the Virginia Company in 1607, had a difficult time until the settlers discovered that by concentrating on a single crop, tobacco, they could buy the goods they needed from England. The little band of religious dissenters who landed at Plymouth in 1620 lost half their number during the first winter and survived only by sheer heroism. But the Massachusetts Bay Company, which founded Boston, was able to profit by the Pilgrims' experience. In 1630 it trans-

ported 900 settlers across the ocean in a large and well-planned operation. Within ten years the population had increased to about 14,000 in Massachusetts and within twenty years there were about 20,000 in New England as a whole. This population had developed a surplus of food for export, and had plenty of fur, fish, and timber to ship back to the mother country. By the end of the century more colonies had been established, either as offshoots of the original settlements or by royal grants to "proprietors," until there were twelve in all (the thirteenth was added in 1732). By 1700 it has been estimated that there were almost 200,000 English settlers in North America, as compared with about 10,000 French. It was already clear that most North Americans would someday speak English.

English and French Colonies

The English colonies were more divided and less well controlled by the home government than the French. New France was under one central administration at Quebec, whereas the English colonies were under twelve separate governments. Each of the twelve eventually elected representative assemblies that controlled local legislation and taxation. The royal governors were not responsible to these assemblies, but, since they were generally dependent on the assemblies for their salaries, their power was effectively limited. In the 1660s Parliament did its best to impose strict mercantilist theories on the colonies—for example, by ruling that certain exports must be sent directly to England in English or colonial ships. These measures caused complaints, and after the Revolution of 1688 the English government gradually became less insistent on asserting its authority. The colonists accepted parliamentary regulation of their trade so long as the regulations were not too strictly enforced, but they became more and more accustomed to running their own affairs to suit themselves.

Without conscious design, the English in the seventeenth century fashioned a new kind of colonial empire in North America, quite different from either the

Codfishing in the waters off Newfoundland, *ca.* 1720.

Portuguese or the Spanish. The Portuguese Empire (and, to a large degree, the Dutch) was based on armed trade. The Spanish Empire was based on the efforts of a ruling class of soldiers, planters, and missionaries to convert the natives and exploit their labor. But the Protestant English (and Protestant Dutch) were never particularly interested in converting the natives. They never felt responsible for the Indians as the Spanish did, partly because there was no possibility of exploiting their labor. So they simply displaced the natives from the land on which they settled. The English transferred a whole European population to a new environment and permitted it to blend the traditional institutions it brought from home with the innovations and improvisations evoked by the new surroundings. Not surprisingly, these innovations tended toward economic, political, and religious freedom. The breeze was blowing in this direction in England, and it was blowing even more strongly in the colonies.

The Russians in Siberia

While the French and the British in North America were pushing westward from the Atlantic seaboard toward the Pacific, the Russians were pushing eastward from the Ural Mountains across Siberia toward the Pacific. The two movements were strikingly similar in many respects, but the Russians had no ocean to cross at the start and they reached the Pacific first. In 1581, groups of Cossacks—"pioneers," or "frontiersmen," who had earlier pushed back the Tartars and Turks and had settled in the lower valleys of the Dnieper, the Don, and the Volga—began to move eastward from the Urals under a leader, Ermak, who became famed in song and story. Like the French in Canada, the Cossacks were mainly in search of furs, particularly sable, and so they followed the dark pine forest, not the steppe to the south. The great rivers of Siberia—the Obi, the Yenisei, and the Lena—flow north into the Arctic Ocean, but in their upper reaches they branch out so that they almost touch one another. Thus the Cossacks could move easily across the continent by water. The movement was not planned or organized. The settlers simply flowed eastward through the sparsely settled wastes of Siberia in search of furs, occasionally stopping to form widely separated settlements, and reached the Pacific in the early 1640s, barely two generations after the movement began. The distance covered was greater than that across North America, but there were no wide mountain barriers until near the end and no serious resistance from natives until the Cossacks met the Chinese in the Amur Valley. There the Russians were checked by a superior, civilized state, and in 1689, by the first treaty concluded between Russia and China, the Russians withdrew from the Amur basin. They remained behind the Stanovoi Mountains for the next 170 years.

Like the English, the Cossacks were in search of freedom as well as furs, and their early communities in Siberia were often wild and lawless, like the later towns of the American "Wild West." But the tsar's government soon reached out across the vast distances to establish its administration and to tax the lucrative fur trade—more like the French than the English government in North America. By 1700 there were perhaps half again as many Russian settlers in Siberia as there were French and British in North America. By the end of the century, Russian traders were venturing across the Bering Strait into Alaska and down the North

A Cossack warrior.

American coastline in search of seals. Thus long before the English colonists in America had reached the Pacific, the Russians, by a combination of individual daring and government backing, had staked out a claim to the northern half of Asia and had even reached out far enough to touch the shores of the Western Hemisphere.

Suggestions for Further Reading

Note: Asterisk denotes a book available in paperback edition.

General Works on the Seventeenth Century

There are several successful attempts at a synthetic treatment of the period. D. Ogg, *Europe in the Seventeenth Century,** 5th ed. (1948), is a sound and interesting narrative of the major developments on the Continent, arranged by country. G. N. Clark, *The Seventeenth Century** (1931), is a more analytical discussion of different aspects of the period: for instance, population, industries, military organization, political thought, science, religion. C. J. Friedrich's volume in the *Rise of Modern Europe* series, *The Age of the Baroque, 1610–1660** (1952), combines narrative and analysis and makes use of recent interpretations of baroque style. C. J. Friedrich and C. Blitzer, *The Age of Power** (1957), is a brief and thoughtful survey of the century, based on Friedrich's larger work. Trevor Aston, *Crises in Europe, 1560–1660* (1965) is uneven, but at its best very good.

Mercantilism and Economic Growth

L. B. Packard, *The Commercial Revolution, 1400–1700* (1927), is the briefest reliable treatment of mercantilism. J. W. Horrocks, *Short History of Mercantilism* (1925), and P. W. Buck, *The Politics of Mercantilism** (1964), are somewhat longer studies. The fullest and best treatment is E. F. Heckscher, *Mercantilism*, 2 vols. (1935). H. Sée, *Modern Capitalism* (trans. 1928), is the best extensive discussion of the subject. F. L. Nussbaum, *History of the Economic Institutions of Modern Europe* (1933), summarizes the work of the great German historian of capitalism, W. Sombart. D. Hannay, *The Great Chartered Companies* (1926), is a good introduction to its subject. J. U. Nef, *War and Human Progress* (1950), argues that war is a detriment, not a stimulant, to technological and economic progress, particularly in this period.

Expansion Overseas

In addition to the works cited for Chapter 18 on geographical discovery, the following are useful on special topics: B. H. M. Vlekke, *The Story of the Dutch East Indies* (1945); C. R. Boxer, *The Dutch Seaborne Empire* (1965); C. Gibson, *Spain in America* (1966); and H. A. Wyndham, *The Atlantic and Slavery* (1935). On the rivalry of France and England in America, the many fascinating volumes of Francis Parkman dating from the 1860s are still worth reading, especially the earlier ones. G. M. Wrong, *The Rise and Fall of New France*, 2 vols. (1928), is the standard modern account. *The Cambridge History of India*, 5 vols. (1922–37), is useful for reference.

France

J. Boulenger, *The Seventeenth Century** (trans. 1920), is a standard one-volume account in English. G. Treasure, *Seventeenth Century France** (1966), is a recent survey. F. C. Palm, *The Establishment of French Absolutism, 1574–1610* (1928), and P. R. Doolin, *The Fronde* (1935), are good special studies. Of the many books on Richelieu, the most trustworthy short account is C. V. Wedgwood, *Richelieu and the French Monarchy** (1949). C. J. Burckhardt, *Richelieu: His Rise to Power** (1964), is a solid piece of work.

England

The classic one-volume account, Whiggish in sympathy and brilliantly written, is G. M. Trevelyan, *England under the Stuarts* (1904, 1946). The standard modern account is G. Davies, *The Early Stuarts, 1603–1660* (1937), in the *Oxford History of England* series. The detailed narrative history of S. R. Gardiner, published in 18 volumes (1863–1903) and covering the years 1603–56, is a major achievement of English historical scholarship to which all later accounts are indebted. C. V. Wedgwood has published three volumes of a history of the Puritan rebellion, *The King's Peace* (1955), *The King's War* (1958), and *A Coffin for King Charles* (1964). D. L. Keir, *The Constitutional History of Modern Britain, 1485–1937** 4th ed. (1950), and J. R. Tanner, *English Constitutional Conflicts of the Seventeenth Century** (1928), together constitute a good introduction to some of the more technical constitutional issues of the period. There are many biographies of Cromwell, but the best is still C. H. Firth, *Oliver Cromwell and the Rule of the Puritans in England* (1900, 1925). W. Notestein, *The English People on the Eve of Colonization, 1603–1630** (1954), is a good introduction to the social history of the period, and B. Willey, *The Seventeenth Century Background** (1934), a good introduction to its intellectual history. A. S. P. Woodhouse, *Puritanism and Liberty* (1938), is a selection of sources illustrating the ferment of democratic ideas during the rebellion. See also W. Haller, *The Rise of Puritanism** (1938), and M. Walzer, *The Revolution of the Saints* (1965).

Germany

There are good chapters on the Thirty Years' War in Ogg and Friedrich (first section, above), also in H. J. Grimm, *The Reformation Era* (1954), and H. Holborn, *A History of Modern Germany: The Reformation* (1959), both listed after Chapter 17. Far and away the best general account in English is C. V. Wedgwood, *The Thirty Years War** (1938). The scholars' argument over how destructive the war was may be followed in S. H. Steinberg's criticism of Wedgwood in *History*, Vol. 32 (1947), pp. 89–102. T. K. Rabb, *The Thirty Years' War** (1964), gives readings on the causes and effects of the war. The Swedish phase of the war is well described by M. Roberts, *Gustavus Adolphus* (1953–58).

20 Absolutism and Constitutionalism, 1660–1715

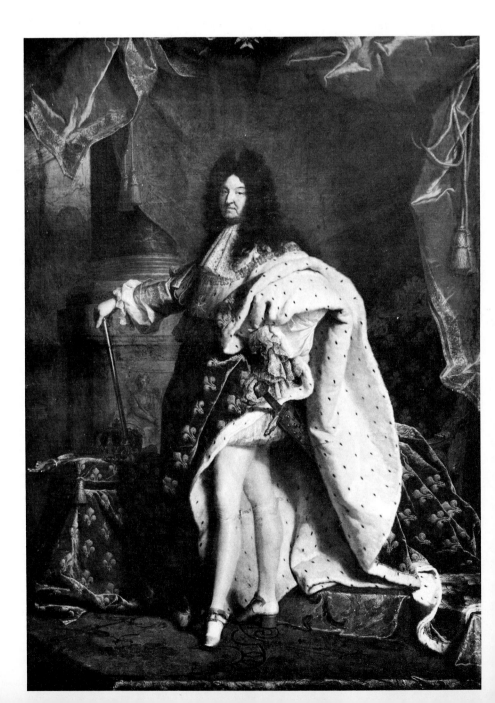

Louis XIV, by Hyacinthe
Rigaud, 1701.

During the latter half of the seventeenth century France was the leading nation in Europe. Its population was twice that of Spain and over four times that of England. Its land was fertile and its commerce and industry were growing.

FRANCE UNDER LOUIS XIV

There were no disturbing arguments over forms of government; absolute monarchy was accepted by almost all Frenchmen as necessary, reasonable, and right. By the Peace of the Pyrenees (1659) the French army had displaced the Spanish as the strongest military machine on the Continent. As time went on, it seemed as if not only French generals, French military engineers, and French diplomatists but French architects, painters, dramatists, and philosophers were the best in Europe. French fashions in dress dominated the Continent, the French language became the leading language of diplomacy and polite conversation, and the French court with its elaborate etiquette and ceremonial became the model for countless smaller courts throughout Europe. As Florence had been the nerve center of the Italian Renaissance and Spain of the Catholic Reformation, so France was the nerve center of late-seventeenth-century politics, diplomacy, and culture.

How much of this predominance is to be attributed to the long reign of Louis XIV is one of those questions that historians can speculate about but never answer. No one doubts that French (and European) history would have run in different channels had Louis never lived—or had he not lived so long. He was born in 1638, became king in 1643, took the reins of power into his own hands in 1661 at twenty-three, and died in 1715 at the age of seventy-seven, leaving the throne to his great-grandson. By temperament and training Louis was the very incarnation of divine-right monarchy—the idea that hereditary monarchy is the only divinely approved form of government, that kings are responsible

to God alone for their conduct, and that subjects should obey their kings as the direct representatives of God on earth. In an age that put its trust in absolute rulers, the achievements of the French people at the peak of their greatness cannot be separated from the personality of their ruler, even if it can be proved that many of those achievements were unrelated to, or even accomplished in spite of, the ruler.

Louis is said to have remarked, "I am the state." Even if the remark is apocryphal, the words reveal more of the true importance of his reign than anything else he said or wrote. Louis XIV set out early in his reign to personify the concept of sovereignty. He dramatized this aim immediately after Mazarin's death by ordering his ministers thereafter to report to him in person, not to a "first minister."

To be the real head of a large and complicated government required long, hard work, and Louis paid the price. His education was poor and he had little imagination, no sense of humor, and only a mediocre intelligence. But he had common sense, a knack of picking up information from others, and a willingness to work steadily at the business of governing. "If you let yourself be carried away by your passions," he once said, "don't do it in business hours." Painstakingly he caught up all the threads of power in his own hands. All major decisions were made in four great councils, which he attended regularly. These decisions were then carried out by professional "secretaries" at the head of organized bureaucracies. In the provinces, the *intendants* more and more represented the direct authority of the central government in justice, finance, and general administration. The old French monarchy imposed its authority through judicial decisions and had frequently consulted local and central assemblies. The new monarchy, begun by Richelieu and perfected by Louis XIV, imposed its authority through executive decisions. Louis reduced the importance of the *parlements*, never summoned the Estates General, and, so far as such a thing was humanly possible in his century, built a government that was himself.

The medal at top, issued in 1661, celebrates Louis' accessibility to his subjects. The medal below was struck in 1685 to commemorate the restoration of military discipline in his reign.

Colbert and the Economy

Colbert, Louis XIV's Controller-General of Finance, systematically ordered the economic life of the country under royal direction. He was an extreme mercantilist; everything he did was consciously or unconsciously meant to strengthen the country for war. He set up high protective tariffs to help home industry, fostered new export industries, encouraged the French colonies in Canada and the West Indies, and did everything he could to develop a powerful navy and a strong merchant marine. Some historians suspect that his minute regulation of industry and commerce did more to hinder than to help the French economy. But until the burden of foreign wars became heavy in the 1680s, national production and wealth were increasing. Colbert also cut down waste and corruption in the collection of taxes, as Sully had once done, but he was unable to make the burden of taxation much more equitable because of the exemptions held or purchased by members of the nobility and the bourgeoisie, the classes best able to pay. During the crisis of Louis' last war an attempt was made to tax these upper classes in order to stave off bankruptcy, but the attempt set no precedent.

The Nobility

The most dangerous potential opponents of royal absolutism, as Louis XIV knew from his own experience during the Fronde, were the members of the nobility. Louis completed Richelieu's work of destroying the political power of the French nobility. He excluded the nobles completely from all responsible positions in government and cheapened their status by increasing their numbers. An army commission came to be almost the only major outlet for a noble's ambition, which meant that the nobles as a class generally constituted a war party at court. All important positions in Louis XIV's government, such as the secretaryships and intendancies, were filled by men of bourgeois or recently ennobled families.

Louis did not attack the social privileges of the nobility; he used them to make the nobles utterly dependent on him. In 1683 he moved the court and government from the Louvre in Paris to Versailles, fifteen miles away. He had hated Paris since the riots of the Fronde, and now in the formal gardens and ornate chateaux of Versailles, which he

Louis XIV on the Duties of a King, 1661

During the early period of his direct rule, Louis XIV prepared notes for the instruction of his son in the art of ruling. He had assistance in this task, and the texts do not necessarily give his exact words. They do express his ideas.

I have often wondered how it could be that love for work being a quality so necessary to sovereigns should yet be one that is so rarely found in them. Most princes, because they have a great many servants and subjects, do not feel obliged to go to any trouble and do not consider that if they have an infinite number of people working under their orders, there are infinitely more who rely on their conduct and that it takes a great deal of watching and a great deal of work merely to insure that those who act do only what they should and that those who rely tolerate only what they must. The deference and the respect that we receive from our subjects are not a free gift from them but payment for the justice and the protection that they expect to receive from us. Just as they must honor us, we must protect and defend them, and our debts toward them are even more binding than theirs to us, for indeed, if one of them lacks the skill or the willingness to execute our orders, a thousand others come in a crowd to fill his post, whereas the position of a sovereign can be properly filled only by the sovereign himself.

. . . of all the functions of sovereignty, the one that a prince must guard most jealously is the handling of the finances. It is the most delicate of all because it is the one that is most capable of seducing the one who performs it, and which makes it easiest for him to spread corruption. The prince alone should have sovereign direction over it because he alone has no fortune to establish but that of the state.

Louis XIV, *Memories for the Instruction of the Dauphin,* ed. by Paul Sonnino (New York: The Free Press, 1970), pp. 63–64.

had built on waste marsh at considerable cost of human lives and treasure, he felt at home. He also felt safe; Versailles was the first royal residence that was completely unfortified. At Versailles, the king lived in an utterly artificial atmosphere, as far removed from reality as Versailles was physically removed from the bustle of Paris. Here the great nobles were compelled to live. Here a ball seemed as important as a battle, and holding the basin for the king's morning ablutions was a job as much to be coveted as commanding the king's armies. Instead of competing for political power, nobles squandered their fortunes and exhausted their energies in jockeying for social prestige.

The regular rectangular shapes of the gardens, the balanced classical lines of the baroque architecture, the bright glint of mirrors and chandeliers, all these seemed to symbolize and emphasize the isolation of Versailles from nature, from the French nation, from the real world. Through all this Louis moved with impassive dignity. Years of self-conscious practice in kingship had given him a kind of public personality—cool, courteous, impersonal, imperturbable—which carried out perfectly the artificiality of the little world at Versailles. At his death he left to his successors a privileged nobility shorn of all political power and responsibility, demoralized by the empty pleasures and petty intrigues of court life, and uneasily aware of its uselessness. It was a dangerous legacy.

Religious Policy

The only other potential opponents of Louis' absolutism were religious groups. The king had his differences with several popes who disliked his Gallican principles, but these quarrels never led to a real breach. Louis was always a good Catholic in a formal sense. He disliked and persecuted the Jansenists, an austere group of Catholic "puritans" who emphasized the teachings of St. Augustine on original sin, the depravity of man, and the need for divine grace. They felt that the Jesuits were far too optimistic about man's ability to work out his own salvation, and far too ready to compromise with the world. Louis, whose confessors

Bishop Bossuet on Absolutism

Jacques Bénigne Bossuet was tutor to Louis XIV's son in the 1670s.

The royal power is absolute. With the aim of making this truth hateful and insufferable, many writers have tried to confound absolute government with arbitrary government. But no two things could be more unlike. . . . The prince need render an account of his acts to no one. . . . Without this absolute authority the king could neither do good nor repress evil. . . . God is infinite, God is all. The prince, as prince, is not regarded as a private person: he is a public personage, all the state is in him; the will of all the people is included in his. As all perfection and all strength are united in God, so all the power of individuals is united in the person of the prince. What grandeur that a single man should embody so much! . . . Behold this holy power, paternal and absolute; behold the secret cause which governs the whole body of the state, contained in a single head: you see the image of God in the king, and you have the idea of royal majesty. God is holiness itself, goodness itself, and power itself. In these things lies the majesty of God. In the image of these things lies the majesty of the prince.

From Jacques Bénigne Bossuet, "Politics Drawn from the Very Words of Scripture," in James Harvey Robinson, ed., *Readings in European History* (Boston: Ginn, 1906), Vol. II, pp. 275–76.

were Jesuits, thought the Jansenists subversive (they had been condemned by the pope) and impertinent (they disapproved of his numerous mistresses). After 1680, though never a particularly religious man, he seems to have become increasingly concerned about the fate of his own soul. When his queen, Maria Theresa, died in 1683, he gave up his mistresses and secretly married Madame de Maintenon, a pious Catholic whose parents were Huguenots. In 1685 he shocked Protestant Europe by revoking the Edict of Nantes, by which Henry IV had granted religious toleration to the Huguenots.

There were about a million Huguenots out of a total population of perhaps eighteen million in France at the opening of Louis XIV's reign. After Richelieu deprived them of their military and political privileges, they had become good citizens and had remained loyal to the crown during the Fronde. Many were successful in industry and the professions, though few had attained the civil and military positions that were theoretically open to them. The French Catholic clergy had long tried to persuade Louis XIV that the continued exercise of the Protestant religion in France was an insult to his dignity and authority, and as the king became more concerned about his salvation the idea of atoning for his sins of the flesh by crushing heresy became more attractive to him. The Edict was "interpreted" more and more strictly. Protestant children were declared of age at seven and converted to Catholicism, and any attempt by their parents to win them back was punished by imprisonment. Money was offered to converts, Protestant chapels were destroyed, and troops were quartered on prominent Huguenots to make life miserable for them. Finally Louis, aided and abetted by his Jesuit advisers, announced that since all the heretics had finally been reconverted to Catholicism there was no further need for the Edict of Nantes and it was therefore revoked. Protestant churches and schools were closed, and all Protestant children were baptized as Catholics. The Revocation was enforced by imprisonment, torture, and condemnation to the galleys, but many Huguenots continued to practice their faith in secret. Others fled to England, the Dutch Netherlands, Brandenburg, and the New World. The industry and skill of the 200,000 or so Huguenots who escaped contributed appreciably to the economic life of their new homes. To France the Revocation brought both economic and moral loss.

There were only two other examples of such brutal treatment of religious minorities in the seventeenth century: the systematic impoverishment and degradation of the Irish Catholics by their English conquerors, and the ruthless suppression of Bohemian Protestantism by the Habsburgs. But in both these cases, unlike that of France, national hatred complicated religious differences. The Revocation of the Edict of Nantes was an anachronistic act of religious intolerance that gained Louis XIV little and lost him much.

Arts and Literature

To dramatize his conception of kingship and to underscore the dependence on the monarch of all other persons and institutions in the state, Louis chose as his emblem Apollo, the sun god. The symbol of the sun, on whose rays all earthly life is dependent, was worked into the architecture and sculpture of the palace of Versailles. The Sun King patronized the arts and gave historians some reason to call his reign the "Augustan Age" of French culture. As befitted such a patron, the prevailing taste was classical, insisting on form, order, balance, and proportion. The ideals of literature and art were "order, neatness, precision, exactitude"—and these were presumed to be the ideals of all reasonable men of all ages.

Pierre Corneille (1606–84) was the father of French classical tragedy. In 1636 he had written *Le Cid*, the first of his powerful dramas that glorified will power and the striving for perfection. Corneille was still writing when Louis XIV began his personal reign, but he was soon eclipsed by his brilliant younger contemporary, Jean Racine (1639–99). Racine wrote more realistically about human beings in the grip of violent and sometimes coarse passions, bringing French tragedy to its highest point of perfection in the years between 1667 and 1677. Then he underwent a religious conversion and renounced playwrighting as an immoral occupation. Some who thrilled to his and Corneille's tragedies had little respect for the comedian Molière (1622–73), but Molière's wit and satire became the unsurpassable model for future French dramatists. From 1659 to his

Cartoon from 1686 showing a "missionary" of the king (an armed dragoon) "converting" a Huguenot to Catholicism.

The emblem of the Sun King.

death in 1673 he was the idol of audiences at Versailles. All three playwrights concentrated on portraying types, not individuals—the hero, the man of honor violently in love, the miser, the hypocrite—embodiments of human passions and foibles who belonged to no particular time or place. As a result, French classical drama of the age of Louis XIV could be understood and appreciated by people everywhere, and French taste in writing came to be the dominant taste of other countries as well. So it was with architecture and the other arts. The baroque style, which ruled the design and decoration of the palace at Versailles, was intelligible and exportable. French artistic and literary standards became the standards of cultivated Europeans everywhere.

The Wars of Louis XIV

Richelieu and Mazarin had begun the process of strengthening the French army, but French military power reached its peak under Louis XIV. Le Tellier and his son Louvois were the ministers of war for almost fifty years. They subordinated the aristocratic officer class to the royal authority, developed a supply system, coordinated infantry and artillery, and, like Gustavus Adolphus, supplied the soldiers with uniforms. Vauban, one of the great military engineers of history, invented the fixed bayonet and perfected the art of building—and of destroying—fortifications. All in all, Louvois provided

his master with the largest and best-equipped army in Europe: 100,000 men in peace and up to 400,000 in war.

Strengthening the army provided the king with great temptations to use his power in foreign wars. War would please the nobles, who profited by it and who had little outlet for their ambitions at home. War would exercise and justify the enormous standing army. Above all, successful war would enhance the glory of the monarch, raise him still further above his subjects, and perhaps make him the arbiter not only of France but of Europe as well. No one better than Louis XIV exemplified a nineteenth-century historian's dictum, "All power tends to corrupt, and absolute power corrupts absolutely." For half a century Europe was ravaged by wars that were started to satisfy the megalomania of the French king. As Louis' thirst for power grew beyond all rational bounds, so did his enemies' fear of him.

The aims of Louis' earlier wars were relatively limited and understandable. With Spain's power broken and the Empire in a state of collapse, he wanted to annex the Spanish Netherlands (later Belgium), Franche-Comté, and bits of western German territories. He fought two wars for these objectives, but each time, after early victories he found himself thwarted by an alliance of other powers. By 1678 he had gained only Franche-Comté and a few border towns in Flanders.

Caricature of Molière as an actor.

Engraving of a performance of *Le Malade imaginaire,* Molière's last play (1673). Molière died on stage on the fourth night of the performance.

The palace at Versailles (1668). Louis XIV is shown arriving in a carriage.

For a time Louis tried legal chicanery in place of bullets to gain more territory. French courts called Chambers of Reunion were set up to "reunite" to France any land that at any time had been a dependency of a French territory. This process gave Louis control of the independent Protestant republic of Strasbourg in 1681, and it was long before European indignation subsided or Strasbourg became a contented part of France. The Revocation of the Edict of Nantes in 1685 was further evidence to European statesmen of Louis' intemperance, and in 1686 the defensive League of Augsburg was formed by the emperor, Spain, Sweden, and several German states. Europe was already at war when William of Orange, ruler of the Dutch Netherlands and Louis' most implacable enemy, became King William III of England in 1689. The circle was closed around France when the English and the Dutch joined the League.

This time France was on the defensive. At the very outset, in 1688, the French united their enemies by perpetrating one of the most senseless atrocities of the century, the systematic devastation of the Palatinate for no good political or military reason just before the occupying French troops withdrew. The War of the League of Augsburg was waged in India and America as well as in Europe, so it may be called the first of the modern world wars. After ten years of fighting, France agreed to the Peace of Ryswick (1697), by which France managed to retain its gains up to 1678 but was forced to renounce nearly all accessions after that date except Strasbourg. England came out of the war considerably stronger as a naval and military power; France came out of it a weaker power than it had been a decade earlier.

The War of the Spanish Succession, 1701–14

At the turn of the century all the fears and hatreds that had been built up during a generation of fighting were concentrated in a fourth struggle, the War of the Spanish Succession (1701–14). This war, like that of 1688–97, was fought in America and India as well as in Europe. In its origins and its course, the older motives of dynastic ambition and preservation of the balance of power were mixed with the newer motives of commercial advantage and national sentiment. Religion now played no important part whatever.

In 1698 Charles II of Spain, who had for thirty years been a kind of walking

452

medical exhibit of half a dozen fatal diseases, was finally dying. He was the last of the Habsburgs who had ruled Spain since 1516, and he had no direct heirs. The question was whether the Spanish Empire would fall to some member of the Austrian Habsburg family or to some member of the French Bourbon dynasty (both Louis XIV's mother and wife were Spanish Habsburg princesses) or would be partitioned or dismembered in some way. The English and the Dutch had obvious reasons for keeping France from gaining control of the Spanish colonial trade or of the Spanish Netherlands. Louis seemed willing to compromise and twice concluded secret treaties with the English and the Dutch to partition the Spanish dominions, but when news of the second treaty reached Madrid the dying king lost his temper. In order to preserve the Spanish Empire intact as a bulwark of Catholicism, he made a will leaving all his dominions to a grandson of Louis XIV. This grandson was proclaimed King Philip V of Spain shortly after the death of Charles II in November 1700.

Louis XIV soon decided to tear up the treaties by which he had accepted a more modest share of the Spanish Empire. He recognized the will of Charles II and sent French troops into the Spanish Netherlands. In 1701 William III of England concluded the Grand Alliance of the Hague by which the English, the Dutch, and the Austrian Habsburg emperor bound themselves to fight until they had ended the threat of Bourbon control of Spain and of the Spanish colonies. Louis XIV had made his last and most arrogant bid for the dominance of Europe, but this time he was forced to fight for France's life against enemies who proved as arrogant and unyielding as he. Within a few years the large allied forces under the brilliant command of Prince Eugene of Savoy and the English Duke of Marlborough had beaten the French in four bloody battles (Blenheim, 1704; Ramillies, 1706; Oudenarde, 1708; Malplaquet, 1709). The English navy had trounced the French at sea, and the English had seized Gibraltar. An allied army had even dethroned Philip V in Spain for a time.

Louis XIV, his country exhausted,

THE CONQUESTS OF LOUIS XIV 1661–1715

ENGLISH CHANNEL

ARTOIS
PICARDY
ÎLE DE FRANCE
NORMANDY
CHAMPAGNE
ALSACE
BRITTANY MAINE
ORLÉANAIS
ANJOU TOURAINE
BERRY
NIVERNAIS
FRANCHE-COMTÉ
POITOU
AUNIS BOURBON-NAIS BURGUNDY
MARCHE
SAINT-ONGE ANGOUMOIS LIMOUSIN AUVERGNE LYONNAIS
DAUPHINY
GUYENNE AND GASCONY
ORANGE C. OF VENAISSIN
NAVARRE LANGUEDOC PROVENCE
BÉARN
FOIX MEDITERRANEAN SEA
ROUSSILLON

☐ France before 1668
▦ Acquisitions by the Treaty of Aix-la-Chapelle, 1668
▨ Acquisitions by the Treaty of Nimwegen, 1678
▥ Acquisitions by the Treaty of Utrecht, 1713

0 MILES 100

sued for peace on almost any terms, only to be met by an allied demand that he contribute French troops to expel his own grandson from Madrid. This was too much for even a badly beaten monarch and he refused, backed by a rising tide of national feeling in France. A similar national reaction in Spain in favor of their new Bourbon monarch, Philip V, resulted in the defeat of English and Austrian troops there. In 1710 a victory of the Tories over the Whigs, who had been the war party in England, brought in a government in London favorable to peace. And finally in 1712 the French won their only important victory of the war. In the end the allies paid the price for asking too much from Louis at the moment when he was almost helpless. The Peace of Utrecht (1713–14), which settled the war, was somewhat more favorable to France than it might have been if it had been signed four years earlier. Here at the very end of his career, the balance of power seemed to work in Louis XIV's favor by preventing the elimination of France from the ranks of the great powers.

Officer and musketeer of the French Guard, late seventeenth century.

The Peace of Utrecht, 1713–14

In theory, the Peace of Utrecht gave the French the prize that they had sought at the beginning of the war. Philip V remained on the throne of Spain, but only on condition that the crowns of Spain and France should never be worn by the same monarch. In every other aim, however, the French were thwarted. They gave up all conquests east of the Rhine, failed to win the Spanish Netherlands, and lost their bid for control of the Spanish colonial trade. England was the chief winner. England took Newfoundland, Acadia (Nova Scotia), and Hudson's Bay Territory from France, and Gibraltar and Minorca from Spain. In addition, the English received the *Asiento*—the right to supply black slaves to the Spanish colonies, a privilege that proved very lucrative and provided an excuse for a large-scale smuggling trade with the Spanish Empire.

England came out of the war rich and powerful, in a position to dominate international commerce and with the strongest navy in Europe. France came out of it still a great nation, but with its people badly exhausted by high taxation and its government bankrupt and unpopular. The Austrian Habsburgs gained by being given the Spanish Netherlands (which now became the Austrian Netherlands), as well as Milan, Naples, and Sicily. Austria thus replaced Spain as the ruling power in Italy. Two new smaller powers, Brandenburg-Prussia and the Duchy of Savoy, came out of the war with increased territories and heightened prestige as a reward for having been on the winning side. A century and a half later Prussia was to unify Germany, and Savoy, as the Kingdom of Sardinia, was to take the lead in the unification of Italy. The Dutch kept the Scheldt River closed, thus blocking the trade of Antwerp, the chief port of the Austrian Netherlands. But they had suffered from the long strain of fighting against the French for half a century and were soon to disappear from the ranks of the great powers.

The Peace of Utrecht ended the first attempt by a European state to establish an overwhelming predominance of power since the days of Philip II of Spain. When Louis XIV died in 1715, rulers outside France breathed a sigh of relief; it was even said that the common people of his own land "openly returned thanks to God." His bid for European hegemony had been defeated by the workings of the balance-of-power principle, but the seeds of future war were unfortunately still deep in the European soil.

ENGLAND: THE EMERGENCE OF A PARLIAMENTARY MONARCHY

While Louis XIV was putting the finishing touches on the institution of absolute monarchy in France, the English, without any very clear idea of where they were headed, were completing the foundation of a constitutional monarchy controlled by Parliament.

The restoration of the king, Parliament, and the Anglican Church in 1660 had established a kind of equilibrium between the crown and Parliament, but it was soon evident that it was a very unstable balance. Who was really to control the government—the king or the wealthy landowners and merchants who dominated Parliament? What was the religious settlement to be, and who was

The House of Commons, on the Great Seal of England, 1651.

to have the last word in making it? Who was to control foreign policy? These three main questions of the past two generations—the questions of politics, religion, and foreign policy—still awaited final answers. It took almost two more generations of domestic intrigue and foreign war for the answers to be found.

Charles II, 1660–85

Charles II was quite unlike his father—witty, worldly-wise, attractive, a man of easy morals and shrewd political sense. He had lived long in exile in France, and his cousin, Louis XIV, was his model. He would have liked to restore England to Catholicism and to set up an absolute monarchy on the French model, but he was too intelligent to ignore the difficulties in his way and too cautious to persist in the face of determined opposition. He was resolved not to risk exile or execution. He knew that if his goal was to be reached, it would be by intrigue, manipulation, and compromise, not by force or by open proclamation of his aims. The result was twenty-five years of infinitely complex party politics and secret diplomacy in which the issues were never very clear to the people or to members of Parliament, or even to the king's ministers.

Cavalier Parliament, 1661–79

Parliament held a commanding position at the beginning of the reign. The "Cavalier Parliament," which met in 1661 and was not dissolved until 1679, was dominated by the landed nobility and gentry, who were now restored to their ancient influence in both local and national government. Both groups were strongly royalist for the moment, both determined to stamp out all remnants of religious and political radicalism. But at the same time they were not willing to see the crown recover any real financial independence of Parliament. In place of the old idea that "the king should live of his own," Parliament now granted Charles a regular income from customs and excise duties, but it was not enough. Charles found that he could not meet even the ordinary expenses of govern-

ment, let alone the expenses of his extravagant mistresses, from his regular revenue. And there was certainly no money for foreign war unless Parliament approved the objectives. So for a time at least, Charles had to let Parliament have its way under the leadership of his father's adviser, Edward Hyde, Earl of Clarendon.

Parliament also had the last word in the religious settlement. The Cavalier Parliament was as strongly pro-Anglican as it was pro-royalist. In a series of statutes passed between 1661 and 1665 and known as the "Clarendon Code," Puritans who dissented from the established church were excluded from local government and Puritan ministers were rooted out of the Anglican clergy. Later legislation made it illegal for a dissenter to sit in Parliament, to serve in the army or navy, or to attend the universities at Oxford or Cambridge. Behind this attempt to discourage dissent was the fear that Puritans were inevitably political radicals. But while the Clarendon Code lowered the social position and narrowed opportunities for dissenters, it did not greatly decrease their numbers. Presbyterians, Congregationalists, Baptists, and Quakers (also Methodists a century later) formed permanent but peaceful minority groups. The dissenters remained antagonistic to the ruling Anglican majority, but they were even more bitterly opposed to Catholicism.

Charles did not like the Clarendon Code. He would have preferred a policy that tolerated both Puritans and Catholics, but Parliament would not stand for this. In 1672 Charles issued a "Declaration of Indulgence," which suspended the operation of the laws against both groups. But the next year Parliament forced him to withdraw the declaration and accept a severe Test Act excluding all but Anglicans from civil and military office. To the Anglican gentry in Parliament, Puritans were still radicals and Catholics still traitors.

Foreign Policy

Two natural calamities, an outbreak of plague in 1665 and a fire that destroyed much of London in 1666, contributed to general unrest. Uneasiness increased as king and Parliament drifted apart over foreign policy. In 1665 Parliament forced Charles into a commercial war with the Dutch but did not give him enough money to win it. When victories failed to develop, Clarendon was unfairly held responsible and was exiled. After Louis XIV began his attacks on the Spanish Netherlands in 1667, the ordinary Englishman began to see the military power of Catholic France as more of a threat than the commercial rivalry of the Protestant Dutch. But to Charles II Louis was still the ideal ally—powerful, wealthy, and an old personal friend.

Pepys' Account of the Great Fire of London, September 2–6, 1666

The fire started near the river, spread to warehouses full of combustible materials, and destroyed most of the old city of London, including St. Paul's Cathedral. This gave Christopher Wren the opportunity to build his famous churches. Samuel Pepys was an eyewitness to the fire and recorded its events in his diary.

[Pepys heard of the fire and took a boat down the Thames.] Every-body was endeavoring to remove their goods, and flinging them into the river or bringing them into lighters; poor people staying in their houses till the fire touched them, and then running into boats. And the poor pigeons, I perceived, were loth to leave their houses, but hovered about the windows and balconys till they burned their wings and fell down. Nobody, to my sight, endeavoring to quench it, but only to remove their goods and leave all to the fire—the wind mighty high and driving it into the city and everything, after so long a drought, proving combustible, even the very stones of the churches.

[That evening Pepys and his wife went out on the river.] We went as near the fire as we could for smoke and all over the Thames; with one's face in the wind, you were almost burned with a shower of fire-drops. This is very true; so that houses were burned by these drops and flakes of fire [even when] three or four—nay five or six—houses from another. When we could endure no more at the water, we went to a little ale-house on the Bankside and there saw the fire grow . . . as far as we could see up the hill of the city, in a most horrible malicious bloody flame, not like the fine flame of an ordinary fire. We stayed till we saw the fire as only an entire arch of fire from this to the other side of [London] bridge and in a bow up the hill for an arch of above a mile long. It made me weep to see it—the churches, houses and all on fire and flaming at once, and a horrid noise the flames made, and the cracking of houses at their ruin.

From *The Diary of Samuel Pepys* (many editions), entry for September 2, 1666.

In 1670 England once more allied itself with France against the Dutch, and Charles negotiated with Louis one of the most notorious deals in the history of English foreign policy, the secret Treaty of Dover. By this agreement Charles promised to declare his Catholicism and to reconvert England to Catholicism in return for French money and, if necessary, French troops. Probably Charles himself was not sure how far he meant to go, but at the least he was ready to adopt a pro-French foreign policy. Between 1675 and 1681 four more secret agreements were concluded between Charles and Louis in which Charles promised he would thwart Parliament's anti-French moves in return for subsidies from France. The close understanding between Charles and Louis leaked out and gradually built up English fears of Catholicism and French dominance. The landed classes represented in Parliament were suspicious of Charles, far less royalist in sentiment than they had been in 1661, and ready to give way to panic if any incident should excite their fear of France and popery.

Whigs and Tories

In 1678 these accumulated fears were fanned into flame by a lurid incident known to history as the Popish Plot. A thoroughly disreputable character named Titus Oates concocted a story, accepted by almost the whole country, that there was a Jesuit plot afoot to murder the king and put his Catholic brother James, the Duke of York, on the throne with French help—"a damnable and hellish plot," Parliament called it, "for assassinating and murdering the king and rooting out and destroying the Protestant religion." Civil war seemed about to break out again.

A "Country Party" led by the Earl of Shaftesbury campaigned at the polls and supported a bill to exclude the Duke of York from the succession to the throne. An Anglican and royalist "Court Party" rallied to the support of Charles II and his brother, though at first without very much enthusiasm. Members of the first group were called Whigs (a name hitherto applied to fanatical Scottish Presbyterians); members of the second group were called Tories (a name for Catholic outlaws in Ireland). The Whigs controlled the three brief Parliaments that followed the dissolution of the Cavalier Parliament in 1679, and innocent men went to their deaths for complicity in the Popish Plot. But the Whig leaders soon overplayed their hand; public opinion swung back in favor of the king, and it was now the turn of innocent Whigs to suffer. By 1681 Shaftesbury had fled abroad, the inventors of the Popish Plot were disgraced or executed, and Charles was stronger than ever before. Until his death four years later he ruled without Parliament, thanks to Louis' subsidies, with his brother James by his side.

The origin of political parties in the modern sense—groups organized for the purpose of electioneering and controlling government through a representative assembly—lies in these chaotic years of English history. Instead of civil war, the eventual outcome was the "two-party system," which came to be characteristic of English and American politics. Whigs and Tories were the remote political heirs of the Parliamentarians and royalists of the 1640s. In turn they became the ancestors of the Liberals and Conservatives, the Democrats and Republicans, of two centuries later.

James II, 1685–88

The Duke of York, who succeeded Charles II as James II in 1685, was a very different sort of person from his brother—a bigoted convert to Catholicism without any of Charles' political shrewdness or tendency to compromise. Within three short years (1685–88) he managed to infuriate almost every group of any importance in English political and religious life, and in the end he provoked the revolution that Charles had succeeded in avoiding. Made overconfident by early successes, he introduced Catholics into the high command of both army and navy and camped a standing army a few miles from London. He surrounded himself with Catholic advisers and attacked Anglican control of the universities. He claimed the power to suspend or dispense with acts of Parliament. In a vain attempt to win the support of Puritans as well as Catholics, he issued a Declaration of Indulgence along the lines of his brother's. By revoking borough charters and browbeating sheriffs he tried to ensure the election of a Parliament favorable to his policies. Louis XIV's Revocation of the Edict of Nantes in 1685 had already terrified Protestants in England. They held back as long as James' immediate heir was a Protestant, but their fears became unbearable when the hope of a Protestant succession was suddenly destroyed by the unexpected birth of a son to James' Catholic queen.

The "Glorious Revolution" of 1688

In spite of the intense political tension, civil war did not break out in 1688 as it had in 1642. Englishmen still remembered the horrors of civil war, and this time there was only one side. James had literally no support of any significance, except for a handful of personal friends. He had alienated both Anglicans and nonconformists, Tories and Whigs, nobles and common people. The result, therefore, was a bloodless "revolution," a thoroughgoing political overturn that, as historians look back on it, answered all the main questions of the century in favor of a limited, or parliamentary, monarchy and established the constitutional pattern of English public life that has persisted to the present time.

James II had two daughters by his first wife (Clarendon's daughter), both of whom remained Protestants. The elder, Mary, was married in 1677 to the stadtholder of the Dutch Republic, William of Orange, who was Louis XIV's outstanding Protestant opponent on the Continent. In June 1688 a group of prominent and representative Englishmen, both Whigs and Tories, invited William to cross the Channel and save the Protestant cause in England. In the following November William landed on the southern coast of England with a Dutch army and marched slowly on London. There was almost no resistance. James II fled to France and a Convention Parliament (an irregular assembly of men who had had parliamentary seats) declared that James had "abdicated" the throne by his flight. It then invited

Engraving of James II, after a painting by Kneller, 1688.

William and Mary to become joint sovereigns. A "Bill of Rights" was passed and the "Glorious Revolution" was accomplished.

The chief result of the Revolution was the establishment of parliamentary sovereignty over the crown. Parliament had made a king and could regulate the right of succession to the throne. Though William was a strong-willed man, especially in matters of foreign policy, he knew that Parliament had the final say. And though the supporters of James II and his son intrigued and even staged two abortive rebellions, there was no second Restoration. Parliament could criticize, influence, and eventually make the government's policy.

The Bill of Rights emphatically denied the king's right to suspend acts of Parliament or to interfere with the ordinary course of justice. It furnished a base for the steady expansion of civil liberties in the generation after 1688. Religious toleration and freedom from arbitrary arrest were established by law; censorship of the press was quietly dropped. The king had to summon Parliament every year because he could not pay or control his armed forces without parliamentary consent. These regular meetings strengthened the parties and made the king dependent on their support. In 1707 the monarch vetoed a parliamentary bill for the last time.

Struggles for control of policy were now no longer between king and Parliament, but between factions in Parliament. The Revolution did not establish democracy, but it did establish control by the wealthy landed proprietors and merchants over both the central and local organs of English government. Generally speaking, the greater noble landowners, the bankers and the merchants, and most dissenters were Whigs, while the smaller gentry, the Anglican parish clergy, and some great lords were Tories. But parties were still loosely organized, and small factions with selfish interests often held the balance of power. England was governed by shifting alliances among leaders of the propertied classes.

The Cabinet System

It took over a century for parliamentary leaders to work out a smooth and efficient way to run the government. The ultimate answer (after 1784) was to be the "cabinet system"—that is, government by a committee of leaders of the majority party in Parliament, holding the chief executive offices in the government, acting under the leadership of a "prime minister," and acknowledging primary responsibility to Parliament rather than to the crown for their actions. During the reigns of William and Mary (1689–1702) and Mary's sister, Queen Anne (1702–

14), the first fumbling moves were made that led to such a system, though parliamentary leaders had as yet no sense of their goal, and monarchs still considered ministers to be responsible to them rather than to Parliament. The privy council had long been too large and unwieldy for effective action, so that a "cabinet council," or inner circle of important ministers, had developed under Charles II. The members of this "cabinet" slowly found that it was better to discuss major questions among themselves and to present a united front to the monarch on matters of policy. Sometimes a leading member of the "cabinet" was referred to as "prime minister." In order to gain Parliament's indispensable support in war or peace, both William and Anne occasionally found that it was better to choose their ministers not from both parties but from the majority party. By the time Queen Anne died in 1714 it had become evident that the real government of England was slowly falling into the hands of a cabinet of ministers who controlled a parliamentary majority, often by bribery, and felt themselves ultimately responsible to the political interests of this majority.

Religious Toleration

The Revolution also produced a certain measure of religious toleration. Broad-mindedness was becoming fashionable in educated circles, and both Anglicans and Puritans were now more afraid of Catholic France than they were of each other. Puritans had supported Anglicans against James II, and King William, who came from the most tolerant country in Europe, insisted on a religious truce. The result was the "Toleration Act" of 1689, which allowed dissenters to worship as they pleased and to educate their clergy and laity in schools of their own. Dissenters were still legally excluded from all civil and military offices, however, and there was no repeal of the long series of anti-Catholic statutes, although they were not enforced with any great rigor after 1689. Protestant fear that a Catholic might succeed to the throne was finally quieted by the Act of Settlement of 1701, which provided that

the sovereign should always be an Anglican. The act also settled the succession, in case James II's two daughters should die without children, on the descendants of that daughter of James I who had married the ill-fated elector of the Palatinate before the Thirty Years' War. In this way the elector of Hanover came to the throne in 1714, when Queen Anne died without issue, thus bringing the Stuart dynasty to a close.

War against France

A third result of the Revolution was to unite crown and Parliament on foreign policy as they had never been united under the first four Stuarts, and thus to turn the energies of a generation of Englishmen from domestic conflict to foreign war. Once on the throne, King William had no difficulty bringing England into the Grand Alliance against Louis XIV, who was sheltering James II in exile. Parliamentary monarchy soon demonstrated

Medal of Queen Anne (1701–14), and her signature.

Contemporary engraving of the Battle of Malplaquet, 1709, at which the British defeated the French in a bloody battle.

that it was a more formidable foe than the absolute monarchy of the Stuarts had been. The English government was able to raise money to fight its wars in a way that was barred to all other European governments except the Dutch. The founding of the Bank of England in 1694 was an important event in the history of English public finance. Within a few days of its founding, it had raised over a million pounds of investors' money that it promptly lent to the government at 8 percent interest. So long as the government continued to pay the interest, the bank made no demand for repayment of this loan. Thus the present permanent, or "funded," national debt began. The merchants and tradesmen, large and small, who invested their money in the bank obviously had confidence in the government, and their investment bound them still more firmly to support the revolutionary settlement.

Throughout the next century English wealth combined with English sea power was to give the island kingdom a striking power out of all proportion to its area and population. During the reigns of William and Mary and of Anne, trade, which was more and more the foundation of English wealth, increased considerably. The Peace of Utrecht (1713) gave English sea power, the guarantor of English trade, an almost unrivaled position. The solution in 1689 of the chief political and religious differences between crown and Parliament touched off an almost explosive release of English energies that by 1763 had rocketed England to the hegemony of Europe.

Ireland and Scotland

The Revolution also did something to further the unification of the British Isles, though indirectly. England, Ireland, and Scotland all had the same king from 1603 on, but union went no further than the common crown. The two smaller kingdoms, especially Ireland, suffered greatly during the seventeenth century through involvement in England's religious and political divisions. The native Irish were Catholic to a man, and the Protestant English both despised them and feared them as potential allies of the Catholic Spanish and French. By settling Protes-

Anti-Catholic woodcuts showing "horrors" of the rebellion by Irish Catholics (1689).

tant colonists in Ulster, James I began the policy of creating a Protestant majority in the northeastern region of Ireland. But the Ulster Protestants were Presbyterians and soon became anti-Stuart, while the rest of the Irish were generally loyal to the Stuart dynasty, and for that reason suffered cruelly under Cromwell. After the Revolution, James II tried to fight his way back to his throne by way of Ireland. He was defeated at the Battle of the Boyne (1689), an event whose memory still stirs up bitter feelings between Catholics and Protestants in Ulster. James' defeat led to a savage and systematic persecution of the Catholic Irish by English (and Irish) Protestant landlords, comparable only to Louis XIV's brutal treatment of the Huguenots. The Irish were exploited and bled white economically, their priests were persecuted, and their Parliament was reserved for Protestants only.

The Scots had somewhat better fortune in the end, although they too suffered by being involved in England's troubles through the century. Scotland had gained little by giving a king to England in 1603. It remained a poor but proud neighbor of a larger kingdom, excluded from the benefits of English trade, jealously guarding its own law and its own Parliament, and firmly defending its Presbyterian Church against Anglican attacks. Although it had been the Scots who touched off the Puritan Rebellion against Charles I, there was strong attachment to the native Stuart dynasty in Scotland, especially among Catholic clansmen of the Highlands. After 1649 and again after 1689 Scotland became a base for risings in support of the Stuarts. The Scots accepted the Revolution of 1688, but they did not accept the Act of Settlement of 1701. They threatened to choose a separate king of their own—possibly the exiled pretender James II—in case James' last daughter, Anne, died without issue. This frightened the English into serious negotiations. In 1707 an organic union between the two kingdoms was finally agreed upon and was confirmed by an Act of Union. Scotland retained its own law and its established Presbyterian religion, but it surrendered its separate Parliament in return for representation in the English Parliament. Scottish nationalists were (and still are) angry over their loss of independence, but Scotland gained much in the next century by becoming an integral part of the Kingdom of Great Britain. Scottish merchants, administrators, and philosophers were to play a prominent part during the eighteenth century in building the British Empire and in furthering the Enlightenment.

John Locke

The Puritan Rebellion and the Glorious Revolution together constituted the first of those revolutions in modern western states that ended absolute divine-right monarchy and eventually put the middle classes in control of government. English leaders did their best to insist to the outside world in 1688–89 that they were doing nothing new or revolutionary at all, but they never succeeded in persuading foreigners that they were merely conservative supporters of ancient English liberties. Europe was more interested in the interpretation of the Revolution by John Locke (1632–1704), a friend of the Earl of Shaftesbury, the founder of the Whig Party. In *Of Civil Government: Two Treatises* (1690)

Locke set down in plain, common-sense fashion the general principles underlying the long English struggle for limited monarchy that culminated in the Revolution of 1688. Even if the logic was not always clear, the reasonableness of the discussion had great influence throughout the eighteenth century.

Locke directed his attack explicitly against the divine-right theory of monarchy, and implicitly against the more pragmatic absolute theory of Thomas Hobbes. He began with the rights to "life, liberty, and property," which he said all men possess naturally, and went on to insist that the sole reason for establishing any government is to preserve these rights. Legislative and executive powers are to be strictly separated; if the executive becomes tyrannical and invades the rights of individuals, the people must curb it through their representative assembly—or if all else fails, they may revolt and set up a new government. In other words, an ultimate right of revolution always resides in the people, and the dissolution of government does not necessarily mean the dissolution of society. Locke's book was probably written before 1688 as a sort of program for revolution, but it was not

John Locke (1632–1704), champion of the "natural" rights of man.

Locke on Government by Consent

Cf. "Bishop Bossuet on Absolutism," p. 449

Men being, as has been said, by nature all free, equal, and independent, no one can be put out of this estate and subjected to the political power of another without his own consent, which is done by agreeing with other men, to join and unite into a community for their comfortable, safe, and peaceful living, one amongst another, in a secure enjoyment of their properties, and a greater security against any that are not of it. . . . When any number of men have so consented to make one community or government, they are thereby presently incorporated, and make one body politic, wherein the majority have the right to act and conclude the rest. . . . Absolute, arbitrary power, or governing without settled standing laws, can neither of them consist with the ends of society and government, which men would not quit the freedom of the state of Nature for, and tie themselves up under, were it not to preserve their lives, liberties, and fortunes, and by stated rules of right and property to secure their peace and quiet.

From John Locke, *Of Civil Government: Two Treatises*, 1690 (New York: Everyman, 1924), pp. 164–65, 186.

published until after the Revolution and so naturally became a kind of apology for what had been done. Inalienable rights, government by consent, separation of powers, the right of revolution—these were the ideas that Locke implied were at the heart of the Glorious Revolution. These were the ideas that seemed self-evident truths to Americans in 1776 and to Frenchmen in 1789 and that formed a link between the English, the American, and the French revolutions.

EASTERN EUROPE
1648–1721

The economy of early modern Europe was divided into two sharply defined halves by an imaginary line running north from the head of the Adriatic Sea, around the Bohemian mountains, and down the Elbe River to the North Sea. West of this line was an area that was increasingly affected by the growth of towns and trade. The majority of the population still lived on the land, but most peasants were free workers and many of them small landowners. Most serfs in the West had become agricultural laborers for pay, and most feudal nobles had become landlords who hired labor for wages (particularly in England) or simply lived on rents. Though still a minority, the bourgeoisie were increasingly influential in society and politics.

East of the line was a society still largely agrarian and feudal, an area of few large towns and an insignificant bourgeoisie. Here in Hungary, Bohemia, Poland, Prussia, and Russia, the landed estates were larger and the landed nobility more powerful politically than in the West. During the sixteenth and seventeenth centuries the nobles of eastern Europe managed to reduce the great majority of the peasants to a state of serfdom in which the peasant was bound to the land and forced to work from two to five days a week for his lord. One reason for this drive to enslave the peasant was that grain prices were rising in western markets and eastern landlords had every inducement to increase the production of their estates. Another reason was that the governments of eastern Europe were either dominated by nobles, as in Hungary and Poland, or favorable to the growth of serfdom because it supported the nobles who served the state, as in Prussia and Russia. In western Europe, command of money was increasingly the key to power and influence; in the East, ownership of land and command of compulsory services were still the secrets of power.

Warfare was as common as in the West, and much more dangerous. States with no natural frontiers on the flat plains of central and eastern Europe could easily be wiped out. Modernized armies were needed, but such armies could be created only by strong, centralized administrations and supported only by effective tax systems. Neither centralization nor taxation was easy. Eastern rulers were facing roughly the same obstacles to the growth of centralized government that western rulers had faced two centuries and more earlier: a powerful landed nobility, a church that held itself above dynastic interests and owned a large portion of the wealth of the land, an agrarian economy with limited commerce and infant industries, a bourgeoisie still too small to bear the weight of heavy taxation, and an ignorant and exploited peasantry tied to the land and thus incapable of meeting the need of new industries for labor. To build a "modern" state in the face of these difficulties was beyond the capacities of all but the ablest rulers.

The Holy Roman Empire

The one large political organization bridging eastern and western Europe was the Holy Roman Empire. But although there was still an emperor, and a diet, which met "perpetually" at Regensburg after 1663, the Empire was a political fiction. It had no central administration, no system of imperial taxation, no standing army, no common law, no tariff union, not even a common calendar. The Peace of Westphalia had recognized the sovereignty of the individual states, as well as the right of France and Sweden to take part in the deliberations of the diet. In the welter of political units—free

Division of Eastern and Western Europe

Crown of the Holy Roman Empire of the German Nation, used from 961 to 1792.

cities, ecclesiastical principalities, counties, margravates, and duchies, together with one kingdom (Bohemia)—that made up the Empire, almost every petty princeling fancied himself a Louis XIV and fashioned a court modeled as closely as possible on Versailles. Already the Empire fitted Voltaire's description a century later as "neither Holy, nor Roman, nor an Empire."

The ruling families of a few of the larger states—Bavaria, Saxony, Hanover, Brandenburg, and Austria—were trying hard to expand their territories by war or marriage and to gain royal titles. Augustus the Strong of Saxony, in addition to fathering more than 300 children, managed to get himself elected king of Poland in 1696. In 1701 the elector of Brandenburg obtained the emperor's consent to style himself king in Prussia. And in 1714 the elector of Hanover became king of England. But only two great powers eventually grew out of the wreck of the Empire. These were Austria and Brandenburg-Prussia.

The Habsburgs and Austria

The attempt of Emperor Ferdinand II (1619–37) to revive and strengthen the Empire under Habsburg control was defeated in the Thirty Years' War. The Habsburgs thereafter turned to a policy that Ferdinand had also furthered: consolidating and expanding the hereditary lands of the family in Austria and the Danube Valley. Thus a centralized Habsburg monarchy might be developed that could hold its own with the states of the West. The Emperor Leopold I (1658–1705) was the chief architect of this policy, aided, and at times prodded, by some capable civil servants and one remarkable general, Prince Eugene of Savoy.

To weld a centralized monarchy together, Leopold had to reduce three separate areas—Austria, Bohemia, and Hungary—to some semblance of unity and obedience. In the Duchy of Austria and neighboring Tyrol, his lawyers were able to establish his ascendancy over a feudal nobility whose economic position was still strong. Bohemia, it will be remembered, had been reduced to obedience to

Vienna early in the Thirty Years' War. A new nobility owing its titles to the Habsburg ruler replaced the old, and the crown of Bohemia, previously elective, was made hereditary in the Habsburg family in 1627.

The real problem was Hungary. Although the Habsburgs had usually been the elected monarchs of the kingdom since early in the sixteenth century, hardly a third of Hungary was actually in Habsburg hands. The rest was either directly or indirectly ruled by the Ottoman Turks. To establish their authority in Hungary, the Habsburg monarchs in Vienna had to deal not only with the powerful Hungarian nobility and the Hungarian Protestants but with the Turks and the French as well. The nobles were wealthy and unruly; the Protestants were numerous and inclined to side with the Turks against the Catholic Habsburgs. The Ottoman Empire was not the power it had been in the sixteenth century, but since 1656 it had been undergoing a revival under a vigorous line of grand viziers of the Kiuprili family, who in the 1660s began a new thrust up the Danube Valley directed at their old enemies, the Habsburgs. Louis XIV, also an

Emperor Leopold I (above) and Prince Eugene of Savoy, Habsburg commander, painting by Kupezky.

inveterate enemy of the Habsburgs, allied himself with the Turks and Hungarian rebels against his Austrian foes. Thus building a monarchy in the Danube Valley was as much a foreign as a domestic problem.

The Siege of Vienna, 1683

The crisis came in 1683. In July of that year a Turkish army of more than 100,000 laid siege to Vienna. For two months the fate of Austria seemed to hang in the balance. Then volunteers began to flow in from all over the Continent to help the emperor in his extremity. The greatest pope of the century, Innocent XI, contributed moral and material aid, and King John Sobieski of Poland arrived with an army that helped rout the Turks by September. The retreat continued year after year as the impetus of Europe's last crusade carried on down the Danube Valley, until Eugene of Savoy broke Turkish military power at the battle of Zenta (1697).

The Peace of Carlowitz in 1699 gave the Habsburgs full control of Hungary. The Hungarian Protestants were crushed; many of them were executed for treason. The landowning nobility was left in full control of its serfs and in possession of many of its old privileges, in return for recognizing the ultimate sovereignty of the chancellery at Vienna. The Habsburgs were thus content with what one historian calls "a loose framework of centralized administration." They left local administration much as they found it, but they had established a strong monarchy in the Danube Valley where none had existed before.

The Treaties of Ryswick (1697) and Carlowitz (1699) marked the appearance on the European stage of two new great powers: England and Austria. Each had risen in response to Louis XIV's bid to make himself the heir of Habsburg power in Spain and Germany. The two illustrated how diverse great powers could be in the seventeenth century: England, a parliamentary monarchy controlled by a commercial and landed aristocracy, its strength based on commerce and sea power; Austria, a bureaucratic monarchy with agriculture and a standing army its most conspicuous sources of

strength. At about the same time two more powers were just beginning to appear, each as distinct and different as England and Austria. These were Brandenburg-Prussia and Russia.

The Rise of Brandenburg-Prussia

The story of the rise of the Hohenzollerns in northern Germany is somewhat parallel to that of the Habsburgs in the South, except that the Hohenzollerns started with less and had farther to go. Their achievements owed proportionately more to the genius and patience of one man, Frederick William (1640–88), called the Great Elector.

The Hohenzollerns had been margraves of Brandenburg since 1417 (a margrave was count of a "mark," or frontier province). To this small territory around Berlin they had added by inheritance two other areas: Cleves and some neighboring lands on the Rhine (1614), and the Duchy of Prussia on the Baltic coast to the northeast (1618). When the Thirty Years' War broke out there was nothing to suggest that the ruler of these three scattered territories had any brighter future than a dozen other German princes. His lands had no natural boundaries, no traditional ties with each other, poor soil, few resources, and sparse population, about a million and a half in all. Furthermore, they were especially hard hit by the Thirty Years' War. Swedish and Imperialist armies tramped back and forth across Brandenburg without hindrance. Berlin lost over half its population. And the Great Elector's dominions as a whole probably lost almost one-third of their people—a loss that took forty years to make up.

The Great Elector, 1640–88

Frederick William was twenty years old when he became elector in 1640 during the later years of the Thirty Years' War. Though he was a devoted Calvinist, he nevertheless respected the Lutheranism of his subjects and was genuinely tolerant in an age of intolerance and fanaticism. The helplessness of Brandenburg during the war taught him that his first and foremost task must be the de-

The castle of the Hohenzollerns (detail from a seventeenth-century engraving).

Frederick William, the Great Elector, as a young man; painting by his contemporary, Mathias Czwiczeic.

velopment of an army, and to this end he set himself with unrelenting effort.

"A ruler is treated with no consideration if he does not have troops and means of his own," he advised his son in 1667. "It is these, Thank God! which have made me considerable since the time that I began to have them."

In 1640 he had a poorly equipped and ineffective army of 2,500 men. Before the end of the war in 1648 he had increased it to 8,000, and by his death in 1688 he had a peacetime force of 30,000, which was once expanded in wartime to 40,000. It was something of a miracle for a state with the meager population and resources of Brandenburg-Prussia to produce such a large, well-equipped, and well-trained standing army in so short a time. In forty years (1648–88) Brandenburg had become the strongest military power in Germany except for Austria. If there was any explanation, it was the single-minded devotion of the Great Elector to this goal and to any political, social, or economic policy that would help him reach it.

The first thing he had to do was to establish his authority over the Estates of Brandenburg and Prussia, which had almost complete control of taxation. In Brandenburg the Great Elector was strong enough to imitate the practice of the king of France by simply continuing to raise taxes that had once been granted

by the Estates, which were never summoned again after 1653. In Prussia the townsmen were more stubborn and the Junkers (or nobles) more unruly. Their leaders turned to Poland for support, and Frederick soon had a fight on his hands. The fight ended only after he had executed the ringleaders of the resistance. In the end Frederick set up a taxation system for the support of his army that was common to all his territories, administered by civil servants of his own choosing, and independent of local control. The nobility were shorn of their power in the Estates and pressed into service to the Hohenzollern state as officers in the army. In return, the power of the Junkers over their serfs on their own estates was left untouched. Military strength, not social betterment, was the Great Elector's objective.

It could be argued, however, that much social betterment came indirectly from his building of a strong army, even if the Prussian peasants were sinking deeper into serfdom. The devastation of war was even worse than aristocratic oppression, and Frederick William protected a whole generation from invasion. He used his army as a weapon in diplomacy rather than in war by selling his support to one side or another in return for subsidies. The subsidies helped pay for the army, and the alliances seldom required much fighting. By pursuing this policy, the Great Elector and his immediate successors made substantial territorial gains. For example, by playing off Sweden against Russia, the Hohenzollerns gained Stettin and Pomerania in 1720. There was little sentiment and much shrewdness in this foreign policy, which showed its results in the steady growth of the army and the territorial expansion of the state.

Frederick William's economic policy was designed to develop his lands to the point where they could support his army without the need for foreign subsidies. He did much to revive and improve agriculture after 1648, and much to encourage industry and commerce. His tolerant policies made Brandenburg a haven for religious refugees—persecuted Lutherans, German Calvinists, and, above all, French Huguenots after the Revocation of the Edict of Nantes in 1685. These immigrants, together with Dutch, Swiss, and other newcomers, brought new skills in agriculture and industry, helped increase the population, and added considerably to the strength of the state. He welcomed even the more radical Protestant sects and the Jews, drawing the line only at admitting the Jesuits, whom he considered too intolerant.

The recognition of the Great Elector's son as King Frederick I in 1701 symbolized the appearance of a new power in Europe. Prussia (as the Hohenzollern lands came to be known) had devoted relatively more of its population, its resources, and its energies to military purposes than had any other German state during the later seventeenth century. It has been said that in Prussia the army created the state. The army was, in fact, the first institution common to all the elector's lands, and its bureaus were the models for many organs of the later civil government. But while the needs of the army were especially important in Prussia, they played a significant role in the

development of every great power in Europe except England.

Sweden

While Prussia was growing in strength, its neighbors, Sweden and Poland, were declining, for different reasons. Sweden had burst upon the European horizon as a military power of first rank during Gustavus Adolphus' invasion of Germany (1630–32). During the latter part of the century the Baltic became a Swedish lake, and a Swedish empire grew up on both sides of the inland sea all the way from the Gulf of Finland to the North Sea. Iron ore and agriculture were the Swedes' chief resources, a technically superior musket their chief military advantage.

Swedish power, however, rested on shaky foundations. The country had a population of less than 2 million—not much larger than Prussia and smaller than the Dutch Republic. Its lines of empire were overextended, and its enemies—from Russia and Poland to Prussia and Denmark—were hungry for revenge.

When young Charles XII (1697–1718) came to the throne, a coalition of Russia, Poland, and Denmark pounced upon his Baltic territories. Charles XII proved to be a military genius and crushed his enemies in a series of lightning campaigns. But he became intoxicated by success and engaged in political adventures that far exceeded his country's resources. He marched deep into Russian territory and was totally defeated at Pultava in 1709. He failed to gain Turkish support, though he spent some years at the Ottoman court seeking an alliance. Finally, he lost his life in a raid on Norway in 1718. In the peace settlements of 1719–21, the Swedish empire outside Sweden was divided among Hanover, Denmark, Prussia, and Russia. Sweden settled down gracefully enough in the eighteenth century to its earlier role of second-class power.

Poland

The case of Poland was quite different, though the results were somewhat similar. Poland, formed in 1386 by the

THE BALTIC: A SWEDISH LAKE   1621–1721

Swedish territory, 1621-1721

Swedish gains and losses, 1621-1721

MILES 0 — 300

ARCTIC OCEAN

TRONDHJEM, 1658-60

1645

FINLAND

KARELIA, 1617-1721

Bergen

Christiania

Viborg, 1721

INGRIA, 1617-1721

Narva

BOHUS, 1658

Stockholm

Novgorod

ÖSEL, 1645

ESTONIA, 1561-1721

HALLAND 1658

GOTHLAND, 1645

LIVONIA, 1629-1721

SCANIA 1658

Riga

Moscow

NORTH SEA

Copenhagen DENMARK

BALTIC SEA

Memel, 1629-35

Smolensk

Pillau, 1629-35

Königsberg

Vilna

Lübeck

Danzig

Bremen Hamburg

Stettin

Elbing, 1629-35

BREMEN VERDEN, 1648-1719

Berlin

HITHER POMERANIA, 1648-1720

Route of Charles XII

Warsaw

Dresden

POLAND

union of the crowns of Poland and Lithuania, was, after Russia, the largest state in Europe. Polish prosperity and culture had reached their peak in the sixteenth century, when the Polish people, linked by their Roman Catholic religion to western Europe, had felt some of the effects of the Renaissance, the Protestant revolt, and the Catholic Reformation. By the beginning of the seventeenth century, however, economic and political decline had set in. The Polish monarchy had always been elective. Until about 1572 the nobles had usually elected the legal heirs of their monarchs, but after this they began to choose anyone whom they believed they could control. By 1700 the real power in Poland lay in the hands of the nobility. The monarchy was almost powerless, although petty German princes still sought election to gain the prestige of a royal title. The peasants were the most depressed in Europe, sunk deep in serfdom. There was almost no bourgeoisie, since the towns had not flourished. Political power was concentrated in the diet, which by now represented only the nobility, since representatives of the towns no longer dared to attend.

The diet was notorious for its futility; one negative vote (the *liberum veto*) could block any action. Moreover, by using the *liberum veto* any member might "explode" the diet—that is, dissolve the diet and wipe out everything it had done up to that moment. Of fifty-seven diets held in the century after 1652, all but nine were so "exploded"—one by a member who simply wanted to see what would happen. If legislation did succeed in running the gauntlet of this national assembly, there was still no way of getting it enforced in the provincial assemblies of lesser nobles or on the private estates of the landed barons. John Sobieski (1674–96), a native Pole of high integrity who made a serious effort to lead the country out of its weakness, was the last great

king of Poland. After him the Polish crown became simply the prize of foreign intrigue, and Poland started down the path that led to extinction at the hands of more powerful neighbors at the end of the eighteenth century.

Russia

Throughout the seventeenth century there was no great power east of Sweden, Poland, and the Ottoman Empire. The Grand Duchy of Moscow had fallen on evil days after the death of Ivan the Dread in 1584. Disputes about the succession to the tsar's crown led to a "Time of Troubles," and the accession of the Romanovs, who were to rule Russia from 1613 to 1917, at first did little to strengthen the state. In the 1650s a near revolution was provoked by a reforming patriarch of the Orthodox Church who ordered that the ritual and liturgy be revised in order to bring them closer to the original Greek text of the Bible. This order exasperated vast numbers of the uneducated masses to whom the Slavonic texts were sacrosanct. For many years after, "Old Believers" resisted the official religious policy of the government in spite of executions and exile.

Russia was a victim state through most of the century, often unable to defend its frontiers against invading Swedes, Poles, and Turks, and still cut off from access to either the Baltic or the Black Sea. English merchants had made contact with Moscow in the 1550s through the White Sea, and German merchants were even more active in the capital. But while Russia absorbed some of the technology (especially the military technology) of the West, it remained relatively untouched by cultural changes in the rest of Europe. Renaissance, Reformation, and scientific revolution, with all the ferment they brought to the West, remained almost unknown to the peoples living east of Catholic Poland.

Medals celebrating the Treaty of Eternal Peace between Russia and Poland in 1686. Top: King John Sobieski; bottom: personification of Poland and Russia.

Peter the Great, 1689–1725

In 1689 one of the most remarkable rulers in all European history came to power in Russia at the age of seventeen. He was a giant of a man, nearly seven feet tall (his enormous boots are still proudly preserved in the Kremlin), with large, skillful hands, inexhaustible energy, insatiable curiosity, and a hot temper. As a boy he had loved to play at war. He had also spent much of his time with the Dutch and Germans who lived in the "German Quarter" of Moscow, listening and learning. In these early years the great passion of his later life seems to have been born: to make Russia a great power by rapidly westernizing its technology, its civil and military institutions, and its popular customs. At his death in 1725 he had aggrandized, upturned, and exhausted his country and had earned the name by which he was to be known to later history: Peter the Great.

Peter's plans at first developed slowly. Using his old-fashioned army, he failed to capture Azov at the mouth of the Don from the Turks in 1695. Next year, after he had built a fleet on the river with Dutch help, Azov fell. Peter had learned a lesson: In order to build a navy and to modernize an archaic army, he would first have to learn a great deal from the West. From 1696 to 1698, thinly disguised as a private citizen, Peter visited Holland, England, and Germany. Here he learned how an utterly different society built its ships, made its munitions, ran its government, and conducted its diplomacy. He alternately shocked and amazed the Dutch and English who came to know him. Direct, spontaneous, and naive in temperament, he always had to try to do things for himself. He worked in the shipyards, eagerly questioned everyone he met on western technology, and caroused through the night in drunken orgies with his Russian companions. He hired over 700 technicians of various sorts to return with him to Russia.

In Vienna word reached him of a revolt of the *streltsi*, the barbarous and undisciplined palace guard, which to Peter represented everything backward and reactionary about Russia. (The *streltsi* were in league with the "Old Believers" and were better at staging palace revolutions than at fighting an enemy.) Peter hastened back to Moscow and made a fearful example of the rebels, executing over a thousand of them and using torture on a scale that shocked even his countrymen, who were used to brutality. At the same time he forbade the wearing of beards and long robes by any Russian, as a sign of his determination to westernize even the personal habits and costumes of his subjects. His subjects wore beards because God was presumed to wear a beard and man was made in His image. But to Peter, beards symbolized the old Russia of reaction, rebellion, and religious fanaticism. The clean-shaven look was western. Typically, the tsar himself took a hand in shaving some of his courtiers.

There was nothing particularly original about what Peter did to reform the military, political, and social institutions of his country. He borrowed his ideas and techniques from what other statesmen were doing at the time in France, England, the Dutch Republic, Brandenburg, and Sweden. But his methods were more casual and informal, more brutal and ruthless, than were those of western countries.

An overwhelming defeat by the Swedes at Narva in 1700 spurred on Peter's efforts to improve his army. With the help of foreign officers and advisers he had trained a formidable force of over 100,000 by 1709, the year he annihilated Charles XII's forces at Pultava. At the time of his death the army numbered over 200,000 in a population of about 8 million. Years of warfare against the Turks were unsuccessful, and even Azov was lost once again. But decisive victories came in the North. In the Great Northern War Peter gained territory on the Gulf of Finland that had once belonged to Sweden. This gave him the "window on the sea," the direct contact with western Europe through the Baltic, that was his primary aim.

To man his army, Peter developed a conscription system. To pay for it was harder, since he could not borrow money. As expenses increased, he and

Contemporary cartoon of Peter cutting off the beard of a Russian noble. Those who wanted to keep their beards had to pay a tax and carry a license (shown below).

his advisers taxed anything and everything they could think of: births, marriages, caskets, graves, and beards, among other things. By the end of his reign the combined burdens of heavy taxation, conscription for the army, and forced labor for industry and for building had resulted in a measurable decline in the population.

Political reforms followed military reforms, though more slowly. Peter's method of governing was informal and haphazard. To get something done, he would dash off a hastily written order and set up a commission to carry it out. Slowly, toward the end of his reign, some order was brought out of the resulting chaos. The first provincial governments were set up; the numerous commissions were brought under supervisory "colleges"; and a "senate," or central administrative body, was instituted to interpret the tsar's orders (which were sometimes confusing) and to carry out his will. A secret police also appeared to provide a check on all officials.

In Russia the imperial government did more and individuals or nonofficial groups did less than in any other European country. After 1700 no new patriarch was appointed, and the church was strictly subordinated to the state under a civilian official. When new industries were needed to support the army, government contractors founded them, using forced labor (serfs and criminals) granted by the tsar. One of Peter's most herculean achievements was to compel the ancient hereditary nobility to serve the state. He ordered many of the sons of the nobility to study abroad, then compelled them as well as their parents to serve for life in the army, in the government, or in industry. At the same time he enlisted commoners for the service of the state, giving them land and titles of nobility. He thus created a "service nobility" out of older and newer classes. To support this service nobility, he allowed them a free hand in dealing with the serfs on their lands. A census for tax purposes resulted in greatly increasing the number of serfs in Russia by classifying doubtful cases as servile. After 1762 the nobles were freed from the obligation of service to the state, but it took another century

for the peasants to become free from the galling form of serfdom prevailing in Russia. In central Europe a serf was usually bound to the land, but in Russia he could be sold apart from the land like a slave and was generally at the mercy of his master—a fact that made it easier for new industries to acquire forced labor but degraded the Russian serf to a level even below that of his counterpart in Germany and Austria.

In 1707 Peter moved the seat of his government to a new city that he had built on conquered territory at the eastern end of the Gulf of Finland and had named in honor of his patron saint. St. Petersburg was a perfect symbol of his work as a whole. It was a city unlike Moscow, without roots in the country's past, built new on a marsh by forced labor. The nobles were ordered to build houses in it and merchants were ordered to settle in it. This seaport city looked westward to Germany, Holland, and western Europe, not to the interior as landlocked Moscow had for centuries. The nobility and civil servants hated it at first, but in the end it became their capital—the political center of what has

Peter the Great, by Aert de Gelder.

been called "a government without a people," and the social center of a westernized aristocracy out of all touch with the Russian peasant. As Versailles came to stand for the France of Louis XIV, so St. Petersburg (later called Petrograd and then Leningrad) came to stand for the Russia of Peter the Great—a powerful autocracy with few vital connections with the people.

Historians still differ sharply in estimating the value of Peter's work, but on some things they are fairly well agreed. The older Russian institutions were bankrupt, and western influences were beginning to have their effect even before Peter appeared on the scene. Peter hastened processes of change that were almost certain to have come in any case. He cannot be blamed for all the evil results that followed, since many of them (such as the intensification of serfdom) had their roots deep in the past and owed much of their growth to Peter's successors. Two things he did accomplish: He transformed Russia from a victim state into a great power, and he involved it irrevocably with the future development of Europe. Since his time, Russia has always been a factor in the European balance of power. Peter's westernizing policy ultimately provoked a strong nationalistic and orthodox reaction, leaving Russia divided to the present day between deep suspicion of everything foreign and eager admiration of western technology and culture. But never again was Russia able to turn its back on Europe.

Even more important than Peter's accomplishments were Peter's methods. His example created a tradition of dynamic autocracy. To future tsars and future dictators his reign was to be the classic example of what might be accomplished by a ruthless and demonic will.

CONCLUSION

The half-century between 1660 and 1715 thus saw significant changes in the political and social structure of Europe. Absolute divine-right monarchy reached the apogee of its development in the France of Louis XIV and was imitated from Madrid to St. Petersburg. It is difficult to imagine two more different personalities than Louis XIV of France and Peter of Russia, but their aims were essentially similar. A few smaller peoples like the Swiss had quietly rejected monarchy in favor of republican government, and the Dutch had become wealthy and powerful as a republic. But it took the English Revolution to demonstrate to Europe that there was a practical alternative to absolute monarchy that could serve great powers as well as small. So by 1715 the political alternatives of absolutism and constitutionalism were each embodied in a great power. At the same time there were important shifts of power within the European state system. The French bid for predominance failed, provoking the rise of England and Austria as great powers. Two great empires of the sixteenth century, the Spanish and the Ottoman, were in decline. Two peoples of limited resources and numbers, the Dutch and the Swedes, had bid strongly for great-power status in the mid-seventeenth century, but by 1715 their strength was spent. Two new powers had appeared in the East to join the balance, the small military Kingdom of Prussia and the vast semibarbarous Tsardom of Russia. The rivalries of these states—England versus France, France versus Austria, Austria versus Prussia, Austria and Russia versus the Ottoman Empire—were to become the dynamic elements in eighteenth-century war and diplomacy.

Suggestions for Further Reading

Note: Asterisk denotes a book available in paperback edition.

General The best general accounts of the period are F. L. Nussbaum, *The Triumph of Science and Reason, 1660–1685** (1953), and J. B. Wolf, *The Emergence of the Great Powers, 1685–1715** (1951), both in the *Rise of Modern Europe* series, with useful bibliographies. These are particularly helpful as introductions to the history of eastern Europe, on which it is hard to find good reading in English. R. Hatton, *Europe in the Age of Louis XIV** (1969), is excellent on the social history of the period. A general study of an important subject begins with this period: Sir Ernest Barker, *The Development of Public Services in Western Europe, 1660–1930* (1944). On the general theme of this chapter, see J. N. Figgis, *The Divine Right of Kings** (1896, 1922); C. J. Friedrich and C. Blitzer, *The Age of Power** (1957); and F. D. Wormuth, *The Origins of Modern Constitutionalism* (1949).

France under Louis XIV

There are good chapters on Louis' reign in Ogg and Boulenger (Chapter 19). Two excellent short surveys are L. B. Packard, *The Age of Louis XIV** (1914), and M. P. Ashley, *Louis XIV and the Greatness of France** (1946). J. B. Wolf, *Louis XIV* (1968), is a good biography. A. Guérard, *The Life and Death of an Ideal: France in the Classical Age** (1928), is a more thought-provoking and comprehensive discussion, including both politics and culture within its scope. J. E. King, *Science and Rationalism in the Government of Louis XIV, 1661–1683* (1949), is an important study. On economic history, the three books of C. W. Cole are the best introduction: *French Mercantilist Doctrines Before Colbert* (1913), *Colbert and a Century of French Mercantilism,* 2 vols. (1939), and *French Mercantilism, 1683–1700* (1943). C. Hill, *Versailles* (1925), is one of many books on the life of the court. W. H. Lewis, *The Splendid Century** (1954), is a recent popular account of all aspects of the reign, full of fascinating material. The best guides to the literary history of the period are the various works of A. A. Tilley.

England

G. N. Clark, *The Later Stuarts, 1660–1714* (1934), in the *Oxford History of England,* is a particularly fine synthesis. A more detailed narrative history of the period may be found in three books, all more or less Whig in sympathy: D. Ogg, *England in the Reign of Charles II,** 2 vols. (1934); the same author's *England in the Reign of James II and William III* (1955); and G. M. Trevelyan, *England under Queen Anne,* 3 vols. (1930–34). A. Bryant, *Charles II* (1931), is more pro-Stuart. The most recent interpretation of the whole period of revolution in England is C. Hill, *The Century of Revolution, 1603–1714* (1961). There is a good modern biography of James II by F. C. Turner (1948), but none of William III. Sir John Pollock, *The Popish Plot* (1903, 1945), is the standard investigation of a tangled historical problem. On the economic history of the period, there is a good special study, *The Bank of England,* by Sir John Clapham, 2 vols. (1944), and a masterly brief sketch by Sir George Clark, *The Wealth of England, 1496–1760* (1947). C. H. Wilson, *England's Apprenticeship, 1603–1763* (1965), is a remarkable study of England's emergence as a great power. Pepys' Diary is the most deservedly famous contemporary account of the Restoration period. It is perhaps read best in the abridgment of O. F. Morshead, *Everybody's Pepys* (1926).

Eastern Europe

In addition to the general accounts in Nussbaum and Wolf (first section, above), two books are very helpful as an introduction to the problems of eastern Europe: S. H. Cross, *Slavic Civilization Through the Ages* (1948), and O. Halecki, *Borderlands of Western Civilization* (1952). For Germany as a whole, see H. Holborn, *A History of Modern Germany, 1648–1840* (1964). On Habsburg history, P. Frischauer, *The Imperial Crown* (1939), follows the history of the house to 1792 and is mostly concerned with personalities. H. F. Schwarz, *The Imperial Privy Council in the Seventeenth Century* (1943), is concerned with constitutional matters. On Prussia, S. B. Fay, *The Rise of Brandenburg-Prussia to 1786** (1937), is very brief but also very good. J. A. R. Marriott and C. G. Robertson, *The Evolution of Prussia* (1915), is more detailed. F. Schevill has written an admiring biography of Frederick William, *The Great Elector* (1947). R. N. Bain, *Scandinavia: A Political History* (1905), and O. Halecki, *History of Poland** (1943), are useful national histories. J. A. R. Marriott, *The Eastern Question* (1917, 1940), is a reliable survey of the slow disintegration of the Ottoman Empire and of the resulting repercussions in Europe. The classic larger history of Russia is by V. O. Kliuchevsky; the standard Marxist account is by M. N. Pokrovsky. There are good one-volume histories by G. Vernadsky, rev. ed. (1944), Sir Bernard Pares, new ed. (1953), and B. H. Sumner, rev. ed. (1947). B. H. Sumner, *Peter the Great and the Emergence of Russia** (1950), is a well-informed and judicious short account. Kliuchevsky's *Peter the Great* (1958) is an English version of an older but still useful book. R. J. Kerner, *The Urge to the Sea: The Course of Russian History* (1942), contains a valuable account of Russian expansion eastward to the Pacific. J. Blum, "The Rise of Serfdom in Eastern Europe," *American Historical Review,* Vol. LXII (July 1957), is a masterly examination of the differences in the economic development of eastern and western Europe. See also his *Lord and Peasant in Russia** (1961).

21

The Scientific Revolution and the Enlightenment

All the above named Instruments as Telescopes of all lengths, Microscopes single and double, Perspectives great and s[...] Reding Glasses of all Sizes, Magnifying Glasses, Multiplying Glasses, Triangular Prisms, Speaking Trumpetts, Spectacles fi[...] to all ages, And all other sorts of Glasses, both Concave and Convex.

Until the seventeenth century the growth of civilized man's knowledge about the natural world around him had been slow, fumbling, and discontinuous. He had made many individual observations of natural phenomena and had derived some useful generalizations from these observations. But many generalizations were poorly stated and others were entirely erroneous. "Experiments" in the modern sense were all but unheard of, and most people felt that scientific speculation was both unsure and impractical.

THE SCIENTIFIC REVOLUTION

By the eighteenth century a startling change had occurred. A large body of verifiable knowledge about nature had accumulated and has continued to accumulate at an increasing rate down to our own day. This knowledge has had revolutionary effects. Human society today has at its disposal more food, clothing, and shelter, faster ways of moving about the globe, quicker means of communicating across great distances, and more power than anyone could have dreamed of before about 1600. The characteristic mark of our civilization is that it is a "scientific civilization," and this quality began to be noticeable in the seventeenth century.

Discussion of a new method of inquiry—we call it the scientific method—began in the universities in the late thirteenth and fourteenth centuries and came to fruition in western Europe after 1600. The new method was essentially a combination of two elements: careful observation and controlled experimentation, and rational interpretation of the results of this observation and experimentation, preferably by use of mathematics. In Professor Whitehead's words, science is "a vehement and passionate interest in the relation of general principles to irreducible and stubborn facts."

When Galileo and others began to apply this method in physics and astronomy, other brilliant "discoveries" followed. These discoveries fired the imagination and enthusiasm of European thinkers. Scientific societies were organized, scientific journals began to appear, and "chain discoveries," each one resting on the results of the one preceding it, made their appearance. Science, hitherto the pursuit of occasional lonely individuals, became a social enterprise and has continued so to the present. Furthermore, it became fashionable. The humanists had been little interested in science, but Newton's work made a profound impression on every writer in Europe. Finally, the gap between the theories of the scholar and the practical knowledge of the technician began to close.

The Medieval Universe

Precisely *why* all this took place when and where it did is still a puzzle. The one thing that can be said is that ever since the twelfth century the people of western Europe had been interested in scientific problems. But the medieval answers to these problems were not very stimulating. For example, it was generally believed that the universe was a finite sphere with the earth at the center. Between the center and the outermost limits were nine transparent spheres that carried the stars, the planets, the sun, and the moon in their daily revolutions around the earth, which remained motionless. On earth all was change, corruptibility, and decay. In the heavens all was perfection and incorruptibility—the perfect sphericity of sun and moon, the unvarying circular motion of the heavenly bodies, and the music of the spheres produced by their motion. And so what was the rule on earth was not the rule in the heavens. There was an earthly physics and a heavenly physics, and the laws of the one were not those of the other.

Even in the Middle Ages, however, not all men were satisfied with this relatively simple picture of the universe. In the thirteenth and fourteenth centuries a small but increasing number of scholars began to question existing explanations. Many of them were Franciscans, inspired perhaps by their founder's sensitive feeling for nature. Stimulated by the current study of Greco-Arabic science, a group of teachers at Oxford and Paris began to apply mathematical reasoning to problems of physics and astronomy, such as

Trade card advertising scientific instruments, 1683.

The Scientific Revolution

ALFRED NORTH WHITEHEAD

A brief and sufficiently accurate description of the intellectual life of the European races during the succeeding two centuries and a quarter up to our own times is that they have been living upon the accumulated capital of ideas provided for them by the genius of the seventeenth century. . . . It is the one century which consistently, and throughout the whole range of human activities, provided intellectual genius adequate for the greatness of its occasions. . . . The issue of the combined labors of four men [Descartes, Galileo, Huyghens, and Newton] has some right to be considered as the greatest single intellectual success which mankind has achieved.

HERBERT BUTTERFIELD

The so-called "scientific revolution," popularly associated with the sixteenth and seventeenth centuries, but reaching back in an unmistakably continuous line to a period much earlier still . . . outshines everything since the rise of Christianity and reduces the Renaissance and Reformation to the rank of mere episodes, mere internal displacements, within the system of medieval Christendom.

From Alfred North Whitehead, *Science and the Modern World* (New York: Macmillan, 1925), pp. 57-58, 67; Herbert Butterfield, *The Origins of Modern Science* (London: Bell, 1949), p. vii.

accelerated motion. Their speculations were continued by professors at the University of Padua in the fifteenth and sixteenth centuries. At Padua, a center of medical training for three centuries, the proper method of studying nature was vigorously debated in the course of arguments about Aristotle. Medieval universities kept interest in science alive, and the first faint beginnings of the scientific revolution were seen in Oxford, Paris, and Padua.

Most Europeans of 1500, however, did not question the standard Greek authorities. The normal state of everything in the universe was a state of rest: Things moved only if they were pushed or pulled by a mover—so said Aristotle. Galen, in the second century, had described the anatomy of the human body so convincingly that doctors still saw the human organs through his eyes. Ptolemy in the same century had worked out such an ingenious mathematical explanation of the observed irregularities in the movements of the planets that no one in 1500 thought it could be improved upon.

All motion in the heavens was circular, Ptolemy assumed, but there were smaller circles, or "epicycles," whose centers moved around the circumference of larger circles, and on the circumferences of these smaller circles the planets moved. It took about eighty epicycles to do the job, but the system worked quite well in explaining the observed phenomena. There seemed to be very little reason at the close of the Middle Ages to try to improve on either the observations or the theories of these ancient writers.

The Background of Change

In the fourteenth, fifteenth, and sixteenth centuries, however, certain forces in European society were preparing the way for a change in the general view of nature. Artisans and craftsmen were becoming more skilled in their techniques. The invention of the lens and the development of the glass industry, to take but one example, gave the promise of vastly extending man's powers of observing natural processes. New techniques in shipbuilding led to voyages of discovery, which in turn stimulated interest in nature and turned men's attention to problems of navigation.

The Renaissance, with its emphasis on literature and art, was in some ways antiscientific. But humanism stimulated a passionate interest in man. Leonardo's studies of the anatomy of the body and Machiavelli's studies of the anatomy of society owed much indirectly to humanism. Furthermore, humanistic study revealed conflicting opinions among the ancients on matters of science, just at the moment when the authority of Galen and Ptolemy was becoming shaky for other reasons. Anatomical studies by artists and the increasing practice of dissection suggested that Galen had made mistakes in observation. Growing skill in mathematics exposed the clumsiness of Ptolemy's explanations. In the opening years of the sixteenth century, conditions were ripe for change.

1543: Vesalius and Copernicus

In 1543 two notable scientific works heralded the end of medieval science and the beginnings of a revolution in western man's conception of nature. Vesalius' *On the Structure of the Human Body* was for its day a marvelously careful description of human anatomy based on direct observation in dissection. Vesalius did not free himself completely from the authority of Galen, nor was there much theory in his book. But it was an influential example of the power of observation. Copernicus' *On the Revolutions of the Heavenly Bodies* was a brilliant mathematical treatise which showed that the number of Ptolemy's epicycles could be reduced to 34 if one assumed that the earth turned on its axis once a day and moved around the sun once a year. Unlike Vesalius, Copernicus was no observer. He learned during his study at Padua in the early years of the century that there was an ancient opinion that the earth moved, and he found that this assumption made everything simpler to explain mathematically. Since medieval theory decreed that "nature always acts in the simplest ways," the simpler explanation must be the truer. And so with no experimental or observational proof, Copernicus presented his readers with a theory of a universe in which the earth was no longer the center. The experimental and the theoretical sides of the modern scientific method were perfectly exemplified in Vesalius' and Copernicus' books, but they were not yet conjoined in one man or one work.

In 1600 a monk named Giordano Bruno was burned at the stake for preaching that the universe was not finite but infinite in extent, that it was filled with numberless suns and planets like our own, and that God was equally in every planet or atom in the cosmos. Bruno had been inspired by Copernicus, although Copernicus himself believed in the finite sphere of the fixed stars and the uniqueness of the earth. This intuition of the infinity of the universe spread gradually among scientists.

Bacon and Descartes

Two major prophets of the Scientific Revolution were Francis Bacon (1561–1626) and René Descartes (1596–1650). Bacon, an English lawyer, statesman, and essayist, waged a vigorous battle in his books against the deductive method of Scholasticism, which started from premises usually taken on authority and then deduced all the logical consequences. This method might help men to organize truths already known, he said, but it could never help them to discover new truths. Only inductive reasoning, which starts from direct observations of phenomena and goes on to develop the principles that explain these observations, can produce new truth. Bacon was as interested in controlling nature as in knowing its processes. He pictured an imaginary society of scientists whose end was to benefit mankind by conducting hundreds of experiments and discovering useful facts. Bacon failed to appreciate the importance of mathematical models in theoretical analysis (he was unconvinced by Copernicus), and although he praised experimentation, he performed

Medieval cosmos based on the earth-centered Ptolemaic conception. Ptolemy's view of the universe was a closed and defined system that seemed so perfectly put together that it was not criticized for fourteen centuries—until the discoveries of Copernicus and Galileo.

Scientific revolutionaries of the seventeenth century: Francis Bacon (top) and René Descartes.

almost no experiments. Nevertheless, his writings did dramatize the importance of empirical research. The founding in 1662 of the Royal Society of London, the first scientific society in England, owed much to Bacon's inspiration, and in a sense he was the remote ancestor of the great research laboratories and research teams of today.

Descartes, a French mathematician and philosopher, was a more important figure than Bacon, but he lacked Bacon's intuitive understanding of the need for careful observations. To Descartes, the excitement of science lay in mathematical analysis and theory. In a famous autobiographical account, he told how the literature and philosophy he studied as a youth left him unsatisfied because they reached no certain conclusions, how mathematics charmed him by its precision and certainty, and how he set out to discover a "method of rightly conducting the reason and discovering truth in the sciences." In November 1619, in a moment of intuition, he saw the exact correspondence between geometry and algebra: the truth that any equation can be translated into a curve on a graph, and that any regular curve can be translated into an equation. This intoxicating vision suggested to him a new way of grasping ultimate truth. If only men would systematically doubt all notions based on authority or custom and start with clear and precise ideas they know to be true, the whole universe might be deduced from a few simple principles and thus comprehended as clearly as the coordinate geometry he had discovered.

Descartes was one of the first to believe that science could save humanity. His enthusiasm was infectious, but he moved too fast. He reduced the universe, including the body of man, to a mathematically intelligible machine. To do this he had to take mind out of the world of matter entirely and define it as a separate substance that comprehended the world of matter but did not exist in it. His generalizations in astronomy, physics, and anatomy were often premature, and his passion for system building went beyond his capacity to check by experiment. But his enthusiasm for scientific "method," his belief that everything could be reduced to mathematical terms, and his insistence on systematic doubt of all earlier theories left a profound mark on the thinking of scientists in the next two centuries. Descartes made it easier for his successors to reject old ideas, and they gradually came to accept his belief that the language of science must be mathematics.

Experiment and Mathematics

Both Bacon and Descartes were over-optimistic. Bacon thought that a generation of determined experimentation would establish a solid structure of knowledge about the universe. Descartes thought that a universal science could be deduced fairly soon from a few basic mathematical axioms. He also believed that the universe was much less complicated than it is; it was one of Descartes' pupils who described the world as a gigantic piece of clockwork.

Meanwhile, experimentation and mathematics were developing slowly and steadily in the hands of a growing host of scientists. William Gilbert used what little was known of the mysterious force of electricity to deduce that the earth itself was a great magnet (1600). William Harvey, who had studied at Padua, proved that the blood must circulate from arteries to veins to heart to lungs and back to heart and then arteries again by measuring the amount of blood actually pumped out by the heart in a minute and arguing that it must go somewhere (1628). Later in the century the new microscope revealed the tiny capillaries that actually connect arteries to veins. Torricelli, Pascal, and others investigated the ancient proposition that "nature abhors a vacuum," a proposition that had been firmly believed by everyone from Aristotle to Descartes. In order to prove the falseness of the proposition, the new investigators created vacuums in test tubes, invented the barometer, and discovered the pressure of the atmosphere. All these advances evidenced a growing precision in observation and an increasing sophistication both in controlling experiments and in quantifying their results.

At the same time mathematics was

making rapid strides. The invention of decimals and of logarithms early in the century facilitated calculation; Pascal inaugurated the study of probability; and at the end of the century Newton and Leibniz crowned the work of many others by simultaneously inventing the calculus, which provided the first method of analyzing regularly accelerating or decelerating motion.

Kepler

It was in astronomy and physics that observational techniques and mathematical methods found their most fruitful union. The German astronomer Johannes Kepler (1571–1630) was troubled by discrepancies in Copernicus' theory, which he nevertheless believed to be true. He worked from the observations of his master Tycho Brahe, which were far more accurate than those available to Copernicus. Copernicus had clung to the old belief that all heavenly bodies moved in circles. But to Kepler it was obvious that the planets' orbits were not circles. For years he worried about the geometry of these orbits and finally tried the ellipse. The properties of the ellipse had been studied since the time of the Greeks, and Kepler quickly saw that his solution fitted the observations. The planets' orbits, he announced, are elliptical, with the sun in one of the two foci of the ellipse. Further, a line from the sun to a planet sweeps out equal areas of the ellipse in equal times, and the cube of the distance of each planet from the sun is proportional to the square of the time of its revolution. Here was astounding proof of the intuition of Descartes and others that nature in some mysterious sense was mathematical. A geometrical figure, studied for centuries as pure theory, was found to "fit" the facts of nature. The implication was that nature was perhaps really a machine, intelligible to careful observers equipped with the tools of mathematics.

Galileo

The first fruits of Kepler's work appeared in 1609. During the same year an Italian, Galileo Galilei (1564–1642), pro-

Harvey Discovers the Circulation of the Blood (1629)

Since calculations and visual demonstrations have confirmed all my suppositions, to wit, that the blood is passed through the lungs and the heart by the pulsation of the ventricles, is forcibly ejected to all parts of the body, therein steals into the veins . . . flows back everywhere . . . from small veins into larger ones, and thence comes at last into the vena cava and to the auricle of the heart; all this too in such amounts that it cannot be supplied from the ingesta [food] and is also in greater bulk than would suffice for nutrition.

I am obliged to conclude that in all animals the blood is driven around a circuit with an unceasing, circular sort of motion, that this is an activity of the heart which it carries out by virtue of its pulsation, and that in sum it constitutes the sole cause for the heart's pulsatile movement.

From C. C. Gillispie, *The Edge of Objectivity* (Princeton: Princeton University Press, 1960), p. 71.

fessor at Padua and Pisa, turned a newly invented instrument, the telescope, on the heavens and soon afterward published an account of what he saw. The changeless perfection and perfect sphericity of the heavenly bodies had dissolved before his gaze. The moon had craters and mountains; there were moving spots on the sun; there were rings around Saturn; and Jupiter proved to have four moons of its own. A bright new star had already appeared and been noted in 1572, and in 1577 a new comet had cut a path through what should have been crystalline spheres. The finite, spherical universe of the Middle Ages was shattered, and thoughtful men suspected strongly that they were looking out into boundless space, sparsely populated by stars like the sun and possibly by other solar systems as well. The old distinction between terrestrial and celestial physics was apparently dissolving. The moon and sun were not perfect globes and the stars were not changeless. Perhaps the same forces and laws operated both on earth and in the heavens. Nor was the earth any longer the motionless center of the universe. The earth was a planet circling the sun like Jupiter or any other, and round about the solar system were infinite, silent spaces.

Two of Galileo's telescopes.

This was too much for obscurantists in the Church. The Copernican theory had been denounced in 1616, and in 1632 Galileo himself was condemned by the Roman Inquisition, threatened with torture, and forced to recant. Nevertheless, his brilliantly written dialogues contributed mightily to the overthrow not only of Ptolemy in favor of Copernicus, but also of Aristotle in favor of a new physics.

Galileo's physics was inspired by the speculations of the fourteenth-century Franciscans, but he went much further and was much more accurate in developing mathematical formulas to describe the laws of motion. He worked out the law of falling bodies. The result was a simple mathematical formula again: The distance covered increases as the square of the time. He saw that the path followed by a projectile is a regular curve, a parabola, produced by the operation of two forces on the projectile—the initial impetus and the pull of the earth. He came close to formulating the key concept of modern mechanics, the law of inertia: that all bodies tend to remain at rest or to continue in motion in straight lines unless acted upon by outside forces. From this deceptively simple proposition—so fundamentally different from Aristotle's conception of motion as the result of some mover's action—was to spring the law of gravitation. Galileo came within an ace of discovering it, but the honor was to be reserved for one who was born in the year he died, 1642.

Newton

It was the genius of an Englishman, Sir Isaac Newton (1642–1727), that related Kepler's astronomy to Galileo's physics, destroyed all distinction between celestial and terrestrial physics, and accomplished at least part of Descartes' dream of establishing a "universal science." The basic intuition came to Newton while he was still a student in his twenties at Cambridge University. The thought occurred to him that the force that keeps the moon from flying off at a tangent and bends it into an orbit about the earth must be exactly the same force that pulls an apple from its branch to the ground. There must be a universal force of attraction between every body in the universe, and this force must be calculable—even if we do not know exactly what it is in itself. Newton's earliest calculations came close enough to mathematical proof to persuade him that it was in truth the same force that operated on the moon and the apple, and that this force varied "directly as the product of the masses" involved and "inversely as the square of the distance" separating the bodies. For some time he seems to have lost interest in his "law," but twenty years later a scientist friend, Edmund Halley, urged him to work out and publish his theory. Newton developed the necessary mathematics (the calculus) to prove his theory to his own satisfaction and published his conclusions, in Latin, in *The Mathematical Principles of Natural Philosophy* (1687). This proved to be one of the most influential books ever written in the history of science as well as in the history of human thought.

To scientists Newton's law of gravitation provided a single, simple explanation of a growing mass of data in astronomy and physics and laid the foundations of future research in both these sciences. Further, Newton gave scientific method its classic formulation in his "Rules of Reasoning":

> In experimental philosophy (i.e., science) we are to look upon propositions collected by general induction from phenomena as accurately or very nearly true, notwithstanding any contrary hypotheses (theories) that may be imagined, till such time as other phenomena occur, by which they may either be made more accurate or liable to exceptions.

Newton's support of the experimental, or inductive, approach was aimed at the premature generalizing of Descartes and his followers. But obviously he did not underestimate the value of mathematical theory, as Bacon had. In Newton the slow growing together of empirical observation and rational interpretation reached full maturity.

The Newtonian Universe

To the layman, who learned about Newton's work through popularizers, a new universe began to open up. It was a far cry from the small and finite medieval universe. It was a universe in which the significant objects were bodies or masses moving about in infinite space in response to regularly operating forces. Mass, force, and motion were the key concepts, and mathematics was the means of understanding them. Medieval man had been obsessed by the question "Why?" and had felt he understood whatever he encountered in nature once he had discovered its end or purpose. Seventeenth-century scientists limited themselves to asking "How?" and were satisfied when they found what appeared to be the regular patterns in natural processes. The world of Kepler, Galileo, and Newton was a vast machine, working according to laws that could be mathematically expressed, laws that were intelligible to anyone who followed the proper experimental and mathematical methods.

What was the place of God and of man in this universe? We shall see what the answers to this question were in the next century. But here it must be observed that no seventeenth-century scientist of prominence thought that he was reading God or man out of the universe. Descartes considered himself a good Catholic and was apparently not troubled by the dangers inherent in his sharp separation of the world of matter from the world of mind. Newton spent most of his energy in his later years in religious speculation. Contradictions were not necessarily evident to the first modern scientists and their readers.

Still, the religious view of life was weakening in the later seventeenth century, and the development of science was in part the result of this decline. The charters of the scientific societies and academies that sprang up throughout Europe during the century usually contained clauses stating that purely theological or political discussion would not be tolerated and that "ultimate" or "final" causes were no part of the group's concern. In the earliest history of the Royal Society of London, published in 1667, it is clear that scientific discussions offered a peculiar attraction to thoughtful men during a fanatical and bitter civil war like the Puritan Rebellion. Science

was impartial politically and theologically; it did not stir men's tempers; it would not start religious wars; and above all, it was useful—it could benefit mankind. Scientific truth was an alternative to theological truth that was more verifiable, more practical, more peaceful—or so at least some men argued. It was more than coincidence that modern science arose in a century that saw Europe's last violent struggles over religion.

One supremely sensitive philosopher felt the religious awe implicit in the new mechanistic picture of the universe. This was an obscure Dutch lens grinder, Baruch Spinoza (1632–77). To Spinoza the new universe of mass, force, and motion, operating in strict obedience to inexorable laws, was God. There was no need, he thought, to consider God as above, behind, or beyond nature. God is not a "free cause" apart from natural law. He is not "Creator" or "Redeemer." He is natural law. "God never can decree, nor ever would have decreed, anything but what is; God did not exist before his decrees, and would not exist without them." Nature is "a fixed and immutable order," with "no particular goal in view." Man, like everything else, is part of this order. So Spinoza could write a book called *Ethics Demonstrated in the Geometrical Manner* and say, "I shall consider human activities and desires in exactly the same manner as though I were concerned with lines, planes, and solids." The wise man contemplates this natural order with serenity and delight. This was Spinoza's religion. Naturally such arguments were called atheistical, and Spinoza was considered a dangerous radical by his contemporaries.

For most men, however, the new science did not destroy the traditional religion. Rather it compelled them to consider the religious significance of a greatly expanded and complicated universe. The telescope was revealing the immense size of the cosmos, displacing the earth and even the sun from the center of the universe. The microscope was beginning to reveal the wonders of the world's minutiae—the capillaries, the bacteria, the cells, the foundations of life. No one felt the two infinites—the infinitely great and the infinitesimally small —so keenly or speculated so profoundly

Newton's design for a reflecting telescope.

about their religious significance as Blaise Pascal (1623–62). "The whole visible world is only an imperceptible atom in the ample bosom of nature," he wrote. The universe, he said, is "an infinite sphere, the center of which is everywhere, the circumference nowhere." "The eternal silence of these infinite spaces frightens me." Yet to examine a mite—"with its minute body and parts incomparably more minute, limbs with their joints, veins in the limbs, blood in the veins, humors in the blood, drops in the humors, vapors in the drops"—is equally astonishing. "What is man in nature? A Nothing in comparison with the Infinite, an All in comparison with the Nothing, a mean between nothing and everything." And yet man is greater than anything in the universe because he comprehends all this, and because Christ died on the cross for him. In this way, Pascal related the new universe to Christianity. Other Christians were not so concerned about the new science, and other scientists were not so concerned to articulate a Christian interpretation.

THE CULTURE OF THE SEVENTEENTH CENTURY

The Baroque Style in Art

The age of the scientific revolution was also the age of the "baroque" style in art—a style that sprang up in the later sixteenth century, reached its climax about the middle of the seventeenth, and came to its end around the middle of the eighteenth. The term *baroque* was invented by eighteenth-century critics who regarded seventeenth-century art as a grotesque corruption of Renaissance art. But modern critics consider the baroque a great achievement; one of them has called it "the high-water mark of European creative effort." As a style it is difficult to define because it reflected all the contrasts and contradictions of seventeenth-century culture in general: its religious ecstasy and its sensual worldliness, its credulity and its rationalism, its violence and its respect for order. Ba-

View of the baroque interior of the church at Weiss in Germany.

roque painters and sculptors were influenced by all these contradictions. They portrayed voluptuous women in repose, military heroes in battle, and saints in ecstasy with equal skill and zest.

In general, the dominant notes of the baroque were a sense of tension and conflict and a liking for the grandiose and dramatic. The conflicts of man and the universe, of man and man, and of man within himself were conceived on a more heroic, and often a more tragic, scale than they had been in the Renaissance. Renaissance painters and writers had been interested in man himself. Baroque painters and writers were fascinated by man in his environment—typical men torn by conflicting passions, confronted by human and supernatural enemies, buffeted by elemental forces beyond their control.

There were instructive parallels between the thought-worlds of the artists and the thought-worlds of the scientists of the period. To Galileo and Newton, bodies or masses moving through space in response to conflicting forces such as gravitation and centrifugal force were the objects of study. To the great French dramatists of the age—Corneille, Racine, and Molière—the objects of study were typical human beings acting and reacting in response to conflicting passions such as love and duty. Baroque painters were intrigued by space. Vermeer portrayed figures in a space that was bathed and suffused with light; Rembrandt spotlighted them in the midst of darkened space; and others pictured them floating through apparently infinite space (to baroque artists the supernatural was natural). The scientists' concern with "mass, force, and motion" seems closely related to the painters' and poets' concern with men caught in the tension between elemental forces in their whole natural or supernatural environment. The typical hero of baroque literature, it has been said, is Satan in Milton's *Paradise Lost*—swayed by colossal passions, moving through vast three-dimensional spaces, commanding many of the natural forces in the universe, but ultimately checked and frustrated by God.

The most typical product of baroque architecture was the royal palace: Versailles in France, Schönbrunn in Austria,

or Blenheim, Marlborough's regal residence in England. The style was fundamentally Renaissance classical, but grander, more ornate, and more complicated. These palaces were designed to be the stage settings of worldly greatness. The vast reception rooms, the halls of mirrors, the great sweeping staircases, and the long vistas of the formal gardens were designed to enhance the drama of royalty and aristocracy. Even the churches of the period—such as Bernini's colonnades framing St. Peter's in Rome—suggested the majesty of God rather than his mercy.

But it was the operas that originated in Italy early in the seventeenth century that were the most original creation of the baroque. The union of dramatic action and a simpler musical style was a great popular success, and opera continued to grow as a distinct form of art down to the twentieth century. The grandiose and palatial stage settings (sometimes outdoors), the dramatic conflicts of the action, and the emotive power of the music exactly suited the taste of the period. Italian composers led the way until the end of the seventeenth century: Monteverdi, the father of the opera, Frescobaldi, Scarlatti, and Vivaldi. But an Englishman, Henry Purcell, wrote the most moving opera of the century, *Dido and Aeneas* (1687).

Opera singers of the baroque period. Detail from a drawing for an opera setting by Ludovico Burnacinia, Vienna, 1674.

SEVENTEENTH-CENTURY THOUGHT ABOUT MAN

The seventeenth century developed conceptions about man that were based on Renaissance views but went beyond them. These conceptions may be conveniently summed up under three heads: individualism, relativism, and rationalism tempered by empiricism. We are speaking here of the thought of the most adventurous and best-educated minds, not of the many, whose thought-world was still conventional and in many ways "medieval."

Individualism

Radical thinkers of the seventeenth century took an increasingly individualistic view of man in society. The most intense Christian piety of the period—whether it was the Catholic devotion preached by St. François de Sales, the stern conscience of Puritans and Jansenists, or the warm inner conviction of German Pietists—was highly individualistic. The trend was equally evident in political theory. The fashion was to start with the individual and then to ask how society and the state could have originated and how they could be justified. Supporters of the divine right of kings were still numerous, but advanced thinkers were arguing that the state was based on a contract, either explicit or implicit, between the people and the ruler. Some, like Hobbes, argued that this contract, once made, was irrevocable. Others, like Locke, insisted that if the ruler broke the terms of the contract, which were usually thought to provide for good government, the people might depose him and set up a new ruler in his place. This idea of a "political contract" between ruler and people had some basis in the Old Testament and had been reinforced by feudal "contracts" between lords and vassals. It had been revived as a fighting idea by religious minorities when they were resisting the tyranny of rulers.

As time went on, the idea of a "social contract" took its place by the side of the "political contract." This was the idea that society itself was the result of a voluntary agreement among individuals who had been absolutely independent in their original "state of nature." The two ideas were mixed, somewhat confusedly, in Locke and later theorists. In both contracts, the individual with his rights and his natural independence logically came first; then came society or the state. In contrast, the Middle Ages had thought of society as an organism or a "body" in which individuals were mere "members." The more radical thinkers of the seventeenth century were coming to think of society as an artificial organization of independent individuals based on voluntary agreement or consent.

Relativism

The greatest thinkers of the Middle Ages were sure that the people of Chris-tendom were God's chosen people and that the truth had been revealed once and for all to Christians. During the sixteenth and seventeenth centuries humanism, the voyages of discovery, and the development of science greatly weakened this assurance.

Humanism had shaken this assurance by revealing Greco-Roman civilization in clearer historical perspective. Here—in a society long since dead, but still alive in its literature, its art, and its historical records—was an alternative to the medieval Christian view of life. Modern historical studies—history, archeology, philology—were born during the Renaissance and were carried on with even greater skill during the seventeenth century. This steady development of the "historical sciences," as they would be called today, slowly impressed upon thoughtful Europeans that there had been other societies in other times with values, beliefs, and institutions quite different from those of the present. Thus the idea of relativism in time was born and grew. What had been right behavior for a Roman was perhaps not right behavior in other times.

The idea of relativism in space resulted from the geographical discoveries, as we have seen. The discovery in America of societies far less civilized than Europe and of societies in Asia more civilized in many respects than Europe had the effect of shaking European provincialism. Perhaps the "noble savages" of the New World were happier than the more cultured but more corrupt Christians of Europe. Perhaps Christians had something to learn from Persian sages and Chinese philosophers. Each society had different standards; was any set of standards absolutely right? So at least increasing numbers of Europeans began to think in the seventeenth and eighteenth centuries.

As the temporal and geographical horizons of the European imagination widened, the vision of man's place in nature was complicated by scientific discovery, as we have seen in considering Bruno and Pascal. European Christians were not unique in time and space, as they had once thought; nor, perhaps, was man himself unique.

The intellectual results of historical study, geographical exploration, and scientific discovery are best seen in the work of Pierre Bayle (1647–1706), the great scholarly skeptic of the later seventeenth century. Bayle, originally a Huguenot, was briefly converted to Catholicism, but he renounced all orthodox belief when his brother died in a dungeon during an attempted forced conversion. He took up residence in the relatively tolerant Dutch Netherlands and devoted the latter part of his life to a crusade against superstition, religious intolerance, and dogmatism in general. In 1697 he published a huge rambling book, a *Historical and Critical Dictionary*, which had enormous influence on eighteenth-century thinkers. Into this book he poured all the relativism and skepticism that he had acquired through his extensive historical study, his amateur knowledge of science (he was an admirer of Descartes), and his personal experience. He argued that atheists might be good citizens and that there was no necessary connection between a man's religious beliefs and the way he behaved. He insisted that there is nothing more abominable than to make conversions by force. He ridiculed the idea that stars and planets could influence human life and mercilessly attacked superstition on every front. He distrusted all historical authorities, including the writers of the Old Testament, unless he was sure that their account of events was inherently credible. His test of truth was reason—and few if any accounts of miracles met this test. All in all, Bayle was the most thoroughgoing skeptic and the most destructive critic of his generation.

Rationalism and Empiricism

The leading thinkers of the seventeenth century were predominantly rationalistic. Reason was the faculty that distinguished man from the beast, and the triumphs of seventeenth-century science proved that reason could be trusted. And so the conclusion was drawn that the man of reason could know and understand the world into which he was born if he made the right use of his mind.

This optimistic attitude was reflected in the growing belief in "natural law." The idea of a law of nature that served as a standard of moral behavior for all men at all times in all places originated with the Stoics and was developed by medieval scholars. During the Renaissance and the Reformation this idea went into eclipse, but the discovery of scientific "laws of nature" (like Kepler's laws of planetary motion) helped to revive the belief that natural laws of human behavior also existed. Cicero had given the idea classic formulation: "There is in fact a true law—namely, right reason—which is in accordance with nature, applies to all men, and is unchangeable and eternal. By its commands this law summons men to the performance of their duties; by its prohibitions it restrains them from doing wrong." This law was implanted in the minds of men by God himself. Its content was hazy, but it was understood to include respect for life and property, good faith and fair dealing, giving each man his due. These principles could always be discovered by reason, just as reason could discover the proof of a geometrical proposition. Hugo Grotius, in his book *On the Law of War and Peace* (1625), turned to the law of nature in an attempt to find some basis for a "law of nations" that would transcend the religious fanaticisms of the Thirty Years' War. And in more general terms, if natural law is the same for all men, then it lessens the contradictions caused by the relativism in time and space that was perplexing seventeenth-century men.

The most influential example of this kind of thinking was John Locke's faith that there are certain "natural rights" vested in every individual in the "state of nature," notably life, liberty, and property. From this it follows logically, as conclusion from axiom, that men form societies and set up governments mainly to preserve these rights. Descartes had hoped to be able to deduce the universe from a few central mathematical principles; Locke in his *Second Treatise of Government* assumed that he could deduce society and government from a few simple axioms about man and natural law.

This enthusiastic rationalism in the study of man and society was qualified

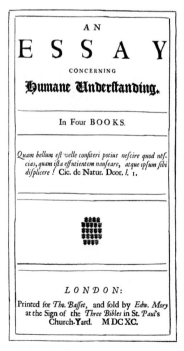

Title page of John Locke's *Essay Concerning Humane Understanding,* 1690.

by an undercurrent of empiricism, of respect for sense-experience. Here again Locke led the way in his *Essay Concerning the Human Understanding.* Many of its readers thought that it did for the study of man what Newton had done for the study of nature. Locke argued that all our ideas come from experience. The mind at birth is a *tabula rasa,* a clean slate, on which our sense-experiences gradually imprint conceptions. There are no "innate ideas," and no self-evident axioms (as Descartes had assumed). The mind and its ideas can be explained only by the outside forces that act upon it.

This was the purest empiricism. Locke hoped that it would provide a weapon for getting rid of all the superstitions and prejudices that cluttered men's minds, but it could destroy many things besides superstitions, including some of Locke's own doctrines. Logically, Locke's theory of the mind did away with original sin (which was held to be born into all men), with revelation (which did not come through the senses), with mathematical axioms, and with all "natural rights" (which were obviously innate and not based on experience). And so the rationalism of Locke's theory of society clashed with the empiricism of his theory of the mind—as the mathematical tendency clashed with the fact-finding tendency in seventeenth-century study of man in general. The eighteenth century was to inherit both: a strong faith in reason and natural law, together with a firm confidence in the value of sense-experience. Out of these two a new blend was to come in the "Enlightenment."

THE ENLIGHTENMENT

The task that the leading thinkers of the eighteenth century set themselves was to popularize the methods and principles of seventeenth-century natural science and

An assembly of *philosophes:* Voltaire (1), Adam (2), Abbé Maure (3), d'Alembert (4), Condorcet (5), Diderot (6), and Laharpe (7). Contemporary engraving by Jean Huber.

to apply these methods and principles to God, man, and society. Scientific discovery continued, but the work that attracted the most brilliant writers of the age was that of applying the new scientific methods to long-festering human ills—economic, social, political, and ecclesiastical. Their concern was not so much to discover new truth about nature as to use the methods of natural science to reform society.

The eighteenth century's own name for this movement was the "Enlightenment." This term suggested the dawn of an age of light after a long night of darkness—the darkness of ignorance, superstition, intolerance, and slavery to the past. This new light was the light of science, as the poet Alexander Pope suggested:

Nature and nature's laws lay hid in night;
God said, "Let Newton be," and all was light.

Although there were "enlightened" writers and readers in every country of Europe from Russia to Spain and from England to Italy, the movement was centered in France, and more particularly in Paris. There were good reasons for this. After the death of Louis XIV (1715) the French government became steadily more inept and ineffective, while the social tension between the privileged aristocracy and the less privileged, but powerful, wealthy middle class became more acute. Many leaders of the Enlightenment were of the middle class, and their writings often reflected middle-class interests. These men of letters were angered by bureaucratic stupidity and aristocratic arrogance; they wanted to get rid of privilege and obscurantism. They learned to write with clarity and wit so that they influenced not only their fellow-bourgeois but many members of the nobility as well. Government censors were either stupid or secretly in accord with critics of society. They could stop only the most blatant attacks; they were quite incapable of checking the criticism and satire that poured from the presses, particularly in the second half of the century.

For someone interested in ideas, Paris

Voltaire on Superstition

Almost everything that goes beyond the adoration of a Supreme Being and submission of the heart to his orders is superstition. One of the most dangerous is to believe that certain ceremonies entail the forgiveness of crimes. Do you believe that God will forget a murder you have committed if you bathe in a certain river, sacrifice a black sheep, or if someone says certain words over you? . . . Do better, miserable humans; have neither murders nor sacrifices of black sheep. . . .

Notice that the most superstitious ages have always been those of the most horrible crimes. . . . The superstitious man is ruled by fanatics and he becomes one himself. On the whole, the less superstition, the less fanaticism, and the less fanaticism, the fewer miseries.

Translated from Voltaire, *Dictionnaire philosophique* (Reproduction of edition of 1776. Paris: Editions de Cluny, n.d.), III, pp. 218–25.

was the most exciting place in Europe during the eighteenth century. Here the intellectuals were in close touch with one another, excited by the feeling that they were helping to guide a revolution of ideas without precedent in European history, and bound together in a crusade to put an end to all the barbarities and absurdities of the old order. Such an intellectual conspiracy could develop only in Paris, capital of the largest and most civilized state in Europe. Other countries were too small, too backward, or, in the case of England, too complacent to become major centers of "enlightened" thought and agitation.

Voltaire

As a movement the Enlightenment is often dated from Voltaire's visit to England (1726–29). Voltaire (1694–1778)—his real name was François Marie Arouet— became the central figure and moving spirit of the Enlightenment, in part at least as a result of this trip. He already had reason to dislike the old regime in France, having been imprisoned for a short time in the Bastille. In England he read Newton and Locke, and he sensed the relative freedom of English society compared with his own. After his return to France he published his *Philosophical Letters on the English* (1733), in which he passed on to his readers Newton's main principles in watered-down form, as well as Locke's theories of human nature and political freedom. He skillfully contrasted the rationality of Newton's method and the reasonableness of the English way of life with the more unreasonable aspects of church, state, and society in France.

These letters set the tone of "enlightened" propaganda in France for the next half-century or so. They were "philosophical"—that is to say, they reflected on the facts of life to discover their meaning and they searched constantly for general principles that might be useful to mankind as a whole. And so the men of the Enlightenment called themselves *philosophes*, observers of the human scene with breadth of view and a sense

of the practical. They were popularizers in the best sense of the word, crusaders for the application of the best intellectual tools of the century to the most vexatious social problems of their own day. Voltaire was the greatest of them—the most prolific, the wittiest, the most readable, and perhaps the angriest. His prime targets were religious intolerance, religious bigotry, and superstition. The close union in France of religious persecution and theological obscurantism with a capricious monarchical despotism exasperated him.

"Ecrasez l'infâme" (crush the infamous thing), he cried, in letters, pamphlets, stories, and satires. In an essay on "religion" he described a vision he had had of a desert covered with piles of bones, the bones of "Christians slaughtered by each other in metaphysical quarrels." He went on to report a "philosophical" conversation with the shades of Socrates and Jesus, who both deplored the spectacle he had just seen. And he attacked intolerance in his own day as vigorously as the barbarism of the past.

When Voltaire died in 1778, he was the literary dictator of Europe, the first writer to have made a fortune from the sale of his own writings. He was buried in Paris in a ceremony worthy of a king.

Montesquieu

Another leading figure of the Enlightenment, Montesquieu (1689–1755), tried to institute a "social science" by applying the methods of the natural sciences to the study of society. In *The Spirit of the Laws* (1748) he suggested that forms of government were related to climate and other environmental factors, and he tried to discover what form of government best fitted a given set of environmental conditions. The book was not "scientific" by later standards, but it was the first serious attempt to relate a civilization to its environment. (Voltaire later elaborated the concept in his *History of Civilization*, 1754.) Montesquieu, like Voltaire, was impressed by Locke's theories about the English constitution. As a French nobleman he wished to limit the excesses of royal absolutism. He concluded that the ideal political form was a separation and balance of powers

Historical Relativism in Montesquieu: The Effects of Climate and Geography

In Asia they have always had great empires; in Europe these could never exist. Asia has larger plains; it is cut out into much larger divisions by mountains and seas . . . and the rivers being not so large form more contrasted boundaries. Power in Asia, then, should be always despotic; for if their subjugation be not severe they would soon make a division inconsistent with the nature of the country.

In Europe natural divisions form many nations of moderate extent, in which ruling by laws is not incompatible with the maintenance of the state: on the contrary, it is so favorable to it that without this the state would fall into decay. It is this that has formed a genius for liberty that renders every part extremely difficult to be subdued and subjected to a foreign power. . . .

Africa is in a climate like that of the south of Asia and is in the same servitude. America, being lately destroyed and repeopled by the nations of Europe and Africa, can scarcely display its genuine spirit, but what we know of its history is very conformable to our principles. . . .

Monarchy is more frequently found in fertile countries and a republican government in those which are not so, and this is sometimes a sufficient compensation for the inconveniences they suffer by the sterility of the land. Thus the barrenness of the soil of Attica established a democracy there.

From Charles de Secondat de Montesquieu, *The Spirit of the Laws*, Book XVII, Chs. 6, 7; Book XVIII, Ch. 1 (in the Bohn Standard Library edition), Vol. I, pp. 289–91.

within government. This conclusion was to have great influence on the authors of the American Constitution.

Diderot
and the Encyclopedia

A third major figure of the Enlightenment was Denis Diderot (1713–84), co-editor of a huge *Encyclopedia* designed to sum up human knowledge and provide a kind of handbook of enlightened philosophy for the educated world. Diderot was an enthusiast for science, and he saw the relationship between science and technology more clearly than most of the *philosophes*. The plates showing machinery and industrial processes are one of the most remarkable features of the *Encyclopedia*. Diderot was also full of confidence in man and his abilities, a kind of prophet of a this-worldly religion of man. His interests were reflected in the titles and content of the *Encyclopedia*, which appeared in thirty-five volumes over the course of thirty years (1751–80). Much of the most trenchant writing of Diderot, Voltaire, and other *philosophes* was done in articles for the *Encyclopedia*. The book succeeded in becoming a bible of the "enlightened" everywhere. Through it ran faith in man's reason, pride in his accomplishments, contempt for his follies, and confidence in his future.

Leading Ideas
of the Enlightenment

There were many other leaders of the Enlightenment, but, rather than list names, it is more fruitful to outline the main ideas on which these people agreed and to sketch the relation of their ideas to religion and to social thought. These ruling ideas may be summed up in five words, each of which bore a heavy freight of meaning in the eighteenth century: reason, nature, happiness, progress, and liberty.

The eighteenth century believed as passionately in reason as the seventeenth, but with a difference. Voltaire's "reason" relied more on experience and less on mathematics than Descartes'. It was a weapon of skeptical inquiry based on observed facts (or what he thought were facts) rather than an instrument of deduction from axioms. To the men of the Enlightenment, reason was the alternative to superstition and prejudice; it was the only sure guide to the principles that governed man and nature. Man's reason could discover the fundamental rationality of the universe, and it could also make human society more sensible. The *philosophes*, as shown by their writing for the *Encyclopedia*, were less interested in "pure science" than in its applications, less concerned with system building than with specific reforms. Reason was now

A plate from Diderot's pictorial *Encyclopedia* illustrating different kinds of domestic spinning devices, from the clumsy spindle and distaff (fig. 1, at left) to the more productive treadle-operated spinning wheel (fig. 2).

a pragmatic instrument, applicable not only to astronomy and physics but to agriculture, government, and social relations as well.

"Nature" was one of the favorite words of the Enlightenment. It was not always clear just what the *philosophes* meant by it, but it was clear enough that to nearly all of them "nature" or "the natural" were the proper standards for measuring God and man. If a thing was according to "nature," it was reasonable and therefore good. Voltaire and his contemporaries brought the idea of natural law to the peak of its prestige and the beginning of its decline. One of them devised this definition of natural law:

> The regular and constant order of facts by which God rules the universe; the order which his wisdom presents to the sense and reason of men, to serve them as an equal and common rule of conduct, and to guide them, without distinction of race or sect, towards perfection and happiness.

There is order and law, then, throughout the universe—laws of economics, of politics, of morality, as well as of physics and astronomy. These laws can be discovered by reason. Men may ignore or defy them but they do so at their peril.

To the enlightened the way to happiness lay in conformity to nature and nature's laws. The man who broke nature's laws was looked on by the enlightened of the eighteenth century somewhat as the heretic who broke God's laws was looked on by the clergy in the Middle Ages, as a rebel against the order of the universe.

The end in view now was happiness, not salvation—happiness here in this world, not joy in the next. The Enlightenment was thoroughly secular in its thinking. When Jefferson included "the pursuit of happiness" along with life and liberty as an inalienable human right, he was expressing the general agreement of the enlightened. The tendency of medieval Christianity to ignore misery in this life because it would be compensated for in the next angered the *philosophes,* who insisted that Christian ideals, if they were worth anything at all, must be realized here and now. Voltaire and his fellows were humanitarians. They abominated torture and cruelty, slavery and the callous treatment of the insane. An Italian, Beccaria, was the first to point out that savage penalties do not stop crime and to demand more rational treatment of criminals. The *philosophes* were also cosmopolitan and even pacifist in temper. Some of the bitterest passages ever written about the insanity of war and the absurdity of blind patriotism were penned by Voltaire. The "happiness" that he and others talked about was often materialistic. But it corresponded closely with Christ's injunction to feed the hungry, clothe the naked, and visit the sick and imprisoned. To the enlightened this was far more important than saving anything so vague as one's own soul.

The *philosophes* were the first sizable group of educated Europeans to believe in progress. They took the older Christian idea of the spiritual progression of mankind from Creation through the Incarnation to the Last Judgment and secularized it. The progress of civilization, they believed, was now out of God's hands and in man's own. Once man had found the clue to discovering and using nature's laws in government, economics, and technology, progress was sure, inevitable, and swift. Both man and society were perfectible. Time was on man's

Key Words in History

If we would discover the little backstairs door that for any age serves as the secret entranceway to knowledge, we will do well to look for certain unobtrusive words with uncertain meanings that are permitted to slip off the tongue or the pen without fear and without research; words which, having from constant repetition lost their metaphorical significance, are unconsciously mistaken for objective realities. In the thirteenth century the key words would no doubt be *God, sin, grace, salvation, heaven,* and the like; in the nineteenth century, *matter, fact, matter-of-fact, evolution, progress;* in the twentieth century, *relativity, process, adjustment, function, complex.* In the eighteenth century the words without which no enlightened person could reach a restful conclusion were *nature, natural law, first cause, reason, sentiment, humanity, perfectibility.* In each age these magic words have their entrances and their exits. And how unobtrusively they come in and go out! We should scarcely be aware either of their approach or their departure, except for a slight feeling of discomfort, a shy self-consciousness in the use of them.

From Carl L. Becker, *The Heavenly City of the Eighteenth-Century Philosophers* (New Haven: Yale University Press, 1932), p. 47.

side, they thought, not against him or even indifferent to him.

This was a major revolution in western thought. The Middle Ages could not have conceived of purely secular progress unrelated to God. Men of the Renaissance still felt themselves inferior to the heroic Greeks and Romans. But in a literary battle between "ancients" and "moderns" that began in 1687 the idea appeared that the "moderns" were as good as, and probably better than, the "ancients." By 1750 a French *philosophe* and economist, Turgot, suggested that the essential element in history was man's slow struggle upward to his crucial discovery of the scientific method. In 1794 Condorcet, a mathematician under sentence of death during the French Revolution, wrote a *Sketch for a Historical Picture of the Progress of the Human Mind,* which summed up all the optimism of his century. He saw "the strongest reasons for believing that nature has set no limit to the realization of our hopes" and foresaw "the abolition of inequality between nations, the progress of equality within nations, and the true perfection of mankind." Progress, he concluded, was now "independent of any power that might wish to halt it" and "will never be reversed." The scientific method cannot be lost, scientific knowledge of natural law will accumulate, and so progress can never cease. It was an intoxicating vision, a vision shared by the vast majority of the enlightened.

All the French *philosophes* were concerned about liberty. They were acutely aware of the limitations on liberty that prevailed inside France: restrictions on freedom of speech, freedom of religion, freedom of trade, freedom to choose a job, and freedom from arbitrary arrest. Looking at England through slightly rose-colored glasses, they envied Englishmen their economic, political, and religious liberty. Their concern about liberty was potentially the most explosive part of their thinking, but almost none of them felt that violence was necessary. Their belief in liberty was tied to their belief in reason. Reason would soon reveal the true natural laws governing everything from trade and government to religion. The artificiality of French soci-

ety, French government, and French religious practices would become evident, and a benevolent despotism, enlightened by this knowledge, would set things right. Or so at least Voltaire and the majority of the Encyclopedists believed.

The Enlightenment and Religion

These ideas inevitably affected the religious thought of Europe. The fashionable belief among educated persons in the eighteenth century came to be Deism, the belief in a God who is Creator but not Redeemer. Like a watchmaker who designs and constructs a complicated piece of machinery to keep perfect time, so God created the universe and started it going and then stepped aside to let it run according to its natural laws. God does not concern Himself with redeeming men or society. The essence of religion is awe and reverence before the rationality and perfection of the universe—a feeling reflected in the hymns of Isaac Watts, which are still sung in many Protestant churches. To a Deist (Voltaire was a good example) all talk of revelation or miracle, all belief in the special intervention of God in the natural order, was false. All dogma and ritual were superstition, since man needed only his reason to understand God. The heart of natural religion was the morality common to all mankind. "Light is uniform for the star Sirius," Voltaire wrote, "and for us moral philosophy must be uniform." Obviously, Deism tended to undermine orthodox Christianity and to substitute for it a rational belief in God as First Cause and natural law as man's moral guide. A few of the French *philosophes* went further and pushed beyond Deism to atheism. Baron d'Holbach, for example, argued that there is nothing but matter in the universe, that man himself is a conglomeration of atoms, and that everything that happens is determined by natural law. But in the end many Protestants were able to find a compromise between Christian beliefs and the Enlightenment's rationalism, humanitarianism, and tolerance. The result in the nineteenth century was Protestant Liberalism.

Others reacted against Deism in the direction of more intense piety. To the enlightened, religious fervor of any sort savored of the fanaticism that had caused the wars of religion, and so all enthusiasm was frowned on. But Deism could be understood only by the educated, and its cold rationality had no appeal to emotional natures. Hence the wide popularity of two warmly emotional Protestant movements, Pietism in Germany and Methodism in England and America. Both emphasized the importance of inner religious experience, of individual "conversion." Pietism was a second and milder Protestant Reformation, directed this time not against the pope but against both the dogmatically orthodox and those who were inclined to Deism in Germany. Individualistic, tolerant, and unconcerned about creeds or ceremonies, the Pietists attracted followers among both Catholics and Protestants.

John Wesley (1703–91) was the leader of a somewhat parallel revival of a warm, personal Christian piety in England in the years following his conversion in 1738. Finding his efforts resisted by the respectable Anglican clergy, he took his message directly to the people, addressing huge congregations outdoors or in remote chapels, teaching them to sing their way to heaven with the hymns of his brother Charles, and sending out streams of pamphlets from his printing presses to the congregations he had established. In the end Wesley was forced to establish a new denomination outside the Anglican Church—the Methodist (originally a term of derision directed at the "methodical" piety of Wesley's followers). Methodism touched thousands upon thousands of Englishmen at home and in the colonies who cared nothing for the arid intellectualism of many of the Anglican clergy in the eighteenth century. More than one historian has suggested that it was Methodism that kept the English lower classes from turning to revolutionary violence during the first impact of the Industrial Revolution.

Social and Political Thought

The *philosophes* were interested in social and political problems, but they were reformers not revolutionists. Their formula for reform was simple: Discover by reason and experience the natural laws that should operate in any given situation, clear away all artificial obstacles to their operation, and the result will be progress toward happiness and freedom. The first "economists" in the modern sense used this formula to launch an attack on mercantilism. In 1758 François Quesnay published his *Economic Survey*, which argued for the existence of natural economic laws that must be allowed to operate freely. In 1776 the Scot Adam Smith published his *Wealth of Nations*, which argued in parallel fashion that all nations would be wealthier if they removed restrictions on trade and let the natural law of supply and demand govern the exchange of commodities. Quesnay was primarily interested in agriculture and Smith in commerce, but both came to the same conclusion: that economic laws, like other natural laws, should be respected, that interference

John Wesley preaching in a private house.

with these laws is dangerous, and that the greatest happiness and freedom come from allowing these laws to operate freely.

The same line of reasoning in political theory led to the theory of enlightened despotism. The *philosophes* hoped that divine-right monarchy would become benevolent monarchy, that monarchs would gradually become "enlightened" (or perhaps engage enlightened *philosophes* as advisers) and so govern their people according to natural law rather than according to their own caprice. To Voltaire and most of his fellows, government should be for the people but not necessarily by the people. A smaller group believed that reason pointed in the direction of a constitutional monarchy like the English, a government based on natural rights and contract, with a separation of powers as a further guarantee of political liberty. Finally, to enlightened despotism and constitutional government there was added a third theory, the theory of democracy, still too radical to be of much immediate influence but of enormous importance for the future. This was the theory obscurely but excitingly preached in *The Social Contract* (1762) by Jean Jacques Rousseau (1712–78).

Rousseau

Rousseau, a native of Geneva, turned up in Paris after a troubled and wandering youth, came to know Diderot and others of the *philosophes,* and for a time tried to become one of them. He was never easy in their company, however. He trusted reason, but he relied even more on emotion. He trusted nature, but to him nature was the unspoiled simplicity of precivilized man, "the noble savage." In a kind of conversion that he experienced in 1749, he became convinced that mankind had lost more than it had gained by cultivating the arts and sciences, and so he surrendered his faith in progress. He grew more and more irritated by the artificiality of Paris society and finally broke with his former friends. Voltaire thought him mad, and Rousseau was haunted in his miserable later years by the illusion that he was being persecuted by everyone.

Rousseau on the Social Contract

The problem is to find a form of association . . . in which each, while uniting himself with all, may still obey himself alone, and remain as free as before. This is the fundamental problem of which the Social Contract provides the solution: . . . the total alienation of each associate, together with all his rights, to the whole community. . . . Each man, in giving himself to all, gives himself to nobody. . . . Each of us puts his person and all his power in common under the supreme direction of the general will, and, in our corporate capacity, we receive each member as an indivisible part of the whole. . . . In order that the social compact may not be an empty formula, it tacitly includes the undertaking, which alone can give force to the rest, that whoever refuses to obey the general will shall be compelled to do so by the whole body. This means nothing less than that he will be forced to be free.

From Jean Jacques Rousseau, *The Social Contract* (New York and London: Everymans, 1913), Book I, Chs. 6, 7, pp. 14-18.

Rosseau was the great critic of the Enlightenment. By temperament he was a shy and sensitive misfit who vainly wanted "to belong." Deep down he knew himself to be good, but he felt that he had been corrupted and humiliated by an artificial society to which he did not and could not belong. To what kind of society or state could he give himself, then? Only to a society in which there were no hereditary rulers, no privileged aristocracy, no one with any right to lord it over others, none but those who had freely consented to become members of the society and had given up to the group all their individual rights. Perhaps Rousseau had an idealized Geneva in mind as he wrote *The Social Contract*—a community in which all the citizens knew and trusted each other—in which the minority accepted the majority's view with good grace because both felt themselves part of the same community. At any rate, he developed a theory of liberty as willing obedience to laws that the individual himself had helped to make as an active and loyal citizen, even though he might have been in the minority on any given issue. Locke and Montesquieu had thought that the way to obtain political liberty was to guarantee individual rights and to separate the organs of government so that no one of them could gain unrestricted control. Rousseau thought he would never feel free until he could find

Jean Jacques Rousseau.

a community to which he could give up everything, on condition that all others did the same. In such a community there would be no division between rulers and ruled; the people would rule themselves. What magistrates there were would be mere servants of the community who could be instantly removed if they failed to carry out the people's will. If the people really governed themselves there should be no checks and balances, no separation of powers, no protection of rights.

Rousseau was picturing democracy in its purest and simplest form: a tight-knit community of loyal and active citizens, unhampered by any checks on their collective will because they unreservedly accepted this general will as their own. His book was highly abstract and difficult to understand. But when revolution actually flared up in France after his death, *The Social Contract* came into its own. It was not a work of the Enlightenment; its full force could be felt only in the new age of democratic revolution, nationalism, and Romanticism. And when romantic nationalism reached its peak, Rousseau could be used to justify dictatorship (which after all is supposed to embody the common will) as well as democracy.

So the two centuries that saw the Scientific Revolution and the Enlightenment might well be called the most revolutionary centuries in western intellectual history. The true watershed between what we call "medieval" and "modern" thought about God, man, and nature runs somewhere through these two centuries. The world of Luther and Loyola, of Charles V and Philip II, was still organically related to the Middle Ages. The world of Newton and Locke, of Voltaire and Rousseau, was unmistakably the father of our own.

ARTS AND LETTERS IN THE EIGHTEENTH CENTURY

The pervasive faith in the rationality, intelligibility, and order of the universe displayed by the scientists and philosophers of the age was reflected in the art and literature of the later seventeenth and early eighteenth centuries. Rationalism blended easily with classicism. The regularity and harmony of Newton's universe seemed to accord with the balance and proportion that Greek architects had admired as artistic ideals and with the rationality and restraint that the leading Greek and Roman writers had held up as literary ideals. The dictators of literary and artistic taste at the close of the seventeenth century were classicists, and when *philosophes* like Voltaire wrote dramas they accepted classical standards as unquestioningly as Corneille and Racine. Architects accepted classical rules of balance and unity with equal zeal in the "Georgian" buildings of England and the beautifully proportioned Place de la Concorde in Paris. Enthusiasm for classical antiquity reached its post-Renaissance climax in 1748 when the remains of the Roman city of Pompeii were discovered in startlingly well-preserved condition under the lava of Mt. Vesuvius.

An Age of Prose

The age of reason was an age of prose. Essays, satirical tales, novels, letters, and histories were the characteristic literary forms of the eighteenth century. Authors bent their energies to description and narrative rather than to suggestion and imagination. The essays of Addison and Steele, which began to appear in 1709, sketched a delightful picture of English rural society, while Jonathan Swift's *Gulliver's Travels* (1726) and Voltaire's *Candide* (1759) were more biting and satirical commentaries on human society. As the century progressed, the novel emerged as the favorite form of literary expression; the most mature example was Henry Fielding's *Tom Jones* (1749). Besides fiction, men read philosophy, economics, and history—of which Edward Gibbon's majestic *History of the Decline and Fall of the Roman Empire* (1788) was the most enduring example. Everything that could be done in prose—argument, satire, realistic description, historical narrative—was tried and done well by some French or British writer.

The elegance and aristocratic flavor of eighteenth-century society can be seen in its painting, and especially in the portraits, which were the most characteristic form of the art. The delicate-featured and exquisitely groomed women who look coolly down on the observer, and the worldly, sometimes arrogant, faces of their husbands under their powdered wigs suggest the artificiality of their society and sometimes the hardness of their characters. Furniture, tableware, and the great town and country houses of wealthy merchants and nobles reflect the same elegance and aristocratic spirit.

Not all the books, the arts, and the crafts were meant for the enjoyment of the aristocracy, however. The eighteenth century saw the appearance of the first newspapers, written for a wide audience of educated readers. William Hogarth (1697–1764) made engravings of his realistic satirical sketches of English lower-class society and sold them by the thousands. Above all, the novelists, the dramatists, and the musicians began to appeal to a middle-class audience that went far beyond the limits of the aristocracy. After the 1770s the plays and operas in Paris were apt to have a keen, satirical edge and to be directed at bourgeois listeners. The heroes and heroines of the novels were more often of middle-class origins than either upper- or lower-class. Music began to move from the aristocratic salon into the public auditorium.

Music

The greatest cultural achievement of the eighteenth century was its music. The musical world of the early eighteenth century was dominated by two great Germans: Johann Sebastian Bach (1685–1750) and George Frederick Handel (1685–1759) (who spent most of his life in England). Together they realized all the dramatic and emotive possibilities of the baroque style: Handel in his oratorios for chorus and instruments, Bach in his richly varied works for keyboard instruments, chamber groups, orchestras, and choruses. In the latter part of the century the orchestra, which had originated in the seventeenth century, was expanded and strengthened, the pianoforte invented, and music brought more and more into touch with a wider public. Joseph Haydn (1732–1809), who wrote for both chamber groups and orchestras, developed the musical forms known as sonatas and symphonies. The other outstanding musical personality of the latter half of the century, Wolfgang Amadeus Mozart (1756–91), was possibly the most gifted musician who ever lived. An infant prodigy, he lived only thirty-five years and died in poverty, but within this short span of time he produced string quartets, concertos, symphonies, and operas that were masterpieces of invention and form.

The Beginnings of Romanticism

Beneath the dominant tendency to respect rational structure and classical balance, however, there were countercurrents of revolt. Some evidence of these currents was seen in Pietism and Methodism, and in Rousseau's distrust of an exclusive reliance on reason. More clearly than Rousseau, the Scottish philosopher David Hume (1711–76) criticized reason as a method of knowing truth and defended the validity in human experience of feeling, conscience, and habit. French and English novelists developed sentimentalism to a fine art, putting their heroines through heart-rending misfortune and mistreatment and trying at every turn to arouse the reader's anger, pity, love, or terror. The most influential example was Samuel Richardson's 2,000-page tear-jerker, *Clarissa Harlowe* (1748), which influenced Rousseau in writing his *Nouvelle Héloise* (1761). The strange, the unusual, the offbeat, and the fantastic began to come into fashion. Gothic architecture and literature began to be appreciated once more, and a collection of poems (1762) ostensibly by a medieval poet named Ossian was very popular, though it turned out to be a forgery.

In Germany, which never came totally under the sway of the French Enlightenment, a "Storm and Stress" movement in literature emphasized the great elemental emotions and denied the supremacy of reason. Johann Gottfried

Wolfgang Amadeus Mozart, unfinished painting by Joseph Lange.

von Herder (1744–1803) worked out a philosophy of history that emphasized the uniqueness and peculiarity of each nation or race, the individuality of its genius, and the falsity of any view that denied this uniqueness in the name of universal reason. Johann Wolfgang von Goethe (1749–1832) at the start of his long literary career published *The Sorrows of Young Werther* (1774), a morbid tale ending in a suicide, which appealed to lovers of sentiment and sensibility. The greatest philosopher of the age, Immanuel Kant (1724–1804), a man who never traveled more than a few miles from Königsberg, his native city in East Prussia, launched a powerful attack on the rationalism of his age as too narrow and too dogmatic. Starting from David Hume's criticism of reason, Kant distinguished carefully between speculative (or scientific) reason and practical (or moral) reason in his very difficult book, *Critique of Pure Reason* (1781). The effect of his work was to enable Christians and idealists to make a new case for religion and morality based upon the fact of man's conscience.

Taken together, these various tendencies heralded the beginnings of what was to be called Romanticism. The "Age of Reason" thus contained within itself the seeds of an age that would rely for its artistic, philosophical, and even social insight on emotion and conscience rather than on reason.

Suggestions for Further Reading

Note: Asterisk denotes a book available in paperback edition.

General   J. H. Randall, *The Making of the Modern Mind* (1926, 1940), is the most successful one-volume survey of the course of western thought, by a philosopher with a sense for historical context. To Randall, "the modern mind" is essentially the scientific mind. C. Brinton, *Ideas and Men* (1950)—the material since the Renaissance has been published as *The Shaping of the Modern Mind** (1953)—is a more informally written and engaging narrative by a historian. Both books are particularly good on the seventeenth and eighteenth centuries. P. Smith, *A History of Modern Culture, 1543–1776,** 2 vols. (1930–34), is full of fascinating material on everything from political theory and science to magic and witchcraft but does little to develop a synthesis. G. R. Sabine, *A History of Political Theory* (1938), is the most penetrating one-volume survey, particularly full on English political thought in the seventeenth century and French in the eighteenth. A. O. Lovejoy, *The Great Chain of Being** (1936), is a classic account of the underlying western conception of the universe as a hierarchical structure of being, from the Greeks to the nineteenth century. Maurice Ashley, *The Golden Century* (1968), is a well-written survey of seventeenth-century social and cultural history.

The Scientific Revolution   E. A. Burtt, *The Metaphysical Foundations of Modern Physical Science** (1924, 1955), and A. N. Whitehead, *Science and the Modern World** (1925, 1948), are famous philosophical inquiries into the origins of modern science, not easy reading, but rewarding to the serious student. A. R. Hall, *The Scientific Revolution** (1954), is the best modern account, well informed and critical. H. Butterfield, *The Origins of Modern Science, 1300–1800** (1949), is a more readable discussion of the subject for the lay reader written by a general historian. Alexandre Koyré writes absorbingly about the cosmological implications of the "revolution" in *From the Closed World to the Infinite Universe** (1957). C. C. Gillispie, *The Edge of Objectivity** (1960), is a brilliantly written essay on the growth of objectivity in the study of nature from Galileo to Einstein. R. G. Collingwood traces the chief western conceptions of the natural order from the Greeks to the present in *The Idea of Nature** (1945). C. J. Singer, *From Magic to Science** (1928), is still valuable for its interpretation of the origins of modern science. On the social background of scientific development, three books are particularly valuable: M. Ornstein, *The Role of Scientific Societies in the Seventeenth Century* (1928); D. Stimson, *Scientists and Amateurs: A History of the Royal Society* (1948); and G. N. Clark, *Science and Social Welfare* *in the Age of Newton* (1937). There are biographies and special studies, too numerous to list here, of every scientist mentioned in the text. But two studies of a famous case are worth noting: G. de Santillana, *The Crime of Galileo** (1955), and F. S. Taylor, *Galileo and the Freedom of Thought* (1938). The effect of scientific discovery on literature is the theme of M. Nicolson, *Science and Imagination** (1956).

Culture of the Seventeenth and Eighteenth Centuries

There is no full and reliable discussion in English on the baroque style in art, the basic studies being in German. The best introductions are in C. J. Friedrich, *The Age of the Baroque** (1952), and Chapter 6 of H. Leichtentritt, *Music, History, and Ideas* (1938). Friedrich's book, together with succeeding volumes in the *Rise of Modern Europe* series (see listings for Chapters 20 and 22), contain valuable accounts of literary and artistic movements in the two centuries. The Pelican *History of Art** has good studies of individual countries for the period 1600–1880. The latter third of G. N. Clark, *The Seventeenth Century* (1931), is devoted to art, literature, and philosophy. B. Willey's two volumes, *The Seventeenth Century Background** (1934) and *The Eighteenth Century Background** (1940), sketch a broad background for the study of English literature in the period. F. Fosca, *The Eighteenth Century* (1953), is probably the best introduction to the painting of the age. In addition to Leichtentritt (above), M. F. Bukofzer, *Music in the Baroque Era* (1947), is particularly interesting. There is no satisfactory general account of religious developments, but A. C. McGiffert, *Protestant Thought Before Kant* (1911), is a brief reliable account, and the various works of E. Troeltsch mentioned for Chapter 17 are always thought-provoking. M. J. Bradshaw, *The Philosophical Foundations of Faith* (1941), is illuminating on the religious attitudes of prominent seventeenth-century figures like Descartes. M. L. Edwards, *John Wesley and the Eighteenth Century* (1933), is one of many books on Methodism.

Contemporary Literature

The best way, as always, to gain a first-hand knowledge of the thought and feeling of the period is through a study of some of the paintings, the buildings, the literary and philosophical writings, and the musical works of the age. This becomes increasingly easy to do after the sixteenth century because of the availability of reproductions, records and cheap reprints. The student will have to make his own selection, but some of the following should be on any reading list (many editions of each except where specified): Descartes, *Discourse on Method;** Bacon, *New Atlantis;* Pascal, *Pensées;** Galileo, *Dialogue on the Great World Systems,* ed. by G. de Santillana (1953); John Bunyan, *The Pilgrim's Progress;** John Locke, *Second Treatise of Government** and *Essay Concerning Human Understanding;** *Selections from Bayle's Dictionary,* ed. by E. A. Beller and M. D. Lee (1952); Beccaria, *Essay on Crimes and Punishments** (trans. 1953); *The Portable Voltaire,** ed. by B. R. Redman (1949); Rousseau, *Social Contract;** Henry Fielding, *Tom Jones;** Samuel Richardson, *Clarissa* (abridgment, Modern Library, 1950). *The Portable Age of Reason Reader,** ed. by C. Brinton (1956), is an excellent selection of readings from the *philosophes.*

The Enlightenment

The most significant study of the transition from the seventeenth century to the eighteenth, from the Scientific Revolution to the Enlightenment, is P. Hazard, *The European Mind: The Critical Years, 1680–1715** (trans. 1952). There are excellent chapters on the Enlightenment in W. L. Dorn, *Competition for Empire** (1940), and in the *New Cambridge Modern History,* Vol. VII (1957), by A. Cobban. The most searching interpretation of the movement as a whole is E. Cassirer, *The Philosophy of the Enlightenment** (1932, trans. 1951), which emphasizes the break with older ways of thinking accomplished by the eighteenth century. C. L. Becker's charming lectures, *The Heavenly City of the Eighteenth-Century Philosophers** (1932), emphasize the continuity with the past. G. R. Havens, *The Age of Ideas: From Reaction to Revolution in Eighteenth-Century France** (1955), is a sound recent study. On the idea of progress, besides Becker, see J. B. Bury, *The Idea of Progress** (1920, 1932); R. F. Jones, *Ancients and Moderns** (1936); and C. Frankel, *The Faith of Reason: The Idea of Progress in the French Enlightenment* (1948). C. R. Cragg, *Reason and Authority in the Eighteenth Century* (1964), is an excellent account of the Enlightenment on the English side of the Channel, and D. Mornet, *French Thought in the Eighteenth Century* (1929), of enlightenment on the other. P. Gay, *The Enlightenment: An Interpretation** (1966–69), is an attempt to pull all aspects of the movement together. For the political thought of the *philosophes,* see K. Martin, *French Liberal Thought in the Eighteenth Century** (1929); and for the historical thought of Voltaire, Robertson, Hume, and Gibbon, see J. B. Black, *The Art of History* (1926).

Source of Illustrations

Index

Index

Ambrose, St., 114, 119

America: discovery of, 398–99 (*see also* Latin America; North America; United States of America)

American Civil War, 627–29

American colonies, 440–43, 508–10, 517–19

American Federation of Labor, 630, 730

American Revolution, 518–20

American Tragedy, An (Dreiser), 742

American War of Independence, 519–20, 588

Amiens Cathedral, 233

Amorites, 7, 11

Amos, 18, 19–20

Amsterdam, 365, 407

Anabaptists, 384, 385, 390, 405

anarchism, 591, 617, 662

Anaxagoras, 45

Andhra dynasty, 131

Angkor Wat, temple of, 323

Angles (*see* Anglo-Saxons)

Anglicanism, 385–87, 424, 425, 426, 427, 454, 459, 490

Anglo-Egyptian Sudan, 681

Anglo-French Entente, 689, 692

Anglo-German Heligoland Treaty, 687

Anglo-Russian Entente, 684, 689

Anglo-Saxon Chronicle, 200, 212

Anglo-Saxons, 115, 116, 143, 144, 152–53, 155, 188, 199–202

Angola, 816

Anjou, 235, 239

Anjou, Duke of, 406

Ankara, battle of, 316

Anna Comnena, quoted, 307

Annam, 323

Anne, Queen of England, 422, 458, 459, 501

Anne of Austria, 419, 421

Anschluss, 765–67

Anti-Comintern Pact, 760

Anti-Corn Law League, 566–67

Antigone (Sophocles), 44

Antigonus, King of Macedon, 51

Antioch, 52, 159, 305

anti-Semitism, 756, 758

Antoninus Pius, Roman Emperor, 87

Antony, Mark, 75–77

Antwerp, 365, 407

ANZUS treaty, 813

apartheid, 816

Apollinaris, Sidonius, quoted, 114

Apollonius of Rhodes, 52

Apology, The (Plato), 46

appeasement policy, 768

Apuleius, 95

Aquinas, St. Thomas, 250, 262–65, 293, 303, 353

Aquitaine, 156, 181, 267

Aquitaine, Duke of, 268

Arab Empire, 167–76, 301–05

Arab League, 814

Arabia, 168, 317

Arabic numerals, 132, 301

Arabs, 117, 735, 791, 813–14

Aragon, 367, 368, 402

Arakcheiev, Alexis, 556

Aramaeans, 16

Arcadius, Roman Emperor, 114–15

Arch of Constantine, 118

archbishops, 106, 373

Archimedes of Syracuse, 53, 123

architecture: Athenian, 42; Babylonian, 6; baroque, 449, 450, 451, 481; Christian, 120, 171–72, 221–22, 262, 291; Egyptian, 10–11, 15; 18th-century, 492; Flamboyant Gothic, 291; Gothic, 221–22, 232, 262–63, 291, 493; Greek, 31; Indian, 129, 328; Italian, 345; Moslem, 174, 303, 325; 19th-century, 743; Prussian, 515; Renaissance, 355, 356; Roman, 66, 92, 94, 161–62; Romanesque, 222; Turkish, 317; 20th-century, 743; U.S., 631

Argentina, 632

Arianism, 114, 144, 145, 155

Aristarchus of Samos, 53

aristocracy, 276; in 18th century, 497, 499, 503; feudal, 191–95; Greek, 32–33, 49; Roman, 58 (*see also* nobility; social classes)

Aristophanes, 44, 46

Aristotle, 46, 49, 53, 145, 167, 245, 247, 264, 293, 299, 300, 302, 353, 474, 478

arithmetic (*see* mathematics)

Arius, 108, 114

Arkwright, Richard, 573

Armenia, 173

Arminius (Herman), 81

Armstrong, Neil A., 827

army: Anglo-Saxon, 201; Arab, 303; Assyrian, 21; Byzantine, 303; English, 282, 284; feudal, 192; French, 366, 448, 449, 451, 533–34; Greek, 34; Persian, 24; Prussian, 465, 504, 506–07; Roman, 62–63, 80, 98–99, 103, 104, 109–10; Russian, 468, 498; Spartan, 37, 47; Swedish, 431; Swiss, 290

Arnold, Matthew, 671

Arouet, François Marie (*see* Voltaire)

art: Assyrian, 21–22; baroque, 480–81; Byzantine, 177, 299–300; Chinese, 136–37; Christian, 120; Etruscan, 57; Gothic, 233; Greek, 42; Hellenistic, 52; Indian, 129, 132–33, 323; Moslem, 317; Renais-

sance, 355–59; Roman, 66, 94–95, 117–18, 120 (*see also* painting; sculpture)

Arthasastra, 129

Articles of Confederation, 624

Artois, Charles Philippe, Count of, 528, 556 (*see also* Charles X, King of France)

Asia (*see* specific country)

Asia Minor, 12, 13, 17, 27–29, 64, 72, 124, 161, 166–67, 299, 304, 316

Asian and Pacific Council, 813

Asian-African conferences, 817

Asiento, 453

Asoka, King of Magadha, 128–30

Association of Southeast Asia, 813

Assyrian Empire, 16, 21–22

astrolabe, 395

astrology, 245

astronomy, 45, 96, 198, 245; Arabic, 168, 301; Indian, 132; in Middle Ages, 473, 474; 17th-century, 477, 478; 16th-century, 475

Aswan Dam, 813

atheism, 489

Athens, 24, 27, 35, 39, 48, 54, 57, 64, 70, 96; Golden Age, 40–46; Peloponnesian War, 46–47

Atlantic Charter, 785, 789

Atomic Energy Commission, 791

atomic weapons, 784–85, 791, 811, 828

Atoms for Peace Program, 829

Attila, King of the Huns, 116

Attlee, Clement, 787, 797

Augsburg, League of, 452

Augsburg, Peace of, 382, 393, 429

Augustenburg, Duke of, 607

Augustine, St. (Bishop of Hippo), 115, 119, 144, 449

Augustine, St. (of Canterbury), 153

Augustus, Roman Emperor, 79–83, 89

Augustus II, King of Poland (the Strong), 463

Aurelian, Roman Emperor, 100, 103

Auschwitz, 778

Ausgleich, 604, 617

Austerlitz, battle of, 539

Australia, 614, 633, 813

Austrasia, 156

Austria, 291, 402, 430, 659–61, 716; *Anschluss*, 765–67; Crimean War, 596, 598; in 18th-century, 454, 499, 504, 506–12, 515–17, 532, 533; Italian War, 601–02, 606; Napoleonic Wars, 536, 538–39, 541; in 19th-century, 546, 549, 554, 555, 557, 559, 562–66, 568, 596, 601–04, 606–09, 612, 674, 675–78, 687; postwar (1919–1939), 727–28, 731, 755, 759; in 17th century, 438, 463–64, 470;

Charlemagne, 156, 182–87, 192, 301
Charles I, Emperor of Austria, 660, 703, 708
Charles I, King of England, 424, 425–26, 428, 430
Charles I, King of France, 187
Charles II, King of England, 427, 455
Charles II, King of Spain, 452–53
Charles III, King of Spain, 512
Charles IV, Holy Roman Emperor, 361
Charles V, Holy Roman Emperor, 367–68, 370, 379, 381, 386, 402, 405
Charles V, King of France, 288
Charles VI, Holy Roman Emperor, 504
Charles VI, King of France, 285, 366
Charles VII, King of France, 285, 288–89, 366
Charles VIII, King of France, 366
Charles IX, King of France, 411
Charles X, King of France, 557
Charles XII, King of Sweden, 466, 468
Charles Albert, King of Sardinia, 562–63
Charles of Anjou, 261, 366
Charles the Bold, Duke of Burgundy, 366
Charles the Great (see Charlemagne)
Charles Martel, 156, 176, 179, 180, 181, 192
Charles of Orléans, 292
Charlotte, Grand Duchess of Luxembourg, 801
Charter Oath, 641
Chartist Movement, 567
Chartist Petition of 1848, 566
Chartres Cathedral, 233
Chaucer, Geoffrey, 266, 282, 292, 293, 355
Chavez, Cesar, 830
Cheap Clothes and Nasty (Kingsley), 590–91
Cheka, 747
Chiang Kai-shek, 737, 738, 765, 793
child labor, 577, 578, 582
Chile, 632, 807
Chilperic I, King of the Franks, 147
Ch'in, 137
Chin dynasty, 334
China, 3, 248, 444, 715; ancient, 123–24, 133–41; Chou dynasty, 134–37; Confucianism, 135–36; exploration, 295, 395; First World War, 711; Han dynasty, 137, 139–41, 330; Manchu dynasty, 636, 638, 640; Ming dynasty, 339; Mongols in, 310–12, 336–38; in 19th century, 614, 621, 636–39; nomad rulers, 140–41; Opium War,

636–37; postwar (1919–1939), 737–38, 760, 764–65, 779; revolution of 1911, 640; science in, 293, 294; Shang dynasty, 134; Sino-Japanese War, 638–39, 642, 688; Sui dynasty, 329; Sung dynasty, 310, 334–36; Taiping Rebellion, 638; T'ang dynasty, 329–34 (*see also* Nationalist China; People's Republic of China)
Chola kingdom, 322
Chou dynasty, 134–37
Chou En-Lai, 821
Christian Democratic Party, Italian, 801
Christian Democratic Union, German, 800
Christian Socialism, 590–91, 652
Christianity, 18, 117, 159; beginnings of, 89–91; in China, 338; doctrine of the Trinity, 108; early organization of, 106; Islam and, 172; in Japan, 341; Mongols and, 311–12; Monophysitism, 164; neoplatonism and, 96; in Roman Empire, 100, 104, 106–09, 112; spread of, 140, 214; Zoroastrianism and, 24 (*see also* names of religions)
Chronicle of Moissac (tr. Bryce), 185
Chu Hsi, 334, 339
Chu Teh, 737
Chuang Tzu, quoted, 136
churches (*see* architecture, Christian; cathedrals)
Churchill, Sir Winston, 774, 782, 785, 787, 797; quoted, 776
Cicero, Marcus Tullius, 71–72, 75, 76, 82, 96, 350, 351, 483
Cid, Le (Corneille), 450
Cimon, 42
Cistercian Order, 219
cities (*see* city-states; towns; urbanization)
City of God, The (St. Augustine), 115, 119
city-states: Greek, 33–35, 46–49; Italian, 346–48; Mesopotamian, 6–8; Philistine, 16; Roman, 88
Civil Constitution of the Clergy, 530
Civil Rights Act of 1964, 804
civil service: in China, 330, 335, 336, 339; in Roman Empire, 87
civil war: American, 627–29; in China, 140, 737, 765; in England, 285, 368, 426; in France, 288, 411–13; in Greece, 789, 791; in India, 133; in Netherlands, 406; in Nigeria, 816; in Pakistan, 811; in Roman Republic, 74; in Russia (15th century), 315; in Spain, 762–64; in U.S.S.R., 748

Civilization of the Renaissance in Italy, The (Burckhardt), 352
Clarendon, Edward Hyde, Earl of, 455, 456
Clarendon Code, 455
Clarissa Harlowe (Richardson), 493
Clark Memorandum, 737
classical economists, 580–81
classicism, 492
Claudius, Roman Emperor, 84–85
Cleisthenes, 38
Clemenceau, Georges, 655, 703, 709, 710
Clement V, Pope, 271, 272
Clement VII, Pope, 278, 363, 385, 386
Cleopatra, Queen of Egypt, 76, 77
clergy, 249; appointment of, 369–70; bourgeoisie and, 230; Charlemagne and, 183, 184, 186; in 16th century, 373–74; taxation of, 243, 254, 261, 262, 270, 369–70 (*see also* bishops)
Clermont, Council of, 217
Cleveland, Grover, 685
Cleves, 464
Clive, Robert, 509
clock, invention of, 295
Clouds, The (Aristophanes), 44
Clovis, King of the Franks, 154–55
Cluny, 214, 219
Cobden–Chevalier treaty, 599
Code (Justinian), 165
Code of Hammurabi, 7
Code Napoléon, 537, 540
coexistence, 796, 817, 818, 821, 829
coinage: invention of, 30; Roman, 118
Colbert, Jean Baptiste, 442, 448
Cold War, 796–97, 803, 810, 817–21; beginnings of, 789–90; in Far East, 792–93; United Nations and, 791
Coligny, Gaspard de, 411, 412
collectivization, 751
Colombia, 686
Colombo Plan for Cooperative Development, 813
Colonial Reformers, 633
colonies: Belgian, 681, 815; British, 439–43, 502, 508–10, 517–19, 633–35, 679–82, 684, 687–88, 737, 798, 816; Dutch, 439–41, 681; French, 439–42, 508, 509, 599–600, 679–81, 684, 736, 798–99; German, 679, 684, 710; Greek, 30; Italian, 681; in North America, 440–43, 502, 508–10, 517–19; Portuguese, 439–40, 443, 816; Russian, 443–44, 683–84; Spanish, 439–40, 555; U.S., 684–86, 737 (*see also* imperialism)
Colosseum, Rome, 92, 94
Columban, St., 155
Columbus, Christopher, 293, 363, 368, 398

Fort Duquesne, 509
Fort Sumter, 627
Fourier, Charles, 585, 586
"Fourteen Points," 708, 709, 710, 713
Fourth Crusade, 307–08
France, 144, 229, 295; American War of Independence, 519–20; Capetian dynasty, 191; Congress of Vienna and, 546; Crimean War, 596, 597, 599; in 18th century, 499–503, 507–11, 517, 519–20; Enlightenment, 485–87; feudalism, 191–95, 209; First World War, 694–95, 699–704, 707, 709–12; in 14th and 15th centuries, 271–72, 287–89, 366; Franco-Prussian War, 609–12, 656; Hundred Years' War, 281–82, 288–89, 366; India and, 328; under Louis XIV, 447–54; mercantilism, 438; in Mexico, 628; under Napoleon I, 536–42, 598–603; under Napoleon III, 609; in 19th century, 546, 555–57, 559, 560, 568, 574, 576, 582, 584–85, 595–603, 609–12, 628–29, 639, 651–52, 655–57, 677–81; postwar (1919–1939), 716–21, 725–26, 728–29, 731, 733, 761, 762, 765, 767–69; postwar (1945–1973), 786, 790, 798–800, 813, 818, 819, 829, 830; religious wars in, 411–13; Second World War, 773–75, 781; in 17th century, 417–22, 438, 447–52, 470; in 16th century, 411–13; in 13th century, 254–56, 268–70; Thirty Years' War, 432–33; towns, 208, 209; in 12th century, 238–40; in 20th century, 656–57, 688–91; War of the League of Augsburg, 452; War of the Spanish Succession, 453–54 (see also French Republic; French Revolution)
Franche-Comté, 451
Francis, St., 249
Francis I, Emperor of Austria, 549
Francis I, King of France, 370
Francis II, King of France, 411
Francis Ferdinand, Archduke of Austria, 660, 661, 693, 694
Francis Joseph I, Emperor of Austria, 564, 602, 604, 660, 703
Franciscan Order, 249–50, 252, 254, 264, 400, 473
Franco, Francisco, 759, 763–64
François de Sales, St., 482
François-Poncet, André, quoted, 756
Franconia, 195
Franco-Prussian War, 609–12, 656
Franco-Russian Alliance, 687
Frankfurt Constitution, 566

Franks, 116, 143, 152, 175–76; Carolingian Empire, collapse of, 187–91; Charlemagne and, 182–87; invasions against, 188–89, 191; papacy and, 179–81; rise of, 153–56
Fredegonda, Queen of the Franks, 147
Frederick, Elector of Saxony, 379
Frederick I, Holy Roman Emperor (Barbarossa), 240–42, 278, 306
Frederick I, King of Prussia, 466
Frederick II, Holy Roman Emperor, 243, 255, 259–62
Frederick II, King of Prussia (the Great), 504, 506–11, 512, 514–15
Frederick V, Elector of the Palatinate, 429, 430
Frederick William, Elector of Brandenburg (the Great Elector), 464–66
Frederick William I, King of Prussia, 504, 506
Frederick William III, King of Prussia, 539, 546, 549
Frederick William IV, King of Prussia, 565–66, 604, 606
Free Democratic Party (FDP), 800
French Community, 799
French East India Company, 439, 508, 509
French Indochina, 600, 812
French Republic: First, 532–46; Second, 561–62; Third, 647, 655–57, 733–34; Fourth, 798–99; Fifth, 799
French Revolution: 1789–1799, 522–36, 545, 550, 552, 588; 1830, 556–57
French Union, 799
Frescobaldi, Girolamo, 481
Freud, Sigmund, 740, 743
friars, 249–50 (see also monasticism)
Friedland, battle of, 539
Friedrich, Caspar David, 550
Frisia, 181
Frisians, 155
Fronde, 421, 426, 448, 449
Fugger, Jakob, 365
Fulcher of Chartres, 218
Fulton, Robert, 575
functionalism, 743
fundamentalism, 669

G

Gadsden Purchase, 625
Gagarin, Yuri, 827
Galbert of Bruges, 191
Galen, 96, 474
Galicia, 155, 513, 563, 702, 703, 705
Galilee, 88

Galileo Galilei, 264, 293, 294, 473, 477–79, 481
Gama, Vasco da, 363, 397, 399
Gambetta, Léon, 600
Gandhi, Indira, 810, 811
Gandhi, Mohandas K., 736, 810
Ganges Valley, 320
Gapon, Georgy Father, 664
Garibaldi, Giuseppe, 563, 602–03
Gasperi, Alcide de, 801
Gastein, Convention of, 607
Gaul, 60, 61, 80, 100, 116, 143, 153–54; Roman conquest of, 73–74, 88
Gaulle, Charles de, 798, 799
General Italian Federation of Labor, 652
Geneva Summit Conference, 818
Genghis Khan, 310, 313, 336
Genoa, 207, 229, 546
Gentile, Giovanni, 755
George, Henry, 632
George I, King of England, 502
George II, King of England, 502, 508
George III, King of England, 511, 512, 519
George IV, King of England, 558
Gerbert (see Sylvester II, Pope)
German Confederation, 546, 547, 565, 606, 607
German Democratic Republic (see East Germany)
German Federal Republic (see West Germany)
Germanic kingdoms, 142–56, 160; Carolingian dynasty, 156; Franks, rise of, 153–56; judicial system, 146–48; migrations, 115–16; Ostrogothic kingdom in Italy, 144–46; Roman Catholic Church in, 149–52; Romans and, 81, 87, 98, 109, 113–14; social classes, 146
German-Roman Empire (see Holy Roman Empire)
Germany, 60, 229, 454, 652, 659; in 11th century, 202; in 15th century, 289, 291; First World War, 694–95, 699–712, 748; in 14th century, 289–90; 1900–1913, 688–91; in 19th century, 546, 559, 568, 574, 576, 584, 606, 608–12, 618, 639, 657–59, 675–79, 684, 687, 688; Ottonian Empire, 196–99; papal-Hohenstaufen feud, 259–62; postwar (1919–1939), 713–21, 725–27, 731, 732, 755–59, 761–69; postwar (1945–1973), 786–88; Roman Catholic Church in, 216–17; Second World War, 773–78, 781–83; in 17th century, 429–33, 435; in 10th

P

Pacification of Ghent, 406
Pact of Steel, 769
painting: baroque, 481; Chinese, 335; Christian, 120; Dutch, 414; 18th-century, 493; Flemish school, 293; Impressionism, 671; Indian, 129, 133; Italian, 300, 345; Japanese, 340; medieval, 293; Renaissance, 355–59; Romantic, 550; 17th-century, 414; 16th-century, 414; Spanish, 414; 20th-century, 743; U.S., 631
Pakistan, 325, 791, 810–11, 813, 814
Palestine, 4, 6, 13, 14, 15, 72, 596, 791, 814; Arabic conquest of, 173; Balfour Declaration, 735; Hebrew conquest of, 18–19; Persian Empire, 23
Palmer, R. R., quoted, 499, 512
Panama, 686
Panama Canal, 686
Panama Scandal, 655, 656
Pan-American Conference (1889), 631
Panchatantra, 132
pan-Germanism, 756, 768
panics of 1873 and 1893, 630
Panipat, battles at, 325, 326
Pan-Slav Congress, 563
pantheism, 126
Pantheon, Rome, 94
papacy: Anagni, assault at, 271; authority, 112, 151, 242–44, 360; Babylonian captivity, 22, 272, 344; conciliar movement, 360–61, 362; English break with, 386–87; Franks and, 179–81, 184–85; Great Schism, 359–60; Hohenstaufens, feud with, 257, 259–62; Holy Roman Empire and, 196–97; independence of, 215–17; monarchy and, 179–81, 215–17, 362, 369–70; prestige of, 272; Renaissance, 362–63, 373; in 16th century, 388; in 12th and 13th centuries, 242–44, 271–72; in 20th century, 754
Papal States, 243, 260, 262, 272, 278, 347, 373, 549, 554, 603
paper, invention of, 332
Papinian, 99
Paradise Lost (Milton), 481
Parallel Lives of Famous Greeks and Romans (Plutarch), 96
Pareto, Vilfredo, 740–41, 755
Paris: in 18th century, 485; in French Revolution, 527, 529; Peace Conference (1856), 596–97, 601; Peace Conference (1919), 709–11; Peace Conference (1946), 787; Peace of (1763), 511; University of, 247, 411, 473, 474

Paris Commune, 533, 611, 650, 651, 656
parishes, 182
Parkman, Francis, 621
parlements, 255–56, 411, 447, 503, 517
Parliament, English: cabinet system, 458–59; Cavalier, 455; under Cromwell, 427; development of, 287; early, 258–59; in 14th century, 287; Long, 425–26, 427; Model Parliament, 268; monarchy and, 369; in 19th century, 558; in 17th century, 454–60; under Stuarts, 424–26; in 13th century, 267–68; under Tudors, 423–24
Parliament Bill of 1911, 653
Parma, Alessandro Farnese, Duke of, 406, 410, 413
Parmenides, 48
Parnell, Charles, 653
Parthenon, 42
Parthians, 74, 76, 80–81, 87, 98
Pascal, Blaise, 414, 476, 477, 480, 482
Pashitch, Nicholas, 694
Past and Present (Carlyle), 590
Paston, John, 276
Paston, Margaret, quoted, 276
Patay, battle of, 285
patricians, 58
patronage, 624
Paul, St., 90
Pavlov, Ivan, 740
Peace of God, 214, 218
Pearl Harbor, 779
peasants, 205–06, 254, 373, 462; Austrian, 516, 563; Chinese, 140, 330; Egyptian, 9; English, 201; under feudalism, 193–95; French, 523, 524, 527, 528, 534, 599; German, 565; Greek, 32–33; Indian, 323–24; Polish, 467; Prussian, 465, 515; rebellions of, 277, 280, 283, 288, 380–81, 560; Roman, 110, 111; Russian, 313–14, 469, 470, 512–13, 615, 616–17
Peasants' Rebellion of 1381, 280, 283
Peasants' Rebellion of 1524–25, 380–81
Pechenegs, 311
Peking, 638
Peloponnesian League, 37, 38, 40, 47
Peloponnesian War, 46–47
People's Party, U.S., 631
People's Republic of China, 787, 792, 793, 799. 807, 809–13, 818, 819, 821, 829, 830
Pepys, Samuel, quoted, 456
Pergamum, Kingdom of, 51, 52
Pericles, 41–42, 45, 47
Permanent Court of International Arbitration, 686
Perry, Matthew, 341, 640

Pershing, John J., 707
Persia, 4, 51, 54, 109, 174, 176, 683, 684; Arabic conquest of, 173; Mongols in, 311
Persian Empire, 8, 22–24, 26, 40, 46, 98, 161, 165–66
Persian Wars, 37–40, 44–45
Peru, 400, 632
Pescadores Islands, 639
Pétain, Henri Philippe, 702, 774
Peter, St., 90
Peter I, Tsar (the Great), 468–70, 504, 513
Peter III, Tsar, 511, 512
Peterloo Massacre, 550
Petition of Right, 425
Petrarch, Francesco, 350, 352; quoted, 351
Petrograd Soviet of Workers' and Soldiers' Deputies, 705, 706
Petronius, 95
phalanges, 585, 586
pharaohs, 9–11, 15
Pharisees, 89–90
Pharsalia (Lucan), 95
Pharsalus, battle of, 74
Phidias, 42
Philip, King of Macedon, 49–50
Philip I, King of Spain, 367
Philip II, King of France (Augustus), 237, 239–40, 254, 306, 307
Philip II, King of Spain, 381, 387, 388, 402–05, 408–10, 412
Philip IV, King of France (the Fair), 268–71
Philip V, King of Spain, 453–54, 503
Philip VI, King of France, 288
Philip of Hohenstaufen, 243
Philippines, 684, 686, 737, 783, 812, 813
Philistines, 16, 19
philology, 482
philosophes, 486, 487, 488, 490, 491, 529, 550, 578, 586, 589
Philosophical Letters on the English (Voltaire), 485–86
Philosophical Radicals, 579, 582
philosophy, 293; Arabic, 301, 302–03; Byzantine Empire, 299; Chinese, 134–36, 334; Christian, 262–64; 18th-century, 493, 494; Enlightenment, 487–89; 14th-century, 318; Greek, 44, 45–46, 48; Hellenistic Era, 53; Indian, 126; 19th-century, 577–81, 665; Roman, 96; 17th-century, 481–84; 13th-century, 262–64; 20th-century, 831
Philotheus of Pskov, Abbot, quoted, 315
Phoenician alphabet, 17, 31, 168
Phoenicians, 16–17; Assyrian conquest of, 21; Persian Empire, 23

physics, 245, 264, 293; Arabic, 301; in Middle Ages, 473, 474; 17th-century, 477–78; 20th-century, 742 (*see also* mathematics; science)

Physics and Politics: Thoughts on the Application of the Principles of Natural Selection and Inheritance to Political Science (Bagehot), 667

picketing, 584

Picasso, Pablo, painting by, 743

Pico della Mirandola, Giovanni, 353, 357, 359

pictographs, 134

Piedmont-Sardinia, 64, 454, 546, 549, 556, 562–63, 596, 601–03

Pietism, 482, 490, 493

Pilate, Pontius, 90

Pillnitz, Declaration of, 532

Pilsudski, Joseph, 727

Pippin II, 156

Pippin III, 179–82, 192

Pirandello, Luigi, 743

Pisa, 207, 229

Pissaro, Camille, 671

Pitt, William, 510, 511

Pitt, William (the Younger), 538

Pius II, Pope, 362

Pius VII, Pope, 537, 549

Pius IX, Pope, 562, 563, 669

Pizarro, Francisco, 400

Place de la Concorde, Paris, 492

plague, 275, 280

Plan XVII, 700

Planck, Max, 742

Plataea, battle at, 39

Plato, 46, 48, 96, 167, 299, 300, 353

Platonic Academy, 353

Platt Amendment, 686

Plautus, 66

plebeians, 58, 59–60

Plehve, Vyacheslav, 662

Plekhanov, Georgi V., 663

Pliny the Younger, 87, 95–96

Plombières agreement, 601, 602, 607

Plutarch, 75, 96

Plymouth, Massachusetts, 442

Pobedonostsev, Constantine, 662

Poe, Edgar Allan, 621

poetry: Byzantine, 299; Chinese, 333; Greek, 31; Latin, 82; medieval, 233–34, 264–65; Roman, 95 (*see also* literature)

Poincaré, Raymond, 694, 717, 725, 726

Poitiers, battle at, 176

Poitou, 239

Poland, 229, 422, 462, 716, 727, 821; in 18th century, 504, 513–14; First World War, 702, 712; in 14th century, 312–13; in 19th century, 546, 558, 559; partitions of, 513–14; postwar (1919–1939), 748, 759, 761,

786, 787; postwar (1945–1973), 789, 808–09; Second World War, 769, 773; in 17th century, 466

Polignac, Prince Auguste Jules de, 557

Politburo, 750

political theory: 18th-century, 490–91; Renaissance, 354; 17th-century, 428 (*see also* Marxism)

pollution, 826

Polo, Marco, 312; quoted, 338

Polybius, 56

polycentrism, 821

Polyptique de l'Abbe Irminon (ed. Guerard), 192

Pomerania, 465

Pompadour, Mme. de, 503, 509

Pompeii, 3, 492

Pompey, 71, 72, 74

Pompidou, Georges, 800

Pontiac, 518

Poor Law, 583

Pope, Alexander, quoted, 485

popes (*see* papacy)

Popish Plot, 456–57

"Popular Front," French, 734

population: growth of, 205, 577, 796; Malthus on, 580–81; Roman, 91; in 20th century, 825–26, 829

Populists, 631, 684

Port Arthur, 639, 787

Portsmouth, Treaty of, 642, 686

Portugal, 328, 339, 367, 432, 759, 790, 814, 816–17; colonization by, 439, 443; in 18th century, 533; exploration by, 295, 396–98; mercantilism, 438; in 19th century, 554, 555

Portuguese Guinea, 816

positivism, 665

Poteidaea, 47

Potsdam Conference, 785, 787, 788

power loom, 573

Pragmatic Sanction of Bourges, 362, 366, 369, 504, 507

pragmatism, 632

prehistoric man, 3–5

Presbyterianism, 383, 424, 426, 455, 460, 461

Prescott, William H., 621

priests (*see* clergy)

Prince, The (Machiavelli), 354, 355

Princip, Gavrilo, 694

Principles of Geology (Lyell), 666

printing: Chinese, 332–33; 15th-century, 364; invention of, 295; movable type, 333

Progress and Poverty (George), 632

Progressive Party: German, 658; U.S., 684

prohibition, 730

protectionism, 630, 654, 661, 721

Protestant Liberalism, 489

Protestant Reformation, 363, 370, 388; in England, 385–87; in Germany, 378–82; radicals in, 384–85; significance of, 389–90; in Switzerland, 382–83

Protestant Union, 429, 430

Protestantism, 387, 390; Louis XIV and, 449–50; science and, 669; Thirty Years' War, 429–33 (*see also* Calvinism; Lutheranism; Methodism; Presbyterianism; Protestant Reformation)

Proudhon, Pierre-Joseph, 591

Proust, Marcel, 742

Provence, 187

Prussia, 229, 454, 462, 546; Crimean War, 596, 598; in 18th century, 499, 504, 506–11, 514–15, 532, 533; Franco-Prussian War, 609–12; mercantilism, 438; Napoleonic Wars, 536, 538–39, 540–41; in 19th century, 549, 559, 565–66, 582, 596, 598, 604–12, 657; in 17th century, 466, 470; War of 1866, 607–09

psychoanalysis, 740

psychology, 740, 743

Ptolemy, astronomer, 96, 396, 474, 478

Ptolemy I, King of Egypt, 51

Puerto Rico, 686

Pugachev, Emelyan, 512

Pullman strike of 1894, 631

Punic Wars, 63–64

Punjabis, 811

Purcell, Henry, 481

Puritan Rebellion, 425–26, 461

Puritanism, 383, 387, 424, 455, 459, 482

putting-out system, 435, 571, 574

pyramids, 9, 10, 15

Pyrenees, Peace of the, 433, 447

Pyrrhus, King of Epirus, 61, 62

Pythagoras, 45

Q

Quadruple Alliance, 548

Quakers, 384, 385, 455

Quebec, 633

Quebec Act of 1774, 519

Quebec Conference, 785

Quemoy, 819

Quesnay, François, 490

Qur'an (*see* Koran)

R

Racconigi Agreement, 691

Rachmaninov, Sergei, 743

racialism, 668, 747

Racine, Jean, 450, 481, 492

Radetzky, Joseph, 563

Radical Protestantism, 384–85

Radical Socialist Party, French, 734
radium, isolation of, 669
railroads, 574–76, 613, 630, 662–63
Rajputs, 320, 322, 326, 327
Raleigh, Sir Walter, 440
Ramayana, 126
Ramillies, battle of, 453
Rapallo, Treaty of, 717
Raphael, 359
Rasputin, Gregory, 664, 665, 703
rationalism, 263–64, 483–84, 492, 545, 550, 554
realism, 292, 293, 355–56, 670
Realpolitik, 603, 605, 675, 676
reason, 45, 483, 487–88, 489, 494, 743
rebellion: Boxer, 639, 686; Indian, 634–35; of Moriscoes, 404; of peasants, 277, 280, 283, 288, 380–81, 560; Puritan, 425–26, 461; of Russian *streltsi,* 468; Satsuma, 641 (*see also* civil war; revolution)
Reconquista, 367
Reconstruction Acts, 629
Redistribution Bill, 653
Reed, John, quoted, 706
Reflections on the Revolution in France (Burke), 531, 553
Reform Act of 1867, 653
Reform Bill of 1832 (*see* Great Reform Bill of 1832)
Reformation (*see* Catholic Reformation; Protestant Reformation)
Reformed Church, 383
Regulation Act of 1773, 634
Reichsrat, 604, 659, 756–57
Reichstag, 608, 657, 658
"Reign of Terror," 534–35
Reinsurance Treaty, 678, 687
relativity, theory of, 669, 742
religion: Babylonian, 8; Chinese (*see* Buddhism; Confucianism; Taoism); Christian (*see* Christianity); Darwinism and, 668–69; Egyptian, 9–10, 15; Enlightenment and, 489–90; Etruscan, 57; Greek, 35–37, 43, 65–66; Hebrew, 17–21; Hellenistic Era, 53–54; Indian (*see* Buddhism; Hinduism); Japanese, 340, 641; mystery, 53–54, 104–06; in 19th century, 668; Persian, 23; Roman, 65–66, 96, 100, 104–09; Romanticism and, 551; science and, 479–80; in 20th century, 831; Zoroastrianism and, 23–24 (*see also* Greek Orthodox Church; Islam; Protestant Reformation; Protestantism; Roman Catholic Church)
religious toleration, 327, 390, 413, 458, 459, 516
Rembrandt van Rijn, 414, 481
Remembrance of Things Past (Proust), 742

Remus, 58
Renaissance, 352–59; of 12th century, 219–25
Renan, Ernest, 667, 669
Renoir, Auguste, 671
reparations, 710–11, 718, 720–21, 729, 787
Report on the Affairs of British North America (Durham), 633
Republic (Plato), 48–49
Republic, The (Bodin), 417
Republican Party, U.S., 626, 733
Rerum novarum (Leo XIII), 652
Restoration, 427–29
Reuchlin, Johann, 376–77
Reuter, Julius, 575
revisionism, 649–50
revivalism, 350
revolt (*see* rebellion; revolution)
Revolt of the Masses, The (Ortega y Gasset), 739
revolution: American, 518–20; Chinese, 640; 1820–1829, 545, 549, 554–56; 1830–1833, 556–59; 1848–1849, 559–68; French (*see* French Revolution); Glorious, 457–62, 470; Hungarian, 808–09, 819; Polish, 808; Russian (1905), 663–64; Russian (1917), 704–07; theory of, 665–67, 669; Turkish, 690
Rhee, Syngman, 793, 813
Rhineland, 710, 761
Rhodes, Cecil, 681, 688
Rhodes, island of, 51, 52
Rhodesia, 798, 816
Ricardo, David, 580, 581
Ricci, Matteo, 339
Richard I, King of England, 237, 239, 306, 307
Richard II, King of England, 282–84, 287
Richardson, Samuel, 493
Richelieu, Armand de, 419–21, 422, 425, 428, 432, 447, 449, 451
Riddle of the Universe at the Close of the Nineteenth Century, The (Haeckel), 665
Riga, peace of, 748
Rilke, Rainer Maria, 742
Rio Treaty, 806
"Roaring Twenties," 729–30
Robespierre, Maximilien, 532, 534, 535
Rocco, Alfredo, 755
Rochau, A. L. von, quoted, 605
Rockefeller, John D., 630, 667
Rocroi, battle of, 432
Roger II, King of Sicily, 210
Roman Catholic Church: Babylonian Captivity, 272, 278, 279, 344; Catholic Reformation, 387–89; centralization of organization, 242; in

England, 152–53, 455–57, 459; feudalism and, 192; in 15th century, 359; financial system, 254, 373–74; First Crusade, 217–19; in France, 530, 537–38, 656; Franks and, 179–81; in Germanic kingdoms, 149–52; in Germany, 657, 758; Great Schism, 277–79, 344, 359–60; Greek Orthodox Church and, 167, 300; heresy and, 143–45, 249, 361–62; in Holy Roman Empire, 196–97, 199; Huguenots and, 411–13, 449–50; indulgences, 373–74, 377–78, 379; Inquisition, 245, 252, 367, 389, 549, 551; Investiture Conflict, 215–17, 240, 301; in Ireland, 450, 460; mendicant orders, 249–50; monasticism, 150–52, 373; in 19th century, 551; parish system, 182; reforms, 249–50, 279–80, 375–77; science and, 669; secular control, 215; in 16th century, 373–78; in Spanish Empire, 401; in 13th century, 243–45, 249–50, 252, 254, 259–62; Thirty Years' War, 429–33; in 12th century, 219–20, 242–43; universities and, 247 (*see also* Christianity; Jesuits; papacy)
Roman Empire, early, 78–100: art, 94–95; Augustus, principate of, 79–83; Christianity, beginnings of, 89–91; cultural centers of, 54; economy, 93–94, 99, 100; "five good emperors," 86–87; Flavian emperors, 85–86; at height of power, 85–97; Jews in, 88–89; Julio-Claudian emperors, 83–85; law, 96–97; literature, 95–96; philosophy and theology, 96; in second century, 87–88; social class, 91–93, 100; in third century, 97–100; weaknesses, 97–100
Roman Empire, late, 102–20; art, 117–18, 120; Constantine, reign of, 107–09; decline of, 112–17; Diocletian, reign of, 103–04; economy, 104, 110–12; in fourth century, 109–12; literature, 117–20; religion, 104–07, 112 (*see also* Eastern Roman Empire; Holy Roman Empire)
Roman Republic, 58–77, 355; beginning of, 58; Caesar, rise of, 72–75; collapse of, 68–72; First Triumvirate, 72–74; Great Latin War, 59, 61; Italy, conquest of, 60–63; overseas expansion of, 63–68; political reform, 59–60; Punic Wars, 63–64; Second Triumvirate, 75–77
Romance of the Rose (Lorris and Meung), 265–66
Romanov dynasty, 467

Romanticism, 492, 493–94, 545, 550–54, 621, 655, 670, 671, 743, 747

Romanus IV, Byzantine Emperor, 304

Rome, 56, 603, 612; origins of, 57–58; sack of (410), 115, 119; sack of (1527), 388 (*see also* Roman Empire; Roman Republic)

Rome-Berlin Axis, 762

Rommel, Erwin, 775

Romulus, 58

Röntgen, Konrad, 742

Roosevelt, Franklin D., 733, 764, 782, 785; quoted, 17, 732

Roosevelt, Theodore, 642, 668, 685, 686

Roosevelt Corollary, 686, 737

Rosen, Baron Roman Romanovich, 642

Rousseau, Jean Jacques, 491, 493, 550; quoted, 491

Royal Oak, 773

Royal Society of London, 476, 479

Ruhr, 658, 774; French occupation of, 717, 720, 726

Rule of St. Benedict (tr. Gasquet), 150

Rumania, 556, 563, 597, 676, 678, 692, 716, 787, 789; First World War, 700, 703, 707; postwar (1919–1939), 759, 768

Runnymede, 237

Ruskin, John, 671

Russia, 370, 462, 466, 652; autocratic state, rise of, 313–16; Byzantine influence on, 300–01; China and, 444; Congress of Vienna, 546–47; Crimean War, 596–98, 616; in 18th century, 499, 504, 509–11, 512–14; explorations of, 443–44; First World War, 694–95, 699–707; Mongols in, 309–15; Napoleonic Wars, 538–41; 1900–1913, 689–92; in 19th century, 556–59, 564, 574, 576, 595–98, 612, 615–18, 628, 639, 662, 675–78, 683; under Peter the Great, 468–70; revolution (1905), 663–64; revolution (1917), 704–07; Russo-Japanese War, 642, 664, 683, 686, 688; Russo-Turkish War, 676; in 17th century, 443–44, 467; in 20th century, 663; vikings in, 189–90 (*see also* Union of Soviet Socialist Republics)

Russia Company, 436

Russian Orthodox Church, 313, 467

Russian Revolution, 704–07

Russo-Japanese War, 642, 664, 683, 686, 688

Ruthenians, 563

Rutherford, Ernest, 742

Rykov, Alexei, 749, 752

Ryswick, Peace of, 452, 464

S

Saar, 658, 710

sabotage trials, 751

Sadowa, battle of, 607, 609

Sailendra dynasty, 323

St. Albans historians, 233

St. Bartholomew's Day Massacre, 412

St. Denis, church of, 221–22

St. Germain, Treaty of, 712

St. Helena, Island of, 542

St. Petersburg, 469–70

St. Sophia Church, Constantinople, 161

Sainte-Chapelle, Paris, 232

Saint-Simon, Count Henri de, 585

Saite dynasty, 9

Sakhalin, Island of, 642

Saladin, 306

Salisbury, Robert Gascoyne-Cecil, Lord, 652, 653, 687

Sallust, 82

Samarkand, 175

Samnites, 61

Samoa, 631, 684, 686

Samuel, 19

samurai, 341, 641

San Francisco Conference, 793

San Stefano, Treaty of, 676

Sankara, 324

Sanskrit language, 13, 124

Santa Anna, Antonio López de, 632

Sappho of Lesbos, 31, 35

Sarajevo, 661, 693, 694

Saratoga, battle of, 520

Sardinia (*see* Piedmont-Sardinia)

Sargon, 6

Sasanids, 98

Satsuma Rebellion, 641

Satyricon (Petronius), 95

Saudi Arabia, 813

Saul, King of the Hebrews, 19

Saul of Tarsus (*see* Paul, St.)

Savonarola, Girolamo, 376

Savoy, 187, 454, 601, 602

Saxons, 183, 191, 195 (*see also* Anglo-Saxons)

Saxony, 181, 187, 195, 196, 430, 463

Scandinavia (*see* Denmark; Norway; Sweden)

Scarlatti, Alessandro, 481

Scharnhorst, Gerhard von, 540

Schlesinger, A. M., Jr., quoted, 820

Schleswig-Holstein, 606–07

Schlieffen, Alfred von, 695

Schlieffen Plan, 695, 700, 701

Schliemann, Heinrich, 28

Schoenerer, Georg von, 660

scholarship: Arabic, 301–02; Byzantine, 318; Chinese, 331; Japanese, 340; Moslem, 318; Renaissance, 352–53; in 13th century, 262–64 (*see*

also education; Humanism; universities)

scholasticism, 224, 346

Schönberg, Arnold, 743

Schönbrunn palace, 481

schools (*see* education; universities)

Schuman, Robert, 799

Schuman Plan, 802

Schurz, Carl, quoted, 565

Schuschnigg, Kurt von, 766

Schwarzenberg, Prince Felix, 564, 604

science, 45, 198; Arabic, 301–02; 18th-century, 485; 14th-century, 318; Hellenistic Era, 52–54; medieval, 245–46, 293–94, 473; 19th-century, 665–69; religion and, 479–80; Renaissance, 359; 17th-century, 473–80; 20th-century, 742

scientific revolution, 473–80

scientific socialism, 585, 588

Scipio Africanus, 64

Scotland, 143, 266, 281, 425; Calvinism in, 409; in 17th century, 460–61; union with England, 461

sculpture: baroque, 481; Christian, 120; Gothic, 265; Greek, 31–32, 42; Indian, 131, 133; Italian, 345; medieval, 293; Renaissance, 355, 356; Roman, 66, 94–95

"Sea Beggars," 406, 409

"sea-peoples," 16

SEATO (*see* Southeast Asia Treaty Organization)

Sebastopol, 596

Second Balkan War, 692

Second Crusade, 220, 306

Second French Empire, 598–600, 618

Second Industrial Revolution, 592, 647, 648–49, 665

Second International, 650

Second Reform Bill of 1867, 614, 617

Second Treatise of Government (Locke), 483

Second Triumvirate, 75–77

Second World War, 773–85

secret police: German, 757; Italian, 754; Russian, 747

Sedan, battle of, 610

Selective Service Act, 779

Seleucid Empire, 51, 54, 64, 131

Seleucus I, 51

Seljuks, 304, 316

Semites, 6–7, 8, 168

senatorial class, Roman, 67, 69, 92–93

Seneca, 85, 95

Sentences (Peter Lombard), 224

September massacres, 533

Septimius Severus, Roman Emperor, 98

Serbia, 660, 676, 678, 691, 692, 694–95, 700, 709

Serbs, 555, 563

Steele, Richard, 492
Stein, Baron Heinrich vom, 540
Stephen II, Pope, 181
Stettin, 465
Stimson Doctrine, 760
Stinnes, Hugo, 658
Stoicism, 53, 96, 97, 105, 483
Stolypin, Peter, 664
Stone Age, 4–5
"Storm and Stress" movement, 493–94
Strafford, Thomas Wentworth, Earl of, 425, 428
Straits Convention of 1841, 595
Stransky, J., quoted, 783
Strasbourg, 452
Strategic Arms Limitation Talks (SALT), 829
Strauss, David Friedrich, 669
Strauss, Richard, 743
streltsi, 468
Stresemann, Gustav, 717–19
Stuart, House of, 424, 459–61
Study of History, A (Toynbee), 741
submarine warfare, 702, 704, 707, 781
Sudan, 679–81, 687, 688, 736
Sudetenland, 728, 767–68
Suetonius, 95
Suez Canal, 614, 636, 736, 813, 814, 819
"Suffragettes," 647, 648
suffrage, 647; in Austria, 659, 660; in England, 559, 614, 647, 725; in France, 530, 562, 647; in Germany, 647; in Italy, 647, 661; in Japan, 738; in Prussia, 604; in U.S., 621, 624
Suger of St. Denis, Abbot, 220–22, 223
Sui dynasty, 329
Suleiman the Magnificent, 370
Sulla, 70–71, 72
Sullivan, Louis, 631, 743
Sully, Maximilien, 418–19, 448
Sumerians, 6
Summa Contra Gentiles (Thomas Aquinas), 263
Sun King (*see* Louis XIV, King of France)
Sun Yat-sen, 640, 737
Sung dynasty, 310, 334–36
Supreme Soviet, 749–50
Suttner, Bertha von, 659
Suzdal, 311
Swabia, 195
Sweden, 370; mercantilism, 438; in 17th century, 466, 470; Thirty Years' War, 431–32
Swift, Jonathan, 492
Swinburne, Algernon, 292

Swiss Confederation, 290
Switzerland, 187, 289–90, 432, 538, 546, 647
Sybil (Disraeli), 590
"Syllabus of the Principal Errors of our Times, A" (Pius IX), 669
Sylvester II, Pope, 197–98
Sylvius, Aeneas (*see* Pius II, Pope)
Symbolism, 671
syndicalism, 591, 662
Synthetic Philosophy (Spencer), 667
Syracuse, 30, 47
Syria, 4, 6, 13, 50, 64, 72, 124, 161, 174, 304, 317, 735, 799; Arabic conquest of, 173; Assyrian conquest of, 21; Monophysitism, 164; Persian Empire, 23

T

Tacitus, Cornelius, 95
Taff Vale decision, 654
Taikwa reforms, 341
Taiping Rebellion, 638
Taiwan, 813
Takahira, Baron Kogoro, 642
Talleyrand, Charles de, 546, 547
Talmud, 89
Tamerlane, 316, 326–28
Tamils, 322
Tanais, 30
T'ang dynasty, 329–34
Tannenberg, battle of, 702
Taoism, 136, 331, 334
Tarawa, 783
Tarentum, 61
Tarik, 175
Tartars, 443
taxation: American colonies, 517; Austrian, 516; Brandenburg-Prussia, 465; of clergy, 242, 254, 261, 262, 270, 369–70; English, 236, 257, 268, 283, 425, 566; French, 268–69, 366, 419, 438, 448, 526, 537; Indian, 325; Roman, 85–86; Russian, 469; in 17th century, 438
Taylor, A. J. P., quoted, 676
technology, 124, 294–95 (*see also* science)
Teheran Conference, 782, 785
telegraph, 575
telescope, 477, 479
temperance, 621
Tennis Court Oath, 526
Terence, 66
Tertullian, 112
Test Act, 455, 558
Texas, 625
textile industry, 207, 285, 435, 573
Thackeray, William Makepeace, 670

Thailand, 130, 812, 813
Themistocles, 39, 41
Theocritus, 52
Theodora, Empress, 159, 164
Theodore of Tarsus, 153
Theodoric, King of the Ostrogoths, 116, 144, 145
Theodosius, Roman Emperor, 114, 119
Theologia Germanica, 279
theology, 112, 162, 164, 223, 224; in 14th century, 318; Islamic, 172; Roman, 96 (*see also* religion)
Theory of the Leisure Class, The (Veblen), 632
Thermopylae, pass at, 38–39
Thierry, King of the Franks, 155
Thiers, Adolphe, 610
Third Communist International (*see* Comintern)
Third Crusade, 306–07
Thirty Years' War, 421, 429–33, 435, 463, 464
Thomas à Kempis, 292
Thomas Aquinas, St. (*see* Aquinas, St. Thomas)
Thrace, 307
Three Emperors' League: 1872, 675–76; 1881, 677, 678
Three Impostors: Moses, Jesus, and Mohammed, The, 260
Thucydides, 42, 66
Thyssen, August, 658
Tiberius, Roman Emperor, 81, 83, 84
Tibet, 130, 812
Tientsin, Treaties of, 638
Tigris-Euphrates Valley, 5
Timur the Lame (*see* Tamerlane)
Tirpitz, Alfred von, 691, 692
tithes, 182
Titian, 359
Tito, Marshal, 808
Titus, Roman Emperor, 86, 92
Tocqueville, Alexis de, 621, 647; quoted, 561, 622
Tokugawa shogunate, 341
Toleration Act of 1689, 459
Tolstoy, Leo, 670
Tom Jones (Fielding), 492
Tongking, 323
Torah, 89
Tordesillas, Treaty of, 399
Tories, 457, 458, 502, 558 (*see also* Conservative Party, British)
Torricelli, Evangelista, 476
totalitarianism, 724, 744, 746–69
Toulouse, Count of, 218
Toulouse Lautrec, Henri de, 670
towns: 11th-century, 207–08; 14th-century, 275–77; gilds, 231; gov-

A 3
B 4
C 5
D 6
E 7
F 8
G 9
H 0
I 1